The Cache Coherence Problem in Shared-Memory Multiprocessors

Software Solutions

IEEE Computer Society Press

Jon T. Butler
Editor-in-Chief, Advances in Computer Science and Engineering

---

SELECTED TITLES

Splash 2: FPGAs in a Custom Computing Machine
Duncan A. Buell, Jeffrey M. Arnold, and Walter J. Kleinfelder

Surviving the Design of a 200 Mhz RISK Microprocessor: Lessons Learned
Veljko Milutinović

The Cache Coherence Problem in Shared-Memory Multiprocessors: Software Solutions
Igor Tartalja and Veljko Milutinović

Executive Briefings

Controlling Software Development
Lawrence Putnam and Ware Myers

The Cache Coherence Problem in Shared-Memory Multiprocessors

Software Solutions

Igor Tartalja
Veljko Milutinović

IEEE
COMPUTER SOCIETY PRESS
50 YEARS OF SERVICE • 1946-1996

Los Alamitos, California

Washington • Brussels • Tokyo

Library of Congress Cataloging-In-Publication Data

Tartalja, Igor.
    The cache coherence problem in shared-memory multiprocessors: software solutions / Igor Tartalja,
Veljko Milutinović
        p.   cm.
    Includes bibliographical references.
    ISBN 0-8186-7096-7
    1. Memory management.   2. Multiprocessors.   3. Cache memory.   4. Systems software.
I. Tartalja, Igor.   II. Title.
QA76.9.M45T37   1996
005.4 ' 2—dc20
                                                                                        95-10025
                                                                                           CIP

Published by the
IEEE Computer Society Press
10662 Los Vaqueros Circle
P.O. Box 3014
Los Alamitos, CA 90720-1264

IEEE Computer Society Press Order Number BP07096
IEEE Catalog Number EH0423-4
Library of Congress Number 95-10025
ISBN 0-8186-7096-7

Additional copies can be ordered from

IEEE Computer Society Press
Customer Service Center
10662 Los Vaqueros Circle
P.O. Box 3014
Los Alamitos, CA 90720-1264
Tel: (714) 821-8380
Fax: (714) 821-4641
Email: cs.books@computer.org

IEEE Service Center
445 Hoes Lane
P.O. Box 1331
Piscataway, NJ 08855-1331
Tel: (908) 981-1393
Fax: (908) 981-9667
mis.custserv@computer.org

IEEE Computer Society
13, avenue de l'Aquilon
B-1200 Brussels
BELGIUM
Tel: +32-2-770-2198
Fax: +32-2-770-8505
euro.ofc@computer.org

IEEE Computer Society
Ooshima Building
2-19-1 Minami-Aoyama
Minato-ku, Tokyo 107
JAPAN
Tel: +81-3-3408-3118
Fax: +81-3-3408-3553
tokyo.ofc@computer.org

Technical Editor: Dharma P. Agrawal
Assistant Publisher: Matt Loeb
Manager, Press Product Development: Catherine Harris
Acquisitions Assistant: Cheryl Smith
Advertising/Promotions: Tom Fink
Production Editor: Lisa O'Conner
Cover Art: Alex Torres
Printed in the United States of America by KNI, Incorporated

The Institute of Electrical and Electronics Engineers, Inc.

CONTENTS

Preface

The problem of cache coherence (consistency) has been studied for almost two decades now, and so far most of the solutions introduced have been on the hardware level. A representative set of papers dealing with hardware issues of the cache coherence problem has been selected and presented in a companion IEEE Computer Society Press book *The Cache Coherence Problem in Shared Memory Multiprocessors: Hardware Solutions*, edited by M. Tomašević and V. Milutinović.

Intensive work on the development of software mechanisms for coherence maintenance began in the second half of the 1980s. Almost all software solutions (except some trivial ones) are developed through academic research and implemented only in prototype machines. Thus we have found that the field of software techniques for maintaining the cache coherence is wide open for future research and development. This book is viewed as a selection of papers dealing with state-of-the-art software solutions for cache coherence maintenance in shared-memory multiprocessors. As such, this selection is a near complement with the selection given in the previously mentioned Tomašević-Milutinović book.

This book is intended for readers who are experienced in computer engineering but uninitiated in the topic of cache coherence. In our opinion, the selection of papers in this book will satisfy readers who wish to gain an in-depth understanding of the problem, as well as those interested in a comprehensive, relatively broad overview. We think that this book will be of special interest for both categories of multicomputer investigators and designers: computer architects and compiler writers. Because it includes most of the representative approaches to the software coherence maintenance, as well as a number of efforts in the related performance evaluation field, this book may also be used as a software coherence reference handbook for advanced undergraduate and typical graduate students in multiprocessing and multiprogramming areas.

Most of the preparational work for this IEEE Computer Society Press book was completed prior to November 1993; that is why some recent references are not reprinted. Instead, we have only listed them as suggestions for further reading.

This book summarizes our half-decade long research and education efforts in the field of software coherency. Our research views are built into this book (the initial research efforts were supported by NCR Corporation.) Our educational views have been expressed through numerous conference tutorials (at some of the leading conferences in the field) and in house presentations (for some of the leading industry in the field), both in the USA and Europe.

In addition to this book, we have prepared a set of transparencies for a 6-hour tutorial presentation. These transparencies include carefully prepared step-by-step examples for a number of approaches covered in the book. For more information, interested readers are welcome to contact the authors by e-mail (etartalj@ubbg.etf.bg.ac.yu) or (emilutiv@ubbg.etf.bg.ac.yu).

The selected papers (27) for this tutorial are organized into five chapters. Each chapter is devoted to a separate topic, although we are aware that some of the papers could have been classified into two, or maybe even more, chapters. Short editors' introductions are given for the entire book, and then for each chapter separately.

I. Tartalja and V. Milutinović
November 1995

Introduction

Shared-memory multiprocessors with private cache memories are widely used as natural and efficient parallel architectures to support the relatively simple programming model based on data sharing. Meanwhile, when two or more processors with private caches share changeable data, the problem of cache coherence (consistency) arises. After a processor changes the value of a variable in its private cache memory, copies of the same variable in other caches become stale and should be invalidated or updated before consumption. One frequently cited definition of cache coherence was given in the Censier and Feautrier paper [CENSI78].

In the beginning, the problem was solved at the hardware level. Most of the hardware schemes for coherence maintenance belong to one of two large groups: *snoopy* schemes (surveyed and compared in [ARCHI86]) and *directory* schemes (surveyed and compared in [AGARW88]). The field of hardware solutions to the cache coherence problem is properly covered in a number of surveys such as the papers written by Stenström [STENS90], Tomašević and Milutinović [TOMA94a, TOMA94b], and Lilja [LILJA93]; the paper [LILJA93] is included in the first chapter of this tutorial. A representative selection of papers dealing with hardware solutions to the problem is given in the companion IEEE Computer Society Press book *The Cache Coherence Problem in Shared-Memory Multiprocessors: Hardware Solutions*, edited by Tomašević and Milutinović [TOMAŠ93].

During the second half of the previous decade, a considerable research effort was made in the direction of software solutions to the cache coherence problem. Although the transparency of the coherence problem, inherently provided by hardware schemes, is sacrificed if the software approach is applied, software maintenance of coherence may be chosen for a number of reasons.

First, software methods are considered to be relatively less expensive to implement. Although a number of software schemes need some hardware support, the complexity of that hardware support is usually considerably less than the complexity of hardware used to maintain coherence without software help. Second, contemporary research (presented in the last two chapters) clearly indicates that the performance of a coherence scheme strongly depends on the multiprocessor workload characteristics. Consequently, either the hardware approach or the software approach can demonstrate better performance, depending on the environment and the application. Software schemes are potentially more efficient (than hardware schemes) for a class of applications characterized by a relatively low level of sharing. Third, all software schemes, according to many serious studies, are scalable. One general feature of software schemes is self-invalidation. By preventing incoherence conditions (sometimes very conservatively), software schemes eliminate the need for processors to communicate because coherence is permanently maintained. This reduces the network traffic and makes the software schemes well scalable.

In most software schemes, decisions about coherence actions may be made both statically (during the program compilation) and dynamically (during the program execution). However, in this book, software schemes for coherence maintenance will be classified as either static or dynamic. The static schemes are primarily based on compile-time program analysis and insertion of specialized coherence maintenance instructions into the code of the analyzed program. The dynamic schemes are primarily based on the detection of incoherence at the execution time and immediate reinforcement of appropriate actions. Static schemes are incorporated into parallelizing optimizing compilers, while dynamic schemes are incorporated into operating system kernels (primitive operations on the kernel level, for synchronization and/or mutual exclusion, are now extended with the cache coherence maintenance related code).

Our intention for this book was to incorporate all representative approaches to software coherence maintenance from the open literature, as well as a selection of representative techniques for performance evaluation. It should be noted that some papers, dealing with analytic or simulation modeling of coherence schemes clearly conclude that (in several application domains) software schemes are comparable in performance with hardware schemes, and become superior to hardware schemes for workloads characterized by migratory data and a relatively low level of sharing. Although the software solutions, in spite of their relatively low cost, have not been implemented in commercial systems so far, we think that this conclusion will command the attention of multiprocessor architects and designers, not only in academia, but in industry as well.

This book, containing a set of 27 selected papers, is organized as follows. The first chapter contains four *introductory readings*, to give a brief overview of the cache coherence problem, and particularly of the software solutions to the problem. The second chapter includes selected *static software cache coherence schemes*, while the third chapter contains *dynamic software cache coherence schemes*. The last two chapters cover the area of performance evaluation. Chapter 4 introduces *techniques for modeling and performance evaluation of cache memories and cache coherence maintenance mechanisms*, while Chapter 5 presents three existing *performance evaluation studies of cache coherence schemes*.

Each chapter is preceded by a concise editors' introduction. All of these introductions are organized in the same manner: the first paragraphs are to introduce the topic and the succeeding paragraphs briefly present the included papers—each paper is described by a separate paragraph. The editors' introductions for Chapters 2 and 3 represent subsets of the surveys given in the originally developed survey paper for this book. This educational methodology has proved efficient for this type of tutorial text. Editors' introductions are recommended for the first quick reading, while the related surveys of the schemes are for later, detailed reading.

Some papers, originally scheduled for inclusion in this book, have been excluded owing to space limitations. These papers have been moved into the category named suggestions for further reading, organized separately for each chapter.

References

[AGARW88] Agarwal, A. et al., "An Evaluation of Directory Schemes for Cache Coherence," *Proc. 15th Ann. Int'l Symp. Computer Architecture,* IEEE CS Press, Los Alamitos, Calif., 1988, pp. 280–289.

[ARCHI86] Archibald, J., and Baer, J.-L., "Cache Coherence Protocols: Evaluation Using a Multiprocessor Simulation Model," *ACM Trans. Computer Systems,* Vol. 4, No. 4, Nov. 1986, pp. 273–298.

[CENSI78] Censier, L.M., and Feautrier, P., "A New Solution to Coherence Problem in Multi-cache Systems," *IEEE Trans. Computers,* Vol. C-27, No. 12, Dec. 1978, pp. 1112–1118.

[LILJA93] Lilja, D., "Cache Coherence in Large-Scale Shared-Memory Multiprocessors: Issues and Comparisons," *ACM Computing Surveys,* Vol. 25, No. 3, Sept. 1993, pp. 303–338.

[STENS90] Stenström, P., "A Survey of Cache Coherence Schemes for Multiprocessors," *Computer,* Vol. 23, No. 6, June 1990, pp. 12–24.

[TOMAŠ93] Tomašević, M., and Milutinović, V., *The Cache Coherence Problem in Shared-Memory Multiprocessors: Hardware Solutions,* IEEE CS Press, Los Alamitos, Calif., 1993.

[TOMA94a] Tomašević, M., and Milutinović, V., "Hardware Approaches to Cache Coherence in Shared-Memory Multiprocessors: Part 1," *IEEE Micro,* Vol. 14, No. 5, Oct. 1994, pp. 52–59.

[TOMA94b] Tomašević, M., and Milutinović, V., "Hardware Approaches to Cache Coherence in Shared-Memory Multiprocessors: Part 2," *IEEE Micro,* Vol. 14, No. 6, Dec. 1994, pp. 61–66.

Chapter 1
Introductory Readings

This chapter includes the papers intended to introduce the reader inexperienced in the field of cache coherence maintenance in shared-memory multiprocessors to the topic. Also, the chapter contains the main contributions to the surveying and the classifying efforts within the field.

The first short paper, "How to Make a Multiprocessor Computer that Correctly Executes Multiprocess Programs," written by Lamport and widely cited in the literature, introduces the notion of "sequential consistency"—a conservative model of memory access ordering that guarantees the correctness of a multiprocess program on a multiprocessor. This paper defines the requirements that must be satisfied by a multiprocessor to be sequentially consistent.

The second paper, "Synchronization, Coherence, and Event Ordering in Multiprocessors," written by Dubois, Scheurich, and Briggs, presents three closely related topics in the multiprocessor world. This paper gives a broad overview of hardware-level and software-level synchronization mechanisms, presents a number of techniques for coherence maintenance, and discusses two major categories of logical behavior of shared-memory multiprocessors based on the strong or weak ordering of events.

The third paper, "Cache Coherence in Large-Scale Shared-Memory Multiprocessors: Issues and Comparisons," written by Lilja, addresses some issues of interest for deeper understanding of the cache coherence maintenance problem. Such issues as coherence detection strategy or coherence enforcement strategy are crucial for any coherence maintenance mechanism (snooping, directory-based, compiler-directed) and may significantly affect the performance of a multiprocessor.

The fourth paper, originally developed by the editors of this book, "A Survey of Software Solutions for Maintenance of Cache Consistency in Shared-Memory Multiprocessors," concentrates exclusively on software schemes. Although the survey is, in our opinion, broad enough to include most relevant software solutions, we expect that the presentation is sufficiently detailed for proper understanding of the mechanisms and characteristics of the approaches surveyed. We also propose a flexible classification of software solutions to the problem, apply the classification criteria on the existing software schemes, and attempt to generalize the classification.

Suggestions for Further Reading

Adve, S.V., and Hill, M.D., "Weak Ordering—A New Definition," *Proc. 17th Ann. Int'l Symp. Computer Architecture*, IEEE CS Press, Los Alamitos, Calif., 1990, pp. 2–14.

Adve, S.V., and Hill, M.D., "A Unified Formalization of Four Shared-Memory Models," *IEEE Trans. Parallel and Distributed Systems*, Vol. 4, No. 6, June 1993, pp. 613–624.

Chaiken, D., et al., "Directory-Based Cache Coherence in Large-Scale Multiprocessors," *Computer*, Vol. 23, No. 6, June 1990, pp. 49–58.

Gharachorloo, K., et al., "Memory Consistency and Event Ordering in Scalable Shared-Memory Multiprocessors," *Proc. 17th Ann. Int'l Symp. Computer Architecture*, IEEE CS Press, Los Alamitos, Calif., 1990, pp. 15–26.

Protić, J., Tomašević, M., and Milutinović, V., "A Survey of Distributed Share -Memory Systems," *Proc. Hawaii Int'l Conf. System Sciences*, Vol. 1, IEEE CS Press, Los Alamitos, Calif., 1995, pp. 74–84.

Smith, A.J., "Cache Memories," *ACM Computing Surveys*, Vol. 14, No. 3, Sept. 1982, pp. 473–530.

Stenström, P., "Reducing Contention in Shared-Memory Multiprocessors," *Computer*, Vol. 21, No. 11, Nov. 1988, pp. 26–37.

Stenström, P., "A Survey of Cache Coherence Schemes for Multiprocessors," *Computer*, Vol. 23, No. 6, June 1990, pp. 12–24.

Sweazey, P., and Smith, A.J., "A Class of Compatible Cache Consistency Protocols and Their Support by the IEEE Futurebus," *Proc. 13th Ann. Int'l Symp. Computer Architecture*, IEEE CS Press, Los Alamitos, Calif., 1986, pp. 414–423.

Teller, P., "Translation-Lookaside Buffer Consistency," *Computer*, Vol. 23, No. 6, June 1990, pp. 26–36.

Tomašević, M., and Milutinović, V., *The Cache Coherence Problem in Shared-Memory Multiprocessors: Hardware Solutions*, IEEE CS Press, Los Alamitos, Calif., 1993.

Tomašević, M., and Milutinović, V., "Hardware Approaches to Cache Coherence in Shared-Memory Multiprocessors: Part 1," *IEEE Micro*, Vol. 14, No. 5, Oct. 1994, pp. 52–59.

Tomašević, M., and Milutinović, V., "Hardware Approaches to Cache Coherence in Shared-Memory Multiprocessors: Part 2," *IEEE Micro*, Vol. 14, No. 6, Dec. 1994, pp. 61–66.

Yen, W.C., Yen, D.W.L., and Fu, K.-S., "Data Coherence Problem in a Multicache System," *IEEE Trans. Computers*, Vol. C-34, No. 1, Jan. 1985, pp. 56–65.

How to Make a Multiprocessor Computer That Correctly Executes Multiprocess Programs

Leslie Lamport

Abstract—Many large sequential computers execute operations in a different order than is specified by the program. A correct execution is achieved if the results produced are the same as would be produced by executing the program steps in order. For a multiprocessor computer, such a correct execution by each processor does not guarantee the correct execution of the entire program. Additional conditions are given which do guarantee that a computer correctly executes multiprocess programs.

Index Terms—Computer design, concurrent computing, hardware correctness, multiprocessing, parallel processing.

A high-speed processor may execute operations in a different order than is specified by the program. The correctness of the execution is guaranteed if the processor satisfies the following condition: the result of an execution is the same as if the operations had been executed in the order specified by the program. A processor satisfying this condition will be called *sequential*. Consider a computer composed of several such processors accessing a common memory. The customary approach to designing and proving the correctness of multiprocess algorithms [1]–[3] for such a computer assumes that the following condition is satisfied: the result of any execution is the same as if the operations of all the processors were executed in some sequential order, and the operations of each individual processor appear in this sequence in the order specified by its program. A multiprocessor satisfying this condition will be called *sequentially consistent*. The sequentiality

Manuscript received September 28, 1977; revised May 8, 1979.
The author is with the Computer Science Laboratory, SRI International, Menlo Park, CA 94025.

of each individual processor does not guarantee that the multiprocessor computer is sequentially consistent. In this brief note, we describe a method of interconnecting sequential processors with memory modules that insures the sequential consistency of the resulting multiprocessor.

We assume that the computer consists of a collection of processors and memory modules, and that the processors communicate with one another only through the memory modules. (Any special communication registers may be regarded as separate memory modules.) The only processor operations that concern us are the operations of sending fetch and store requests to memory modules. We assume that each processor issues a sequence of such requests. (It must sometimes wait for requests to be executed, but that does not concern us.)

We illustrate the problem by considering a simple two-process mutual exclusion protocol. Each process contains a *critical section*, and the purpose of the protocol is to insure that only one process may be executing its critical section at any time. The protocol is as follows.

process 1

 a := 1;

 <u>if</u> b = 0 <u>then</u> critical section;

$$a := 0$$

    else ··· <u>fi</u>

process 2

b := 1;

if a = 0 then critical section;

b := 0

else $\cdots$ fi

The else clauses contain some mechanism for guaranteeing eventual access to the critical section, but that is irrelevant to the discussion. It is easy to prove that this protocol guarantees mutually exclusive access to the critical sections. (Devising a proof provides a nice exercise in using the assertional techniques of [2] and [3], and is left to the reader.) Hence, when this two-process program is executed by a sequentially consistent multiprocessor computer, the two processors cannot both be executing their critical sections at the same time.

We first observe that a sequential processor could execute the "b := 1" and "fetch b" operations of process 1 in either order. (When process 1's program is considered by itself, it does not matter in which order these two operations are performed.) However, it is easy to see that executing the "fetch b" operation first can lead to an error—both processes could then execute their critical sections at the same time. This immediately suggests our first requirement for a multiprocessor computer.

Requirement R1: Each processor issues memory requests in the order specified by its program.

Satisfying Requirement R1 is complicated by the fact that storing a value is possible only after the value has been computed. A processor will often be ready to issue a memory fetch request before it knows the value to be stored by a preceding store request. To minimize waiting, the processor can issue the store request to the memory module without specifying the value to be stored. Of course, the store request cannot actually be executed by the memory module until it receives the value to be stored.

Requirement R1 is not sufficient to guarantee correct execution. To see this, suppose that each memory module has several ports, and each port services one processor (or I/O channel). Let the values of "a" and "b" be stored in separate memory modules, and consider the following sequence of events.

1) Processor 1 sends the "a := 1" request to its port in memory module 1. The module is currently busy executing an operation for some other processor (or I/O channel).
2) Processor 1 sends the "fetch b" request to its port in memory module 2. The module is free, and execution is begun.
3) Processor 2 sends its "b := 1" request to memory module 2. This request will be executed after processor 1's "fetch b" request is completed.
4) Processor 2 sends its "fetch a" request to its port in memory module 1. The module is still busy.

There are now two operations waiting to be performed by memory module 1. If processor 2's "fetch a" operation is performed first, then both processes can enter their critical sections at the same time, and the protocol fails. This could happen if the memory module uses a round robin scheduling discipline in servicing its ports.

In this situation, an error occurs only if the two requests to memory module 1 are not executed in the same order in which they were received. This suggests the following requirement.

Requirement R2: Memory requests from all processors issued to an individual memory module are serviced from a single FIFO queue. Issuing a memory request consists of entering the request on this queue.

Condition R1 implies that a processor may not issue any further memory requests until after its current request has been entered on the queue. Hence, it must wait if the queue is full. If two or more processors are trying to enter requests in the queue at the same time, then it does not matter in which order they are serviced.

Note. If a fetch requests the contents of a memory location for which there is already a write request on the queue, then the fetch need not be entered on the queue. It may simply return the value from the last such write request on the queue. □

Requirements R1 and R2 insure that if the individual processors are sequential, then the entire multiprocessor computer is sequentially consistent. To demonstrate this, one first introduces a relation $\rightarrow$ on memory requests as follows. Define A $\rightarrow$ B if and only if 1) A and B are issued by the same processor and A is issued before B, or 2) A and B are issued to the same memory module, and A is entered in the queue before B (and is thus executed before B). It is easy to see that R1 and R2 imply that $\rightarrow$ is a partial ordering on the set of memory requests. Using the sequentiality of each processor, one can then prove the following result: each fetch and store operation fetches or stores the same value as if all the operations were executed sequentially in any order such that A $\rightarrow$ B implies that A is executed before B. This in turn proves the sequential consistency of the multiprocessor computer.

Requirement R2 states that a memory module's request queue must be serviced in a FIFO order. This implies that the memory module must remain idle if the request at the head of its queue is a store request for which the value to be stored has not yet been received. Condition R2 can be weakened to allow the memory module to service other requests in this situation. We need only require that all requests *to the same memory cell* be serviced in the order that they appear in the queue. Requests to different memory cells may be serviced out of order. Sequential consistency is preserved because such a service policy is logically equivalent to considering each memory cell to be a separate memory module with its own request queue. (The fact that these modules may share some hardware affects the rate at which they service requests and the capacity of their queues, but it does not affect the logical property of sequential consistency.)

The requirements needed to guarantee sequential consistency rule out some techniques which can be used to speed up individual sequential processors. For some applications, achieving sequential consistency may not be worth the price of slowing down the processors. In this case, one must be aware that conventional methods for designing multiprocess algorithms cannot be relied upon to produce correctly executing programs. Protocols for synchronizing the processors must be designed at the lowest level of the machine instruction code, and verifying their correctness becomes a monumental task.

REFERENCES

[1] E. W. Dijkstra, "Hierarchical ordering of sequential processes," *Acta Informatica,* vol. 1, pp. 115–138, 1971.
[2] L. Lamport, "Proving the correctness of multiprocess programs," *IEEE Trans. Software Eng.,* vol. SE-3, pp. 125–143, Mar. 1977.
[3] S. Owicki and D. Gries, "Verifying properties of parallel programs: an axiomatic approach," *Commun. Assoc. Comput. Mach.,* vol. 19, pp. 279–285, May 1976.

Synchronization, Coherence, and Event Ordering in Multiprocessors

Michel Dubois and Christoph Scheurich

Computer Research Institute, University of Southern California

Fayé A. Briggs

Sun Microsystems

Multiprocessors, especially those constructed of relatively low-cost microprocessors, offer a cost-effective solution to the continually increasing need for computing power and speed. These systems can be designed either to maximize the throughput of many jobs or to speed up the execution of a single job; they are respectively called *throughput-oriented* and *speedup-oriented multiprocessors*. In the first type of system, jobs are distinct from each other and execute as if they were running on different uniprocessors. In the second type an application is partitioned into a set of cooperating processes, and these processes interact while executing concurrently on different processors. The partitioning of a job into cooperating processes is called *multitasking*[1]* or *multithreading*. In both systems global resources must be managed correctly and efficiently by the operating system. The problems addressed in this article apply to both throughput-

*Multitasking is not restricted to multiprocessor systems; in this article, however, we confine our discussion, with no loss of generality, to multitasking multiprocessors.

> **Efficient multiprocessing depends on a harmonious blend of synchronization, coherence, and event ordering in a system that provides the user with a simple logical model of concurrency behavior.**

and speedup-oriented multiprocessor systems, either at the user level or the operating-system level.

Multitasked multiprocessors are capable of efficiently executing the many cooperating numerical or nonnumerical tasks that comprise a large application. In general, the speedup provided by multitasking reduces the turnaround time of a job and therefore ultimately improves the user's productivity. For applications such as real-time processing, CAD/CAM, and simulations, multitasking is crucial because the multiprocessor structure improves the execution speed of a given algorithm within a time constraint that is ordinarily impossible to meet on a single processor employing available technology.

Designing and programming multiprocessor systems correctly and efficiently pose complex problems. Synchronizing processes, maintaining data coherence, and ordering events in a multiprocessor are issues that must be addressed from the hardware design level up to the programming language level. The goal of this article is not only to review these problems in some depth but also to show that in the design of multiprocessors these problems are intricately related. The definitions and concepts presented here provide a solid foundation on which to reason about the logical properties of a specific multiproces-

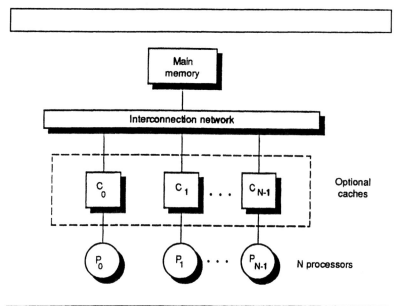

Figure 1. A shared-memory multiprocessor with optional private caches. The interconnection network may be either a simple bus or a complex network.

sor and to demonstrate that the hardware adheres to the logical model expected by the programmer. This foundation aids in understanding complex but useful architectures such as multiprocessors with private caches or with recombining interconnection networks (Figure 1).[2] Other important issues, such as scheduling and partitioning, have been addressed in a previous survey article.[3] Readers who are not familiar with the concept of cache memory should consult the survey by Smith.[4]

Basic definitions

The instruction set of a multiprocessor usually contains basic instructions that are used to implement synchronization and communication between cooperating processes. These instructions are usually supported by special-purpose hardware. Some primary hardware functions are necessary to guarantee correct interprocess communication and synchronization, while other, secondary hardware functions simplify the design of parallel applications and operating systems. The notions of synchronization and communication are difficult to separate because communication

primitives can be used to implement synchronization protocols, and vice versa. In general, *communication* refers to the exchange of data between different processes. Usually, one or several sender processes transmit data to one or several receiver processes. Interprocess communication is mostly the result of explicit directives in the program. For example, parameters passed to a coroutine and results returned by such a coroutine constitute interprocess communications. *Synchronization* is a special form of communication, in which the data are control information. Synchronization serves the dual purpose of enforcing the correct sequencing of processes and ensuring the mutually exclusive access to certain shared writable data. For example, synchronization primitives can be used to

(1) Control a producer process and a consumer process such that the consumer process never reads stale data and the producer process never overwrites data that have not yet been read by the consumer process.

(2) Protect the data in a database such that concurrent write accesses to the same record in the database are not allowed. (Such accesses can lead to the loss of one or more updates if two processes first read the data in sequence and then write the

updated data back to memory in sequence.)

In shared-memory multiprocessor systems, communication and synchronization are usually implemented through the controlled sharing of data in memory.

A second issue addressed in this article is *memory coherence*, a system's ability to execute memory operations correctly. Censier and Feautrier define a coherent memory scheme as follows: "A memory scheme is coherent if the value returned on a Load instruction is always the value given by the latest Store instruction with the same address."[5] This definition has been useful in the design of cache coherence mechanisms.[4] As it stands, however, the definition is difficult to interpret in the context of a multiprocessor, in which data accesses may be buffered and may not be atomic. Accesses are buffered if multiple accesses can be queued before reaching their destination, such as main memory or caches. An access by processor i on a variable X is atomic if no other processor is allowed to access any copy of X while the access by processor i is in progress. It has been shown that memory accesses need not be atomic at the hardware level for correct execution of concurrent programs.[6,7] Correctness of execution depends on the expected behavior of the machine. Two major classes of logical machine behavior have been identified because they are common in existing multiprocessor systems: the *strongly ordered* and the *weakly ordered* models of behavior.[7] The hardware of the machine must enforce these models by proper ordering of storage accesses and execution of synchronization and communication primitives. This leads to the third issue, the *ordering of events.*

The strictest logical model for the ordering of events is called *sequential consistency*, defined by Lamport. In a multiprocessor *sequential consistency* refers to the allowable sequence of execution of instructions within the same process and among different concurrent processes. Lamport defines the term more rigorously: "[A system is sequentially consistent if] the result of any execution is the same as if the operations of all the processors were executed in some sequential order, and the operations of each individual processor appear in this sequence in the order specified by its program."[8]

Since the only way that two concurrent processors can affect each other's execution is through the sharing of writable data and the sending of interrupt signals, it is

10

the order of these events that really matters. In systems that are sequentially consistent we say that events are strongly ordered.

However, if we look at many systems (transaction systems, for example), it becomes clear that sequential consistency is often violated in favor of a weaker condition. In many machines it is often implicitly assumed that the programmer should make no assumption about the order in which the events that a process generates are observed by other processes between two explicit synchronization points. Accesses to shared writable data should be executed in a mutually exclusive manner, controlled by synchronizing variables. Accesses to synchronizing variables can be detected by the machine hardware at execution time. Strong ordering of accesses to these synchronizing variables and restoration of coherence at synchronization points are therefore the only restrictions that must be upheld. In such systems we say that events are weakly ordered. Weak ordering may result in more efficient systems, but the implementation problems remain the same as for strong ordering: strong ordering must still be enforced for synchronizing variables (rather than for all shared writable data).

We can infer from this discussion that synchronization, coherence, and ordering of events are closely related issues in the design of multiprocessors.

Communication and synchronization

Communication and synchronization are two facets of the same basic problem: how to design concurrent software that is correct and reliable, especially when the processes interact by exchanging control and data information. Multiprocessor systems usually include various mechanisms to deal with the various granules of synchronizable resources. Usually, low-level and simple primitives are implemented directly by the hardware. These primitives are the basic mechanisms that enforce mutual exclusion for more complex mechanisms implemented in microcode or software.

Hardware-level synchronization mechanisms. All multiprocessors include hardware mechanisms to enforce atomic operations. The most primitive memory operations in a machine are Loads and

```
        {Processor 1:}
        A:=0
        .
        .
        A:=1                            /* event S1(A) */
LAB1:   If (B =1) goto LAB1            /* event L1(B) */
        <critical section>
        A:=0

        {Processor 2:}
        B:=0
        .
        .
        B:=1                            /* event S2(B) */
LAB2:   If (A =1) goto LAB2            /* event L2(A) */
        <critical section>
        B:=0
```

Figure 2. Synchronization protocol using two shared variables, *A* and *B*.

Stores. With atomic Loads and Stores complex synchronization protocols can be built. Figure 2 depicts a simple protocol. Before a processor can enter its critical section, it sets its control variable (*A* for processor 1 and *B* for processor 2) to 1. Hence, for both processors to be in their critical sections concurrently, both *A* and *B* must equal 1. But this is not possible, since a processor cannot enter its critical section if the other processor's control variable equals 1. Therefore, the two processors cannot execute their respective critical sections concurrently. This simple protocol can be deadlocked, but the problem can be remedied.[8] Such protocols are hard to design, understand, and prove correct, and in many cases they are inefficient.

More sophisticated synchronization primitives are usually implemented in hardware. If the primitive is simple enough, the controller of the memory bank can execute the primitive at the memory in the same way it executes a Load or a Store, at the added cost of a more complex memory controller. This is typically the case for the Test&Set and the Full/Empty bit primitives described below. Interprocessor interrupts are also possible hardware mechanisms for synchronization and communication. To send a message to another process currently

running on a different processor, a process can send an interrupt to that processor to notify the destination process.

A common set of synchronization primitives consists of Test&Set(lock) and Reset(lock). The semantics of Test&Set and Reset are

TEST&SET(lock)
{ *temp* ← lock; lock ← 1;
return *temp*; }
RESET(lock)
{ lock ← 0; }

The microcode or software will usually repeat the Test&Set until the returned value is 0. Synchronization at this level implies some form of busy waiting, which ties up a processor in an idle loop and increases the memory bus traffic and contention. The type of lock that relies on busy waiting is called a *spin-lock*.

To avoid spinning, interprocessor interrupts are used instead. A lock that relies on interrupts instead of spinning is called a *suspend-lock* (also called *sleep-lock* in the C.mmp[1]). This lock is similar to the spin-lock in the sense that a process does not relinquish the processor while it is waiting on a suspend-lock. However, whenever it fails to obtain the lock, it records its status in one field of the lock and disables all interrupts except interprocessor interrupts. When a process frees the lock, it signals all waiting processors through an interprocessor interrupt. This mechanism prevents the excessive interconnection traffic caused by busy waiting but still consumes processor cycles. Spin-locks and suspend-locks can be based on primitives similar to Test&Set, such as Compare&Swap.

The Compare&Swap(r1,r2,w) primitive is a synchronization primitive in the IBM 370 architecture; r1 and r2 are two machine registers, and w points to a memory location. The success of the Compare&Swap is indicated by the flag z. The semantics of the Compare&Swap instruction are

COMPARE&SWAP(r1,r2,w)
  { $temp \leftarrow w$; if ($temp = $ r1)
  then {$w \leftarrow$ r2; $z \leftarrow 1$;}
  else {r1 $\leftarrow temp$; $z \leftarrow 0$;}
  }

Test&Set and Compare&Swap are also called *read-modify-write* (RMW) primitives. A common performance problem associated with these basic synchronization primitives is the complexity of locking protocols. If N processes attempt to access a critical section at the same time, the memory system must execute N basic lock operations, one after the other, even if at most one process is successful. The NYU Ultracomputer[2] and the RP3 multiprocessor[9] use the Fetch&Add(x,a) primitive, where x is a shared-memory word and a is an increment. When a single processor executes the Fetch&Add on x, the semantics are

FETCH&ADD(x,a)
  { $temp \leftarrow x$; $x \leftarrow temp + a$;
  return $temp$; }

The implementation of the Fetch&Add primitive on the Ultracomputer is such that the complexity of an N-way synchronization on the same memory word is independent of N. The execution of this primitive is distributed in the interconnection network between the processors and the memory module. If N processes attempt to Fetch&Add the same memory word simultaneously, the memory is updated only once, by adding the sum of the N increments, and a unique value is returned to each of the N processes. The returned values correspond to an arbitrary serialization of the N requests. From the processor and memory point of view, the result is similar to a sequential execution of N Fetch&Adds, but it is performed in one operation. Consequently, the

Fetch&Add primitive is extremely effective in accessing sequentially allocated queue structures and in the forking of processes with identical code that operate on different data segments. For example, the following high-level parallel Fortran statement[10] can be executed in parallel by P processors if there is no dependency between iterations of the loop:

DOALL $N = 1$ to 100
  < code using N>
ENDDO

Each processor executes a Fetch&Add on N before working on a specific iteration of the loop. Each processor will return a unique value of N, which can be used in the code segment. The code for each processor is as follows (N is initially loaded with the value 1):

$n \leftarrow$ FETCH&ADD (N,1)
while ($n \leq 100$) do
  { <code using N>
    $n \leftarrow$ FETCH&ADD (N,1);
  }

In the HEP (Heterogeneous Element Processor) system, shared-memory words are tagged as *empty* or *full*. Loads of such words succeed only after the word is updated and tagged as full. After a successful Load, the tag can be reset to empty. Similarly, the Store on a full memory word can be prevented until the word has been read and the tag cleared. These mechanisms can be used to synchronize processes, since a process can be made to wait on an empty memory word until some other process fills it. This system also relies on busy waiting, and memory cycles are wasted on each trial. Each processor in the HEP is a multistream pipeline, and several process contexts are present in each processor at any time. A different process can immediately be activated when an attempt to synchronize fails. Very few processor cycles are wasted on synchronization. However, the burden of managing the tags is left to the programmer or the compiler. A more complex tagging scheme is advocated for the Cedar machine.[3]

Software-level synchronization mechanisms. Two approaches to synchronization are popular in multiprocessor operating systems: semaphores and message passing. We will discuss message passing in the next section. Operations on semaphores are P and V. A binary semaphore has the values 0 or 1, which signal acquisition and blocking, respectively. A counting semaphore can take any integer

value greater than or equal to 0. The semantics of the P and V operations are
$P(s)$
  { if ($s > 0$) then
    $s \leftarrow (s - 1)$;
    else
    { Block the process and append it
     to the waiting list for s;
     Resume the highest priority process in the READY LIST;}
  }

$V(s)$
  { if (waiting list for s empty) then
    $s \leftarrow (s + 1)$;
    else
    { Remove the highest priority process blocked for s;
     Append it to the READY LIST;}
  }

In these two algorithms shared lists are consulted and modified (namely, the Ready List* and the waiting list for s). These accesses as well as the test and modification of s have to be protected by spin-locks, suspend-locks, or Fetch&Adds associated with semaphore s and with the lists. In practice, P and V are processor instructions or microcoded routines, or they are operating system calls to the process manager. The process manager is the part of the system kernel controlling process creation, activation, and deletion, as well as management of the locks. Because the process manager can be called from different processors at the same time, its associated data structures must be protected. Semaphores are particularly well adapted for synchronization. Unlike spin-locks and suspend-locks, semaphores are not wasteful of processor cycles while a process is waiting, but their invocations require more overhead. Note that locks are still necessary to implement semaphores.

Another synchronization primitive implemented in software or microcode is Barrier, used to "join" a number of parallel processes. All processes synchronizing at a barrier must reach the barrier before any one of them can continue. Barriers can be defined as follows after the task counter Count has been initialized to zero:

BARRIER(N)
  { count : = count + 1;
  if (count $\geq N$) then
  { Resume all processes on barrier queue;

*The Ready List is a data structure containing the descriptors of processes that are runable.

Table 1. Synchronization, communication, and coherence in various multiprocessors.

Multiprocessor	Number of processors	CPU architecture	Hardware primitives	Cache	Coherence scheme
IBM 3081	≤ 4	IBM 370	Compare&Swap (CS, CDS), Test&Set (TS)	Write-back	Central table
Synapse N + 1*	≤ 32	Motorola 68000	Compare&Swap (CAS), Test&Set (TAS)	Write-back	Distributed table/ bus watching
Denelcor HEP*	100s	Custom	Full/empty bit	No cache	
IBM RP3†	100s	IBM ROMP	Fetch&Op (e.g., Fetch&Add)	Write-back	No shared writable data in cache
NYU Ultracomputer†	100s		Fetch&Add	Write-back	No shared writable data in cache
Encore Multimax	≤ 20	National Semiconductor 32032	Test&Set ("interlocked" instructions)	Write-through (two processors share each cache)	Bus watching
Sequent Balance 8000	≤ 12	National Semiconductor 32032	Test&Set (spin-lock using lock cache and bus watching)	Write-through	Bus watching

*Commercial machines no longer in production.
†Experimental prototype.

Reset count; }
    else
    Block task and place in barrier queue;
}

The first N-1 tasks to execute Barrier would be blocked. Upon execution of Barrier by the Nth task, all N tasks are ready to resume. In the HEP each task that is blocked spin-locks on a Full/Empty bit. The Nth task that crosses the barrier writes into the tagged memory location and thereby wakes up all the blocked tasks. This technique is very efficient for executing parallel, iterative algorithms common in numerical applications.

Interprocess communication. In a shared-memory multiprocessor, interprocess communication can be as simple as one processor writing to a particular memory location and another processor reading that memory location. However, since these activities occur asynchronously, communication is in most cases implemented by synchronization mechanisms. The reading process must be informed at what time the message to be read is valid, and the writing process must know at what time it is allowed to write to a particular memory location without destroying a message yet to be read by another process. Therefore, communication is often implemented by mutually exclusive accesses to mailboxes. Mailboxes are configured and maintained in shared memory by software or microcode.

Message-based communication can be synchronous or asynchronous. In a synchronous system the sender transmits a message to a receiving process and waits until the receiving process responds with an acknowledgment that the message has been received. Symmetrically, the receiver waits for a message and then sends an acknowledgment. The sender resumes execution only when it is confirmed that the message has been received. In asynchronous systems the sending process does not wait for the receiving process to receive the message. If the receiver is not ready to receive the message at its time of arrival, the message may be buffered or simply lost. Buffering can be provided in hardware or, more appropriately, in mailboxes in shared memory.

A summary of synchronization and communication primitives for different processors is given in Table 1.

Coherence in multiprocessors

Coherence problems exist at various levels of multiprocessors. Inconsistencies (i.e., contradictory information) can occur between adjacent levels or within the same level of a memory hierarchy. For example, in a cache-based system with write-back caches, cache and main memory may contain inconsistent copies of data.[4] Multiple caches conceivably could possess different copies of the same memory block because one of the processors has modified its copy. Generally, this condition is not allowable.

In some cases data inconsistencies do not affect the correct execution of a program (for example, inconsistencies between memory and write-back caches may be tolerated). In the following paragraphs we identify the cases for which data

13

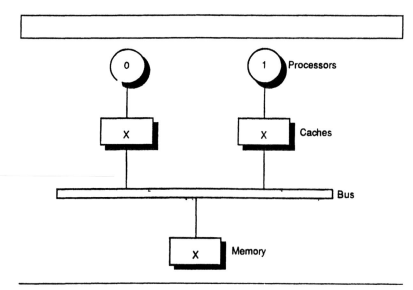

Figure 3. Cache configuration after a Load on X by processors 0 and 1. Copies in both caches are consistent.

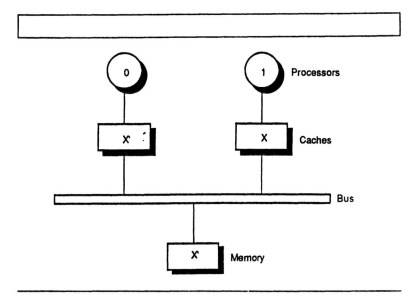

Figure 4. Cache configuration after a Store on X by processor 0 (write-through cache). The copies are inconsistent.

inconsistencies pose a problem and discuss various solutions.

Conditions for coherence. Data coherence problems do not exist in multiprocessors that maintain only a single copy of data. For example, consider a shared-memory multiprocessor in which each CPU does not have a private memory or cache (Figure 1 without optional caches). If Loads, Stores, and RMW cycles are atomic, then data elements are accessed and modified in indivisible operations. Each access to an element applies to the latest copy. Simultaneous accesses to the same element of data are serialized by the hardware.

Cache coherence problems exist in multiprocessors with private caches (Figure 1 with optional caches) and are caused by three factors: sharing of writable data, process migration, and I/O activity. To illustrate the effects of these three factors, we use a two-processor architecture with private caches (Figures 3-5). We assume that an element X is referenced by the CPUs. Let $L_j(X)$ and $S_j(X)$ denote a Load and a Store by processor j for element X in memory, respectively. If the caches do not contain copies of X initially, a Load of X by the two CPUs results in consistent copies of X, as shown in Figure 3. Next, if one of the processors performs a Store to X, then the copies of X in the caches become inconsistent. A Load by the other processor will not return the latest value. Depending on the memory update policy used in the cache, the cache level may also be inconsistent with respect to main memory. A write-through policy maintains consistency between main memory and cache. However, a write-back policy does not maintain such consistency at the time of the Store; memory is updated eventually when the modified data in the cache are replaced or invalidated. Figures 4 and 5 depict the states of the caches and memory for write-through and write-back policies, respectively.

Consistency problems also occur because of the I/O configuration in a system with caches. In Figure 6 the I/O processor (IOP) is attached to the bus, as is most commonly done. If the current state of the system is reached by an $L_0(X)$ and $S_0(X)$ sequence, a modified copy of X in cache 0 and main memory will not have been updated in the case of write-back caches. A subsequent I/O Load of X by the IOP returns a "stale" value of X as contained in memory. To solve the consistency problem in this configuration, the I/O processor must participate in the cache coherence protocol on the bus. The configuration in Figure 7 shows the IOPs sharing the caches with the CPUs. In this case I/O consistency is maintained if cache-to-cache consistency is also maintained; an obvious disadvantage of this scheme is the likely increase of cache perturbations and poor locality of I/O data, which will result in high miss ratios.

Some systems allow processes to migrate—i.e., to be scheduled in different processors during their lifetime—in order to balance the work load among the processors. If this feature is used in conjunction with private caches, data inconsistencies can result. For example, process A, which runs on CPU_0, may alter data contained in its cache by executing $S_0(X)$ before it is suspended. If process A migrates to CPU_1 before memory has been updated with the most recent value of X, process A may subsequently Load the stale value of X contained in memory.

It is obvious that a mere write-through policy will not maintain consistency in the system, since the write does not automatically update the possible copies of the data contained in the other caches. In fact, write-through is neither necessary nor sufficient for coherence.

Solutions to the cache coherence problem. Approaches to maintaining coherence in multiprocessors range from simple architectural principles that make incoherence impossible to complex memory coherence schemes that maintain coherence "on the fly" only when necessary. Here we list these approaches from least to most complex:

(1) A simple architectural technique is to disallow private caches and have only shared caches that are associated with the main memory modules. Every data access is made to the shared cache. A network interconnects the processors to the shared cache modules.

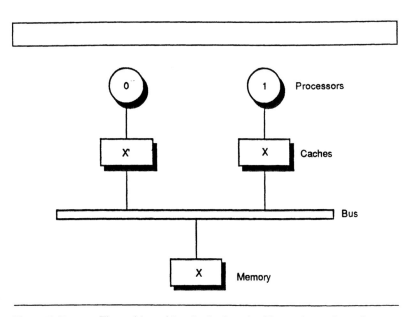

Figure 5. Same as Figure 4 but with write-back cache. The copies are inconsistent.

(2) For performance considerations it is desirable to attach a private cache to each CPU. Data inconsistency can be prevented by not caching shared writable data; such data are called *noncachable*. Examples of shared writable data are locks, shared data structures such as process queues, and any other data protected by critical sections. Instructions and other data can be copied into caches as usual. Such items are referred to as *cachable*. The compiler must tag data as either cachable or noncachable. The hardware must adhere to the meaning of the tags. This technique, apparently

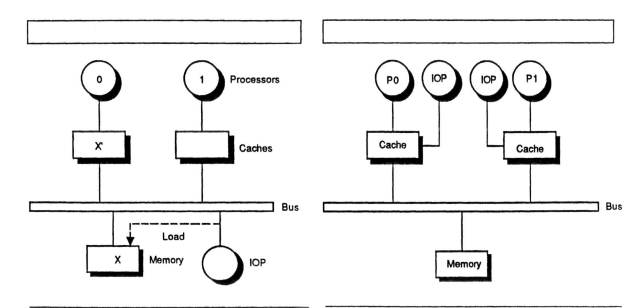

Figure 6. IOPs are attached to the bus and bypass the cache.   Figure 7. IOPs are attached to the caches.

15

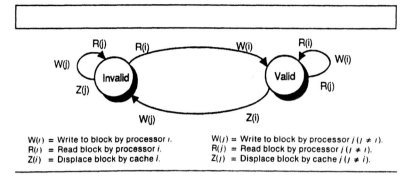

W(i) = Write to block by processor i.
R(i) = Read block by processor i.
Z(i) = Displace block by cache i.

W(j) = Write to block by processor j (j ≠ i).
R(j) = Read block by processor j (j ≠ i).
Z(j) = Displace block by cache j (j ≠ i).

Figure 8. State diagram for a given block in cache i for a write-through coherence protocol.

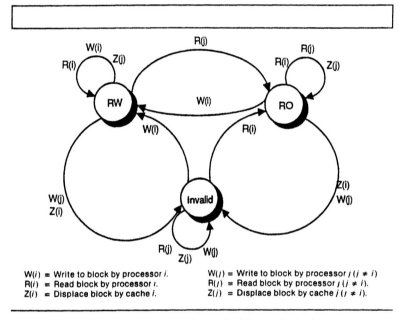

W(i) = Write to block by processor i.
R(i) = Read block by processor i.
Z(i) = Displace block by cache i.

W(j) = Write to block by processor j (j ≠ i).
R(j) = Read block by processor j (j ≠ i).
Z(j) = Displace block by cache j (j ≠ i).

Figure 9. State diagram for a given block in cache i for a write-back coherence protocol.

simple in principle, must rely on the detection within each CPU that a block is cachable or not. Such a detection can be made in a virtual memory environment by tagging each page. The tag is stored in entries in the CPU's translation buffers. Translation buffers (TBs) are similar to caches, but they store virtual-to-physical address translations.

(3) If all shared writable data are declared noncachable, the performance may be degraded appreciably. If accesses to shared writable data always occur in critical sections, then such data can be cached. Only the locks that protect the critical sections must remain noncachable. However, to maintain data consistency, all data modified in the critical section must be invalidated in the cache when the critical section is exited. This operation is often referred to as a *cache flush*. The flushing operation ensures that no stale data remain in the cache at the next access to the critical section. If another cache accesses the data via the acquisition of the lock, consistency is maintained. This scheme is adequate for transaction-processing systems in which a shared record is acquired,

updated in a critical section, and subsequently released. It works for write-through caches; for write-back caches, the design is more complex.

(4) A scheme allowing shared writable data to exist in multiple caches employs a centralized global table[5] and is used in many mainframe multiprocessor systems, such as the IBM 308x. The table stores the status of memory blocks so that coherence enforcement signals, called *cache cross-interrogates* (XI), can be generated on the basis of the block status. To maintain consistency, XI signals with the associated block address are propagated to the other caches either to invalidate or to change the state of the copies of the referenced block. An arbitrary number of caches can contain a copy of a block, provided that all the copies are identical. We refer to such a copy as a *read-only copy* (RO). To modify a block present in its cache, the processor must own the block with read and write access. When a block is copied from memory into cache, the block is tagged as exclusive (EX) if the cache is the only cache that has a copy of the block. A block is owned exclusively with read and write (RW) access when it has been modified. Only one processor can own an RW copy of a block at any time. The state IN (invalid) signals that the block has been invalidated.

The centralized table is usually located in the storage control element, which may also incorporate a crossbar switch that connects the CPUs to the main memory. To limit the accesses to the global table, local status flags can be provided in the cache directories for the blocks that reside in the cache. Depending on the status of the local flags and the type of request, the processor is allowed to proceed or is required to consult the global table.

(5) In bus-oriented multiprocessors the table that records the status of each block can be efficiently distributed among processors. The distributed-table scheme takes advantage of the broadcasting capability of the bus. Typically, consistency between the caches is maintained by a bus-watching mechanism, often called a *snoopy cache controller*, which implements a cache coherence protocol on the bus. In a simple scheme for write-through caches, all the snoopy controllers watch the bus for Stores. If a Store is made to a location cached in remote caches, then the copies of the block in remote caches are either invalidated or updated. This scheme also maintains coherence with I/O activity. Figure 8 depicts a state diagram of the block state changes depending on

the access type and the previous state of the block. A similar scheme was applied in the Sequent Balance 8000 multiprocessor, which can be configured with up to 12 processors.

The efficiency of the hardware that maintains coherence on the fly is vital. Recognizing that the Store traffic may contribute to bus congestion in a write-through system, Goodman proposed a scheme called *write-once*, in which the initial Store to a block copy in the cache also updates memory.[11] This Store also invalidates matching entries in remote caches, thereby ensuring that the writing processor has the only cached copy. Furthermore, Stores can be performed in the cache at the cache speed. Subsequent updates of the modified block are made in the cache only. A CPU or IOP Load is serviced by the unit (a cache or the memory) that has the latest copy of the block.

Multiprocessors with write-back caches rely on an ownership protocol. When the memory owns a block, caches can contain only RO copies of the block. Before a block is modified, ownership for exclusive access must first be obtained by a read-private bus transaction, which is broadcast to the caches and memory. If a modified block copy exists in another cache, memory must first be updated, the copy invalidated, and ownership transferred to the requesting cache. Figure 9 diagrams memory block state transitions brought about by processor actions. The first commercial multiprocessor with write-back caches was the Synapse N + 1.

Variants of the cache coherence bus protocols have been proposed. One scheme, proposed for the Spur project at the University of California, Berkeley, combines compile-time tagging of shared and private data and the ownership protocol. In another system, the Xerox Dragon multiprocessor, a write is always broadcast to other caches and main memory is updated only on replacement. These bus protocols are described and their performances compared in an article by Archibald and Baer.[12]

Advantages and disadvantages. Although scheme 1 provides coherence while being transparent to the user and the operating system, it does not reduce memory conflicts but only the memory access latency. Shared caches, by necessity, contradict the rule that processors and caches should be as close together as possible. I/O accesses must be serviced via the shared caches to maintain coherence.

Tagging shared writable data fails to alleviate the coherence problem caused by I/O accesses.

There are a number of disadvantages associated with scheme 2, which tags data as cachable or noncachable. The major one is the nontransparency of the multiprocessor architecture to the user or the compiler. The user must declare data elements as shared or nonshared if a concurrent language such as Ada, Modula-2, or Concurrent Pascal is used.[13] Alternatively, a multiprocessing compiler, such as Parafrase,[10] can classify data as shared or nonshared automatically. The efficiency of these approaches depends respectively on the ability of the language to specify data structures (or parts thereof) that are shared and writable and of the compiler to detect the subset of shared writable data. Since in practical implementations a whole page must be declared as cachable or not, internal fragmentation may result, or more data than the shared writable data may become noncachable.

Tagging shared writable data also fails to alleviate the coherence problem caused by I/O accesses. Either caches must be flushed before I/O is allowed to proceed, or all data subject to I/O must be tagged as noncachable as well. Depending on the frequency of I/O operations, both approaches reduce the overall hit rate of the caches and hence the speedup obtained by using caches.

Another common drawback of tagging shared writable data rather than maintaining coherence on the fly is the inefficiency caused by process migration. Caches must be flushed before each migration or process migration must be disallowed at the cost of limiting scheduling flexibility.

Scheme 3—flushing caches only when synchronization variables are accessed—has performance problems. In practice the whole cache has to be flushed, or else the data accessed in a critical section must be tagged in the cache. I/O must also be preceded by cache flushing. Note that the programmer must be aware that coherence is restored only at synchronization points.

Scheme 3 appears to be attractive only for small caches.

Scheme 4 solves the problems caused by I/O accesses and process migration. However, a global table that must be accessed by all cache controllers can become a bottleneck, even when XIs are filtered by hardware. But the main problem of this coherence scheme is the distance between the processors and the global table. As processors become faster, the access latency of the table becomes a limiting factor of system performance; in particular, when cache access times are very fast, the time penalty for a miss (*miss penalty*) must be minimized.

By distributing the table among the caches, the last scheme partly solves the problems of table access contention and latency. However, the complexity of the bus interface unit is increased because it has to "watch" the bus. Furthermore, since the scheme relies on a broadcast bus, the number of processors that can be interconnected is limited by the bus bandwidth.

Ping-pong effect. In systems with caches employing scheme 4 or 5, the execution of synchronization primitives, such as atomic read-modify-write memory cycles, can create additional access penalties. If two or more processors are spinning on a lock, RMW cycles that cause the lock variable to bounce repeatedly from one cache to another are generated. This can be aggravated by clustering different locks into a given block of memory. However, if RMW operations are implemented carefully, spin-locks can be efficient.

Let us illustrate the ping-pong problem by an example and discuss techniques for reducing system performance degradations. In this example we will assume the use of the Test&Set(lock) instruction; however, the problem can occur with other primitives. The traditional segment of code executed to acquire access to a critical section via a spin-lock is the following:

while (TEST&SET(lock) = 1) **do** nothing;
   /* spin-lock with RMW cycles */
   < execute critical section >
RESET(lock);
   /* exit critical section */

Assume that each processor has a private write-back cache and that three or more processors attempt to access the critical section concurrently. If processor P_0 succeeds in acquiring the lock, the other processors (P_1 and P_2) will spin-lock and cause the modified lock variable to be invalidated in the other processors' caches for each access to the lock. As a result of the invalidation of the modified lock variable, the block is transferred to the requesting cache—a significant penalty. The modification is a result of the writing in the last part of the RMW memory cycle.

One technique for avoiding the ping-pong effect is to use the following segment of code in place of the while statement in the previous code segment:

repeat
    while (LOAD(lock) = 1) **do** nothing;
        /* spin without modification */
until (TEST&SET(lock) = 0);

In this segment of code the lock is first loaded to test its status. If available, a Test&Set is used to attempt acquisition. However, while a processor is attempting to acquire the lock, it "spins" locally in its cache, repeating the execution of a tight loop made of a Load followed by a Test. This spinning causes no invalidation traffic on the bus. On a subsequent release of the lock, the processors contend for the lock, and only one of them will succeed. The ping-pong problem is solved; spin-locks can therefore be implemented efficiently in cache-based systems.

Ping-ponging also occurs for shared writable variables. A typical example is the index N in the Doall loop described earlier, in the section on hardware-level synchronization mechanisms. Unless the implementation of Fetch&Add is carefully designed, accesses to the index N create a "hot spot,"[9] which in a cache-based system results in intense ping-ponging between the caches. The careful implementation of synchronization primitives and the creation of hot spots in cache-based systems are research topics that deserve more attention.

Strong and weak ordering of events

The mapping of an algorithm as conceived and understood by a human programmer into a list of machine instructions that correctly implement that algorithm is a complex process. Once the translation has been accomplished, however, it is relatively easy in the case of a uniprocessor to understand what modifications of the machine code can be made without altering the outcome of the execution. A compiler, for example, can resequence instructions to boost performance, or the processor itself can execute instructions

out of order if it is pipelined. This is allowable in uniprocessors, provided that hardware mechanisms (interlocks) exist to check data and control dependencies between instructions to be executed concurrently or out of program order.

If a processor is a part of a multiprocessor that executes a concurrent program, then such local dependency checking is still necessary but may not be sufficient to preserve the intended outcome of a concurrent execution. Maintaining correctness and predictability of the execution of concurrent programs is more complex for three reasons:

(1) The order in which instructions belonging to different instruction streams are executed is not fixed in a concurrent program. If no synchronization among instruction streams exists, then a very large number of different instruction interleavings is possible.

(2) If for performance reasons the order of execution of instructions belonging to the same instruction stream is different from the order implied by the program, then an even larger number of instruction interleavings is possible.

(3) If accesses are not atomic (for example, if multiple copies of the same data exist, as is the case in a cache-based system, and if not all copies are updated at the same time, then different processors can individually observe different interleavings during the same execution. In this case the total number of possible execution instantiations of a program becomes still larger.

To illustrate the possible types of interleavings, we examine the following three program segments to be executed concurrently by three processors (initially $A = B = C = 0$, and we assume that a Print statement reads both variables indivisibly during the same cycle):

Local dependency checking is necessary, but it may not preserve the intended outcome of a concurrent execution.

P1	P2	P3
a: $A \leftarrow 1$	c: $B \leftarrow 1$	e: $C \leftarrow 1$
b: Print BC	d: Print AC	f: Print AB

If the outputs of the processors are concatenated in the order P1, P2, and P3, then the output forms a six-tuple. There are 64 possible output combinations. For example, if processors execute instructions in program order, then the execution interleaving a,b,c,d,e,f is possible and would yield the output 001011. Likewise, the interleaving a,c,e,b,d,f is possible and would yield the output 111111. If processors are allowed to execute instructions out of program order, assuming that no data dependencies exist among reordered instructions, then the interleaving b,d,f,e,a,c is possible and would yield the output 000000. Note that this outcome is not possible if processors execute instructions in program order only.

Of the 720 (6!) possible execution interleavings, 90 preserve the individual program order. We have already pointed out that of the 90 program-order interleavings not all six-tuple combinations can result (i.e., 000000 is not possible). The question remains whether out of the 720 non-program-order interleavings all six-tuple combinations can result. So far we have assumed that the memory system of the example multiprocessor is access atomic; this means that memory updates affect all processors at the same time. In a cache-based system such as depicted in Figure 1, this may not be the case; such a system can be nonatomic if an invalidation does not reach all caches at the same time.

In an atomic system it is easy to show that, indeed, not all six-tuple combinations are possible, even if processors need not adhere to program order. For example, the outcome 011001 implies the following: Processor P1 observes that C has been updated and B has not been updated yet. This implies that P3 must have executed statement e before P2 executed statement c. Processor P2 observes that A has been updated before C has been updated. This implies that P1 must have executed statement a before P3 executed statement e. Processor P3 observes that B has been updated but A has not been updated. This implies that P2 must have executed statement c before P1 executed statement a. Hence, e occurred before c, a occurred before e, and c occurred before a. Since this ordering is plainly impossible, we can conclude that in an atomic system, the outcome 011001 cannot occur.

The above conclusion does not hold true

18

in a nonatomic multiprocessor. Let us assume that the actual execution interleaving of instructions is a,c,e,b,d,f. Let us further assume the following sequence of events: When P1 executes b, P1's own copy of B has not been updated, but P1's own copy of C has been updated. Hence, P1 prints the tuple 01. When P2 executes d, P2's own copy of A has been updated, but P2's own copy of C has not been updated. Hence, P2 prints the tuple 10. When P3 executes f, P3's own copy of A has not been updated, but P3's own copy of B has been updated. Hence, P3 prints the tuple 01. The resulting six-tuple is indeed 011001. Note that all instructions were *executed* in program order, but other processors did not *observe* them in program order.

We might ask ourselves whether a multiprocessor functions incorrectly if it is capable of generating any or all of the above-mentioned six-tuple outputs. This question does not have a definitive answer; rather the answer depends on the expectations of the programmer. A programmer who expects a system to behave in a sequentially consistent manner will perceive the system to behave incorrectly if it allows its processors to execute accesses out of program order. The programmer will likely find that synchronization protocols using shared variables will not function. The difficulty of concurrent programming and parallel architectures stems from the effort to disallow all interleavings that will result in incorrect outcomes while not being overly restrictive.

Systems with atomic accesses. We have shown in an earlier work[14] that a necessary and sufficient condition for a system with atomic memory accesses to be sequentially consistent (the strongest condition for logical behavior) is that memory accesses must be performed in the order intended by the programmer—i.e., in program order. (A Load is considered performed at a point in time when the issuing of a Store from any processor to the same address cannot affect the value returned by the Load. Similarly, a Store on X by processor i is considered performed at a point in time when an issued Load from any processor to the same address cannot return a value of X preceding the Store.) In a system where such a condition holds, we say that storage accesses are *strongly ordered*.

In a system without caches a memory access is performed when it reaches the memory system or at any point in time

Figure 10. Concurrent program for three processors accessing shared variables.

Processor 1	Processor 2	Processor 3
$S_1(A)$	$L_2(A)$	$L_3(B)$
	$S_2(B)$	$L_3(A)$

when the order of all preceding accesses to memory has become fixed. For example, if accesses are queued in a FIFO (first in, first out) buffer at the memory, then an access is performed once it is latched in the buffer. When a private cache is added to each processor, Stores can also be atomic in the case of a bus system because of the simultaneous broadcast capability of the buses; in such systems the invalidations generated by a Store and the Load requests broadcast by a processor are latched simultaneously by all the controllers (including possibly the memory controllers). As soon as each controller has taken the proper action on the invalidation, the access can be considered performed.

Buffering of access requests and invalidations also become possible if the rules governing sequential consistency are carefully observed. With extensive buffering at all levels, and provided that the interconnection and the memory system have sufficient bandwidth, the efficiency of all processors may be very high, even if the memory access latency is large compared to the processor cycle time. Two articles present more detailed discussions of the buffering of accesses and invalidations in cache-based multiprocessors.[7,15]

In a weakly ordered system the condition of strong ordering is relaxed to include accesses to synchronization variables only. Synchronization variables must be hardware-recognizable to enforce the specific conditions of strong ordering on them. Moreover, before a lock access can proceed, all previous accesses to nonsynchronization data must be allowed to "settle." This means that all shared memory accesses made before the lock operation was encountered must be completed before the lock operation can proceed. In systems that synchronize very infrequently, the relaxation of strong ordering

to weak ordering of data accesses can result in greater efficiency. For example, if the interconnection network is buffered and packet-switched, the interface between the processor and the network can send global memory requests only one at a time to the memory if strong ordering is to be enforced. The reason for this is that in such a network the access time is variable and unpredictable because of conflicts; in many cases waiting for an acknowledgment from the memory controller is the only way to ensure that global accesses are performed in program order. In the case of weak ordering the interface can send the next global access directly after the current global access has been latched in the first stage of the interconnection network, resulting in better processor efficiency. However, the frequency of lock operations will be higher in a program designed for a weakly ordered system.

Systems with nonatomic accesses. In a multiprocessor system with nonatomic accesses, it has been shown that the previous condition for strong ordering of storage accesses (and sequential consistency) is not sufficient.[14]

Example 1. In a system with a recombining network[2] the network can provide for access short-circuiting, which combines Loads and Stores to the same address within the network, before the Store reaches its destination memory module. For the parallel program in Figure 10—$S_i(X)$ and $L_i(X)$ represent global accesses "Store into location X by processor i" and "Load from location X by processor i," respectively—such short-circuiting can result in the following sequence of events:

(1) Processor 1 issues a command to store a value at memory location A.

19

(2) Processor 2 reads the value written by processor 1 "on the fly" before A is updated.

(3) Because of the successful read of A in step 2, processor 2 issues a command to write a value at memory location B.

(4) Processor 3 reads the value written by processor 2; it reflects the updated B.

(5) Processor 3 reads memory location A and an old value for A is returned because the write to A by processor 1 has not propagated to A yet.

Each processor performs instructions in the order specified by the programmer, but sequential consistency is violated. Processor 2 implies that step 1 has been completed by processor 1 when it initiates step 3. In step 4 processor 3 recognizes that implication by successfully reading B. But when processor 3 then reads A, it does not find the implied new value but rather the old value. Consequently, processor 3 observes an effect of step 1 before it is capable of observing step 1 itself.

Example 2. In a cache-based system where memory accesses and invalidations are propagated one by one through a packet-switched (but not recombining) network, the same problem as in the previous example may occur. Initially, all processors have an RO copy of A in their cache.

(1) Processor 1 issues a command to store a value at memory location A. Invalidations are sent to each processor with a copy of A in its cache. (For simplicity we assume that the size of a cache block is one word.)

(2) Processor 2 reads the value of A as updated by processor 1, because the invalidation has reached its cache; processor 1 writes the data back to main memory and forwards a copy to processor 2.

(3) Because of the successful read of A in step 2, processor 2 issues a command to write a value at memory location B, sending invalidations for copies of B.

(4) Processor 3 reads the value written by processor 2; it reflects the updated B, because the associated invalidations have propagated to processor 3.

(5) Processor 3 reads memory location A and an old value for A is returned because the invalidation for A caused by processor 1 has not yet propagated to the third processor's cache.

Again each processor executes all instructions in program order. Furthermore, a processor does not proceed to issue memory accesses before all previous invalidations broadcast by the processor have been acknowledged. Yet the same problem occurs as in the previous example; sequential consistency is violated. This is the case because invalidations are essentially memory accesses. Because invalidations are not atomic, the system is not strongly ordered.

User interface

The discussion in this article shows that the issues of synchronization, communication, coherence, and ordering of events in multiprocessors are intricately related and that design decisions must be based on the environment for which the machine is destined. Coherence depends on synchronization in some coherence protocols because the user has to be aware that synchronization points are the only points in time at which coherence is restored. Strict ordering of events may be enforced all the time (strong ordering) or at synchronization points only (weak ordering).

At the user level most features of the physical (hardware) architecture are not visible. The instruction set of each processor and the virtual memory are the most important system features visible to the programs. Depending on the features of the physical architecture that are visible to the programmer, the task of programming the machine may be more difficult, and it may be more difficult to share the machine among different users.

Nontransparent coherence or ordering schemes. A sophisticated compiler may succeed in efficiently detecting and tagging the shared writable data to avoid the coherence problem. Such a compiler may also be able to make efficient use of synchronization primitives provided at different levels. The compiler may be aware of access ordering on a specific machine and generate code accordingly. It is not clear that compiler technology will improve to a point where efficient code can be generated for these different options.

If a program is written in a high-level concurrent language, the facility to specify shared writable data may not exist in the language, in which case we must still rely on the compiler for detecting the minimum set of data to tag as noncachable. It should be emphasized that perfectly legal programs in concurrent languages that allow the sharing of data, generally will not execute correctly in a system where events are weakly ordered.

User access to synchronization primitives. Programmers of concurrent applications may have in their repertoires different hardware- or software-controlled synchronization primitives. For performance reasons it may be advisable to let basic hardware-level synchronization instructions be directly accessible to users, who know their applications and can tailor the synchronization algorithm to their own needs. The basic drawback of such a policy is the increased possibility of deadlocks, resulting from programming errors or processor failure. Spin-locks and suspend-locks consume processor cycles and bus cycles. Therefore, such locks should never be held for a long time. Ideally, a processor should not be interruptible during the time that it owns a lock; for example, one or several processors may spin forever on a lock if the process that "owns" the lock has to be aborted because of an exception. In a virtual-machine environment the user process does not have any control over the interruptibility of the processor, and thus a process can be preempted while it is owning a lock. This will result in unnecessary, resource-consuming spinning from all other processes attempting to obtain the lock.

A solution to this problem is the task-force scheduling strategy,[1] in which all active processes of a multitask are always scheduled and preempted together. Another solution is the implementation of some kind of time-out on spinning. The drastic solution to all these problems is to involve the operating system in every synchronization or communication, so that it can include these mechanisms in its scheduling policy to maximize performance.

Making a multiprocessor function correctly can be a simple or an extremely difficult task. Basic synchronization mechanisms can be primitive or complex, wasteful of processor cycles or highly efficient. In any case the underlying hardware must support the basic assumptions of the logical model expected by the user. In a strongly ordered system such an assumption usually is that the system behaves in a sequentially consistent manner.

Increased transparency comes at the cost of efficiency and increased hardware complexity. But traditional and significant advantages such as the ability to protect users against themselves and other users, ease of programming, portability of programs, and efficient management of shared resources by multiple users are strong arguments for the designers of general-purpose computers to accept the hardware complexity and the negative effect on performance. The designers of general-purpose machines will probably prefer coherence enforcement on the fly in hardware, strong ordering of memory accesses, and restricted access to synchronization primitives by the user.

On the other hand, for machines with limited access by sophisticated users, such as supercomputers and experimental multiprocessor systems, the performance of each individual task may be of prime importance, and the increased cost of transparency may not be justified.

The challenge of the future lies in the ability to control interprocess communication and synchronization in systems without rigid structures. Efficient multiprocessing will be provided by systems in which synchronization, coherence, and logical ordering of events are carefully analyzed and blended together harmoniously in the context of efficient hardware implementations. It is necessary, however, to provide the programmer with a simple logical model of concurrency behavior. When multiprocessors do not conform to the concept of a single logical model, but rather must be viewed as a dynamic pool of processing, storage, and connection resources, the control in software over communication and synchronization becomes a truly formidable task. The concepts of strong and weak ordering as defined in this article correspond to two widely accepted models of multiprocessor behavior, and we believe that future designs will conform to one of the two models. □

Acknowledgment

Through many technical discussions, William Collier of IBM Poughkeepsie helped shape the content of this article.

References

1. A.K. Jones and P. Schwarz, "Experience Using Multiprocessor Systems—A Status Report," *Computing Surveys*, June 1980, pp. 121-165.

2. A. Gottlieb et al., "The NYU Ultracomputer—Designing an MIMD Shared Memory Parallel Computer," *IEEE Trans. Computers*, Feb. 1983, pp. 175-189.

3. D. Gajski and J.-K. Peir, "Essential Issues in Multiprocessor Systems," *Computer*, June 1985, pp. 9-27.

4. A.J. Smith, "Cache Memories," *Computing Surveys*, Sept. 1982, pp.473-530.

5. L.M. Censier and P. Feautrier, "A New Solution to Coherence Problems in Multicache Systems," *IEEE Trans. Computers*, Dec. 1978, pp.1112-1118.

6. W.W. Collier, "Architectures for Systems of Parallel Processes," IBM Technical Report TR 00.3253, Poughkeepsie, N.Y., Jan. 1984.

7. M. Dubois, C. Scheurich, and F. Briggs, "Memory Access Buffering In Multiprocessors," *Proc. 13th Int'l Symp. Computer Architecture*, June 1986, pp. 434-442.

8. L. Lamport, "How to Make a Multiprocessor Computer That Correctly Executes Multiprocess Programs," *IEEE Trans. Computers*, Sept. 1979, pp. 690-691.

9. G.F. Pfister et al., "The IBM Research Parallel Processor Prototype (RP3): Introduction and Architecture," *Proc. 1985 Parallel Processing Conf.*, pp. 764-771.

10. D.A. Padua, D.J. Kuck, and D.H. Lawrie, "High-Speed Multiprocessors and Compilation Techniques," *IEEE Trans. Computers*, Sept. 1980, pp. 763-776.

11. J.R. Goodman, "Using Cache Memory to Reduce Processor-Memory Traffic," *Proc. 10th Int'l Symp. Computer Architecture*, June 1983, Stockholm, Sweden, pp. 124-131.

12. J. Archibald and J.-L. Baer, "Cache Coherence Protocols: Evaluation Using a Multiprocessor Simulation Model," *ACM Trans. Computer Systems*, Nov. 1986, pp. 273-298.

13. G.R. Andrews and F.B. Schneider, "Concepts and Notations for Concurrent Programming," *Computing Surveys*, Mar. 1983, pp. 3-43.

14. M. Dubois and C. Scheurich, "Dependency and Hazard Resolution in Multiprocessors," Univ. of Southern Calif. Technical Report CRI 86-20.

15. C. Scheurich and M. Dubois, "Correct Memory Operation of Cache-Based Multiprocessors," *Proc. 14th Int'l Symp. Computer Architecture*, June 1987, pp. 234-243.

Cache Coherence in Large-Scale Shared-Memory Multiprocessors: Issues and Comparisons

DAVID J. LILJA

Department of Electrical Engineering, University of Minnesota, Minneapolis, Minnesota 55455

Due to data spreading among processors and due to the cache coherence problem, private data caches have not been as effective in reducing the average memory delay in multiprocessors as in uniprocessors. A wide variety of mechanisms have been proposed for maintaining cache coherence in large-scale shared-memory multiprocessors, making it difficult to compare their performance and implementation implications. To help the computer architect understand some of the trade-offs involved, this paper surveys current cache coherence mechanisms and identifies several issues critical to their design. These design issues include: (1) the *coherence detection strategy*, through which possibly incoherent memory accesses are detected either statically at compile-time, or dynamically at run-time; (2) the *coherence enforcement strategy*, such as updating or invalidating, used to ensure that stale cache entries are never referenced by a processor; (3) how the *precision of block-sharing information* can be changed to trade-off the implementation cost and performance of the coherence mechanism; and (4) how the *cache block size* affects the performance of the memory system. Trace-driven simulations are used to compare the performance and implementation impacts of these different issues. Additionally, *hybrid* strategies are presented that can enhance the performance of the multiprocessor memory system by combining several different coherence mechanisms into a single system.

Categories and Subject Descriptors: B.3.2 [**Memory Structures**]: Design Styles—*Cache Memories*; C.1.2 [**Computer Systems Organization**]: Multiple Data Stream Architectures: *MIMD*; C.5.1 [**Computer System Implementation**]: Large and Medium Computers

Additional Key Words and Phrases: Adaptive, block size, cache coherence, comparison, consistency, directory, memory disambiguation, shared memory, tagged directory, version control

1. INTRODUCTION

The sequence of memory addresses generated by a program typically exhibits the properties of *temporal* and *spatial* locality [Smith 1982]. Temporal locality, or locality in time, means that memory addresses recently referenced by a program are likely to be referenced again in the near future. Spatial locality means that the addresses referenced by a program in a short period of time are likely to span a relatively small portion of the entire address space. For example, some programs frequently operate on large data structures in which the consecutive elements of the structure are located in sequential memory locations. Thus, the

This work was supported in part by the National Science Foundation under grant CCR-9209458 and by the research funds of the Graduate School of the University of Minnesota.

"Cache Coherence in Large-Scale Shared-Memory Multiprocessors: Issues and Comparisons" by D.J. Lilja from *ACM Computing Surveys*, Vol. 25, No. 3, Sept. 1993, pp. 303–338. Copyright © ACM, Inc. 1993. Reprinted by permission.

CONTENTS

———————◆———————

memory addresses generated by a program to access such structures are likely to be clustered into a small range of the address space. Private data caches, which are small, fast memories physically located near a processor, exploit these memory-referencing properties to reduce the average time required to access the larger main memory. By temporarily storing in the cache a copy of a value from the main memory that is being actively referenced by a program, caches amortize the time required to copy the memory location from the slower main memory into the faster cache over several references to the same (temporal locality) and nearby (spatial locality) memory locations.

In a shared-memory multiprocessor such as that shown in Figure 1, private data caches have been shown to be quite effective in reducing the average delay to access the shared memory [Gottlieb et al.

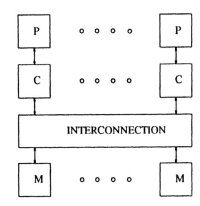

P = processor C = private data cache M = memory module

Figure 1. Shared-memory multiprocessor architecture.

1982; Pfister et al. 1985]. Caches have not provided the same level of memory performance improvement in multiprocessors as in uniprocessors, however, since the data referenced by a program in a multiprocessor is distributed among the processors. This data spreading reduces the processors' locality of reference, thus reducing the effectiveness of the caches. Additionally, since multiple copies of a shared-memory location can be resident in several different caches simultaneously, the private data caches introduce a *coherence* problem in which it is possible for the different cached copies to have different values at the same time. It is the responsibility of the cache coherence mechanism to ensure that whenever a processor reads a memory location, it receives the correct value.

This paper examines mechanisms for maintaining cache coherence in large-scale shared-memory multiprocessors, such as the New York University Ultracomputer [Gottlieb et al. 1982], the University of Illinois Cedar [Kuck et al. 1986], the IBM RP3 [Pfister et al. 1985], the Alliant FX-series [Perron and Mundie 1986], and the Stanford DASH [Lenoski et al. 1992]. The remainder of this section defines the cache coherence problem and presents an overview of three different types of mechanisms proposed to solve this problem. Additionally, a new frame-

23

work is presented that identifies the primary factors affecting the implementation cost and the performance of the cache coherence mechanisms. Section 2 describes a trace-driven simulation methodology that is used to illustrate the performance effects of these different factors. Since large-scale parallel machines frequently are used to execute numerical application programs, the simulation comparisons presented in Section 3 use memory traces produced by a multiprocessor emulator executing several different numerical programs. While the use of these applications may bias the simulation results, the issues presented are important to any shared-memory multiprocessor system, regardless of the application programs executed by the system.

1.1 Problem Definition

There are two important, related aspects to the cache coherence problem. The first, which is briefly discussed next, is the model of the memory system presented to the programmer. The second important aspect, and the primary focus of the remainder of this survey, is the mechanism used by the system to maintain coherence among the caches and the main memory.

1.1.1 Consistency Models

One definition of a system with coherent caches is a system that guarantees that "the value returned on a Load instruction is always the value given by the latest Store instruction with the same address" [Censier and Feautrier 1978]. The difficulty with this definition is that the meaning of "latest" is not precisely defined when the loads and stores occur on different processors that are running asynchronously with respect to each other. Due to delays and buffering in different portions of the processor-memory interconnection network, and within the processors and memories themselves, each processor and each memory module can observe a different ordering of events. The *consistency model* of a multiprocessor defines the programmer's view of the time ordering of events that occur on different processors. These events include memory read and write operations, and synchronization operations. As fewer assurances are made by the system to the programmer regarding the order of events, there is a greater potential to overlap operations from different processors with each other, and with other operations within the same processor, and thereby increase the system performance. However, the cost of this greater performance is the added burden on the programmer (or on the compiler) to ensure that any dependences between operations are not violated.

From the programmer's view of the memory system, the *sequential* consistency model defines a strict ordering of the execution sequence of memory operations allowed within a processor and among processors. Specifically, a multiprocessor system is said to be sequentially consistent if "the result of any execution [of the program] is the same as if the operations of all the processors were executed in some sequential order, and the operations of each individual processor appear in this sequence in the order specified by its program" [Lamport 1979]. With this consistency model, each access to the shared memory must complete before the next shared-memory access can begin. Also, all memory operations are executed in the order defined by the program. This strong ordering of memory accesses imposes a severe performance penalty by greatly limiting the allowable overlap between memory operations issued by an individual processor, and by other processors.

The *weak-ordering* consistency model [Dubois et al. 1988] relaxes the guaranteed ordering of events of the sequential consistency model to allow for greater overlap of memory reads and writes. With the weak model, only memory accesses to programmer-defined synchronization variables are guaranteed to occur in a "sequentially consistent" order. All memory references by different processors to shared data variables between accesses to synchronization variables (i.e., between *synchronization points*) can occur in any arbitrary order. Thus, in a system with a weak-ordering model, the programmer can make no assumptions about the ordering of events between synchronization points. To prevent nondeterministic operation, each processor must guarantee that all of its outstanding shared-memory accesses are completed before issuing a synchronization operation. Similarly, the synchronization operation must be completed before any subsequent shared-memory operations can be issued.

In addition to relaxing the ordering constraints on data references, the *release* consistency model [Gharachorloo et al. 1990] weakens the ordering constraints on synchronization variables by splitting the synchronization operation into separate *acquire* and *release* operations. The *acquire* operation is issued by a processor when it wishes to obtain exclusive access to some shared-memory object. To prevent interference with another processor that may currently have exclusive access to the shared object, the processor must wait for the *acquire* operation to complete before initiating any references to the shared memory. The *release* operation, on the other hand, is used to give up exclusive access to a shared-memory object. To ensure than any changes made by the processor to the shared object are actually performed in the shared memory before exclusive access is surrendered, the processor must wait for all of its shared-memory accesses to complete before issuing the release operation. This splitting of the synchronization operation into two separate phases allows this consistency model to achieve a greater overlap of the memory operations issued by all of the processors than either the weak or sequentially consistent models. To quantify the effect of this additional overlap, several studies have examined the performance improvement that can be obtained by using these relaxed consistency models [Gharachorloo et al. 1991; Gupta et al. 1991; Torrellas and Hennessy 1990; Zucker and Baer 1992].

1.1.2 Cache Coherence

A related problem to the memory consistency model, and the primary focus of this survey, is the mechanism used by the system to ensure that processors do not access stale data. In a shared-memory multiprocessor, each of the processors can directly access any location in the common memory address space using a single read (load) or write (store) instruction. Since each processor has a private data cache, a copy of the same shared-memory location may be present in one or more of the caches at the same time. When a shared-memory location is written by any processor, the fact that the value in that location has been changed must be propagated to all of the processors with a cached copy of the location to ensure that none of them uses a stale version.

For example, consider a system with three processors, each with a private data cache, in which the sequence of reads and writes shown in Figure 2(a) are performed. After the first two reads have been completed at t_2, the caches of both processors P_0 and P_1 will contain the value of 12 for the variable stored at memory location X, as shown in Figure 2(b). At time t_3, processor P_0 writes to this memory location changing its value to 16. In a system without a cache coherence mechanism, this value will be updated only in P_0's cache so that when P_1 rereads X at time t_4, it will read the old value 12 from its cache, as shown in Figure 2(c). Similarly, processor P_2 also will read the old value since the main memory has not been updated with the latest value written by P_0. The cache coherence mechanism is necessary to ensure that the stale values of X in the other processors' caches and in the main memory (i.e., the value 12) will not be propagated to future read operations.

1.1.3 Relationship between Consistency Models and Coherence

A useful way of viewing the relationship between the memory consistency model and the cache coherence mechanism is

Time	P_0	P_1	P_2
t_1	read X		
t_2		read X	
t_3	write 16,X		
t_4	read X	read X	read X

(a) Sequence of reads and writes.

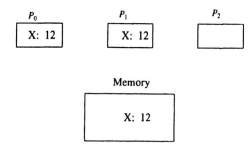

(b) Cache contents after the read at time t_2.

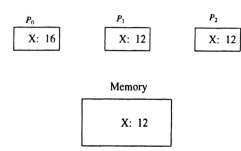

(c) Cache contents after the reads at time t_4.

Figure 2. An example of the cache coherence problem.

that the coherence mechanism ensures that all of the caches see all of the writes to a *specific* block in the same logical order. The consistency model, on the other hand, defines for the programmer the order of writes to *different* blocks as perceived by each of the processors. That is, if the programmer follows the rules of the consistency model for the system being used, the coherence mechanism forces the value returned by any load operation to be the value guaranteed by the consistency model.

In a system that guarantees sequential consistency, for instance, the coherence mechanism ensures that the effects of each write operation to a shared-memory location are propagated to all of the caches before the next write to that same location by any processor can proceed. These accesses are said to be *strongly ordered* [Dubois et al. 1988]. In a system with a weakly ordered consistency model, on the other hand, only accesses to pre-defined synchronization variables are strongly ordered. The ordering of accesses to shared-data memory locations by different processors can occur in any order. The processors must then ensure that they do not proceed across a synchronization point until all of the memory accesses they have issued have been acknowledged by the coherence mechanism. Thus, this weak-ordering consistency model ensures that the data values in the caches are coherent only at synchronization points. Examples of the relationship between different consistency models and different coherence mechanisms are presented next.

1.2 Overview of Cache Coherence Mechanisms

A variety of mechanisms have been proposed for solving the cache coherence problem. The optimal solution for a given multiprocessor system depends on several factors, such as the size of the system (i.e., the number of processors), the anticipated usage of the system, and the desired system cost. The following three subsections present an overview of the operation of the three main types of coherence mechanisms.

1.2.1 Snooping Coherence

Snooping coherence mechanisms rely on a low-latency, shared interconnection among the processors and the memory modules, such as a common bus, that allows each processor to monitor all transactions to the shared memory. As a processor "snoops" on the other processors' memory references, it can detect when a block that it has cached has been changed by another processor. It then invalidates [Goodman 1983; Katz et al.

1985; Papamarcos and Patel 1984] its cached copy so that its next reference to the block will force a cache miss, and thus the current value will be obtained from memory, or from another cache. Alternatively, it can directly update [McCreight 1984; Thacker et al. 1988] its cached copy with the new value available on the bus. Since the shared bus typically broadcasts the effects of each write operation to a shared-memory location to all of the caches in the same cycle as the write itself, these snooping coherence mechanisms typically implement a strongly ordered consistency model.

While these snooping mechanisms are relatively simple to implement, the shared bus can become a severe performance bottleneck. To reduce the contention on a single bus, the Wisconsin Multicube [Goodman and Woest 1988] proposed an n-dimensional grid of buses with the processors located at the crosspoints of the buses and the memory modules at the ends. The additional buses provide greater memory bandwidth at the expense of a more complicated coherence protocol. Another approach [Archibald 1988; Wilson 1987] clusters the processors on smaller, separate buses, and maintains coherence among processors within each cluster. An additional hierarchy of buses is introduced to maintain intercluster coherence. Yet another approach adds a special coherence bus [Bhuyan et al. 1989; Marquardt and Al Khatib 1989] to remove the coherence-updating data traffic from the normal data read operations on the primary memory bus.

Since all of these schemes use additional buses to increase the bandwidth between the processors and the shared memory, their performance ultimately will be limited by the bus contention when there are too many processors, and by the difficulty of physically constructing these long, high-speed buses. Consequently, it appears that the snooping coherence schemes are limited to use in relatively small-scale multiprocessor systems. Since the focus of this survey is primarily on large-scale multiprocessors,

the snooping coherence schemes are not considered further.

Another method of avoiding the bus saturation problem is to replace the bus with an interconnection network, such as a multistage Omega network, a mesh, a fat tree, or a hypercube. These networks provide higher bandwidth between the processors and the memory modules than a shared bus, but they also increase the delay to access memory. This longer delay intensifies the need for the private caches, but by eliminating the mechanism through which processors monitor the shared-memory transactions, the networks compound the coherence problem. Both hardware directory mechanisms and compiler-directed approaches have been suggested for maintaining coherence in these systems.

1.2.2 Directory Coherence

With a directory-based coherence scheme [Tang 1976; Yen et al. 1985], a processor must communicate with a common directory whenever the processor's action may cause an inconsistency between its cache and the other caches and memory. The directory maintains information about which processors have a copy of which blocks since several processors may have a copy of the same block cached at the same time. Before a processor can write to a block, it must request exclusive access to the block from the directory. Before the directory grants this exclusive access, it sends a message to all processors with a cached copy of the block forcing each processor to invalidate its copy. After receiving acknowledgments from all of these processors, the directory grants exclusive access to the writing processor. When a processor tries to read a block that is exclusive in a different processor, it will send a miss service request to the directory. The directory then will send a message to the processor with the exclusive copy telling it to write the new value back to memory. After receiving this new value, the directory sends a copy of the block to the requesting processor. Directory schemes differ in how much information they maintain about shared blocks, where that information is stored, and whether invalidating or updating is used to ensure coherence, resulting in differences in memory requirements and performance. These trade-offs are discussed further in Section 3.

By waiting for the invalidation and write-back acknowledgments for all writes to a shared-memory location before letting a processor proceed with a write, the directory implements a strongly ordered consistency model. A weakly ordered consistency model can be implemented with a directory by having the directory delay the writing processor only when it is accessing a synchronization variable. This approach then puts the burden on the processor to ensure that before it proceeds across a synchronization point it has received acknowledgments from the directory for all of the writes it has issued to shared-data memory locations. Since this weakened consistency model delays processor writes only to synchronization variables, it will produce higher performance than the strongly ordered model.

1.2.3 Compiler-Directed Coherence

Compiler-directed coherence mechanisms determine at compile-time which cache blocks *may* become stale. Special instructions then are inserted into the generated code to be executed by each of the processors to prevent them from using this possibly stale data. One of the simplest of these compiler-directed coherence mechanisms [Veidenbaum 1986] uses *indiscriminate invalidation* of the data caches to enforce coherence with a weakly ordered consistency model. This coherence mechanism assumes a *doall* parallel loop model of execution [Polychronopoulos 1988] in which there are no dependences among the iterations of the loop. Thus, all of the iterations can be executed simultaneously on multiple independent processors. The parallel loop terminates when all of the iterations have completed executing. Processors may be reassigned to iterations at the entry and exit points of the parallel loop. These points are called the *loop boundaries*.

At the start of each parallel loop, each processor first executes a *cache-invalidate* instruction to begin the execution of the loop with an empty cache. Each processor also executes a *cache-on* instruction to allow all references to shared-writable variables to be cached during the execution of the loop. The caches are write-through so that all writes to shared-memory locations are propagated directly to the global shared memory. At the end of the parallel loop, each processor again invalidates its entire cache to prevent stale entries from propagating into the next section of the program. Incoherent accesses are thereby prevented since the weakly ordered consistency model used with this coherence mechanism guarantees coherent caches only at loop boundaries. Since the caches are invalidated at the loop boundaries, and since the current value is only in the main memory, coherence is assured. Similar schemes have been suggested for the RP3 machine [Brantley et al. 1985] and the Ultracomputer [Edler et al. 1985]. These simple approaches tend to invalidate more cache entries than are necessary to maintain coherence, and thus they may reduce the memory system performance when compared to a directory mechanism. More sophisticated compiler-directed mechanisms with better performance than this simple mechanism are described in Section 3.1.2.

1.3 Factors Affecting Coherence Mechanisms

The most important consideration in choosing a cache coherence mechanism for a multiprocessor usually is its performance, or how effective it allows the caches to be in reducing the average delay when fetching data from memory. Another important consideration is the implementation cost, typically measured by how much memory is required to store the cache block sharing information, and by the complexity of the control logic.

28

The different coherence schemes have significantly different trade-offs in cost and performance, making it difficult to evaluate the alternatives. The primary issues affecting the cache coherence mechanisms can be summarized as:

(1) The *coherence detection strategy*, that is, the strategy by which the coherence mechanism detects a possibly incoherent memory access, which can be done either dynamically at runtime, or statically at compile time.

(2) The *coherence enforcement strategy*, such as updating or invalidating, that is used to ensure that stale cache entries are never referenced by a processor.

(3) How the *precision of block-sharing information* can be changed to trade-off the implementation cost and the performance of the coherence mechanism.

(4) How the *cache block size* affects the performance of the memory system.

This paper surveys the state of the art in cache coherence mechanisms in the context of the above issues. Trace-driven simulations are used to compare how these different issues affect the performance and implementation costs of the different coherence mechanisms. Additionally, hybrid strategies are discussed that combine several different coherence mechanisms into a single system to improve the memory-referencing performance. These comparisons should help the computer architect understand some of the trade-offs involved in the various coherence alternatives.

2. COST AND PERFORMANCE MODELING

The most accurate method of determining the performance of a specific computer design, or for proving the validity of a new architectural approach, is to build it. Unfortunately, actually building a complete computer system is very time consuming and expensive. It also requires the designer to select specific values for architectural parameters, such as the data cache size and the cache block size, without knowing what reasonable values of the parameters may be for the new system. Therefore, before actually committing an idea to hardware, it is desirable to explore the limits of the design space using mathematical analysis or simulation. A large number of potential design options can be quickly examined by analytically modeling the system and varying the desired parameters. Analytic models are of limited usefulness when comparing cache coherence mechanisms, however, due to the assumptions that must be made concerning memory-referencing patterns and data sharing. To provide more realistic results while still maintaining flexibility in choosing system parameters, the performance evaluations presented in this survey use trace-driven simulations.

2.1 Trace-Driven Simulation

An address trace for a multiprocessor is a record of the sequence of memory addresses generated by the processors as they execute a program. There are several different methods of generating these traces [Stunkel et al. 1991]. For example, it is possible to instrument an actual computer system to record the memory references as they are generated by the program. This approach has the advantages of being very accurate, very fast, and able to monitor operating system execution as well as a user program. Its main disadvantages are the cost and difficulty of building the hardware monitor, and the complexity of instrumenting all of the processors in a multiprocessor system. It also limits the simulation to using traces from a specific implementation of a computer system, which may be substantially different from the system to be studied.

Another method that has many of the advantages of hardware monitoring to generate traces is to alter the microcode of a processor to generate traces as it executes the instructions. This approach also can trace operating system activity, and it is relatively fast; but it requires a substantial effort to rewrite the microcode. Also, it is not applicable to processors without microcode, or to those that have their microcode in read-only memory. As more parallel computer systems use hardwired processors, this technique will become less useful.

Software-based techniques have been suggested to avoid some of the difficulties of the hardware-monitoring and microcode-based approaches. In some processors, it is possible to generate an interrupt after the execution of every instruction. The interrupt routine then produces the trace information for the current instruction. Another approach is to modify a program's source code or executable object code to produce a trace as the program executes. Both of these methods can generate traces without significantly slowing down the traced system, but they can introduce significant timing distortions into the trace due to the interrupts and due to the additional trace generation instructions. They also are limited to the instruction set of the specific processor used to execute the program.

The most flexible method of generating traces, and the one used in this survey, is to simulate the execution of the entire multiprocessor system. The primary disadvantage of this approach is that it is quite slow since the simulator must model all of the operations of all of the hardware elements of the processors. This explicit modeling of all operations, however, produces accurate traces, and it allows the simulation of any architectural feature, especially those that may not exist in a real machine.

Starting with application programs written in Fortran (described in Section 2.3), the Alliant compiler [Perron and Mundie 1986] is used to automatically find the parallel loops and to generate parallel assembly code. This assembly code then is executed by a multiprocessor emulator to produce a trace of the memory addresses generated by each of the p processors. This multiprocessor system uses an execution model in which each parallel loop is followed by a sequential

section of the program so that execution alternates between p processors executing a parallel section of the program and a single processor executing a sequential section. The memory traces from the p processors are completely interleaved into a single trace such that during the execution of a parallel section of the program, an address generated by processor i is followed by an address generated by processor $i + 1$, and so on, modulo p. During the execution of sequential sections of the program, processor 0 generates all of the memory references. In an actual system, timing differences between the processors due to cache misses, network and memory contention, and synchronization delays may produce a different ordering of the references, but this interleaving, which represents a valid ordering, highlights the effects of data sharing in the cache coherence mechanisms used in these simulations. Thus, this ordering provides a rigorous test of the different coherence mechanisms.

Since the simulation is very time consuming, it is limited to executing relatively short programs compared to those that could be executed on actual hardware. Additionally, these simulations are for one program running at a time, thus ignoring the effects of multiple programs sharing the system and the effects of the operating system. The simulations also prohibit task migration. In spite of these limitations, this trace-driven methodology provides an adequate means of comparing the performance of the different coherence mechanisms.

2.2 Machine Model

The interleaved memory trace drives a multicache simulator to determine the miss ratio and the cache-memory network traffic. A fully associative data cache with a random replacement policy is used in each processor to eliminate the confounding effects of set associativity conflicts. The long execution time required to perform the simulations limited the size of the application programs' data sets. To maintain a realistic relationship between the size of the data set and the size of the data cache, a data cache of 8 KB is used in each of the 32 processors, unless otherwise noted.

Since this system assumes that all instructions are only read, they can never cause coherence problems. Consequently, all instruction references are ignored. This multiprocessor architecture uses a separate synchronization bus for distributing the next available iteration values when scheduling loop iterations and for performing the barrier synchronization at the end of the parallel loops. With this architecture, synchronization variables are never cached with the data, and, since this study is concerned primarily with the effect of the cache coherence mechanism on data references, accesses to synchronization variables are not considered in these simulations. It should be noted, however, that synchronization variables stored in memory can be heavily shared. Heavy sharing of a single memory location by many different processors can cause memory *hot spots* [Pfister et al. 1985], which may make it undesirable to cache synchronization variables [Dubois et al. 1988]. Special hardware or software can be added to the system to improve access to synchronization variables [Anderson 1990; Goodman et al. 1989; Kruskal et al. 1986], but the analysis of these techniques is beyond the scope of this survey.

The $p = 32$ processors are connected to the shared memory via a packet-switched multistage interconnection network. Network traffic from a processor to the memory, such as a miss service request or write-back data, uses the forward network, while traffic from the memory to a processor, such as an invalidation command or fetched data, uses the separate reverse network. Both the forward and reverse networks use 32-bit data paths. Each packet between the memory modules and the processors requires a minimum of two words (eight bytes). The first word contains the source and destination module numbers plus a code for the operation type, and the sec-

ond word contains the actual memory address. Additional words are needed for the actual data values fetched and written. Table 1 details the actions required for each type of memory reference, along with the generated network traffic, when using the $p + 1$-bit full directory [Censier and Feautrier 1978]. This directory structure is described more fully in Section 3.3.1.

2.3 Test Programs

Six numerical application programs written in Fortran were used to generate the parallel memory traces for these simulations. *Arc3d* and *flo52* both analyze fluid flows. The *trfd* program uses a series of matrix multiplications to simulate a quantum mechanical two-electron integral transformation. *Simple24* is a hydrodynamics and heat flow problem using a 24-by-24-element grid. The *pic* program uses a particle-in-cell technique to model the movement of charged particles in an electrodynamics application. The *lin125* program is the Linpack benchmark using a 125-by-125-element matrix. The problem sizes and outer loop counts were reduced in these programs so that the entire program could be simulated in a reasonable period of time.

The memory-referencing characteristics of the test programs are summarized in Table 2 for $p = 32$ processors, and a cache block size of $b = 1$ word. The blocks were classified by examining the traces and determining how many processors accessed each block. The *private* blocks are those that are referenced by the same processor throughout the program's execution with no references by any other processor. The *shared-writable* blocks are referenced by two or more different processors, at least one of which writes the block. Finally, the *shared read-only* blocks are blocks that are referenced by more than one processor, but are never written. The percentages do not sum to 100 since the table does not show the statistics for the shared read-only blocks.

As shown in this table, fewer than 40% of the unique blocks referenced by *arc3d*,

Table 1. Memory Operations and Resulting Network Traffic (b = Number of Words per Block. Word Size = 4 Bytes)

Memory Operation	Forward traffic (bytes)	Reverse traffic (bytes)
Read hit.		
(none)	-	-
Read miss, block *shared* in one or more caches. or only in memory.		
miss service	8	8+4b
Read miss, block *exclusive* in another cache.		
miss service	8	8+4b
write-back	8+4b	8
Write hit, block *shared* in one or more caches.		
processor requests exclusive access from directory	8	-
directory sends invalidation messages	-	8 * #cached
processors acknowledge invalidations	8 * #cached	-
directory acknowledges writing processor	-	8
Write hit, block *exclusive* in this cache.		
(none)	-	-
Write miss, block only in memory.		
miss service	8	8+4b
Write miss, block *shared* in one or more caches.		
processor requests exclusive access from directory	8	-
directory sends invalidation messages	-	8 * #cached
processors acknowledge invalidations	8 * #cached	-
directory acknowledges writing processor	-	8
Write miss, block *exclusive* in another cache.		
miss service	8	8+4b
write-back	8+4b	8

Table 2. Memory-Referencing Characteristics of the Test Programs (Blocks = Number of Unique Single-Word Data Blocks Referenced by the Program. Refs = Number of Memory References Made to the Blocks)

Prog	Total		Private		Shared-writable	
	blocks	refs	%blks	%refs	%blks	%refs
arc3d	53733	6603772	55.6	48.9	38.1	48.9
pic	100087	8765261	77.0	57.0	22.9	34.8
simple24	10759	4251420	10.7	56.5	88.8	43.1
trfd	1478	5877557	11.2	14.9	88.8	70.5
flo52	115331	10000000	82.3	77.1	17.7	22.5
lin125	21041	10000000	21.7	1.2	78.3	94.4

flo52, and *pic* are shared-writable, and fewer than half of their total references are made to these blocks. Most of their references are to private and read-only blocks, and thus do not cause any coherence actions. In contrast, more than 78% of the blocks referenced by *simple24*, *lin125*, and *trfd* are shared-writable, although only *trfd* and *lin125* have more than half of their references to these blocks. These different sharing characteristics provide for a broad range of

memory performance in the simulations to highlight the strengths and weaknesses of the different coherence mechanisms.

2.4 Performance Metrics

The two most important measures of performance for a memory system are the latency and the bandwidth. The *average memory latency* is the time from when a processor issues a memory read operation until the data requested is available to the processor, averaged over all memory references. If the requested data is resident in the cache, the latency is simply the cache access time, which typically is one cycle. If the data is not in the cache, however, a miss service request is generated and sent to the memory system. The average memory delay can be approximated as $T_{ave} = (1 - m)T_{cache} + mT_{miss}$ where m is the cache miss ratio ($0 < m \leq 1$); T_{cache} is the time required to access the cache on a hit; and T_{miss} is the time required by the memory system to service the miss. The value of this miss service time is a function of the intrinsic delay in the memory modules, the time required to propagate the request through the network, and the additional time required to perform any necessary coherence operations. The network delay is a function of the total traffic in the network. High network traffic increases the probability that there will be collisions in the network, which then can increase the miss service time. Because of the dependence of the miss service time on specific parameters of the system, such as the memory access delay, this survey uses the miss ratio as a first-order indication of the expected memory performance.

The *bandwidth* of the interconnection network determines how many data bytes per unit time can be transferred between the memories and the processors. To prevent the network from becoming a performance bottleneck, it is important to provide sufficient bandwidth, but it can be expensive to provide the wide data paths and the fast components needed for a high-bandwidth network. Maintaining coherence in this type of system can require many messages for each memory request, which can put a significant load on the network. As a result, the cache coherence protocol should try to minimize the network traffic by maintaining a low miss rate and by reducing the number of messages required to maintain coherence. The simulations presented in this survey use the average number of bytes transferred per memory request as an indication of the network bandwidth requirements for the different coherence mechanisms.

The total execution time of a program takes into account the trade-offs between the miss ratio and the network traffic, and it is the performance measure that is most interesting to the user of a multiprocessor system. To understand the impact of architectural decisions on the performance of the different coherence mechanisms, however, it is useful to separate the overall performance into the individual factors that contribute to this performance. As a result, the miss ratio and the average network traffic are the metrics used in this survey to compare the different design factors that comprise a cache coherence mechanism. This author feels that examining these two metrics directly provides greater insight into the trade-offs in the coherence mechanisms than by simply comparing total execution times.

3. PERFORMANCE IMPACTS

This section uses the trace-driven simulation model described in the previous section to examine the impact on performance and on implementation cost of the primary design factors affecting cache coherence mechanisms. Descriptions of the different coherence mechanisms are also provided.

3.1 Coherence Detection Strategy

There are several interrelated factors that determine the performance of a cache coherence mechanism. One of the most important factors is *when* the mechanism performs *coherence detection* —either dynamically at run-time, or statically at compile-time. The dynamic coherence detection strategies solve the coherence problem by examining the actual memory addresses generated by a program at run-time and by dynamically keeping track of which processors have a copy of which blocks. In contrast, the static coherence schemes try to predict which memory addresses *may* become stale by analyzing the program's referencing behavior when it is compiled.

It is important to distinguish the *implementation* of a coherence mechanism from its method of determining when a shared-memory location is stale. While the statically detected coherence mechanisms necessarily are software based since they rely on a compiler, they also need some hardware support to maintain the current state information about the memory locations. Thus, it is not precisely correct to refer to these mechanisms as "software-only" coherence mechanisms. Similarly, mechanisms that dynamically detect the need for coherence actions use hardware to monitor the actual memory addresses, but they also can be augmented with compilers and other software to produce hybrid schemes, as described in Section 4. This survey distinguishes the two major classes of coherence mechanisms as *dynamically detected* and *statically detected* instead of as hardware and software mechanisms.

3.1.1 Memory Disambiguation

The ability to *disambiguate memory references*, that is, the ability to determine if two different memory accesses actually refer to the same physical location in memory, is critical to providing a high-performance cache scheme. The primary advantage of the dynamic detection schemes is that by examining the actual memory addresses being referenced, they are able to perfectly disambiguate these accesses. Statically detected coherence schemes, however, must rely on the im-

precise disambiguation performed by the compiler. For example, consider the following sequence of references to the array A( ):

S_1. P_1 read: ...   = A(f(.))

            ...

S_2. P_2 write: A(g(.)) =   ...

            ...

S_3. P_1 read: ...   = A(h(.))

In this sequence of memory references, the read in statement S_1 loads an element of array A( ) into processor P_1's cache. The particular element read is determined by the value of function f(.), which may be anything that produces a valid index into the array. Typically it is some function of the loop count. If functions f(.) and g(.) map into the same memory location, the write in statement S_2 causes the corresponding element in P_1's cache to become stale since it no longer contains a copy of the current value. If function h(.) in statement S_3 also maps to the same memory location, P_1 will attempt to read this stale value, unless it is first invalidated or updated. Determining whether or not some action is required in this case is the crux of the cache coherence problem [Cheong 1988b].

For static coherence detection, a data dependence test [Banerjee 1988; Lichnewsky 1988; Li 1990] can be used to determine if the three functions never refer to the same element, in which case no coherence action is necessary, or to determine if the same element is always referenced by the three statements so that some coherence action must be taken. Unfortunately, the data dependence tests often are too imprecise to determine whether the elements are always the same or always different. In this case, static coherence mechanisms must err on the conservative side by assuming that they are the same element and then inserting the appropriate coherence actions into the generated code.

A related memory disambiguation problem for static coherence detection mechanisms occurs with procedure calls, functions, and subroutines. The name of a variable inside of a procedure most likely will be different than the name of the variable passed to the procedure. To provide precise dependence analysis, the compiler must perform interprocedural analysis to track variable names across procedure boundaries and thereby determine if a particular memory reference may cause a coherence problem. In many programming languages, this interprocedural analysis can be very difficult to perform, in which case the coherence mechanism may have to take an extremely pessimistic approach and invalidate the entire data cache at the entry and exit points of each procedure [Cheong and Veidenbaum 1988a; 1989]. Procedure calls provide no problem for the dynamic coherence detection schemes since they examine the actual memory addresses at run-time and have no indication that a procedure call has even occurred.

3.1.2 Static (Compile-Time) Coherence Detection Mechanisms

The indiscriminate invalidation schemes discussed in Section 1.2.3 [Veidenbaum 1986; Brantley et al. 1985, Edler et al. 1985] are more conservative than is necessary to ensure coherence in that they invalidate cache entries that are not actually stale. This overinvalidation then produces unnecessarily high miss ratios. More complex schemes determine at compile-time which particular cache blocks may become stale, and when they may be stale, and then invalidate these specific entries before they are accessed. Subject to the memory disambiguation limitations of the compiler, these schemes are able to preserve at least some temporal locality between parallel loops.

For example, the *fast, selective invalidation* scheme [Cheong and Veidenbaum 1988a] associates a *change* bit with each cache block. This bit is set true by the *cache-invalidate* instruction inserted by the compiler at each parallel loop boundary to indicate that the block may have been changed during the current loop. The *memory-read* instruction forces a cache miss when it references a block with its *change* bit set to true. This miss ensures that the current copy of the block is fetched from the main memory. The *change* bit then is reset to false when the data block is loaded into the cache. Subsequent *memory-read* references to the same block will see this reset *change* bit and will generate a cache hit since the cached copy is now assured of being up to date.

Another memory-referencing instruction, called the *cache-read* instruction, ignores the *change* bit when it accesses a memory location. It is used to reference a shared-writable location that is guaranteed by the compiler to be up to date in the cache in the current parallel loop, and therefore can be treated as a cache hit. In addition to the *change* bit, this coherence mechanism requires a *valid* bit for each cache block, but no *dirty* bit is required since it uses a write-through strategy. Because each processor is responsible for maintaining coherence in its own cache, no state information is required in the main memory.

Improvements to this fast, selective invalidation scheme use version numbers [Cheong and Veidenbaum 1989] or timestamps [Min and Baer 1989] to determine whether or not a cache entry is up to date when it is referenced. In the version control mechanism [Cheong and Veidenbaum 1989], for instance, each processor maintains a *current version number* (*CVN*) in a separate local memory within the processor for each variable used in a program. For each parallel loop, the compiler predetermines which variables may have been written by any processor during the loop. It then generates instructions that are executed by each processor at the end of a parallel loop to increment the CVN values for these variables. This change in the CVN value indicates to subsequent memory references that a new version of this variable may have been created.

In addition to maintaining one CVN entry per program variable, each cache entry has an associated *birth version number* (*BVN*). The BVN value is set equal to the corresponding CVN value when the referenced variable is first loaded into the cache from the shared memory. When a variable is written, its BVN is set to the new version number, CVN + 1. Because of this defined relationship between the BVN and CVN values, a read reference to a memory location will be a cache hit if and only if BVN ≥ CVN. If BVN < CVN, however, the cached copy may be stale, and the current value must be loaded from the main memory.

3.1.3 Dynamic (Run-Time) Coherence Detection Mechanisms

With dynamic coherence detection, the memory addresses actually generated by the program are examined at run-time to provide perfect memory disambiguation. An example of a coherence mechanism with dynamic detection is the p + 1-bit full directory (Censier and Feautrier 1978]. (Other directory configurations are discussed in Section 3.3.) With this directory, two bits per cache block encode one of three states for each of the blocks in the caches. The *invalid* state means that the block is empty and will cause a cache miss when it is referenced. When a block is shared by several processors, it must be in the *shared read-only* state in each processor to prevent any processor from modifying the block without first requesting *exclusive* access from the directory. A processor is free to update a block in the *exclusive* state since it is assured of having the only copy of the block. The directory in each memory module maintains p *valid* bits and a single *exclusive* bit for each block in the module. If the *exclusive* bit is reset, up to p *valid* bits may be set to indicate which processors have a copy of the block in the *shared read-only* state. If the *exclusive* bit is set for a block, a single *valid* bit will be set to point to the processor that has the only copy of the block, which must be in the *exclusive* state.

3.1.4 Performance Comparisons

The trace-driven simulation methodology described in Section 2 is used to quantify the effect of the coherence detection strategy on the memory system performance. Specifically, the performance of the p + 1-bit full directory [Censier and Feautrier 1978] is compared to the compiler-directed version control coherence mechanism [Cheong and Veidenbaum 1989]. The range of performance of the version control scheme is estimated using three different levels of compiler technology, as summarized in Table 3. The *simple* compiler has imprecise memory disambiguation in that it maintains one version number (i.e., one CVN entry) for an entire array. With this compiler, a write to any element of an array creates a new version of the entire array. Furthermore, this compiler cannot track variable names across subroutine boundaries so that the entire data cache is invalidated at the entry and exit points of each subroutine.

The other extreme of compiler performance for the version control mechanism assumes an *ideal* compiler with perfect memory disambiguation and perfect interprocedural analysis. This compiler maintains a unique CVN entry for each element of every array, and it never invalidates the caches at subroutine boundaries. It models the best possible performance of the version control scheme, but it is probably impossible to implement this perfect memory disambiguation in an actual compiler. The *realistic* compiler compromises between these two extremes with imprecise memory disambiguation, but perfect interprocedural analysis. It should be pointed out that at the end of every parallel loop, the CVN values of every variable that may have had a new version created in that loop must be incremented. The ideal compiler may perform significantly more CVN updates at the end of each parallel loop than the other two compilers since it has to update a CVN value for every array element that was written, instead of a single CVN update per array. The time required to perform this updating adds directly to the average memory delay, which may be significant for large arrays.

Because of the imprecise nature of

Table 3. Compilers Used for the Version Control Simulations

Compiler	Action at subroutine boundaries	Number of *CVN* entries
simple	clear caches	one per array
realistic	ignore subroutine boundaries	one per array
ideal	ignore subroutine boundaries	one per array element

Table 4. Miss Ratio (Percent) for Static and Dynamic Detection Strategies

Program	Directory			Version Control				
				simple overall	realistic overall		ideal	
	read	write	overall			read	write	overall
arc3d	15.0	8.0	23.0	41.6	30.2	19.3	8.3	27.6
pic	8.8	8.9	17.7	32.9	25.9	8.0	8.1	16.1
simple24	9.4	3.1	12.5	63.5	56.0	12.6	3.2	15.8
trfd	10.9	1.5	12.4	42.0	18.0	13.9	4.1	18.0
flo52	1.1	0.8	1.9	44.2	44.1	2.7	1.1	3.8
lin125	5.7	4.2	9.9	9.5	9.4	5.9	0.2	6.1

compile-time data dependence tests, and because of the information hiding in procedures, coherence mechanisms that rely exclusively on the compiler to disambiguate memory references tend to invalidate more cache entries than are actually necessary to maintain coherence. By tracking the actual memory addresses, dynamic directory mechanisms can invalidate only those blocks that are actually stale, which, as shown in Table 4, can cause the directory mechanism to have a lower overall miss ratio than the ideal compiler-directed version control mechanism for the *arc3d*, *simple24*, *trfd*, and *flo52* programs. The directory has slightly higher miss ratios than the ideal implementation of version control for *pic* and *lin125* primarily due to the high number of write misses produced with the directory.

These extra write misses occur because in these two programs, a large, shared array is repeatedly written by different processors during different portions of the programs' execution. When the array is written for the first time, it is marked as exclusive in the writing processor's cache. When another processor tries to over-write this same location, it misses and must request exclusive access from the directory. These misses can be prevented by allocating a new array so as not to overwrite the same array multiple times, but this approach will require additional memory space. With the version control mechanism, the compiler detects that these write references will not cause coherence violations, and thereby reduces the number of write misses. The performance of the *simple* compiler tends to be poor compared to the other compilers and compared to the directory since it invalidates all of the caches at every subroutine boundary. The *realistic* compiler has slightly better performance than the simple compiler because it can look beyond subroutine boundaries, but its miss ratio generally still is higher than that of the ideal compiler due to its imprecise memory disambiguation.

A major advantage of the static coherence detection mechanisms is that by making each processor responsible for maintaining coherence in its own cache using self-invalidation, interprocessor communication is limited to that required to service the cache misses. The

Table 5. Network Traffic for Static and Dynamic Detection Strategies (Bytes Per Reference)

Program	Directory			Version Control		
	miss	invalidate	total	simple	realistic	ideal
arc3d	4.59	5.40	9.98	8.32	6.04	5.52
pic	3.53	4.47	8.00	6.58	5.18	3.23
simple24	2.43	2.44	4.87	12.7	11.2	3.17
trfd	2.48	2.27	4.75	8.40	3.61	3.61
flo52	0.39	0.40	0.79	8.83	8.81	0.76
lin125	1.99	1.99	3.98	1.90	1.87	1.22

dynamic mechanism, on the other hand, sends many messages between the directory and the processors which increases the congestion in the interconnection network compared to the static mechanism and thereby may increase the memory latency. As shown in Table 5, the total network traffic for the ideal compiler in the version control mechanism is approximately the same as the network traffic required to service only the misses with the directory. These similar traffic requirements are expected since these two approaches have similar miss ratios. However, this table also shows that the network traffic required by the directory for the invalidation messages approximately doubles the total network traffic over that required for servicing only the misses. The simple and realistic compilers in the version control approach produce higher network traffic than the ideal compiler since they have significantly higher miss ratios. Even with these higher miss ratios, though, the network traffic they produce can be less than the total network traffic produced by the directory since they generate no invalidation messages.

In summary, the primary advantage of dynamic coherence detection is its perfect memory disambiguation. By knowing precisely those addresses being referenced, the dynamic mechanism invalidates only those cache blocks that are actually stale. This exact invalidation generally produces lower miss ratios than a mechanism that statically detects coherence violations. Additionally, the dynamic detection mechanism is completely transparent to procedure boundaries, while the static coherence detection mechanism requires good interprocedural analysis to match the performance of the dynamic mechanism. The primary advantage of static detection mechanisms is that they produce lower network traffic than the dynamic mechanisms since they do not require any invalidation messages. Similar results to the simulations presented here have been reported in other studies comparing compiler-directed and directory-based coherence mechanisms [Adve et al. 1991; Lilja 1991; Min and Baer 1990].

3.2 Coherence Enforcement Strategy

Another factor affecting the performance of a multiprocessor memory system is the actual method used by the coherence scheme to ensure that no processor accesses a stale-memory location. The simplest approach is to make all shared-writable memory locations *noncacheable* so that there can never by multiple copies [Lilja et al. 1989]. However, since references to shared-writable variables can constitute a large fraction of the references made by a program (see Table 2), bypassing the cache for all references to these memory locations can significantly reduce performance. Two other coherence enforcement strategies always allow shared-writable memory locations to be cached, but either *update* or *invalidate* stale-cache entries before they are referenced again. With an update approach, the new value of the shared location is distributed to all processors with a copy of the block whenever it is written by any processor. The advantage of this approach is that it prevents an additional miss if the cache block is reused by a processor with a cached copy after it has been written by another processor. A significant disadvantage is the additional network traffic produced by the potentially large number of update messages.

Instead of updating cached copies when they are changed, the invalidation strategy marks all cached copies as *invalid* within the cache to force the processor to miss the next time it references that block. This approach reduces the network traffic compared to the update strategy, but it does introduce the extra delay of another miss if the block is reused. Invalidation schemes can be classified as either *self-invalidation* or *directed-invalidation*. With self-invalidation, the compiler inserts extra instructions into the generated code to force the processor to invalidate some or all of its data cache before it accesses a stale entry. With directed-invalidation, some outside agent, such as a directory, forces a processor to invalidate a specific block in its cache at a specified time.

3.2.1 Performance Comparisons

In a system in which all of the processors are connected with a shared bus, an update protocol is implemented by having each write to a shared-memory location write-through to the bus to broadcast the new value to all of the processors [McCreight 1984; Thacker et al. 1988]. In the system used in this survey, however, the bus is replaced by a multistage interconnection network. Since this type of network does not support broadcasting, coherence updates are implemented using individual messages. For example, when a processor writes to a shared-memory location, a message containing the new value is sent to the directory. The directory then sends a message containing the new value to each processor with a cached copy of the block instructing the processors to update their copies. The processors respond with an acknowl-

edgment to the directory, which then acknowledges the processor that performed the initial write. With this approach, updates of written blocks are sent only to processors that actually have a cached copy instead of being broadcast to all of the processors. The invalidation-based directory coherence simulator described in Section 2.2 is modified to use this update-based protocol.

Table 6 compares the miss ratios produced by a directory coherence scheme using either updating or invalidating for three different cache sizes. In the infinite cache, blocks are never replaced due to lack of cache space. Consequently, with an update strategy in an infinite cache, once a block is moved into the cache, it is never removed. The number of misses in this configuration then is simply the number of misses required to bring each block into the cache the first time. That is, the number of misses is the same as the number of unique blocks referenced, and it is the minimum number of misses that can be produced for the given programs. Comparing the invalidation strategy in the infinite cache with the update strategy shows how the invalidations required to maintain coherence increase the miss ratio due to the sharing of cache blocks by different processors. In particular, it demonstrates the performance effect of requiring exclusive access to a block in order to write to the block. Since updating allows writes to blocks that are shared, updating typically produces a lower miss ratio than invalidating. As the cache size is reduced, the miss ratio increases for both updating and invalidating since there is no longer enough space in the caches to store all of the referenced blocks.

The network traffic statistics in Table 7 show that the cost of the lower miss ratio with updating is the considerably higher network traffic it produces compared to the traffic produced by invalidating. This table separates the network traffic into that required to move the data into a cache on a miss, and into that required to maintain coherence, which is either the update traffic or the invalidate

Table 6. Miss Ratio (Percent) for Updating and Invalidating Coherence Enforcement Strategies

Program	Cache size (bytes)					
	4K		16K		∞	
	inv	up	inv	up	inv	up
arc3d	26.8	16.0	19.9	6.73	18.0	1.7
pic	28.6	26.9	8.4	6.8	7.8	1.4
simple24	13.5	6.4	11.2	3.6	9.3	0.73
trfd	12.4	0.39	12.4	0.38	12.4	0.38
flo52	2.1	1.7	1.9	1.4	1.8	1.4
lin125	10.0	1.7	10.0	1.6	10.0	1.6

Table 7. Network Traffic (Bytes Per Reference) Due to Cache Misses and Due to Coherence Enforcement for Updating and Invalidating

Program	Strategy	Cache size (bytes)					
		4K		16K		∞	
		miss	coh	miss	coh	miss	coh
arc3d	invalidate	5.36	5.56	3.97	5.17	3.61	5.13
	update	3.21	12.6	1.34	15.0	0.34	16.2
pic	invalidate	5.72	3.35	1.68	2.26	1.56	2.78
	update	5.39	7.69	1.36	8.87	0.29	10.1
simple24	invalidate	2.69	2.39	2.23	2.49	1.86	2.68
	update	1.27	7.37	0.71	.7.54	0.15	7.96
trfd	invalidate	2.49	2.27	2.49	2.27	2.49	2.27
	update	0.08	52.3	0.08	52.3	0.08	52.3
flo52	invalidate	0.43	0.45	0.37	0.42	0.36	0.31
	update	0.35	5.23	0.29	5.40	0.27	6.39
lin125	invalidate	1.99	1.88	1.99	1.88	1.99	1.89
	update	0.34	27.1	0.32	27.3	0.32	27.4

traffic. The miss traffic for updating is always less than that generated by invalidating since its miss ratio is lower than the miss ratio with invalidating. However, the component of the network traffic due to coherence actions is roughly 2 to 25 times greater for updating that invalidating since updating produces some network traffic on every write to a shared-memory location. The invalidation strategy, on the other hand, produces coherence traffic only when a processor first requests exclusive access to a block, or when a write-back is required. Subsequent writes to the same block by the same processor generate no additional traffic.

How the differences in network traffic and miss ratios translate to overall memory delay depends on the implementation details of each individual system. For instance, given a high-bandwidth network, an updating strategy probably will produce lower average memory delays than invalidating since updating has the lowest miss ratio. The high traffic produced by updating may be easily handled by the network without increasing the memory delay. However, if the interconnection network is the system bottleneck, as it is likely to be in many systems, then invalidating may produce the best overall performance in spite of its relatively higher miss ratio since it produces the lowest network traffic.

3.2.2 Adaptive Coherence Enforcement

In addition to the effect these implementation details have on performance, the sharing characteristics of a program also can affect the relative performance of updating and invalidating. In some programs, an invalidation strategy may produce the best performance, while in other programs, an updating strategy may be best [Eggers and Katz 1989b; Karline et al. 1986]. For instance, if a shared block tends to be written by only a single processor, but read by many processors, distributing the new values of the block produced by each write using an updating strategy will reduce the miss ratio when compared to an invalidating strategy. If a block is written many times by a single processor between reads by other processors, however, an invalidating strategy will tend to reduce the unnecessary network traffic that would be produced by an updating strategy. Furthermore, the sharing characteristics of a single block may change over the course of a program's execution making updating the best choice for some references to the block, while other references to the same block may produce better performance using invalidating. To adjust the coherence enforcement strategy to the potentially changing sharing patterns of each block, several *adaptive* coherence schemes have been proposed.

The competitive snoopy cache [Karline et al. 1986] initially updates all shared copies of a block by broadcasting writes to these blocks over the shared bus. If a processor has not referenced its copy of the block after a specified number of writes, it invalidates its cached copy so that it no longer requires the block updates. Similarly, the EDWP coherence scheme [Archibald 1988] dynamically switches from an updating strategy to an invalidating strategy by keeping track of the number of writes made to each block. After three writes are made to a block by the same processor with no intervening reads by other processors, the block is assumed to be no longer actively shared, and all of the cached copies are invalidated. These two approaches thus attempt to dynamically adjust the coherence enforcement strategy based on the program's run-time behavior.

The Munin system [Bennett et al. 1990] implements a coherence mechanism that uses the compiler to categorize each object referenced by the program into a coherence type, and it then adjusts the coherence enforcement strategy to each particular type. For example, a data object that is determined to be mostly read is copied to each processors' cache as it is referenced, but an object that is alternately read and written may have a single copy moved among the processors instead of being copied. Another adaptive coherence strategy [Mounes-Toussi 1993] examines the program at compile-time to estimate the cost of using updating or invalidating for each write reference to a shared memory block. Each reference then is tagged with the lowest-cost coherence enforcement strategy to be used at run-time. Simulation studies of this approach indicate that by switching enforcement strategies for each shared block, it can obtain the low miss ratios of an updating coherence strategy while generating the low network traffic of an invalidating strategy, thereby achieving the best of both enforcement strategies. Additionally, since the compiler can look ahead in a program to predict future memory-sharing patterns, this compiler-assisted adaptive scheme tends to produce lower miss ratios and lower network traffic than the adaptive schemes that switch enforcement strategies using only run-time information.

3.3 Precision of Block-Sharing Information

Coherence schemes that dynamically determine which memory references need coherence actions have access to the memory addresses only as the program generates them. Since it is impossible for the hardware to predict how the blocks will be shared, the coherence mechanism must track the state and sharing characteristics of every memory block referenced by the program. The number of memory bits needed to store this information can be enormous. *Exact* mechanisms, such as the $p + 1$-bit full directory [Censier and Feautrier 1978], maintain enough state information about the sharing of blocks to know exactly which processors have a copy of which blocks. When a block needs to be invalidated, these exact mechanisms send invalidation messages only to those processors that actually have a cached copy of the block. *Imprecise* mechanisms, such as the n-pointer plus broadcast directory [Agarwal et al. 1988], reduce the amount of stored information, but occasionally must resort to broadcasting invalidation messages to all processors, even those without a cached copy of the affected block. These broadcasts can significantly increase the memory traffic in the interconnection network. Some recently proposed *tagged* directories further reduce the directory memory requirements by maintaining sharing information only for blocks that are actually cached. The following subsections describe the various directories, and present current models [Lilja 1991] for comparing the number of memory bits needed by each directory to maintain the cache-block-sharing information.

3.3.1 Traditional Directories

In the traditional directories, memory bits are associated with each block in the memory modules to maintain the current state of the block and to store information about which processors have a cached copy of each block. The $p + 1$-bit full directory [Censier and Feautrier 1978], for example, encodes three states for each cached block using two state bits per cache block. In the *invalid* state, the block is empty or not up to date. In the *shared*, *read-only* state, the block is shared and can only be read by all processors. A processor with a block in the *exclusive* state is assured of having the only copy. Thus, it can both read and write the block. The directory maintains an additional p *valid* bits and a single *exclusive* bit for each block in the memory, where p is the number of processors. The total number of bits dedicated to storing coherence information in this scheme is $p[m(p + 1) + 2c]$, where m is the total number of blocks in the memory modules, and c is the total number of blocks in the caches.

The broadcast directory [Archibald and

Baer 1984] maintains only the *valid* and *exclusive* state bits for each block in the memories and the caches, for a total of $2p(m + c)$ bits. Because it maintains only this limited information, this directory must broadcast all of its invalidation messages to all of the processors. These broadcasts can be very time consuming in a system with a complex interconnection network, such as a multistage network, since these networks typically do not support broadcasting. Additionally, these broadcasts increase the average memory delay compared to the full directory due to the increased network congestion. The primary advantage of this directory structure is its low memory requirements for storing the block-sharing information.

The n-pointers plus broadcast scheme [Agarwal et al. 1988] reduces the need for broadcasting by maintaining n pointers with each memory block to point to the first n processors that request a copy of the block. When a block needs to be invalidated, invalidation messages can be sent only to the processors with a cached copy of the block. If more than n processors attempt to simultaneously share the same block, the directory sets a *broadcast* bit to indicate that invalidations must be broadcast to all of the processors. This approach thereby trades-off memory requirements with the need to broadcast. Each of the n pointers in each of the entries in this directory requires $\log_2 p$ bits to point to any processor, plus a bit for each pointer to indicate if it contains a valid processor number. Additionally, each entry requires the single *broadcast* bit plus an *exclusive* bit. Finally, each block in the data caches requires two state bits, making a total of $p[2c + m(2 + n + n \log_2 p)]$ bits dedicated to maintaining coherence for this directory structure.

The *linked-list* directory [James et al. 1990] reduces the size of the directory compared to the full-directory structure without requiring broadcasts by maintaining a linked list from the directory to each of the processors having a cached copy of a block. A doubly linked list typically is used so that normal cache block

42

replacements may be performed within a processor without communicating with other processors. When a block is invalidated due to a coherence operation, the invalidation command is propagated from one end of the list to every processor that has a copy of the block. This single-ended propagation eliminates the potential race condition that exists if invalidations were propagated simultaneously from both ends. The total number of coherence bits required in this linked list directory is $p[3c + 2m + 2(c + m)\log_2 p]$ since each pointer in each memory block and in each cache block requires $\log_2 p$ bits to point to a processor, plus an extra bit to point back to memory. Additionally, two state bits are used in each cache block, and an *exclusive* bit is needed for each memory block.

3.3.2 Tagged Directories

In the traditional directories described in the previous section, memory bits for pointing to a processor with a cached copy of a block are statically associated with each block in the main memory. Thus, the total number of coherence bits is proportional to the size of the memory. The *tagged directories* take advantage of the observation that only blocks actually cached in one or more processors need to be allocated pointers. In these directories, pointers are dynamically associated with memory blocks using an address tag field only as the blocks are moved from the memory to a cache. With this approach, the number of coherence pointers is proportional to the size of the data caches, which are significantly smaller than the main memory. A variety of different configurations can be used to maintain the coherence pointers themselves, such as those used in the full $p + 1$-bit directory, the n-pointers directory, or the linked-list directory discussed in the previous section. Additionally, several other possible tagged-directory structures are described below.

The *pointer cache* tagged directory [Lilja 1991] maintains one pointer of $\log_2 p$ bits with each address tag of $\log_2 m$ bits. This structure allows multi-ple entries in the directory to have the same address tag. When n processors share the same block, n distinct pointer entries will be allocated in the directory with the same address tag, but pointing to different processors. The maximum number of processors that can share a block with this scheme is limited by the associativity, a, of the pointer cache itself. When more than a processors try to share a block, or when the entire pointer cache overflows, a free pointer is created by randomly choosing an active pointer and invalidating the selected block in the indicated processor.

The total number of bits needed to store sharing information with this pointer cache is $[r(\log_2 m + \log_2 p + 2) + 2c]p$, where r is the number of entries in each pointer cache. Typical values of r required for good performance are discussed in the next section. This bit count includes the $\log_2 m$ address tag bits, the $\log_2 p$ processor pointer bits, the pointer valid bit, and the exclusive state bit needed for each pointer, plus the two state bits needed for each block in the data cache. No additional coherence bits are needed in the shared memory since the tagged directories store this sharing information only when a block is actually cached.

The *tag cache* directory [O'Krafka and Newton 1990] is a variation of the pointer cache idea that uses two levels of caches in the directory. The first level of the tag cache associates n pointers with each address tag. When a block is shared by more than n processors, the corresponding entry in the tag cache is overflowed to the second-level tag cache. This second-level cache uses the $p + 1$-bit structure of the full directory for each address tag. Overflows of this second-level tag cache are handled by invalidating a randomly selected entry to be reused by another block. The number of bits dedicated to maintaining coherence with this directory structure is $p[r_1(\log_2 m + n \log_2 p + 2) + r_2(\log_2 m + p + 2) + 2c]$ where r_1 and r_2 are the number of entries in the two levels of the tag cache.

The *coarse vector* tagged directory [Gupta et al. 1990] incorporates a mode bit into each pointer entry to force the directory controller to interpret the pointer in one of two different ways. If the mode bit is reset, then the v pointer bits are interpreted as n direct pointers to processors. Since $\log_2 p$ bits are required to uniquely identify a processor, each entry can point to $n = \lfloor v/\log_2 p \rfloor$ unique processors. If more than n processors attempt to simultaneously share the same block, the mode bit is set to indicate that the pointer bits should be interpreted as pointing to one of the p/g clusters, where there are g processors per cluster. That is, when the mode bit is set, the ith bit of the v pointer bits will be turned on to indicate that at least one of the processors in the ith cluster has a copy of the shared block. Invalidation messages then will be sent to all of the processors in each cluster that has its corresponding bit set in the tag cache entry. The total number of bits needed for coherence with this directory structure is $r_{cc} p[\log_2 m + max(p/g, \log_2 p) + 3] + 2cp$, where r_{cc} is the number of entries in the tag cache. The max function is needed to ensure that at least one complete processor number of $\log_2 p$ bits can be stored in the v bits.

The *LimitLESS* directory, which was proposed as part of the Alewife project [Chaiken et al. 1991], uses hardware and software to implement a combination of the n-pointers per address tag structure of the previously discussed tag cache, plus the $p + 1$-bit full directory. Specifically, when more than n processors attempt to share a block, an interrupt service routine is invoked to emulate the complete sharing information of the full directory. Since it is assumed that more than n processors will attempt to share the same block infrequently, the performance of this combined hardware/ software approach should be comparable to that of the other tagged directories.

3.3.3 Cost and Performance Comparisons

There are two primary components of the hardware implementation cost of a cache coherence mechanism: (1) the control logic required to implement the mecha-nism and (2) the number of memory bits needed to store the cache-block-sharing information. It is difficult to quantify the control logic cost of the different coherence mechanisms without detailed circuit designs since the complexity of this logic can vary considerably. With detailed designs, the implementation cost can be measured as the VLSI chip area needed to implement the control logic, for instance, but this comparison is beyond the scope of this survey. Instead, the amount of memory used to store coherence information is used for an approximate comparison of the implementation cost since it can be a significant portion of the total cost of implementing the mechanism.

To compare the memory requirements of the different coherence mechanisms, the memory overhead is defined to be the ratio of the total number of bits dedicated to coherence functions divided by the total number of data bits in both the main memories and the data caches [Lilja 1991]. The total number of data bits in the system is $D = pbw(m + c)$, where p is the number of processors; b is the number of words in each block; w is the number of bits per word; m is the number of blocks in each of the p memory modules; and c is the number of blocks in each of the p caches. If N_x is the number of bits dedicated to coherence functions for a particular coherence scheme, the corresponding overhead is $O_x = N_x/D$.

Table 8 shows the memory overhead for several different directories that maintain different amounts of block-sharing information. In this table, the memory overhead is normalized to the number of blocks in the data cache, c. The ratio of the number of pointer cache entries in each memory module, r, to the number of blocks in each data cache is $s = r/c$, and $k = m/c$ is the ratio of the number of blocks in memory, m, to the number of blocks in the data caches.

A 4-way set associate pointer cache is used to provide a fair comparison of a realistic pointer cache implementation. An invalidation on overflow policy is used to create free pointers when the pointer cache overflows. A random replacement

Table 8. Normalized Memory Overhead for the Directory Mechanisms

Scheme	Overhead, O_x
1. $(p+1)$-bit full directory	$\dfrac{k(p+1)+2}{bw(k+1)}$
2. 2-bit broadcast directory	$\dfrac{2}{bw}$
3. n-pointer + broadcast directory	$\dfrac{k(2+n+n\log_2 p)+2}{bw(k+1)}$
4. Linked list directory	$\dfrac{2(k+1)\log_2 p+2k+3}{bw(k+1)}$
5. Pointer cache directory	$\dfrac{s[\log_2(kc)+\log_2 p+3]+2}{bw(k+1)}$

policy is used in both the pointer caches and in the fully associative data caches. The word size is $w = 32$ bits with $p = 32$ processors, and the data cache block size is $b = 1$ word. Typical cache memory sizes are in the range of 64 KB (2^{16}) words to 256 KB (2^{18}) words, and a typical memory module may contain from 2 MB (2^{21}) words to 16 MB (2^{24}) words. Thus, typical values of $k = m/c$, which is the ratio of the number of blocks in each memory module to the number of blocks in each data cache, are in the range of 8 to 256. The following simulations use $k = 256$. The data cache again is $c = 8$ KB in each of the $p = 32$ processors.

The network traffic generated by the different directories is shown in Figure 3(a–f) plotted against their respective overheads. The number of pointer entries available in the pointer cache tagged directory, r, relative to the number of blocks in the data cache, c, is varied from $s = r/c = 1/32$ to $s = 2/1$, doubling with each data point. When s is small, there are not enough pointers available to point to all of the processors that try to share cache blocks. As a result, pointers frequently must be reused by randomly choosing an active pointer and invalidating the block in the processor to which it points. These frequent pointer invalidations produce a large number of invalidation messages, which then generate a large amount of network traffic. In all of the programs tested, a pointer is usually available when one is needed when the number of pointers available in the pointer cache is the same as the number of blocks in the data caches (i.e., $s = 1$). This one-to-one ratio usually is adequate because the memory references tend to be uniformly distributed among all of the memory modules. Thus, requests for pointers also tend to be uniformly distributed.

Even with this pointer cache size of $s = 1$, the memory overhead of the pointer cache directory is significantly smaller than the overhead of the other directories. The 2-bit broadcast directory has the next lowest memory overhead since it stores only 2 bits for each block in the memory. However, it does not maintain precise information about which processors have cached copies of blocks, forcing it to broadcast all of its invalidation messages. These broadcasts

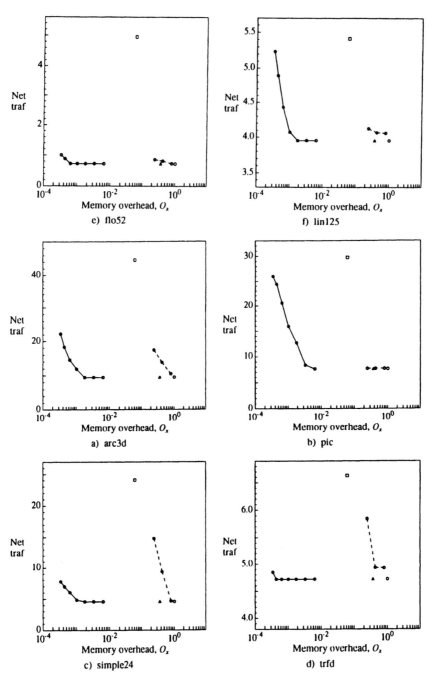

solid line = pointer cache tagged directory, $s=1/32, 1/16, 1/8, 1/4, 1/2, 1/1, 2/1$
square point = 2-bit broadcast
triangle point = linked list
dashed line = n-pointer plus broadcast, $n=1,2,4$
circle point = full directory

Figure 3. The effect of the precision of block-sharing information (memory overhead) on network traffic.

produce extremely high network traffic compared to the other directories. The overhead of the n-pointer directory increases in direct proportion to n, the number of pointers it has available per block. It produces very high network traffic when $n = 1$ since it must resort to broadcasting whenever more than one processor attempts to share the same block. Since fewer than four processors typically attempt to share the same block at the same time in most of these traces (and in many other programs [Agarwal et al. 1988; Eggers and Katz 1988; Weber and Gupta 1989]), $n = 4$ pointers often is sufficient to reduce the network traffic of this mechanism to be approximately the same as that of the full directory. The network traffic of the linked-list directory is the same as that for the full directory since both send invalidations only to those processors that actually have a cached copy of the block. Its memory overhead is less than that of the full directory, however, since it maintains fewer total pointers.

The miss ratio of the pointer cache tagged directory follows a curve similar to its network traffic. With a small pointer cache, many active blocks are invalidated to obtain free pointers. When these active blocks are again referenced, they force the processor to miss. When the size of the pointer cache increases to $s = 1$, the data cache miss ratio improves to be the same as the full directory. The other directories all produce identical data cache miss ratios since they all allow up to p processors to simultaneously cache the same block. The precision of block-sharing information each maintains (i.e., the memory overhead) affects only the number of invalidation messages they need to generate, and thus affects only the total network traffic and not the miss ratio.

While the network traffic and the miss ratio produced by the linked-list scheme is the same as that produced by the full directory, the average memory latency of the linked-list scheme is expected to be higher than that of the directory. This longer delay occurs because the entire linked list for a shared block must be traversed when the block is invalidated. This list traversal time adds directly to the delay for the write that triggered the invalidation when a strongly ordered consistency model is used. With a weakly ordered model, however, much of this delay may be hidden. With a full-directory scheme, on the other hand, the generation and sending of all of the invalidation messages can be pipelined to further reduce the memory delay.

These simulations demonstrate that the memory overhead of the directory mechanisms is directly related to the precision of the block-sharing information they maintain and is inversely related to the corresponding memory traffic. That is, more information must be stored in order to reduce the network traffic. However, a tagged cache directory can provide the low network traffic of a full directory while using very little memory since it maintains the sharing information only for blocks that are actually cached. The additional cost of the tagged directory compared to a traditional directory is the relatively more complex control logic it requires.

3.4 Cache Block Size

The cache *block size*, also called the *line size*, is the number of consecutive memory words updated or invalidated as a single unit. The *fetch size*, on the other hand, is the number of words moved from the main memory to the cache on a miss. While these two parameters do not have to be the same, the following discussion assumes that a single block is fetched per miss. Increasing the number of words in a cache block can reduce the miss ratio because of the high probability that memory locations physically near recently referenced locations will be referenced in the near future (i.e., spatial locality). When the block size becomes too large, the miss ratio increases since the probability of using the additional fetched data becomes smaller than the probability of reusing the data replaced. The block size that minimizes the average memory delay generally is smaller than the block size that minimizes the miss ratio because the additional time required to transfer the larger blocks can overwhelm the latency to receive the first word [Przybylski et al. 1988; Smith 1987].

In addition to allowing a cache to exploit spatial locality, another advantage of blocks larger than a single word is that they reduce the memory overhead of the directory coherence mechanisms. Since pointer information is maintained only for blocks and not for individual words, Table 8 shows that the cache coherence memory overhead is inversely related to the block size. For example, doubling the block size will cut the overhead in half. This relationship is not true for the compiler-directed coherence mechanisms, such as version control, however, since they still need a dirty bit per word, independent of the block size.

Unfortunately, cache blocks larger than a single word can introduce *false sharing* in which two nonshared words end up occupying the same block. For instance, when a loop scans through an array, the *stride* is the array subscript increment from one iteration to the next. If the stride is one, consecutive elements of the array will be accessed by consecutive iterations of the loop. If the iterations are distributed sequentially across the processors, consecutive array elements will be referenced by different processors. When the cache block size is greater than one array element, and the array elements are arranged linearly in memory, many processors will need a copy of the same block, causing a large amount of sharing. This type of sharing is referred to as false sharing since the processors are not actually sharing data, but are sharing memory blocks due to the placement of the array elements in memory. As long as the processors only read the array, this sharing is not harmful, but when a processor attempts to write to an element when using an invalidation protocol, all the copies of the written block will be invalidated, even though not all of the elements are changed. In the worse case, every write to the shared block will cause an invalidation, and every read will be a cache miss, so that blocks will *ping-pong* between caches. As a result, the processor miss ratios and ·the memory network traffic increase compared to a system with a block size of one word, thereby increasing the average memory delay.

To eliminate the false-sharing problem, many dynamic coherence schemes use small blocks, in which case they lose the potential benefits of exploiting spatial locality [Agarwal and Gupta 1988; Eggers and Katz 1989a; Goodman 1983; Lee et al. 1987]. The statically detected coherence schemes also tend to favor small block sizes. With block sizes larger than one word, the compiler must know the block size, and it must control the placement of the data in the memory. If the compiler ignores the block size, false sharing can introduce dependences between otherwise independent program statements. These hidden dependences then can cause incorrect program execution since coherence will not be correctly maintained. The solution to this problem is to use one-word blocks or to restrict data placement so that each block containsonly one unique variable name. For arrays, this restriction has little effect beyond some fragmentation in the last block allocated to the array, but if large blocks are used, a substantial amount of memory space may be wasted on scalar variables since only one variable can be assigned to a block.

3.4.1 Performance Effects

Figure 4 demonstrates how the cache block size affects the network traffic and miss ratio for the $p + 1$-bit full directory. The other directory schemes are not shown since they have similar behavior, and the version control scheme is not simulated with block sizes larger than one word due to compiler limitations. Each word is four bytes, and the block size is varied from 1 to 16 words (4 to 64 bytes). The fetch size is set to one block, so that one complete block is fetched on a miss. The parallel loop iterations are

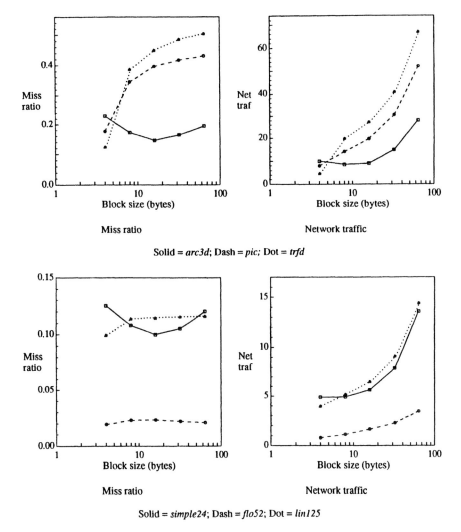

Miss ratio

Network traffic

Solid = *arc3d*; Dash = *pic;* Dot = *trfd*

Miss ratio

Network traffic

Solid = *simple24*; Dash = *flo52*; Dot = *lin125*

Figure 4. Effect of cache block size on miss ratio and network traffic (bytes/reference).

scheduled with iteration 1 executing on processor 0, iteration 2 on processor 1, and so on. (The effects of different scheduling strategies have been discussed elsewhere [Lilja 1992].)

The lowest miss ratios for *arc3d* and *simple24* occur with a block size of four words, indicating that there is some spatial locality that can be exploited in these programs when using this scheduling strategy. As the block size is increased, however, the larger blocks begin to evict blocks that are still in use, which then increases the miss ratio. For the other programs tested, the lowest miss ratios are produced with single-word blocks due to significant amounts of false sharing with blocks larger than a single word.

Figure 4 also shows that the total network traffic increases as the block size increases. Figure 5 separates this network traffic into the component required to move the blocks into the caches on a miss and into the component required to

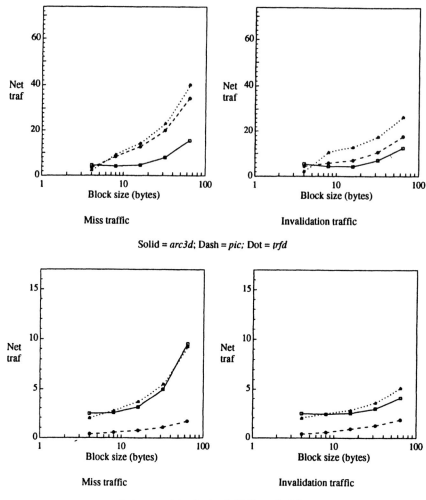

Figure 5. Components of total network traffic due to cache misses and due to invalidations from data sharing.

send the invalidation messages from the directory to the individual processors. For the *arc3d* and *simple24* programs, the network traffic due to misses is relatively flat as the block size increases from 4 to 16 bytes. Since in these two programs the miss ratio decreases as the block size increases to 16 bytes, there are fewer blocks fetched, but each block is larger. The result is that the miss traffic remains approximately constant until the miss ratio begins to increase when the block size is greater than 16 bytes. The invalidation traffic produced by these two programs decreases slightly as the block size increases from 4 to 16 bytes indicating that there is little false sharing until the block size is larger than 16 bytes. This reduction in invalidation traffic shows that the caches are exploiting the available spatial locality, which also is reflected in the reduced miss ratios.

In the other programs, the miss traffic increases significantly as the block size is increased due to the combination of higher miss ratios 'and the fetching of larger blocks. The increases in the invalidation traffic with the larger blocks for these programs shows that the increases in the miss ratios are due, at least in part, to the false-sharing effect. That is, as the block size is increased there is more false sharing, which then requires more invalidations to maintain cache coherence. It is interesting to note that the invalidation traffic generally contributes about half as much to the total traffic as does the miss traffic. Thus, the larger blocks tend to cause more network traffic than the traffic produced by the additional invalidation messages from the false-sharing effect.

4. HYBRID TECHNIQUES

The use of the different cache coherence mechanisms is not mutually exclusive in that several of the different mechanisms can be combined into a single system. This section presents several such hybrid mechanisms.

4.1 Compiler Assistance for Reducing the Directory Size

By allocating pointers to blocks only as they are referenced, the tagged directories can significantly reduce the memory requirements of a directory-based cache coherence scheme. They still waste some directory resources, however, by allocating pointers to blocks that cannot cause coherence problems, such as blocks that are never written or are never shared. To reduce the number of pointers allocated, it is possible to use the compiler to mark all private and read-only blocks as not needing coherence enforcement. Several studies [Agarwal and Gupta 1988; Eggers and Katz 1988; Lilja et al. 1989; Weber and Gupta 1989] have shown that a substantial fraction of all blocks referenced by a program may be private or read-only, and thus they could be marked as not needing coherence enforcement.

When used with a tagged directory, this compiler marking can significantly reduce the number of pointers needed in a given program and can thereby substantially reduce the required directory size [Lilja and Yew 1991]. More complex compile-time analysis techniques can mark each individual memory reference as needing a pointer allocated or not [Nguyen et al. 1993]. This more precise marking can reduce the time a pointer is needed for a specific shared-memory location, thereby allowing pointers to be reused more frequently than with no marking. This frequent reuse further reduces the size of the directory needed to maintain a given level of memory performance.

4.2 Combining Multiple Coherence Mechanisms

The DASH distributed shared-memory multiprocessor prototype developed at Stanford University [Lenoski et al. 1990; 1992] incorporates two different dynamic coherence mechanisms, a snooping bus and a directory, and two different coherence enforcement mechanisms, invalidating and updating, into a single system. The processors in this system are divided into groups, or *clusters*, with four high-performance MIPS R3000 processors in each cluster. Cache coherence within each cluster is maintained using a bus-based snooping protocol [Papamarcos and Patel 1984]. Coherence among clusters, in contrast, is maintained using a directory-based invalidation protocol where the directory appears to be another processor on the snooping bus in each cluster.

An interesting feature of this directory is that, in addition to the standard invalidation protocol, it also supports two different update mechanisms. The first is an *update-write* operation in which the new data produced by the write is directly distributed to all processors with a cached copy of the block being written. The sharing information stored in the directory is used to determine which processors need to be updated. The second update mechanism is called the *deliver* operation. With this operation, the processor writing to a block writes into the cache using the invalidate protocol. When it has completed its sequence of writes, it issues a *deliver* instruction specifying which clusters should receive a copy of the block. The directory then sends a copy to each of the specified clusters, and the directory is updated appropriately. This write mechanism is useful when the desired destination clusters are unlikely to have a copy of the block already cached, thereby making the *update-write* inadequate.

4.3 Compiler-Plus-Directory Coherence Mechanism

While the version control [Cheong and Veidenbaum 1989] and timestamp [Min and Baer 1989] coherence mechanisms keep extra state information in each cache to help preserve temporal locality between parallel tasks, another mechanism that combines static and dynamic coherence detection [Chen and Veidenbaum 1991] keeps this extra state information in a directory in the memory modules. The directory monitors the memory references generated by the program and dynamically updates its state to precisely determine which caches contain which memory blocks, and whether the blocks have been modified. At the parallel task boundary, each processor sequentially scans through its cache and invalidates the cache entries that the stored directory information specifies should be invalidated. Of course, this sequential scan could significantly increase the execution time of the program, but this coherence mechanism may be able to reduce the network traffic compared to a conventional directory. Unlike a conventional directory-based coherence mechanism, this approach uses the directory only to ensure that all cached blocks are updated with the correct state at the parallel-task boundary, and not to perform dynamic invalidations. Consequently, it implicitly implements a weakly ordered consistency model.

4.4 Extending the Memory Hierarchy into the Network

Instead of using the interconnection network for only moving data between the memory modules and the caches, it is possible to extend the memory hierarchy into the network itself. It may be possible to simplify the cache coherence mechanism and to simultaneously improve performance by caching data within the switches of the network. For example, the Memory Hierarchy Network (Mizrahi et al. 1989] adds a local memory to each switch in the network to cache the data being referenced by the processors that are connected to the switch. Additionally, the switches maintain a distributed directory of where data is stored in the system. To simplify the coherence mechanism, only a single copy of a block is allowed in the system. This single copy then migrates through the network as it is referenced by the different processors.

One of the critical parameters in this type of system is the block migration policy. This policy determines when a shared block should migrate and how far up the network it should move. Simulations of this network with different migration policies have indicated that distributing the directory throughout the network can significantly improve the performance of the memory system, while storing data at intermediate levels of the network has much less of an impact on performance. Additional research is needed to fully evaluate this idea of extending the memory system into the interconnection network, but early results suggest that it is an approach that may be able to significantly improve multiprocessor memory performance.

5. CONCLUSIONS

Using private data caches in a shared-memory multiprocessor can significantly reduce the average time required to access memory, but these private caches introduce the complexity of the cache coherence problem. This survey has identified several important architectural issues that affect the performance and implementation cost of a cache coherence mechanism. Trace-driven simulations have been used to quantify the performance impact of these different issues. These architectural issues affecting the cache coherence mechanism are the coherence detection strategy, the coherence enforcement strategy, the precision of block-sharing information, and the cache block size.

5.1 Coherence Detection Strategy

The coherence detection strategy determines when and how memory references are disambiguated to detect that a possible incoherence exists among the data caches and the main memory. The dynamic coherence detection mechanisms examine the actual memory addresses generated at run-time. The resulting perfect memory disambiguation produces low miss ratios, but the dynamic mechanisms tend to have relatively high network traffic due to the messages required to maintain coherence. The static coherence detection schemes, in contrast, examine memory references at compile-time. Since these techniques rely on imprecise compiler-based data dependence tests to disambiguate memory references, they tend to invalidate more cache entries than are necessary to maintain coherence, and thus produce miss ratios that are higher than the dynamic mechanisms. The self-invalidation used by the static mechanisms tends to compensate for their lower miss ratios by reducing the network traffic compared to that produced by dynamic coherence detection strategies.

5.2 Coherence Enforcement Strategy

After detecting a possibly incoherent memory access, the cache coherence mechanism must prevent the stale data value from being referenced by a processor. The invalidation coherence enforcement strategy forces processors to invalidate blocks within their caches. If the block is referenced again, a miss will be generated which will cause the processor to fetch the current value of the block either from the main memory or from another processor. With an update enforcement strategy, the new value of a block created by a write operation is automatically distributed to all processors with a cached copy of the block. When these processors reference the block again, they do not generate another miss service request. As a result, the update strategy tends to produce lower miss ratios than the invalidate strategy. The lower miss ratio of updating comes at the expense of its significantly higher network traffic when compared to invalidating, however.

5.3 Precision of Block-Sharing Information

The amount of block-sharing information that is maintained by the coherence mechanism has a direct impact on the implementation cost of the mechanism, as measured by the number of memory bits required to store the sharing information, and a direct impact on the performance of the memory system. To reduce the memory requirements, the coherence mechanism, such as the n-pointer plus broadcast directory, can store a relatively small amount of information about which processors have a copy of a cached block. The mechanism then must resort to broadcasting of the invalidation messages when the number of processors sharing a block overflows the available resources. This approach trades-off lower memory overhead with higher network traffic when compared to a directory that stores complete sharing information. However, recently proposed tagged-directory schemes can achieve very low memory overhead by storing sharing information only for those blocks that are actually cached. These directories still can maintain low network traffic since they are able to store sufficient sharing information for each cached block.

5.4 Cache Block Size

An important factor affecting the performance of the memory system is the cache block size, which is the number of words stored in the cache as a single unit. The use of cache blocks larger than a single word may allow the processors to exploit the spatial locality typical of memory-referencing behavior. However, memory references in a multiprocessor system tend to be spread out among the processors which reduces the available spatial locality compared to a uniprocessor system. Additionally, blocks larger than a single word introduce the false-sharing problem which tends to make multiprocessor systems favor small cache block sizes. In some application programs, it may be possible to reduce the miss ratio by using multiword blocks, but simulation studies suggest that single-word blocks minimize the network traffic by reducing both the miss service traffic and the invalidation traffic.

5.5 Summary

Finally, it is important to point out that it is possible to incorporate several different cache coherence mechanisms into a single system. For instance, the DASH prototype has demonstrated a coherence mechanism that incorporates both a bus-based snooping coherence mechanism and a directory-based coherence mechanism, and it gives the programmer a choice of both updating and invalidating coherence enforcement strategies. Additionally, it is possible to use compile-time information to augment the performance of a coherence mechanism, for instance, to reduce the size of the directory by reducing the number of coherence pointers that need to be allocated and by reducing the time they need to be active. Since each of the factors affecting the cache coherence mechanism produce different trade-offs in terms of miss ratios and network traffic, it is likely that these hybrid approaches will provide the best opportunity for increasing the performance and reducing the implementation cost of the cache coherence mechanism in large-scale shared-memory multiprocessors.

ACKNOWLEDGMENTS

Thanks to Farnaz Mounes-Toussi for generating the data used to compare the updating and invalidating coherence enforcement strategies, and to Hector Garcia-Molina, Dick Muntz, and the anonymous referees for their considerable efforts in reviewing the early drafts of this survey. Their insightful comments and suggestions helped to significantly improve the focus and clarity.

REFERENCES

ADVE, S. V., ADVE, V. S., HILL, M. D., AND VERNON, M. K. 1991. Comparison of hardware and software cache coherence schemes. In the *International Symposium on Computer Architecture*, 298–308.

AGARWAL, A., AND GUPTA, A. 1988. Memory-reference characteristics of multiprocessor applications under MACH. In *ACM SIGMETRICS Conference on Measurement and Modeling of Computer Systems*. ACM, New York, 215–225.

AGARWAL, A., SIMONI, R., HENNESSY, J., AND HOROWITZ, M. 1988. An evaluation of directory schemes for cache coherence. In the *International Symposium on Computer Architecture*, 280–289.

ANDERSON, T. E. 1990. The performance of spin lock alternatives for shared-memory multiprocessors. *IEEE Trans. Parall. Distrib. Syst. 1*, 1 (Jan.), 6–16.

ARCHIBALD, J. K. 1988. A cache coherence approach for large multiprocessor systems. In the *ACM International Conference on Supercomputing*. ACM, New York, 337–345.

ARCHIBALD, J., AND BAER, J.-L. 1984. An economical solution to the cache coherence problem. In the *International Symposium on Computer Architecture*, 355–362.

BANERJEE, U. 1988. *Dependence Analysis for Supercomputing*. Kluwer Academic Publishers, Norwell, Mass.

BENNETT, J. K., CARTER, J. B., AND ZWAENEPOEL, W. 1990. Adaptive software cache management for distributed shared memory architectures. In the *International Symposium on Computer Architecture*, 125–134.

BHUYAN, L. N., LIU, B.-C., AND AHMED, I. 1989. Analysis of MIN-based multiprocessors with private cache memories. In the *International Conference on Parallel Processing*. Vol. 1, Architecture, 51–58.

BRANTLEY, W. C., MCAULIFFE, K. P., AND WEISS, J. 1985. RP3 processor-memory element. In the

International Conference on Parallel Processing, 782–789.

CENSIER, L. M., AND FEAUTRIER, P. 1978. A new solution to coherence problems in multicache systems. *IEEE Trans. Comput.* C-27, (Dec.), 1112–1118.

CHAIKEN, D., KUBIATOWICZ, J., AND AGARWAL, A. 1991. LimitLESS Directories: A scalable cache coherence scheme. In the *International Conference on Architectural Support for Programming Languages and Operating Systems*, 224–234.

CHEN, Y.-C., AND VEIDENBAUM, A. V. 1991. A software coherence scheme with the assistance of directories. In the *ACM International Conference on Supercomputing*. ACM, New York.

CHEONG, H., AND VEIDENBAUM, A. 1989. A version control approach to cache coherence. In the *ACM International Conference on Supercomputing*. ACM, New York, 322–330.

CHEONG, H., AND VEIDENBAUM, A. V. 1988a. A cache coherence scheme with fast selective invalidation. In the *International Symposium on Computer Architecture*, 299–307.

CHEONG, H., AND VEIDENBAUM, A. V. 1988b. Stale data detection and coherence enforcement using flow analysis. In the *International Conference on Parallel Processing*. Vol. I, Architecture, 138–145.

DUBOIS, M., SCHEURICH, C., AND BRIGGS, F. A. 1988. Synchronization, coherence, and event ordering in multiprocessors. *Computer 21*, 2 (Feb.), 9–21.

EDLER, J., GOTTLIEB, A., KRUSKAL, C. P., MCAULIFFE, K. P., RUDOLPH, L., SNIR, M., TELLER, P. J., AND WILSON, J. 1985. Issues related to MIMD shared-memory computers: The NYU Ultracomputer approach. In the *International Symposium on Computer Architecture*, 126–135.

EGGERS, S. J., AND KATZ, R. H. 1989a. The effect of sharing on the cache and bus performance of parallel programs. In the *International Conference on Architectural Support for Programming Languages and Operating Systems*, 257–270.

EGGERS, S. J., AND KATZ, R. H. 1989b. Evaluating the performance of four snooping cache coherency protocols. In the *International Symposium on Computer Architecture*, 2–15.

EGGERS, S. J., AND KATZ, R. H. 1988. A characterization of sharing in parallel programs and its application to coherency protocol evaluation. In the *International Symposium on Computer Architecture*, 373–382.

GHARACHORLOO, K., GUPTA, A., AND HENNESSY, J. 1991. Performance evaluation of memory consistency models for shared-memory multiprocessors. In the *International Conference on Architectural Support for Programming Languages and Operating Systems*, 245–257.

GHARACHORLOO, K., LENOSKI, D., LAUDON, J., GIBBONS, P., GUPTA, A., AND HENNESSY, J. 1990. Memory consistency and event ordering in scalable shared-memory multiprocessors. In the *International Symposium on Computer Architecture*, 15–26.

GOODMAN, J. R. 1983. Using cache memory to reduce processor-memory traffic. In the *International Symposium on Computer Architecture*, 124–131.

GOODMAN, J. R., AND WOEST, P. J. 1988. The Wisconsin Multicube: A new large-scale cache-coherent multiprocessor. In the *International Symposium on Computer Architecture*, 422–431.

GOODMAN, J., VERNON, M., AND WOEST, P. 1989. A set of efficient synchronization primitives for a large-scale shared-memory multiprocessor. In the *International Conference on Architectural Support for Programming Languages and Operating Systems*, 64–73.

GOTTLIEB, A., GRISHMAN, R., KRUSKAL, C. P., MCAULIFFE, K. P., RUDOLPH, L., AND SNIR, M. 1982. The NYU Ultracomputer—Designing a MIMD, shared-memory parallel machine. In the *International Symposium on Computer Architecture*, 27–42.

GUPTA, A., HENNESSY, J., GHARACHORLOO, K., MOWRY, T., AND WEBER, W.-D. 1991. Comparative evaluation of latency reducing and tolerating techniques. In the *International Symposium on Computer Architecture*, 254–263.

GUPTA, A., WEBER, W.-D., AND MOWRY, T. 1990. Reducing memory and traffic requirements for scalable directory-based cache coherence schemes. In the *International Conference on Parallel Processing* Vol. I, Architecture, 312–321.

JAMES, D. V., LAUNDRIE, A. T., GJESSING, S., AND SOHI, G. S. 1990. Scalable coherent interface. *Computer 23*, 6, (June), 74–77.

KARLINE, A. R., MANASS, M. S., RUDOLPH, L., AND SLEATOR, D. D. 1986. Competitive snoopy cacheing. In the *Symposium on Foundations of Computer Science*, 244–254.

KATZ, R., EGGERS, S., WOOD, D. A., PERKINS, C., AND SHELDON, R. G. 1985. Implementing a cache consistency protocol. In the *International Symposium on Computer Architecture*, 276–283.

KRUSKAL, C. P., RUDOLPH, L., AND SNIR, M. 1986. Efficient synchronization on multiprocessors with shared memory. In the *ACM Symposium on Principles of Distributed Computing*. ACM, New York, 218–228.

KUCK, D. J., DAVIDSON, E. S., LAWRIE, D. J., AND SAMEH, A. H. 1986. Parallel supercomputing today and the Cedar approach. *Science 231* (Feb. 28), 967–974.

LAMPORT, L. 1979. How to make a multiprocessor computer that correctly executes multiprocess programs. *IEEE Trans. Comput.* C-28, 9, (Sept.), 690–691.

LEE, R. L., YEW, P.-C., AND LAWRIE, D. J. 1987. Multiprocessor cache design considerations. In the *International Symposium on Computer Architecture*, 253–262.

LENOSKI, D., LAUDON, J., GHARACHORLOO, K., WEBER, W.-D., GUPTA, A. HENNESSY, J., HOROWITZ, M., AND LAM, M. S. 1992. The Stanford DASH Multiprocessor. *Computer 25*, 3 (Mar.), 63–79.

LENOSKI, D., LAUDON, J., GHARACHORLOO, K., GUPTA, A., AND HENNESSY, J. 1990. The directory-based cache coherence protocol for the DASH multiprocessor. In the *International Symposium on Computer Architecture*, 148–159.

LI, Z., YEW, P.-C., AND ZHU, C.-Q. 1990. An efficient data dependence analysis for parallelizing compilers. *IEEE Trans. Parall. Distrib. Syst. 1*, 1 (Jan.), 26–34.

LICHNEWSKY, A., AND THOMASSET, F. 1988. Introducing symbolic problem solving techniques in the dependence testing phase of a vectorizer. In the *International Conference on Supercomputing*.

LILJA, D. J. 1992. Prefetching and scheduling interactions in shared memory multiprocessors. In the *Midwest Electrotechnology Conference*, 84–87.

LILJA, D. J. 1991. Processor parallelism considerations and memory latency reduction in shared memory multiprocessors. Rep. No. 1136, Center for Supercomputing Research and Development, Univ. of Illinois, Urbana.

LILJA, D. J., AND YEW, P.-C. 1991. Combining hardware and software cache coherence strategies. In the *ACM International Conference of Supercomputing*. ACM, New York 274–283.

LILJA, D. J., MARCOVITZ, D. M., AND YEW, P.-C. 1989. Memory referencing behavior and a cache performance metric in a shared memory multiprocessor. Rep. No. 836, Center for Supercomputing Research and Development, Univ. of Illinois, Urbana.

MARQUARDT, D. E., AND ALKHATIB, H. S. 1989. C2MP: A cache-coherent, distributed-memory multiprocessor system. In *Proceedings of Supercomputing '89*, 466–475.

MCCREIGHT, E. M. 1984. The Dragon Computer System, an early overview. In the *NATO Advanced Study Institute on Microarchitecture VLSI Computers*, 83–101.

MIN, S. L., AND BAER, J.-L. 1990. A performance comparison of directory-based and timestamp-based cache coherence schemes. In the *International Conference on Parallel Processing*. Vol. I, *Architecture*, 305–311.

MIN. S. L., AND BAER J.-L. 1989. A timestamp-based cache coherence scheme. In the *International Conference on Parallel Processing*. Vol. I, *Architecture*, 23–32.

MIZRAHI, H. E., BAER, J.-L., LAZOWSKA, E. D., AND ZAHORJAN, J. 1989. Extending the memory hierarchy into multiprocessor interconnection networks: A performance analysis. In the *International Conference on Parallel Processing*. Vol. I, *Architecture*, 41–50.

MOUNES-TOUSSI, F. 1993. An adaptive cache coherence enforcement strategy with compiler assistance. M.S. Thesis, Dept. of Electrical Engineering, Univ. of Minnesota, Minneapolis.

NGUYEN, T. N., LI, Z., AND LILJA, D. J. 1993. Efficient use of dynamically tagged directories through compiler analysis. In the *International Conference on Parallel Processing*.

O'KRAFKA, B. W., AND NEWTON, A. R. 1990. An empirical evaluation of two memory-efficient directory methods. In the *International Symposium on Computer Architecture*, 138–147.

PAPAMARCOS, M. S., AND PATEL, J. H. 1984. A low-overhead coherence solution for multiprocessors with private cache memories. In the *International Symposium on Computer Architecture*, 348–354.

PERRON, R., AND MUNDIE, C. 1986. The architecture of the Alliant FX/8 Computer. In *IEEE COMPCON*. IEEE, New York, 390–393.

PFISTER, G. F., BRANTLEY, W. C., GEORGE, D. A., HARVEY, S. L., KLEINFELDER, W. J., MCAULIFFE, K. P., MELTON, E. A., NORTON, V. A., AND WEISS, J. 1985. The IBM research parallel processor prototype (RP3): Introduction and Architecture. In the *International Conference on Parallel Processing*, 764–771.

POLYCHRONOPOULOS, C. D. 1988. Toward autoscheduling compilers. *J. Supercomput.*, 2, 297–330.

PRZYBYLSKI, S., HOROWITZ, M., AND HENNESSY, J. 1988. Performance tradeoffs in cache design. In the *International Symposium on Computer Architecture*, 290–296.

SMITH, A. J. 1987. Line (block) size choice for CPU cache memories. *IEEE Trans. Comput. C-36*, 9 (Sept.), 1063–1075.

SMITH, A. J. 1982. Cache memories. *ACM Comput. Surv. 14*, 3 (Sept.), 473–530.

STUNKEL, C. B., JANSSENS, B., AND FUCHS, W. K. 1991. Address tracing for parallel machines. *Computer 24*, 1 (Jan.), 31–38.

TANG, C. K. 1976. Cache design in the tightly coupled multiprocessor system. In the *AFIPS Conference Proceedings, National Computer Conference*. AFIPS, Arlington, Va., 749–753.

THACKER, C. P., STEWART, L. C., AND SATTERTHWAITE, E. H. 1988. Firefly: A multiprocessor workstation. *IEEE Trans. Comput. 37*, 8 (Aug.), 909–920.

TORRELLAS, J., AND HENNESSY, J. 1990. Estimating the performance advantages of relaxing consistency in a shared-memory multiprocessor. In the *International Conference on Parallel Processing*. Vol. I, *Architecture*, 26–33.

VEIDENBAUM, A. V. 1986. A compiler-assisted cache coherence solution for multiprocessors.

In the *International Conference on Parallel Processing*, 1029–1036.

WEBER, W.-D., AND GUPTA, A. 1989. Analysis of cache invalidation patterns in multiprocessors. In the *International Conference on Architectural Support for Programming Languages and Operating Systems*, 243–256.

WILSON, A. W. 1987. Hierarchical cache/bus architecture for shared memory multiprocessors.

In the *International Symposium on Computer Architecture*, 244–252.

YEN, W. C., YEN, D. W. L., AND FU, K.-S. 1985. Data coherence problem in a multicache system. *IEEE Trans. Comput. C-34*, 1 (Jan.), 56–65.

ZUCKER, R. N., AND BAER, J.-L. 1992. A performance study of memory consistency models. In the *International Symposium on Computer Architecture*, 2–12.

Received September 1991; final revision accepted March 1993.

Software Cache Consistency in Shared-Memory Multiprocessors

A Survey of Approaches and Performance Evaluation Studies

Igor Tartalja and Veljko Milutinović
Department of Computer Engineering
School of Electrical Engineering
University of Belgrade
POB 816
11000 Belgrade, Yugoslavia

E-mail:{etartalj, emilutiv}@ubbg.etf.bg.ac.yu

Abstract

This paper represents a comprehensive survey of software solutions for maintenance of cache consistency in shared-memory multiprocessor systems. The lack of widely known, acceptably systematic, and flexible classification in this research field has been our basic motivation for this work. We have proposed here a classification based on a set of ten carefully selected criteria that we considered most relevant. Existing solutions have been described and decomposed on the basis of this classification. Different solutions correspond to various points of an abstract multidimensional criterion-space. Such a generalized approach enables the points corresponding to nonexistent, but potentially useful solutions to be noticed and selected for exploration. Finally, an overview of papers dealing with performance evaluation of software solutions has been given. Different evaluation techniques have been presented and compared, using representative examples.

1. Introduction

Shared-memory multiprocessor systems represent an efficient architectural support for applications characterized by significant data sharing among parallel processes. The efficiency of these systems can be significantly improved if cache memories are used. The presence of cache memories is important for two reasons: first, because of the speed difference between the processor and the main memory; second, because of the access contention for both the interconnection network and the memory modules. A shared cache [YEH83] overcomes the speed gap, but not the access contention. Private caches enable most of the memory references to be satisfied locally, thereby reducing the contention both on the interconnection network and the memory modules.

One problem inherent to the use of private cache memories is potential inconsistency of the memory system. If several processes on several processors access the shared data, several copies of shared data will exist in private cache memories. If these data are changeable, a change made by one processor renders the other copies out of date. These stale copies should either be invalidated or modified before some other processor uses them. This problem has been studied for at least two decades. Consequently, a variety of possible solutions to the problem have been proposed. Two major approaches are the hardware and the software maintenance of the consistency of private caches.

Hardware approaches make consistency maintenance fully transparent for all levels of software, thereby simplifying the programming model of the multiprocessor system with private cache memories but increasing the hardware complexity of the system. One recent survey of hardware approaches is given in [TOMA94a, TOMA94b]; most of the related papers are classified and reprinted in the IEEE Computer Society Press book {TOMAŠ93}.

Software approaches [WULF72, GOTTL82, PFIST85, BRANT85, EDLER85, SMITH85, CHERI86, VEIDE86, MCAUL86, LEE87b, CHEON88, CYTRO88, CHEON89, MIN89, BENN90b, TARTA92, CHEON92, LOURI92, CHIUE93, DARNE93] lift the transparency of the problem above the operating system level or the compiler level. This complicates the programming model to some extent, but decreases the complexity of the hardware support. Also, software approaches tend to be more efficient than hardware approaches in a class of nonnumeric applications characterized by predominantly migratory data [ADVE91]. This survey of software approaches can be treated as the continuation of the effort that started with the above-mentioned survey of hardware approaches [TOMA94a, TOMA94b].

The motivation to do the classification and the survey presented in this paper comes from the lack of a wide, systematic, and flexible classification and a corresponding survey of software solutions. Existing survey papers in the field of cache consistency focus mostly on hardware solutions. For example, papers [ARCHI86] and [EGGER88] present and compare (using simulation methodologies) hardware schemes based on snooping. Paper [AGARW88] gives a survey and an evaluation of hardware schemes based on directories. Papers [TOMA94a, TOMA94b] contain the most comprehensive survey of hardware solutions. Paper [STENS90] contains both hardware and software solutions, but the solutions included are not detailed and many recent software solutions are missing. A similar statement applies to paper [LILJA93]. Paper [CHEON90] gives a comparative analysis of three software schemes based on compiler assistance—all three were developed by Cheong and Veidenbaum. Paper [MIN92] contains an overview of software solutions and proposes one relatively narrow classification of software solutions.

In this paper we propose a set of criteria for the classification of software solutions. Existing software solutions are presented in the context of these criteria.

After that, the proposed classification is generalized through the introduction of an abstract space of relevant criteria. Each specific software solution is associated with one specific point (specified with multiple coordinates) of the multidimensional criterion space. This type of generalization marks the points with no known associated solution. Some of these points correspond to solutions that are potentially useful under the circumstances.

In addition, this paper contains a survey of representative efforts in the domain of performance evaluation of software solutions [MIN90, TARTA92, OWICK89, ADVE91]. The efforts presented include both analytical (using mathematical models) and empirical (using simulation models) analyses, as well as comparisons of software and hardware solutions.

The paper is organized as follows. The second section defines the cache consistency problem in the context of software solutions. The third part proposes a set of classification criteria, defines the basic classes of software solutions, and mentions typical examples for each class. The fourth part contains a broad survey of existing solutions based on the above mentioned classification. The fifth part introduces a generalization of the above classification and points to some potentially useful solutions not yet found in the open literature. The sixth part contains a survey of efforts related to performance evaluation and comparison of software solutions.

2. Approaches to Classification of Cache Consistency Schemes

One of the most widely cited definitions of memory system consistency (coherency) is the Censier–Feautrier definition from [CENSI78]. It states that "a memory scheme is coherent if the value returned on a load instruction is always the value given by the latest store instruction with the same address." This definition allows copies of shared data to contain different values temporarily. It is only important that the value is updated before it is read. The ability to delay consistency maintenance activities to the moment when they are necessary decreases the frequency of consistency maintenance activities and consequently the system overhead. Most software solutions exploit this possibility.

The most common criterion used for classification is the placement of the consistency maintenance mechanism—either in the hardware or in the software. Hardware solutions make the consistency problem completely transparent to the user and to all software levels. Software solutions make the consistency problem visible either to the operating system or the compiler. The virtual machine accessible to the programmer that uses the compiler or the operating system primitive operations must be consistent. This classification has a drawback because some solutions are hybrid by nature, and not always easy to classify according to the hardware/software division line. The consistency maintenance algorithms in software are implemented more or less with hardware support. On the other hand, some authors [SKEPP95, DAHLG95] offer compiler-level optimizations for hardware solutions. Still, this paper starts from the hardware/software division, primarily in conformance with the widely adopted basic classification of [STENS90] and [TOMA94a, TOMA94b].

Instead of the hardware/software criterion, other criteria could serve as well for the classification of cache consistency maintenance solutions in shared-memory multiprocessor systems. These include, but are not limited to, the following:

1. **Dynamic versus static.** If consistency maintenance activities are planned at the execution time, the solution is dynamic. All hardware solutions, as well as the solutions predominantly implemented on the operating system level, belong to this group. If the consistency maintenance activities are planned at the compile time, the solution is static. All compiler solutions belong to this group.

2. **Centralized versus distributed.** If the consistency maintenance data (such as directories in some hardware solutions) are kept at a centralized site, the solution is centralized. If the consistency maintenance data (such as descriptions of cache line states in some solutions with snooping) are kept in a distributed fashion, the solution is distributed.

3. **With communications versus without communications.** If the consistency maintenance activities imply communications among processors, as is typically the case with hardware solutions, the solution is "with communications." If the consistency maintenance activities are performed without any communications among processors, as is typically the case with software solutions, the solution is "without communications." On a related issue, Min and Baer [MIN90] classify the existing schemes to those (a) without invalidation (such as the write-update snoopy schemes), (b) with induced invalidation (such as write-invalidate snoopy schemes or directory-based schemes), and (c) with self-invalidation (such as software schemes based on compiler assistance).

4. **Scalable versus nonscalable.** All software schemes that we are aware of, as well as some directory-based hardware schemes, are characterized by good scalability. Snoopy schemes are characterized by poor scalability and are applicable only in multiprocessors with a relatively small number of processors.

3. A Proposal for the Classification of Software Schemes

Of the papers that treat, among other issues, the classification of software solutions, the most complete is that by Min and Baer [MIN90]. Their classification is based on several criteria (some of which we have accepted and reproduced in this paper) and encompasses a relatively small number of existing solutions. It will be referred to here as the Min–Baer classification. This paper proposes a set of 10 criteria which are believed to be broad enough to create clear distinctions among most of the existing software solutions. Given criteria are not fully orthogonal, that is, some criteria are derived from another ones. The classification method is flexible enough to permit widening of the criterion set by adding new criteria if and when so required by a newly generated solution. For each criterion, we define a set of corresponding classes. Each class is illustrated with examples from the open literature (a reference to the original paper is included). Also, a "wild card" class is introduced, referred to as (*), which can be associated with any criterion. If a given criterion is irrelevant for some solution, it will be assumed that the solution is marked as (*) in relation to that criterion.

Criterion #1:	**Dynamism (D).** Decisions about what consistency maintenance activities to take can be made at compile time (statically) or at run time (dynamically).
Classes:	Static schemes (s), as in [WULF72, VEIDE86, CHEON89], or dynamic schemes (d), as in [SMITH85, BENN90b, TARTA92].
Comment:	In this work, only the schemes that require absolutely no compile time analysis are designated as dynamic schemes. Consequently, some of the schemes that make invalidation-related decisions at run time, but also perform some compile time analysis are classified as static schemes.

Criterion #2:	**Selectivity (S).** Explicit consistency maintenance activities (such as invalidation) can be done on the entire cache memory (that is, without any spatial discrimination) or on only a portion of the cache memory (that is, selectively).
Classes:	Indiscriminative schemes (i), as in [VEIDE86], or selective schemes (s), as in [CHEON88, CYTRO88, TARTA92].
Comment:	The schemes referred to as selective are characterized by a wide range of granularity of data which can be the subject of the consistency maintenance activities. For example, in the case of the IBM RP3 [BRANT85], a wide plethora of objects, all of them of different sizes, can be the subject of the invalidation actions. The granularity differences are not reflected through this criterion; however, another criterion (to be introduced later) covers the granularity issue.

Criterion #3:	**Restrictiveness (R).** The consistency maintenance activities can be performed for preventive purposes (conservatively) or only when absolutely necessary (restrictively).
Classes:	Conservative schemes (c), as in [VEIDE86, SMITH85], or restrictive schemes (r), as in [CHEON89, TARTA92].
Comment:	This criterion could result in a fine division having more than two classes. One could introduce a measure called the "level of restrictiveness," defined as the ratio of absolutely necessary consistency maintenance activities to the total number of consistency maintenance activities performed, averaged over a number of benchmark programs. In an absolutely restrictive scheme, this ratio would be equal to 1.

Criterion #4:	**Adaptivity (A).** The consistency maintenance algorithm can be fixed or adaptable to the characteristics of the access patterns to data objects.
Classes:	Fixed schemes (f), as in [SMITH85, CYTRO88, CHEON89, TARTA92], or adaptive schemes (a), as in [BENN90b].
Comment:	So far, only one adaptive scheme appears in the open literature [BENN90b]; thus no need exists to introduce a finer measure

called the "level of adaptivity." However, as time goes by and other adaptive schemes are introduced, a need may arise for such a measure.

Criterion #5: **Locality (L).** The consistency maintenance algorithm may reduce misses strictly locally (interblock reduction) or globally (intrablock reduction).

Classes: Local schemes (l), as in [SMITH85, VEIDE86], or global schemes (g), as in [CHEON89, TARTA92].

Comment: Obviously, this criterion is an extension of the restrictiveness criterion and is irrelevant for the absolutely conservative schemes (those without any reduction of misses).

Criterion #6: **Granularity (G).** The size and structure of the unit object varies from one consistency maintenance algorithm to the other.

Classes: Line (l), also referred to as "cache line" or "cache block" as in [CHEON89]; page (p), as in [WULF72, SMITH85]; segment (s), as in [TARTA92]; or flexible object (f), as in [BRANT85, BENN90b].

Comment: To some extent, this criterion extends the selectivity criterion. In the case of fully indiscriminative schemes, this criterion is irrelevant.

Criterion #7: **Blocking (B).** The basic program block in the consistency maintenance process varies in size and structure from one algorithm to the other.

Classes: Critical region (c), as in [SMITH85, TARTA92]; epoch (e), as in [MCAUL86, VEIDE86, LEE87, CHEON89, MIN89]; subroutine (s), also referred to as "procedure" as in [CYTRO88]; or the entire program (p), as in [WULF72].

Comment: Actually, terms such as "computational unit" [MCAUL86], "loop" [VEIDE86], "epoch" [LEE87, MIN89], "task level" [CHEON89], and the like, refer to the issue which is essentially the basic consistency block. Consequently, one entire class was introduced to encompass all these cases.

Criterion #8: **Positioning (P).** Instructions to implement the consistency maintenance algorithm can be positioned at various places in the program.

Classes: Entry/exit into/from the critical region (e), as in [SMITH85, TARTA92]; loop boundary (b), as in [VEIDE86, CHEON89]; source/sink of the data dependency (d), as in [CYTRO88]; or interrupt procedure (i), as in [CHERI86].

Comment: Some of the schemes do comparisons at each reference (using specialized hardware support), which can also be treated as a consistency maintenance activity. However, this criterion considers only the special instructions for consistency maintenance (invalidate, flush, post, and the like).

Criterion #9: **Updating (U).** The main memory can be updated either at the time of cache write or after some delay.

Classes:	Write-through (t), as in [CHEON89]; write-back (copy-back) (b), as in [CYTRO88, BENN90b]; hybrid (h), which implies both write-through AND write-back, as in [SMITH85]; or alternative (a), which implies either write-through OR write-back, as in [TARTA92].
Comment:	One should notice the difference between the hybrid schemes which (as in [SMITH85]) offer write-through for private data and write-back for shared data, on one hand, and alternative schemes which (as in [TARTA92]) propose that one or the other approach be used exclusively.

Criterion #10:	**Checking (C).** Conditions of inconsistency can be checked using several techniques.
Classes:	Checking the data type or the reference type (r), as in [WULF72, LEE87a, MIN89]; program structure analysis (s), as in [BRANT85, VEIDE86]; data dependency analysis (d), as in [CYTRO88]; run-time information comparison (c), as in [CHEON89]; or monitoring of the traffic on the interconnection network (m), as in [CHERI86].
Comment:	The classification based on this criterion should be treated conditionally. Some schemes include more than one technique for detection of inconsistency. For example, this is the case with the scheme in [CHEON88]. In such cases, the schemes are classified according to the technique that dominates. However, for completeness, the presence of other techniques will be indicated accordingly (using slashes, as in c/+s+d+r/).

4. An Overview of Software Schemes

This section contains a relatively broad overview of existing software schemes for maintenance of consistency among private cache memories. Using the criteria and the classes introduced in the previous section, a (10-element) set of attributes is associated with each scheme presented. These attributes determine the place of a given scheme in the proposed classification. In accordance with the (first) dynamism criterion, this section is divided into two subsections. One deals with static schemes and the other with dynamic schemes.

For consistency of presentation, each scheme description of this section includes the following elements:

(a) Information about the authors and the home institution of their research, the project of which that research was a part, and the major references to the original work.

(b) The essence of the contribution, or the major characteristic of the research, in succinct form.

(c) Description of the scheme, in which the level of detail is related to the impact of the scheme, its relevance to the class under consideration, and the amount of data available through the open literature.

(d) Final discussion of the scheme (advantages, disadvantages, and possibly a discussion of some specific issues).

(e) At the end, the 10-element descriptor vector is given, thus defining the place of the scheme within the overall classification used in this work.

4.1. Static Schemes

Static schemes predominantly rely on program analysis at compile time. Analysis points to potential causes of inconsistency, and additional information is added to the program to avoid fatal inconsistency errors during the program execution. This additional information includes, but is not limited to, issues such as marking of data, marking of references, and insertion of special instructions. This analysis (and related actions) eliminates the need for processors to communicate during the execution of the critical parts of the code, thereby making static schemes well scalable. On the other hand, static solutions degrade system performance because the precise prediction of memory conflicts due to cache inconsistency is not possible (actions are performed on the basis of some kind of "worst-case" analysis, not on the basis of "deterministic-optimum" analysis).

4.1.1. The C.mmp page marking from Carnegie-Mellon University

Wulf and Bell [WULF72] from Carnegie-Mellon University, working on the C.mmp project, were among the first to notice the problem of multiple values of shared variables existing concurrently in private cache memories of different processors in a multiprocessor system. The essence of the proposed method for the maintenance of cache consistency is in keeping the read-write shared data out of the cache at all times.

Only the read-only shared pages can be cached in the private cache memories. This is particularly the case with pages that contain shared instructions. Pages are marked as "cachable" using a bit reserved for this purpose in the relocation registers.

This scheme is extremely conservative, thereby permitting relatively easy realization but decreasing the processing power considerably [OWICK89].

Classification: (D:s,S:*,R:c,A:f,L:*,G:p,B:p,P:*,U:*,C:r).

4.1.2. The Ultracomputer program structure analysis from New York University

Gottlieb and his coauthors [GOTTL82, GOTTL83], Edler with his coauthors [EDLER85], and McAuliffe in his PhD thesis [MCAUL86] proposed the approach for software maintenance of cache consistency in the Ultracomputer multiprocessor developed at New York University. The essence of the approach is that the caching of read-write shared data is permitted in the intervals of the program execution when the read-write shared data are used exclusively by one processor.

The Ultracomputer supports two instructions for software managing of cache memories. These instructions are inserted into the user code at compile time. The Release instruction frees one cache memory entry without copying the data (from that entry) into the main memory. This means that the Release instruction prevents memory traffic. According to [GOTTL83], the main memory is updated according to the write-back approach. In a later paper [EDLER85], a combined approach is used: write-back for private data and write-through for shared data. Independently of cache consistency maintenance, the Release instruction can be used, at the exit from a begin-end block, to free the space in cache that was used by the local variables. In the context of cache consistency maintenance, the read-write shared variables are kept in cache only during the time intervals when it is guaranteed that they will be accessed only for read. At the end of these intervals, the variable has to be removed from the cache, using the Release instruction, and marked as noncachable. The second of the two cache consistency maintenance instructions is the Flush instruction which copies data from the cache memory entry into the main memory without erasing the entry. For private data, the Flush instruction must be executed when blocking a task, because the execution of the task may continue on another processor. For data shared by a parent-task and its child-tasks, instructions Flush and Release are executed before the spawn operation. The variable that was private before a new task was created now becomes shared and must be marked as noncachable; however, its value in the main memory is up to date. After the child-tasks are completed, the parent task can continue to work with the same variable, treating it as a private, and therefore cachable, variable. The first next reference to that variable will place its current value into the cache. All activities described here can be performed on the segment level or on the cache level.

This scheme is less conservative than the Wulf–Bell scheme. Still, this caching scheme has no restrictiveness in the invalidation of shared data. The scheme supports only the locality of references within "safe" intervals. The consistency maintenance related instructions can be made selective with the segment-level granularity; however, something like that would slow them down due to the required scan through cache directory.

Classification: (D:s,S:s,R:c,A:f,L:l,G:s,B:e,P:b,U:h,C:s).

4.1.3. The RP3 flexible invalidation from the IBM T.J. Watson Research Center

Brantley, McAuliffe, and Weiss [BRANT85], as well as Pfister and coauthors [PFIST85], proposed a cache consistency maintenance scheme similar (but more flexible with respect to granularity of data) to the one from the NYU Ultracomputer. The research was done at the IBM T.J. Watson Research Center and was intended for the IBM's RP3 multiprocessor.

At compile time, shared data are marked as cachable if they are used exclusively in the given program block. Data marked as noncachable in one program block may become cachable in the next program block, and vice versa. Also at compile time, data are marked as volatile or not, which helps in the efficient management of the temporary cachable data. In short, all data exhibit two attributes: cachability and volatility. These attributes are also specified on the level of segment and page descriptors for specific segments and specific pages. They are also applied to segment tables and page tables. Moreover, the RP3 includes a number of different data invalidation instructions: line invalidation, page invalidation, segment invalidation, user space invalidation, supervisor space invalidation, and invalidation of all volatile data (which can exist in many different segments or pages). The main memory is updated using the write-through approach.

In general, the cache consistency maintenance strategy of the IBM RP3 scheme is still very conservative; however, its selective invalidation is more flexible in the sense that the granularity of the invalidation can be varied. Consequently, in the case of the IBM RP3 scheme, the software designer can use more powerful "tools" in an effort to minimize the probability that a data item is "expelled" from the cache, although it may be needed later.

Classification: (D:s,S:s,R:c,A:f,L:l,G:f,B:e,P:b,U:t,C:s).

4.1.4. Cache on/off control from the University of Illinois

Veidenbaum [VEIDE86] proposed a relatively simple static software scheme for cache consistency maintenance in the Cedar multiprocessor at the University of Illinois. The scheme assumes a program structure based on parallel/serial loops, which are widely used to express parallelism in numeric applications. The essence of the scheme is that compiler inserts special-purpose instructions for cache consistency maintenance only at loop boundaries and at subroutine call points.

Assuming that the main memory value of the shared variable is current, which is achieved here using the write-through approach, incoherence occurs when a value fetched from the cache is different from the value in the main memory. According to this definition, Veidenbaum gives a formal proof of the lemma about the necessary conditions for inconsistency. When processor Pj (j=1,2,...) fetches the variable X, the inconsistency will happen if (1) the value of the variable X is present in the cache memory of the processor Pj, and (2) the new value of X is placed into the main memory by the processor Pk (k≠j, k=1,2,...) after the processor Pj had accessed the variable X last time. Detection of the necessary conditions of inconsistency can be based on the data dependency graph. As indicated in Figure 1, the inconsistency will happen if the following is satisfied: (1) Pj executes instruction S1 which writes into or reads from X; (2) another processor Pk (k≠j) executes instruction S2 which writes a new value into X; and (3) Pj executes instruction S3 which reads from X again.

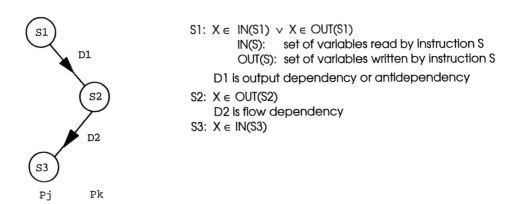

S1: $X \in IN(S1) \lor X \in OUT(S1)$
      IN(S):   set of variables read by instruction S
      OUT(S): set of variables written by instruction S
    D1 is output dependency or antidependency
S2: $X \in OUT(S2)$
    D2 is flow dependency
S3: $X \in IN(S3)$

Figure 1. Data dependency graph containing the conditions of inconsistency.

Instructions for cache consistency maintenance are as follows: (1) Flush (or Invalidate according to [CHEON90]), which deletes the contents of the entire cache (indiscriminative invalidation); (2) Cache-on, which enables the cache, that is, enables all references to go through the cache; (3) Cache-off, which disables the cache, that is, forces all references to bypass the cache. The proposed cache coherence maintenance algorithm is applied at compile time—each instruction in the program is examined, and where necessary, the above-mentioned cache consistency maintenance instructions are inserted before, inside, or after the loops as well as before/after procedure calls, as follows:

1. DoAll: There is no data dependency between different iterations of the loop, thus there is no inconsistency hazard. Consequently, cache memory can be enabled. The loop is expanded with Cache-on and Flush instructions, so each processor, at the beginning of the iteration which is assigned to that particular processor, enables its own cache and deletes the old contents.

2. DoAcross: Parallelization is possible with additional synchronization required to cope with the data dependency between different iterations. Consequently, conditions of inconsistency can arise, and the Cache-off instruction should be inserted in the loop. However, the cache could be enabled. In that case, the Flush instruction should be inserted after the synchronization-related wait-on-semaphore operation in the appropriate iteration on the processor which contains the sink of data dependency. With respect to other details, the treatment of the DoAcross loop is the same as the treatment of the DoAll loop.

3. Serial loop: Cache memory can be enabled because the loop is entirely executed on one processor. This is the consequence of the fact that the structure of data dependencies between iterations disables any parallelization. Instructions Cache-on and Flush have to be inserted before the loop.

4. DoEnd: If the cache was enabled before the loop and disabled in the loop, the Cache-on instruction is inserted after the loop. If the cache was enabled before the loop and enabled (fully or partially) in the loop (because the loop was of the type DoAll or DoAcross), the Flush instruction is inserted after the exit from the loop.

5. Call: Instruction Cache-off is inserted before the call; if the cache is enabled before the call, instructions Cache-on and Flush are inserted after the call.

As can be seen, the algorithm includes no analysis of individual data dependencies for each particular instruction. It only does the preventive disabling and flushing of the cache at the boundaries of those loop types in which the nonconsistency condition can be created. Consequently, this algorithm is very conservative, its restrictiveness of invalidation is very low, and the invalidation is indiscriminative.

Classification: (D:s,S:i,R:c,A:f,L:l,G:*,B:e,P:b,U:t,C:s).

4.1.5. Program analysis and reference marking from the University of Illinois

Lee, Yew, and Lawrie [LEE87a, LEE87b] proposed a scheme based on the static analysis of program structure and marking of individual references. The research was done at the University of Illinois.

The approach starts from the notion of epoch, which refers either to a parallel loop or to a piece of sequential code between two parallel loops. First, the program is analyzed and segmented into a sequence of epochs. Second, for each data item, its cachability status is marked for each epoch separately (the cachability status of a data item may change from one epoch to the other). The marking is done at compile time, using Paraphrase, a parallelizing Fortran compiler. Within an epoch, all references to a variable accessed by a number of processors, but for at least by one processor for write, are marked as noncachable (references to other variables are marked as cachable). References marked as noncachable bypass the cache at execution time and access the main memory directly. At the end of each epoch, the invalidation of the cache contents is done, so that the processor obtains up-to-date values from the main memory at the next reference to the variable. The main memory is updated using the write-back approach.

This algorithm efficiently supports the intraepoch localities. However, the cache is flushed at the end of each epoch, which means that the interepoch localities are not supported and the performance of the scheme is degraded.

Classification: (D:s,S:i,R:c,A:f,L:l,G:*,B:e,P:b,U:b,C:r/+s/).

4.1.6. Fast selective invalidation from the University of Illinois

Cheong and Veidenbaum [CHEON88] proposed another software scheme for consistency maintenance which also originated from research done at the University of Illinois. The speed of invalidation in this scheme is close to that of indiscriminative invalidation, but its selectivity is such that it results in a better hit ratio.

It is assumed that the value of a variable in shared memory is always valid because the write-through approach is used. Also, it is assumed that the synchronization variables are not cached. Each word in cache has a change bit associated with it. When set, this bit indicates that the word is potentially invalid (in another paper, which originated from the same research [CHEON90], this bit is defined in the inverse way). When a new line is entered into the cache, the corresponding change bits are set to 0 (zero). Also, a cache write sets this bit to 0. The Invalidate instruction only sets the change bits to 1—it does not perform the actual invalidation. The setting of change bits is done in one cycle for all change bits in the cache. That is why the invalidation is as fast as in the case of indiscriminative invalidation. At compile time, the Invalidate instructions are inserted at the critical places in the program (loop boundaries), in the same way as in a previously described scheme [VEIDE86]. Also, each word in cache has a clear bit associated with it. This bit, when set, indicates that nothing was read/written from/into the corresponding word. The Clear-cache instruction sets the clear bits of the entire cache memory to 1 (one), which brings the cache into the initial clear state. Marking of references is done at compile time, as follows. All references that can be guaranteed not to fetch an invalid data copy are marked as cache-read. Other references are marked as memory-read. The marking algorithm is applied to each procedure separately. It is assumed that the cache is always cleared at the beginning of a procedure (using the Clear-cache instruction). References to data that are only read within a procedure are marked as cache-read; also, all references to read-write data coming chronologically prior to the first write to the same data are marked as cache-read. Other references are marked according to specific rules. For cache hit, not only must the address and validity tags match, but also the reference must be either a cache-read or a memory-read with the change bit set to 0.

In this scheme, the invalidation instructions are inserted into the program statically. The same applies for marking of references. However, the Invalidate instruction here only points to the occurrence of a situation in which stale contents may appear in cache memory. Decisions about actual invalidations are made at execution time. The hit is prevented only for those memory-read references with the change bit in the accessed word set. This approach has two benefits. First, invalidation has no impact on cache-read references; that is, the invalidation is selective. Second, when a variable is read more than once within a single iteration of a DoAll loop, although all reads are marked as memory-read, the invalidation will refer to the first read only; the other reads will be satisfied in the cache memory (intraepoch restrictive invalidation). However, the algorithm for inserting the Invalidate instruction is conservative—preventive invalidation is done at the boundaries of parallel loops (interepoch conservative invalidation).

Classification: (D:s,S:s,R:c,A:f,L:l,G:l,B:e,P:b,U:t,C:c/+s+d+r/).

4.1.7. Programmable cache from the IBM T.J.Watson Research Center

Cytron, Karlovsky, and McAuliffe [CYTRO88] proposed a solution for cache consistency maintenance in shared-memory multiprocessors that is based on a detailed static analysis of data dependencies for all instructions in the program. The authors were with the IBM T.J. Watson Research Center and the University of Illinois at the time when the work was published.

As in other static schemes, special instructions for cache memory management are inserted into the program at compile time, as follows: (1) Post is the instruction that passes the value of the local data copy into the location of the original data in main memory; (2) Invalidate is the instruction that destroys the local data copy; and (3) Flush is the instruction that performs a combination of the previous two instructions. A write-back cache memory is assumed, one which is large enough so that replacement of lines can be neglected. The line size is equal to one memory word. Each address in the global address space is marked in one of the following three ways: (a) Cachable—data copies on these addresses can exist in private cache memories at all times (read-only shared data and private data); (b) Temporarily cachable—data at these addresses can be placed into the cache memory, and the compiler is responsible for making decisions about when these data are to be flushed or invalidated (read-write shared data); (c) Noncachable—data from these locations are not allowed to be placed into the cache memory (shared data with activity dynamics such that the consistency maintenance does not pay off, due to a relatively large overhead). The cachability status of an address is determined in three steps: first, all variables are marked as

Temporarily cachable; second, the locations where the cache management instructions are to be inserted are determined; and third, the variables that require no consistency maintenance are marked as Cachable, while those accessed only after invalidation are marked as Noncachable; other variables remain Temporarily cachable (these would require a special analysis to determine how profitable it would be to perform the consistency maintenance activity for each particular variable). The proposed algorithm relies on some information obtained from the parallelizing compiler, such as information about the ability to parallelize a loop (if the loop is parallel or serial), the data dependency graph, and the like. Instruction Post(X) is inserted after the instruction that writes into a shared variable X if it (the instruction that writes) is a source of the crossing flow dependency. The term crossing refers to the case in which the sink of the dependency can be executed on another processor. Also, if the variable X is inter-procedurally live after the procedure under analysis, the instruction Post(X) is inserted after the last write to X within the same procedure. Hence, the instruction Write is followed by the instruction Post(X) in the case of the following sequence:

$$Write\ (Pi,X) \rightarrow Read(Pj,X) \quad (j \neq i)$$

The authors propose two different algorithms for insertion of the instruction Invalidate. The first one is less complex. It is linearly dependent on the number of flow dependencies in the analyzed program. However, it can generate unnecessary invalidations because it is based on a conservative invalidation strategy: Invalidate (X) is inserted before each reading of the variable X if the variable X is a sink of a crossing flow dependence. Also, if a shared variable X has been defined before the entry into the procedure, the Invalidate(X) instruction is inserted before the first reading of the variable X in the procedure. Hence, instruction Invalidate(X) is inserted before the read operation when the above-mentioned write-read sequence exists. However, it would be enough to invalidate the variable X before the second reading, only when the following sequence exists:

$$Ref(Pj,X) \rightarrow Write\ (Pi,X) \rightarrow Read(Pj,X) \quad (j \neq i)$$

Consequently, the authors propose a better, but more complex algorithm for insertion of the invalidation instructions (an algorithm quadratically dependent on the number of flow dependencies). The Invalidate(X) instruction is inserted before the sink of the crossing flow dependency if the source of the analyzed flow dependency acts as a sink in at least one output dependency, or in at least one antidependency, in relation to the variable X. Instruction Flush(X) generates both operations—the passing of X into the shared memory and the invalidation of X in cache memory (of the processor that executed the instruction). Instruction Flush is inserted after the source of the direct dependency, substituting for the instructions Post and Invalidate when such substitution can be done without causing unnecessary misses.

This scheme is very restrictive to the invalidations within a procedure. This is due to the fact that both the program structure analysis and the data dependency analysis are performed at compile time. However, the problem of unnecessary invalidations on the interprocedure level is still there.

Classification: (D:s,S:s,R:r,A:f,L:g,G:l,B:s,P:d,U:b,C:d/+s+r/).

71

4.1.8. Version control from the University of Illinois

Cheong and Veidenbaum [CHEON89] proposed a scheme that represents an improvement of their "fast selective invalidation" scheme. The new scheme was also developed at the University of Illinois. It is based on the static analysis of the parallel program tasking structure and a dynamic control of the variable version using appropriate hardware support.

The essence of the approach is in the notion that, whenever a write is made to a shared variable, a new "version" of its contents is formed. In the case of DoAll loops, there is no data dependency between iterations (iterations of the DoAll loop form tasks on the same level of the task execution graph), and there is no hazard of another processor needing the new version of the shared variable. Therefore, no consistency maintenance related activities are needed within a DoAll loop—a temporary inconsistency of the memory system is allowed. However, before the processor passes the task level boundary, the most recent version of the variable in cache must be stored into the main memory. Each processor keeps a private information about the current version of each shared variable (scalar or vector) in its local memory. For that purpose, a current version number (CVN) is maintained. When passing to the next task level (for example, after the exit from a DoAll loop), processors execute the instructions (inserted by the compiler, based on the static program analysis) for incrementing the CVN for all variables being written at the previous task level. At the same time, each cache line contains a field with the information about the birth version number (BVN). The BVN is updated at the loading of each cache line from main memory. After a read miss and the loading of the cache line, BVN is equal to CVN. At each cache write, BVN is made equal to CVN + 1 (the number of the next version). At each access to a shared data item in cache, CVN and BVN are compared. If BVN is smaller than CVN, the data item in cache is stale, and the access is declared a miss. If BVN is equal to or greater than CVN, the data item in cache is valid, and the access is declared a hit (after a write to a variable, BVN = CVN + 1, and BVN is greater than CVN on the same task level).

The version control scheme [CHEON89] demonstrates a better performance than the previous two schemes [VEIDE86 and CHEON88] because it respects the temporal locality of references over the task execution level boundary [CHEON90]. A direct consequence of this is an increased hit ratio. This advantage is paid for by a more complex hardware support for consistency maintenance in comparison to other schemes.

Classification: (D:s,S:s,R:r,A:f,L:g,G:l,B:e,P:b,U:a,C:c/+s/).

4.1.9. Timestamps from the University of Washington

Min and Baer [MIN89, MIN92], from the University of Washington, proposed, independently of Cheong and Veidenbaum, a scheme which is essentially similar to the version control scheme.

Each shared data structure is assigned a counter, which is incremented at the end of each epoch in which the data structure can be modified. Each word in cache is assigned a "timestamp." This timestamp is set to "counter + 1" when that word is modified. At the access to cache memory, a word is valid if the value of the timestamp is equal to or greater than the value of the corresponding counter. The Min-Baer counter corresponds to the Cheong–Veidenbaum CVN, and the Min-Baer timestamp corresponds to the Cheong–Veidenbaum BVN. The Min–Baer epoch corresponds to the Cheong–Veidenbaum task level.

The primary difference between the timestamps approach and the version control approach lies in the fact that Min and Baer also propose a very sophisticated algorithm of marking references, which better supports the localities between dependent tasks in a DoAcross loop.

Classification: (D:s,S:s,R:r,A:f,L:g,G:l,B:e,P:b,U:t,C:c/+s+r/).

4.1.10. Generational approach from the State University of New York at Stony Brook

Chiueh [CHIUE93] proposed an improvement of the idea about control of shared-data versions. His consistency scheme takes care of the current generation of tasks using a levelized task graph, instead of the separate management of each variable version. The work was performed at the State University of New York at Stony Brook.

Each cache line is extended with a valid generation number (VGN) field. On the other hand, a new register, to indicate the current generation number (CGN) of tasks, is added to each processor register set. At the end of each task, where a shared variable was written, the appropriate instruction to modify the appropriate VGN field in the cache line is inserted by compiler. The VGN field is set to the generation number, when this variable is written again by an arbitrary processor; thus, the VGN field indicates the last generation number, until the appropriate shared variable can be considered as valid. When a task is scheduled to a processor, CGN is written into the CGN register of that processor, to indicate the current generation of the task. An access to a shared variable X is treated as a hit, if $VGN(X) \geq CGN$.

Compared to the Cheong-Veidenbaum version control scheme or the Min-Baer timestamping scheme, this generational approach simplifies the hardware support. Instead of a local table for each processor to keep information on the global current version of each shared variable, only one additional register (CGN) is used here. Additionally, the Chiueh's approach naturally overcomes some inherent problems of the version control scheme, such as DoAccross loop handling or inefficiency caused by conditional writes.

Classification: (D:s,S:s,R:r,A:f, L:g,G:l,B:e,P:b,U:t,C:c/+s+r/)

4.1.11. One-bit time stamps from Rice University

Darnell and Kennedy [DARNE93], from Rice University, proposed a new scheme based on timestamping. Their scheme requires considerably less complex hardware support then appropriate schemes [CHEON89] and [MIN89], although it achieves at least the same hit ratio.

One bit, called "epoch bit," is associated with each cache line and notifies any arbitrary access to the cache line during current epoch of the program execution. All epoch bits are reset at each epoch boundary. Invalidate instructions are inserted statically by compiler at the end of each epoch (before reset of the epoch bits). Invalidation can be related to the whole array (conservative analysis of the program) or only to some parts of the array that have been written during the current epoch. In run time, these instructions actually invalidate only the cache lines that have not been accessed during the epoch. Invalidate instruction practically copies the epoch bit to the valid bit.

As it has been shown through simulation study, this scheme has nearly always a better hit ratio than the scheme proposed by Min and Baer [MIN89]. Hardware support, on the other hand, is very simple—each cache line is enlarged with one bit (epoch) and no additional bits are required in instructions or private memory.

Classification: (D:s,S:s,R:r,A:f,L:g,G:l,B:e,P:b,U:*,C:c/+s/).

4.2. Dynamic solutions

Like hardware solutions, dynamic software solutions maintain the consistency of private caches entirely at run time. They are implemented in the kernel of the operating system. Consequently, they do not contribute to compiler complexity (in static schemes, one multiprocessor system requires a number of different compilers—one for each language). Since the consistency maintenance decisions are performed at execution time, dynamic approaches do not require preventive actions; thus it is possible to carry out only absolutely necessary actions. Dynamic approaches are difficult to apply when the parallelism is modeled via parallel loops. Consequently, dynamic solutions are not suitable for numeric applications, which are primarily based on a programming model characterized by parallel loops. On the other hand, dynamic solutions offer a natural solution for nonnumeric concurrent applications, which are frequently based on a programming model with an explicit management of sharing (using critical regions, monitors, or similar mechanisms).

4.2.1. One time identifiers from the University of California at Berkeley

Smith [SMITH85] proposed a solution for dynamic maintenance of cache consistency that is entirely based on the application of operating-system-level primitive operations for control of exclusive access to critical regions. This research was done at the University of California at Berkeley.

In the case of conventional page-organized memory, the hashing function is used at each access to a page to calculate the real page address from the virtual page address. To avoid unnecessary repetitions of this operation, a translation lookaside buffer (TLB) can be introduced. This buffer is a cache in which the address tag contains the virtual page address and the data field contains the real page address. Smith proposed that each TLB entry and each line in the processor cache be expanded with another field which provides a unique marking of a shared data page. This field is referred to as OTI (one-time identifier). When a new TLB entry is loaded, a new and unique value is placed into its OTI field. This value is read from a special incrementing register. When an entry for a shared page is accessed for the first time, the entry is loaded into the cache from the main memory. At the same time, the OTI field value from the TLB is passed to the OTI field in the cache. All subsequent accesses to this variable check the value of the OTI field in cache for a match with the value of the OTI field in the TLB. If a match occurs, the access is treated as a hit; otherwise it is a miss. After the exit from a critical region, the processor executes the instructions that invalidate all TLB entries of the pages that belong to shared data being protected by the just-exited critical region. At the first next access to shared data, the corresponding TLB entry is loaded again, and a new value for the OTI field is obtained. This allows all later accesses to stale data to be treated as misses because the value of the OTI field in the TLB is different from the value of the OTI field in the cache. Next, Smith proposed a selective write-through, as follows. Updating of shared data is done with the write-through approach (which guarantees that the main memory is always updated for shared data), while the updating of the private data is done using the write-back approach.

The advantage of the OTI scheme is the complete decentralization of cache consistency maintenance, as is the case with most static schemes and not the case with most hardware schemes. Consistency is maintained at each processor autonomously, without any communications with other processors in the system. However, the scheme requires a relatively complex hardware support (the OTI extension in the TLB and the cache, comparators for the OTI fields, and so forth). Also, at the exit from a critical region no possibility remains for restriction in executing the invalidation instructions (here, the invalidation is done as a preventive action).

Classification: (D:d,S:s,R:c,A:f,L:l,G:l,B:r,P:e,U:h,C:c).

4.2.2. Consistency on interrupt request from Stanford University

Cheriton, Slavenburg, and Boyle [CHERI86] proposed a combined hardware–software solution for the maintenance of cache consistency in virtually addressed private cache memories. This research was done at Stanford University and was a part of the VMP multiprocessor project. The essence of the solution is in the hardware-based determination of the inconsistency conditions and generation of the interrupt request, followed by the software-based activities aimed at consistency maintenance.

This scheme is based on the concept of virtual memory. Page faults are determined in hardware, whereas fetching of new pages from the secondary memory is done in software. The proposed cache memory page size is relatively large (up to 512 bytes), and the proposed hardware for the transfer of data blocks is relatively fast (40 Mbytes/sec). Consequently, cache memory misses are relatively rare and can be processed in software on the operating-system level. The same concept is extended into the domain of cache consistency maintenance. The hardware-based bus monitor detects the inconsistency conditions and informs the local processor about that, by issuing an interrupt request. In response, the processor executes the interrupt routine and performs the consistency maintenance activities (within the interrupt routine). The same consistency maintenance mechanism is used both for the shared pages and the pages that contains entries of the page table. The main memory is viewed as a sequence of cache page frames. A page can be in one of two states: shared or private. In the shared state, the page frame contains the most recently written page value, while the local cache memories can contain copies of that particular page. In the private state, only one cache memory contains a copy of the page. Each bus monitor maintains a private table of actions. For each page frame, this table defines the activity to be done by the monitor when the address from that page appears on the bus. If the corresponding page is not in the processor's private cache memory, no action is needed. If the page in the cache memory is shared, the monitor ignores all read-shared requests; all read-private and assert-ownership requests have to be aborted, followed by an interrupt to the local processor (during the processing of that interrupt request, the processor invalidates the page in cache memory). If the page in cache memory is private, the monitor has to abort the transaction and issue an interrupt request for each transaction related to that page (during the processing of that interrupt, if the page is dirty, the processor performs a write-back into the main memory; if the transaction is read-private or assert-ownership, the processor invalidates the page in cache; if the transaction is read-shared, the processor changes the page state into shared). The processor that was performing the aborted transaction detects the abortion and starts the transaction again. As the authors briefly summarize, using this protocol, a request for a shared copy of a shared page is satisfied immediately. A request for a shared copy of a private page results in an abortion of the transaction and the relinquishing of ownership. Consequently, the processor that requested the page is allowed to succeed in the next try. A request for a private copy of a shared page is satisfied immediately, but it induces the invalidation of all cache copies of that page. A request for a private copy of a private page is aborted but causes the relinquishing of ownership, which allows success on the next try.

The exclusively hardware-based detection of inconsistency conditions results in a very restrictively applied invalidation; however, the size of the cache page (which must be relatively large so that interrupts related to misses are relatively rare) makes the invalidation poorly selective in the case of shared data of fine granularity.

Classification: (D:d,S:s,R:r,A:f,L:g,G:p,B:p,P:i,U:b,C:m).

4.2.3. Conditional invalidation from the University of Belgrade

The authors of this survey, in their paper [TARTA92], proposed a class of dynamic software schemes for maintenance of cache consistency based on testing for inconsistency conditions at the entry into a critical region, thereby avoiding unnecessary invalidations. The work was performed at the University of Belgrade in cooperation with the NCR Corporation.

Consistency maintenance activities are performed at the entry into /exit from the critical region (the program code region with exclusive access to the shared data segment). Of the three schemes they proposed, the "version verification" scheme is the most invalidation-restrictive, and the one that utilizes the existing interregional locality of references the best. At the entry into the critical region, the real version of the shared segment (information from the shared-segment table) is explicitly compared with local and private information about the most recently used segment version. If the versions do not match, selective invalidation of the shared segment is done. If the shared memory is updated using the write-back approach, the updating of the shared-segment original (in main memory) is done at the exit from the critical region.

A simulation analysis has shown the advantages of the restrictively applied invalidation, even if the number of processors is relatively small (up to 16). This is especially the case if the mostly-read shared segments predominate.

Classification: (D:d,S:s,R:r,A:f,L:g,G:s,B:r,P:e,U:a,C:c).

4.2.4. Adaptive software cache management from Rice University

Bennett, Carter, and Zwaenepoel [BENN90a, BENN90b] proposed a dynamic adaptive software maintenance of consistency for the Munin system at Rice University. Munin supports several consistency maintenance mechanisms, and in each case uses the one that best fits the prevailing class of shared objects for that particular case (the access type is relevant when making the decision about the specific mechanism to use).

Generally, in distributed shared memory (DSM) systems [PROTI95] the memory inconsistency problem exists because the virtual address space is physically distributed on several local memories. Consequently, one memory address can be mapped into a number of memory modules. Munin is a program system that makes this problem completely transparent for the application. For the purpose of memory consistency maintenance, the programmer informs the system about the expected way of access to shared objects. The classes of objects are (a) write-once, (b) private, (c) write-many, (d) result, (e) synchronization, (f) migratory, (g) producer-consumer, (h) read-mostly, and (i) general read-write. A study [BENN90b] has shown that the number of general read-write objects is relatively small. It was also shown that parallel programs behave differently in different phases of their execution. Except in the initialization phase, most of the accesses are of the read type. Finally, it was noticed that the average period between two accesses to synchronization objects is considerably longer than the average access period for other shared objects.

In addition to traditional mechanisms for consistency maintenance in DSM systems (replication, invalidation, migration, and remote load/store), Munin supports one new mechanism—delayed update. When a process modifies a shared-data item, the new value is not immediately sent to remote servers to update their copies. Instead, the sending is postponed until the first next synchronization, and all changes are sent in one package. Between the synchronizations, each process forms its own queue of delayed updates. This queue is flushed at the time of the next synchronization.

Some objects are written only once (at the initialization), and later only read. These objects are maintained by replication and accessed only locally. Private objects are those accessible to all processes, but they are accessed by one processor only. Accesses to private objects are local, and they are not managed by Munin. The write-many objects are those being written into many times between two synchronization points. The delayed update mechanism proves to be very efficient for the consistency maintenance of these objects (weak consistency). The result objects collect the writes from several processes and make them available for reading to only one process. The delayed update mechanism is very useful here, as well. For the synchronization objects, the consistency is maintained using the distributed locks mechanism. Migratory objects are accessed in one time interval by one process only (within the critical region). Consistency is achieved efficiently if, at the exit from the critical region of one process, the object and the associated distributed lock for that critical region are migrated onto the processor to execute the first next process from the waiting queue for the corresponding critical region. The producer-consumer objects are those being written into by one process and being read by a number of other processes. The consistency is maintained by the so-called *eager object movement* to the processors that need them before the actual need arises (and the related request is issued). The mostly-read objects are replicated and then maintained by updating via broadcast after the writes which are relatively rare. The general read-write objects are those that cannot be put into any of the previously described classes. Consistency of these objects is maintained through a mechanism based on the Berkeley Ownership scheme for consistency maintenance of cache memories.

The adaptivity of this consistency scheme (based on the dynamic nature of objects) has a very positive impact on the overall performance of the system and the application. Simulation studies [BENN90b] have shown that, for a given application (such as Quicksort), this adaptive method can decrease the bus traffic by more than 50 percent compared to the conventional hardware write-update, and more than 85 percent compared to the write-invalidate mechanism.

Classification: (D:d,S:s,R:r,A:a,L:g,G:f,B:p,P:*,U:*,C:*).

5. Generalization of the Proposed Classification

The set of criteria introduced earlier in the paper enables each software solution to be described with a set of attributes. These attributes are related to the 10 criteria and correspond to different possible classes of the applied criteria. A 10-tuple of attributes was associated with each of the presented solutions. The proposed classification method can be easily generalized through the introduction of an abstract space of criteria. Each one of the presented solutions can be treated as a point in such a space.

The coordinates of the multidimensional discrete space of criteria correspond to the chosen criteria, and the discrete values on these coordinates correspond to the classes of the applied criteria, that is, to the attributes. The number of criteria determines the dimension of the space. The number of classes for each criterion determines the number of discrete values that exist on the corresponding coordinate.

If the abstract space is described with a sufficiently large number of criteria (complete space), each point corresponds to one of the existing solutions. If the abstract space is described with a smaller number of criteria (reduced space), one point may correspond to a larger number of existing solutions. This situation indicates either that some important criterion was not taken into consideration or that the solutions are practically the same (such as [CHEON89] and [MIN89]) or semantically similar (such as [MIN89] and [CHIUE93]), but different in implementation, resulting in different performance and/or complexity. On the other hand, if some criterion is not relevant for some solution, the axes related to this criterion must be extended so that the value (attribute) is "irrelevant." This action prevents the propagation of the solution over all points along the coordinate of the irrelevant criterion. Thus all points in the complete space come into one-to-one correspondence with the existing solutions, and the classification boils down to positioning a given solution to a given point in the space.

For example, Figure 2 shows a reduced three-dimensional (3D) space formed from the first three criteria (dynamism, selectivity, and restrictiveness). Some points in this reduced space correspond to several solutions; however, only one representative solution is shown. For example, the point (s,s,r) contains not only the scheme from [CHEON89], but also the schemes from [CYTRO88] and [MIN89]. In addition, the point (d,s,r) contains not only the scheme from [TARTA92], but also the scheme from [BENN90b].

If the coordinates of the space are treated as discrete and bounded, as is the case with the abstract criterion space discussed here, the total possible number of points in this space is given by

$$Q = \prod_{i=1}^{N} C_i \qquad (1)$$

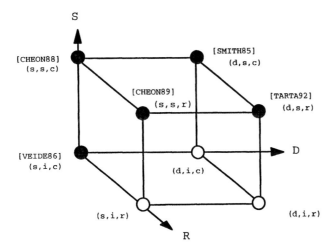

1. Dynamism (D): static (s) or dynamic (d)
2. Selectivity (S): indiscriminative (i) or selective (s)
3. Restrictiveness (R): conservative (c) or restrictive (r)

Figure 2. An example of a reduced 3D abstract criterion space.

where C_i refers to the number of classes for the ith criterion ($I = 1,...,N$). According to equation (1), the number of theoretically different software schemes for the concrete case of the 10-criterion abstract space presented here, is $Q=40,960$. Of course, this number should be considered as an illustration for one possible classification, not as a general conclusion.

The combinations of attributes (N-tuples of attributes) that correspond to nonexisting solutions are referred to as "free points." Some of these free points can serve as guides to new solutions that are potentially useful. (Some of the free points correspond to solutions that make no sense; and of those that do make sense, some may not be very useful in given circumstances.) It should be noted that, given the characteristics of classes that describe a new solution, one could roughly estimate the performance of the solution without analyzing its details.

A relatively large number of new and potentially useful solutions could be found in the "plane" of adaptive static schemes. Using the semantic information about the access methods to a shared object, appropriate instructions could be inserted into the code at compile time to support the mechanism that is "optimal" for the given access method.

6. Evaluation Studies of Software Schemes

This section is devoted to an overview of existing evaluation studies of software solutions. Most of these are aimed at the following two issues: (a) obtaining a better understanding about the impact of various parameters (especially the workload related parameters) on the performance of software solutions and (b) gaining an impression about the real bottlenecks of software solutions. In addition, one of our goals is to present different methods for evaluation of software solutions.

The following evaluation studies have been selected for presentation here: (a) one simulation analysis based on real address traces [MIN90], (b) one simulation study based on the probabilistic synthetic workload [TARTA92], (c) one analytical study based on the mean value analysis (MVA) model [OWICK89], and (d) one analytical study that compares hardware directory-based schemes and software static schemes [ADVE91]. Each study is presented in two paragraphs, first describing the method and conditions and the second describing the main results and conclusions.

In [MIN90], Min and Baer compared a hardware scheme based on a centralized full-map directory, developed by Censier and Feautrier with a static software scheme based on timestamps developed by Min and Baer. In a follow-up paper, it was shown that the static software scheme based on timestamps demonstrates a lower miss ratio than do other static software schemes [MIN92]. The comparison in [MIN90] is based on simulation with three address traces of three different applications in which the model of parallelism is expressed through parallel DoAll loops (the program paradigm is referred to as SPMD—single program multiple data). At run time, the program forms a sequence of epochs. One epoch can have multiple instances, as is the case with epochs in which DoAll loops are executed—each instance represents one iteration and is executed on a different processor. The simulation was done both for the prescheduled processes (the ith iteration of DoAll is executed on the processor (i mod P)+1, and the serial code between two loops is always on the same processor) and for the randomly scheduled processes (the processor that executes an instance of an epoch is randomly selected). The following performance measures were shown: (a) miss ratio, (b) write traffic, and (c) network traffic. All of these performance measures were viewed as functions of the number of processors in the system.

For the analyzed applications, the miss ratio was about the same for both schemes for any number of processors. In general, the miss ratio is an increasing function of the number of processors because the larger the number of processors, the greater the probability that one processor writes to a location between two successive reads from the same location by another processor. However, the larger the number of processors, the lower the probability of benefiting from interiteration locality because the iterations are spread over a larger number of processors. For two out of three analyzed applications, the miss ratio is considerably higher if the iterations are randomly distributed because the ability to re-use the cache contents outside the epoch boundary is lost. The opposite behavior was noticed with just one out of three applications. The write traffic is considerably higher with the software scheme (compared to the hardware scheme) and is fairly independent of the number of processors and the process scheduling policy. The relatively large write traffic of the software scheme is a consequence of the write-back of dirty lines at the end of each instance of one epoch. The network traffic is larger with the hardware scheme because it is directory-based. Also, the network traffic increase as a function of the number of processors is faster with the hardware scheme (compared to the software scheme). This is because the traffic increase is related to the inductive invalidation typical of hardware schemes in general, whereas the software schemes are characterized by self-invalidation, which has no impact on the network traffic. With software schemes, the increase of the network traffic is minimal when the number of processors goes up. This is because the write traffic and write misses have a relatively small impact on the network traffic.

In [TARTA92], the authors presented the results of their study of the impact of the restrictiveness of invalidation conditions on processing power. They used a modified Archibald–Baer model of the probabilistically synthesized workload. The modifications consist of the introduction of (a) new parameters that model the spatial and the processor locality as well as (b) an operating system model that is rather simplified, but adequate for this purpose. The authors first propose a class of schemes referred to as the selective and conditional self-invalidation class (SCSIC). The schemes of this class differ only in the restrictiveness of the invalidation conditions. The schemes are compared on a realistic multiprocessor simulator having a 32-bit bus and a set-associative cache of a relatively small size with several words per cache line. The selected performance measures are (a) the average number of invalidations during the passage through a critical region, (b) cache hit ratio, and (c) the processing power. All performance measures were treated as functions of the number of processors in the system. An important parameter in the entire analysis is the probability that, in a given passage through the critical region, the shared data are only read (Pr-o). This parameter has an important impact on the overall performance of all SCSIC schemes.

The preliminary results of the simulation analysis demonstrate the advantages of the restrictively applied invalidation, even in systems with only 16 processors. The advantage is higher when the value of the parameter (Pr-o) is higher, which is obvious. However, what is not obvious is the quantitative value of the real advantage. When the number of processors is as low as 16 and the value of Pr-o is equal to 0.95, the advantage is more than 5 percent for the scheme with the most restrictive invalidation (verification of the segment version) compared with a similar, OTI-like scheme. For a much larger number of processors, which is more realistic for future systems, the advantage is expected to be considerably higher.

In [OWICK89], Owicki and Agarwal used the analytical MVA model for performance comparison of four representative schemes for the maintenance of cache consistency. The chosen schemes include the following: (a) Base—a scheme with no consistency maintenance, which defines the upper limit for performance; (b) No-cache—a very conservative scheme that does not allow the caching of pages with shared data (this scheme corresponds to the scheme proposed for the C.mmp [WULF72]); (c) Software-flush—a more sophisticated scheme based on static program analysis and insertion of the flush instruction (this scheme corresponds to the scheme from [CYTRO88] and [CHEON88]); and (d) Dragon [ATKIN84]—one of the best hardware schemes based on snooping and write-broadcast. The developed analytical model includes the system model, the workload model, and the contention model. The system model defines the number of cycles required for each given operation in hardware. The workload model defines the frequencies (probabilities) of specific actions. For example, ls refers to the probability that the instruction is a load or store, shd refers to the probability that load or store use shared data, and apl refers to the number of references to a shared data item before it is flushed from the cache using the flush instruction. The contention model determines the additional time spent due to the contention on the common bus or the multistage interconnection network. The basic performance measure used in this research is processing power. It is viewed as a function of the number of processors in the system. For each relevant parameter, three values are used: low, medium, and high. If the impact of one parameter is studied, the value of that parameter is varied from low to high, while the values of all other parameters are kept at the medium value.

For the common bus case, the analysis has shown that the No-cache scheme has the worst performance and the Dragon scheme the best. Also, it was shown that the software schemes are relatively sensitive to the changing values of the ls, shd, and apl parameters. For low values of parameters ls and shd, the performance of the Software-flush scheme is comparable with that of the Dragon scheme. For medium and high values of these parameters, the Dragon scheme has an advantage. The software schemes show an increased sensitivity to the apl parameter. For relatively high values of this parameter ($apl = 25$) the performance of the Software-flush scheme is even better than the performance of the Dragon scheme. For the multistage interconnection network case, the analysis has shown that the processing power of the software schemes increases linearly with the number of processors, which is an indication of the high level of scalability of these schemes.

In [ADVE91], the authors compared the directory-based hardware schemes with static software schemes. Their applied analytical method starts from a general program behavior model, which specifies the access dynamics for different classes of shared data. The following classes of shared data have been observed: (a) passively shared objects (the shared read-only data, and the shared read-write data actually accessed by one processor only), (b) mostly-read objects, (c) frequently read-written objects, (d) migratory objects (the data being accessed within critical regions), and (e) synchronization objects (for example, the lock of the critical regions). The model includes high-level parameters and low-level parameters. The high-level parameters include (a) the fraction of memory accesses related to data references (f_{data}), (b) the fraction of data references related to private data (f_{pvt}), (c) the fraction of shared references related to a particular class of data (f_{PS}, f_{MR}, f_{RW}, f_{MIG}), (d) the fraction of accesses to mostly-read ($f_{w/MR}$) or read-written ($f_{w/RW}$) data that are writes, (e) the runtime average number of read accesses by a processor to a mostly-read data element between consecutive compiler-inserted invalidations executed on that element by the same processor (l_{MR}), (f) the average number of read accesses by a processor to a frequently read-written data element between potential writes by other processors (l_{RW}), (g) the mean number of processors that access a data element of appropriate data class between consecutive actual writes to that element (n_{MR} and n_{RW}), and so on. These high-level parameters are independent of the cache consistency scheme, describe the workload, and enable different classes of data to be analyzed independently of each other with respect to their impact on the efficiency of a given scheme. The low-level parameters for the hardware scheme in [AGARW88] include (a) the fraction of references that are read misses or write misses to lines in shared ($p_{r/sh}$ or $p_{w/sh}$) or modified ($p_{r/mod}$ or $p_{w/mod}$) state, (b) the probability that invalidations are sent individually ($p_{ind.inv}$), and (c) the average number of processors to which individual invalidations are sent (n_{inv}). The low-level parameters for the software scheme in [CYTRO88] include (a) the fraction of references that are read (p_r) or write (p_w) misses and (b) the fraction of references that are posts (p_{post}) or invalidates (p_{inv}). All low-level parameters used in direct comparison of different schemes are derived from the general high-level model, and therefore the comparisons are expected to be fair. These low-level parameters serve as input data into the approximate MVA model of the scheme being analyzed. In this study, the basic performance measure is the processor efficiency. It is defined as the "average fraction of time each processor spends executing locally out of its cache."

For different classes of data, the paper gives the contours of the constant ratio of software to hardware efficiency method. From these contours, one can easily identify the parameter domains where the software scheme exhibits an advantage in comparison with the hardware scheme, and vice versa. For the class of migratory data, the software scheme is always more efficient. For the class of mostly-read objects, the software scheme is slightly better only for very small values (close to 1) of the average number of compiler-inserted invalidates done by a processor in the interval between two successive actual writes into the given data item, averaged over the intervals when the processor does execute such invalidates ($ratio_{MR}$). Larger values of the parameter $ratio_{MR}$ correspond to a larger number of unrealized potential writes that cause unnecessary invalidations. For larger values of the $ratio_{MR}$ parameter ($ratio_{MR} \geq 3$), a relatively small value of the parameter l_{MR} ($l_{MR}=1$), and a fraction of the mostly-read objects $f_{MR}>0.2$, the hardware scheme is more 20 percent better than the software scheme. However, for a larger value of the parameter l_{MR} ($l_{MR} \geq 8$), the hardware scheme is less than 20 percent better than the software scheme for almost all values of $ratio_{MR}$ and $f_{MR}<0.85$; therefore, the software scheme is comparable in performance with the hardware scheme for a much lower production cost. In general, the software scheme is relatively sensitive to changes of the parameter l_{MR}. On the other hand, the hardware scheme is sensitive to the changes of the parameters $f_{w/MR}$ and n_{MR}. For the frequently read-written data class with the expected fraction in real applications $f_{RW}<0.2$, it was concluded that the software scheme is also comparable with the hardware scheme because it is within the 20 percent range of the hardware scheme performance. Finally, the paper deals with an impact of reduction in the hit ratio (due to the conservative analysis of memory conflicts typical of static software schemes) on the software/hardware scheme efficiency ratio. If the values of all relevant parameters are set in such a way that the hardware and the software scheme are equal in performance, the following interesting impact of the hit ratio reduction is observed. If the hit ratio reduction is more than 15 percent, the hardware scheme is more than 20 percent better in performance. If the reduction of the hit ratio is 10 percent, the hardware scheme is about 10 percent better in performance. However, if the hit ratio reduction is less than 5 percent, and if most of the potential writes are actually executed, the performance advantage of the software scheme goes up to about 20 percent.

It should be underlined here that the study by Adve et al. [ADVE91] uses the term "software schemes" to mean only the static software schemes. However, dynamic software schemes merit attention as well, for a number of reasons. For example, the imprecise prediction of memory conflicts and potential writes at compile time, which can significantly degrade the performance of static schemes, is not an issue with the dynamic schemes. Also, in the case of nonnumeric applications characterized by tasks communicating through exclusive usage of shared variables inside critical regions—where dynamic software schemes (as [SMITH85] or [TARTA92]) offer a natural solution by virtue of the dominance of migratory data objects—a relatively good performances can be expected.

7. Conclusions

This paper represents an effort to encompass and classify the existing work in the field of software-based algorithms for the maintenance of cache consistency in shared-memory multiprocessor systems. A set of 10 classification criteria is proposed. Each criterion results in several classes. These classes serve as attribute values for description and classification of existing approaches.

The basic criterion, the dynamism of the approach, is used to divide the surveyed schemes into two essential groups: (a) static, which do the program analysis for detection of inconsistency conditions at compile time, and (b) dynamic, which detect the inconsistency conditions at run time.

After the field is broadly surveyed and the correspondence between schemes and attributes is established, a generalization of the proposed classification is introduced. It is based on an N-dimensional criterion space. Each scheme that is essentially different from other existing schemes corresponds to a point in that space. This generalization allows the following to be accomplished:

- With the state of the art in the field, it can be detected that some solutions are essentially the same (because they belong to the same point in the criterion space), although they are declared as formally different (because they have been introduced independently of each other in time and space).
- With the development of the field, it can be determined if a set of criteria (and related classes) is defined widely enough so that essentially different solutions can be associated with different points in the space.
- With respect to future contributions in the field, the "empty" points in the criterion space can serve as guides toward new solutions (as was the case with the Mendeleev periodic classification system in chemistry).

Through a careful inspection of the criterion space, one can recognize that a part of the criterion space that corresponds to static and adaptive schemes is "empty" at the time. This means that some potentially good new solutions can be found in this part of the criterion space, thus encouraging research in that direction.

Finally, the paper gives a survey of performance evaluation studies in the field of software-based consistency maintenance. Representative evaluation techniques and their basic results have been described in two different domains: (a) simulation analysis based on the real address traces or the synthetic workload models, and (b) analytical evaluation based on MVA models.

The presented studies also yield good insight into the real performance differences between software and hardware schemes for different values of technology- and application-related parameters. One especially important conclusion is that in several applications (mostly, but not only, those characterized by migratory data) software schemes demonstrate better performance. It is expected that in real implementations, this performance advantage may be even slightly higher because the complexity of hardware support for software schemes is relatively low. Consequently, VLSI systems that utilize software schemes potentially have a slightly better internal timing, and operate with a slightly faster system clock.

8. References

[ADVE91]   Adve, S.V., et al., "Comparison of Hardware and Software Cache Coherence Schemes," *Proc. 18th Ann. Int'l Symp. Computer Architecture,* ACM Press, New York, N.Y., 1991, pp. 298–308.

[AGARW88]   Agarwal, A., et al., "An Evaluation of Directory Schemes for Cache Coherence," *Proc. 15th Ann. Int'l Symp. Computer Architecture,* IEEE CS Press, Los Alamitos, Calif., 1988, pp. 280-289.

[ARCHI86]   Archibald, J., and Baer, J.-L., "Cache Coherence Protocols: Evaluation Using a Multiprocessor Simulation Model," *ACM Trans. Computer Systems,* Vol. 4, No. 4, Nov. 1986, pp. 273–298.

[BENN90a]   Bennett, J.K., Carter, J.B., and Zwaenepoel, W., "Munin: Distributed Shared Memory Based on Type-Specific Memory Coherence," *Proc. 1990 Conf. Principles and Practice of Parallel Programming,* 1990, pp. 168–176.

[BENN90b]   Bennett, J.K., Carter, J.B., and Zwaenepoel, W., "Adaptive Software Cache Management for Distributed Shared Memory Architectures," *Proc. 17th Ann. Int'l Symp. Computer Architecture,* IEEE CS Press, Los Alamitos, Calif., 1990, pp. 125–134.

[BRANT85]   Brantley, W.C., McAuliffe, K.P., and Weiss, J., "RP3 Processor-Memory Element," *Proc. 1985 Int'l Conf. Parallel Processing,* IEEE CS Press, Los Alamitos, Calif., 1985, pp. 782–789.

[CENSI78]   Censier, L.M., and Feautrier, P., "A New Solution to Coherence Problem in Multicache Systems," *IEEE Trans. Computers,* Vol. C-27, No. 12, Dec. 1978, pp. 1112–1118.

[CHERI86]   Cheriton, D.R., Slavenburg, G.A., and Boyle, P.D., "Software-Controlled Caches in the VMP Multiprocessor," *Proc. 13th Ann. Int'l Symp. Computer Architecture,* IEEE CS Press, Los Alamitos, Calif., 1986, pp. 366–374.

[CHEON88]   Cheong, H., and Veidenbaum, A.V., "A Cache Coherence Scheme with Fast Selective Invalidation," *Proc. 15th Ann. Int'l Symp. Computer Architecture,* IEEE CS Press, Los Alamitos, Calif., 1988, pp. 299–307.

[CHEON89]   Cheong, H., and Veidenbaum, A.V., "A Version Control Approach to Cache Coherence," *Proc. Int'l Conf. Supercomputing 89,* ACM Press, New York, N.Y., 1989, pp. 322–330.

[CHEON90]   Cheong, H., and Veidenbaum, A.V., "Compiler-Directed Cache Management in Multiprocessors," *Computer,* Vol. 23, No. 6, June 1990, pp. 39–47.

[CHEON92]   Cheong, H., "Life Span Strategy—A Compiler-Based Approach to Cache Coherence," *Proc. 1992 Int'l Conf. Supercomputing,* ACM Press, New York, N.Y., 1992, pp. 139–148.

[CHIUE93]   Chiueh, T.-C., "A Generational Algorithm to Multiprocessor Cache Coherence," *Proc. 1993 Int'l Conf. Parallel Processing,* Vol. 1, CRC Press, Boca Raton, Fla., 1993, pp. 20–24.

[CYTRO88]   Cytron, R., Karlovsky, S., and McAuliffe, K.P., "Automatic Management of Programmable Caches," *Proc. 1988 Int'l Conf. Parallel Processing,* Penn State Press, University Park, Pa., 1988, pp. 229–238.

[DAHLG95]   Dahlgren, F., Skeppstedt, J., and Stenström, P., "Effectiveness of Hardware-Based and Compiler-Controlled Snooping Cache Protocol Extensions," *Proc. Int'l Conf. High-Performance Computing,* 1995, (to appear).

[DARNE93]   Darnell, E., and Kennedy, K., "Cache Coherence Using Local Knowledge," *Proc. Supercomputing '93,* ACM Press, New York, N.Y., 1993, pp. 720–729.

[EDLER85]   Edler, J., et al., "Issues Related to MIMD Shared-Memory Computers: The NYU Ultracomputer Approach," *Proc. 12th Ann. Int'l Symp. Computer Architecture,* IEEE CS Press, Los Alamitos, Calif., 1985, pp. 126–135.

[EGGER89]   Eggers, S.J., and Katz, R.H., "Evaluating the Performance of Four Snooping Cache Coherency Protocols," *Proc. 16th Ann. Int'l Symp. Computer Architecture,* ACM Press, New York, N.Y., 1989, pp. 2–15.

[GOTTL82]   Gottlieb, A., et al., "The NYU Ultracomputer—Designing a MIMD, Shared-Memory Parallel Machine (Extended abstract)," *Proc. 9th Ann. Int'l Symp. Computer Architecture,* IEEE CS Press, Los Alamitos, Calif., 1982, pp. 27–42.

[GOTTL83]   Gottlieb, A., et al., "The NYU Ultracomputer—Designing an MIMD, Shared Memory Parallel Computer," *IEEE Trans. Computers,* Vol. C-32, No. 2, Sept. 1983, pp. 175–189.

[LEE87a]   Lee, R.L., Yew, P.-C., and Lawrie, D.H., "Multiprocessor Cache Design Considerations," *Proc. 14th Ann. Int'l Symp. Computer Architecture*, ACM Press, New York, N.Y., 1987, pp. 253–262.

[LEE87b]   Lee, R.L., "The Effectiveness of Caches and Data Prefetch Buffers in Large-Scale Shared Memory Multiprocessors," PhD thesis, TR 670, Center of Supercomputing Research and Development, Univ. of Illinois at Urbana-Champaign, Aug. 1987.

[LILJA93]   Lilja, D., "Cache Coherence in Large-Scale Shared-Memory Multiprocessors: Issues and Comparisons," *ACM Computing Surveys*, Vol. 25, No. 3, Sept. 1993, pp. 303–338.

[LOURI92]   Louri, A., and Sung, H., "A Compiler Directed Cache Coherence Scheme with Fast and Parallel Explicit Invalidation," *Proc. 1992 Int'l Conf. Parallel Processing*, Vol. 1, CRC Press, Boca Raton, Fla., 1992, pp. 2–9.

[MCAUL86]   McAuliffe, K., "Analysis of Cache Memories in Highly Parallel Systems," PhD Thesis, TR 269, Courant Institute of Mathematical Sciences, New York University, May 1986.

[MIN89]   Min, S.L., and Baer, J.-L., "A Timestamp-Based Cache Coherence Scheme," *Proc. Int'l Conf. Parallel Processing*, Vol. 1, Penn State Press, University Park, Pa., 1989, pp. 123–132.

[MIN90]   Min, S.L., and Baer, J.-L., "A Performance Comparison of Directory-Based and Timestamp-Based Cache Coherence Schemes," *Proc. 1990 Int'l Conf. Parallel Processing*, Vol. I, Penn State Press, University Park, Pa., 1990, pp. 305–311.

[MIN92]   Min, S.L., and Baer, J.-L., "Design and Analysis of a Scalable Cache Coherence Scheme Based on Clocks and Timestamps," *IEEE Trans. Parallel and Distributed Systems*, Vol. 3, No. 1, Jan. 1992, pp. 25–44.

[OWICK89]   Owicki, S., and Agarwal, A., "Evaluating the Performance of Software Cache Coherence," *Proc. 3rd Int'l Conf. Architectural Support for Programming Languages and Operating Systems*, ACM Press, New York, N.Y., 1989, pp. 230–242.

[PFIST85]   Pfister, G.F., et.al., "The IBM Research Parallel Processor Prototype (RP3): Introduction and Architecture," *Proc. 1985 Parallel Processing Conf.*, IEEE CS Press, Los Alamitos, Calif., 1985, pp. 764–771.

[PROTI95]   Protić, J., Tomašević, M., and Milutinović, V.," A Survey of Distributed Shared Memory Systems," *Proc. 28th Ann. Hawaii Int'l Conf. System Sciences*, Vol. 1, IEEE CS Press, Los Alamitos, Calif., 1995, pp. 74–84.

[SKEPP95]   Skeppstedt, J., and Stenström, P., "A Compiler Algorithm that Reduces Read Latency in Ownership-Based Cache Coherence Protocols," *Proc. Int'l Conf. Parallel Architectures and Compilation Techniques*, 1995, pp. 69–78.

[SMITH85]   Smith, A.J., "CPU Cache Consistency with Software Support and Using One Time Identifiers," *Proc. Pacific Computer Communication Symp.*, 1985, pp. 142–150.

[STENS90]   Stenström, P., "A Survey of Cache Coherence Schemes for Multiprocessors," *Computer*, Vol. 23, No. 6, June 1990, pp. 12–24.

[TARTA92]   Tartalja, I., and Milutinović, V., "An Approach to Dynamic Software Cache Consistency Maintenance Based on Conditional Invalidation," *Proc. 25th Ann. Hawaii Int'l Conf. System Sciences*, Vol. 1, IEEE CS Press, Los Alamitos, Calif., 1992, pp. 457–466.

[TOMAŠ93]   Tomašević, M., and Milutinović, V., *The Cache Coherence Problem in Shared-Memory Multiprocessors: Hardware Solutions,* IEEE CS Press, Los Alamitos, Calif., 1993.

[TOMA94a]   Tomašević, M., and Milutinović, V., "Hardware Approaches to Cache Coherence Problem in Shared-Memory Multiprocessors, Part 1," *IEEE Micro,* Vol. 14, No. 5, Oct. 1994, pp. 52–59.

[TOMA94b]   Tomašević, M., and Milutinović, V., "Hardware Approaches to Cache Coherence Problem in Shared-Memory Multiprocessors, Part 2," *IEEE Micro,* Vol. 14, No. 6, Dec. 1994, pp. 61–66.

[VEIDE86]   Veidenbaum, A.V., "A Compiler-Assisted Cache Coherence Solution for Multiprocessors," *Proc. 1986 Int'l Conf. Parallel Processing,* IEEE CS Press, Los Alamitos, Calif., 1986, pp. 1029–1036.

[WULF72]   Wulf, W.A., and Bell, C.G., "C.mmp—A Multi-Mini Processor," *Proc. Fall Joint Computer Conf.,* IEEE Press, New York, NY, 1972, pp. 765–777.

[YEH83]   Yeh, P.C.C., Patel, J.H., and Davidson, E.S., "Shared Cache for Multiple-Stream Computer Systems," *IEEE Trans. Computers,* Vol. C-32, No. 1, Jan. 1983, pp. 38–47.

Chapter 2
Static Software Cache Coherence Schemes

In this book, we consider as "static" all of the software schemes that are predominantly based on the program analysis at compile time. In static schemes, the algorithms for detection of incoherence conditions are incorporated into the compiler. Compile-time analysis results in the insertion of additional instructions into the analyzed code and, in some solutions, in the marking of data references and/or data structures. Prediction of potential incoherence at compile time prevents communication among processors at run time (which characterizes the hardware schemes) and consequently reduces the network traffic. On the other hand, the compile-time prediction of actual cache incoherence events cannot be absolutely precise, and thus some static solutions are unnecessarily conservative. A number of papers dealing with compiler-based coherence maintenance were selected for this chapter.

As an introductory reading to the field of static software schemes, we suggest the paper written by Cheong and Veidenbaum, "Compiler-Directed Cache Management in Multiprocessors." This paper represents a detailed survey of the three schemes developed by the authors, but does not cover the entire field of static software coherence maintenance.

Brantley, McAuliffe, and Weiss, in their paper "RP3 Processor-Memory Element" (a follow-up to the work of Pfister et al., reported in "The IBM Research Parallel Processor Prototype (RP3): Introduction and Architecture"), mention briefly an approach to software cache coherence maintenance that permits a change of cachability status of shared data between the execution of program segments. When the read-write shared (noncachable) data change their status to read-only data, caching is enabled. The approach is very similar to the NYU Ultracomputer approach reported earlier (see the paper by Gottllieb et al. and the McAuliffe PhD thesis in Suggestions for Further Reading). The IBM RP3 prototype was developed at the IBM T.J. Watson Research Center. In general, the cache coherence maintenance strategy of the IBM RP3 scheme is still very conservative; however, its selective invalidation is more flexible in the sense that the granularity of data to be invalidated can be varied.

Veidenbaum proposes, in the paper "A Compiler-Assisted Cache Coherence Solution for Multiprocessors," a relatively simple static software scheme for cache coherence maintenance in the Cedar multiprocessor at the University of Illinois. In comparison with the previous paper, where a solution to the coherence problem is just mentioned, Veidenbaum precisely elaborates a coherence maintenance algorithm. The scheme assumes the program structure based on parallel/serial loops, which are widely used to express parallelism in numeric applications. The essence of the scheme is that the compiler inserts special-purpose instructions for cache coherence maintenance only at loop boundaries and at subroutine call points. As can be seen, the algorithm includes no analysis of individual data dependencies for each particular instruction. It does the preventive disabling and flushing of the cache only at the boundaries of those loop types in which the incoherence condition can arise.

Cheong and Veidenbaum, in the paper "A Cache Coherence Scheme With Fast Selective Invalidation," propose another software scheme for coherence maintenance which originated from research done at the University of Illinois. The speed of invalidation is close to that of indiscriminative invalidation, but its selectivity is such that it allows a better hit ratio. Although the algorithm for inserting the Invalidate instruction is conservative, preventive invalidation is done at the boundaries of parallel loops (intercycle conservative invalidation).

Cytron, Karlovsky, and McAuliffe, in the paper "Automatic Management of Programmable Caches," propose a solution for cache coherence maintenance in shared-memory multiprocessors that is based on a detailed static analysis of data dependencies for all instructions in the program. The authors were with the IBM T.J. Watson Research Center and with the University of Illinois at the time when the work was published. This scheme is very restrictive to the invalidations within a procedure. This is due to the fact that both the program structure analysis and the data dependency analysis are performed at compile time. However, the problem of unnecessary invalidations on the interprocedure level remains.

Cheong and Veidenbaum, in the paper "A Version Control Approach to Cache Coherence," propose a scheme that represents an improvement of their "fast selective invalidation" scheme. It was also developed at the University of Illinois. The scheme is based on the static analysis of the parallel program tasking structure and a dynamic control of the variable version, using appropriate hardware support. Compared with the previous two schemes by the same authors, the version control scheme demonstrates a better performance because it respects the temporal locality of references over the task execution level boundary. A direct consequence of this is an increased hit ratio. This advantage is paid for by more complex hardware support for coherence maintenance.

Min and Baer, in the paper "Design and Analysis of a Scalable Cache Coherence Scheme Based on Clocks and Timestamps," propose, independently of Cheong and Veidenbaum, the "timestamps" scheme, which is very similar to the version control scheme. The basic difference between the timestamps approach and the version control approach lies in the fact that Min and Baer also propose a very sophisticated marking of references, which better supports the localities between dependent tasks in a DoAcross loop. This research was done at the University of Washington.

Chiueh, in the paper "A Generational Algorithm to Multiprocessor Cache Coherence," proposes a substitution for the current version table (needed in the Cheong-Veidenbaum version control scheme for separated version maintenance of all shared data) with only one register that keeps information on current task generation. For each shared variable, the last generation (level in the task graph) where the shared variable can be considered as valid is statically determined. The work was performed at the State University of New York at Stony Brook.

Darnell and Kennedy, in the paper "Cache Coherence Uisng Local Knowledge," propose a new timestamping scheme based on one-bit timestamps. Their scheme requires a considerably simpler hardware support than the Min-Baer's timestamping or the Cheong-Veidenbaum version control scheme. However, the Darnell-Kennedy scheme yields nearly always a better hit ratio than the Min-Baer scheme. This research was done at Rice University.

Suggestions for Further Reading

Abraham, S.G., and Hudak, D.E., "Compile-Time Partitioning of Iterative Parallel Loops to Reduce Cache Coherence Traffic," *IEEE Trans. Parallel and Distributed Systems*, Vol. 2, No. 3, July 1991, pp. 318–328.

Cheong, H., and Veidenbaum, A.V., "Stale Data Detection and Coherence Enforcement Using Flow Analysis," *Proc. 1988 Int'l Conf. Parallel Processing*, Penn State Press, University Park, Pa., 1988, pp. 138–145.

Cheong, H., "Life Span Strategy—A Compiler-Based Approach to Cache Coherence," *Proc. 1992 Int'l Conf. Supercomputing*, ACM Press, New York, N.Y., 1992, pp. 139–148.

Gottlieb, A., et al., "The NYU Ultracomputer—Designing an MIMD, Shared Memory Parallel Computer," *IEEE Trans. Computers*, Vol. C-32, No. 2, Sept. 1983, pp. 175–189.

Lee, R.L., "The Effectiveness of Caches and Data Prefetch Buffers in Large-Scale Shared Memory Multiprocessors," PhD thesis, TR 670, Center of Supercomputing Research and Development, Univ. of Illinois at Urbana-Champaign, Aug. 1987.

Lee, R.L., Yew, P.-C., and Lawrie, D.H., "Multiprocessor Cache Design Considerations," *Proc. 14th Ann. Int'l Symp. Computer Architecture*, ACM Press, New York, N.Y., 1987, pp. 253–262.

Lilja, D.J., and Yew, P.-C., "Combining Hardware and Software Cache Coherence Strategies," *Proc. 1991 Int'l Conf. Supercomputing*, ACM Press, New York, N.Y., 1991, pp. 274–283.

Louri, A., and Sung, H., "*A Compiler Directed Cache Coherence Scheme with Fast and Parallel Explicit Invalidation*," *Proc. 1992 Int'l Conf. Parallel Processing*, Vol. 1, CRC Press, Boca Raton, Fla., 1992, pp. 2–9.

McAuliffe, K., "Analysis of Cache Memories in Highly Parallel Systems," PhD thesis, TR 269, Courant Institute of Mathematical Sciences, New York University, May 1986.

Min, S.L., "Memory Hierarchy Management Schemes in Large Scale Shared-Memory Multiprocessors," Univ. of Washington, 1989.

Wulf, W.A., and Bell., C.G., "C.mmp—A Multi-Mini-Processor," *Proc. Fall Joint Computer Conference*, IEEE CS Press, Los Alamitos, Calif., 1972, pp. 765–777.

Compiler-Directed Cache Management in Multiprocessors

Hoichi Cheong and Alexander V. Veidenbaum

University of Illinois at Urbana-Champaign

I n recent years, multiprocessor architecture has assumed an important role in high-speed computing as a way of increasing performance over that of uniprocessor systems. However, as the number of processors increases, the memory access time — the time for data and instructions to travel between the shared memory and the processors — increases due to memory conflicts and the limited throughput of the interconnection media.

A cache memory can reduce the average memory access time. However, before we can use private caches in large-scale multiprocessor systems, we must solve the *cache coherence* problem. The coherence problem arises if several caches can contain a copy of the same memory location and a read from one of them is not guaranteed to produce the latest value of the location. In this article, we discuss why we need to find alternatives to hardware-based cache coherence strategies for large-scale multiprocessor systems. Then, we present three different software-based strategies that share the same goals and general approach.

Why study software-managed caches? Several hardware schemes have been proposed for cache coherence enforcement in multiprocessor systems. Most of them only apply to bus-based sys-

Large-scale multiprocessor systems need alternatives to hardware-based cache coherence strategies. This article presents three software-based strategies that have common objectives.

tems.[1] Others use a directory scheme, either centralized or distributed,[2] to maintain coherence. Bus architectures are not scalable to a large number of processors. Neither can the bus-based approach be used in systems using multistage interconnection networks. The central directory is a serious performance bottleneck and also is not

scalable to a large number of processors. The distributed directory schemes that require a presence vector with a bit-per-processor per memory line are not scalable.

The only viable scheme is a distributed directory scheme that does not require the presence vector.[2] Without knowing the identity of the caches that contain a line, this scheme has to use a broadcast to all caches when the line status changes or an up-to-date line is requested. Broadcasting reduces bandwidth of the interconnection network. This directory scheme requires complicated protocols that can cause latency to increase considerably.

On the surface, the cache coherence problem can be solved easily if shared data are not cached. However, as pointed out in the work by F. Darema-Rogers et al.,[3] shared-data accesses account for a large portion of global memory accesses. If shared data are not cached, the performance will suffer.

We are interested only in strategies suitable for shared-memory multiprocessor systems with interconnection networks and a large number of processors. Of all the schemes mentioned above, only one scheme might suit such a system. Therefore, we need an alternative. A scalable, efficient cache coherence scheme for large-scale systems must:

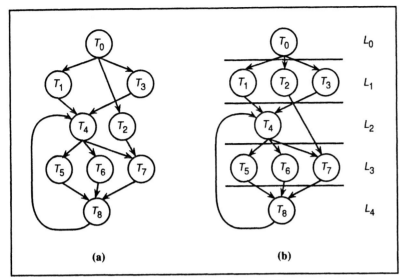

Figure 1. An example of a task graph (a) and its levels (b).

(1) eliminate runtime communication for coherence maintenance,

(2) require the cost of hardware for coherence maintenance to be a very slow-growing function of the number of processors only, not the memory size, and

(3) reduce the total time needed to invalidate cache lines.

We believe compiler assistance can help us accomplish the above goals. The first requirement can be achieved by using compile-time analysis to obtain information on accesses to a given line by multiple processors. Such information can allow each processor to manage its own cache without interprocessor runtime communication. This will also allow us to achieve the second goal. Compiler-directed management of caches implies that a processor has to issue explicit instructions to invalidate cache lines. However, if done a line at a time, the total time for maintaining coherence becomes excessive. To achieve the third goal requires using schemes with special hardware support to invalidate stale data efficiently so the time cost is independent of the number of invalidated lines.

These attributes are the essence of the three software-based schemes discussed in this article. The observation central to all of these schemes is that the contents of private caches and the shared memory can differ as long as incorrect data are not used

by a processor. This observation relaxes the requirement used in hardware-based schemes that every write must be made known to all caches that contain a copy of a line. Therefore, it eliminates the need for communication.

A parallel task-execution model and task graph. We will concentrate on maintaining cache coherence in the execution of parallel Fortran programs. We assume that the execution of a parallel program (parallelized from a sequential program or written in a parallel language) is represented by tasks, each executed by a single processor. Task migration is not allowed. Tasks independent of each other can be scheduled for parallel execution. Dependent tasks will be executed in the order defined by program semantics. The execution order of dependent tasks is enforced through synchronization.

The dependence relationship among tasks, and hence the execution order, can be described by a task graph, $G = \{E, T\}$, a directed graph where E is a set of edges and T is a set of nodes. A node, $T_i \in T$, represents a task, and a directed edge, $e_{i,j} \in E$, represents that some statements in T_j depend on other statements in T_i (see Figure 1a). T_i in such a case is called the parent node of T_j, and T_j is called the child node of T_i.

Task nodes are combined into a single node using the following criterion: Two nodes T_i and T_j connected by an edge e_{ij} can be combined into one node if T_i is the only

parent node of T_j, and T_j is the only child node of T_i.

The task graph can be divided into levels $L = \{L_0, \ldots L_n\}$, where each L_i is a set of tasks such that the longest directed path from T_0, the starting node, to each of the tasks in the set has i edges (see Figure 1b). Tasks on the same level are not connected by any directed edges. Therefore, tasks on the same level perform no write accesses or read-writes to the same data by different processors. Such tasks can be executed in parallel without intertask synchronization.

Let us assume that parallelism in a program is expressed in terms of parallel loops. A parallel loop specifies starting execution of iterations of the loop by multiple processors. In a *Doall* type of parallel loop, all such iterations are independent and can be executed in any order. In a *Doacross* type loop, there is a dependence between iterations. In terms of tasks, one or more iterations of a Doall loop are bundled into a task. In a Doacross loop, one iteration is a task, and synchronization exists between tasks.

Assumptions. We assume a weakly ordered system.[4] While it does not guarantee sequential consistency, the program model is quite simple and has performance much higher than for strongly ordered systems. In terms of our task-execution model, this implies that the values written in a task level must be deposited in the shared memory before the task-level boundary can be crossed.

For clarity, the following discussion focuses on parallel task execution without intertask dependence. However, the cache coherence schemes we'll discuss in this article can be applied to parallel execution with intertask synchronization.

We don't address the questions of line sizes and write policy in this article. We will assume a line size of one word and the write-through policy. However, the schemes presented can be adapted to different line size and write policies.

The algorithms we present have been implemented in the Parafrase restructurer[5] and the resulting code used for simulations. Because Parafrase does not perform interprocedural analysis, we only compile-simulate one subroutine at a time, even though our analysis can be done interprocedurally. Because of this, a subroutine is assumed to start with an empty cache.

The memory references of a program consist of instruction fetches, private-data accesses, and shared-data accesses. Only the latter require coherence enforcement for writable data. Private data may only become a problem if task migration is considered. We assume that instruction, private data, and shared read-only data accesses can be recognized at runtime and will not be affected by the cache coherence mechanism.

A simple invalidation approach

Low invalidation overhead and simplicity characterize the first scheme for maintaining cache coherence.[6] The scheme assumes the value in the shared memory is always current and defines an incoherence as a condition in which

(1) a processor performs a memory fetch of a value X, and
(2) a cache hit occurs, but the cache has a value different from that in memory.

An incoherence cannot occur if the access is a store. Note that we require a processor to try to fetch X; otherwise, the fact that the memory and the cache have different values is not an error. The necessary conditions for the cache incoherence to occur on a fetch of X require that

(1) a value of X is present in the cache of processor P_j, and
(2) a new value has been stored in the shared memory by another processor after the access by P_j that brought X into the cache.

The above conditions can be formulated in terms of data dependencies, and a compiler can then check for a dependence structure that might result in coherence violations. This is rather complex, however, because the test will have to be performed for every read reference. In addition, the data dependence information does not specify whether the references involved are executed by different processors. To simplify the analysis and to get the processor information, we propose to use the type of parallel loop. The compiler has already performed data dependence analysis to determine the loop type, and processor assignment is part of the loop execution model. Let us consider programs with Doall and Doacross loops. By definition, any dependence between two statements inside a Doall loop is not across iterations, but cross-iteration dependencies are present in Doacross. It follows that a statement S_i in a Doall dependent on a statement S_j in

the same loop is executed on the same processor as S_j. In a Doacross loop, two statements with a cross-iteration dependence are executed on different processors, whereas statements with a dependence on the same iteration are executed on the same processor.

A cache management algorithm. Let us assume that the following instructions are available for cache management:

Invalidate. This instruction invalidates the entire contents of a cache. Using resettable static random-access memories for valid bits, this can be accomplished in one or two clocks with low hardware cost.
Cache-On. This instruction causes all global memory references to be routed through the cache.
Cache-Off. This instruction causes all global memory references to bypass the cache and go directly to memory.

The cache state, on or off, must be part of the processor state and must be saved/restored on a context switch. Processes are created in the cache-off state.

The algorithm uses loop types for its analysis as follows:

(1) A Doall loop has no dependencies between statements executed on different processors. Therefore, any shared-memory access in such a loop can be cached. Caching is turned on.
(2) A serial loop is executed by a single processor, and shared-memory accesses can be cached. Caching is turned on.
(3) Doacross or recurrence loops do have cross-iteration dependencies. Therefore, conditions for incoherence can be true. Caching is turned off.
(4) An Invalidate instruction is executed by each processor entering a Doall or a Doacross. The processor continuing execution after a Doall also executes an Invalidate instruction. In terms of a task graph, these points are equivalent to task-level boundaries.

Consider the program example in Figure 2. At the beginning, every processor executes the Cache-On instruction. Note that cache management instructions inserted in parallel loops are executed once by every participating processor, not on every iteration of such a loop.

The algorithm is presented in Veidenbaum.[6] The correctness of the algorithm is proven by showing that the conditions necessary for an incoherence to occur are

```
Cache_on
Doall i = 1, n
    Invalidate
    Y(i)= .
        = W(i)... Y(i)
    .
        = ... X(i)
    .
enddo
Invalidate
    .
    .
Doall j = 1, n
    Invalidate
    .
        = W(j)... Y(j)
    X(j) = ...
    .
enddo
Invalidate
    .
    .
Doall k = 1, n
    Invalidate
        = W(k)
        = ... X(k)
    .
        = ... Y(k)
    . .
enddo
Invalidate
Doserial i = 1, n
    .
        = ... X(i)
    .
        = ... X(f(i))
enddo
```

Figure 2. Program example.

not satisfied in programs processed by the algorithm.

This algorithm preserves all temporal locality at each task level. It satisfies the three requirements set out for a scalable coherence scheme.

Improving the cache management algorithm. In this section, we describe directions for possible extensions of the cache management algorithm, such as allowing caching to be used in some Doacross loops and reducing the number of cache invalidations by doing a more detailed analysis.

94

```
Doall i = 1, n
    invalidate        /* an invalidate-
        cache to reset the change bits */
    Y(i)= .
        = W(i)... Y(i) /* cache-reads */

        = ... X(i) /* cache-read */
        .
enddo
invalidate        /* an invalidate-cache
        to reset the change bits */
        .
        .
        .
Doall j = 1, n
    invalidate        /* an invalidate-
        cache to reset the change bits */
        .
        = W(j)... Y(j) /* cache-reads */
    X(j) = ...
        .
enddo
invalidate        /* an invalidate-cache
        to reset the change bits */
        .
        .
        .
Doall k = 1, n
    invalidate        /* an invalidate-
        cache to reset the change bits */
        = W(k)        /* cache-read */
        = ... X(k) /* memory-read */
        .
        = ... Y(k) /* cache-read */
        .
enddo
invalidate        /* an invalidate-cache
                to reset the change bits */
Doserial i = 1, n
        .
        = ... X(i) /* memory-read */
        .
        = ... X(f(i)) /* memory-read */
        .
enddo
```

Figure 3. Program example.

A Doacross loop is executed by assigning successive iterations to different processors (modulo the number of processors available). The cross-iteration dependencies that exist in a Doacross are thus between statements executed by different processors. Synchronization primitives have to be used between these processors to ensure that dependencies are satisfied, for example, the classical P and V primitives. A straightforward solution is to issue an Invalidate instruction after the P by each processor executing a statement depending on a statement executed by another processor. Since the shared memory has the current value after the V instruction and the cache does not have anything, the value will be fetched out of global memory. Otherwise, the Doacross loops can be treated the same way as the Doall loops by the cache management algorithm. The most interesting case of Doacross is one with other loops nested in it. In such a case, the inner loops take full advantage of caches. Invalidation has to be done after such loops, anyway.

The simplified algorithm we presented does not directly check the conditions necessary for incoherence. It may be possible to detect that the necessary conditions are not satisfied for any reference in a loop. In such a case, invalidation does not have to be performed in or after the loop. Other cases are a loop such that all the data used in the loop has been invalidated by an earlier Invalidate instruction or one where all the data written is invalidated by a later Invalidate before being used.

The fast selective invalidation scheme

The simple scheme we discussed above is not selective in enforcing coherence. It is not selective in either analysis or hardware used to identify and invalidate only stale cache copies. An obvious drawback is that valid cache lines cannot stay in cache across task-level boundaries; therefore, temporal locality is limited. We now try to improve performance by considering individual references in the analysis phase. We also introduce special hardware to enforce coherence on a reference by reference basis.

The fast selective invalidation scheme[7] chooses to enforce coherence at the point of a read reference (load). The idea is to make sure that every read reference will deliver only nonstale cache data to the processor; otherwise, the up-to-date copy from the global memory will be used.

Every read reference (load) to shared memory in a program will be classified and marked by the compiler as either memory-read or cache-read. Each load by a processor is tagged according to the compiler marking. Read references are marked cache-read if the cache resident copy is guaranteed up to date. Read references will be marked as a memory-read if the cache resident copy might have become stale.

A processor will generate different types of memory operand fetches at runtime according to the classification. A cache controller treats a cache-read as a read in a conventional uniprocessor cache. A memory-read implies reading a potentially stale copy, therefore an up-to-date copy will be loaded.

Consider the example in Figure 3. Recall that all processors executing a subroutine start with an empty cache. Read references will be marked as follows: Read accesses to the data elements of W are marked cache-reads because W is read-only. Accesses to Y are also cache-reads because the writes to Y do not have existing copies of data elements to turn stale. Accesses to X before the write in the second loop are cache-reads because they precede all writes to the X data elements. Accesses in the third and the fourth loop are memory-reads because they might access words loaded in the first loop but turned stale by the write in the second loop.

If the compiler can mark only the stale accesses as memory-read, a simple approach would treat the memory-read as a default miss and use the global memory copy. However, the marking is done for each individual read reference with respect to writes by other processors. It might happen that two references marked memory-read are accessing the same location in the same task. In this case, the second reference can use the data in the cache. For example, in the last loop of Figure 3, $X(f(i))$ may access data brought into the cache by the reference to $X(i)$.

To avoid the unnecessary memory access for the later reference, the following special hardware is introduced: A status bit called the *change* bit is added to each cache word. The bit is set when a line is loaded into the cache and reset at task-level boundaries. An access marked memory-read will first check if both the valid and the change bits are true. This will indicate a hit. Otherwise a miss occurs. An Invalidate instruction resets the change bits of all lines. It is inserted in the same places as in our first coherence scheme.

Cache operation. Valid and change bits are associated with each cache word. The change bits are reset at each task-level boundary by the processor starting a task. The change bit is set when a word is written into the cache on a read miss or a write.

A memory-read to a cache word with a false change bit is a default miss, but it will be treated as a conventional cache access with a true change bit. Therefore, the status of the bit can distinguish the first memory-read or the memory-reads following a write from other accesses to the same line in the same task.

An Invalidate instruction resets the change bits, and it will be inserted in the program by the same algorithm as in the simple invalidation scheme of the last section.

Used in a traditional sense, the valid bit implies that nothing has been loaded/stored in the cache line and will cause a default miss. A load or store operation sets the valid bit of an individual cache word. The processor can issue a Clear-Cache instruction to reset all the valid bits and an Invalidate instruction to reset all the change bits using resettable SRAMs.

A cache hit is a function of four Boolean variables:

(1) matched (true on address tag match and false otherwise),
(2) cacheread (true if an access is a cache-read and false for memory-read),
(3) change (true for a reset change bit and false for reset change),
(4) valid (true for a set valid bit and false for a reset valid bit).

Given these variables, a cache hit is represented by

Hit = *matched* $\wedge$ *valid* $\wedge$
      (*cacheread* $\vee$ ($\overline{cacheread}$ $\wedge$ *change*))

Reference marking scheme. We rely on a parallel Fortran compiler such as Parafrase[5] to insert the Invalidate instruction at appropriate places in the instruction stream and to identify and mark references as cache-read or memory-read. We discuss the reference marking scheme below (a more detailed discussion can be found in Cheong and Veidenbaum[8]).

The marking of read references is based on the order of the read-write accesses and the task-level boundaries. Flow analysis[8] is used to carry out such marking

The marking algorithm can be summarized as follows: References to read-only variables within a subroutine are marked cache-read. For variables that are both read and written within the subroutine, all references to a variable preceding the first write to that variable are marked cache-read. The remaining read references are marked according to the following rule: In a parallel execution graph, for each task level L_j that contains a write to a data element, if an

access to the data element exists in $i < j$ levels, all read references to the data element in task levels $k > j$ should be marked memory-read. The rest of the read references should be marked cache-read.

The above rule is based on the same necessary conditions as defined in the section entitled "A simple invalidation approach." The compiler algorithm to mark the references depends on flow analysis to detect the necessary conditions. The analysis detects the order of individual read and write references with respect to task-level boundaries that represent the entry and exit points of parallel loops in the flow graph. References to array variables are analyzed by name only, that is, without considering the subscripts, because it is impossible to analyze accesses to individual array elements in the general case across task-level boundaries.

Summary. The fast selective invalidation scheme is selective by doing the analysis for individual references and by using hardware that can invalidate individual lines. Selective invalidation covers both read-only (*W* in the example) and read-write *Y* and *X*) variables that are accessed by cache-reads. It preserves more temporal locality than the simple invalidation approach that invalidates at least all cache copies of read-write variables at each task boundary.

It is fast because, instead of sequentially invalidating each cache line, it accomplishes invalidation by resetting the change bit. Using resettable SRAMs, one Invalidate instruction can reset the change bits of all cache lines. Therefore, the time cost to invalidate stale copies is negligible. The actual invalidation occurs when a word is accessed by a miss induced by the state of the change and valid bits. It incurs no time penalty, as compared to explicitly issuing an instruction to invalidate a cache line or even a page. Other methods aimed at selective invalidation either do not achieve the same level of selective invalidation[9] or require sequential invalidation[10] (for a detailed discussion, see Cheong and Veidenbaum[8]).

Overall, however, this scheme is still not selective enough. Relying on compile-time detection alone, the scheme is forced to be conservative. Even though temporal locality exists across task levels, it cannot be exploited by memory-read references. More selective invalidation methods, and hence better temporal locality, are the target of the next coherence maintenance scheme.

The version control scheme

The goal of preserving temporal locality across task-level boundaries is only satisfied for references marked cache-read in the fast selective scheme. Once a reference is marked as a memory-read, all references to the same variable on successive task levels also have to be marked memory-read. The first access to such variables in each task on a new level causes a default miss. To prevent the loss of this type of temporal locality, the version control scheme is used.

General ideas. The order of writes to a variable (or memory address) from different tasks is completely determined by the task-execution graph, even if it cannot be determined at compile time. Only one task at a time can write the variable. The writes to a variable in one task theoretically produce a different version of the variable than the writes in other tasks.

Multiple writes to a variable within a task produce only one version because only the value of the last write to a variable will ever be read by other tasks — and only by tasks at subsequent task levels. Thus, at the end of a task execution, only one new version is produced for each variable written within the task.

A version of a variable produced in a task is the new version of the variable to be used at subsequent levels. It can be used by the task that generated the new version, but no other task at this level can use this version of the variable. After the processor finishes the task and moves to a subsequent level, the new version becomes the current version. The current version of the variable contains the up-to-date value to be used until generation of the next version. Each cache copy of a variable in the system must belong to a particular version.

For the scheme to be practical, an array is considered a single variable. Even though a task may write to only a part of an array, a new version is nevertheless assigned for the entire array. If multiple tasks on the same task level write to an array, the writes altogether produce only one new version. A new version of an array variable can still be used in every task at the level where the variable is written because tasks are guaranteed to use disjoint subsets of the array elements.

A processor maintains an integer called the current version number for each variable (scalar or array). The value of the

```
Doall i = 1, n
  Y(i)= .
      = W(i)... Y(i)
      .
      = ... X(i)
      .
enddo
Increment CVN for Y, ...
      .
      .
      .
Increment CVN for ...
Doall j = 1, n
      .
      = W(j)... Y(j)
  X(j) = ...
      .
enddo
Increment CVN for X...
      .
      .
      .
Increment CVN for ...
Doall k = 1, n
      = W(k)
      = ... X(k)
      .
      = ... Y(k)
      .
enddo
Increment CVN for ...
Doserial i = 1, n
      .
      = ... X(i)
      .
      = ... X(f(i))
      .
enddo
```

Figure 4. Program example.

CVN of a variable represents the version of the variable that the processor must use. Each processor updates its own CVNs independently of all other processors using compiler-generated instructions. The general idea is to increment CVNs of all variables written at a task level when the processor moves to the next level. CVNs are kept in a separate local memory. Since each array needs only one CVN, the local memory is small.

Each cache line contains an additional tag called a birth version number. The BVN of the cache line represents a particular version to which the cache copy belongs. The BVN tag is loaded with the value of CVN on a read miss or CVN+1 on a write.

The version scheme performs the following tasks:

(1) runtime comparison of the BVN of a cache line and the CVN of the variable to determine if the access is a hit,
(2) the tagging of each cache line with a BVN, and
(3) proper maintenance of the CVNs.

Given adequate hardware support, these tasks can be achieved with minimal time cost to the system.

Cache management with version numbers. At each reference, hardware compares the CVN and the BVN to avoid stale cache copies. When a cache line is loaded from the global memory, the corresponding CVN of the variable is copied into the BVN field of the cache line. When a cache line is written, the BVN field of the cache line will be set to the new version number of the variable, that is, CVN+1. The BVN of the cache line is checked against the CVN of the variable when the copy is read.

A cache line with a BVN less than the CVN of the variable is a stale cache line. When this is detected, a cache miss will be generated and the up-to-date value will be loaded from the global memory. Cache lines the processor writes will have their BVN equal to the new version number. On a subsequent task level, such cache lines will be identified by the equality of the CVN and the BVN. At the current level, the lines have BVN > CVN.

CVNs of all variables written on a task level are incremented by a processor when it moves to the next task level. The processor performs this by accessing the CVNs from its local memory. The updates of the CVNs in each processor are done independently, without communication overhead and with little computational overhead.

The CVNs of the same variable kept by different processors do not have to agree. The fact that the BVN of the copy is less than the CVN of the variable, not the exact difference of the two numbers, is sufficient for maintaining cache coherence.

Version update. In this section, we describe the version update of a variable in terms of what is done at compile time and what is done at runtime. For simplicity, let us assume an acyclic task-execution graph (the general case is discussed in Cheong and Veidenbaum[11]). A set of variables Var_i that the tasks at level L_i can write to is computed at compile time and used to update the CVNs of these variables at runtime. When a processor finishes a task at level i and is ready to execute a task at level $i + k$, it needs to increment the CVN of each variable that could have been modified on level i and the levels that the processor skips, that is,

$$\bigcup_{j=0}^{j=k-1} Var_{i+j}$$

If a variable is written by another processor at any of the levels skipped, the CVN of the variable will always be larger than the BVN of the corresponding cache line of this processor.

There are two ways of dealing with level skipping. One is to allow a processor to skip levels and then apply updates defined by the compiler for each of the skipped levels separately. This requires the processor to calculate or to be notified of the number of levels skipped. Another way is to disallow level skipping and require each processor to at least update the CVNs upon crossing each level boundary.

The same program example as in previous schemes illustrates version update operations (see Figure 4). If variable Y is updated in the first loop and X in the second loop, their CVNs will be increased in every processor at the end of the loops, respectively. As can be seen in Figure 4, the version control scheme preserves more temporal locality than previous schemes. For variable X, if a processor writes to some $X(j)$s in the second loop, it will reference these copies in its own cache as cache hits in the third loop and the fourth loop. Had the fast selective invalidation scheme been used, first accesses to these copies in these loops would have been default misses.

Hardware support. The version control coherence scheme requires the following hardware support to reduce the overhead:

(1) A *version manager* to maintain the CVNs of each variable in a fast local memory. A CVN is addressed by an identity (ID) number assigned to each variable at either compile time or link time. The version manager can execute two instructions — Increment for a given CVN or Reset for all CVNs — issued by its processor.
(2) The identity number of a variable. This is issued by the processor with every

memory reference. The ID field for each variable can be part of the address of the memory reference, such as a segment number in a segmented memory system, or it can be an extension of the address. In the latter case, 16 bits will be sufficient for most programs.

(3) A field in each cache tag that contains the BVN. All BVNs can be reset by a processor instruction.

Before a program execution starts, the CVNs are set to 1 and the BVN field in each cache line is set to 0. Given a finite size of CVN and BVN, an overflow might occur that would require a processor to reinitialize the BVN for all cache copies and the CVN of the variable. The larger the size of the numbers, the fewer such resets needed. However, too large a size increases the hardware cost.

Figure 5 illustrates a simplified view of the hardware block diagram. In parallel with the cache read operation, the ID number in the address is used to retrieve the CVN from the version manager's memory. The retrieved CVN is compared with the BVN of the cache line. The comparison of the CVNs and the BVN is carried out in parallel with the tag comparison of the cache access. Also, loading an up-to-date copy from the global memory and loading the correct CVN into the version field of the cache line can be done in parallel.

When a missed cache line is brought into the cache, its BVN is set to the CVN of the variable. Hence, the correct version number will be written to the BVN field of the up-to-date cache line read from the global memory.

A write operation will update the cache line and update the BVN field of the cache line with the CVN+1. The suboperations associated with a cache write can be carried out in parallel.

Extension to multilevel caches. The version control coherence scheme can be extended to systems with multilevel cache memories. For multilevel caches, hardware schemes rely on protocols in which invalidation signals traverse levels of caches. To reduce such global traffic, an additional restriction called the "inclusion property" is imposed such that an ancestral cache knows if a copy of its line is present in its descendent caches (the ones closer to processors). The inclusion property also requires a line to be present in an ancestral cache for it to be present in a descendent cache. The version control scheme has the

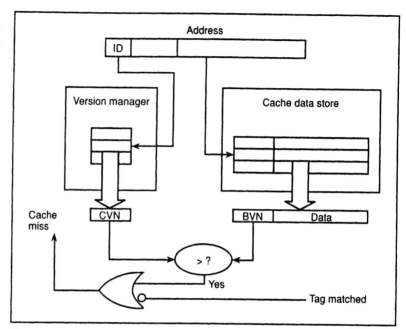

Figure 5. Hardware support for version control.

advantage that the inclusion property does not need to be maintained, since no invalidation signals need to be sent among caches.

The version control scheme is extendible to multilevel caches by implementing version tags (BVNs) in all the cache memories. The same criteria to determine hits or misses as in the single-level version control scheme apply to caches at all levels. The multilevel case only differs from the single-level case in that the CVNs of the same variable must be consistent among all version managers. Otherwise, a copy shared by two processors might be considered up to date by one processor with a smaller CVN and treated as stale by another with a larger CVN. Uniform CVNs can be obtained by requiring each processor to perform updates of CVNs without skipping levels.

The same mechanism that guarantees that values written on a task level are deposited to the shared memory before crossing the task-level boundary now also guarantees depositing of the values in all caches on a path from a processor to memory. This assures that an up-to-date value is read by a task from an intermediate-level cache after crossing the task-level boundary.

Summary. A reference that would be marked memory-read under the fast selective scheme and would force a default miss

right after a task-level boundary can be a cache hit in the version control scheme. More intertask temporal locality is preserved.

Using version numbers, a processor can distinguish the up-to-date cache lines written or loaded by the processor itself from lines possibly modified by other processors. Temporal locality is preserved across task-level boundaries. Neither the simple invalidation scheme nor the fast selective invalidation scheme can preserve this temporal locality. As described earlier, the simple invalidation scheme preserves temporal locality for shared variables only within a task level.

As for the fast selective scheme, temporal locality across task levels is preserved for all variables accessed by references marked cache-read but not by accesses tagged memory-read. The version control scheme does not change the version number of a shared variable until a task level is reached on which it is written. Between levels where the variable is written, the corresponding cache lines are not invalidated once loaded into a cache.

Each processor communicates with its version manager, but this does not add to interprocessor traffic. No communication between processors is required. The number of version update operations is relatively small because one update per processor is needed for a variable written in a task level regardless of the number of writes in the task level and the number of data elements of the variables. Min and Baer[12] independently proposed a similar idea.

Comparison of schemes

To compare the performance of the three schemes, trace-driven simulations were conducted on numerical benchmark routines listed in Table 1. The architecture simulated consisted of processors with private caches connected to interleaved shared-memory systems through interconnection networks. Split instruction/data caches are used with a data cache size of 8,192 words. Coherence block size of one word is still used, but the size of a transfer block is varied. Each processor has an unlimited number of registers. Two system sizes, 32 and 512 processors, are simulated. Only three of the seven benchmark routines used show significant speedup improvement going from the 32- to the 512-processor system.

Benchmark routines (Table 1) are parallelized by Parafrase. The parallelized Fortran routines were interpreted to extract the shared-memory traces. The resulting traces are simulated by a cache simulator.

The metric used for comparison is the shared data hit ratio. As mentioned in the "Assumptions" section, instructions and private data do not cause coherence problems and can be cached as in a uniprocessor cache. In our simulations, coherence enforcement is not applied to instructions and private data.

Each of the schemes invalidates some up-to-date cache lines. To determine the amount of unnecessary invalidation, we obtained the hit ratio for an ideal coherence scheme. In this scheme, each processor knows exactly which of its cache lines have become stale at the end of each task level due to writes by other processors.

Tables 2 and 3 show the simulated ratios for the benchmark routines in Table 1. The column subheadings SI, FS, VC, and IR represent the simple invalidation scheme, the fast selective scheme, the version con-

Table 1. Benchmark programs.

Subroutines No.	Name	Program Name and Description
1	Newrz	Simp2: New velocity computation and volume change in a Lagrangian hydrodynamics program.
2	Ux	Vortex: A PDE solver.
3	Cg	A conjugate gradient matrix solver (for Ax=b).
4	Cmslow	Baro: Nonlinear tendency computation in a barometer program.
5	Lblkern	A kernel of experimental physics computation.
6	Step	Arc3D: Computational fluid dynamics.
7	Parmvr	Pic: Particle in cell program.

Table 2. Simulated data hit ratios for shared data in a 32-processor system.

Sub. No.	Block size of 1				Block size of 2				Block size of 4			
	SI	FS	VC	IR	SI	FS	VC	IR	SI	FS	VC	IR
1	35.04	42.66	52.40	52.40	65.99	70.23	75.26	75.26	82.09	84.37	87.04	87.04
2	91.05	91.06	91.06	91.06	94.22	94.22	94.22	94.22	95.78	95.79	95.79	95.79
3	21.30	38.25	84.19	86.68	59.17	67.99	91.82	93.48	78.60	83.15	95.77	96.85
4	39.84	53.39	58.22	76.79	63.60	73.82	76.04	86.44	75.86	84.22	85.52	91.36
5	2.91	44.70	61.94	63.40	25.08	66.52	77.65	80.93	37.44	78.52	86.79	90.79
6	93.79	93.82	93.82	93.82	94.46	94.47	94.47	94.48	97.84	97.86	97.86	97.87
7	47.00	48.77	49.73	49.83	72.06	74.32	74.71	74.77	86.32	86.77	87.01	87.04

(Sub.: Subroutine; SI: simple invalidation scheme; FS: fast selective invalidation scheme; VC: version control scheme; IR: ideal data hit ratio)

Table 3. Simulated data hit ratios for shared data in a 512-processor system.

Sub. No.	Block size of 1				Block size of 2				Block size of 4			
	SI	FS	VC	IR	SI	FS	VC	IR	SI	FS	VC	IR
1	15.84	34.62	40.59	40.59	37.62	52.88	55.45	55.45	43.56	59.62	62.38	62.38
2	32.45	49.05	49.14	49.46	48.99	65.53	65.63	65.96	57.10	73.64	73.75	74.06
6	28.57	36.24	55.45	73.77	51.01	56.44	69.99	86.11	63.20	66.88	78.28	92.54

(Sub.: Subroutine; SI: simple invalidation scheme; FS: fast selective invalidation scheme; VC: version control scheme; IR: ideal data hit ratio)

trol scheme, and the ideal data hit ratio, respectively, for different transfer block sizes of one, two, and four words. The average differences (over the number of routines in the table) of hit ratios obtained with each scheme and the ideal hit ratios are 13.26 percent, 5.19 percent, and 1.57 percent, respectively, for the simple invalidation scheme, the fast selective invalidation scheme, and the version control scheme on 32 processors. The average differences for the system with 512 processors are 21.7 percent, 10.61 percent, and 4.65 percent.

The simple invalidation scheme is capable of preserving temporal locality only within each task level. Depending on the program structure and granularity, the simple invalidation scheme delivered a wide range of data cache hit ratios. The fast selective invalidation approach can preserve some temporal locality across task levels, especially for variables for which the access pattern is dominated by a sequence of reads followed by writes. For this reason, the fast selective scheme can improve upon some of the benchmarks on which the simple invalidation scheme did not do well.[7] However, for variables whose access pattern is of alternating read and write accesses, the fast selective invalidation scheme cannot exploit most of the intertask-level temporal locality. The version control scheme provides by far the highest data hit ratio among all three schemes,[11] simply because most of the intertask-level temporal locality can be exploited by the version control mechanism.

Compiler-directed cache coherence strategies provide a viable alternative for cache system design in large-scale multiprocessors. The compiler-directed strategies expose multiprocessor cache management to the compiler and achieve cache coherence with independently managed caches and the hardware cost that grows very slowly as a function of the number of processors only. The most important advantage of independently managed caches is the elimination of interprocessor communication for coherence maintenance.

The three proposed schemes differ in the complexity of the hardware required. The schemes offer a range of cache performance at different costs. Detailed performance evaluation will be needed to select the most cost-effective scheme for a given system. ∎

Acknowledgments

We want to thank the referees for many constructive comments that helped improve this article.

This work is supported in part by the National Science Foundation under Grant No. US NSF MIP-8410110, NASA Ames Research Center Grant No. NASA NCC 2-559, the US Department of Energy under Grant No. US DOE DE-FG02-85ER25001, and IBM.

References

1. P. Sweazey and A.J. Smith, "A Class of Compatible Cache Consistency Protocols and Their Support by the IEEE Futurebus," *Proc. 13th Int'l Symp. Computer Architecture*, Vol. 14, No. 2, June 1986, pp. 414-423.

2. J. Archibald and J.-L. Baer, "An Economical Solution to the Cache Coherence Problem," *Proc. 11th Int'l Symp. Computer Architecture*, June 1984, pp. 355-362.

3. F. Darema-Rogers, G.F. Pfister, and K. So, "Memory Access Patterns of Parallel Scientific Programs," Tech. Report RC 12086 (No. 54146), IBM T.J. Watson Research Center, Yorktown Heights, N.Y., Sept. 1986.

4. M. Dubois, C. Scheurich, and F.A. Briggs, "Buffering in Multiprocessors," *Proc. 13th Int'l Symp. Computer Architecture*, Vol. 14, June 1986, pp. 434-442.

5. D.J. Kuck et al., "The Structure of an Advanced Vectorizer for Pipelined Processors," *Computer Software and Applications Conf. (CompSAC 80)*, Oct. 1980, pp. 709-715.

6. A.V. Veidenbaum, "A Compiler-Assisted Cache Coherence Solution for Multiprocessors," *Proc. 1986 Int'l Conf. Parallel Processing*, Aug. 1986, pp. 1,029-1,036.

7. H. Cheong and A.V. Veidenbaum, "A Cache Coherence Scheme with Fast-Selective Invalidation," *Proc. 15th Int'l Symp. Computer Architecture*, CS Press, Los Alamitos, Calif., Order No. 861, June 1988, pp. 299.

8. H. Cheong and A.V. Veidenbaum, "Stale Data Detection and Coherence Enforcement Using Flow Analysis," *Proc. 1988 Int'l Conf. on Parallel Processing*, CS Press, Los Alamitos, Calif., Order No. 889, Vol. I, Aug. 1988, pp. 138-145.

9. A.J. Smith, "CPU Cache Consistency with Software Support and Using One-Time Identifiers," *Proc. Pacific Computer Communications Symp.*, Seoul, Korea, Oct. 1985, pp. 153-161.

10. R. Cytron, S. Karlovsky, and K.P. McAuliffe, "Automatic Management of Programmable Caches," *Proc. 1988 Int'l Conf. Parallel Processing*, CS Press, Los Alamitos, Calif., Order No. 889, Vol. II, Aug. 1988, pp. 229-238.

11. H. Cheong and A.V. Veidenbaum, "A Version Control Approach to Cache Coherence," *Proc. Int'l Conf. Supercomputing 89*, CS Press, Los Alamitos, Calif., Order No. 2021, June 1989, pp. 322-330.

12. S.L. Min and J.-L. Baer, "A Timestamp-Based Cache Coherence Scheme," *Proc. 1989 Int'l Conf. Parallel Processing*, CS Press, Los Alamitos, Calif., Order No. 1935, Vol. I, Aug. 1989, pp. 23-32.

RP3 Processor-Memory Element

W. C. Brantley, K. P. McAuliffe, J. Weiss

IBM T. J. Watson Research Center
Yorktown Heights, NY 10598

Abstract: RP3 is a parallel processor prototype being developed at the IBM Yorktown Heights Research Facility. The system consists of 512 Processor-Memory Elements (PMEs) and an interconnection network. Each PME contains an IBM 801-like microprocessor, memory-mapping unit, 32K-byte cache, vector floating-point unit, an I/O interface, 4 Mbytes of memory, a performance monitor, and an interface to a high-performance bipolar interconnection network. The purpose of this paper is to describe the components that comprise the PME and some of the issues involved in designing specific components. The paper also describes special functions included in the RP3 architecture that facilitate the use of RP3 for a wide range of applications.

1.0 Introduction

The RP3 Processor-Memory Element (PME) is a high-performance engine designed for use in a multi-purpose MIMD parallel processor. It includes a processor, memory-mapping unit, cache, vector floating-point unit, I/O interface, 4 Mbytes of memory, and a performance monitoring device (see Figure 1). A PME's components are constructed mainly from field-effect transistor logic. The PME communicates with other PMEs via an interconnection network constructed from bipolar logic [15]. Also included in the PME are switch interfaces. These components provide logic-level conversion and request/response packet-size conversion between the PME and the network switches.

The PME components (with the exception of the switch interface) are similar to the components found in traditional uniprocessors; in fact, some of the PME components were designed for uniprocessor systems. Our processor is a standard (proprietary) 32-bit microprocessor. We chose to use a standard processor instead of designing a special "parallel" microprocessor in order to concentrate on the architectural requirements for parallel processing.

Extending traditional uniprocessor components to function effectively in a multi-purpose parallel processor is an arduous task. Applications targeted for RP3 were analyzed to determine the architectural features necessary to provide correct execution. Other features that enhance system performance without violating correctness were also studied. Trade-offs were made among algorithmic requirements, hardware complexity, and hardware error-detection and recovery. The architectural features required for the correct execution of programs in a parallel environment are: atomicity of loads and stores to primitive data types, atomicity of coordination primitives, and sequential consistency [12].

The following section describes what we mean by sequential consistency. The subsequent section describes the addressing structure of RP3. The remaining sections describe how the above requirements and how features that provided enhanced performance are integrated into the PME. In order to maintain continuity, the description is done on a PME component-by-component basis.

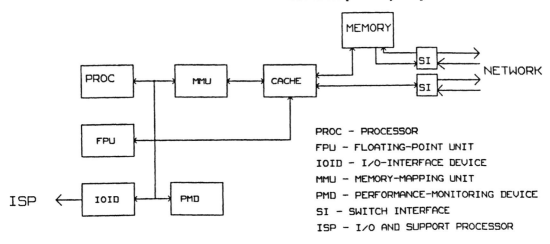

Figure 1. Processor-Memory Element Data Flow.

2.0 Sequential Consistency

By sequential consistency we mean that the results of a set of concurrently executing tasks comprising a program produce the same results as if the tasks were run in some arbitrary sequential order. Collier [2] lists three conditions for maintaining sequential consistency: uniprocessor order, coherence, and program order. **Uniprocessor order** is defined as requiring that loads and stores to the *same* location generated by a *single* processor be serviced at memory in the order determined by the task being executed on the processor. **Coherence** is defined as requiring that the value returned from a processor's load reflect the last value stored at that address by any processor. **Program order** is defined as requiring that loads and stores to shared data be serviced at memory in the order determined by the program, independent of the number of tasks comprising the program.

Uniprocessor order and coherence alone are not sufficient to ensure sequential consistency. Consider Example 1, a program composed of two tasks running on PME_1 and PME_2, respectively. The tasks are communicating via a shared variable A. The shared variable X is used as a semaphore to indicate valid data in A. Assume that shared data cannot be cached; thus coherence is maintained by definition. Uniprocessor order is trivially maintained by PME_1 since the stores are to distinct locations. Uniprocessor order is guaranteed by PME_2 because of the control dependence on X. Sequential consistency, however, may be violated since the stores from PME_1 may be serviced in reverse order. The violation occurs if the store to X is serviced, followed by the servicing of the loads of X and A by PME_2, while the store to A by PME_1 is delayed.

```
Assume X=A=0 initially and X and A are
stored in different PME memories.

    PME₁              PME₂
    A := 1     loop: if X=0 goto loop
    X := 1           b := A

Sequential consistency is violated if
b=0 at termination.
```

Example 1

From the definitions above it is clearly possible for the hardware to guarantee program order by limiting the number of outstanding requests to shared data to one. Any number of requests to private (non-shared) data can be concurrently outstanding provided they are serviced by memory in the order they were issued. Note that uniprocessor order and program order is maintained trivially if the processor is not capable of having more than one concurrently outstanding request at a time.

3.0 Address Structure

The RP3 address translation is performed in two levels: a segment/page mapping and an interleave transformation. Because of the two-level translation three address representations are required: virtual (before translation), real (after segment/page, before interleaving), and absolute (the result of the entire translation process). These representations and their relationships are described in this section.

A virtual address identifies a location within a supervisor's or user's virtual address space. A virtual address is composed of three fields: segment index, page index, and page offset as shown below.

SEGMENT INDEX	PAGE INDEX	PAGE OFFSET
0 9	10 17	18 31

A segment/page mapping is applied to the virtual address to produce a real address plus additional transformation information. The real address does not necessary imply a physical address within memory; rather, it is an intermediate representation. The additional transformation information is an interleave amount [15].

The interleave amount and the real address are inputs to the interleave transformation. The interleave transformation is essentially a right rotate, where the interleave amount specifies the number of bits of the real address that are rotated. The result of this rotation is called the absolute address. The absolute address is composed of two fields: PME number and memory offset as shown below.

PME NUMBER	MEMORY OFFSET
0 9	10 31

The PME number identifies the memory to which a request is transmitted. The memory offset specifies the location to be accessed within a memory.

The interleave amount can range from 0 to the base 2 logarithm of the maximum number of PMEs in the system. The interleave range for RP3 is 0 to 9. An interleave amount of n results in consecutive addresses within a page to be interleaved across 2^n memories since the n most rapidly changing bits are rotated into the PME field of the absolute address. When the interleave amount is zero, the real and absolute addresses are identical. The variable interleaving amount facilitates the partitioning of RP3 into submachines for testing new operating systems and for fault-tolerance.

Figure 2 shows the RP3 address structure. The figure shows the address representation for nontranslated addresses as well as translated addresses. Nontranslated address processing is described in Section 6.

Prior to the interleave transformation the real address can be optionally hashed (the option is set during system configuration). The hashing is a page-dependent one-to-one reordering of addresses within a page. The purpose of the hashing function is to improve system performance by uniformly distributing interleaved addresses across the memories regardless of the access pattern within the virtual address space. If the interleave amount is zero, no hashing is performed. We chose to make hashing an option in order to conduct experiments on the effectiveness of hashing in large parallel processors.

4.0 The Processor

The processor used in the PME is a state-of-the-art 32-bit microprocessor based on the 801 [16] philosophy of single-cycle instruction execution. Our processor differs from other RISC processors ([14,8,9]) in that the PME processor has a large instruction set. The processor has the ability to prefetch; i.e., issue a memory request and then continue execution until the datum is needed. The prefetch

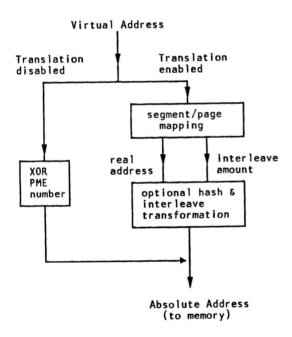

Figure 2. Address translation process on RP3.

ability provides a performance enhancement since the average effective latency of a shared-memory access is reduced. The average effective latency of shared memory is further reduced by acknowledging stores immediately rather than waiting until they are serviced at a memory.

Since the processor was not designed to be used in parallel systems we augmented its instruction set to include special coordination, serialization, and cache control (see Section 7.3) functions. The coordination functions, comprising several fetch-and-ops (e.g. fetch-and-add), are used for process coordination and synchronization [6,7] (see Section 8 for a list of the supported fetch-and-op functions). Since the coordination functions are not part of the processor instruction set, an instruction sequence is used to initiate a fetch-and-op; the sequence specifies an address, data, and the function to be applied to the address. Atomicity of the instruction sequence cannot be guaranteed by the hardware since interrupts can occur between instructions in the sequence. However, once the fetch-and-op is initiated, the read-modify-write operation is performed atomically at the memory. To provide logical atomicity at the processor, the external registers containing the address and data of the fetch-and-op must be saved and restored during context switches as if they were processor registers.

In addition to the fetch-and-op functions, PME supports interprocessor interrupts for coordination and synchronization of processes. A processor can cause an interrupt to be generated at any other processor by invoking an interprocessor-interrupt function; a set of processes can be interrupted by a sequence of such invocations, one for each processor. The interrupt is generated by sending an "interrupt request" through the network directed at a memory (in the same way a load or store is transmitted). The target memory forwards the interrupt to its associated processor. Two different interrupt levels are supported: interrupt highest level and interrupt lowest level. The primary use of the interprocessor interrupt is asynchronous communication. This function is especially useful in maintaining a producer-consumer relationship between the sending and target processors. Another use is processor initialization and restart.

Since the processor prefetches and since up to 16 concurrently outstanding stores are supported, program order may be violated which, in turn, violates sequential consistency. To guarantee sequential consistency the PME restricts, by default, the number of its outstanding requests to shared data to one. The limitation of one outstanding request to shared data is sufficient in general, but it is overly restrictive in a number of cases (e.g. chaotic relaxation) and degrades performance. Thus, functions have been added to permit a programmer or compiler to control the serialization of access to shared data. The functions used for software serialization control are called "fence" functions. A programmer uses the fence functions to access counters in the cache containing the number of outstanding requests (see Section 7.3). If serialization is required, the programmer "busy waits" on a counter until it reaches zero.

5.0 The Floating-Point Unit

The floating-point unit (FPU) performs arithmetic operations on both vectors and scalars. Vector operation are of the form memory-to-memory; scalar operations are of the forms: register-to-register, register-to-memory, and memory-to-register (the registers are internal to the FPU). Operations that apply a scalar to a vector are also supported. The arithmetic operations include addition, subtraction, multiplication, division, and comparison. The operands can be either single or double precision. Double-precision loads and stores are atomic operations at the memories; however, the processor bus is only 32 bits wide. When the FPU issues a double-precision request it adds a special attribute to the request. The cache will interpret this attribute and perform the necessary function to ensure the request is treated as an atomic operation at the memory.

A floating-point operation is initiated by the processor. The processor loads the FPU with the operation to be performed, the (starting) address of the operands, and, if a vector operation is to be performed, a stride and length. Once the FPU has been initiated, the FPU fetches and stores operands and performs the arithmetic function independently and asynchronously to the processor. When an operation is completed, the FPU can signal the processor via an interrupt or by setting a completion flag in the FPU-status register which the processor can monitor.

The performance of the FPU is governed by several factors:

1. Operand location: Operations on vectors resident in cache execute several times faster than operations performed on operands stored in shared memory.

2. Control-register reload: Scalar-operation time can be dominated by the number of internal FPU parameters (e.g. operand addresses) that must be changed by the processor between successive operations. Software can be optimized to reduce this overhead, since all FPU control-registers are "sticky"; i.e., the values are not destroyed during a operation.

3. Vector length: This has minimal effect, since little pipelining is performed; typically, a vector length of less than 20 is sufficient to reach 90% of peak performance.

4. Peak bus-bandwidth: The FPU, processor, and I/O interface device share a common bus, so contention can limit performance. Without contention, bandwidth limits peak performance to 1.5 Mflops/PME for

single precision and to 0.9 Mflops/PME for double precision.

The FPU can also be used to move blocks of data asynchronously with processor operation. This function can be used with message passing or to implement a "local/global" paging mechanism.

6.0 The Memory-Mapping Unit

The memory-mapping unit (MMU) performs virtual-to-real address translation by a segment/page mapping. Translation is performed using a high-speed translation-lookaside buffer (TLB) consisting of 128 entries. The TLB has a set-associative organization with a set size of two. When a TLB miss occurs, TLB reload is performed by hardware; however, the hardware reload can be disabled, allowing experimentation with other translation architectures. An LRU algorithm determines which entry is to be replaced during a reload.

In addition to providing memory protection during the segment/page mapping, the MMU provides additional translation information unique to RP3 and special attributes pertaining to the datum being accessed. The additional translation information is in the form of an interleave amount. The cache applies the interleave amount to the real address in a interleave transformation. The result of the interleave transformation is called the absolute address. This transformation permits memory to be dynamically partitioned between sequential and interleaved memory.

The special attributes provided during MMU translation specify a datum's *cacheability* and the datum's *volatility* in the cache. The cacheability attribute controls whether the datum may be cached. The volatility attribute is used in managing temporarily cacheable data (described in Section 7.3). The cacheability and volatility attributes are specified in both the segment and page descriptors. Having the attributes on both levels permits flexibility in the way a datum is to be treated in the storage hierarchy (e.g. an entire segment could be marked as cacheable except for one page which is marked as noncacheable). The attributes also apply to the segment and page tables.

If address translation is disabled, the MMU XORs the most significant bits of the virtual address with the PME number to produce the absolute address (no hashing or interleaving is performed and the data is noncacheable). The predominant use of this feature is to permit a processor to access memory on its own PME during initialization and interrupt handling. An XOR is used instead of an OR to allow a processor to access all of the PME memories when translation is turned off. An add operation could have been used; however, the XOR requires less hardware with no loss of function.

7.0 The Cache

The performance of parallel processors employing a shared memory is limited by the memory access-time due to network latency. However, analogous to reducing the effective memory access-time in uniprocessor systems, a memory hierarchy can be used in these parallel processors -- the hierarchy comprising a cache associated with each PME, local memory, and a large shared memory. The inclusion of the cache reduces the effective memory access-time to the average of the shared memory and the cache access times. The indiscriminate use of a cache, however, may introduce memory-coherence violations.

Two different solution techniques can be used to ensure coherence in the memory hierarchy: run-time checks or compile-time checks. Run-time coherence checks are performed by hardware in a centralized or distributed fashion. Maintaining coherence by hardware introduces serialization; how the serialization is manifested is dependent on the implementation [18]. Since run-time checks introduce serialization they are not suitable for large parallel systems. Compile-time coherence checks tag a datum as either cacheable or noncacheable. Although compile-time checks are static (the cacheable/noncacheable attribute is determined during compilation), the attributes are not restricted from being changed between program segments. Between two program segments the usage of a datum may change from shared read-write to read-only, thus the datum changes from noncacheable to cacheable.

Since compile-time checks provide flexibility and contain no inherent serial bottlenecks, cache coherence in RP3 is maintained by software. The use of compile-time checks necessitates the inclusion of processor instructions that control the cache. These instructions enable the software to invalidate data in the cache whenever necessary (e.g. prior to process migration). To maintain an adequate level of performance, the cache invalidations must be performed efficiently for a large number of logical data blocks. This is discussed further in the following sections.

7.1 Cache Placement

The RP3 cache could be placed in three different positions with respect to address translation: before virtual-to-real translation -- "virtual" cache; before real-to-absolute translation -- "real" cache; or after real-to-absolute translation -- "absolute" cache. The placement of the cache affects system performance and the ability to provide effective cache-invalidation functions. Discussed below are the advantages and disadvantages of each cache placement.

A virtual cache provides the most flexibility with respect to invalidating logical blocks of data; i.e., any consecutive virtual address range can be invalidated by the processor issuing a single command. The cache performs the invalidation by sweeping through the cache directory once, invalidating any cache line in the given range. A virtual cache facilitates a one-cycle data response; data can be returned to the requestor the cycle following the request. A major disadvantage of a virtual cache is the synonym problem [17]: two or more virtual addresses may map into the same real address. Other disadvantages include the necessity to maintain a process identifier in the directory and the high cost of caching segment and page descriptors.

A real cache has the advantage of being able to support a variety of invalidation functions; however, it is more restrictive than a virtual cache with respect to invalidation, since the largest block of consecutive addresses that can be invalidated in a single sweep through the cache is a page. A single-cycle real cache can be obtained if the directory lookup is overlapped with translation. This implies that the minimum page size is a function of the the number of cache congruence classes; this becomes a disadvantage if the number of congruence classes is large. Another advantage is that a real cache can hold segment and page descriptors. A disadvantage of the real cache is that the interleave amount must be a part of the tag comparison since the result of the virtual to real address translation is a real address plus an interleave amount. This is necessary since identical real addresses can be mapped to different absolute addresses using different interleave amounts. A real cache, like the virtual cache, has a synonym problem: it is possible for different real addresses to be mapped to the same absolute address using different interleave amounts.

The absolute cache does not have any synonym problems. It does, however, provide the least flexibility with respect to cache invalidation since consecutive real addresses are not mapped onto consecutive absolute address after interleaving. The absolute cache also is not capable of returning data in one cycle since segment/page translation and interleaving must occur before the cache is accessed.

Since a single-cycle cache is an important performance criterion, the absolute cache was rejected. For our anticipated applications, we feel that the real cache is the best compromise. The real cache, although somewhat restrictive in the variety of invalidation functions that may be supported, introduces fewer synonym problems. Although two real addresses could potentially be mapped onto the same absolute address using two different interleave amounts, we do not expect this to occur; in fact, we expect the operating system to disallow such occurrences.

7.2 Cache Organization

Since multiple devices (the processor, FPU, and I/0 interface) can issue data requests to the cache, the cache design must minimize the penalty of a miss. To facilitate this objective the RP3 cache is designed to be lockup free [10];i.e., the cache continues to satisfy other requests while a cache line is being fetched to satisfy a miss. The lockup-free design increases the utilization of each of the devices by reducing the effective memory access time. The cache also permits the devices to prefetch requests without the penalty of locking out loads and stores if the prefetch causes a miss. The cache supports up to eight misses concurrently.

The cache is organized as two pipelined stages: directory lookup and tag comparison/data response. To obtain a single-cycle response for cache hits, the directory lookup is overlapped with MMU translation. The address-mapping algorithm is set-associative, size two, with 1024 lines per set. A larger set size would provide better performance [17], but I/O-pin limitations restricted the design to a set size of two. The line size is 16 bytes; thus the total cache size is 32k bytes.

A line size of 16 bytes is considered small for a uniprocessor cache consisting of 32k bytes [17], but our studies indicate that a small cache line provides better system performance in large parallel systems [13]. This inconsistency is due to the high cost of fetching a cache line in a parallel system. The smaller miss ratio (thus increased performance) obtained by using a larger line size is offset by the larger network latency due to increased conflicts because of long messages. Furthermore, although a small line size provides a less than optimal miss ratio during cold start [3], the line size has less of an effect on the miss ratio once the cache has filled. In fact a small line size is preferable to a large line size once the cache has achieved steady state since a small line size is less likely to pollute the cache with extraneous data.

When a cache miss occurs, two double-word memory requests are issued to fetch the cache line; if interleaving is in effect, the requests are directed to different PMEs. A cache line is fetched using two memory requests to minimize network queuing delays (the queuing delays in the network are quadratic in the request size [11]). To support this line fetching scheme, a cache-directory entry maintains residency bits on a partial-line basis. A cache hit is based on the residency of the datum being accessed, not on the residency of the entire cache line. If a cache miss occurs on a cache line that has been requested but not yet received, the cache locks-up until the "missed" data returns. The contents of a cache-directory entry are:

Tag	F	R1	R2	R3	R4	MD	US

Tag Most significant bits of real address and interleave amount.

F Filling bit; when set indicates that the cache line is being fetched.

Ri Four residency bits. Ri is set when word i is resident.

MD Volatile data bit; when set, the line has volatile data.

US Indicates user or supervisor.

The RP3 cache uses a store-through update policy. Although store-through produces a larger amount of network traffic than store-in (sometimes referred to as store-back), our simulations show that the RP3 interconnection network has sufficient bandwidth to handle the increased traffic with only a slight loss in system performance. The performance lost was traded for cache simplicity. A store-through cache has the advantage that the network traffic is relatively constant. A store-in cache, on the other hand, may generate less traffic overall, but it suffers from periodic congestion in the network caused by copy-backs necessary to update main memory during context switches or at termination of subtasks.

Store misses are handled using a store-allocate-no-fetch (SANF) policy. When a store miss occurs, a cache line is allocated and the modified datum is written into cache. The remainder of the cache line is not fetched. If a subsequent load causes a miss for the line, the line is fetched. The SANF policy reduces the overhead of process initiation (especially for stack oriented languages).

7.3 Special Cache Functions
Special functions have been added to the cache to ensure correct operation in a parallel environment. These functions include fence counters, time-out counters, network-routing control, and cache-invalidation functions. The fence counters count the number of outstanding memory requests to ensure sequential consistency. A counter is maintained for each of all processor requests, processor requests to shared data, FPU requests, and requests issued by the I/O subsystem. Enforcement of sequential consistency can be performed implicitly by hardware or explicitly by a user. Consistency is maintained in hardware by allowing only one request to be outstanding to a shared memory location. Software can maintain consistency by accessing the counters using special processor functions and "busy waiting" on the counters.

The time-out counters are used to monitor the time a request has been outstanding. The primary function of these counters is for fault detection. If the time-out counter associated with an outstanding request "goes off" the request is assumed lost and the service processor is notified. The time-out counter are also used for performance monitoring (see Section 8.0)

106

The cache also specifies the routing path of a request through the network. Typically, requests are transmitted over a preferred path; however, the cache can be configured to route requests over an alternate path in order to avoid switch failures. Before transmitting the request, the cache will examine the destination. If the request's destination PME is the same as the source, the cache will bypass the interconnection network routing the request directly to the memory on its PME (such a request is termed a local memory access).

The cache supports several invalidation functions. Each type is performed by a single sweep through the directory. The following sets of data can be invalidated: a cache line, a page, all user space, all supervisor space, or volatile data. Volatile data are used to indicate temporarily cacheable pages and/or segments. When temporarily cacheable data are require to be invalidated, a single "invalidate volatile data" function is issued by the processor. This function is more powerful than page or segment invalidates since volatile data can be from several different segments and pages.

8.0 Memory
Each PME has 2 or 4 Mbytes of storage. Thus, the total amount of memory in a full-scale, 512-way, RP3, not including caches, is 1-2 Gbytes. The memory is sophisticated in that it performs the arithmetic functions needed to support the various fetch-and-op functions. The supported fetch-and-ops are: fetch-and-add, fetch-and-and, fetch-and-or, fetch-and-min, fetch-and-max, fetch-and-store (swap), and fetch-and-store-if-zero (compare with 0 and swap). The memory also provides error correction and refresh logic.

In addition the memory provides support of interprocessor interrupts. Since the network is bipartite [15], there is no direct processor-to-processor communication path. Thus, an interprocessor interrupt is directed to the memory on the same PME containing the processor to be interrupted. When the memory receives an interprocessor interrupt, the memory acknowledges the sender and signals the cache (on the same PME as the memory) to generate an interrupt to the processor.

9.0 Performance Monitoring
Since RP3 is an experimental machine, performance monitoring has been integrated into the system by the addition of a monitoring device in each PME. The device monitors such events as processor bus activity, TLB misses, cache misses, and local/remote memory accesses. The device also samples memory latency, number of outstanding requests, network request types, and routing paths.

The performance-monitoring device (PMD) can be controlled by the processor or the I/O interface device. Thus, monitoring can be completely transparent to the processor or an application can monitor itself to determine the relative performance of particular algorithms the application uses. The PMD is flexible in that it can be programmed to monitor user, supervisor, or both user and supervisor activity. The sample rate is also programmable.

10.0 I/O-Interface Device
I/O for RP3 is provided through a special I/O subsystem. A PME is connected to the I/O subsystem via an I/O-interface device (IOID) which is physically attached to the processor bus. The IOID is a slave to the I/O subsystem, providing the interface between the PME and the subsystem. On behalf of the I/O subsystem, the IOID generates the necessary memory requests to perform the I/O operations. I/O operations are capable of running asynchronously with processor execution. The IOID is also used for hardware diagnostics, initial program load, initialization of the PME via LSSD [4], and obtaining the measurement data from the PMD.

11.0 Summary
A major goal of the RP3 project is to provide a powerful and flexible vehicle for the study of parallel architectures and parallel algorithms. To meet this goal the PME was designed to function in a multi-purpose parallel processor, capable of supporting a variety of computational models. To function in such an environment the PME design includes architectural features that are required for parallel processing plus features that enhance system performance.

An extant microprocessor was chosen as the PME processor. We feel that this was an appropriate design decision in that we were able to concentrate on other design issues instead of designing yet another microprocessor. Functions external to the microprocessor were added to provide the following essential functions: interprocessor coordination functions, hardware serialization primitives, and cache control functions.

Acknowledgements

We are grateful to the following people who have participated in the definition of the RP3 PME: J. Anthony, M. Cassera, D. George, W. Groh, R. Jackson, W. Kleinfelder, A. Norton, E. Melton, G. Pfister, D. Rathi, M. Tsao, and S. Wakefield. Also, we would like to thank the the following people who are contributing to the RP3 project: T. Agerwala, G. Almasi, J. Brody, R. Bryant, F. Darema-Rogers, M. Elliott, A. Goyal, A. Gottlieb, J. Hall, S. Harvey, Y. Hsu, B. James, M. Kumar, O. La Maire B. Lau, D. Lee, H. Liberman, M. Malek, P. Meehan, E. Melton, A. Moretti, R. Mraz, E. Nowicki, C. Osekoski, D. Ostapko, M. Pullen, T. Richardson, K. So, J. Stone, C. Tan, P. Teller, M. Thoennes, F. Tsui, W. White and M. Wong. We would also like to acknowledge the contributions of others in the Data Systems, General Technology, System Technology, and Federal Systems Divisions of IBM and members of the NYU Ultracomputer Project. Lastly, we would like to thank Ron Cytron and Harold Stone for their comments during the preparation of this paper.

References

[1] Blodgett, A. J. and Barbour, D. R., "Thermal Conduction Module: A High-Performance Multilayer Ceramic Package", *IBM J. of Research and Development,* vol. 26 No. 1, January, 1982, pp.30-36.

[2] Collier, W. W., "Principles of Architecture for Systems of Parallel Processors", *IBM Technical Report,* TR 00.3100, Poughghkeepsie, March 1981.

[3] Easton, M. C. and Fagin, R., "Cold-Start vs. Warm-Start Miss Ratios and Multiprogramming Performance", *CACM,* Vol 21, No. 10, pp. 866-872.

[4] Eichelberger, E. B. and Williams, T. W., "A Logic Design Structure for LSI Testability", *Proc. of the 14th Design Automation Conf.,* 1977, pp. 426-468.

[5] Gottlieb, A., Grishman, R., Kruskal, C. P., McAuliffe, K. P., Rudolph, L., and Snir, Marc, "The NYU Ultracomputer -- Designing an MIMD Shared Memory Parallel Computer", *IEEE Trans. on Computers,* February 1983, pp.175-189.

[6] Gottlieb, A., Kruskal, C. P., "Coordinating Parallel Processors: A partial Unification", *Computer Architecture News* October 1981, pp. 16-24.

[7] Gottlieb, A., Lubachevsky, B. D., and Rudolph, L., "Coordinating Large Numbers of Processors", *ACM TOPLAS,* January 1982.

[8] Hennessy, J. L., Jouppi, N., Baskett, F., and Gill, J., "MIPS: A VLSI Processor Architecture", *Proc. CMU Conference on VLSI Systems and Computations,* October, 1981.

[9] Hennessy, J. L., Jouppi, N., Baskett, F., and Gill, J., "Hardware/Software Trade-offs for Increased Performance", *Proc. Architectural Support for Programming Languages and Operating Systems,* March, 1982.

[10] Kroft, D. "Lockup-free Instruction Fetch/Prefetch Cache Organization", *Proc. 8th Annu. Symp. Computer. Arch.* 1981, pp. 81-88.

[11] Kruskal, C. P. and Snir, M., "Some Results on Multistage Interconnection networks for Multiprocessors", Courant Institute, NYU, NY, Ultracomputer Note 41.

[12] Lamport L., "How to Make a Multiprocessor Computer That Correctly Executes Multiprocess Programs", *IEEE Trans. on Computers,* Vol. C-28, 1979, pp. 690-691.

[13] Norton, A. and Pfister, G., "A Methodology for Predicting Multiprocessor Performance", *Proc of 1985 Int. Parallel Processing Conf,* August 1985.

[14] Patterson, D. A. and Sequin, C. H., "RISC-I: A Reduced Instruction Set VLSI Computer Architecture", *Proc of the Eighth Annual Symp. on Computer Architecture,* Minneapolis, Minn., May, 1981.

[15] Pfister, G. F., Brantley, W. C., George, D. A., Harvey, S. L., Kleinfelder, W. J., McAuliffe, K. P., Melton, E. A., Norton, V. A., and Weiss J. "The IBM Research Parallel Processor Prototype (RP3): Introduction and Architecture", *Proc of 1985 Int. Parallel Processing Conf,* August 1985.

[16] Radin, G., "The 801 Minicomputer", *IBM Journal of Research and Development,* Vol. 27, No. 3, May 1983, pp. 237-246.

[17] Smith, A. J., "Cache Memories", *Computing Surveys,* Vol. 14, No.3, September 1982, pp.473-530.

[18] Yen, W. C., Yen, W. L., and Fu, K.-S., "Data Coherence Problem in a Multicache System", *IEEE Trans. on Computers,* Vol. C-34, No. 1, January 1985, pp. 56-65.

A COMPILER-ASSISTED CACHE COHERENCE SOLUTION FOR MULTIPROCESSORS

Alexander V. Veidenbaum

Center for Supercomputing Research and Development
University of Illinois at Urbana-Champaign
Urbana, Illinois, 61801

Abstract -- The existing solutions to multiprocessor cache coherence problem are not suitable, in our opinion, for systems with a large number of processors. We propose a new solution in which a compiler generates cache management instructions. Conditions necessary for cache coherence violation are defined. The structure of a program and its dependence graph are used to detect when these conditions become true, and the instructions to enforce coherence are generated. No communication between processors is required at run-time to enforce coherence. The correctness of the solution is proved.

Introduction

Several multiprocessor architectures have been built or are being built that can truly be called large-scale ([4], [5], [14], [2]). They can have several hundred processors sharing memory and all working on solving a single problem. Such multiprocessors are characterized by a long memory access time making the use of cache memories very important. However, a cache coherence problem makes the use of caches difficult. In this paper we discuss the proposed solutions to the cache coherence problem and why they may not be suitable for a large-scale multiprocessor. We propose a different solution that relies on a compiler to manage the caches. We define conditions necessary for a data incoherence to occur. A restructuring compiler, such as Parafrase [0], can be used to detect when such conditions arise and to generate cache management instructions to enforce coherence.

Existing solutions to the cache coherence problem

Let us examine the proposed solutions to the cache coherence problem (see [18]) for use on large-scale multiprocessors. The solutions can be divided into the following groups:

(1) Solutions based on a single shared resource.
These include a central directory scheme of [15] and a shared cache scheme of [17].
A large number of processors can not access the shared resource without severe performance degradation. That's why these solutions are not extendable to large-scale multiprocessors.

(2) Bus-based solutions.
An example of such a solution is that of Goodman [6].
These solutions are also using a shared resource, the bus, and could have been considered in the first group. We put them in a separate group because they seem to us capable of supporting a larger number of processors then the solutions in the first group, but not hundreds of processors on a single bus.

(3) Cacheability attribute processed during virtual address translation.
This scheme was used in C.mmp [3]. Again a central resource, shared page tables, can be identified in this solution. The overhead of changing the cacheabilty attribute seems large to us for a truly extendable solution.

In addition, most modern processors contain a translation buffer (TLB) acting as a cache for page table entries. When a cache attribute needs to be changed all of the TLBs need to be updated. Therefore, we may have solved the data cache coherence problem, but we have created a TLB coherence problem.

A variant of this solution has been proposed which allows the cacheability of read-only data. In this case the attribute is never changed during the execution of a program. This solution is restrictive and may not allow a large number of references to be cached.

Multiprocessor architecture

The architecture we are interested in is a shared-memory multiprocessor. It consists of a global shared memory, a global interconnection network, and proces-

This work was supported in part by the National Science Foundation under Grants No. US NSF DCR81-10110 and DCR84-06916, and the US Department of Energy under Grant No. US DOE DE-FG02-85ER25001.

sors with private caches. The only way of exchanging data between processors is through the shared memory. The block diagram of this architecture is given in Figure 1.

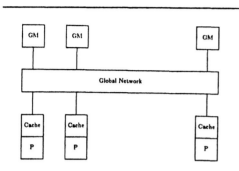

Figure 1. Multiprocessor architecture.

Interconnection network

We assume the interconnection network to be of the shuffle-exchange type. The network has a unique path from any input to any output port. The order of accesses by a given processor to a given memory location is preserved by the network.

Cache organization

We assume that a cache is a physical address cache, using the "Write-through" policy, and having a block size of one. We also assume that on context switch the system ensures the correctness of cache contents. Other details of cache organization will be presented in the following sections.

Definitions

The following notation is used in this paper:
(1) S_i - statement i of a program,
(2) P_j - processor j of a multiprocessor,
(3) C_j - private cache of processor P_j,
(4) $M[X]$ - the contents of a memory location of a variable X,
(5) $C_j[X]$ - the value of X contained in the cache of processor P_j,
(6) X^s - a store of X,
(7) X^f - a fetch of X,
(8) X^a - an access to X, i.e either a fetch or a store.
In some cases we may qualify the access type by a processor that performed the access as follows: $X^{a(P_j)}$.
(9) $(Y)^*$ - zero or more repetitions of Y.

Data dependencies

The definitions of this section follow those of [8] and [16] which should be consulted for any additional information on dependence analysis.
For each statement S_i we define two sets, IN and OUT.

-- $IN(S_i)$ is a set of variables the statement uses.

-- $OUT(S_i)$ is a set of variables the statement generates.

The following types of dependencies are defined between two statements S_i and S_j if there is a flow of control path from S_i to S_j and S_i precedes S_j on that path.

-- S_j is data flow dependent on S_i if the set $IN(S_j) \cap OUT(S_i)$ is not empty.

-- S_j is data antidependent on S_i if the set $IN(S_i) \cap OUT(S_j)$ is not empty.

-- S_j is output dependent on S_i if the set $OUT(S_j) \cap OUT(S_i)$ is not empty.

-- S_j is control dependent on a conditional statement S_i if its execution depends on the execution of S_i and the path chosen after that.

If the two statements are both enclosed by DO loops a dependence may exist on some but not all iterations of the enclosing loops. Also, a dependence may exist between S_i executed in one iteration and S_j executed in another iteration of a loop. Such a dependence is called a cross-iteration dependence. The data dependence information can be represented by a graph on the statements of a program, called a data dependence graph.

Loop types

A program can have any of the following four loop types:

(1) A DOALL loop - a loop which does not have any cross-iteration dependencies [11].

(2) An R(N,1) loop - a loop solving a first-order linear recurrence [8].

(3) A DOACROSS loop - a loop that has a dependence graph cycle but can be executed in a pipelined fashion [13].

(4) A serial loop - a loop with a dependence graph cycle where pipelined execution is not possible.

The type of a loop is determined by the dependence graph of statements nested in it. The first three types of loops can be executed on multiple processors to achieve performance improvement.

A memory reference sequence

A memory reference sequence X for a memory loca-

110

tion of a variable X is an ordered sequence of accesses generated by a program as observed at the memory:

$$X = X^s ((X^f)^* (X^s)^*)^*$$

Any access X^a generated by a program can be identified by a sequence number i giving the position of X^a in $\mathbf{X}$. We use a subscript i to indicate the sequence number, X^a_i. Let us assume that the sequence number is know a priori for any access.

For a serial program the sequence is unique for a given set of input data. For a deterministic parallel program the sequence is unique except for possible permutations in any of the fetch subsequences.

The model of computation we use assumes that the following two conditions are satisfied at any time T when a processor generates X^a_i:

A1. $M[X] = X^s_j$, where $j < i$ and $\forall$ k, $j < k < i$: X^a_k was a fetch,

A2. If X^a_i is a store then $\forall$ j, $j < i$: X^a_j has been performed.

In other words, the value in the shared memory is always current. All the stores preceding the current access have been completed but none of the following stores have been completed. This is necessary to keep things "simple" in the system where the only way of communicating between processors is through shared memory. These conditions a equivalent to enforcing the data dependence constraints between the statements. We assume that the ordering is enforced through the use of synchronization primitives.

Cache incoherence

We define an incoherence as a condition when:

1. a processor P_j performs a memory fetch X^f_i

and

2. $M[X] \neq C_j[X]$ at such time.

An incoherence cannot occur if X_i is a store. Note that we require a processor to try to fetch X, otherwise the fact that the memory and the cache have different values is not an error.

Using the notion of the reference sequence let us define the necessary conditions for the cache incoherence to occur.

Lemma 1

The two conditions necessary for a cache incoherence to occur at processor P_j issuing X^f_i, are:

C1. $C_j[X] = X^{a(P_j)}_l$, where $l < i$ and X^a_l was the last access to X by P_j.

C2. $\exists$ k, $l < k < i$: $M[X] = X^{s(P_m)}_k$, where j≠m. (If more then one such stores took place let X^s_k be the one with largest sequence number.)

That is, a value of X is present in the cache of P_j (C1), and a new value has been stored in the shared memory by another processor since the last access by P_j (C2).

Proof

(1) The first condition must be true, for if it is not true the value is fetched out of GM and is therefore correct.

(2) Let us assume that an incoherence occurred on $X^{f(P_j)}_i$, i.e. $M[X] \neq C_j[X]$ at that time, but C2 is not true. Let us also assume that this is the first time any of the conditions {A1, A2, C1, C2} we specified are not satisfied.
C2 being false means:

$$M[X] = X^{s(P_m)}_k,$$
where $k \geq i$ or $k \leq l$ or j=m.

If $j = m$ then the value in the cache is that stored by processor j. Since it was the last store before X^f_i we have $M[X] = C_j[X]$, which is not true. Therefore j≠m.
If $k > i$ then condition A2 has not been satisfied when the store of X^s_k occurred since not all the preceding accesses have been made. We assumed that this was the first time any of the conditions were false, but found that A2 must have been false earlier. Therefore, $k \leq i$.
k cannot be equal to i since X_k is a store and X_i is a fetch.
k cannot be equal to l since this will imply j=m which we have shown is false.
For the case of $k < l$ we have two possibilities: X_l is a store or X_l is a fetch. If X_l is a store then $M[X] = C_j[X]$ when X_l is issued since no other processors store into X after X_l and neither does P_j. If X_l is a fetch we again have $M[X] = C_j[X]$. Since the contents of memory and the cache are not equal, k cannot be less then l.
It follows then that C2 is a necessary condition for the incoherence to occur.□

Corollary

Cache incoherence cannot occur on a variable that is assigned only once during program execution.

The proof follows from the fact that the conditions C1 and C2 of Lemma 1 cannot be true at the same time.

Detecting the necessary conditions

Our goal is to have the restructuring compiler

detect the conditions of Lemma 1 and generate the cache management instructions. The power of restructuring compilers is in the ability to perform the data dependence analysis. Therefore, let us express the conditions necessary for cache incoherence to occur in terms of data dependencies. It follows from Lemma 1 that:

(1) The value of X has to be in the cache of processor P_j. This implies that a statement S_{i_1} was executed by P_j such that X belongs to $IN(S_{i_1})$ or X belongs to $OUT(S_{i_1})$.

(2) A different processor has computed a new value of X. This implies that a statement S_{i_2} was executed by P_k such that X belongs to $OUT(S_{i_2})$, $k \neq j$.

(3) Finally, an incoherence can only occur if P_j is fetching X. This implies a statement S_{i_3} is executed by P_j such that that X belongs to $IN(S_{i_3})$.

From the above, S_{i_2} depends on statement S_{i_1}, and statement S_{i_3} depends on statement S_{i_2}. One of the following two dependence graphs are possible:

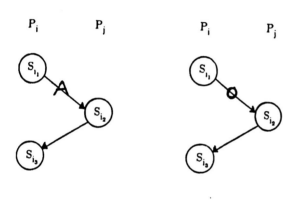

In addition to the above dependence structure, it is necessary that S_{i_2} be executed on a different processor. How can we detect that? We propose to use the loop type information for this purpose. (If other types of parallelism are being exploited they can be taken care of in a similar fashion.) Recall that only three of the four types of loops we are dealing with can be executed on multiple processors. Let us concentrate on DOALL and DOACROSS loops. We assume that one or more consecutive iterations of such a loop are assigned to a processor. By definition, any dependence between two statements inside a DOALL loop is not across iterations, but there are cross-iteration dependences in DOACROSS. It follows that a statement S_i in a DOALL dependent on a statement S_j in the same loop is executed on the same processor as S_j.

In a DOACROSS loop, two statements with a cross-iteration dependence are executed on different processors, while statements with a dependence on the same iteration are executed on the same processor.

Using the above we first construct a simplified algorithm using only the loop type information. We then extend it to consider the dependence structure and the flow of control.

A cache management algorithm

Let us assume that the following instructions are available for cache management:

Flush. This instructions invalidates the entire contents of a cache.

Cache_on. This instruction causes all global memory references to be routed through the cache.

Cache_off. This instruction causes all global memory references to by-pass the cache and go directly to memory.

In addition, the cache state, on or off, must be part of the processor state and has to be saved/restored on context switch. Processes are created in the cache-off state.

The algorithms uses loop types for its analysis as follows:

(1) A DOALL loop does not have any dependencies between statements executed on different processors. Therefore condition C2 of Lemma 1 is false, and any shared memory access in such a loop can be cached.

(2) A serial loop is executed by a single processor, and hence condition C2 of Lemma cannot be true.

(3) A DOACROSS or an R(N,1) loops do have cross-iteration dependencies. Therefore condition C2 can be true. Initially, let us just turn caches off in such loops.

The algorithm is shown in Figure 2. The algorithm turns cacheing on and off, depending on the type of loop a program enters. (Note that cache management instructions inserted in parallel loops are executed once by every participating processor.) Conditions for incoherence are checked at loop boundaries. In addition, procedure and function calls which may have parallel loops in called routines are considered. The algorithm does not really consider individual dependencies or look for the dependence structure satisfying conditions of Lemma 1. It states that within certain loop types (or nests of this type) the conditions cannot be satisfied or cacheing is not allowed.

The algorithm is simple enough to be executed either at compile time or at run time. At compile time we know which loops can be executed on multiple processors, but whether they will be executed as such depends on run-time processor allocation. At run time we know which loops get multiple processors. For example, if a DOACROSS is serialized we can turn the cacheing on during the whole time the loop is executed.

```
cache_state := on
insert Cache_on, Flush
For every statement in a program do
        case(statement type)
            of(DO)
                    case(DO type)
                        of(DOALL)
                                insert Cache_on, Flush after
                                        the DO statement
                                push(cache_state)
                                cache_state := on
                        of(serial)
                                if cache_state = off
                                then  insert Cache_on, Flush before
                                                the DO statement
                                fi
                                push(cache_state)
                                cache_state := on
                        of((DOACROSS, R(N,1))
                                insert Cache_off after the DO statement
                                push(cache_state)
                                cache_state := off
                    endcase
            of(DOEND)
                    do_type := type of DO for which this is DOEND
                    old_cstate := cache_state
                    cache_state := pop()
                    if cache_state=on AND old_cstate=off
                    then  insert Cache_on after DOEND
                    fi
                    if      cache_state=on
                        AND
                            do_type={DOALL,DOACROSS,R(N,1)}
                    then  insert Flush after DOEND
                    fi
            of(CALL)
                    insert Cache_off before the CALL statement
                    if cache_state = on
                    then  insert Cache_on, Flush after
                                    the CALL statement
                    fi
        endcase
enddo
```

Figure 2. The cache management algorithm

Correctness proof

We will prove the correctness of the algorithm by showing that the conditions necessary for an incoherence to occur are not satisfied in programs processed by the algorithm. The conditions necessary for an incoherence on a variable X to occur when executing a statement S_i are:

CC1:   Statement S_i depends on statement S_j through a variable X.

CC2: S_i is executed by processor P_l and S_j is executed by processor P_m, $l \neq m$.

CC3:   X is in the cache C_l prior to the execution of S_i and $C_l[X] \neq X^{s(P_m)}$.

A general loop structure enclosing statements i and j is shown in Figure 3. Note that a statement not in any loop can be represented by a statement enclosed in a serial loop with one iteration. Therefore some of the loops shown in Figure 3 can be removed to obtain simpler cases.

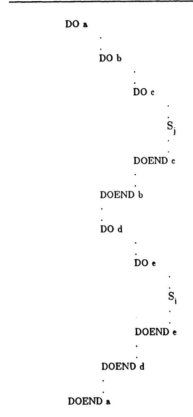

Figure 3. Program structure

We have to show that for every path in the control flow graph of our program between S_j and S_i one of the conditions above is false for any S_i. A note about loops with GOTOs exiting the loop: we assume such loops have a single exit path regardless of how the loop was exited. This is usually required for correct synchronization, while it also simplifies the analysis of control flow between loops in our proof.

Let us consider the innermost loop DO_e enclosing S_i. Three cases are possible:

(1) DO_e is a DOACROSS or an R(N,1) loop.
    In this case a Cache_off instruction is issued by every processor executing the iterations of the DO_e.

113

Therefore, X will be fetched from memory when S_1 is executed. This is equivalent to CC3 being false.

(2) DO_e is a DOALL loop.

In this case a Flush instruction is issued by every processor executing iterations of DO_e. Therefore CC3 is false.

(3) DO_e is a serial loop.

Consider all the loops enclosing S_1 between DO_e and DO_d. Let us skip all loops e, ..., k+1 that are serial to DO_k, $k \leq d$, such that:

A. DO_k is a DOACROSS.

In this case S_1 is enclosed by a nested set of serial loops DO_e through DO_{k+1}. The nested set is executed on one processor and a Flush instruction is executed before the DO_{k+1} according to the Algorithm 1. Therefore CC3 is false.

B. DO_k is a DOALL.

In this case a Flush instruction is executed by every processor executing iterations of DO_k. Since all of the loops DO_{k+1} through DO_e are serial, every processor executing S_i has executed a Flush instruction. Therefore CC3 is false.

C. Otherwise DO_k is a serial, i.e. all of the loops DO_d through DO_e are serial.

Now let us consider the loop type of DO_a:

α DO_a is a DOACROSS.

In this case a Flush instruction is executed before DO_d according to Algorithm 1. Since S_i is executed by the same processor, CC3 is false.

β DO_a is a DOALL or a serial loop.

In this case we have to consider the loops enclosing S_j.

I) DO_b through DO_c are all serial.

In this case both loop nests DO_b through DO_c and DO_d through DO_e are serial. Since they are nested in a DOALL or a serial loop they will be executed on the same processor. Hence condition CC2 cannot be true for statements S_i and S_j.

II)   Otherwise consider the outermost loop DO_k, $b \leq k \leq c$, that is not serial, i.e. it is a DOALL, a DOACROSS, or an R(N,1). In this case a Flush instruction is executed after $DOEND_k$ by the same processor that is to execute S_i. Therefore CC3 is false.

Finally, let us consider CALL statements. Suppose S_j is a subroutine or function CALL.

In this case a called routine may have loops in it enclosing the statement actually generating X. In addition, the called routine may not have any cache management instruction in it (that is why we turn cacheing off before a call). However, in all but one of the cases considered in the proof a Flush or Cache_off instruction is performed by a processor that executes S_i. Therefore, CC3 is false when S_i is executed regardless of the type of statement of S_j.

The one case that does not have the cache flushed is $C.\beta II$. In that case S_i and S_j are executed by the same processor, and there is no Flush on any path between the two statements. The algorithm inserts a Flush instruction after a CALL statement taking care of this case.□

Improving the cache management algorithm

In this section we describe the extensions of the cache management algorithm. The first one allows cacheing to be used in DOACROSS loops. The second and third attempt to reduce the number of cache flushes by doing a more detailed dependence and flow analysis.

(1) Cacheing of data inside DOACROSS loops.

A DOACROSS loop is executed by assigning successive iterations to different processors (mod the number of processors available). The cross-iteration dependencies that exist in a DOACROSS are thus between statements executed by different processors. Synchronization primitives have to be used between these processors to ensure that dependencies are satisfied (say, the classical P and V primitives).

A straight-forward solution is to issue a Flush instruction after the V by each processor executing a statement depending on a statement executed by another processor. Since the shared memory has the current value after the V instruction and the cache does not have anything, the value will be fetched out of global memory. Otherwise the DOACROSS loops can be treated the same way as the DOALL loops by the cache management algorithm.

A more interesting solution is possible for architectures that support memory access combined with synchronization, such as [7] or [5]. In this case we can identify exactly which word requires synchronization and invalidate just one word, not the entire cache. Cache controller design has to be modified to allow invalidation of individual words, preferably as part of a synchronized fetch. The correct value is fetched from memory and can be put in the cache. Any subsequent unsynchronized fetch will use the value out of the cache.

114

The processor performing a synchronized store does not have to do anything special, just write the data through to shared memory.

The last solution requires a synchronized data access for every variable on which a cross-iteration dependence exists. Any attempt to minimize the number of synchronization primitives, as proposed by [12], or use of implied synchronization may result in an incorrect execution of a program.

(2) The simplified algorithm we presented does not really look for the dependence structure implied by the Lemma 1 conditions. Specifically, it does not check the existence of a statement bringing a variable into a cache prior to the execution of the two statements with a dependence on two different processors. An incoherence cannot occur if such a statement does not exist. In such a case it is not necessary to invalidate the contents of a cache.

Consider a DOACROSS loop with cacheing enabled. Assume each processor executing this loop performed a Flush instruction just after it entered the loop. Let us know consider a statement S_i that uses a variable X generated in another iteration of the DOACROSS. If we examine all the flow of control paths from the first statement in a loop to S_i and determine there are no generations or uses of X on any of them then we do not have to invalidate X in the cache before S_i (a single assignment condition). If the above is true for all the cross-iteration dependencies in the loop we do not need a Flush instruction in this DOACROOS.

This technique can be extended to analyze the whole program to avoid Flushing after every parallel loop.

(3) The algorithm uses data dependence information indirectly, through loop types. A beginning and end of a parallel loop are synchronization points it detects and uses to issue cache management instructions. This synchronizes all dependencies from statements in such loops to statements outside of such loops. However, this synchronization point may be located much earlier than the statement using the data. Another synchronization point may exist later in the program that takes care of an earlier one. For example, consider the program segment in Figure 4. If no statement in DOALL$_b$ has dependence arcs to statements in DOALL$_c$ or any code between the two loops, and the flow of control always goes through DOALL$_c$ after passing through DOALL$_b$, a Flush is not necessary after DOALL$_b$.

The correctness proof can be easily extended to include the algorithm improvements shown in this section.

```
DO a
    .
    .
    DOALL b
    .
    DOEND b
    .
    DOALL c
    .
    DOEND c
DOEND a
```

Figure 4. Program example.

Conclusions

We have presented a solution to the cache coherence problem in which a restructuring compiler generates cache management instructions. An algorithm to do that is presented and its correctness proved. In this solution each processor manages its own cache without any additional communication with other processors. The cache management instructions are very simple, affect only the processor issuing them and have a small fixed cost. Finally, the total number of such instructions issued by any processor is a function of loop bounds and loop structure of a program, not of the number of processors used or the number of stores in the program. That is why we believe the solution is scalable to multiprocessors of any size.

Acknowledgments

We thank all the members of the Cedar project who discussed this proposal with us, especially Madhu Sharma, Dave Padua, Rich Barton, Dan Sorensen, and Hoichi Cheong.

References

[1] Utpal Banerjee, "Data Dependence in Ordinary Programs," M.S. Thesis, University of Illinois at Urbana-Champaign, DCS Report No. UIUCDCS-R-76-837, November, 1976.

[2] W. Crowther et al, "Performance measurements on 128-node Butterfly(TM) parallel processor" Proceedings of the 1985 International Conference on Parallel Processing, pp. 531-540, 1985.

[3] S.H. Fuller and S.P. Harbison, "The C.mmp multiprocessor," Department of Computer Science, Carnegie-Mellon University, Technical Report, 1978.

[4] A. Gottlieb, R. Grishman, C.P. Kruskal, K.P. McAuliffe, L. Rudolph, and M. Snir, "The NYU Ultracomputer -- Designing an MIMD Shared-Memory Parallel Machine," IEEE Trans. on Computers, Vol. C-32, No. 2, pp. 175-189, February 1983.

115

[5] Daniel Gajski, David Kuck, Duncan Lawrie, and Ahmed Sameh, "Cedar -- a Large Scale Multiprocessor," Proceedings of the 1983 International Conference on Parallel Processing, pp. 524-529, August, 1983.

[6] J.R. Goodman, "Using cache memory to reduce processor-memory traffic," Proceedings 10th International Symposium on Computer Architecture, pp.124-131, June, 1983.

[7] "Heterogeneous Element Processor Principles of Operation," HEP technical documentation series, Denelco, part. no.9000001, February, 1981.

[8] David J. Kuck, "The Structure of Computers and Computations," Volume 1, John Wiley and Sons, New York, 1978.

[9] D.J. Kuck, R.H. Kuhn, B. Leasure, and M. Wolfe, "The Structure of an Advanced Vectorizer for Pipelined Processors," Fourth International Computer Software and Applications Conference, October, 1980.

[10] D. H. Lawrie, "Access and Alignment of Data in an Array Processor," IEEE Transactions on Computers, vol. C-24, no. 12, pp. 1145-1155, December, 1975.

[11] S. F. Lundstrom and G. H. Barnes, "Controllable MIMD Architecture," Proceedings of the 1980 International Conference on Parallel Processing, pp. 19-27, 1980.

[12] S.P. Midkiff, "Compiler Generated Synchronization for High Speed Multiprocessors", M.S. Thesis, University of Illinois at Urbana-Champaign, May 1986

[13] D.A. Padua Haiek, "Multiprocessors: Discussions of Some Theoretical and Practical Problems," Ph.D. Thesis, University of Illinois at Urbana-Champaign, DCS Report No. UIUCDCS-R-79-990, November 1979.

[14] G.F. Pfister et al, "The IBM Research Parallel Processor Prototype," Proceedings of the 1985 International Conference on Parallel Processing, pp. 764-772, 1985.

[15] C. K. Tang, "Cache system design in the tightly coupled multiprocessor system," Proceedings AFIP National Computer Conference, vol.45, pp.749-753, 1976.

[16] Michael J. Wolfe, "Optimizing Supercompilers for Supercomputers," Ph.D. Thesis, University of Illinois at Urbana-Champaign, 1982.

[17] W.C. Yen, J.H. Patel, E.S. Davidson. "Shared cache for multiple-stream computer systems," IEEE Trans. on Computers, Vol. C-34, No. 1, pp. 56-65, January, 1983.

[18] W. C. Yen, D. W. L Yen, and K. S. Fu, "Data Coherence Problem in a Multicache System," IEEE Trans. on Computers, Vol. C-34, No. 1, pp. 56-65, January 1985.

A Cache Coherence Scheme With Fast Selective Invalidation

Hoichi Cheong *and* Alexander V. Veidenbaum

Center for Supercomputing Research and Development
University of Illinois at Urbana–Champaign
Urbana, Illinois, 61801

Abstract

Software–assisted cache coherence enforcement schemes for large multiprocessor systems with shared global memory and interconnection network have gained increasing attention. Proposed software–assisted approaches rely on either indiscriminate invalidation or selective invalidation to invalidate stale cache lines. The indiscriminate approach combined with advanced memory hardware can quickly invalidate the entire cache but may result in lower hit ratios. The selective approach may achieve a better hit ratio. However, sequential selection and invalidation of cache or TLB entries is time consuming. We propose a new solution that offers the fast operation of the indiscriminate invalidation approach and can selectively invalidate cache items without extensive run–time book–keeping and checking. The solution relies on the combination of compile–time reference tagging and individual invalidation of potentially stale cache lines only when referenced. Performance improvement over an indiscriminate invalidation approach is presented.

1. Introduction

Efficiently managed private cache memories can lead to major improvements in the performance of large scale multiprocessor systems. Private caches serve not only to improve memory access time but also to reduce traffic in the interconnection network. Congestion in the network and memory components of multiprocessors like Cedar, RP3 and the Ultracomputer will lead to serious performance degradation.

In a multiprocessor system with private caches, more than one copy of data may exist. To ensure that all processors use the most up–to–date copy of a data item, it is essential that any modifications to it be reflected in the caches of all processors which may use the data. Efficiently maintaining coherence among private caches in very large multiprocessors is a formidable task. Most existing cache coherence enforcement schemes suitable for such systems rely on software support. However, not all these

This work is supported in part by National Science Foundation under Grant No.US NSF DCR84–10110, the U.S. Department of Energy under Grant No. US DOE DE–FG02–85ER25001, and IBM Corporation.

approaches are suitable for parallel numerical programs, and those that are suffer from the limitations discussed below.

Software–based cache coherence enforcement schemes rely on invalidation of potentially stale copies of data. Two classes of invalidation schemes have been proposed in the literature: (1) indiscriminate invalidation, and (2) selective invalidation. The indiscriminate invalidation scheme invalidates the entire cache while the selective invalidation scheme identifies individual cache data items which are potentially stale. Since the latter scheme involves a sequential invalidation of data, it is likely to be much slower than the former.

We believe that invalidation schemes used in existing software–assisted cache coherence enforcement schemes are inefficient. Our goal is to achieve constant time invalidation while limiting the number of data items invalidated. In this paper, we present a cache coherence enforcement scheme in which all references are marked at compile time but invalidation decisions are made when the data is actually referenced. It is different from other schemes that invalidate cached variables at the end of some intervals in program execution. This new invalidation approach is as fast as indiscriminate invalidation and achieves a better hit ratio.

The next section of this paper includes a short survey of existing approaches to cache coherence enforcement. In Section 3, a detailed description of our approach is given with a comparison to the existing software–supported methods. In section 4, simulation results are presented and compared to the simulation results of an indiscriminate invalidation scheme.

2. Existing Cache Coherence Schemes

Several algorithms have been proposed for cache coherence enforcement in multiprocessor systems. Most of them apply only to bus–based systems [Good83, McCr84, PaPa84, RuSe84, Katz85] and some are a subset of the protocol for the proposed Futurebus standard [SwSm87]. These cache coherence strategies rely on monitoring the bus accesses and are not applicable to systems with multistage interconnection networks. In this paper, we are interested only in strategies suitable for multiprocessor systems with multistage interconnection networks and shared global memory. We restrict the use of the term "multiprocessor systems" to these systems.

Tang proposed a central directory scheme [Tang76], which is applicable to multiprocessor systems. Several variants of this scheme have also been proposed [CeFe78, ArBa84]. The central directory scheme maintains the status of each cache line and the identities of the cache units which contain the line. A *store controller* controls the communication among the caches and the shared global memory. Accesses to shared variables and cache misses have to go through the *store controller*. The *store controller*, in turn, orders individual cache units to effect necessary changes to the status of corresponding cache lines or to supply the up-to-date copy of a memory line. The central directory forces such accesses and corresponding communication to be serialized. Furthermore, it is expensive to build when the number of processors becomes large.

Censiur and Feautrier adopted a distributive approach. Instead of using a central directory, each memory line has a status field and a bit vector. Each bit corresponds to a cache unit in which the memory line may reside. Store control is distributed to each memory module. While serialization of accesses and communication is not completely eliminated, it only occurs on accesses to a common memory module. The length of the bit vector makes this scheme costly to implement on a large-scale system.

Archibald and Baer proposed a scheme to reduce the cost of the bit vector. Instead of the bit vector, they use two bits to represent the status of a memory line. However, the exact identities of cache units in which the memory line reside are lost. The store controllers, as a result, have to broadcast to every cache unit both cache line status changes and requests for up-to-date copies. Such broadcasts essentially take up available network bandwidth in large-scale systems.

Preserving cache transparency to user programs is a major goal of the above approaches. To achieve this goal, the exact status of a memory line is determined entirely at run-time. However, the price is paid in the form of forced serialization of accesses or communication, or occupying available network bandwidth.

It becomes apparent that an efficient cache coherence scheme for large-scale systems needs to reduce the communication cost at run-time. One possibility is to determine the status of memory lines based on program analysis rather than entirely at run-time. Software-based schemes proposed in [BrMW85, EGKM85, Smit85, Veid86, LeYL87] use such an approach and will be discussed in the following section.

2.1. Software-Assisted Cache Coherence Schemes

In these approaches, determination of when existing cache copies turn stale is made prior to run-time. Based on the analysis by a compiler or a preprocessor, invalidation instructions are inserted in a source program. When the program is executed, the processor will issue instructions to invalidate cache lines. To reduce the run-time communication cost in enforcing cache coherences, stale cache copies are usually invalidated but not updated immediately. The invalidated copies will be updated during subsequent read misses to these cache line. These approaches use one or more of the following techniques: write-through store policy, software-directed invalidation of cache memory, and compiler-assisted marking of variable references.

2.1.1. The One-Time-Identifier Approach

Smith has proposed a scheme [Smit85] that associates a one-time-identifier (OTI) with each translation lookaside buffer (TLB) entry and each cache line. The OTI is used to distinguish between stale and current copies of shared variables. A new OTI value is generated by a counter for each new TLB entry. When a shared variable is loaded into the cache, the OTI value of the corresponding TLB entry becomes the OTI value of the cache line. Cache hits on shared variables require that the OTI value of the cache line matches that of the corresponding TLB entry.

The processor issues an *invalidate TLB entry* instruction for each page in a write-shared region when the processor is about to give up access to the region. This ensures that, after accesses by other processors, a subsequent access to each page in the same region will cause the TLB to be reloaded with a new entry and a new OTI value. A mismatch between the old OTI value of a stale cache line and the current OTI value of the reloaded TLB entry will cause a miss. Since Smith's algorithm uses write-through to store the shared data, the miss will force the processor to access the up-to-date copy from the main memory.

Some disadvantages of this scheme are apparent. First, the attempt to avoid over invalidation and unwanted misses might itself cause unwanted misses. Reloading a TLB entry of a shared page may be caused by the replacement policy rather than by the invalidation scheme. Reloading a TLB entry results in a new OTI value. A cache line in the corresponding page, although not necessarily stale, will have an older OTI value and any reference to it will be considered a miss. Secondly, invalidation of shared page entries in the TLB is carried out sequentially. Finally, the implementation of the OTI costs cache memory space and may be more expensive than other software-based approaches.

2.1.2. Invalidation Using Program Structure

The algorithm proposed by Veidenbaum [Veid86] relies on a compiler to insert invalidate-cache instructions at places where a reassignment of processors will take place. These locations are identified as parallel loop boundaries of a program. Write-through is used to maintain the up-to-date copies of variables in the global memory.

Indiscriminate invalidation of the entire cache is used to prevent processors from getting stale copies of the data from the cache. Indiscriminate invalidation requires memory technology to support a one clock invalidation of the entire chip. No marking of pages or variables is needed in the algorithm. A more detailed algorithm with a correctness proof was provided in [Veid86] and simulated cache performance results for numerical programs appeared in [ChVe87].

This approach requires minimal hardware assistance when compared to other algorithms in this section. All shared variables except synchronization primitives are cacheable in this algorithm. The main disadvantage of this approach is the possibility of unnecessary misses due to the indiscriminate invalidation.

2.1.3. RP3 and NYU Ultracomputer

The RP3 and the NYU Ultracomputer strategies [BrMW85, EGKM85, McAu87] are similar and the following discussion focuses mainly on the NYU approach [McAu87].

A program is viewed as a collection of *computational units*. Computational units can be executed in parallel if there are no data dependences [Bane76] among units. A compiler determines whether a variable is cacheable or non-cacheable in a computational unit when it is executed in parallel with others. Synchronization variable are not cacheable.

A variable used by a computational unit X is regarded as cacheable if in the parallel execution of X with other units, it is only written by X. At the end of each computational unit's execution, all cacheable variables that are shared among different computational units are invalidated from the cache. Any modifications to the shared variables in the cache must be reflected in the main memory (by write-through). This implies that all shared variables in the cache are considered stale after a computational unit execution. Since, at the beginning of each computational unit, the cache in a processor is free of shared variables, a processor will not access stale cache copies. The invalidation functions are implemented by stepping through the cache directory [McBM85].

2.1.4. Reference Marking

The approach of [LeYL87] uses a compiler to tag each variable reference with a cacheable/noncacheable attribute. A write-back cache is used. A program is segmented into units called *epochs* which are either parallel loops or serial code between parallel loops. A reference to a variable in an epoch is marked non-cacheable if the variable in that epoch is read by more than one processors and written by at least one processor. Invalidation of the cache at the end of epochs, enables the processor to avoid stale copies of data and to get the up-to-date values from the main memory.

This scheme [Lee87] also advocates the same indiscriminate invalidation as the Veidenbaum's. Consequently, it suffers from the same disadvantage as the algorithm in [Veid86], that of unnecessary misses.

2.2. Summary of Software-Supported Schemes

The advantage of the software-supported schemes is that they have no run-time communication overhead in enforcing cache coherence. However, the price is paid in terms of cache misses due to accesses to unnecessarily invalidated cache lines. To reduce such misses, it is important to minimize the number of necessary invalidations. Invalidation strategies and maintenance of the up-to-date copies of data in the shared global memory are crucial to software-based cache coherence schemes [Smit85]. The following section discusses how these two issues are handled in the above software-based schemes.

2.2.1. Write-Policy Issues

An important aspect of software-based approaches is that an updated copy of a modified variable must be written to the shared global memory before it is referenced by other processors. A write-back policy does not appear to be a good choice for the following reasons. The main advantage of write-back in a uniprocessor system is to reduce memory traffic in the case of multiple writes to a cache word. Modified data is only written to the main memory if the cache line is replaced. Modified data in multiprocessor systems must be identified and written to the global memory before the next invalidation or synchronization operation. This is a time consuming process that can occur many times before the cache word is replaced. Another problem with write-back is the burst of network traffic created whenever a write-back occurs. For the above reasons, three out of the four schemes discussed use some form of write-through policy.

2.2.2. Existing Invalidation Schemes

There are two issues associated with invalidation: (1) when to invalidate and (2) what to invalidate. In dealing with the first issue, the approaches taken by [Veid86, McAu87, Lee87] are very similar. The ends of computational units [McAu87] and the boundaries of parallel loops [Veid86] are identical. The two schemes cause invalidation instructions to be inserted in the same program locations. The definition of epochs of [Lee87] causes invalidations at fewer program locations but more references than necessary are marked non-cacheable.

The approach of [Smit85] works well in a write-shared region. Exclusive accesses to the region are arbitrated by synchronization operations such as P(S) and V(S), or Test-and-Set. However, it is not obvious how this approach can be applied to parallel numerical programs where stale data may arise in program execution without explicitly delimited write-shared regions. Consider a Doall type parallel loop. Processors executing the loop can proceed without communication since there is no data dependence across iterations. However, stale data may be accessed in the execution of loop iterations. The parallel execution of such loops may also cause stale data copies to be read by processors continuing after the loop [ChVe87]. The method of [Smit85] may be modified to work with parallel numerical programs by relaxing the constraint of exclusive access to write-shared regions. However, even if such relaxation can be achieved, the number of points in the program where invalidations are needed will be no less than those in [Veid86] and [McAu87].

Two methods for invalidation are adopted in the schemes: (1) indiscriminate invalidation in [Veid86, Lee87], and (2) selective invalidation in [Smit85, McAu87]. The first method achieves quick invalidation but may cause more misses due to invalidating data that is not stale. The effect of each invalidation on cache behavior is equivalent to that of a cold start. Nevertheless, experiments in [ChVe87] showed that this method can achieve good performance. However, certain program structure can lead to loss of temporal locality and results in low hit ratios.

The second method suffers from the time consuming process of sequential invalidation of cache or TLB entries. Ideally, selective invalidations should be done variable by variable. However, due to the lack of good compile-time algorithms, gross approximations of what should be invalidated are used. For example, all shared cacheable variables are invalidated at the end of each computational unit in [McAu87]. For this reason, even though selective invalidation can, in theory, result in less invalidated variables than the indiscriminate approach, we believe that the number of variables invalidated in [McAu87] is not much less than in the indiscriminate approach in [Veid86]. A simple extension of the scheme of [Veid86] is to invalidate only the read–write variables and keep them in a separate cache. Without the penalty of sequential invalidation, this can result in the same number of variables invalidated as with the [McAu87] scheme. Since one TLB entry potentially corresponds to many cache lines, the OTI scheme if extended to parallel programs as discussed above may result in less items to invalidate than the [McAu87] approach. However, we believe that the number of subsequent misses due to accesses to invalidated cache lines will remain close to the one in the indiscriminate invalidation approach.

In summary, in order to realize the full potential of software–based cache coherence schemes, we need (1) to be more accurate in deciding which variables to be invalidated, and (2) to avoid the time consuming sequential invalidation process. We need better compile–time methods to detect stale cache copies. None of the existing approaches has proposed a good detection algorithm. As a result, the existing selective invalidation approaches do not appear to be much better than the indiscriminate approach as one would expect.

3. The New Approach

Our approach achieves cache coherence by combining and extending existing methods such as the insertion of invalidate–cache instructions in the instruction stream [Veid86], and marking references. It differs from the existing ones in the way invalidation is handled and marked references are affected by the invalidation.

Every reference to shared memory is marked as either *memory-read* or *cache-read*. A read reference will be marked by the compiler as a *memory-read* if the cache resident copy of the data may have become stale. Read references are marked *cache-read* if the cache resident copy

is guaranteed to be up–to–date. Consider for example the program shown in Figure 1. Suppose processor A executes the first and the last serial loops. The Doall loop is executed by more than one processors including Processor A. In the last loop, processor A will have stale copies of parts of the X array which are modified by other processors in the Doall loop. The read of the X array in the first loop is marked *cache-read*, followed by *memory-reads*. Y is marked *cache-read* as it is never modified.

A *change* bit is associated with each cache word. This bit, when true, indicates that the cache word may be stale. The *change* bit is set true by the invalidate instruction (inserted as indicated in the program in Fig. 1.) The status of the *change* bit determines whether a *memory-read* reference is to be treated as a miss or as a hit. A *memory-read* reference is a cache hit if the *change* bit is false, else the reference is treated as a miss. The bit is reset after the data is fetched into the cache. Subsequent

```
doserial i = 1, n
        .
        .
        .
        = ... Y(i)  /* cache-read */

        = ... X(i)  /* cache-read */
        .
        .
        .
enddo
doall j = 1, n
/* an invalidate-cache would be
   inserted here */
        .
        .
        = ... Y(j)  /* cache-read */

   X(j) = ...
        .
        .
        .
enddo
/* an invalidate-cache would be
   inserted here */
doserial k = 1, n
        .
        .
        .
        = ... X(k)  /* memory-read */

        = ... Y(k)  /* cache-read */
        .
        = ... X(k)  /* memory-read */
        .
        .
enddo
```

Figure 1. A program example.

memory-read references to the same data will be served by the cache until the next invalidate–cache instruction. References marked *cache-read* are not affected by the status of the *change* bit.

The proposed scheme permits retention of data for *cache-read* references. This prevents unnecessary misses on accesses after an invalidate–cache instruction. It is different from earlier indiscriminate invalidation schemes in which the entire cache is invalidated. Invalidate–cache instructions in our scheme are used only to signal that stale data might exist in the cache. A cache datum is determined to be truly invalid only at reference time by examining both, the nature of the reference and the state of the *change* bit. This achieves selective invalidation using reference marking and restricting the interpretation of invalidation to individual references. Further, unlike existing selective invalidation schemes, the invalidation is accomplished in constant time.

For the example in Figure 1, the indiscriminate invalidation approach will cause references to array variable Y to be misses in the second and last loops even though they are never modified. In our approach, since the references to array variable Y in the second and the last loops are marked *cache-read* and are not affected by the status of the *change* bit, they will not be treated as misses. Our invalidation scheme thus selectively retains variable Y in the cache. Further, even references marked *memory-read* can be cache hits once the *change* bit is reset. As in the example, the *memory-read* references of the second appearance of $X(k)$ in the last loop will not be misses since the miss prior to that resets the *change* bit of $X(k)$. The references to the first appearance of $X(k)$ in the third loop causes misses since they are marked *memory-read* and the *change* bit is set by the invalidate–cache instruction preceding the loop. These misses of $X(k)$ occur as the cache coherence scheme anticipates since the up–to–date copy of $X(k)$ may not be in the processor's cache.

3.1. Target Architecture and Program Structure

3.1.1. Parallel Program Structure

The system executes programs written or translated into a form with parallel loop constructs. For the sake of clarity, we focus on programs with serial and Doall loops but Doacross loops can also be handled with proper synchronization. Barrier synchronization is employed at the beginning and at the end of all Doall loops. Synchronization variables, themselves, are not cached.

3.1.2. Cache Memory

Clear and change bits

Associated with each cache word are a *clear* bit (similar to the valid bit in the traditional sense) and a *change* bit. If the *clear* bit is set (true), it implies that nothing has been loaded/stored in the cache word. A false (reset) *clear* bit implies that the cache word has been loaded or written into at least once. The status of the *change* bit determines whether a *memory-read* reference is to be treated as a miss or

as a hit (as discussed earlier in this section). *Change* bits for all cache words are set when an invalidate–cache instruction is executed and *clear* bits are set by a clear–cache instruction. A load or store operation resets the *change* and the *clear* bit of the cache word.

Write-policy

We use a write–through policy. The coherence enforcement scheme can be adapted to a variety of write-miss and allocate policies.

Line-fetching

The cache issues a line request for multiple words on a read miss. Line–fetching may cause cache coherence problems when different words of a line are accessed by two processors. We will discuss this in Section 3.3.

3.1.3. Memory Operand Access

We classify data references as either *memory-read* or *cache-read*. The type of each reference is indicated to the cache controller by the processor when a memory operand fetch is issued. More precisely, a *cache-read* reference is a cache hit if the *clear* bit is false and the address tags match. Otherwise, it is a miss. A *memory-read* reference is a cache hit if the *clear* bit is false, the *change* bit is false, and the address tags match. Otherwise, it is a miss.

The state diagram in Figure 2 shows how cache misses and hits are determined. A cache word can be in one of four states determined by the status of its *change bit* and the *clear bit*. State transitions are driven by cache accesses, and the *clear-cache* and *invalidate-cache* instructions. For simplicity, a line size of one word is assumed and a write miss is assumed to update the cache word (a different write miss policy may cause different state transitions).

3.1.4. Additional Instructions

Two additional instructions, (1) invalidate–cache and (2) clear–cache, are required. The invalidate–cache instruction sets true the *change* bit of all cache words. The clear–cache instruction, which is used to provide the processor with a clean cache, sets true the *clear* bit of all cache words. In both cases, the bits are set for the entire cache at once.

3.2. Software Support

We rely on a parallel Fortran compiler such as Parafrase [KKLW80] to insert the invalidate–cache instruction at appropriate places in the instruction stream and also to identify and mark references as *cache-read* or *memory-read*. The algorithm for the former task is discussed in [Veid86]. The reference marking scheme is discussed in the following subsection.

3.3. Reference Marking Scheme

The reference marking scheme identifies references to potentially stale data. We are concerned with references which might access data modified by other processors due

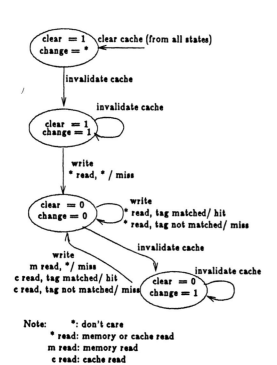

Note: *: don't care
     * read: memory or cache read
     m read: memory read
     c read: cache read

Figure. 2: State changes of a cache word

to parallel program execution. References markings are based on the location of invalidate–cache instructions and information available from def–use chains [AhSU85]. Since we use compile–time analysis, the order in which read and write accesses of a variable occur is determined by flow analysis.

We restrict our discussion of the reference marking scheme to a line fetch size of one word for simplicity. Cases with a line size larger than one will be discussed later.

The reference marking algorithm is applied to one subroutine at a time. A subroutine is assumed to start with a clean cache (the clear–cache instruction is issued upon entry to each subroutine). Variables which are only read, within a subroutine, are considered read–only and references to them are marked *cache–read*. For variables which are both read and written within the subroutine, all references to a variable which precede the first write to that variable are marked *cache–read*. The remaining class of references, that of read accesses following the first write access to the variable, are marked according to the following rules:

Case 1

A read reference is issued by the same processor that performed all the preceding writes. In this case, the reference can be marked *cache–read*. The reason is that the processor can only read either unmodified data or data modified by itself and thus gets the up–to–date copy. A read reference belongs to this category if the read reference and all writes preceding it lie within a pair of consecutive (in the run–time order) invalidate–cache instructions.

Case 2

The read reference is to a variable which has either been modified by the current processor or for which no copy exists in the processor's cache. Such references are also marked *cache–read*. A read reference belongs to this category if (1) all preceding writes to the variable are enclosed within a pair of consecutive invalidate–cache instructions, (2) there are no read references to the variable before the first of the pair of invalidate–cache instructions, and (3) the read reference under consideration appears after the second invalidate–cache instruction. Between the pair of invalidate–cache instructions, the reads of one processor do not depend on the writes of another. Furthermore, since there were no read accesses before this pair, the current processor's cache does not contain a stale copy of the variable after the second invalidate–cache instruction. Consequently, the read reference can be marked *cache–read*.

Case 3

A read reference is to a variable for which a stale copy may exist in the current processor's cache. The reference is marked *memory–read*. A read reference belongs to this category if (1) the preceding writes are separated by at least one invalidate–cache instruction, or (2) all preceding writes are enclosed by a pair of consecutive invalidate–cache instructions but one or more reads precede the first of the pair.

When a line size larger than one is used, additional software or hardware support is required to enforce coherence. A problem arises when two distinct processors access the same cache line but do not use all words in it. This may load words into the cache which dependence analysis can not detect, and therefore can result in coherence violation.

There are two such cases: 1) the locations belong to different variables (array or scalar) or 2) to the same array. For example, consider the execution of an innermost Doall loop. Processor A might load in words as part of a line which will be written by another processor executing an adjacent iteration. When processor A reads the unused words after the Doall loop execution is completed, it can fetch stale data.

The problem can be solved by either hardware or software. One possible software solution is to require different variables be assigned on line boundaries in memory, and the following restriction to be applied to the second case in the marking algorithm:

Case 2a

In addition to the condition tested in Case 2, the read reference can only be marked *cache-read* if there are no read references to the same variable enclosed by the two invalidate–cache instructions. Otherwise, the read reference has to be marked *memory-read*.

This is the approach used in our simulation study. Another possibility is to extend the marking algorithm to detect and mark such cases as *memory-reads*. The analysis has to be extended to cover the problem cases assuming the knowledge of memory allocation.

A possible hardware solution is to use an extra bit per cache word, the *use* bit, to identify a word that is loaded in with a line but is never used. After an invalidate–cache instruction, initial references to such cache words are treated as misses. The application of the *use* bit can be described as follows: The *use* bits of all words in a line are reset when the line is loaded in from the global memory due to a miss. When a word is actually delivered by the cache controller to the processor, the *use* bit is set. After an invalidate–cache instruction (indicated by the *change* bit set), references to a cache word with the *use* bit reset are also treated as misses.

The hardware solution has the disadvantage that a read hit may require the *use* bit to be changed, i.e. a subsequent write operation. This can only happen once per word on its first access after a word is loaded and only on words other than the one causing the miss.

When subroutine calls are present within the current subroutine, one of several alternatives may be pursued. We can expand the subroutine before insertion of invalidate–cache instructions. For subroutines where expansion is not possible, a conservative approach is to mark all references to variables modified by the call as *memory-read* accesses. An invalidate–cache instruction is then inserted right after the call. Alternatively, a clear-cache instruction can be inserted after the subroutine call and the reference marking algorithm is then applied to the following code.

The above conditions used in our algorithm constitute a very restrictive subset of conditions under which references can be marked *cache-read*. A set of more general conditions to determine whether a reference is *cache-read* or *memory-read* is beyond the scope of this paper but is formalized and discussed in detail in [Cheo88].

4. Experimental Results

We implemented our cache coherence enforcement scheme in a compiler and a parallel program simulator. The results are compared to the results obtained using the indiscriminate approach in [Veid86]. We are unable to compare our results to other schemes because neither results nor appropriate simulators are available. However,

Subroutine	Program	Description
Newrz	SIMP2	New velocity computation and volume change in a Lagrangian hydrodynamics program
Step	ARC3D	Computational fluid dynamics
Ux	VORTEX	A PDE solver
Cg		A conjugate gradient matrix solver (for Ax=b)
Cmslow	BARO	Nonlinear tendency computation in a barometer program
Parmvr	PIC	Particle in cell program
Lblkerna		A kernel of experimental physics computation

Table. 1: Benchmark Subroutines.

a qualitative analysis of the advantages of our approach over the others has already been given in the previous section.

In our simulation, we use separate 8K word direct-mapped real-address data and instruction caches. We use line fetching size of one, two, and four words. A tag per word is used in the simulation. A write-through policy is used and the cache word is also updated in a write-hit or write-miss. Parallel program traces are generated by Parafrase [AbKw85].

We used subroutines from several numerical program described in Table. 1. The hit ratios are shown in Table 2a and Table 2b. Table 2b includes the results of only the subroutines that can use a large number of processors (the speedups of using 512 processors over 32 processors for Step, Ux, and Newrz are 7.9, 9.07, and 8.26 respectively). The numbers in the columns with subheading *new* show hit ratios with the new coherence scheme and the ones with *old* as their heading contain the hit ratios with the indiscriminate invalidation scheme. The column headed by *blk n* represents results obtained with *n* as the line size.

We see that the new approach achieves better hit ratios. The hit ratio improvement is program-dependent. We observed earlier in our experiments [ChVe87] that indiscriminate invalidation scheme has lower hit ratios when more processors are available. The reason is the loss of temporal locality due to frequent invalidations between adjacent inner Doall loops. The low hit ratios of Lblkerna with 32 processors, and Newrz, Ux, and Step with 512 processors are due to this reason. The new approach preserves more of the available temporal locality, and the results in these cases show that it is effective and brings the data hit ratios back to a respectable level.

Data Hit Ratios						
Subr.	blk 1		blk 2		blk 4	
	old	new	old	new	old	new
step	94.23	*94.25*	96.32	*96.34*	97.45	*97.46*
lblkerna	2.91	*44.70*	25.08	*66.52*	37.44	*78.52*
ux	91.05	*91.06*	94.22	*94.22*	95.78	*95.79*
cmslow	39.83	*53.39*	63.60	*73.82*	75.86	*84.22*
cg	21.30	*38.25*	59.17	*67.99*	78.60	*83.15*
newrs	35.04	*42.66*	65.99	*70.23*	82.09	*84.37*
parmvr	47.00	*48.77*	72.06	*74.23*	86.32	*86.77*

Table. 2a: Data hit ratio comparison
(32 processors).

Data Hit Ratios						
Subr.	blk 1		blk 2		blk 4	
	old	new	old	new	old	new
step	21.22	*35.42*	37.33	*51.51*	45.53	*59.78*
ux	32.45	*49.05*	48.99	*65.53*	57.10	*73.64*
newrs	15.84	*34.68*	37.62	*52.88*	43.56	*59.62*

Table. 2b: Data hit ratio comparison
(512 processors).

One might ask if the hit ratio increase is entirely due to marking references to read–only variables *cache–read* in the program and never invalidating them. If this is true, a separate read–only data cache might be used together with a much simpler reference marking scheme. However, in our experiments, four out of seven subroutines show that their largest hit ratio increase is primarily due to having marked references to read–write variables as *cache–read*. Table. 3 shows the percentage increase of hit ratio due to references of read–write variables marked *cache–read* and the percentage increase due to references of read–only variables marked *cache–read*. For example, in subroutine Step, 95.0% of the hit ratio increase results from references to read–write variables marked *cache–read*, while one 5.0% of the hit ratio increase is due to references to read–only variables marked *cache–read* data. As can be seen in Table. 3, four out of seven subroutines show that *cache–read* references to read–write variables account for more than 90% of hit ratio increase.

The experimental results show a definite improvement over an indiscriminate invalidation approach. Also, it should be noticed that our reference marking scheme is conservative since def–use give a rather imprecise dependence relationship (name–only). Improvements can be made by using a more sophisticated data dependence analysis. Such improvements will lead to more *cache–read* references while preserving the coherence of the memory hierarchy.

5. Conclusion

In this paper, we have discussed existing cache coherence enforcement schemes for large–scale multiprocessor systems and their suitability for parallel numerical program execution. We proposed a new approach to software–assisted cache coherence enforcement which is free from the drawbacks of earlier schemes. Our scheme is based on (1) compile–time insertion of invalidate–cache instructions, (2) compile–time marking of read references, (3) hardware support for *cache–read* and *memory–read* references, and finally, (4) reference–time checking and invalidation of individual cache items.

The new approach incorporates both, the speed advantage of the indiscriminate invalidation approach as well as the higher hit ratios of selective invalidation approach. The new approach allows stale data to be invalidated only when it is referenced individually, and thus leaves up–to–date cache copies alone. It is conceptually different from existing indiscriminate invalidation approaches where all cache data is made invalid at some fixed points in time. The proposed approach is superior to existing selective invalidation approaches because time–consuming, run–time, sequential checking and invalidation of stale data or TLB entries is avoided. It is also different from existing reference marking schemes in that the marking of the reference alone does not force the access to be treated as a cache miss. Once the stale copy is updated,

Contribution to data hit ratio increases		
(measured at prefetching line size of one)		
Subr.	Read–write	Read–only
step	95.0	5.0*
lblkerna	10.5	89.5
ux	98.5	1.5*
cmslow	15.8	84.2
cg	3.5	96.5
newrs	90.0	10.0*
parmvr	99.3	0.7

Table. 3: Percentage of hit ratio increases
due to *cache–read* references to read–write
and read–only variables respectively
(* with 512 and the rest with 32 processors).

this allows *memory-read* references to access the cache data until the next invalidate–cache instruction. Consequently, we thus save a large number of unnecessary misses by invalidating cache data at reference–time on a need–to–do and individual basis without the extra time penalty of a selective approach.

The hit ratio improvement in our experimental results further demonstrates that software–assisted cache coherence enforcement is not only a feasible solution to large multiprocessor systems but is also a very promising solution.

Acknowledgements

Our thanks to John Fu, Elana Granston and Madhumitra Sharma for their valuable comments.

References

[AbKw85]   Abu-Sufah, W., and Alex Y. Kwok. *Performance Prediction Tools for Cedar: A Multiprocessor Supercomputer.* The 12th Ann. Int. Symp. on Comp. Arch. (June 1985) pp.406–413.

[AhSU85]   Aho, Alfred V., Ravi Sethi and Jeffrey D. Ullman. *Compilers Principles, Techniques, and Tools.* Addison-Wesley, 1985.

[ArBa84]   Archibald, James and Jean-Loup Baer. *An Economical Solution to the Cache Coherence Problem.* 11th Int. Symp. on Comp. Arch. (June 1984) pp.355–362.

[Bane76]   Banerjee, U. *Data Dependence in Ordinary Programs.* M.S. Thesis, Dept. of Computer Science, Report No. 76–837, Univ. of Illinois at Urbana–Champaign (Nov. 1976).

[BrMW85]   Brantley, W. C., K. P. McAuliffe and J. Weiss. *RP3 Processor-Memory Element.* Proc. of the 1985 Int. Conf. on Parallel Processing (1985) pp. 782–789.

[CeFe78]   Censier, L. M. and P. Feautrier. *A New Solution to Coherence Problems in Multicache Systems.* IEEE Trans. Comput., Vol. C–27 (Dec. 1978) pp. 1112–1118.

[Cheo88]   Cheong, H. Ph.D. Thesis, Dept. of Electrical and Computer Engineering, Univ. of Illinois at Urbana–Champaign (1988).

[ChVe87]   Cheong, H. and A. V. Veidenbaum. *The Performance of Software-Managed Multiprocessor Caches on Parallel Numerical Programs.* International Conference on Supercomputing (June 1987).

[EGKM85]   Edler, Jan, Allan Gottieb, Clyde P. Kruskal, Kevin McAuliffe, Larry Rudolph, Marc Snir, Patricia Teller and James Wilson. *Issues Related to MIMD Shared-Memory Computers: The NYU Ultracomputer Approach.* Proc. 12th Int. Symp. on Comp. Arch. (June, 1985) pp. 126–135.

[Good83]   Goodman, James R. *Using Cache Memory to Reduce Processor-Memory Traffic.* Proc. 10th Annual International Symposium on Computer Architecture (June, 1983) pp. 124–131.

[KaEW85]   Katz, R. H., S. J. Eggers, D. A. Wood, C. L. Perkins and R. G. Sheldon. *Implementing a Cache Consistency Protocol.* Proc. 12th Ann. Int. Symp. on Comp. Arch. (June, 1985) pp. 276–283.

[KKLW80]   Kuck, D. J., R. H. Kuhn, B. Leasure and M. Wolfe. *The Structure of an Advanced Vectorizer for Pipelined Processors.* Fourth International Computer Software and Applications Conference (Oct., 1980).

[LeYL87]   Lee, R. L., P. C. Yew and D. H. Lawrie. *Multiprocessor Cache Design Considerations.* The 14th Annual International Symposium on Computer Architecture (June, 1987) pp. 253–262.

[Lee87]   Lee, Roland L. *The Effectiveness of Caches and Data Prefetch Buffers in Large-Scale Shared Memory Multiprocessors.* Ph.D Thesis, Tech. Rep 670, Center of Supercomputing Research and Development, U. of Illinois at Urbana–Champaign (August 1987).

[McAu87]   McAuliffe, Kevin K. Ph.D. Thesis NYU (May, 1987).

[McCr84]   McCreight, Edward M. *The Dragon Computer System: An Early Overview.* Technical Report (June, 1984).

[PaPa84]   Papamarcos, Mark and Janak Patel. *A Low-Overhead Coherence Solution for Multiprocessors with Private Cache Memories.* Proc. 11th Ann. Int. Symp. on Comp. Arch. (June, 1984) pp. 348–354.

[RuSe84]   Rudolph, Larry and Zary Segall. *Dynamic Decentralized Cache Schemes for MIMD Parallel Architectures.* Proc. 11th Ann. Int. Symp. on Comp. Arch. (June, 1984) pp. 340–347.

[Smit85]   Smith, Alan Jay. *CPU Cache Consistency with Software Support and Using "One Time Identifiers".* Proceeding of the Pacific Computer Communications '85 (1985) pp. 153–161.

[SwSm86]   Sweazey, Paul and Alan Jay Smith. *A Class of Compatible Cache Consistency Protocols and Their Support by the IEEE Futurebus.* The 13th Annual International Symposium on Computer Architecture (June, 1986) pp. 414–423.

[Tang76]   Tang, C. K. *Cache System Design in the Tightly Coupled Multiprocessor System.* Proc. AFIP National Computer Conference (1976) vol. 45, pp. 749–753.

[Veid86]   Veidenbaum, Alexander V. *A Compiler-Assisted Cache Coherence Solution for Multiprocessors.* 1986 Proc. ICPP (Aug., 1986) pp. 1029–1036.

Automatic Management of Programmable Caches
(Extended Abstract)

Ron Cytron (*)
Steve Karlovsky (**)
Kevin P. McAuliffe (*)

(*) IBM T. J. Watson Research Center
Computer Science Department
Yorktown Heights, New York 10598

(**) Center for Supercomputing Research and Development
University of Illinois at Urbana-Champaign
Urbana, Illinois 61801

We present algorithms for compiler-directed management of cache memories, where hardware does not keep such memories consistent: caches may contain discrepant values for shared variables. Our algorithms determine when a cached value must update its shared variable, and when a processor's cached value is potentially stale. Although our algorithms are presented in the context of programmable caches, the algorithms apply to a broad class of architectures where hardware does not force coherence among processors' local memories. We present algorithms and results for cache management of automatically parallelized sequential programs. We then consider optimizing the placement of cache management instructions. These optimizations apply to programs with explicitly specified cache management instructions as well as those where such instructions are automatically determined.

1.0 Introduction

As a means of obtaining increased performance, one trend in parallel architecture is to incorporate increasing numbers of processors. To cooperate in solving a problem, these processors must share data. We consider a broad class of architectures comprised of multiple processors connected to multiple memory modules (a global memory) via a multi-cycle interconnection network. Increasing the number of processors in such a system necessarily increases the average latency associated with referencing shared data. To reduce the effective memory latency, a cache can be associated with each processor. The inclusion of processor-specific caches reduces memory latency since the resulting access time is an average of the global memory access time and cache memory access time. Moreover, since the cache services a percentage of all memory requests, network traffic is diminished, thus further reducing the average latency for global memory.

The indiscriminate use of such cache memories can introduce memory coherence problems: distinct processors can view discrepant values for the same global variable. Historically, centralized or distributed hardware cross-interrogation mechanisms enforce coherence: when a processor issues a store to an address, the hardware ensures that the value in the other processors' caches is consistent with the value stored, either by invalidating the address in cache or by updating the cache with the stored value [2, 7, 13]. Maintaining coherence by hardware introduces serialization, the manifestation of which depends on the hardware implementation [22]. Incoherence can be tolerated where discrepant values for a given address are not *observable* by any processor. Although this refinement eliminates some unnecessary serialization, all global memory accesses must be tracked. For large parallel systems, maintaining coherence exclusively in hardware is prohibitive either in cost or in serialization. For this reason, the larger systems have proposed managing caches through software [14, 17, 18]

Although it might appear that the burden of managing the caches has now fallen on the programmer, this paper is devoted to showing how automatic techniques can effectively manage software-controlled caches. Because our methods are based on dependence analysis of sequential programs, our algorithms are easily incorporated into parallelizing compilers. These algorithms have been implemented in PTRAN [4, 16]; the examples shown in this paper demonstrate the results of this implementation.

In the remainder of this section, we state our assumptions and definitions with respect to software-controlled caches and we define our execution model. In Section 2.0, we provide algorithms for determining the placement of cache management instructions (cache control points). Section 3.0 describes optimizing cache management instructions. In Section 4.0, we state our conclusions and describe future work.

(**) This work was supported in part by the National Science Foundation under Grants No. US NSF MIP-8410110, the U. S. Department of Energy under Grant No. US DOE-DE-FG02-85ER25001, and the IBM Donation.

1.1 Software-Controlled Caches

We define a programmable cache as a standard cache memory where certain control mechanisms (see below) can be invoked under software control. For the present discussion, we assume a store-in cache with sufficient size (and mapping power) to avoid any *evictions*.[1] We also assume that the "line size" of the cache is the unit of storage reference (for example, a word). Thus, no data is cached without explicit reference, and no data in cache is ever replaced outside the scope of software control. In Section 4.0, we discuss the implications of evictions, store-through caches, and longer line sizes.

Unlike traditional approaches, we allow incoherence: two processors may reference the same variable, yet view discrepant values for that variable. Thus, we have a storage hierarchy with a uniform address space, referenced through global memory and caches that afford processors an efficient, albeit potentially inconsistent, view of global memory.

Each address within the global address space is marked with cacheability status:

Cacheable: Data at the associated address can always be cached, and software will never demand that such data leave a cache. This marking is appropriate only for read-only data or data that is never shared among processors.

Temporarily cacheable: Data at the associated address can be cached at any reference, but software controls the durations of the data's residency in cache, using the *invalidate* or *flush* instructions described below.

Non-cacheable: Data at the associated address can never be cached. This marking is useful where the overhead associated with managing temporarily cached data becomes excessive.

Under these definitions, data enters a cache when a processor references the associated address, only if that address is marked *cacheable* or *temporarily cacheable*. Because of the store-in and eviction-free assumptions, data leaves a cache only under software control. For temporarily cached data, a processor can issue the following instructions with respect to its own cache:

Post: Data associated with an address is copied back to global memory. The processor's cache retains its copy of the data.

Invalidate: Data associated with an address is marked invalid. Global memory is unaffected since the cached value is *not* copied back to global memory. When the processor next references the associated address, the reference will be satisfied at global memory.

---

(1) An eviction is the removal of a cache line by hardware for the purpose of replacement.

(2) These last two forms of data dependence can often be eliminated by renaming techniques.

Flush: Both of the above operations occur: data is copied back to global memory and marked invalid in the cache.

Although we define the marking and management of cached addresses in terms of individual addresses, implementation considerations have motivated architectures to consider addresses at a coarser granularity. For example, the Ultracomputer project at NYU [12] and the RP3 project at IBM [8] have considered marking cacheability status at the page or segment level as a cost-effective alternative to marking individual addresses. In the current Ultracomputer prototype [14] and in the original treatment of this problem by Veidenbaum [20], post or invalidate instructions issued by a processor apply to the entire cache associated with that processor. The RP3 allows finer grain control of cache invalidation, including line invalidate and temporarily-cacheable-data (marked data) invalidate. Such organizations invite further compile-time optimizations as described in Section 3.0.

1.2 Execution Model

Our execution model consists of a program that has been analyzed by a parallelizing compiler such as PTRAN. Although our algorithms incorporate information obtained through interprocedural analysis, the algorithms themselves examine separately each procedure of a program in turn. In the resulting program, parallelism is achieved (in part) by executing certain loops as *DOALL* loops, where the iterations of such loops can be executed by distinct processors. In general, concurrency can be generated for arbitrary parts of a program, but in this discussion we restrict ourselves to nested DOALL parallelism. The algorithms readily generalize for COBEGIN/COEND constructs.

Each time a DOALL loop is encountered, some number of processors are assigned to execute some number of iterations of that loop. When the iterations are exhausted, the processors assigned to the loop are freed. Thus, a single DOALL loop can be executed multiple times (as shown in Figure 2), but the processors assigned to the DOALL may differ for each execution.

1.3 Notation

Our algorithms use a *scheduling vector* that specifies which loops of a program potentially execute as DOALL loops. For loop i, if $SV(i)$ = 'P', then loop i is a parallel (DOALL) loop; otherwise $SV(i)$ = 'S' and loop i executes sequentially. We also require the *data dependence* graph typically computed by parallelizing compilers. We avoid a detailed discussion of data dependence [6, 9, 21], and focus instead on those aspects relevant to our work. Two statements ST_i and ST_j participate in a *flow dependence* (denoted $ST_i \delta ST_j$) if ST_i can create data that could be consumed at ST_j. Statements ST_i and ST_j participate in an *output dependence*, if both statements write to the same location and ST_j should write last (denoted $ST_i \delta^o ST_j$. Statements ST_i and ST_j participate in an *anti-dependence* (denoted $ST_i \bar{\delta} ST_j$) if ST_i reads data that can subsequently be written by ST_j.[2] For these dependence relations, ST_i and ST_j could be executed on the same or different processors. If they execute on different processors, we assume the compiler has inserted synchronization or has sequenced the computations so that ST_i finishes before ST_j starts [10]. Synchronization, however, is insufficient to honor flow dependences where processors cache values: sometimes a processor must *post* its cached value for access by another processor. Further, we must sometimes *invalidate* stale values in a cache, so that a subsequent reference is correctly resolved in global memory. For clarity, we do not show synchronization operations in our examples.

We use the following notation to describe how processors reference global memory: Let $Write(P_i,X)$ denote a global memory write issued by processor P_i for variable (location) X. Let $Read(P_i,X)$ similarly denote a read, and let $Ref(P_i,X)$ denote an arbitrary reference (read or a write). We use "→" to denote a possible sequence of such operations. For example, notation

$$Ref(P_i,X) \rightarrow Ref(P_j,X)$$

denotes that P_j might reference X after P_i.

2.0 Algorithms

We determine in three steps cacheability and associated coherence requirements.

1. Mark all variables as *temporarily cacheable*.

2. Determine where cache actions (post, invalidate, or flush) are necessary to maintain coherence, using algorithms in the ensuing sections. Given our assumptions with regard to line size and eviction, this determination is *partitionable*: cache management instructions for a given variable are not affected by such considerations for other variables. Thus, each variable can be analyzed separately; the solution over all variables is just the *union* of post and invalidation points.

3. Identify the actual cacheability of variables. For variables that require no cache action, the variables should be marked *cacheable*. Variables that are referenced only after invalidation should be marked *non-cacheable*. A variable whose behavior falls between these two extremes requires analysis to determine the profitability of caching that variable. Such analysis is beyond the scope of this paper.

2.1 Processor-Crossing Dependences

To determine cache control points, our algorithms must determine when the source and sink of a dependence potentially execute in different processors. The dependence analysis in PTRAN yields a collection of fully-refined *direction vectors* for each dependence that cannot be refuted by the decision algorithms [9]. We avoid a detailed discussion of direction vectors [21], and focus on the properties relevant to our discussion. A fully-refined direction vector can be classified as one of the following:

Loop-Carried(i) The dependence is satisfied by sequencing the iterations of some loop i, where loop i surrounds the source and sink of the dependence [6].

Loop-Independent The dependence is implicitly satisfied for the nested DOALL model of parallel execution.[3]

The algorithm shown in Figure 1 determines if a dependence *crosses* processors. For (sourceδsink), the dependence crosses processors if *source* and *sink* potentially execute in different processors.

---

procedure CROSSES? (*source, sink*)

If the dependence is loop-carried (by loop i),
then
    If $SV(i) = $ 'P'
    then return (CROSSES)
    else mark__loop = i
else mark__loop = ICLoop (*source, sink*)

For each loop j such that mark__loop contains loop j and loop j contains either *source* or *sink*,
    if $SV(j) = $ 'P'
    then return (CROSSES)

return (DOES__NOT__CROSS)

Figure 1.   Processor-Crossing Algorithm: ICLoop is a function that returns the innermost common loop of its arguments.

The algorithm of Figure 1 conservatively assumes that a dependence can cross processors where processors are reallocated to iterations. Consider the example of Figure 2.

```
DO i=1 to N
    DOALL j=1 to M
        B(j)    =
        X(j)    =
                =  B(j) + X(j)
                =  B(j-1)
        A(i,j)  =
                =  A(i-1,j)
    ENDDOALL

        =  A(i,f(i))
ENDDO
```

Figure 2.   Dependences Cross

The flow dependences for A are satisfied by the outer sequential loop. However, successive executions of the inner loop cause flow dependences that potentially cross processors, since we make no assumptions about processor allocation to loop iterations. Optimization of this situation is discussed in Section 3.0.

The complexity of this algorithm is $O(\Delta)$, where Δ is the maximum depth of interval (loop) nesting. When invoked by the other algorithms of this paper, the processor-crossing algorithm effectively executes in constant time.

---

(3)   For more general COBEGIN/COEND parallelism, such dependences are satisfied by sequencing certain statements [5]

2.2 Posting Values to Global Memory

The purpose of posting is to keep global memory up-to-date, preventing stale values from being referenced. Our fundamental observation is that the sequence:

$$Write(P_i,X) \rightarrow Read(P_j,X), i \neq j \qquad (1)$$

should cause P_i to post its cache value for X to global memory. The post, in addition to the requisite synchronization or sequencing, guarantees P_j references the correct value for X in global memory. Consider some procedure Q for which parallel loops have been identified. An algorithm that captures observation (1) for procedure Q is shown in Figure 3.

For each statement ST_i that defines variable X,

if X is *interprocedurally live* in Q, and if the definition of X by ST_i reaches any exit of Q,

then POST (ST_i, X)

else consider each flow dependence $ST_i \delta ST_j$ for X.

if CROSSES? (ST_i, ST_j)

then POST (ST_i, X)

Figure 3.   Post Algorithm: POST (ST, V) causes the reference of variable V to be posted upon completion of statement ST.

The first POST is necessary where a procedure may define variables that are used solely by other procedures. For such definitions, no flow dependences *per se* exist in the analyzed procedure. However, interprocedural information indicates whether other procedures use the defined variable, and we do not assume that such procedures execute in the same processor that defines the variable. Intraprocedural information indicates whether the definition can persist to a procedure exit. We therefore conservatively determine that such definitions must be posted to global memory for access by other procedures. The second POST is necessary for intraprocedural flow dependences. Consider the example of Figure 2 with post instructions as shown in Figure 4.

```
DO i=1 to N
    DOALL j=1 to M
        B(j)   =
        POST (B(j))
        X(j)   =
               = B(j) + X(j)
               = B(j-1)
        A(i,j) =
        POST (A(i,j))
               = A(i-1,j)
    ENDDOALL

    = A(i,f(i))
ENDDO
```

Figure 4.   Example

---

(4)   Flow dependences are a subset of def-use arcs.

Note that post instructions have been placed after definitions that participate in flow dependences that cross processors. For each such definition, a post instruction is generated that references the defined location. Thus, the argument to POST must be identical to the variable defined, including any subscript expressions indexing the variable. Note that the assignment to X requires no post: a processor that creates data for X will be the same processor consuming that data.

The complexity of this algorithm is $O(\Delta \times |def \rightarrow use|)$, where Δ is the maximum depth of interval nesting (effectively constant) and $|def \rightarrow use|$ is the number of def-use data flow arcs.[4]

2.3 Invalidating Cache

The purpose of invalidation is to keep cache up-to-date, preventing stale values from being referenced. Although the cache is not actually updated at invalidation time, a subsequent reference to an invalidated address demands that the cache be refreshed from global memory. Our fundamental observation is that the sequence:

$$Ref(P_i,X) \rightarrow Write(P_j,X) \rightarrow Read(P_i,X), j \neq i \qquad (2)$$

could cause processor P_i to have a stale value of X in its cache. In such cases, P_i must invalidate X. We present two solutions for the invalidation problem. Our first solution is conservative with respect to observation (2) above. This solution is analogous to the posting algorithm: invalidation points are determined by examining each dependence in turn. A more precise (and expensive) scheme is considered in Section 2.3.2.

2.3.1 Simple Scheme

As a first approximation to observation (2) above, consider the algorithm shown in Figure 5 as applied to some procedure Q.

For each statement ST_j that uses variable X,

if X is *upwards-exposed* for procedure Q,

then INVALID (ST_j, X)

else consider each flow dependence $ST_i \delta ST_j$ for X.

if CROSSES? (ST_i, ST_j)

then INVALID (ST_j, X)

Figure 5.   Simple Invalidation: INVALID (ST, V) causes a processor to invalidate its cache for variable V prior to executing statement ST.

The first INVALID causes a processor to invalidate its cache of a variable that could be defined by some other procedure; the invalidation occurs before the variable is accessed. Consider a dependence $ST_i \delta ST_j$ on a variable X, for which the algorithm of Figure 3 posts X after ST_i. The second INVALID of Figure 5 determines an invalidation of X before executing ST_j.

Returning to the example of Figure 4, the program shown in Figure 6 shows where invalidations occur.

129

```
DO i=1 to N
   DOALL j=1 to M
      B(j)    =
      X(j)    =
              = B(j) + X(j)
              INVALID (B(j-1))
              = B(j-1)
      A(i,j)  =
              INVALID (A(i-1,j))
              = A(i-1,j)
   ENDDOALL

              INVALID (A(i,f(i)))
   = A(i,f(i))
ENDDO
```

Figure 6.   Invalidations under Simple Scheme

The invalidations for this example essentially occur at the sink of dependences that caused posts in Figure 4. The complexity of this algorithm is therefore $O(\Delta \times |def \to use|)$.

2.3.2 Better Scheme

Unfortunately, excessive invalidations result from applying the algorithm of Figure 5. Returning to the example of Figure 6, the invalidate of $A(i,f(i))$ is unnecessary. Each element of A is defined at most once. Suppose a processor has a value for $A(i,f(i))$ in its cache. If that processor subsequently references that value, then the value can come from cache since no other processor could have defined the value. If the value is missing from cache, then the reference is resolved in global memory. The corresponding definitions would be posted, as determined by the algorithm of Figure 3.

In contrast to observation (2), the simple invalidation algorithm detects the more conservative situation:

$$Write(P_j, X) \to Read(P_i, X), j \neq i$$

We can eliminate invalidation where defined data can reside in at most one cache. The algorithm shown in Figure 7 captures such cases.

For each statement ST_j that uses variable X,

   if X is *upwards-exposed* for procedure Q,

   then INVALID (ST_j, X)

   else consider each flow dependence $ST_i \delta ST_j$ for X.

      if CROSSES? (ST_i, ST_j)

      then if $\exists ST_k$ such that $(ST_i \delta^\circ ST_k$ or $ST_k \bar{\delta} ST_j)$ and CROSSES? (S_k, S_i)

      then INVALID (ST_j, X)

Figure 7.   Better Invalidation

The second INVALID occurs where some processor may read or write the value assigned by statement ST_i. That value could then be stale at the reference by ST_j and thus require invalidation. Using the algorithms of Figure 3 and Figure 7 results in the program shown in Figure 8.

```
DO i=1 to N
   DOALL j=1 to M
      B(j)    =
              POST (B(j))
      X(j)    =
              = B(j) + X(j)
              INVALID (B(j-1))
              = B(j-1)
      A(i,j)  =
              POST (A(i,j))
              = A(i-1,j)
   ENDDOALL

   = A(i,f(i))
ENDDO
```

Figure 8.   Resulting Program

In essence, this better invalidation scheme determines where a processor may safely reference data that was not obtained from global memory since processor reassignment. In Figure 8, processor reassignment occurs for the inner DOALL loop. If the processor executing the outer sequential loop is assigned to an iteration of the inner DOALL loop, then the data for the use $A(i,f(i))$ may reside in cache. Although the dependence could cross processors, no stale accesses result.

As expected, the complexity of this better invalidation algorithm is worse than for the simple invalidation scheme:

$$O(|def \to use| \times (\Delta + \Delta \times (|use \to def| + |def \to def|)))$$

Where the maximum interval depth is considered constant, and where variables fewer definition than use sites, the complexity is essentially $O(|def \to use|^2)$. In practice, this complexity would be noticed only where statements define most variables. Otherwise, the observed complexity should be closer to $O(|def \to use|)$.

2.4 Flush (Post and Invalidate)

In the above discussion, posts were associated with definitions and invalidates with uses. This section examines how the two operations can be combined into a *flush* operation performed after the definition. A flush of X causes X to be posted to global memory and invalidated from the issuing processor's cache. The advantage of separating post and invalidate is that certain uses may benefit from cache accesses, even while other uses of the same variable go to global memory. In the example of Figure 8, the use of $B(i)$ can be resolved in cache while the use $B(i - 1)$ must be satisfied in global memory. If the post and invalidate were combined at the definition ($FLUSH(B(i))$), then the resulting program would forfeit resolving one use of B in cache. We seek a solution where invalidates and posts can be combined without loss of cache utilization. Consider the example shown in Figure 9. Data dependence identifies a processor-crossing flow dependence for X from ST_2 to ST_4, causing the definition to be posted after ST_2 and the use to be invalidated before ST_4. No cache action is required for the dependence from ST_6 to ST_7. Thus, the invalidation inside the DOALL loop can be eliminated in favor of a flush of X after ST_2.

```
ST₁    DO i=1 to N
ST₂       X =
             FLUSH (X)

ST₃       DOALL j=1 to N
ST₄          = X
ST₅       ENDDOALL

ST₆       X =
ST₇          = X
ST₈    ENDDO
```

Figure 9.   Flush Example

The algorithm shown in Figure 10 computes those definitions for which flushes do not sacrifice cache utilization.

---

do while ∃ unexamined flow dependence arcs for variable X

    Pick some arc *defsite* → *usesite*

    Initialize

        DEFSITES = {*defsite*}

        USESITES = {*usesite*}

    Compute the "closure" of the dependence; repeat until no changes to *DEFSITES* or *USESITES*:

        if ∃*newdefsite* ∉ *DEFSITES* such that *newdefsite*δ*usesite* , where *usesite* ∈ *USESITES*,

        then *DEFSITES* = *DEFSITES* ∪ *newdefsite*

        if ∃*newusesite* ∉ *USESITES* such that *defsite*δ*newusesite* , where *defsite* ∈ *DEFSITES*,

        then *USESITES* = *USESITES* ∪ *newusesite*

    if ∀*defsite* ∈ *DEFSITES*,

        POST (*defsite*, X)

    and ∀*usesite* ∈ *USESITES*,

        INVALID (*usesite*, X)

    then

        for each *defsite* ∈ *DEFSITES*, replace POST (*defsite*, X) with FLUSH (*defsite*, X)

        for each *usesite* ∈ *USESITES*, eliminate INVALID (*usesite*, X)

Figure 10.   Flush Algorithm

With the proper data structure, the complexity of this algorithm is $O(|def \to use|)$.

3.0   Optimizations

Although the placement of cache management instructions determined by the algorithms of the preceding section is correct, the resulting programs are not necessarily optimal with respect to cache utilization or program speedup. In this section, we describe how the placement of cache management instructions can be improved. In Section 3.1, we use data flow techniques

to improve cache utilization and to reduce synchronization delay for values posted to global memory. In Section 3.3 we consider how variables with similar cacheability profiles could be grouped together. Single cache instructions could then concurrently manage all members of a group. In Section 3.2, we consider how process formation and processor allocation can influence cache performance. The techniques discussed in this section are of interest for explicitly parallel as well as automatically parallelized programs.

3.1   Data Flow Motion

Here we seek to improve the placement of cache management instructions through "standard" data flow analysis. For a given region of a program, such analysis typically computes [15]:

KILL()	The set of variables for which a definition occurs along every path through the region.
PRESERVE()	The set of variables for which some path through the region contains no definition.
NODEF()	The set of variables for which no definition occurs along any path through the region.

A region that preserves X may or may not define X, but a region that kills X always defines X. Consider two processes P1 and P2 as shown in Figure 11.

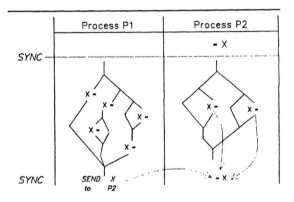

Figure 11.   Problem Statement

Process P1 contains a region of code that *kills* X: every path through P1 contains some definition for X. The region is followed by synchronization, at which point P1 has no more updates for X as far as P2 is concerned. Note that such synchronization could have been explicitly specified in a parallel program. Process P2 begins by referencing X. This reference is either resolved in cache or causes a value for X to be cached in P2. Note that the algorithm of Section 2.3.2 can allow such references to be safely resolved in cache. P2 then executes a region of code that *preserves* X: some path through this region avoids defining X. The preserving region in P2 is followed by a use of X that is reached by the dependence arcs shown in Figure 11. The semantics are as follows: If the region of code in P2 defines X, then the use of X should reference the value computed by P2 (potentially in P2's cache). Otherwise, P2 fails to define X and the use should reference the value created by P1.

131

This scenario is actually a very general setting for our problem. Control flow within process P2 decides whether P2 receives its locally computed value for X or receives a value computed by some other process. When the value comes from another process, P2 must *invalidate* X: the reference to X prior to the synchronization point can result in a stale value for X in P2's cache. Similarly, control flow within P1 decides which definition of X in P1 should reach the last use of X in P2, should P2 fail to define X itself. Although the synchronization point is shown after the region that kills X, we wish to *post* X from the cache of P1 as early, yet as infrequently, as possible. This allows other processors that wait on results from P1 to proceed as soon as possible.

3.1.1 Invalidating

Applying the algorithm of Section 2.3.2 allows references prior to the synchronization point to be resolved in cache. Unfortunately, the use of X by P2 after the synchronization point would be preceded by an invalidation of X, even though some paths assign X prior to the use. We wish to invalidate X only if it has not been updated after the synchronization point. Although hardware could be developed to detect such situations, we wish to explore a software-based solution.

Given that the value for X in P2's cache is stale immediately after the *SYNC* point in Figure 11, P2 could invalidate X after the *SYNC*. Subsequent stores to X by P2 would cause P2's cache to contain the correct value for X. With respect to cache utilization, this scheme is the software equivalent of the "fast selective invalidate" scheme proposed by Cheong and Veidenbaum [11], where a bit associated with each address indicates if the address is referenced after a *SYNC* point. Such a reference causes the cache to be updated, and subsequent references are satisfied by the cache.

In general, invalidation instructions could be moved from a use site to somewhere after the synchronization point for the dependence causing the invalidation, if the following conditions hold:

1. A processor executes the invalidation instruction if the use site is reached.

2. The address(es) referenced at the use site can be generated at the invalidation point.

The first condition allows the invalidation instruction to be moved to any *dominator* of the use site in P2 (where the *SYNC* point is the final dominator).[5] The second condition is easily satisfied for scalars. For arrays, the invalidation must occur for any element that could be referenced at the use. This motivates the need for an invalidation instruction that could be applied to a group of addresses, perhaps contiguous such as those belonging to an array.

An alternative to the wholesale invalidation of such data at dominators would be to place invalidation instructions along the required paths. Consider the example of Figure 12. In Figure 12(a), invalidation always occurs for X, whereas in Figure 12(b), invalidation occurs only if the assignment to X is avoided.

There is another reason for determining the precise placement of invalidation instructions with respect to control flow. A precise invalidate (coupled with a post) corresponds to interprocessor communication, where one processor has finished updating a variable and the invalidating processor must receive the value for that variable. Once the "else" branch in Figure 12(b) is taken, X can be invalidated and the value can be requested from global memory, well in advance of the actual use of X. For processors connected via a multi-cycle interconnection network, the advance staging of such data can dramatically improve performance.

```
INVALID (X)          |
                     |
if ()                | if ()
  then  X = ...       |   then X = ...
  else               |   else INVALID (X)
endif                | endif
  .                  |   .
  .                  |   .
  .                  |   .
  = X                |   = X
     (a)             |        (b)
```

Figure 12.   Where to Invalidate?

This problem can be cast as a data flow problem over the control flow graph of a program. In terms of P2 shown in Figure 11, each node either kills X, preserves X, or fails to define X. The data flow problem then computes a solution that accounts for all paths through P2. The data flow values assigned at a given point E are:

VALID   All paths from the start of P2 to E contain a killing definition or invalidation of X.

NODEF   There are no definitions of X on any path from P2 to E.

PRES   Some path from the start of P2 to E defines, yet fails to kill, X.

Data flow analysis computes a solution for the entry to a node of the control flow graph. The node itself is then examined, and a value is computed for the exit(s) of that node. If *IN* is the data flow value on entry to node N and N can either $KILL(X)$, $PRESERVE(X)$, or $NODEF(X)$, then

$$OUT(N) = f(IN, Action(N))$$

follows:

$$f(VALID, Action(N)) = VALID$$
$$f(PRES, KILL(X)) = VALID$$
$$f(PRES, PRESERVE(X)) = PRES$$
$$f(PRES, NODEF(X)) = PRES$$
$$f(NODEF, KILL(X)) = VALID$$
$$f(NODEF, PRESERVES(X)) = PRES$$
$$f(NODEF, NODEF(X)) = NODEF$$

Where multiple paths meet at entry to a node, the meet of the data flow information is:

---

(5)   The dominators of a node n are those nodes whose execution must have occurred if node n is executed.

```
              Path 2

         Meet |  VALID   NODEF     PRES
      -----------------------------------
              |
    P   VALID | VALID   VALID     PRES
    a         |
    t   NODEF | VALID   NODEF     PRES
    h         |
        PRES  | PRES    PRES      PRES
    1         |
```

Note that *PRES* is *bottom* of the meet lattice, and *NODEF* is *top*.

When the data flow problem has completed, one of two values should prevail at the use of X in P2:

- The value *VALID* signifies that all paths either killed X or could contain the appropriate invalidation instructions. Such instructions are placed on edges carrying the data flow value *NODEF*, where *VALID* meets such edges to produce *VALID*.

- The value *PRES* signifies that some path may or may not define X, and invalidation should be placed at some dominator of the use of X.

This algorithm when applied to the example of Figure 12 places invalidation on the *else* branch of the *if* statement. Consider the example shown in Figure 13.

```
    if ()
    then X =
    else ...    *-- INVALID(X)
    endif

    if ()
    then ....
    else X =
    endif

      = X
```

Figure 13.   Invalidation Placement

The data flow problem places invalidation at the *else* branch of the first *if* statement. The data flow value *VALID* is subsequently propagated to the use of X, signifying that invalidation need not occur at a dominator of the use.

This algorithm is a *rapid* (and therefore *fast*) data flow algorithm [19]. For each variable, the algorithm takes $O(N\alpha(N))$, where N is the number of nodes in the control flow graph of a procedure. Our algorithms require the prior construction of def-use chains, which incurs similar expense.

3.1.2   Posting

In the example of Figure 11, P1 contains a region where every path defines X. At the end of the region, P1 should make its value for X available for process P2. Thus, P1 should post its value for X to global memory. Although the post instruction could occur at the synchronization point terminating the region, we wish to issue the post as early, yet as infrequently, as possible. The post can occur whenever we are certain P1 will

make no further assignment to X. This allows process P2 to proceed before P1 reaches the declared synchronization point. We compute post points by solving a dataflow problem similar to *very busy expressions* [3] over the expression X, where

- all uses of X within the killing region of P1 are ignored

- the synchronization point at the end of P1 is treated as the sole use of X.

Posts can be placed where X is very busy, as shown in Figure 14.

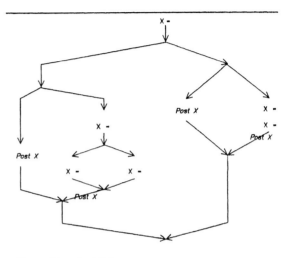

Figure 14.   Post Points

3.2   Processor Allocation

Our execution model contained no assumptions with respect to the allocation of processors within or between DOALL loops. With greater supervision over processor allocation, a compiler could conceivably increase reuse of data in cache. Consider Figure 6. If for each iteration of the outer loop, iterations of the inner loop were assigned to the same processors, then the invalidations would not be necessary. As another example, consider Figure 15.

```
    DOALL i= ...
       A(i) =
    ENDDOALL

    IF () THEN
       DOALL i= ...
          A(i) =
       ENDDOALL
    ENDIF

    DOALL i= ...
          = A(i)
    ENDDOALL
```

Figure 15.   Example for Supervised Processor Allocation

Where processors cannot be repeatedly assigned the same iterations, an invalidation must occur either at the end of the first loop or before the use of A in the last loop. Either invalidation

133

prohibits the values for A computed by the first loop to remain in cache for use by the last loop. The invalidation is extraneous if the second loop does not execute. If iterations are assigned consistently to processors for the second and third loops, then the invalidation optimization algorithm of Section 3.1.1 can place invalidation inside the IF-block. The effects of invalidations can also be reduced by locality-increasing transformations such as *loop fusion* [1].

3.3 Grouping

Invalidation could benefit from a mechanism that allows a set of individual invalidates to be combined into a single *group invalidate*. Consider Figure 6. The invalidations for A are due to the cross processor flow dependences carried by the outer loop. Rather than issuing individual invalidations for each reference $A(i - 1, j)$, a group invalidate for all addresses associated with A could be executed once by each processor assigned to the inner DOALL loop. This mechanism requires hardware assistance, and the optimization of group selection is beyond the scope of this paper.

4.0 Conclusion and Open Problems

The algorithms presented in this paper are sufficiently simple and fast to be implemented in parallelizing compilers. We have implemented the algorithms described in Section 2.0 in PTRAN; the effectiveness of these algorithms has yet to be determined. The following sections describe the effects of relaxing certain assumptions under which the algorithms were developed.

4.1 Line Size

We have thus far assumed that cache activity is regulated at the granularity of an individual storage reference (for example, a word). To exploit locality of reference, many systems organize cache by *lines*, where a single line contains multiple words. When a reference is satisfied by bringing a word into cache, other words associated with the referenced line are also brought into cache. Thus, words can be brought into cache without actually referencing the associated addresses. The algorithms presented in this paper assumed that if a variable is invalidated, only a subsequent reference to that variable could bring the variable back into cache. Optimizations that move an invalidation instruction away from a use are potentially incorrect where an intervening reference indirectly causes the variable to enter cache. Consider the example shown in Figure 16.

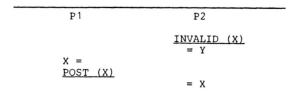

P1	P2
	INVALID (X)
	= Y
X =	
POST (X)	
	= X

Figure 16. Line Size Problems: The reference to Y brings in a value for X if X and Y are in the same cache line.

With the invalidate of X moved away from the use, the use of X in P2 references stale data.

We feel that a strictly software solution to this problem is unreasonable: a compiler would have to know the mapping of variables to lines. We are currently investigating a solution involving hardware assistance. In particular, we postulate the usefulness of an *invalidate if not referenced* instruction. Such an instruction would invalidate data that was prefetched into cache due to its proximity to an actually referenced variable.

For performance considerations, invalidation should be localized within a cache line (applied to specific words) rather than invalidating the entire line. This requires residency bits for each unit of storage reference. To lessen hardware costs, residency could be maintained on a word basis: invalidating a byte would invalidate its associated word.

4.2 Store-in

Although our algorithms were developed for a store-in cache, the techniques also apply to a store-through cache. Obviously, a compiler need not post values to global memory for a store-through cache. However, store-through caches can degrade performance through increased network traffic. In particular, reduction of network traffic through optimized post instructions as considered in Section 3.1.2 is appropriate only for store-in caches.

4.3 Evictions

We have thus far assumed that data leaves a cache only under software control; however, caches typically use a hardware eviction policy. Although our algorithms are still correct, eviction beyond software control raises the following issues:

- Cache management instructions for one variable may affect the cache behavior of other variables. Strictly speaking, our assumptions as to the *partitionability* of cache management problems no longer hold. However, the actual mapping of addresses to cache locations cannot be considered at compile-time (for example, formal parameters).

- The optimization of post instructions involves holding onto cached data until a processor has finished modifying data at a given address. Where such data is prematurely evicted, optimization may suffer and network traffic may be increased.

Thus, adding eviction to our cache model results in potentially decreased performance. The above considerations suggest that even eviction should enter the realm of software control. Where the compiler determines certain data non-evictable, new data cannot cause the eviction of such data until the data is subsequently marked evictable. Cacheable data that conflicts only with non-evictable data would not enter cache on reference.

5.0 Acknowledgements

We thank Fran Allen and Michael Burke for their comments on this work.

Bibliography

1. W. A. Abu-Sufah, D. J. Kuck, and D. H. Lawrie. On the Performance Enhancement of Paging Systems Through Program Analysis and Transformations. *IEEE Trans. on Computer*, C-30(5):341-356, May 1981.

2. Anant Agarwal, Richard Simoni, John Hennessy, and Mark Horowitz. Scalable Directory Schemes for Cache Coherence. *Proceedings of the 15th International Symposium on Computer Architecture*, 1988.

3. A.V. Aho, R. Sethi, and J.D. Ullman. *Compilers: Principles, Techniques, and Tools.* Addison-Wesley, 1986.

4. Fran Allen, Michael Burke, Philippe Charles, Ron Cytron, and Jeanne Ferrante. An Overview of the PTRAN Analysis System for Multiprocessing. *Proceedings of the 1987 International Conference on Supercomputing, Springer-Verlag*, Athens,Greece, 1987. To appear in a special issue of the Journal of Parallel and Distributed Computing.

5. Fran Allen, Michael Burke, Ron Cytron, Jeanne Ferrante, Wilson Hsieh, and Vivek Sarkar. A Framework for Determining Useful Parallelism, IBM T.J. Watson Research Center, July 1988. ACM International Conference on Supercomputing '88.

6. Randy Allen and Ken Kennedy. Automatic Translation of FORTRAN Programs to Vector Form. *ACM Transactions on Programming Languages and Systems*, 9(4):491-592, October 1987.

7. James Archibald and Jean-Loup Baer. An Economical Solution to the Cache Coherence Problem. *11th Int. Symp. on Comp. Arch.*, pages 355-362, 1984.

8. W. C. Brantley, K. P. McAuliffe, and J. Weiss. RP3 Processor-Memory Element. *Proc. 1985 International Conference on Parallel Processing*, pages 782-789, 1985.

9. Michael Burke and Ron Cytron. Interprocedural Dependence Analysis and Parallelization. *Proceedings of the Sigplan '86 Symposium on Compiler Construction*, 21(7):162-175, July 1986.

10. Michael Burke, Ron Cytron, Jeanne Ferrante, Wilson Hsieh, and David Shields. On the Automatic Generation of Useful Parallelism: A Tool and an Experiment, IBM T.J. Watson Research Center, July 1988. ACM SIGPLAN Symposium on Parallel Programming: Experience with Applications, Languages, and Systems.

11. Hoichi Cheong and Alex Veidenbaum. Stale Access Detection and Cache Coherence Enforcement Using a Flow Analysis Approach. *Proceedings of the 1988 International Conference on Parallel Processing*, 1988.

12. Jan Edler, Allan Gottlieb, Clyde P. Kruskal, Kevin P. McAuliffe, Larry Rudolph, Marc Snir, Patricia J. Teller, and James Wilson. Issues Related to MIMD Shared-memory Computers: the NYU Ultracomputer Approach. *Conference Proceedings of the 12th Annual International Symposium on Computer Architecture*, pages 126-135, Boston, Massachusetts, 1985.

13. James Goodman. Using Cache Memory to Reduce Processor-Memory Traffic. *The 10th Int. Symp. Comput. Arch.*, pages 124-131, June 1983.

14. Allan Gottlieb. An Overview of the NYU Ultracomputer Project. in J. Dongarra, editor, *Experimental Parallel Computing Architectures*, North-Holland, 1987. Formerly Ultracomputer Note #100, Courant Institute of Mathematical Sciences, New York University (1986).

15. Matthew S. Hecht. *Flow Analysis of Computer Programs.* Elsevier North-Holland, Inc., 1977.

16. Steven R. Karlovsky. Automatic Management of Programmable Caches: Algorithms and Experience, Center for Supercomputing Research and Development, Urbana, Illinois. 1988. Master's thesis in progress.

17. David J. Kuck, Edward S. Davidson, Duncan H. Lawrie, and Ahmed H. Sameh. Parallel Supercomputing Today and the Cedar Approach. *Science*, 231:967-974, February 1986.

18. G. F. Pfister, W. C. Brantley, D. A. George, S. L. Harvey, W. J. Kleinfelder, K. P. McAuliffe, E. A. Melton, V. A. Norton, and J. Weiss. The IBM Research Parallel Processor Prototype (RP3): Introduction and Architecture. *International Conference on Parallel Processing*, pages 764-771, 1985.

19. Barry K. Rosen. Monoids for Rapid Data Flow Analysis. *Siam Journal of Computing*, 9(1):159-196, February 1980.

20. Alex Veidenbaum. A Compiler-Assisted Cache Coherence Solution for Multiprocessors.. *International Conference on Parallel Processing*, pages 1029-1036, August 1986.

21. Michael J. Wolfe. *Optimizing Supercompilers for Supercomputers*, PhD thesis, University of Illinois at Urbana-Champaign, Urbana, Illinois 1982. Report No. UIUCDCS-R-82-1105.

22. W. C. Yen, D. W. L. Yen, and K.-S. Fu. Data Coherence Problems in a Multicache System. *IEEE Transactions on Computers*, C-34:56-65, January 1985.

A Version Control Approach to Cache Coherence

Hoichi Cheong & Alex Veidenbaum

Center for Supercomputing Research and Development

University of Illinois at Urbana-Champaign

104 South Wright Street

Urbana, Illinois 61801

Abstract

A version control approach to maintain cache coherence is proposed for large-scale shared-memory multiprocessor systems with interconnection networks. The new approach, unlike existing approaches for such class of systems, makes it possible to exploit temporal locality across synchronization boundaries. As with the other software-directed approaches, each processor independently manages its cache, i.e., there is no interprocessor communication involved in maintaining cache coherence. The hardware required per processor in the version control approach stays constant as the number of processors increases; hence, it scales up to larger systems. Furthermore, the new approach incurs low overhead. The simulated results of several schemes for large-scale systems show that the new approach achieves a data cache hit ratio closest to maximum possible.

Keywords: **Software-directed cache coherence, parallel task execution, version control.**

1 Introduction

Cache coherence for shared-memory multiprocessor systems with private caches has received much attention. As large-scale shared-memory systems with interconnection networks (called large-scale systems hereafter) are proposed [12, 4, 11], solutions developed for systems connected by a single system bus [13, 19, 20, 21, 14] are no longer applicable. Other approaches that do not depend on a system bus [23, 5, 2] are usually hampered by high communication cost when applied to large-scale systems.

Several approaches for large-scale systems have focused on software-directed invalidation to maintain cache coherence and are referred to as software-directed approaches. The earlier approaches [22, 24, 18, 17, 16] relied on compile-time knowledge

of parallel programs to determine when to invalidate cache items to prevent the reading of stale cache items. However, these schemes can also invalidate many non-stale cache items and result in low hit ratios. Later approaches made use of the dependence relationship [3] of parallel programs to invalidate cache copies more selectively [8, 9, 10]. Since a compiler cannot accurately predict run-time memory access behavior, these approaches have to make conservative assumptions about which cache items to invalidate. This imprecise prediction leads to limited exploitation of potential temporal locality.

We identify the temporal locality not preserved in the existing schemes, and present a version control approach to enforce cache coherence in large-scale systems. The proposed scheme has the characteristics of software-directed approaches which require no additional communication among processors. With hardware support, it preserves temporal locality better than any existing software-directed approach.

This paper first discusses the software-directed cache coherence schemes. Next, we investigate the cache coherence problem, demonstrate the inadequacy of the existing schemes, and show why temporal locality in parallel execution is not exploited. Finally, we propose a coherence scheme that uses data version control to retain the temporal locality. We will discuss the algorithm and the implementation issues, and present some simulation results.

2 Software-directed Schemes

A cache copy of a variable is *stale* if it does not contain the most recently written value. An access to a stale cache copy is called a *stale access*.

The tasks of cache coherence schemes are (1) to detect stale accesses or predict when a cache copy becomes stale, and (2) to avoid stale accesses or prevent cache copies from turning stale. The software-directed schemes try to achieve such detection or prediction, as much as possible, at compile-time. Detected stale cache copies or cache copies that are predicted to turn stale will be invalidated by the processor at run-time [9]. The advantage of these approaches is that the processors do not need to exchange information about their cache status at run-time. A direct benefit is the reduction of network traffic due to the communication overhead associated with conventional hardware approaches [23, 5, 2].

However, current software-directed schemes are limited in exploiting potential temporal locality in a program. Compile-time prediction and detection do not have enough run-time information to produce a precise result. To avoid incoherence, all the existing compile-time detection algorithms must be conservative. Whenever a precise decision cannot be made, any suspected access or copy is considered stale. The number of such accesses can be large in programs where variables are frequently read and written. Conservative decisions in such cases result in a loss of temporal locality of cache accesses and hence low hit ratio. This motivates the need for more precise schemes.

3 Cache Coherence and Temporal Locality

It is our goal to preserve as much temporal locality in parallel programs as possible. In this section, we will investigate (1) the conditions for the occurrence of stale accesses and stale cache copies in parallel execution, (2) existing software-directed techniques to prevent stale accesses, and (3) the temporal locality loss due to these techniques.

3.1 Parallel Task Execution

We assume that a parallel program (parallelized from a sequential program [15] or written in a parallel language) is divided into tasks that are each executed by a single processor. If two tasks access the same variable and one writes to it, the tasks have a data dependence [3]. Depending on the program semantics, the data dependence can be flow (read after write), anti (write after read) or output (write after write) [3]. Besides data dependence, two tasks can have control dependence such that one task contains a predicate and the execution of the other task is controlled by the predicate. Tasks will be executed in the order defined by the dependences. The execution order of dependent tasks is enforced through synchronization. Tasks that are independent of each other can be scheduled to execute in parallel.

The dependence relationship among tasks and hence the execution order can be described by a task execution graph, $G_e = (T, E)$. G_e has a starting node T_0 and is a directed cyclic graph where E is a set of edges and T is set of nodes. A node T_i represents a task and a directed edge from T_i to T_j, $e_{i,j}$, represents that some statements in T_j depend on other statements in T_i (Figure 1(a)). Hence, $e_{i,j}$ also represents that in the execution order T_i precedes T_j. T_i is an ancestor to T_j if there is a directed path from T_i to T_j. T_i is called an immediate ancestor of T_j, and T_j an immediate descendent of T_i if the path contains only one edge. The execution order represented by the directed edges is a transitive relationship; hence, and edge from T_i to T_j can be removed if T_i remains an ancestor of T_j after the removal. Given two distinct tasks, T_i and T_j and $e_{i,j}$, the two tasks can always be combined into one if T_i is the only immediate ancestor of T_j and T_j is the only immediate descendent of T_i. Thus, an edge is always one of the fan-out edges or the fan-in edges. An example of a G_e is given in Figure 1(a).

The task graph can be divided into levels $L = \{L_0, ..., L_n\}$, where each L_i is a set of tasks with the following property: given

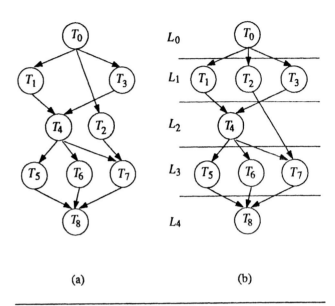

Figure 1. A task graph.

(a)   (b)

any task T_k in L_i, from T_0 to T_k the longest directed path that contains no cycle has exactly i edges (Figure 1(b)). Tasks on the same level are not connected by any directed edges and hence are independent. In other words, for tasks on the same level, no more than one task contains write accesses to the same *variable element* (element for short), i.e., a scalar variable or an array element. Also, no task contains any read access to an element if another task on the same level contains a write access to the same element. Therefore, tasks on the same level can be executed in parallel without inter-task synchronization. This form of parallelism is often encountered in *Doall* loops.

In general, tasks with inter-task dependence can also be executed in parallel provided synchronization and data communication during task execution preserve the correct semantics. For clarity, the following discussion focuses on parallel task execution without inter-task dependence. However, the cache coherence scheme to be proposed in this paper can be applied to parallel execution with inter-task synchronization.

The order of levels describes the execution order of tasks on different levels. The precedence order is preserved if a task can be started only when its dependence on other tasks is satisfied. Let us assume without loss of generality that a task scheduler keeps a list of ready tasks. Available processors take tasks from the ready list and execute them. When a task terminates, the variables modified in the task are all written to the shared global memory, and all its immediate descendant tasks are checked. A task becomes ready to execute and will be put on the ready list if all its predecessors were executed and all tasks on previous task levels are started.

137

3.2 Stale Accesses and Copies

A copy of variable X will turn stale in processor P_i's cache if another processor P_j changes the value of X. This subsection deals with the following important aspects of stale accesses and stale copies: the conditions for the stale accesses and stale copies, and the software-directed coherence schemes to detect and avoid stale accesses and copies.

3.2.1 Occurrence and Detection of Stale Accesses and Copies

The occurrence of stale accesses and stale copies is determined by the execution order of the tasks, and the read and write operations issued by the processors executing the tasks. The following can be observed about parallel program execution:

1. A write to a variable by a processor turns copies of the variable stale in other processors' cache.

2. A processor can never turn it's own cache copy stale.

3. Given a T_i with a write that turns the existing cache copies stale, the copies must have been loaded into the caches in tasks preceding T_i in sequential execution order.

4. Given a T_i with a write that turns cache copies stale, the stale copies can only be accessed in tasks following T_i in sequential execution order.

Observations 3 and 4 are the results of the definition of parallel execution, i.e., there is no dependence among tasks executed in parallel. Thus, for the detection of stale accesses and stale copies, one need not look at the relation of reads and writes within a task. Instead, reads and writes issued in different tasks, particularly the ones that are dependent, are important.

Observations 3 and 4 can be used to detect writes that potentially turn cache copies stale, or accesses to stale copies respectively, without run-time inter-processor communication. A compile-time detection technique based on these observations has been developed [8, 9]. The following notation is used to summarize the above and to help further discussion.

Variable access triples   Let the triple $(P, \text{access-}V, T)$ represent a processor P accessing variable V, a scalar or an array, while executing task T. The prefix to V, "access", denotes the access type, i.e., a write (w), a read (r) or any type of access(a). Thus, $(P_i, \text{r-}X, T_i)$ denotes that processor P_i reads variable X while executing task T_i.

A sequence of triples read from left to right represents the order of accesses to variable X by the tasks in the triples. For example, the following sequence denotes that a processor P_i will have a stale copy of X due to the modification by P_j in T_l if $i \neq j$:

$$(P_i, \text{a-}X, T_k)...(P_j, \text{w-}X, T_l),$$

The following represents that a processor P_i may access a stale copy of X in T_m if $i \neq j$:

$$(P_i, \text{a-}X, T_k)...(P_j, \text{w-}X, T_l)(P_i, \text{r-}X, T_m),$$

A write to a variable within a task can overwrite a stale cache copy. Thus, a stale access, detected by the above observation, can become a nonstale access if it is executed after a write to the same variable element within the task. Data dependence analysis [3] or flow analysis [1] on statements within a task can distinguish such cases.

The compile-time detection scheme in [8, 9] applied to Fortran programs defines task boundaries to be the loop boundaries. By analyzing the flow graph and the dependence relationship of program statements in a subroutine, execution order of the tasks can be established, and the potential stale accesses can be distinguished from nonstale accesses by using Observation 4.

3.2.2 Drawbacks of the Current Approaches

One of the drawbacks of the compile-time detection schemes is that the identity of the processor executing a task may be unknown until run-time. This makes the detection of stale copies less precise, and the worst case is assumed when in doubt. For example, given an execution sequence,

$$(?, \text{a-}X, T_k)...(?, \text{w-}X, T_l)(?, \text{r-}X, T_m),$$

the following execution sequence,

$$(P_i, \text{a-}X, T_k)...(P_j, \text{w-}X, T_l)(P_i, \text{r-}X, T_m),$$

will be assumed at compile-time even though another sequence,

$$(P_i, \text{a-}X, T_k)...(P_j, \text{w-}X, T_l)(P_j, \text{r-}X, T_m)$$

is also likely to occur. The former sequence results in a stale access of X by P_i due to the write operation of P_j. In the latter sequence, P_j does not access a stale copy of X since it reads back what it has just written.

The detection is even less precise for array variables. For example, if X is an array in the above sequences, and the reads of X in T_m are preceded by writes to the same array, compile-time detection schemes cannot always guarantee that the same array elements are being read and written. Thus, all array reads in T_m may have to be considered as stale accesses.

3.2.3 Avoidance of Stale Accesses and Copies

A processor can use one of the two possible invalidation strategies when it is detected that a cache copy will be turned stale: (1) it can invalidate a cache copy before it can be turned stale, or (2) invalidate a stale copy before accessing it. Invalidate instructions can be inserted in the program stream by the compiler based on the detection result. Thus, cache coherence can be preserved without run-time communication.

In the first strategy, to prevent a cache copy from turning stale, a processor that loads in the cache copy will invalidate it after accessing it in the task. For example, consider the following task execution sequence,

$$(?, \text{a-}X[S], T_k)(?, \text{a-}X[R], T_i)...(?, \text{w-}X[\ ], T_l)$$
$$(?, \text{r-}X[\ ], T_m)(?, \text{r-}X[\ ], T_n),$$

where S and R are subsets of subscripts to array X and $S \cap R \neq \{\emptyset\}$. The writes to array $X[\ ]$ in T_l are the ones described in Observations 3 and 4. After accessing $X[\ ]$, if the processors that execute T_k and T_i invalidate their cache copies of $X[\ ]$, the writes in T_l will affect no existing cache copies. However, since it is difficult to find out at compile-time or to keep track of at run-time what a processor has loaded into its cache in a previous task, the processor must invalidate cache copies of variables before the end of each task. Therefore, after loading a cache copy in a task, re-using the up-to-date cache copies in subsequent tasks is impossible [9].

In the second strategy, stale copies are allowed to occur but a processor must invalidate them before using the variable. In

138

the execution sequence of the example above, the processors that execute T_m and T_n need to invalidate their cache copies of $X[\ ]$ before reading them. A processor that accesses $X[\ ]$ before T_l does not invalidate its copies after accessing. Similarly, to the first strategy, the invalidate operations before accesses must be carried out in each task that accesses the variable. Therefore, for a processor executing T_n, re-using the up-to-date copies loaded in T_m is also impossible [9].

3.3 Temporal Locality

A good coherence scheme has to preserve as much temporal locality as possible. There are two kinds of temporal locality in parallel task execution. When the up-to-date copy of a variable is loaded into the cache, the processor can use this copy within the current task without worrying about the copy turning stale. We refer to the re-use of an up-to-date cache copy within a task as *intratask temporal locality*. The cache copy will remain up-to-date until the variable is written by another processor executing a task later in the execution order. Until then, no matter which task is executed by the same processor, the cache copy stays up-to-date. We call this type of re-use of the cache copies *intertask temporal locality*.

Most of the existing cache coherence schemes preserve only intratask temporal locality. Each processor starts a task with a clean cache [24, 17, 16]. Cache coherence is maintained but intertask temporal locality is lost. Another approach is to invalidate only all read-write variables at the end of each task [18]. Intertask temporal locality for such variables is still not preserved.

The fast selective invalidation scheme [8, 9] preserves all intratask temporal locality by using a status bit for each cache word to distinguish a cache copy loaded in the current task from one loaded earlier. It also preserves intertask temporal locality for all read-only variables. Only this scheme preserves some intertask temporal locality for read-write variables.

The essential issue in preserving available temporal locality is to recognize up-to-date copies of the variables and to keep them in the cache as long as possible. The solution requires a processor to keep track of when its cache copies may turn stale and to spare them from being invalidated before turning stale. For example, assume that X is not written in any task between T_i and T_j in the following:

$$... \ (?, \ w\text{-}X, \ T_i)...(?, \ r\text{-}X, \ T_j)$$

If a processor P_i is scheduled to execute T_j and already has a cache copy of X, the copy is either stale or nonstale depending on when it is loaded into the cache. If the copy of X is loaded before T_i and P_i does not execute T_i, it is stale. Otherwise, it must be up-to-date.

Existing software-directed cache coherence schemes fail to capture this distinction and assume the worst case, i.e., that the copy existing prior to T_j is stale in T_j. Thus, for coherence purposes, the copy of X has to be invalidated before its use in T_j. The information to make this distinction is available only at run-time since processor assignment to tasks is not done at compile-time.

To tackle the above problem, a version control method is introduced, and its implementation will be discussed in the following sections.

4 Cache Coherence by Version Control

We propose a scheme that uses version numbers to record the state of existing cache copies, and to detect and to avoid stale accesses.

Consider two tasks that both contain writes to the same variable. The order of such writes from different tasks is determined by the task execution graph. The writes to a variable in one task are said to produce a different version of the variable than the writes in the other task. Each cache copy of a variable in the system must belong to a particular version.

Multiple writes to a variable within a task are considered to produce only one version for the following reason. Only the value of the last write to a variable, within a task, will ever be read by other tasks, and only by tasks executed later in sequential order. Values written before the last write, within the same task, do not exist at the end of the task, and hence need not be considered a new version. Thus, at the end of a task execution, only one new version has been produced for each variable written within the task.

For the scheme to be practical, an array is considered a single variable. Even though a task may write to only a part of an array, a new version is nevertheless considered to be produced for the entire array. If an array is written to by multiple tasks executed in parallel, the writes altogether produce only one new version.

A version of a variable produced in a task is the current version of the variable until a subsequent task, executed in sequential order, produces the next version. The current version of the variable contains the up-to-date value to be used until the generation of the next version.

An integer, called the *Current Version Number (CVN)*, is used to distinguish the different versions of a variable (scalar or array). Each processor maintains its own *CVN* for each variable used in the program in a separate local memory. Since each array needs only one *CVN*, the local memory can easily contain all *CVN*s.

Each cache copy is tagged with a *birth version number (bvn)* field. When the cache copy of a variable is loaded from the global memory, the cache copy has the up-to-date value of the variable. Hence, the corresponding *CVN* of the variable is copied into the *bvn* field of the cache copy. When a variable is written, the *bvn* field of the cache copy will be set to the new version number of the variable, i.e., *CVN* plus one. The *bvn* of the cache copy is checked against the *CVN* of the variable when it is read. A cache copy with a *bvn* less than the *CVN* of the variable is a stale cache copy. When this is detected, a cache miss will be generated and the up-to-date value will be loaded from the global memory.

When a processor has no tasks to execute on a task level, the *CVN* of all the variables modified by any processor on that level will be incremented by one. Hence, the new version number *CVN* (one plus the old value) will be equal to the *bvn* of the cache copy written on that level. On a subsequent task level, the up-to-date cache copy will be recognized by the equality of the *CVN* and the *bvn* and not invalidated. Therefore, intertask temporal locality is preserved.

The version scheme consists of three tasks: (1) proper maintenance of the *CVNs*, (2) tagging each cache copy with a *bvn*, and (3) run-time comparison of the *bvn* of a cache copy and the *CVN* of the variable. We shall show how these tasks can be achieved with minimal time cost to the system, given adequate hardware support.

The most important part of the scheme is how to update the *CVN* of a variable efficiently when a new version is created. The updates of the *CVNs* in each processor can be done independently without communication overhead, and with little computational overhead. In the following subsections, we will describe how to keep track of different versions of a variable, the hardware necessary to support an implementation of the version control scheme, and the implementation issues.

4.1 Version Update

Let us first restrict the discussion to acyclic task execution graphs. A set of variables Var_i that the tasks can write to at level i can be computed at compile-time, and used to update the *CVNs* of these variable at run-time. When a processor finishes a task at level i and is ready to execute a task at level $i+k$, it needs to increment the *CVN* of each variable that could have been modified on level i and the levels that the processor skips, i.e., $\bigcup_{j=0}^{j=k-1} Var_{i+j}$. Provided a variable is written at any level from L_{i+1} through L_{i+k-1}, the *CVN* of the variable will always be larger than the *bvn* of the cache copy of the processor. The processor thus knows whether its cache copies are the up-to-date version of the variable.

The *CVNs* of the same variable kept by different processors do not have to agree. The fact that the *bvn* of the copy is less than the *CVN* of the variable, not the exact difference of the two number, is sufficient for maintaining cache coherence. Therefore, the processors can manage the *CVNs* independently. For details, see [6].

4.2 Version Update for Cyclic Task Graphs

The above discussion assumes that an acyclic static task graph describing the precedence order is available for *CVN* updates. In general, we can have a cyclic task graph built at compile-time. A cyclic task graph includes control flow cycles. The above approach to *CVN* updates applies to a cyclic graph but with additional scheduling constraints discussed below.

A cyclic graph can also be partitioned into levels, at compile-time, by ignoring the backward edges. However, while the scheduler dispatches tasks in a cycle from the static graph, the levels in the cycle are repeated as the cycle is iterated. The following discusses possible approaches of *CVN* updates when cycles are present.

Consider a cycle with nodes at levels L_i through L_{i+k}. Because tasks may take different amounts of time to complete, a processor may pick a task on L_{i+j} at iteration $m+n$ after completing a task on L_{i+l} at iteration m, where $j, l \leq k$. Besides updating

the version numbers of the variables modified on the level L_{i+l} at iteration m, the version numbers for those modified on the levels skipped also need to be updated. Let *VAR* contain all variables that can be written in the tasks on the levels skipped :

$$VAR = \left(\bigcup_{L=i+l+1}^{i+k} Var_L \right) \cup \left(\bigcup_{for\ n-1\ iterations} \left(\bigcup_{L=i}^{i+k} Var_L \right) \right) \cup \left(\bigcup_{L=i}^{i+j-1} Var_L \right)$$

which can be simplified to

$$VAR = \bigcup_{L=i}^{L=i+k} Var_L$$

In other words, for all the iterations skipped, a processor must update no more than the *CVNs* of the variables written at all levels in one iteration. However, by the level number itself, it is difficult to determine how many levels a processor skips. For example, if k and l are equal in the above, it will be unknown to a processor whether it has skipped anything. However, the ambiguity above can be removed if an iteration number is used to distinguish levels in different iterations. When a processor takes a task from L_{i+j} of iteration $m+n$ after one on L_{i+l} of iteration m, the variables modified on the level skipped are given as:

$$VAR = \bigcup_{L=i+l+1}^{i+j-1} Var_L, \qquad if\ j>l+1\ and\ n=0$$

$$VAR = \left(\bigcup_{L=i+l+1}^{i+k} Var_L \right) \cup \left(\bigcup_{L=i}^{i+j-1} Var_L \right), \quad if\ j \leq l\ and\ n=1$$

Finally, for $n > 1$, or $n = 1$ and $j > 1$,

$$VAR = \bigcup_{L=i}^{L=i+k} Var_L$$

which is also the update for skipping the entire cycle.

Another approach to removing the ambiguity is to forbid a processor to skip levels. The *CVN* updates for the variables modified at each level are made into a task, called an *exit* task. Each processor is required to execute an exit task before it starts a task on the next level. The scheduler will not dispatch the tasks on the next level unless all tasks of the level are started. This approach is straightforward but results in less dynamic execution.

4.3 Hardware Support and Implementation Issues

The version control coherence scheme requires the following hardware support:

1. A *version manager* keeps the *CVNs* of each variable in a fast local memory. A *CVN* is addressed by an identity (ID) number assigned to each variable at either compile-time or link time. The version manager executes instructions issued by the processor to increment *CVN* or to reset all *CVNs*.

2. A field in the memory address for each reference contains the identity number (ID) of the variable.

3. Each cache word has a field that contains the *bvn*. All *bvns* can be reset upon a processor instruction.

140

4.3.1 Operation

Before a program execution starts, the *CVNs* are reset to zero, the cache words are invalidated, and the *bvn* field in each cache word is reset to zero. A simplified view of the hardware block diagram is illustrated in Figure 2.

In parallel with the cache read operation, the ID number in the address is used to retrieve the *CVN* from the version manager's memory. The retrieved *CVN* is compared with the *bvn* of the cache copy. The comparison of the *CVNs* and the *bvn* is carried out in parallel with the tag comparison of the cache access. Also, the loading of an up-to-date copy from the global memory and the loading of the correct *CVN* into the version field of the cache word can be done in parallel.

When a missed cache copy of a variable element is brought into the cache, its *bvn* is set to the *CVN* of the variable. Hence, the correct version number will be written to the *bvn* field of the up-to-date cache copy read from the global memory.

Figure 2. Hardware support for version control.

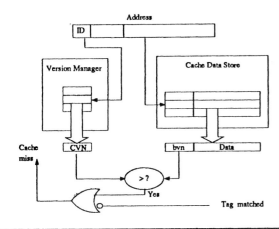

A write operation will update the cache word, and update the *bvn* field of the cache word with the *CVNs* plus one. The suboperations associated with a cache write can be carried out in parallel.

4.3.2 Implementation Issues

To implement the version control scheme, we would like to use existing hardware or require minimal extensions.

ID number Each address needs to include an ID number unique to each variable for fast access of the *CVN*. A segment number in a segmented virtual memory system can be used as an ID if each variable occupies a distinct segment. For scalar variables, either each scalar occupies a segment or multiple scalars share a segment. The former will have the best temporal locality for scalars but higher overheads while the latter will have less temporal locality but lower overheads.

Finite version number size The *CVN* and *bvn* are integers with finite size. When a *CVN* exceeds its maximum value, the version manager has to reset all *CVNs*, and the processor has to invalidate its entire data cache memory and reset all *bvns* before the *CVN* and *bvn* can be used again. The frequency of these operations depends on the size of the version field; however, it is far lower than the invalidation involved in the existing software-directed schemes. To determine the reasonable size of *CVN* requires further study. However, even a small 8-bit *bvn* number for each cache block size of 8 bytes adds only 12.5% of memory space.

The above description uses one *bvn* per cache word to simplify the discussion. To lower the cost, a *bvn* can be used for a cache block with multiple words. In such a case, each word will require a valid bit for the cache write operation. For details, see [6].

4.3.3 Further Optimization

In the above approach, after a cache item written by a processor is replaced out of the cache due to address mapping conflict, the processor will not know that the cache item has been written by itself if the processor happens to read it again in the same task. The *bvn* given to the cache item at the write operation is equal to *CVN+1* but is *CVN* at the subsequent read after the replacement. In such a case, potential temporal locality will be lost. To prevent this loss, compile-time techniques in [8] can be used to distinguish a read-after-write from a read-before-write to the same variable in a task. A read-after-write to the same variable will result in a *bvn* equal to *CVN+1* as opposed to *CVN* with a read-before-write. To implement this, a processor should be able to distinguish these two kinds of read operations and temporal locality is increased at the expense of a more complicated processor.

5 Experimental Results

A compile-time algorithm to implement version control has been implemented for parallel Fortran programs. A flow analysis [1] technique is applied to the program flow graph to compute the Var_i at each level. The version control scheme, using the *CVN* update with *exit* tasks described in Section 4.2, is implemented. The execution trace for the set of kernel subroutines (Table. 1) was generated for 32 and 512 processor cases. The task execution is simulated with cache block sizes of one (blk 1), two (blk 2) and four (blk 4) words. The hit ratio by the Version Control scheme (VC) is compared to the Indiscriminate Invalidation (II) scheme [24] and the Fast Selective (FS) scheme [8]. Also, the ideal (MX) hit ratio of the processor is presented.

The ideal hit ratio is obtained in simulation by invalidating only the stale cache copies. It is equal to the hit ratio obtained when a processor invalidates exactly what other processors write. Since no up-to-date copy is invalidated, the ideal hit ratio is the maximum possible given the same cache organization. In reality, it requires a great deal of inter-processor communication as in the bus-based schemes, or exact analysis to achieve such a hit ratio. In our simulation for the ideal hit ratio, each processor *knows* exactly which cache copies are turned stale and invalidates them accordingly.

Table 1. Benchmark Subroutines.

Subroutines		Original Program and Description
no.	name	
1	Newrz	SIMP2: New velocity computation and volume change in a Lagrangian hydrodynamics program
2	Ux	VORTEX: A PDE solver
3	Cg	A conjugate gradient matrx solver (for Ax=b)
4	Cmslow	BARO: Nonlinear tendency computation in a barometer program
5	Lblkern	A kernel of experimental physics computaion
6	Step	ARC3D: Computational fluid dynamics

Table 2. Data hit ratio comparison and overhead (32 processors).

(Subroutine numbers 5, 4, 3, and 1 denote subroutines lblkern, cmslow, cg, and newrz respectively.)

(a) Data hit ratio comparison.

Sub	Data Hit Ratios											
	blk 1				blk 2				blk 4			
no.	II	FS	VC	MX	II	FS	VC	MX	II	FS	VC	MX
5	2.91	44.70	61.94	63.40	25.08	66.52	77.65	80.93	37.44	78.52	86.79	90.79
4	39.84	53.39	58.22	76.79	63.60	73.82	76.04	86.44	75.86	84.22	85.52	91.36
3	21.30	38.25	84.19	86.68	59.17	67.99	91.82	93.48	78.60	83.15	95.77	96.85
1	35.04	42.66	52.40	52.40	65.99	70.23	75.26	75.26	82.09	84.37	87.04	87.04

(b) Overhead.

sub. no.	5	4	3	1
ohd	2.53%	0.96%	0.58%	0.1%

The same set of benchmark subroutines was used in the study of the Fast Selective scheme [8]. In the current study, we omitted the subroutines in which the Fast Selective Scheme has already achieved close to ideal hit ratio. Also, as in the study of the Fast Selective scheme, only the subroutines that can benefit from a large number of processors were simulated for the 512-processor case.

Table 3. Data hit ratio comparison and overhead (512 processors).

(Subroutine numbers 6, 2, and 1 denote subroutines step, ux, and newrz respectively.)

(a) Data hit ratio comparison.

Sub	Data Hit Ratios											
	blk 1				blk 2				blk 4			
no.	II	FS	VC	MX	II	FS	VC	MX	II	FS	VC	MX
6	28.57	36.24	55.45	73.77	51.01	56.44	69.99	86.11	63.20	66.88	78.28	92.54
2	32.45	49.05	49.14	49.46	48.99	65.53	65.63	65.96	57.10	73.64	73.75	74.06
1	15.84	34.62	40.59	40.59	37.62	52.88	55.45	55.45	43.56	59.62	62.38	62.38

(b) Overhead.

sub. no.	6	2	1
ohd	3.8%	0.17%	1.38%

The results in Tables 2(a) and 3(a) show that version control approach out-performs the other methods as predicted. Given the same tasks executed by the same processor, the version control approach performs at least as well as the existing methods simply because it also preserves intratask temporal locality. The version control approach out-performs the others because it alone preserves intertask temporal locality. Clearly, the performance depends on whether the previous tasks executed by a processor access the same set of array elements and variables as the current task. However, even when this condition is true, the available temporal locality cannot be exploited by any other existing software directed schemes including [22, 18, 17, 16, 10]. Therefore, among all the existing software-directed schemes, the version control approach will achieve data hit ratio the closest to the maximum possible.

We also estimated the overhead of the *CVN* updates as follows. We add together the number of statements, memory data reads, memory data writes, register reads, register writes and the ALU operations, and call the sum *processor operations*. The overhead of the *CVN* updates is expressed as the ratio of twice the number of update operations to the number of the processor operations. The number of operations in address computations is not included. Therefore, the overhead estimation is conservative. It is assumed that the processor takes one unit to issue an update instruction and the version manager takes one unit to increment a *CVN*. The results in percentage are shown in Tables 2(b) and 3(b) with row heading "Ohd".

Tasks executed in parallel usually contain iterations of the same parallel loop. The union of all the variables modified on the level is equal to the variables modified in one task. Also, writes to multiple elements of an array result in only one *CVN* update. Therefore, the overhead of *CVN* updates is small.

6 Conclusion

Smith[22] has previously proposed a *One Time Identifier* approach which uses time discrepancy to maintain cache coherence. However, his work is limited to eliminating incoherence while using exclusively-accessed regions in which accesses are forced to be sequential. Therefore, the *OTI* method is not directly applicable to general parallel execution. Also, coherence is enforced on a page by page basis. Thus, variables contained in pages within an exclusive region, even not modified, will be invalidated after the region. Intertask temporal locality cannot be preserved.

The version control approach is the combination of (1) a natural extension of our stale access and stale data detection methodology and the fast selective invalidation scheme, and (2) a generalized *time identifier* approach. In 'our approach, we manage cache coherence for accesses to each individual variable, not for whole pages. With the new approach, intertask temporal locality for shared read-write variables is preserved. A combination of compiler techniques and hardware support is used to capture run-time information which is used to exploit such temporal locality. This gain of temporal locality is achieved with no extra inter-processor communication, which is an important property of software-directed coherence schemes.

The version control scheme has been shown to achieve hit ratio closest to the idealized hit ratio when compared to existing software-directed cache coherence schemes. Without greater increases in the complexity in hardware or software support, we believe that no other software-directed coherence scheme can achieve a better hit ratio than the version control scheme. Thus, the simulated hit ratio of the version control approach can be used to evaluate existing software-directed schemes or ones yet to be developed.

The hardware cost per processor of the version control approach stays constant. The scheme does not constrain scalability of the system. Even though this scheme incurs additional hardware cost when compared to other software-directed schemes, the temporal locality it preserves makes it worthwhile.

The version control approach can be easily extended to hierarchical cache multiprocessor systems. It can be shown that the version control approach reduces or eliminates communication costs of the existing schemes. The version control approach extended to hierarchical cache systems does not need to satisfy the so-called "inclusion" property that imposes further restrictions on the systems. Extension of version control to hierarchical cache multiprocessor systems is beyond the scope of this paper and is described in detail in [7].

A referee brought to our attention that a time-stamp approach similar to version control has also been proposed independently for systems with one level private caches by a University of Washington group.

7 Acknowledgement

The authors would like to thank John Fu for his valuable suggestions and the referee who shared with the authors his/her insight in the optimization technique.

This work is supported in part by National Science Foundation under Grant No. US NSF MIP-8410110, the U.S. Department of Energy under Grant No. US DOE DE-FG02–85ER25001, NASA Ames Research Center Grant No. NASA NCC 2–559, and IBM Corporation.

Bibliography

[1] Alfred Aho, Ravi Sethi, and Jeffrey Ullman. *compilers Principles, Techniques, and Tools*. Addison-Wesley, 1985.

[2] James Archibald and Jean-Loup Baer. An economical solution to the cache coherence problem. *Proc. of the 11th Annual Int'l. Symp. on Computer Architecture*, pages 355–362, June 5-7, 1984.

[3] Utpal Banerjee. Data dependence in ordinary programs. Technical Report Rpt. No. 76-837, Univ. of Illinois at Urbana-Champaign, Dept. of Computer Sci., Nov., 1976. M.S. thesis.

[4] W. C. Brantley, K. P. McAuliffe, and A. J. Weiss. Rp3 processor-memory element. *Proc. of the 1985 Int'l. Conf. on Parallel Processing*, pages 782–789, August, 1985.

[5] L. M. Censier and P. Feautrier. A new solution to coherence problems in multicache systems. *IEEE Trans. Computers*, C-27(12):1112–1118, December, 1978.

[6] Hoichi Cheong. Towards efficient software-based cache coherence strategies. Technical report, University of Illinois at Urbana-Champaign, 1989. Ph.D. Thesis in progress.

[7] Hoichi Cheong and Alex Veidenbaum. A version control approach to cache coherence in hierarchical cache multiprocessor systems. Technical Report CSRD No. 848, University of Illinois at Urbana-Champaign, Jan 1989.

[8] Hoichi Cheong and Alex Veidenbaum. A cache coherence scheme with fast selective invalidation. *Proc. 15th Annual International Symposium on Computer Architecture*, page 299, June 1988.

[9] Hoichi Cheong and Alexander V. Veidenbaum. Stale data detection and coherence enforcement using flow analysis. *Proceedings of the 1988 International Conference on Parallel Processing*, I, Architecture:138–145, August 1988.

[10] Ron Cytron, Steve Karlovsky, and Kevin P. McAuliffe. Automatic management of programmable caches. *Proceedings of the 1988 International Conference on Parallel Processing*, II, Software:229–238, August 1988.

[11] Jay Edler, Allan Gottlieb, Clyde P. Kruskal, Kevin P. McAuliffe, Larry Rudolph, Marc Snir, Patricia J. Teller, and James Wilson. Issues related to mimd shared-memory computers: the nyu ultracomputer approach. *Proceedings of the 12th International Symposium on Computer Architecture*, pages 126–135, June 1985.

[12] Daniel Gajski, David Kuck, Duncan Lawrie, and Ahmed Sameh. Cedar – a large scale multiprocessors. *Proc. of the 1983 International Conf. on Parallel Processing*, Aug. 1983.

[13] J. R. Goodman. Using cache memory to reduce processor-memory traffic. *Proc. of the 10th Annual Int'l. Symp. on Computer Architecture*, pages 124–131, 1983.

[14] Randy H. Katz, Susan J. Eggers, D. A. Wood, C. L. Perkins, and R. G. Sheldon. Implementing a cache consistency protocol. *Proc. of the 12th Annual Internation Symposium on Computer Architecture*, pages 276–283, June, 1985.

[15] David J. Kuck, Robert H. Kuhn, Bruce Leasure, and Michael Wolfe. The structure of an advanced vectorizer for pipelined processors. *Computer Software and Applications Conference (COMPSAC80)*, pages 709–715, October 1980.

[16] R.L. Lee, P.C. Yew, and D.H. Lawrie. Multiprocessor cache design considerations. *Proc. of the 14th Annual International Symposium on Computer Architecture*, pages 253–262, June, 1987.

[17] Roland L. Lee. The effectiveness of caches and data prefetch bufffers in large-scale shared memory multiprocessors. Technical Report CSRD No. 670, CSRD, University of Illinois at Urbana-Champaign, August 1987.

[18] Kevin P. McAuliffe. Analysis of cache memories in highly parallel systems. Technical Report No. 269, Courant Institute of Mathematical Sciences, NYU, 1986. Ph.D. Thesis.

[19] E. McCreight. The dragon computer system: An early overview. Technical report, Xerox Corp, September 1984.

[20] Mark S. Papamarcos and Janak H. Patel. A low-overhead coherence solution for multiprocessors with private cache memories. *Proc. of the 11th Annual Int'l. Symp. on Computer Architecture*, pages 348–354, June 5-7, 1984.

[21] Larry Rudolph and Zary Segall. Dynamic decentralized cache schemes for mimd parallel processors. *Proc. of the 11th Annual Int'l. Symp. on Computer Architecture*, pages 340–347, June 5-7, 1984. Also, Rpt. No. CMU-CS-84-139, Dept. of Computer Sci., Carnegie-Mellon U., 1984.

[22] Alan Jay Smith. Cpu cache consistency with software support and using "one time identifiers". *Proc. Pacific Computer Communications Symp.*, pages 153–161, Oct. 22-24, 2985.

[23] C. K. Tang. Cache system design in the tightly coupled multiprocessor system. *Proc. NCC*, 45:749–753, 1976.

[24] Alexander Veidenbaum. A compiler-assisted cache coherence solution for multiprocessors. *Proc. of the 1986 Int'l. Conf. on Parallel Processing*, pages 1029–1036, Aug., 1986.

Design and Analysis of a Scalable Cache Coherence Scheme Based on Clocks and Timestamps

Sang Lyul Min, *Member, IEEE*, and Jean-Loup Baer, *Senior Member, IEEE*

Abstract—Shared-memory multiprocessors with a multistage interconnection network have two important weaknesses: slow access to global memory and the absence of an instantaneous broadcast mechanism. The first weakness can be remedied by introducing private caches associated with each processor but efficient enforcement of cache coherence is hindered by the second weakness. This paper proposes a timestamp-based software-assisted cache coherence scheme that does not require any global communication to enforce the coherence of multiple private caches. The proposed scheme is based on a compile-time marking of references and a hardware-based local incoherence detection scheme. The possible incoherence of a cache entry is detected and the associated entry is implicitly invalidated by comparing a clock (related to program flow) and a timestamp (related to the time of update in the cache). This paper also reports on the results of a performance comparison between the proposed timestamp-based scheme and other software-assisted schemes. The comparison is based on a trace-driven simulation using actual traces. The results indicate that the proposed scheme performs significantly better than previous software-assisted schemes especially when the processors are carefully scheduled so as to maximize the re-use of cache contents. This scheme requires neither a shared resource (e.g., sophisticated memory controllers) nor global communication, and is, therefore, scalable up to a large number of processors.

Index Terms—Cache coherence, clock, "dance-hall" architectures, reference marking, timestamp.

I. INTRODUCTION

LARGE scale shared-memory multiprocessors where hundreds or thousands of processors and memory modules are interconnected through an "equidistant" [35] multistage interconnection network have recently been designed and/or implemented. A typical "dance-hall" architecture, where a set of processors is lined up on one side of a processor–memory interconnection network and a set of memory modules lined up on the other side, is shown in Fig. 1. The memory hierarchy consists of private caches C, local memories LM, and a shared global memory M. Examples of such architectures (although possibly without the complete memory hierarchy) include the University of Illinois Cedar machine [15], the BBN Butterfly

Manuscript received July 30, 1989; revised November 25, 1990. This work was supported in part by the National Science Foundation under Grants CCR-8619663, CCR-8702915, and CCR-8904190, Boeing Computer Services, Digit Equipment Corporation (the System Research Center and the External Research Program), and a Fulbright scholarship for S. L. Min.
S. L. Min is with the Department of Computer Engineering, Pusan National University, Pusan 609-735, Korea.
J.-L. Baer is with the Department of Computer Science and Engineering FR-35, Univiversity of Washington, Seattle, WA 98195.
IEEE Log Number 9102436.

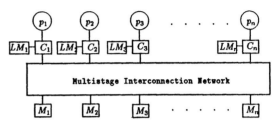

p : Processor
M : Memory module
C : Private cache
LM : Local memory

Fig. 1. Dance-hall type architecture.

multiprocessor [5], the NYU Ultracomputer [18], and the IBM RP3 machine [31].

One of the major problems associated with these architectures is the slow global memory access; thus, the efficient management of local memory and private caches is very important. Local memory is generally used to store code and private data although shared data can be temporarily stored in local memory as in [6]. In some sense, we could say that local memory allows single copy caching. The decision on what will be stored in local memory and for how long, and on what will remain in global memory is entirely done at compile-time. On the other hand, caching in its usual sense is a run-time process. It is automatic in hardware-based caching mechanisms and can be *prevented* in some instances in software-assisted schemes. The use of local memory is not incompatible with that of private caches. On the contrary, they can complement each other. However, in this paper, we restrict ourselves to a study of caching of shared variables.

The presence of multiple private caches introduces the well-known cache coherence problem [7]. Hardware-based protocols to solve the cache coherence problem are well understood in a shared-bus environment (e.g., [17], [22], [32], [37]). However, these solutions cannot be extended to the dance-hall multiprocessors since they make use of the instantaneous broadcast and "snoopy" mechanisms provided by the shared-bus. Software-assisted [10], [25], [27], [33], [38], [40] and directory-based [1], [4], [7], [36], [41] schemes are usually advocated in such an environment.

In this paper, we propose a software-assisted cache coherence scheme which overcomes some of the inefficiencies of previous approaches by using a combination of a compile-time marking of references and a hardware-based local incoherence detection scheme. We also give a performance evaluation of our proposed scheme. In Section II, we give the notation used throughout the paper. Section III reviews previous software-assisted approaches to enforcing cache coherence. In Section IV, a complete description of our approach is given. A correctness proof of our proposed scheme is given elsewhere [29] and is omitted here. Section V gives a quantitative comparison of our scheme with previous approaches. Section VI provides some concluding remarks.

II. DEFINITIONS

Programs written for shared-memory multiprocessors may use explicit parallel constructs or may be conventional sequential programs transformed into equivalent parallel ones by a restructuring compiler or a preprocessor like Parafrase [24], [39], PFC [3], or PTRAN [2]. The parallelism is constrained by data dependences: *flow-dependence*, *anti-dependence*, and *output-dependence* [23]. Let r and r' be read operations and w and w' be write operations in a program. r is defined to be flow-dependent on w if the memory location written by w may be read by r. w is defined to be anti-dependent on r if the memory location read by r may be later written by w. w is defined to be output-dependent on w' if the memory location written by w' may be later overwritten by w.

A data dependence relationship among statements in a program can be graphically represented by a labeled directed multigraph called *data dependence graph*. The nodes of the graph are statements in the program and (S_i, S_j, δ) is in the arc set if and only if S_j is δ-dependent on S_i.

In parallel programs, as in sequential programs, most of the execution time is spent in loops. We distinguish between *serial loops*, *DoAll loops*, and *DoAcross loops*. *serial loops* are loops with inter-iteration delay equal to the execution time of the whole loop body (i.e., iteration i cannot begin until iteration $i - 1$ finishes). *DoAll* loops are loops with the delay equal to 0 (i.e., all iterations of a *DoAll* loop can be executed completely in parallel). *DoAcross* loops [11] have a delay between 0 and the execution time of the loop body caused by inter-iteration dependences. *DoAll* and *DoAcross* loops will also be called *parallel loops*.

We assume that a parallel program is composed of a set of *epochs* [25] which are either parallel loops or serial regions between them. Execution of an iteration of a parallel loop constitutes an instance of the epoch of type parallel loop. A serial region is a special type of epoch which has only one instance. Initially, we assume that only one level of nested Do loops is to be executed concurrently (i.e., only different iterations of a parallel loop can be executed in parallel on multiple processors). In Section IV-D, we will discuss the case where the parallel program may have nested parallelism.

As an example, consider the program segment shown below. It has two epochs, one consisting of the DoAcross loop i and the other consisting of the serial code after the DoAcross loop (i.e., $S \leftarrow 0$ and the serial loop k). The DoAcross loop has two dependences: a flow dependence δ_1 caused by the dependency between $A(i, j)$ (in S_1) and $A(i, j)$ (in S_2) and a flow dependence δ_2 caused by the dependency between $A(i, j)$ (in S_1) and $A(i - 1, j)$ (in S_2).

$$
\begin{aligned}
&\text{DoAcross } i = 1, n_1 \\
&\quad \text{Do } j = 1, n_2 \\
S_1: &\quad\quad A(i, j) \leftarrow \cdots \\
S_2: &\quad\quad \cdots \leftarrow A(i, j) + A(i - 1, j) \cdots \\
&\quad \text{END Do} \\
&\text{END DoAcross} \\
&S \leftarrow 0 \\
&\text{Do } k = 1, n_3 \\
&\quad\quad S \leftarrow S + A(k, 1) \\
&\text{END Do}
\end{aligned}
$$

III. PREVIOUS APPROACHES TO ENFORCING CACHE COHERENCE

In [7], Censier and Feautrier defined *a memory scheme to be coherent if the value returned on a read is the value given by the latest store with the same address*. Most of the previous research done on enforcing cache coherence assumed shared resources such as a shared bus [17], [22], [32], [37] or a directory [4], [7], [36], [41]. These shared resources are, however, a hindrance toward scalability. A shared-bus is saturated as soon as the number of processors sharing it exceeds some threshold (certainly below 100 processors). Directories either grow linearly with the number of processor/cache pairs [7], [36], [41] or, if the encoding is more efficient, the protocols rely on broadcasts [4] that should be avoided in a scalable multiprocessor. We are therefore searching for alternatives that do not assume any shared resource but global memory and that do not use broadcast. Our approach, an instance of a "self-invalidation" cache coherence scheme, is based on software assists and local coherence checks.

The simplest software-assisted cache coherence scheme is to disallow caching of shared read/write data for the entire program [40]. This is accomplished by a compile-time marking of shared variables that are writable as noncacheable. The mechanism is simple but inefficient in the sense that every reference to noncacheable data is to be forwarded to global memory even though the addressed data could be cacheable during parts of the program where it is read-only or accessed exclusively by a single processor.

To overcome this performance penalty, Veidenbaum [38] proposed a scheme that allows changing of the cacheability of data. He identified the conditions necessary to cause cache incoherence. From those conditions, he showed that all global memory references can be routed through private caches inside DoAll loops and serial regions. But caching is prohibited inside loops with inter-iteration dependencies (DoAcross loops). In addition, caches that may potentially contain stale copies of data are flushed at the boundaries of loops. Although this scheme represents an obvious progress over no shared data caching at all, it still suffers from two inefficiencies. First, caching of read-only shared variables and variables that are exclusively accessed by only one processor inside DoAcross loops is disallowed. Second, the blind invalidations at the boundaries of loops flush out many cache entries that hold up-to-date copies of data.

The first inefficiency of Veidenbaum's scheme was partially remedied in the schemes proposed by McAuliffe [27] and Lee

146

[25]. Cacheability of variables is determined on an epoch by epoch basis. If a variable is potentially referenced by more than one processor in a given epoch and at least one of these references is a write, the variable is marked as noncacheable for that epoch. Otherwise, it is marked as cacheable. Although this scheme captures localities within an epoch very well, it still suffers from performance penalties due to the cache flushes at the end of epochs.

Subsequently Cheong and Veidenbaum [9], [10] proposed the *fast-selection invalidation* scheme which is an improved version of Veidenbaum's scheme. Fig. 2 shows the two possible conditions for a stale access [38] on which their reference marking scheme is based. In the first condition, a cache entry is loaded by a write by processor i and becomes stale when another processor j issues a write to the same memory location. The correctness criteria of cache coherence would be violated if processor i were still allowed to access what is now a stale copy in its cache. Similarly a stale access is possible when the cache entry is loaded by a read miss and becomes obsolete by a write from another processor. In their scheme, each read reference is marked at compile-time as either *memory-read* (the reference may potentially access a stale copy in the cache) or *cache-read* (on a hit, it is guaranteed that the cache entry is up-to-date). Notice that since these reference markings are done at compile-time, every reference to a shared variable that could be made after the variable was written by two different processors should be marked as *memory-read* by the compiler (condition 1). Similarly, every reference to a shared variable that could be made after the variable was read by one processor and then written by another processor should also be marked as *memory-read* (condition 2). From the above two conditions, it is easy to see that most read references to shared variables will be marked as *memory-read* by the compiler. In addition to the above compile-time detection scheme for stale accesses, a *change bit* is associated with each word in the cache. Its main purpose is to allow caching of *memory-read* references that occur more than once during an instance of an epoch. The change bits of the entire cache are set at the beginning of each epoch instance. A *cache-read* is executed as usual, irrespective of the change bit. If a *memory-read* is issued and there is a copy of the corresponding memory block in the cache with the change bit set, the cache controller has no idea of whether the copy was loaded after the last write of the memory block or not. Therefore the controller has to take a conservative approach and the request is serviced by the global memory. However, it is possible that the copy was indeed loaded after the last write and is up-to-date. The extraneous *memory read* is due to the limitation of the compile-time analysis. Many more read requests than necessary will be directed to the global memory (recall that most reads from shared variables are marked as *memory-read*). Therefore, the network traffic will be unduly increased and the scalability of the scheme is in question.

A scheme that is very similar to Cheong and Veidenbaum's was independently proposed by Cytron *et al.* [12]. This scheme uses the same compile-time analysis to detect stale accesses and, therefore, suffers from the same scalability problem. In Cytron's version, there is no change bit. Instead, intra-instance

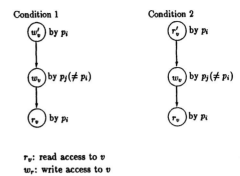

r_v: read access to v
w_r: write access to v

Fig. 2. Conditions for a stale cache access.

localities are captured by carefully moving around invalidation instructions so that cache entries loaded during the current instance are not needlessly invalidated.

The scheme that we propose in the next section has many similarities with the *version control approach* proposed at the same time, and independently, by Cheong and Veidenbaum [8]. We will briefly compare these two schemes at the end of Section IV-C.

For completeness purposes, we mention Smith's *one time identifier* scheme [33] which is more geared toward the caching of variables in critical sections. Table I shows a summary of the software-assisted cache coherence schemes discussed in this section.

IV. TIMESTAMP-BASED CACHE COHERENCE SCHEME

A. Overview

We propose an extension of the previous methods that has as a goal to capture more possibilities for the caching and retention in the caches of shared variables by looking more deeply at inter-epoch localities. Our approach, like those in the previous section, is based on compile-time analysis and, in addition, on hardware support in the form of counters and tag bits in the cache.

The basic idea is as follows. We associate a "clock" (i.e., a counter) with each sharable data structure (array or scalar) of interest. This clock is incremented at the end of each epoch in which the data structure *may* be modified (a decision that is taken at compile-time). We also associate a timestamp with each word (for the time being we assume that the block size is equal to one word) in the cache. This timestamp is set to the value of the relevant clock + 1 when the word is updated in the cache. A reference to a cache word is valid if its timestamp is equal to or greater than its associated clock value.

As an example, let us consider the program segment and the associated data-dependence graph given in Fig. 3. The output-dependence δ_1 is caused by the dependency between $X(f())$ and $X(g())$ and the flow-dependences δ_2 and δ_3 are caused by the dependencies between $X(g())$ and $X(p())$ and between $X(f())$ and $X(p())$, respectively. In Cheong and Veidenbaum's scheme, the reference to array X in S_3 will be marked as *memory-read* and, therefore, will be directed to the global memory. The situation would be about the same in

TABLE I
SUMMARY OF SOFTWARE-ASSISTED CACHE COHERENCE SCHEMES

	Wulf and Bell	Veidenbaum	McAuliffe	Lee	Veidenbaum and Cheong	Cytron *et al.*	Smith
coherence enforcement unit	each variable	all variables	each variable	each variable	each reference	each reference	each page
coherence enforcement region	program	loop	computational unit (CU)	epoch	program	program	critical section
detection of incoherence	usage of variables in a program	loop nesting structure	usage of variables in a CU	usage of variables in an epoch	flow analysis	data-dependence analysis	OTI
invalidation place	—	boundary of loops	boundary of CU's	boundary of epochs	boundary of loops	each reference	end of critical section
global memory update policy	—	write-through	write-back	write-back	write-through	hybrid scheme	write-through (for shared writable data)

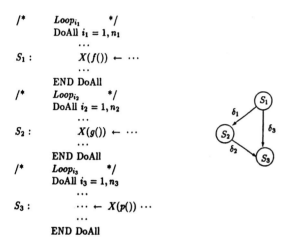

```
/*      Loop_{i_1}     */
        DoAll i_1 = 1, n_1
            ...
S_1 :        X(f()) ← ···
            ...
        END DoAll
/*      Loop_{i_2}     */
        DoAll i_2 = 1, n_2
            ...
S_2 :        X(g()) ← ···
            ...
        END DoAll
/*      Loop_{i_3}     */
        DoAll i_3 = 1, n_3
            ...
S_3 :        ··· ← X(p()) ···
            ...
        END DoAll
```

Fig. 3. Sample program segment which exhibits the inefficiencies of the previous approaches.

```
        if    b()    then    DoAll i_1 = 1, n_1
                                ...
S_1 :                            X(f()) ← ···
                                ...
                             END DoAll
                             DoAll i_2 = 1, n_2
                                ...
S_2 :                            X(g()) ← ···
                                ...
                             END DoAll
                     else    DoAll i_3 = 1, n_3
                                ...
S_3 :                            X(q()) ← ···
                                ...
                             END DoAll
        DoAll i_4 = 1, n_4
            ...
S_4 :        ··· ← X(p())···
            ...
        END DoAll
```

Fig. 4. Another sample program segment showing the inefficiencies of the previous approaches.

Cytron's scheme. In this scheme, the above reference would be preceded by an invalidation instruction and be eventually serviced by the global memory. These are necessary because when there is a corresponding word in the cache it is not known, at compile-time, whether this cached word is stale (i.e., written in $Loop_{i_1}$) or valid (i.e., written in $Loop_{i_2}$).

In our approach, we would associate a clock with the array X. Its initial value is 0 and it is incremented by 1 at the end of each epoch (here parallel loop) in which the variable X is modified (here $Loop_{i_1}$ and $Loop_{i_2}$). After the first loop, the cache blocks corresponding to $X(f())$ would have a timestamp of 1 (0 (clock value) + 1) and after the second loop the cache blocks corresponding to $X(g())$ would have a timestamp of 2 (1 (clock value) + 1). When the statement S_3 is reached, and if there is a corresponding cache word for a reference to $X(p())$, then this cache reference will be valid if the timestamp is 2, corresponding to $X(g())$, and invalid otherwise.

As a second example, consider the program segment given in Fig. 4. Again the reference to array X in S_4 will be directed to the global memory in Cheong and Veidenbaum's scheme since the compiler has to make the conservative assumption

that the Boolean expression $b()$ may evaluate to true. But if clocks and timestamps are maintained in the same way as in the previous example, the reference to the array X in $Loop_{i_4}$ can be satisfied by the cached words if they are loaded into the cache in either $Loop_{i_2}$ in the *then* case or $Loop_{i_3}$ in the *else* case.

The above two examples show that some of the inefficiencies of previous software-assisted cache coherence schemes can be remedied by history information which can be gathered at execution time.

Fig. 5 shows our approach to capturing localities across different epochs. We divide the analysis into two parts: intra-epoch analysis and inter-epoch analysis. The intra-epoch analysis is done at compile-time and results in various markings of references. These markings indicate that 1) for a cache entry to be re-used in future epochs it should be guaranteed that there is no succeeding write reference to the same memory location in the same epoch, and 2) for a read reference to use a cache entry loaded in past epochs it should be guaranteed that the read reference does not have any preceding write to

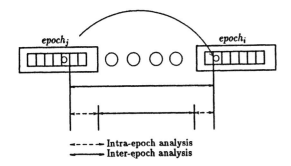

- - - - ▸ Intra-epoch analysis
———— Inter-epoch analysis

Fig. 5. Overall approach to capture inter-epoch localities.

the same memory location in the same epoch. Inter-epoch analysis is performed at execution time using clocks and timestamps as indicated in the previous examples. This inter-epoch analysis detects any intervening write reference to the same memory location between the epoch in which the cache entry was loaded by a processor and the one in which it is accessed by the same processor. The above intra- and inter-epoch analyses, when combined, enable a processor on a read access to a shared variable to detect any write reference to the same variable by other processors since the last update in the associated cache entry in its local cache.

B. Support Mechanism

Our cache coherence scheme requires the following hardware and software support mechanisms.

1) Hardware Support:

- Clock registers

  R_{clock} is the set of n_{clock}-bit clock registers associated with each processor. For each $r_{\text{clock}} \in R_{\text{clock}}$ and v_{clock} of type subrange $0 \cdot\cdot 2^{n_{\text{clock}}} - 1$, the following operations are defined.

  — LOAD-CLOCK r_{clock}, v_{clock} with the semantics $r_{\text{clock}} \leftarrow v_{\text{clock}}$

  — CLEAR-ALL with the semantics: $\forall\ r_{\text{clock}} \in R_{\text{clock}}$, $r_{\text{clock}} \leftarrow 0$

- Cache memory: With each word in the cache, we associate

  — an n_{clock}-bit timestamp.

  — a provisional bit (pb). This bit indicates when the entry has been loaded into the cache ($pb = 1$ loaded during the current instance, $pb = 0$ otherwise).

  — an invalid bit (ib) ($ib = 0$ valid, $ib = 1$ invalid).

Deciding a suitable value for n_{clock} is a tradeoff between the increase in the storage taken up by clocks and timestamps and the reduction in the number of clock or timestamp overflows (cf. end of Section IV-C).

Note that the hardware support is proportional to the cache size while in directory-based schemes, the extra hardware is proportional to the size of global memory. Let us assume a system with N processors and associated caches and N

memory modules. There are M memory blocks/module and C blocks/cache. In both directory and timestamped-based schemes, we need N more sophisticated controllers (N memory controllers in the directory case, N cache controllers in the timestamped one). The amount of tag bits, i.e., the storage overhead, is between $2NM$ (Archibald and Baer's scheme [4]) and $(N + 1)NM$ (Censier and Feautrier's scheme [7]) in directory-based schemes. In the timestamped case, there are ($n_{\text{clock}} + 2$) extra tag bits per block for a total overhead of $NC(n_{\text{clock}} + 2)$. If one assumes M to be one order of magnitude greater than C, the timestamp-based scheme is $10(N + 1)/(n_{\text{clock}} + 2)$ times more economical than Censier and Feautrier's scheme in terms of storage overhead. With $N = 200$ and $n_{\text{clock}} = 16$, the storage overhead of Censier and Feautrier's scheme is two orders of magnitude greater than that of the timestamp-based scheme. Notice that the relative space advantage of the timestamp-based scheme becomes greater as the number of processors in the system is increased. Also note that with 16 bit timestamp, the storage overhead of the timestamp-based scheme is comparable to that of Archibald and Baer's scheme, which is the most space-economic among the directory-based schemes. (See Section IV-C for the rationale behind the 16 bit timestamp.)

2) Software Support: The software support consists of variables associated with shared data structures and a marking mechanism.

We associate a variable v_{clock} of type subrange $0 \cdot\cdot 2^{n_{\text{clock}}} - 1$ with each shared variable v. Its value is typically loaded into one of the clock registers before referencing v. (See the formats for reads and writes given in Section IV-C.)

The reference marking scheme is based on a data-dependence analysis of a parallel program. Various attributes are given to read and write operations. These attributes are used to decide which actions to take for the associated operation at execution time.

Marking of write operations: A reference marking scheme for write operations is required in our scheme for both correctness and efficiency purposes. For correctness purposes, a reference marking is necessary for each write operation. This marking states whether the cache entry just written can be re-used in future epochs. The above decision is based on whether the write reference may have a succeeding write reference to the same memory location from other processors in the same epoch. If a given write operation may have such a succeeding write reference, the resultant cache entry cannot be re-used in future epochs and, therefore, the associated timestamp should not be set to the value of clock + 1.

For efficiency purposes, it is advantageous to know whether it is beneficial to load the cache or to simply bypass it for a given write operation. For example, we would choose the latter alternative if the resultant cache entry cannot be re-used either in future epochs or in the current epoch instance.

From the above considerations, each write operation to a shared variable in a parallel program belongs to zero, one, or both of the following two overlapping classes (cf. Fig. 6; for a more formal definition of the markings, see [29]).

1) $\mathcal{TW}$ (*timestamped* writes)
2) $\mathcal{PW}$ (*provisional* writes).

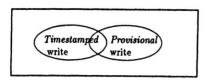

Fig. 6. Containment relationship among various write markings.

A write operation in an epoch belongs to the first class (i.e., is marked as *timestamped-write*, TW) if the memory location written by it cannot be overwritten by writes from different instances of the same epoch. As we will see later, the cache words updated by writes in TW are targeted for reads in later epochs.

A write operation in an epoch belongs to the second class (i.e., is marked as *provisional-write*, PW) if there is at least one potential read in the same instance of the epoch that may read the cache word updated by the PW write. Write operations in PW are targeted for reads in the same instance of the epoch to which they belong.

Write operations which belong to neither of the above two classes are forced to bypass the cache since there are no potential reads from the cache words that might have been updated by them. This not only increases the efficiency of cache storage but also reduces the number of requests the cache controller should handle. The containment relationship among the markings of a write operation is depicted in Fig. 6.

As an example of marking of write operations, let us consider the following DoAcross loop.

```
DoAcross i₁ = 1, n₁
      A(i₁) ← ⋯
      ⋯
      A(i₁ − 1) ← ⋯
      ⋯
      ⋯ ← A(g(i₁)) + ⋯
END DoAcross
```

For ease of explanation, the synchronizations required to satisfy the inter-iteration dependencies are omitted. The first write to the array (i.e., $A(i_1)$) cannot be marked as *timestamped-write* since the memory location written by it can be overwritten by the write to $A(i_1 - 1)$ in the subsequent iteration. It is marked as *provisional-write* if $A(g(k))$ may denote the same memory location as $A(k)$ for some k, $1 \le k \le n_1$ to allow the cache word written by $A(i_1)$ to service the read reference $A(g(i_1))$ generated in the same iteration. The second write to the array A (i.e., $A(i_1 - 1)$) is marked as *timestamped-write* since it is guaranteed that the memory locations written by it will not be overwritten by other writes. If both $A(k - 1)$ and $A(g(k))$ may denote the same memory location for some k, $1 \le k \le n_1$, $A(i_1 - 1)$ is also marked as *provisional-write*.

Marking of read operations: For read operations, we need a slightly more complicated marking scheme than for write operations to handle both cache misses and cache hits. In the case of a miss, a scheme similar to that for write operations is needed to decide whether the resultant cache entry can be re-used in future epochs and whether it is beneficial to load

the cache. In the case when there is a matching word in the cache, we need the same validity analysis as for a write. This leads to the following marking policies for cache loading and cache access.

• *Marking policy on read miss:* On a read miss, we need a policy to decide whether the word fetched from the global memory will be placed in the cache or not and, if so, whether the newly loaded cache entry can be re-used in future epochs. For these purposes, each read operation can be marked as *timestamped-loading* (i.e., TL) and/or *provisional-loading* (i.e., PL). The meanings of *timestamped-loading* and *provisional-loading* are analogous to those of *timestamped-write* and *provisional-write*, respectively. A read operation in an epoch is marked as *timestamped-loading* if the memory location read by it cannot be written by writes in other instances of the same epoch and, therefore, the resultant cache entry can be re-used in future epochs. As in *timestamped* writes, the cache words loaded by reads marked as TL are targeted for reads in later epochs. A read operation in an epoch is marked as *provisional-loading* if there is at least one other potential read in the same instance of the epoch that may access the cache word loaded by the former on a cache miss. In order to use the cache storage effectively, read operations marked as neither *timestamped-loading* nor *provisional-loading* do not load the cache with the word fetched from the global memory on cache misses.

• *Marking on read hit:* As we mentioned before, for a read operation to utilize cache entries loaded in past epochs, it should be guaranteed that it does not have any preceding write to the same memory location in the same epoch. This test is necessary for correctness purposes. On the other hand, for efficiency reasons, it is advantageous to know whether there could be an up-to-date copy in the cache for a given read reference. For example, if it is decided that the cache cannot have an up-to-date copy for a given read reference, it would be beneficial to simply bypass the cache. This bypassing would reduce the number of requests the cache should service.

From the above considerations, each read of a shared variable belongs to zero, one, or both of the following two sets.

1) TR (*timestamped* reads)
2) PR (*provisional* reads).

For a read to be in the set TR, it should be guaranteed that it is not preceded by any write to the same memory location from different instances of the same epoch. Read operations in TR are marked as *timestamped-read* and utilize the cache words updated by *timestamped* writes or loaded by reads marked as *timestamped-loading* on cache misses. The cache word is considered to be up-to-date if its timestamp value is equal to or greater than the current clock value of the corresponding variable.

A read operation r belongs to the second class (i.e., PR) if there is at least one reference (write or read) to the same memory location in the same instance of the epoch that can reach r. This indicates whether it is possible that r may be satisfied by the cache word updated by a *provisional* write to the same memory location or loaded into the cache by another read from the same memory location marked as *provisional-loading* in the same instance of the epoch.

Read operations which belong to neither of the above two classes, called *memory-only* reads, are made to bypass the cache since the request cannot be satisfied by the cache. It cannot be satisfied by cache words updated by *provisional* writes or loaded into the cache by reads marked as *provisional-loading* because there are no such writes or reads in the instance of the epoch to which the request belongs to (otherwise the request would have been marked as *provisional-read*). Neither can it be satisfied by *timestamped* writes or reads marked as *timestamped-loading* because the request can be preceded by a write reference to the same memory location from other epoch instances in the same epoch, that may make the previously loaded cache entry stale. The containment relationship among the markings of a read operation is depicted in Fig. 7.

We give below an example of marking of read operations.

```
DoAcross i₁ = 1, n₁
    A(g(i₁)) ← ···
    ...
    ··· ← A(f(i₁)) + ···
    ...
    ··· ← A(p(i₁)) + ···
END DoAcross
```

Again we omit the synchronizations to simplify the discussion. The first read operation (i.e., $A(f(i_1))$) is marked as *timestamped-read* if $f(k)$, $1 \leq k \leq n_1$ is not equal to any $g(k')$ for $1 \leq k' < k$. If the above condition is satisfied, the read reference $A(f(i_1))$ can access cache words brought in during past epochs. In addition, the read to $A(f(i_1))$ is marked as *provisional-read* if $f(k) = g(k)$ for some k, $1 \leq k \leq n_1$ to take advantage of the case when the cache word written by the reference to $A(g(i_1))$ is read by the reference to $A(f(i_1))$ executed in the same iteration of the parallel loop. The marking of the second read operation (i.e., $A(p(i_1))$) is done similarly.

For cache block loading purposes, the read to $A(f(i_1))$ is marked as *timestamped-loading* if $f(k)$, $1 \leq k \leq n_1$ is not equal to any $g(k')$ for $k < k' \leq n_1$. In this case, it is guaranteed that the cache words loaded into the cache on read misses on $A(f(i_1))$ remain up-to-date at the end of the parallel loop and may be referenced by *timestamped* reads in future epochs. In addition, it is marked as *provisional-loading* if $f(k)$ is equal to $p(k)$ for some k, $1 \leq k \leq n_1$ to take advantage of the case when the cache word loaded by a read miss on $A(f(i_1))$ satisfies the read reference $A(p(i_1))$ generated in the same iteration of the parallel loop. However, the read reference to $A(p(i_1))$ cannot be marked as *provisional-loading* since there is no possible read reference in the same iteration which can be satisfied by the cache word that might have been loaded into the cache on misses on $A(p(i_1))$.

C. Overall Scheme

In the following, we assume that each instance of an epoch is executed on a distinct processor and that the block size of the

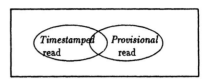

Fig. 7. Containment relationship among various read markings.

cache is equal to one word. We will discuss the consequences of removing these assumptions later in this section.

In our scheme, each write reference to a shared variable has the following format:

r_{clock}	tw	pw	operand specifier

where r_{clock} is the clock register which holds the clock value of the variable being referenced, *tw* stands for *timestamped* write, and *pw* for *provisional* write.

Table II lists the actions taken for possible combinations of the *tw* and *pw* bits for a write to a shared variable. (Recall the tag bits for a cache entry described in Section IV-B1.) The semantics implies a write-through policy. We could have considered a limited write-back policy where dirty cache words are written back to the global memory at the end of each epoch instance but we would have had to add an enforcement of write-backs for variables involved in data dependencies between epoch instances. In [28], a new global memory update policy, called *write-last* policy, was proposed which combines the advantages of the write-through and write-back policies by updating global memory as soon as possible but avoiding duplicate global memory updates.

Notice that for a nontimestamped write the timestamp field is set to r_{clock}. It is because the corresponding memory location may be overwritten by a different processor in the same epoch, thus making stale the newly loaded cache entry.

A read reference to a shared variable has the following format:

r_{clock}	tr	pr	tl	pl	pc	operand specifier

where r_{clock} has the same meaning as before, and *tr* stands for *timestamped* read, *pr* for *provisional* read, *tl* for *timestamped* loading, *pl* for *provisional* loading, and *pc* for *preceded*.

The *preceded* bit (*pc*) is set to 1 at compile-time if the read reference may be preceded by a write to the same memory location in the same epoch. It is set to 0 otherwise.

The condition for a read hit, assuming there is a matching cache block in the cache, is defined as: (the first term in each *and* condition depends on the instruction, i.e., is compiler generated, while the second depends on cache bits set at run-time)

$$(tr = 0 \ \wedge \ pr = 1) \ \wedge \ (ib = 0 \ \wedge \ pb = 1)$$
(*provisional* read)
or

TABLE II
ACTIONS TAKEN FOR A WRITE TO A SHARED VARIABLE

Type of Write		Actions Taken
Memory-only write	$tw = 0$ & $pw = 0$	Update the global memory.
Provisional write	$tw = 0$ & $pw = 1$	if *block miss* then allocate a new cache entry. Update both the global memory and the associated cache entry. $ts \leftarrow r_{clock}$ $pb \leftarrow 1$ if $ib = 1$ then $ib \leftarrow 0$
Timestamped write	$tw = 1$ & $pw = 0$	if *block miss* then allocate a new cache entry. Update both the global memory and the associated cache entry. $ts \leftarrow r_{clock} + 1$ $pb \leftarrow 0$ if $ib = 1$ then $ib \leftarrow 0$
Timestamped & provisional write	$tw = 1$ & $pw = 1$	if *block miss* then allocate a new cache entry. Update both the global memory and the associated cache entry. $ts \leftarrow r_{clock} + 1$ $pb \leftarrow 1$ if $ib = 1$ then $ib \leftarrow 0$

$(tr = 1 \ \wedge \ pr = 0) \ \wedge \ (ib = 0 \ \wedge \ ts \geq r_{clock})$
(*timestamped* read)
or
$(tr = 1 \ \wedge \ pr = 1) \ \wedge \ (ib = 0 \ \wedge \ (pb = 1 \ \vee \ ts \geq r_{clock}))$ (*both*).

If there is a hit and the above Boolean expression is satisfied, the corresponding read reference is satisfied by the cache. Otherwise, the actions taken on a read reference are decided by the loading policy specified by the *tl, pl,* and *pc* bits. The *pc* bit is used to indicate whether on a read marked as *timestamped-loading*, we set the timestamp field of the referenced cache word at clock + 1 ($pc = 1$, i.e., the read may have a preceding write to the same memory location in the same epoch) or at clock ($pc = 0$). Table III specifies the actions taken on a read miss based on the *tl, pl,* and *pc* bits.

An instruction which clears the *provisional* bits of the entire cache is inserted after each DoAll and DoAcross statement. The clock values of the shared variables which may be modified in a parallel loop (i.e., DoAll or DoAcross loop) are incremented by 1 in every processor at the end of the execution of the parallel loop.

At the beginning of a serial region, the processor assigned to execute that region clears the *provisional* bits of the associated private cache. It also increments by 1 the clock values of the shared variables modified by it during the serial region at the end of the serial region. The remaining processors increment the clock values of the shared variables which may be written in the serial region by 1. The instructions doing the above tasks (i.e., checking whether the current processor is the processor assigned to execute the current serial region and incrementing the clocks) are inserted at compile-time.

The invalid bits of the entire cache are set and the clock variables of all the shared variables used in a program are initialized to 0 at the start of the parallel program. In the rare occasion of a clock or a timestamp overflow, the entire contents of the private cache associated with the processor causing the overflow are invalidated and all the clock variables and clock registers in the processor are re-initialized to 0. If we assume n_{clock} to be 16, the above cache flushing and re-initialization would occur once every 2^{16} epoch executions for the worse case.

As mentioned earlier, Cheong and Veidenbaum's *version control approach* [8] and our approach have many similarities. The version control scheme uses a directed graph called *task execution graph* to model the execution of a parallel program. In the graph, each node denotes a task and each directed edge represents a dependency between the two involved tasks. The tasks at the same level in the task execution graph correspond to an epoch in our proposed scheme. Instead of clocks and timestamps, the version control approach uses *current version numbers* and *birth version numbers*. Clocks and version numbers, and timestamps and birth version numbers, are maintained in an analogous way. The main difference between the two schemes is that, by incorporating (and paying the "price" of) more sophisticated reference markings, our proposed scheme has a better chance of capturing localities between dependent tasks that can occur in DoAcross loops.

D. Extensions

Parallel programs with nested parallelism: Our scheme is flexible enough to be applied to programs with nested parallel loops. For this purpose, we define an *era* as a segment of a parallel program delimited by two enclosing *barrier* operations. In this framework, a write is marked as *timestamped-write* if it is guaranteed that the memory location written by it cannot be overwritten in the era to which it belongs by writes from other processes including those that are spawned by itself. A write is marked as *provisional-write* if there is at least one potential read reference of the same memory location that may be issued by the same processor before the next synchronization point. As before, *timestamp-loading* and *provisional-loading* are defined similarly.

For a read to be marked as *timestamped-read*, it should be guaranteed that it is not preceded by any write to the same memory location from other processes in the same era. A read is marked as *provisional-read* if there is at least one preceding reference to the same memory location that may be executed

TABLE III
ACTIONS TAKEN ON A READ MISS

Type of Read		Actions Taken
No loading	$tl = 0$ & $pl = 0$	Fetch from the global memory and do not cache.
Provisional loading	$tl = 0$ & $pl = 1$	Fetch from the global memory and load into the cache. $ts \leftarrow r_{clock}$ $pb \leftarrow 1$ if $ib = 1$ then $ib \leftarrow 0$
Timestamped loading	$tl = 1$ & $pl = 0$	Fetch from the global memory and load into the cache. if $pc = 1$ then $ts \leftarrow r_{clock} + 1$ else $ts \leftarrow r_{clock}$ $pb \leftarrow 0$ if $ib = 1$ then $ib \leftarrow 0$
Timestamped & provisional loading	$tl = 1$ & $pl = 1$	Fetch from the global memory and load into the cache. if $pc = 1$ then $ts \leftarrow r_{clock} + 1$ else $ts \leftarrow r_{clock}$ $pb \leftarrow 1$ if $ib = 1$ then $ib \leftarrow 0$

by the same process after the most recent synchronization point.

As an example, consider the program segment, a single era, shown in Fig. 8. The read operation from array B (i.e., $B(i,n_1)$) is marked as *timestamped-loading* since there is no succeeding write to the array. The read from array A (i.e., $A(i, 1)$), however, cannot be marked as *timestamp-loading* since the memory location read by it will be written by one of its children processes spawned to execute the DoAll loop j. For cache access purposes, both reads are marked as *timestamped-read* since they cannot be preceded by any writes to the same locations from other processes in the era. Similarly, the write to array A inside the DoAll loop j (i.e., $A(i, j)$) is marked as *timestamped-write* since it is guaranteed to be the last write to that particular memory location in the era.

Multiple iterations of a parallel loop executed on the same processor: The possibility that multiple iterations of a parallel loop are executed on the same processor could enhance rather than degrade the performance of our scheme. In this case, it is possible that a read marked as *memory-only* read issued in an iteration of a parallel loop can be satisfied by the cache word updated by a write marked as *timestamped-write* or a read marked as *timestamped-loading* in an earlier iteration of the same parallel loop executed by the current processor. A *memory-only* read request can be satisfied by the cache if $ib = 0 \land ts > r_{clock}$.

This increases the bandwidth requirement of the caches since they must be interrogated even on a *memory-only* read. Caches could be designed so that the interrogation of their entries on a *memory-only* read can be enabled or disabled under program's control at run-time. The default option would be disabled. Enabling would occur if the ratio of the number of processors allocated to a parallel loop over the number of iterations of the loop is small enough.

Block size of the cache larger than one word: There are both advantages and disadvantages in having a cache block size larger than one word. The main advantage of a larger-than-one-word block size is the implicit prefetching of the other words in the block on a cache miss [34]. The prime disadvantage of having a cache with a block size larger than one word in a shared-memory multiprocessor is due to false sharing [14]. In

```
barrier
DoAll i = 1, n₁
   ··· ← B(i, n₁) + A(i, 1)
   DoAll j = 1, n₂
      A(i, j) ← ···
   END DoAll
END DoAll
barrier
```

Fig. 8. Example of parallel program with nested parallelism.

an invalidation-based cache coherence scheme, an invalidation of one word in a cache block invalidates other words in the block as well. This may cause a cascade of invalidations if multiple words in the same block are written by different processors at about the same time. In fact, as observed in [26], large block sizes can penalize performance in the type of architectures that we are studying.

If the block size were larger than one word, all the words in a cache block loaded on a read miss, except the requested one, will be assigned values of $pb = 1$ and $ts = r_{clock}$ if they come from the same variable (e.g., array) and the variable is not modified in the current epoch. Otherwise, the invalid bits of those words are set to 1. It would be an easy task for a compiler to allocate shared variables so that they do not cross the block boundaries. Note that for caches with block size larger than one word, each word in a cache block has its own pb and ib bits. On a write miss, we advocate a variation of a policy in which a block is allocated, the write is reflected in the allocated block only on the referenced words, and the invalid bits of the other words in the block are set to 1.

V. EVALUATION OF SOFTWARE-ASSISTED CACHE COHERENCE SCHEMES

The use of private caches is advocated in many proposed and/or implemented shared-memory multiprocessors to reduce both the average memory access time and the network traffic. As we briefly mentioned in Section I, there are two general approaches to enforcing cache coherence in large-scale shared-memory multiprocessors: directory-based and software-assisted. In a directory-based cache coherence scheme, a directory entry, which is kept in the memory controller, is associated with each memory block. This entry encodes the state of the block. The state is used to decide whether there is a need for invalidations on a given write transaction to the block and if so, to locate the private caches which have a copy of the block to be invalidated. It is also used to tell whether the corresponding memory block is stale or not and if so, to locate the private cache which is guaranteed to have the most current copy of the block. In addition to the state in the global directory, a local state is usually associated with each cache block in private caches. This local state is used to allow a private cache to service most requests from its associated processor without incurring any global actions.

Even though cache coherence schemes based on directories can be quite efficient in yielding a high hit ratio because of their ability to dynamically keep track of the status of each block, the network traffic generated for invalidation requests and for the manipulation of local and/or global state information can be substantial. In our proposed scheme, cache entries are invalidated solely by local processors and no globally-manipulated information is associated either with cache blocks or with memory blocks. This eliminates the extra network traffic at the expense of less efficient caching. An initial performance comparison between our proposed timestamp-based scheme and a directory-based scheme was made in [30]. The results indicated that the timestamp-based scheme generally yields miss ratios comparable to those of the directory-based scheme with less network traffic for parallel programs written in the SPMD (single program multiple data) model of parallel programming where parallelism is expressed in terms of DoAll loops. Detailed results from the comparison are not repeated here and interested readers are referred to [30].

In our comparative study [30], we have used the most efficient (in terms of hit ratio and network traffic) directory scheme. In order to have a fair comparison, we needed to determine the most efficient software-assisted scheme. Therefore, in this section, we evaluate the relative effectiveness of various software-assisted cache coherence schemes. Lee's [25], Cheong and Veidenbaum's [9], [10], and our own timestamp-based cache coherence schemes are chosen since they can exploit an increasing amount of program localities. Notice that Cheong and Veidenbaum's scheme being evaluated in this paper is the fast-selective scheme [9], [10], not the version control scheme [8]. We expect that the performance of the version control scheme would be essentially the same as that of the timestamp-based scheme for parallel programs with only DoAll loops. Our evaluation methodology is trace-driven simulation.

The method used to get parallel traces and the simulator structure are described in Section V-A. Section V-B discusses the sample parallel programs traced. Section V-C presents our simulation results.

A. Methodology

As shown in Fig. 9, the simulation consists of three steps: generation of serial traces with markers, preprocessing, and actual trace-driven simulation.

1) Generation of serial traces: Trace data used in the experiment are obtained by preprocessing traces from serial execution of parallel programs with marking instructions embedded in them. Markers are placed on events of interest such as start of an epoch, end of an instance of an epoch, etc. Since the programs used to generate the traces were written using explicit parallel constructs (e.g., DoAll, END DoAll), the insertion of marking instructions was straightforward. The original serial traces are gathered by *tracer*, a trace generating program run on the VAX architecture under the Ultrix V2.3 operating system [19]. For each memory reference the corresponding trace record contains fields for the type of reference (e.g., read instruction, read data, write data, etc.), storage segment involved (i.e., data segment, stack segment, or instruction segment), the size of the item being referenced, and the memory address.

2) Preprocessing: The original serial traces are restructured through the preprocessing step based on various types of markers as shown in Fig. 10. Attributes required during the actual simulation are assigned to each reference during this step. These include markings of references used in the cache coherence schemes simulated, the value of the associated clock register, etc. (for a complete list, see Table IV). The markings represent an upper bound on the accuracy of data dependence information that could be obtained from a parallelizing compiler. For example, in the program segment shown in Fig. 11 the memory location corresponding to $A(2)$ is marked as cacheable in our experiment for Lee's scheme if the *then* path is taken at execution time during the third iteration of the DoAcross loop. However, the compiler would mark it as noncacheable since the compiler should make the conservative assumption that the *else* path could be taken. This slightly increases the hit ratio of Lee's scheme. These kinds of optimistic markings are used throughout but do not bias the experiment since about the same degree of favor is given to the three schemes evaluated.

In order to remove the degree of freedom brought upon by the sophistication of the register allocation techniques used in the compiler, two different parallel traces from the same serial trace were simulated. The first trace (*unfiltered* version) contains all the references that the original serial trace has. In the second trace (*filtered* version), all the *registerable* references are filtered out. A read reference is defined to be *registerable* if it has at least one preceding reference (either read or write) to the same memory location in the same epoch instance whereas a write is defined to be so if it has at least one succeeding write reference to the same memory location in the same instance. These registerable references represent an upper bound of references that can be captured by registers. Even though the unfiltered trace is more realistic, especially when we do not know how many registers will be used in a compiler, the filtered one allows us to see the importance of inter-epoch locality since the intra-instance locality is captured by the registerable references. We think that the evaluation based on filtered traces becomes more important with the existence of increasingly sophisticated register allocation techniques.

3) Trace-Driven Simulation: Traces restructured by the preprocessing step are used to drive a cache simulator in order to obtain various performance measures such as the hit ratio and

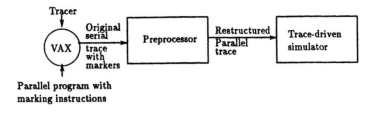

Fig. 9. Overall structure of simulation process.

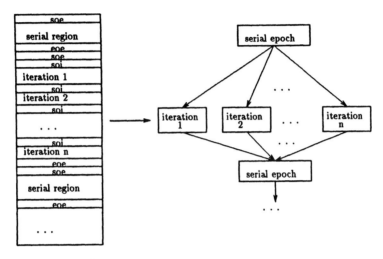

soe: start of epoch
eoe: end of epoch
soi: start of instance

Fig. 10. Restructuring of a serial trace into a parallel trace.

```
DoAcross i = 1, N
      A(i) = ···
      if C(i) > C(i+1) then ··· = A(i)
                        else ··· = A(i-1)
END DoAcross
```

Fig. 11. Example of an optimistic marking.

the amount of network traffic for various cache organizations. The input parameters to the simulator are the cache size, set associativity, type of cache coherence scheme, global memory update policy, replacement policy, number of processors allocated, and processor scheduling policy. A direct-mapped cache with one-word block size, so that false sharing effects are eliminated, is assumed throughout the experiment. Table V shows the ranges of the parameters which define the space actually explored by our experiment. Only data references (both private and shared data references) are simulated since requests for instructions can be handled similarly in the three schemes. The output from the simulator includes the miss ratio for each type of reference and the amount of network traffic. Reasons for cache misses such as block miss, timestamp mismatch, etc., are also provided. We report the above performance figures for only one processor. This is

sufficient because of the self-invalidating nature of the schemes under evaluation.

The actual scheduling of parallel iterations on processors, based on the number of allocated processors, is done when the restructured trace is processed by the simulator. Two different types of scheduling policies are used: pre-scheduling and random scheduling. In the pre-scheduling policy the ith iteration of a parallel loop is executed on processor $i \bmod \mathcal{P}$ where $\mathcal{P}$ is the number of processors allocated. In this policy, it is also assumed that one designated processor called MASTER always executes all the serial regions in the program. In the random scheduling case, whenever there is an instance of an epoch for execution (including a serial region), a processor is randomly selected to execute it.

B. Parallel Programs Traced

Three parallel application programs are used to generate the traces. They follow the same parallel programming paradigm, namely: SPMD (single program multiple data).

The first program, *sim* [20], simulates a multistage interconnection network which serves vector load/store requests from processors to memory modules. The second program, *gauss* [13], uses the Gauss elimination technique to solve the

155

Attribute	Scheme	Type of reference	Condition
noncacheable	Lee's scheme	read & write	if and only if the associated variable is referenced by more than one write process in the epoch to which it belongs and at least one of these references is a write
memory-read	Cheong & Veidenbaum's scheme	read	after the corresponding location is written more than twice in different epochs
cache-read	Cheong & Veidenbaum's scheme	read	if and only if it is not *memory-read*
timestamped-write	timestamp-based scheme	write	if and only if it has no succeeding write to the same location in the same epoch
provisional-write	timestamp-based scheme	write	if and only if there is at least one scheme succeeding read reference to the same location in the same instance
timestamped-read	timestamp-based scheme	read	if and only if it has no preceding write scheme to the same location in the same epoch
provisional-read	timestamp-based scheme	read	if and only if there is at least one preceding reference to the same location in the same instance
timestamped-loading	timestamp-based scheme	read	if and only if it has no succeeding write to the same location in the same epoch
provisional-loading	timestamp-based scheme	read	if and only if there is at least one succeeding read reference to the same location in the same instance
preceded	timestamp-based scheme	read	if and only if there is at least one scheme preceding write reference to the same location in the same epoch
clock value	timestamp-based scheme	read & write	the value of the associated clock register

TABLE V
RANGE OF PARAMETERS USED IN THE EXPERIMENT

Parameter	Range
Scheme	Lee, Cheong and Veidenbaum, timestamp-based
Scheduling policy	pre-schedule, random-schedule
Trace type	unfiltered, filtered
Number of processors	1 2 4 8 16 32 64
Cache sizes	128 256 512 1K 2K 4K 8K 16K 32K ∞ (infinite cache) (in words)

following linear system of equations.

$$a_{11}x_1 + a_{12}x_2 + \cdots + a_{1n}x_n = b_1$$
$$a_{21}x_1 + a_{22}x_2 + \cdots + a_{2n}x_n = b_2$$
$$\cdots$$
$$a_{n1}x_1 + a_{n2}x_2 + \cdots + a_{nn}x_n = b_n.$$

The last application, *mhd*, is a program for the numerical solution of two-dimensional magnetohydrodynamic (MHD) differential equations [16]. The first two programs are written in *pcp*, a parallel extension of the C programming language [21]. The last one is a slightly modified version of the program originally written in HEP Fortran. These programs do not contain any DoAcross loop; this slightly favors the cache coherence schemes with little or no ability to capture inter-iteration locality. Table VI shows a summary of the characteristics of the three traces used in the experiment. In the

table, a value (or contents of a memory location) is considered shared if it is accessed by more than one process.

C. Results

There are three types of temporal localities in parallel programs: intra-instance, inter-instance, and inter-epoch localities. The main difference among the three schemes evaluated here is in their ability to exploit the above types of localities. All three schemes can exploit the first two types, although the amount of inter-instance locality captured by Lee's and Cheong and Veidenbaum's schemes is limited. It is because caching is restricted to references to read-only shared variables in the former case and to read references marked as *cache-read* in the latter. Only Cheong and Veidenbaum's and the timestamp-based schemes can explore inter-epoch locality since in Lee's scheme caches are flushed at the end of each epoch. As we

156

TABLE VI
CHARACTERISTICS OF THE TRACES USED IN THE EXPERIMENT

	sim		gauss		mhd	
	unfiltered	filtered	unfiltered	filtered	unfiltered	filtered
number of instructions traced	7973367	7973367	4470574	4470574	5626036	5626036
number of data references	5855877	1010014	4499205	2096148	1533562	640969
number of data reads	4689713	707285	3792278	1409077	1087221	385378
number of data writes	1166164	302729	706927	687071	446341	255591
number of *registerable* reads	3982428	0	2383201	0	701843	0
number of *registerable* writes	863435	0	19856	0	190750	0
number of epochs	641	641	201	201	73	73
number of serial epochs	161	161	102	102	13	13
number of parallel epochs	480	480	99	99	60	60
number of parallel instances	26080	26080	5049	5049	2148	2148
number of shared values	158351	158351	667009	667009	199898	199898
number of reads to shared values	518462	251569	2354402	1339154	704584	365195

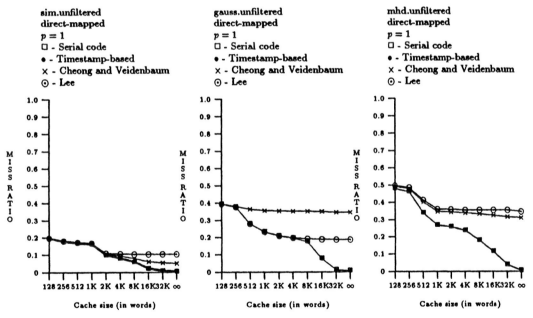

Fig. 12. Miss ratio for single processor case for the original (unfiltered) traces.

mentioned in Section IV-A, the amount of inter-epoch locality captured by Cheong and Veidenbaum's scheme is very limited.

This qualitative assessment is validated by the data shown in Fig. 12 where the miss ratios of the three schemes are shown along with the miss ratio of the serial execution case when the parallel programs happen to be executed on a single processor. The serial execution always yields the highest hit ratio since no cache entry is needlessly invalidated.

For small caches there is not much difference among the three schemes. It is because the three schemes respond well to intra-epoch locality (i.e., intra-instance + inter-instance) which can be captured even with small caches. But the effect of inter-epoch locality becomes the dominant factor once all of the intra-epoch locality is captured by the cache. This is the main reason why Cheong and Veidenbaum's and the timestamp-based schemes yield better hit ratios than Lee's scheme for

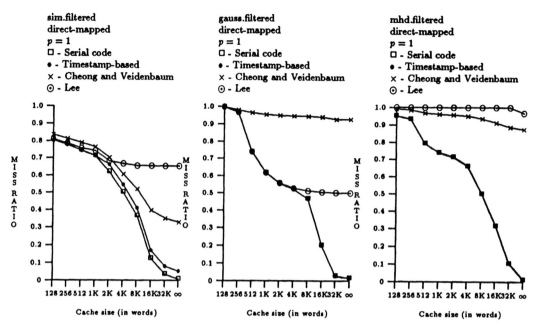

Fig. 13. Miss ratio for single processor case for the filtered traces.

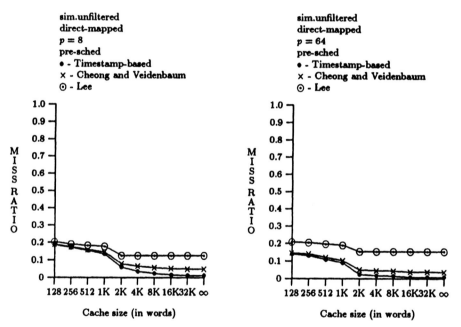

Fig. 14. Miss ratio for the *sim* application for $p = 8$ and $p = 64$ (pre-scheduling case).

larger caches with the exception of the *gauss* program (cf. Fig. 12). In the *gauss* application, however, Lee's scheme yields better hit ratios than Cheong and Veidenbaum's scheme. This is because Lee's scheme can capture more effectively the localities caused by read-only sharing of shared memory locations, in this case read-only sharing of pivot rows, across different iterations of a parallel epoch. Another interesting point to notice is the rapid drop in miss ratios in the *gauss* program when the cache size is increased from 256 words to 512 words in Lee's and the timestamp-based schemes. A careful inspection of the corresponding trace shows that 256

words is the threshold cache size beyond which the localities due to the above read-only sharing are captured by the caches.

The above trends are more apparent if we consider the miss ratios for the same configuration for filtered traces as depicted in Fig. 13. (Recall that in filtered traces the intra-instance localities are captured by registers.) The remaining sole source of locality for Lee's scheme is inter-instance localities due to read-only sharing of shared variables across different instances of the same epoch. This is the reason why Lee's scheme yields miss ratios near one for the *mhd* program in which there is little such read-only sharing. Cheong and Veidenbaum's scheme still

158

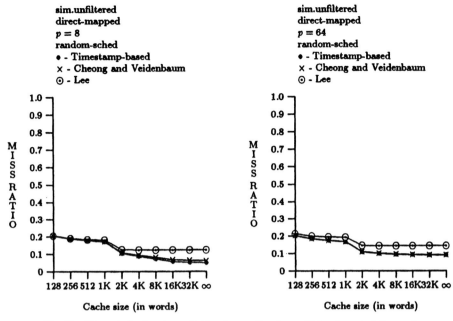

Fig. 15. Miss ratio for the *sim* application for $p = 8$ and $p = 64$ (random-scheduling case).

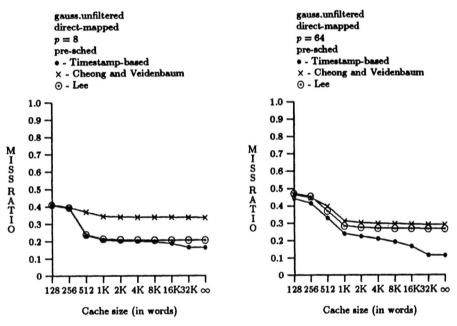

Fig. 16. Miss ratio for the *gauss* application for $p = 8$ and $p = 64$ (pre-scheduling case).

captures some inter-instance and inter-epoch localities but to a limited degree as we can see in the figure. The timestamp-based scheme, however, consistently manages to maintain miss ratios comparable to those of the serial execution case.

The same analysis holds in the multiprocessor simulations for the *sim* and *mhd* programs under a pre-scheduling policy (see Fig. 14 for *sim*; similar data for *mhd* can be found in [28]). This is a consequence of the pre-scheduling which allows shared memory locations written by one processor to be subsequently read by the same processor. In the *sim*

program, the rows of the multistage interconnection network are simulated in parallel for each network cycle and, with pre-scheduling, the same row is always simulated by the same processor. This increases the chance of the reuse of the cache contents before they become stale. A similar behavior occurs in *mhd*. These characteristics provide the timestamp-based scheme ample opportunities to exploit inter-epoch localities.

In general, however, the chances for shared-memory locations written by a processor to be referenced by the same processor before they become stale are decreased as more

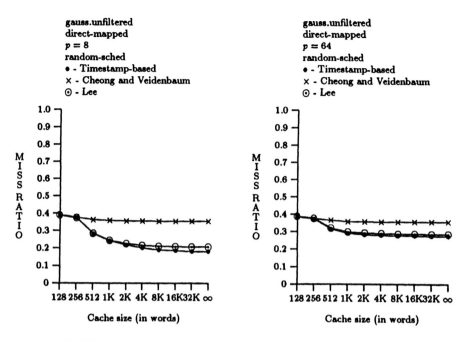

gauss.unfiltered
direct-mapped
p = 8
random-sched
• - Timestamp-based
× - Cheong and Veidenbaum
⊙ - Lee

gauss.unfiltered
direct-mapped
p = 64
random-sched
• - Timestamp-based
× - Cheong and Veidenbaum
⊙ - Lee

Fig. 17. Miss ratio for the *gauss* application for $p = 8$ and $p = 64$ (random-scheduling case).

processors are allocated in the random scheduling case. This is shown in Fig. 15 for the *sim* application. Miss ratios in the random scheduling case are worse than their pre-scheduling counterparts for the *sim* and *mhd* applications. Furthermore, the difference in miss ratios between the timestamp-based scheme and the better of the other two schemes is reduced as more processors are allocated in the random scheduling case as we can see in the figure. One interesting point to notice is that for the timestamp-based scheme the miss ratios of caches are lowered as more processors are allocated for the *sim* and *mhd* applications (cf. Figs. 12 and 14 for *sim*). It is because, as more processors are allocated, the amount of shared data to be cached per processor is reduced, thus reducing the number of misses due to replacements.

On the other hand, as the number of processors is increased, the miss ratios for the *gauss* application are not lower as we can see in Fig. 16. It is because the amount of inter-instance locality, which is one of the main components of cache hits in the *gauss* application, decreases. Also, the hit ratios under pre-scheduling are worse than those obtained under random scheduling for some cache sizes (cf. Figs. 16 and 17). This seemingly anomalous behavior can be explained by looking carefully inside the Gauss Elimination algorithm. The algorithm consists of two major steps: reduction and back substitution. The code segment corresponding to the reduction step is given in Fig. 18. It starts with a parallel reduction with a_{11} as a pivot, i.e., the elements of the first column are zeroed out and the other elements are modified adequately on a row by row basis. The process is then repeated for the (new) second column and so on until the matrix A is reduced to an upper triangular matrix.

Accesses to each row of the matrix A by processors for each invocation of the DoAll loop are shown in Fig. 19,

```
do i = 1, n
    DoAll j = i+1, n
        tmp = a(j,i)
        if (tmp < ε) exit
        a(j,i) = 0.0
        tmp = tmp/a(i,i)
        do k = i+1, n
            a(j,k) = a(j,k) - a(i,k) * tmp
        end do
        b(j) = b(j) - b(i) * tmp
    END DoAll
end do
```

Fig. 18. The reduction step of the Gauss elimination algorithm.

assuming that three processors are allocated and that they are pre-scheduled naively, i.e., processor i executes the ith instance of the DoAll loop on every invocation of the DoAll loop. In the figure, we can notice that each processor reads the row of the matrix A which was last written by some other processor in the previous invocation of the DoAll loop. This drastically reduces the chance of capturing inter-epoch locality since most of the cache contents associated with the matrix A become stale whenever a new step of the reduction is started. Therefore, none of the three cache coherence schemes work well in this situation; this fact is well illustrated in Fig. 20 in which the reasons for misses are shown for the unfiltered gauss trace when eight processors are pre-scheduled (see also Fig. 16 which shows an overall miss ratio of 0.2 to 0.4 depending on the cache size for the 8 processor case). As can be seen, most misses for large caches are due to timestamp mismatch rather than block misses. On the other hand, if we use random scheduling, there is some chance, although small, that elements of the matrix A written by a processor are read by the same processor during the next invocation of the DoAll

Matrix A	1st invocation	2nd invocation	3rd invocation
A_1	p_1^r, p_2^r, p_3^r		
A_2	p_1^r, p_1^w	p_1^r, p_2^r	
A_3	p_2^r, p_2^w	p_1^r, p_1^w	p_1^r
A_4	p_3^r, p_3^w	p_2^r, p_2^w	p_1^r, p_1^w

p_i^r: read by p_i
p_i^w: write by p_i

Fig. 19. Accesses to matrix A by processors when $p = 3$.

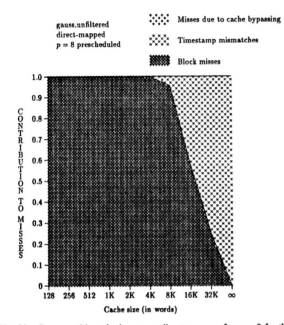

gauss.unfiltered
direct-mapped
$p = 8$ prescheduled

⬚⬚⬚ Misses due to cache bypassing

░░░ Timestamp mismatches

▓▓▓ Block misses

Fig. 20. Decomposition of misses according to sources for $p = 8$ for the unfiltered gauss trace (pre-sched).

Matrix A	1st invocation	2nd invocation	3rd invocation
A_1	p_1^r, p_2^r, p_3^r		
A_2	p_1^r, p_1^w	p_2^r, p_3^r	
A_3	p_2^r, p_2^w	p_2^r, p_2^w	p_3^r
A_4	p_3^r, p_3^w	p_3^r, p_3^w	p_3^r, p_3^w

Fig. 21. Accesses to matrix A by processors in the data-constrained schedule.

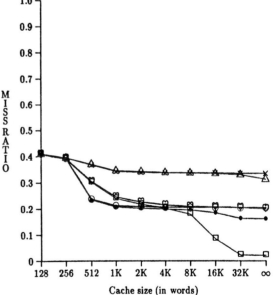

gauss.unfiltered
direct-mapped
$p = 8$
□ - Timestamp-based (data-constrained sched)
△ - Cheong and Veidenbaum (data-constrained sched)
♡ - Lee (data-constrained sched)
• - Timestamp-based (pre-sched)
× - Cheong and Veidenbaum (pre-sched)
⊙ - Lee (pre-sched)

Fig. 22. Miss ratio for $p = 8$ for the unfiltered gauss trace (data-constrained scheduling).

loop. This is the main reason why, in the *gauss* program, the random scheduling yields slightly better hit ratios than the pre-scheduling for some cache sizes.

Naturally, better performance could be achieved by tailoring the scheduling to the application by using some form of *data-constrained* scheduling. Fig. 21 shows such a schedule for *gauss* assuming three processors are allocated. In this schedule, the processor that has executed the kth instance of the DoAll loop during the previous invocation is assigned to execute the $k - 1$th instance to maximize the reuse of the cache entries associated with the array A. The results from the new simulation for 8 processors are compared to those from the pre-scheduling case in Fig. 22.

The results from the data-constrained scheduling case are quite consistent with our expectations. With the new schedule, the timestamp-based scheme yields better hit ratios than in the pre-scheduling and random scheduling cases, especially for large caches. Most of the improvements result from the fact that most of the cache entries associated with the matrix A are now re-used over different invocations of the DoAll loop in the new schedule. On the other hand, the miss ratios from the other two schemes are barely improved because of their limitation

to exploit inter-epoch locality. This enlarges the performance gap between the timestamp-based scheme and the other two schemes. One interesting point to note from the figure is that the miss ratios for the pre-scheduling case are better than those

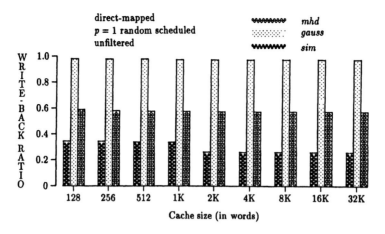

direct-mapped
p = 1 random scheduled
unfiltered

~~~~~~ mhd
········· gauss
~~~~~~ sim

Fig. 23. Ratios of write-back traffic to write-through traffic when $p = 1$.

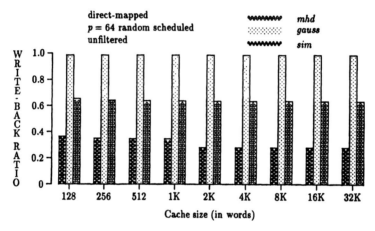

direct-mapped
p = 64 random scheduled
unfiltered

~~~~~~ mhd
········· gauss
~~~~~~ sim

Fig. 24. Ratios of write-back traffic to write-through traffic when $p = 64$.

for the data-constrained scheduling for small caches (< 4K words). This is because, in the new schedule, p_1 (from which we measured the miss ratios) executes fewer iterations of the DoAll loop during the reduction step than in the pre-scheduling case. This, in turn, reduces the amount of inter-instance locality due to the read-only sharing of the pivot rows for p_1, thus yielding lower hit ratios than in the pre-scheduling case. Such an effect would have been minimized if we used a much larger A matrix than that used in the experiment or if the miss ratios were averaged over all processors.

The data gathered by the traces allows us to also provide some information on the potential network traffic. Figs. 23 and 24 depict the ratios of write-back traffic to write-through traffic for different cache sizes for $p = 1$ and $p = 64$, respectively. The three schemes evaluated here are assumed to have the same write-back traffic because the global memory update policy used in one of the schemes can be equally used in the others. The result shows that, except for *sim* the ratio is almost insensitive to cache size. This indicates that few memory locations are written in a single epoch instance in our experiment. The exception for the *sim* program (from 0.33 to 0.26 for $p = 1$ and from 0.34 to 0.28 for $p = 64$) occurs when the cache size is increased from 1K words to 2K

words because of access to some large data structures larger than 1024 words. This can be also seen in Figs. 12, 14, and 15 in which hit ratios for the *sim* program are significantly improved when the cache size is increased from 1K words to 2K words independently of the number of allocated processors and the scheduling policy. The high write-back ratios of the *gauss* application arise because most of the writes are to shared memory locations and these locations are rarely written more than once inside a single instance.

The above results indicate that the write-back policy may reduce the write traffic substantially at the possible expense of transient fluctuations in the network traffic at the end of epoch instances. This, in turn, provides a ground for our write-last global memory update policy that tries to minimize these fluctuations without increasing the network traffic.

VI. Conclusions

The efficient enforcement of coherence of multiple private caches is essential to the effective performance of dance-hall type architectures. In this paper, we propose a self-invalidating cache coherence scheme which overcomes some of the inefficiencies of previous software-assisted schemes. Our approach is based on compile-time marking of read/write operations and on execution time incoherence detection which makes use of locally maintained clocks and timestamps. We show, through trace-driven simulation, that our timestamp-based cache coherence has a better performance (hit ratio) than previous schemes especially when the processors are carefully scheduled so as to maximize the re-use of cache contents. We also investigate the effects of register allocation on cache performance through trace filtering and show that the ability to capture localities across different epochs, the main strong point of our approach, becomes relatively more important as more sophisticated register allocation techniques are applied.

There are numerous open areas for future research. One such area is an integration of the timestamp-based cache coherence scheme into a parallelizing compiler such as Parafrase [24], PFC [3], and PTRAN [2]. We think that such an integration also provides a ground for a fair comparison of software-assisted schemes with directory-based cache coherence schemes and user-controlled local memory. It remains to assess (via simulation of parallel programs) which scheme or which combination of the three schemes is most advantageous in terms of processor utilization and overall throughput.

Another interesting topic for future research is an investigation of multilevel cache hierarchies in which the first level cache employs a software-assisted cache coherence scheme whereas the second level uses a directory-based scheme. This configuration seems to be a nice match since the first level cache will not be disturbed unduly by unrelated coherence events and the second level cache will have a high hit ratio because it is directory-based.

ACKNOWLEDGMENT

The authors thank C. Ebeling, S. Eggers, and R. Cypher for their many helpful discussions. We would also like to thank R. Henry for allowing us to use *tracer* program. Thanks also to E. D. Brooks III for providing us with the parallel programs used to generate the parallel traces. Finally, we want to thank the anonymous referees for their constructive comments.

REFERENCES

[1] A. Agarwal, R. Simoni, J. Hennessy, and M. Horowitz, "An evaluation of directory schemes for cache coherence," in *Proc. 15th Annu. Int. Symp. Comput. Architecture*, June 1988, pp. 280–289.
[2] F. Allen, M. Burke, P. Charles, R. Cytron, and J. Ferrante, "An overview of the PTRAN analysis system for multiprocessing," in *Proc. 1987 Int. Conf. Supercomput.*, June 1987.
[3] J. R. Allen and K. Kennedy, "PFC: A program to convert FORTRAN to parallel form," MASC Tech. Rep. 82–6, Dep. Math. Sci., Rice Univ., Mar. 1982.
[4] J. Archibald and J.-L. Baer, "An economical solution to the cache coherence problem," in *Proc. 12th Annu. Int. Symp. Comput. Architecture*, June 1985, pp. 355–362.
[5] BBN, *Butterfly Parallel Processor Overview*, Version 1, Dec. 1985.
[6] D. Callahan, "A global spproach to detection of parallelism," Rice Univ., Apr. 1987.
[7] L. M. Censier and P. Feautrier, "A new solution to coherence problems in multicache systems," *IEEE Trans. Comput.*, vol. C-27, pp. 1112–1118, Dec. 1978.
[8] H. Cheong and A. Veidenbaum, "A version control approach to cache coherence," in *Proc. 1989 Int. Conf. Supercomput.*, June 1989, pp. 322–330.
[9] ——, "Stale data detection and coherence enforcement using flow analysis," in *Proc. 1988 Int. Conf. Parallel Processing, Vol. I Architecture*, Aug. 1988, pp. 138–145.

[10] ——, "A cache coherence scheme with fast selective invalidation," in *Proc. 15th Annu. Int. Symp. Comput. Architecture*, June 1988, pp. 299–307.
[11] R. Cytron, "Doacross: Beyond vectorization for multiprocessors," in *Proc. 1986 Int. Conf. Parallel Processing*, IEEE, Aug. 1986, pp. 836–844.
[12] R. Cytron, S. Karlovsky, and K. P. McAuliffe, "Automatic management of programmable caches (extended abstract)," in *Proc. 1988 Int. Conf. Parallel Processing, Vol. II Software*, Aug. 1988, pp. 229–238.
[13] G. A. Darmohray and E. D. Brooks III, "Gaussian techniques on shared memory multiprocessor computers," unpublished Tech. Rep., UCRL-97939, preprint.
[14] S. J. Eggers, "Simulation analysis of data sharing in shared memory multiprocessors," Univ. of California, Berkeley, Feb. 1989.
[15] D. Gajski, D. Kuck, D. Lawrie, and A. Sameh, "Cedar—A large scale multiprocessor," *Comput. Architecture News*, vol. 11, no. 1, pp. 7–11, Mar. 1983.
[16] W. Gentzsch, "Vectorization of computer programs with applications to computational fluid dynamics," vol. 8, *Notes on Numerical Fluid Mechanics*, Friedr. Vieweg & Sohn Verlagsgesellschaft mbH, Braunschweig 1984.
[17] J. R. Goodman, "Using cache memory to reduce processor-memory traffic," in *Proc. 10th Annu. Int. Symp. Comput. Architecture*, June 1983, pp. 124–131.
[18] A. Gottlieb, R. Grishman, C. P. Kruskal, K. P. McAuliffe, L. Rudolph, and M. Snir, "The NYU Ultracomputer—Designing a MIMD, shared-memory parallel machine," in *Proc. 9th Annu. Int. Symp. Comput. Architecture*, Apr. 1982, pp. 27–42.
[19] R. R. Henry, "Address and instruction tracing for the VAX architecture," unpublished tech. rep., Aug. 1983.
[20] E. D. Brooks III, "Performance of the butterfly processor-memory interconnection in a vector environment," in *Proc. 1985 Int. Conf. Parallel Processing*, IEEE, Aug. 1985, pp. 21–24.
[21] E. D. Brooks III and G. A. Darmohray, "A parallel extension of C that is 99 % fat free," unpublished tech. rep.
[22] R. H. Katz, S. J. Eggers, D. A. Wood, C. L. Perkinsk, and R. G. Sheldon, "Implementing a cache consistency protocol," in *Proc. 12th Annu. Int. Symp. Comput. Architecture*, June 1985, pp. 276–283.
[23] D. J. Kuck, *The Structure of Computers and Computation*. New York: Wiley, 1978.
[24] D. J. Kuck, R. H. Kuhn, B. Leasure, and M. Wolfe, "The structure of an advanced vectorizer for pipelined processors," in *Proc. Comput. Software Appl. Conf. (COMPSAC80)*, IEEE, Oct. 1980, pp. 709–715.
[25] R. L. Lee, "The effectiveness of caches and data prefetch buffers in large-scale shared memory multiprocessors," Center for Supercomputing Res. and Develop., Univ. of Illinois, CSRD Rep. 670, May 1987.
[26] R. L. Lee, P.-C. Yew, and D. H. Lawrie, "Multiprocessor cache design considerations," in *Proc. 14th Annu. Int. Symp. Comput. Architecture*, June 1987, pp. 253–262.
[27] K. P. McAuliffe, "Analysis of cache memories in highly parallel systems," New York Univ., May 1986.
[28] S. L. Min, "Memory hierarchy management schemes in large scale shared-memory multiprocessors," Univ. of Washington, 1989.
[29] S. L. Min and J.-L. Baer, "A timestamp-based cache coherence scheme," in *Proc. 1989 Int. Conf. Parallel Processing, Vol. I Architecture*, Aug. 1989, pp. 23–32.
[30] ——, "A performance comparison of directory-based and timestamp-based cache coherence schemes," in *Proc. 1990 Int. Conf. Parallel Processing, Vol. I Architecture*, Aug. 1990, pp. 305–311.
[31] G. F. Pfister, W. C. Brantley, D. A. George, S. L. Harvey, W. J. Kleinfelder, K. P. McAuliff, E. A. Melton, V. A. Norton, and J. Weiss, "The IBM Research Parallel Processor Prototype (RP3): Introduction and architecture," in *Proc. 1985 Int. Conf. Parallel Processing*, IEEE, Aug. 1985, pp. 764–771.
[32] L. Rudolph and Z. Segall, "Dynamic decentralized cache consistency schemes for MIMD parallel processors," in *Proc. 12th Annu. Int. Symp. Comput. Architecture*, June 1985, pp. 340–347.
[33] A. J. Smith, "CPU cache consistency with software support and using 'one time identifiers'," in *Proc. Pacific Comput. Commun. Symp.*, Oct. 1985, pp. 22–24.
[34] ——, "Line (block) size choice for CPU caches," *IEEE Trans. Comput.*, vol. C-36, pp. 1063–1075, Sept. 1987.
[35] L. Snyder, "Type architectures, shared memory and the corollary of modest potential," *Annu. Rev. Comput. Sci.*, vol. 1, pp. 289–317, 1986.
[36] C. K. Tang, "Cache design in the tightly coupled multiprocessor system," in *AFIPS Conf. Proc. Nat. Comput. Conf.*, 1976, pp. 749–753.
[37] C. P. Thacker and L. C. Stewart, "Firefly: A multiprocessor workstation," in *Proc. Second Int. Conf. Architectural Support for Programming Languages Oper. Syst.*, Oct. 1987, pp. 164–172.

[38] A. V. Veidenbaum, "A compiler-assisted cache coherence solution for multiprocessors," in *Proc. 1986 Int. Conf. Parallel Proessing*, Aug. 1986, pp. 1029–1036.

[39] M. Wolfe, "Optimizing compilers for supercomputers," Dep. Comput. Sci., Univ. of Illinois at Urbana–Champaign, UIUCDCS-R-82-1105, Oct. 1982.

[40] W. A. Wulf and C. G. Bell, "C.mmp—A multi-mini processor," in *Proc. Fall Joint Comput. Conf.*, Montvale, NJ, Dec. 1972, pp. 765–777.

[41] W. C. Yen, D. W. L. Yen, and K.-S. Fu, "Data coherence problem in a multicache system," *IEEE Trans. Comput.*, vol. C-34, pp. 56–65, Jan. 1985.

A Generational Algorithm to Multiprocessor Cache Coherence

Tzi-cker Chiueh

Computer Science Department
State University of New York at Stony Brook
chiueh@sbcs.sunysb.edu

Abstract

In view of the growing gap between processor speeds and network latency, it becomes increasingly expensive to maintain multi-processor cache consistency via run-time inter-processor communication. Software-controlled cache coherence schemes have the advantage of simplified hardware and the reduction of inter-processor communication traffic. Among previously proposed software-based schemes, those based on the concept of version/timestamp show the most aggressive performance potential. Unfortunately these methods have several implementation and performance problems that prevent them from being practical implementation choices. In this paper, we discuss these problems and describe a generational cache coherence algorithm that eliminates all of these problems. Moreover, the new algorithm can exploit inter-level temporal locality of parallel programs with significantly less hardware support.

1. Introduction

Multi-processor cache consistency maintenance schemes are generally classified into hardware and software categories. Hardware-based cache coherence schemes use run-time inter-processor notifications to update or invalidate stale cached data. For bus-based shared-memory multiprocessors such as Sequent's Symmetry, these notification messages usually account for a large portion of the bus traffic. In some instances, the percentage of consistency-related to total traffic could be as high as 80% [EGGE89]. In larger-scale multiprocessor systems where buses are easily saturated by inter-processor communication traffic, using run-time notification to maintain cache consistency becomes rather inefficient due to the lack of a broadcast medium. On the other hand, in hardware-based cache-consistency schemes, consistency maintenance actions are taken only when inconsistency actually arises at run time, e.g., a shared data write operation. Consequently, the hardware approach typically won't induce over-invalidations or unnecessary updates.

Among the software-controlled cache coherence schemes proposed in the literature, the version-controlled [CHEO89] or time-stamped [MIN89] cache coherence scheme shows the most aggressive performance potential. Since the basic idea of these two schemes is identical, we will only discuss the version-controlled scheme in the following. Cheong's version-controlled cache coherence algorithm is based on the *single assignment* principle. This principle dictates that a variable be assigned only once throughout its lifetime. Whenever a variable is updated, the variable's current version is abandoned and a new version of the variable is created to hold the new value. Under this principle, detecting stale cached data becomes straightforward: A variable's cache copy becomes stale only when there is a write to that variable in other processors. But by the single assignment principle the variable will assume a new name after the write. Consequently the next access to that variable will use its new name and cause a cache miss on the original cached copy due to name mismatch. Despite its conceptual simplicity, this algorithm has certain implementation and performance problems that need to be solved before it can be put to practical use. The

major contribution of this paper is a new software-controlled cache coherence algorithm that is both simpler and free of these performance problems.

The rest of this paper is organized as follows. To motivate the proposed algorithm, we discuss the version-controlled algorithm and its problems in Section Two. In Section Three, a generational cache coherence algorithm is presented, together with the required architectural support. Section Fiour concludes this paper with a summary of the major ideas of this work and pointers for future work.

2. Version-Controlled Cache Coherence Schemes and Its Problems

Before describing the generational algorithm, let's describe our assumed parallel computation model [CHEO89] [MIN89]. A program is either explicitly (i.e., by programmers) or implicitly (i.e., by the compiler) partitioned into tasks. A task is a unit of computation that gets scheduled and assigned to processors for execution at run time. There are data dependency relationships (*true, output,* and *anti* dependency) among tasks. Tasks that are not related by data dependencies are said to be *independent* of each other and can be executed in parallel without synchronization. The data dependency relationships among a program's tasks can be expressed by a directed graph called the task graph [CHEO89]. A task graph's nodes represent tasks while its directed edges represent dependencies. If there is an edge E_{ij} from Node i to Node j, then Task j depends on Task i. Figure 1 shows an example task graph, where, for example, Task Five depends on Task Four. The compiler uncovers independent tasks by *levelizing* the task graph through topological sorting. Nodes at the same level of a levelized task graph are guaranteed to be independent and therefore can be dispatched simultaneously. In Figure 1, Task Two and Task Three are independent of each other.

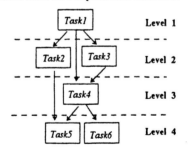

Figure 1 A Levelized Task Graph

If a compiler inserts barrier instructions at the boundaries of consecutive levels of a task graph, only *Doall* loop parallelism is exploited. To exploit the parallelism of *Doacross* loops, a system must be able to dispatch in parallel the tasks at different levels. However, in this case, synchronization instructions must be inserted appropriately to synchronize the execution behavior of concurrent tasks. Although the underlying idea of version-control and time-stamp algorithms are the same, Min's algorithm can exploit *Doacross* loop parallelism by adding extra mechanisms, whereas Cheong's simply can't. In contrast, the proposed generational algorithm can handle both *Doall* and *Doacross* loops in a single framework.

2.1. The Algorithm

Data variables are classified into private, shared read-only, and shared read-write three categories. Only shared read-write variables could cause cache consistency problems. From now on a variable is assumed to be shared read-write unless stated otherwise. A variable can be a scalar, a structure, or an array. Associated with each variable in a program are two numbers: a *current version number* (CVN) and a *birth version number* (BVN). The CVN represents the most up-to-date version number of a variable. The effective address used to access a variable is formed by concatenating the variable's CVN with its original memory address. Each node of a shared-memory multiprocessor maintains a local memory called the *variable ID table*, which keeps track of the CVN's of *all* the variables of a program. Every memory access in the programs has to specify both a variable ID and its address as shown in Figure 2, where the ID is used to index the variable ID table to locate the variable's CVN and to form an effective cache access address.

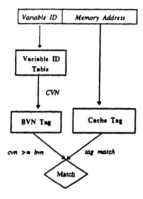

Figure 2   Formation of Effective Cache Access Address

Accordingly, each cached copy of a variable has a BVN in the cache's tag memory that designates the version number immediately after the cache copy is created. A variable's cache copy can be created in two ways: written by a store instruction or brought from main memory upon cache misses. The BVN of a variable's cache copy is set to the variable's CVN if the cache copy is brought from main memory, and is set to CVN+1 if the copy is updated by a write instruction. In a parallel task execution model where barrier instructions are inserted at the level boundaries, a variable can be written by at most one task at each level, possibly more than once. Only the last write to a variable needs an adjustment of the variable's BVN in the cache tag. Before reaching a level barrier, *every* task must increment the CVN's of all the variables that are modified at that level. The set of variables that are modified at any level are assumed to be known at compile time, and these CVN increment instructions are inserted to a program statically.

A cache access is a hit when the cache tag matches the memory address and BVN ≥ CVN. Cheong's algorithm can ensure that accesses to stale cache copies lead to cache misses because stale copies , by construction, have smaller BVN's than the CVN's used to access shared variables. In addition, a variable's cache copy updated at one level by a processor could be accessed by the same processor without cache miss at subsequent levels if no writes to that variable occur in the interim on other processors. Therefore the algorithm can

exploit inter-level temporal locality.

Because each node maintains the CVN's on its local variable ID table, every node is supposed to update the CVN's at the level barrier. As a result, Cheong's algorithm may not be able to guarantee cache consistency when some nodes did not participate in processing tasks at the i-th level and are assigned a task at the j-th level, where j ≥ i. This could take place when the i-th level has fewer independent tasks than the j-th level. In general, this so-called *level skipping* problem can occur when the levels of consecutive tasks assigned on a node are i and i+n (n > 1), respectively. [CHEO89] solves this problem by keeping track of the levels skipped by a node and updating the node's variable ID table *before* assigning a task to that node. Let's use Var_i to denote the set of variables modified at the i-th level. Then the set of variables whose CVN's need to be updated are the set of variables modified from Level i+1 to Level i+n-1, denoted by Mod(i+1, i+n-1):

$$\text{Mod}(i+1, i+n-1) = \bigcup_{j=i+1}^{j=i+n-1} Var_j$$

where $\cup$ is the multi-set union operator, i.e., duplicates are NOT eliminated. If a variable occurs in Mod(i, i+n) X times, its CVN must be incremented X times. The computation of Mod(i, i+n) and the associated CVN updates must occur at run time since processors are dynamically assigned to tasks. In the above discussion, we are assuming an acyclic task graph, the update procedure for cyclic task graphs are even more complex and can be found in [CHEO89].

2.2. Problems

In addition to the level-skipping problem, Cheong's algorithm has several other problems that prevent it from being a practical implementation choice. This prompts us to search for a better approach. The first problem is the run-time overhead associated with updates of current version numbers. In Cheong's algorithm, a task at one level must update the CVN's of all shared variables written at that level, even if the task itself only modifies a subset of the written variables. In addition, *level skipping* could result in more CVN updates *before* a task is assigned to a node. Consequently, although the Cheong's algorithm avoids run-time inter-processor consistency-maintenance communication, a program's tasks have to perform extra work. When this overhead is relatively small, this may seem to be a good tradeoff in the light of the increasing speed gap between processors and interconnection networks.

A[0]=1;

For i = i to A_Dim

*A[i] = A[i-1] * 2;*

⋮

Figure 3   A Doacross Loop

The second problem associated with Cheong's algorithm is that it only works for Doall loops but not for Doacross loops. Consider the Doacross loop in Figure 3. Variable A is written in Iteration I and read in Iteration I+1, and therefore Iteration I+1 is flow-dependent on Iteration I. Suppose Iteration I and I+1 are assigned to Node N and Node M respectively. To exploit Doacross loop parallelism, iterations at different levels, in this case, Iteration I and I+1, are allowed to be dispatched simultaneously. Further assume that there is a copy of A in Node M before this Doacross loop is initiated. If the BVN of A in Node N is l after the write operation in Iteration I, A's CVN in Node M is still $l-1$ when the read access in Iteration I+1 is made. This is because CVN updates are only performed at the end of the tasks that are dispatched simultaneously, and by this time A's new CVN has not yet propagated from Node N to Node M As a result, when Node M accesses A. the stale copy of A seems to be up to date even though it isn't, thus leading to a false hit. Note that synchronization primitives only guarantee the execution order of dependent tasks but don't prevent false hits. Unless special notification mechanisms are provided, Cheong's algorithm can not handle Doacross loops.

The third problem of Cheong's algorithm is related to the finiteness of the version numbers of shared data variables. When a shared variable's version number is overflowed, it becomes impossible to use its version number to detect staleness of the variable's cache copy. One possibility is to reset the overflowed variable's version number to zero. However, this requires a system-wide coordination that resets the variable's CVN's and BVN's in all nodes and in main memory. Exactly how overflow cases are handled are not discussed in [CHEO89] and [MIN89]. There is a fundamental tradeoff between the number of bits allocated to version numbers and the frequency of version number reset operations. The shorter version numbers are, the more frequently version numbers overflow. On a similar vein, Cheong's algorithm also assumes that the variable ID table in each node is always big enough to hold the version numbers of all the shared variables in a given program. Since the number of shared data variables varies from program to program, it is not clear how big the variable ID table should be, and what will happen when variable ID tables are not big enough.

On the performance side, Cheong's algorithm is necessarily conservative. Consider the example in Figure 4, where the entire array A is modified at Level I, one element of A is modified at Level J, and then at Level K, only those elements whose value is greater than 1000 are modified. At compile time, there is no information as to which element of A is modified at level J, and the values of A's elements. Consequently Cheong's algorithm has to make pessimistic assumptions by incrementing the CVN's of A's cached elements in all nodes at the end of Level I. Similar things occur at the end of Level K even though it may well be the case that only a small portion of A are actually modified. Since CVN increments render stale those cache copies that have smaller BVN's, unnecessary CVN updates essentially correspond to over-invalidation in hardware-based cache coherence schemes.

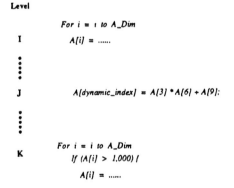

Level

I   *For i = 1 to A_Dim*

       A[i] = ...

J   *A[dynamic_index] = A[3] * A[6] + A[9];*

K   *For i = 1 to A_Dim*

       If (A[i] > 1,000) {

         A[i] = ...

Figure 4   An Example Program

There are two factors that contribute to cache over-invalidation. First, because an aggregate data structure such as an array is treated as an indivisible unit and is allocated a single variable ID, the version numbers of all array elements are implicitly incremented even though only the version numbers of a small portion of the array need to be adjusted. One possible solution is to allocate an ID to each array element, thus allowing a finer-granularity control over the version numbers of individual array elements. However, this approach could potentially aggravate the finite variable ID table problem

described above. Second, due to a lack of run-time information, state-of-the-art data flow analysis techniques can't identify the array elements that are actually modified at a particular level. As a result , over-invalidation is inevitable even if each array element has its own variable ID. This problem can only be solved by more aggressive compile-time data dependency analysis techniques.

Last but not least, Cheong's algorithm requires each memory access in a program to be specified in terms of a memory address AND a variable ID (as shown in Figure 2) This calls for a modification to the instruction set architecture of the host processor.

3. Generational Cache Coherence Algorithm

Through a closer examination, we found that almost all the problems associated with Cheong's algorithm are rooted in the fact that each shared data variable is allowed to have a separate version numbering dynamics. That is, at any point in the program execution, each shared variable is allowed to have a different current version number. As a result, each node has to maintain a variable ID table to keep track of each variable's CVN's, and pays the overhead of updating the CVN's. Suppose, on the other hand, all shared variables conform to a single version numbering scheme, there is no need to maintain individual variable's current version numbers, and the CVN update would be greatly simplified. The proposed generational cache coherence scheme is exactly based on this observation.

3.1. An Example

In Cheong's algorithm, each shared variable has a CVN in the variable ID table and a BVN in the corresponding cache line when it is cached. Because a variable's BVN is incremented each time the variable is written, the version numbers of different variables progress at different paces, depending on the update frequency of each individual variable. The basic idea of our generational cache coherence algorithm is to impose a single version numbering scheme upon a program's shared variables.

Let's call each level of the task execution graph a *generation*, each of which has an associated *generation number*. When a task is dispatched to a node, the task is also assigned a *current generation number* (CGN), which is the number of the generation to which this task belongs. Figure 5(a) shows the set of tasks and the set of variables modified in each generation. Note that each variable is either a scalar or an aggregate data structure. For example, a, b, c, and d are modified by T1 and T2 in the first generation. In our algorithm, the generation number is a replacement of the CVN's in Cheong's algorithm. In addition, each variable's cache line has a *valid generation number* (VGN), which designates the next generation in which the variable will be modified. Figure 5(b) shows the VGN's of a, b, c, d, and e at the end of each generation.

Initially the VGN's of all shared variables are zero; therefore the accesses to a, b , c, and d in the first generation cause cache misses, which bring a copy of each of these variables into the nodes. At the end of the first generation, because a, b, c, and d are modified in this generation, their VGN's need to be adjusted. However, unlike Cheong's algorithm, the VGN's are not simply incremented. Instead a variable's VGN after it is updated is assigned to the number of the next generation in which that variable *may* be written. Intuitively the VGN of a variable denotes the last generation at which the current value of that variable is guaranteed to be up to date. In this example, because a is next written in the third generation, a's VGN becomes 3 at the end of the first generation. Similarly the VGN's of b, c, and d become 2, 4, and 3, respectively. Because e is not modified in the first generation, its VGN remains unchanged. Following the same reasoning, one can deduce that the VGN's of a, b, c, d, and e are <3,3,4,3,4> and <5,5,4,4,4> at the ends of the second and third

167

Generation	Tasks	Modified Variables
1	T1, T2	a, b, c, d
2	T3	b, e
3	T4, T5, T6	a, b, d
4	T7, T8	c, d, e
5	T9	a, b
6	END	

Figure 5(a)   An Example Task Graph and Its Modified Variable Sets

Variable \ Generation	a	b	c	d	e
0	0	0	0	0	0
1	3	2	4	3	0
2	3	3	4	3	4
3	5	5	4	4	4
4	5	5	6	6	6
5	6	6	6	6	6

Figure 5(b)   Assignment of Valid Generation Numbers for Modified Variables in Figure 5(a)

generations, respectively, as shown in Figure 5(b).

When a program accesses a shared data variable, the system concatenates the current generation number with the memory address to form the cache access address. A cache access is a hit if the memory address matches a tag and VGN ≥ CGN. Essentially the current generation number replaces the current version numbers in Cheong's algorithm and is shared by all data variables in the programs. If, for instance, the write to a in the third generation is preceded by a read to a, and the node assigned to do this is the same one that writes to a in the first generation, then the read access is a cache hit because a's VGN is equal to the current generation number. However, if these two writes are performed by different nodes, the read access will be a cache miss.

3.2. The Algorithm

More formally, the generational cache coherence algorithm works as follows. Given a task execution graph as explained in Section One, the compiler levelizes the graph and assigns a generation number to each level. Tasks at a level use the level's generation number as their current generation number (CGN). When a task is dispatched to a node, the task's generation number is loaded into the node's current generation number register. For each variable modified at a particular level, the last write to the variable at that level entails an update of the variable's valid generation number (VGN) in the cache. After a variable is updated, its VGN becomes the generation number of the level at which the next write to that variable may take place. A read access to the cache memory is a hit if the memory address matches the tag and the cache line's VGN is greater than or equal to the node's CGN. A write

access to the cache memory is a hit if the memory address matches the tag.

In the case of a cache miss, the requested cache line is either brought from the main memory or from another CPU. If it is from main memory, then the cache line's VGN is assigned the node's CGN; if from another CPU, then both the cache line and its VGN are copied. When a cache line is replaced, only the data is written back to main memory, but not its VGN. Although this decision could degrade the effectiveness of data caching, there are two reasons for not maintaining VGN's in main memory. First, maintaining VGN's in main memory could significantly increase the hardware requirements of main memory directories because every cache line now needs an extra field for its VGN. Second, by keeping main memory directories as stateless as possible, it is easier to handle VGN overflow as will be explained in the next section. Since a task's generation number is determined at compile time, there is no need to update CGN's. Moreover, since all variables share a CGN at any point in program execution, the hardware overhead for maintaining each individual variable's current generation number is avoided. Only a current generation number register is needed for each node.

Note that the generational algorithm *doesn't* require more data-flow knowledge than Cheong's algorithm. They both require that the set of potential modified variables at each level be known at compile time. For Cheong's algorithm, this knowledge is needed to insert CVN update instructions into the tasks. For our algorithm, it is needed to update the VGN's of the modified variables.

3.3. Discussion

Because our algorithm doesn't need a variable ID table in each node, the problem of finite ID tables and the overhead of updating CGN's are eliminated automatically. However, for a given word size, presumably it is easier for generation numbers than for version numbers in Cheong's algorithm to overflow. This is because the dynamic range of a generation number is dependent on the update frequencies of a program's *all* variables while that of a version number depends on the update frequency of *one* variable. As a result, the word size of generation numbers needs to be larger than version numbers, which in turn implies larger cache tags. On the other hand, because only a single generation number is used for all variables of the tasks at a particular level, it becomes feasible to manage the generation numbers at compile time, which will be discussed in the next section.

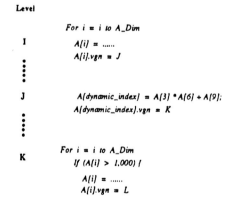

Figure 6   An Example of VGN Update

Most of the performance problems associated with Cheong's algorithm are eliminated by our generational algorithm. We discuss each of them in detail next. First, since all variables share a current generation number, this algorithm doesn't need to pay the overhead of updating individual variable's CGN. Second, this algorithm can exploit the Doacross loop parallelism without extra mechanisms. Consider a Doacross loop as shown in Figure 3, with each iteration flow-dependent on its preceding one except the first one. Let's further assume that the first iteration is assigned the generation number 1, and the second iteration the generation number 2, and so on. At run time, the dispatcher can dispatch as many iterations of this loop as the number of nodes in the system. With proper synchronization, the first read access from Iteration I+1 to the shared variable written in Iteration I will cause a cache miss. The reason is that the shared variable, A[I], if previously cached in the node assigned to run Iteration I+1, should have a VGN equal to I, the generation number of the I-th iteration. But the current generation number register holds I+1, therefore a cache miss occurs. By assigning CGN's to the tasks at compile time, the generational algorithm can exploit parallelism beyond Doall loops without run-time inter-processor communication.

The problem of over-invalidation in Cheong's algorithm can also be solved by the generational algorithm *without* extra hardware. Consider Figure 6, which is similar to Figure 4 except that it is augmented with instructions to update the VGN's of the shared variables. Again A is modified at Level I, J, and K, and K > J > I. At level J, only one element of A is modified but its index is not known at compile time. At the time of the last updates to the array elements of A at Level I, the VGN's of these array elements, in theory, should be J, as shown in Figure 6. However, it is possible to change the VGN's to K and insert the following instruction to the tasks at level I after the update of A[i]'s.

> If (i == dynamic_index)
>   A[i].vgn = J
> else
>   A[i].vgn = K

Note that the compiler doesn't need to know which A's element it is. By moving the VGN's from J to K, more temporal locality in the programs could be exploited. For example, if there are read accesses to A's other elements than *dynamic_index* at Level J+1, they may well hit on the cache because their VGN's are K rather than J.

Similarly, in the case of Level K, where the value of A's element determines whether it should be modified, in this case, the element's value must be greater than 1000. Then the VGN's of A's array elements could still be K at the end of Level I if the following instruction is inserted to the tasks at level I.

> If (i == dynamic_index)
>   A[i].vgn = J
> else If (A[i] > 1000)
>   A[i].vgn = K
>   else
>   A[i].vgn = L

where L is the next generation in which A is modified. Again the compiler doesn't need to acquire extra data-flow knowledge; only a simple form of source-code replication, perhaps with the help of control-flow analysis, is needed to take advantage of a program's temporal locality.

Just as the version-controlled scheme needs to increment BVN's, the generational scheme needs to update VGN's. However, there is a difference. Unless there is a special hardware support, incrementing BVN's requires a read-modify-write instruction sequence, whereas updating VGN's only requires a single write. In addition, since all shared variables use a generational numbering system, elements of an aggregate data structure, e.g., an array, can have different VGN's simultaneously. In other words, unlike the version-controlled scheme, the granularity of cache coherence is decoupled from high-level data structures in the program. This allows a more aggressive exploitation of cache locality.

4. Conclusion

In this paper, we have describe the performance and implementation problems of the by far most aggressive software-controlled cache coherence scheme, version-controlled [CHEO89] and time-stamped [MIN89]. A closer examination of the problems reveals that they are all rooted in the fact that every shared data variable is assigned a separate version number. Based on this observation, we propose a generational algorithm that imposes a uniform version numbering scheme upon the shared data variables of a parallel program. Because of this unified version numbering, most of the hardware cost and performance overhead associated with Cheong's algorithm are eliminated. Moreover, the generational algorithm can exploit the Doacross loop parallelism and can maintain consistency at the granularity of individual array elements without extra hardware costs, thus achieving a better performance over Cheong's algorithm.

Due to space constraints, we didn't report on a new generation number management algorithm and its architectural support [CHIU93]. This algorithm successfully handles the finiteness problem of generation numbers by combining a special generation encoding scheme and a fast reset hardware. Both [CHEO89] and [MIN89] failed to address this issue. Consequently they have to assume a large version number field in each cache line, or to pay a serious performance penalty due to a system-wide invalidation when version numbers overflow.

Because the proposed scheme involves compile-time transformation, a trace-driven simulation study won't provide a meaningful performance evaluation. Currently we are developing a cycle-by-cycle MIMD machine simulator based on the R2000/3000 architecture, which incorporates the hardware features described above, and a parallel compiler that can exploit program parallelism and perform affinity scheduling, as well as manage cache consistency. With these tools in place, we can start to evaluate the performance of the generational algorithm and compare with other hardware/software cache consistency techniques.

REFERENCE

[CHIU93]   T. Chiueh, "A Generational Approach to Software-Controlled Cache Coherence," Technical Report, Computer Science Department, SUNY at Stony Brook, 1993.

[CHEO89] H. Cheong, *Compiler-Directed Cache Coherence Strategies for Large-Scale Shared Memory Multiprocessor Systems*, UILU-ENG-89-8018, CSRD Report No. 953, Ph.D. Thesis, Center for Supercomputing Research and Development, University of Illinois, Urbana-Champaign, December 1989.

[EGGE89] S. Eggers, *Simulation Analysis of Data Sharing in Shared-Memory Multiprocessors*, Report No. UCB/CSD 89/501, Ph.D. Thesis, Computer Science Division (EECS), University of California, Berkeley, April 1989.

[MIN 89]   S. Min, *Memory Hierarchy Management Schemes in Large-Scale Shared-Memory Multiprocessors*, TR 89-08-07, Ph.D. Thesis, Department of Computer Science and Engineering, University of Washington, Seattle, August 1989.

[MIN 89]   S. Min, J. Baer, H. Kim, "An Efficient Caching Support for Critical Sections in Large-Scale Shared-Memory Multiprocessors," IBM RC 15311, 1/4/90, IBM Research Division, T.J. Watson.

Cache Coherence Using Local Knowledge *

Ervan Darnell [†]   Ken Kennedy

Computer Science Department, Rice University, Houston, TX 77251-1892

Abstract

Typically, commercially available shared memory machines have addressed the cache coherence problem with hardware strategies based on global inter-cache communication. However, global communication limits scalability and efficiency.

"Local knowledge" coherence strategies, which avoid global communication at run-time, offer better scalability, at the cost of some additional cache misses. The most effective local knowledge strategies described in the literature are those based on generation timestamps (TS).

We propose a new strategy, TS1, that requires less extra storage than TS, only one extra bit per cache line, and can produce more cache hits by exploiting sophisticated compiler analysis. TS1 handles common synchronization paradigms including DOALL, DOACROSS, and critical sections.

Early results show TS1 is, worst case, slightly slower than TS. Best case, TS1's flexibility allows for significant improvements.

1 Introduction

Data race free programs executing on a shared memory multiprocessor are expected to have the same semantics as if they were executing on a sequential processor. For this to be the case, memory must appear sequentially consistent [10]. Caches on shared memory multiprocessors must have some global knowledge about executing programs otherwise they could fail to preserve sequential consistency by retaining stale values.

Most approaches to the cache coherence problem have focused on hardware mechanisms to maintain coherence. Unfortunately, the overhead of maintaining coherence in hardware can be high; scaling systems based on hardware coherence is a difficult problem [15]. Snoopy cache strategies, which monitor some common bus, are now in common use for small scale systems [16, 18]; however, snoopy strategies are problematic for large-scale machines because such machines cannot be based on a single, central broadcast medium for lack of sufficient bandwidth. Directory strategies [2, 8, 11, 19], in which a directory entry associated with each memory location (or cache line) indicates which processors have cached values for that location, seem more promising for large-scale systems. However, directories can require large amounts of additional storage and directory maintenance operations may substantially increase network traffic.

As an alternative to using a hardware mechanism that supports global communication between caches, a compiler could perform global analysis and augment the code with cache control directives to maintain coherence. This approach does not hinder the scalability of the machine. However, since compiler analysis must be conservative, some valid values will be unnecessarily removed from cache with this approach, thus reducing hit rates.

In this paper, we propose a local knowledge only coherence strategy, TS1 (Time Stamping with 1 bit), that, for a particular granularity of compiler analysis, achieves the best hit rate that any such strategy can at a cost of one additional bit per cache line, sufficient logic to set, reset, or copy this bit to the *valid* bit, and a fast invalidate. We compare TS1 to previous local knowledge only coherence strategies. We show that time-stamping and TS1 achieve the same effect with naive compiler support but that TS1 can more readily utilize improved compiler analysis.

Section 2 provides an overview of some of the terminology we use. Section 3 discusses some of the better previous local strategies. Section 3.5 shows that time stamping strategies provide optimal hit ratios for a given granularity of compiler analysis. Section 4 describes our new strategy for achieving the same effect as time-stamping at lower hardware cost. It also discusses the impact of the accuracy of compiler analysis. Section 5 gives some preliminary results comparing TS and TS1. Section 6 discusses extensions to other types of synchronization. Section 7 concludes and discusses possible future directions.

*This work was supported in part by the National Science Foundation under Cooperative Agreement CCR-9120008 through its research contracts with the Center for Research on Parallel Computation at Rice University.

[†] corresponding author: ervan@cs.rice.edu

```
DOALL I
   A(I)=...        A(2) write allocated on processor 2
ENDDO

DOALL I
   A(I+1)=...      A(2) write allocated on processor 1
ENDDO

DOALL I
   B(I)=A(I)+1     Access stale A(2) on processor 2
ENDDO
```

Figure 1: Example of stale access in the absence of coherence control

2 Definitions and framework

Fork-join programs are composed of a series of *epochs*[4]. Each *epoch* consists of one or more *instances* which run in parallel. Each epoch is either a (fork-join) parallel loop with no internal synchronization, e.g. a Fortran DOALL, or a serial region between parallel loops. Serial regions can be nested serial loops and/or those parts of serial loops enclosing parallel loops. A serial region is an *epoch* with one *instance*.

The instances (iterations) of a parallel loop are scheduled on processors at run time. The compiler must assume that a given instance could be executed on any processor. All coherence strategies known to us make this assumption. If scheduling is known at compile time, a different set issues arises and different techniques are applicable.

We regard non-unit cache line size aliasing as an orthogonal problem. Our discussion assumes that the cache line size is one word.

Staleness occurs when a location is accessed on processor p_i, written subsequently on processor $p_j, j \neq i$, and read again still later on processor p_i (without its cache being updated to reflect the new value). For example, in figure 1, if processor p_i gets iteration i, the reference to A(2) in the last epoch would be stale (without coherence). Any additional references that happen between the first and second epochs will not change the situation. If A(2) were written on p_i between the second and third epochs (not shown in the figure) it would again be valid (on p_i) without coherence control.

Numerous previous authors have tried to capture this notion in various analytical ways [4, 6, 9]. Here we simply note the dynamic behavior that causes staleness without addressing its detection at compile time.

Coherence is maintained by making sure that values are communicated between caches when necessary. Values are updated from cache to main memory either by using write-thru cache or write-back cache trigged by synchronization events. Values are moved from main memory to cache on demand when they are not found in the cache. Stale values are removed from caches at the correct time so that subsequent reads will load the new values. This removal may be done by anything from explicit operating system calls that the compiler inserts to the hardware failing to register a hit because of some combination of bits.

2.1 Semantics of fork-join

The semantics of fork-join, e.g. DOALL, parallelism is that the fork-join loop be data race free; there can be no carried dependence, i.e. a value cannot be written in one instance (iteration) and read on another within the same epoch (DOALL).

A value can be read on several processors in the same epoch so long as none write it. The lack of carried dependence might be proven by the compiler or asserted by the programmer. In either case, it has the following important implication: If a value, x, is accessed in epoch e on p_i it will be coherent in epoch $e + 1$ on p_i without any coherence control or communication with main memory. This is true because x being accessed on p_i during e means that it could not have been written on p_j during e. By the definition of staleness, x is still coherent in epoch $e + 1$ on p_i.

The same value being read on different processors during epoch e does not present a problem because it cannot be written on any processor during epoch e. These properties are trivially preserved by serial regions.

2.2 Local versus global knowledge

To avoid staleness, each cache must account for what is written by every processor, including those to which it is not directly connected. This set of writes can be exactly the locations written or any approximating superset. If this global knowledge of what is written is shared at run time, we would characterize it as a *global strategy*. Global strategies are usually thought of as hardware strategies, e.g. snoopy caches [16, 18] and directory based caches [2, 11, 19]. Other global strategies, e.g. OS level page strategies [17], are software strategies.

Cache misses have four causes: initial loading, cache size, cache organization (e.g. associativity), and invalidation to preserve coherence between processors (sharing induced). Coherence strategies are concerned only with the last category, sharing induced misses. No currently existing global strategy causes a logically unnecessary sharing miss. They are in that sense optimal. The drawback of global strategies is the that scalability is impaired by the cost of maintaining global knowledge at run time.

If no global knowledge is shared at run time, then coherence must rely on locally collected knowledge plus whatever global knowledge was collected at compile time. Previous local knowledge strategies have been referred to in the literature as software [4, 6] or hardware [14] strategies depending on whether *most* of the work was done in software or hardware. We consider all of these strategies to be similar and refer to them collectively as *local strategies*.

A local strategy will likely never result in a globally optimal hit ratio for a processor because some useful runtime knowledge will be unavailable. The effectiveness of local strategies can vary widely depending on the program being run and the strategy being used. The principal advantage of local strategies is that they are scalable because no global knowledge need be com-

```
DOALL I=1,N
   A(I)=...
ENDDO

DOALL I=1,N
   IF (c1) A(I+1)=...
ENDDO

DOALL I=1,N
   B(I)=A(I)+1
ENDDO
```

Figure 2: Global versus Local coherence

```
DOALL I=1,N
   A(I)=...
ENDDO

DOALL I=1,N
   A(I)=A(I)+...
ENDDO

DOALL I=1,N
   B(I)=A(I)+1
ENDDO
```

Figure 3: Dynamic versus static coherence

municated at run time to maintain coherence. They rely on what *could* happen not what *does*. We use *could* happen to mean that the compiler cannot disprove it.

The fundamental limitation of local strategies is that if an *instance* (task) could write a value (and it cannot be determined for certain at compile time), other *instances* must assume that it has. A task need make no assumptions about what it itself does because sufficient marking bits can be used locally to make whatever determinations are useful regardless of the incompleteness of compiler analysis.

Figure 2 gives an example of where a local strategy would fail to achieve the same hit ratio as a global strategy. If condition c1 is always false (for a given execution) but is not analyzable by the compiler, all potential reuse of cached values of A between the first and third epochs will be lost using a local strategy but preserved using a global strategy.

2.3 Dynamic versus static coherence

Local strategies are either static or dynamic. Static local strategies decide which cache lines to invalidate and when that invalidation should occur, using only compile time knowledge. In contrast, dynamic strategies can use run time information as well; which data actually gets invalidated depends on the actual execution path of the program. This comes in two forms, knowing (part of) the processor schedule and intra-instance control flow. Dynamic strategies take advantage of reuse that exists only because of a particular run time schedule. Static strategies must assume worst case scheduling (though they can still exploit some inter epoch reuse).

Dynamic strategies strictly improve on static strategies. Any static strategy can be changed to a dynamic strategy that will not cause any more sharing misses and will usually do much better. The trade-off is that dynamic strategies require some additional hardware support to handle marking bits. Static strategies require no hardware support other than the ability to invalidate cache lines under software control. Static strategies can be used on some existing machines, such as the BBN TC2000[6, 7].

Figure 3 shows an example for which static strategies are inherently inefficient. The value of A written

in the first epoch cannot be allowed to reach the third epoch. Since the second epoch (with the write) *might* have a different schedule than the first, an invalidate must remove the value from cache that was loaded in the first epoch. This will cause either the read in the second epoch or the third epoch to miss (depending on where the invalidate occurs). But if the schedules for all epochs are actually the same at run time this would be unnecessary. A dynamic strategy could recognize this and preserve reuse in both the second and third epochs.

3 Previous approaches

We briefly survey some previous local strategies in order to give credit to previous authors in this area and to show what improvement TS1 makes. Knowing the different approaches helps for understanding the core issues of local strategies and not being distracted by often disparate implementation approaches. Those aspects of previous strategies not directly concerned with coherence are covered in section 6.3.

3.1 Fast Selective Invalidation

One of the first strategies was Fast Selective Invalidate (FSI) [4]. FSI determines at compile time which references access shared variables that might have been previously written. These are designated *memory reads*. For *memory reads* to be cache hits they must be found in the cache and have a special *epoch* bit set (originally called a change bit). Accesses to shared variables set the *epoch* bit. All of the *epoch* bits are reset at every epoch boundary. With this strategy, no shared value crosses an epoch boundary in cache, ensuring that caches are coherent. The penalty is that no inter-epoch reuse is preserved for shared variables. FSI is a static strategy.

3.2 Life Span Strategy

Life Span Strategy (LSS) [3] is an improvement over FSI. Instead of resetting the *epoch* bit after every epoch, the *epoch* bit for a given cache line is reset after the end of the next epoch. This is implemented with an extra bit in each line, the stale bit, that marks the passage of one epoch boundary. Thus any referenced value is preserved into next epoch. This is valid by DOALL semantics as previously noted (section 2.1). LSS is a dynamic strategy.

The LSS paper describes an extension to preserve a value in cache for any fixed number of epochs. The number of epochs it survives must be determined at compile time. Its maximum value is the shortest path (in number of epochs) that could be taken before another write. The actual path between writes at run time could be much longer. The count is stored in unary so that updating the count can be done with a shift and checking for validity can be done by examining the last bit. Values which are not referenced will eventually be removed from cache. If, in practice, values stay in cache for only a few epochs due to cache size limitations, a small number of bits can be used for the extended LSS at no great cost. Additional bits would not help because the values would already be evicted before the count runs out.

3.3 Parallel Explicit Invalidation

Parallel Explicit Invalidation (PEI) [12] works by combining an invalidate with each write instruction. Writing an element in an array invalidates everything in the array except for the element itself. This achieves coherence because anything written on a different processor will be removed from the cache of this processor before the next epoch (sufficient dummy writes are added to make sure this invariant is maintained in the presence of uncertain control flow and serial epochs). The PEI strategy preserves inter-epoch reuse by leaving the value written on this processor in cache. PEI is a dynamic strategy.

The implementation uses a bit mask to control the region invalidated. This requires that write instructions have enough additional bits to contain the mask. It does, however, allow for essentially constant time invalidation. It also allows for many special cases to be handled with more precision (assuming the compiler analysis is sufficient). In some instances, it can improve on the hit ratio time-stamping would achieve. However, in general, it fails to preserve intra-epoch reuse when there are multiple references to the same array in one instance. Those values that are lost to intra-epoch reuse are also lost to inter-epoch reuse. The use of an *epoch* bit alone would not suffice to prevent this. For PEI to achieve good results, arrays, or in the worst case, each dimension of an array, must occupy an amount of memory equal to a power of two.

3.4 Time Stamping

Time stamping (TS) strategies [4, 14] are more effective at preserving reuse than any of the previously mentioned strategies. For a given quality of compiler analysis, it is impossible to achieve a better hit ratio with any other local strategy. The trade-off is that they require several extra bits per cache line, extra bits per memory access instruction, several extra counters per processor, and extra logic in the cache controller. Time stamping is a dynamic strategy.

In time stamping, there is a counter (referred to as a clock) for each array which tracks the number of epochs in which the array was possibly written. Each processor has a copy of all of the clocks. At the *end* of an epoch, each processor increments its clocks for each array that might have been written during that epoch on *any* processor. This requires no global communication. The clock value for an array represents the last epoch where the array could have been written.

Each cache line has a time stamp. When a value is accessed, its time stamp is set to what the current clock value for its array will be in the next epoch. Example, if the current clock value for array A is 5, a write to A(1) is loaded into cache with a time stamp of 6 because the clock will be incremented at the end of this epoch. A read of A(1) in a loop with no write would set the time stamp to 5 because the clock will not be incremented at the end of the epoch.

A value becomes stale when its time stamp is less than the corresponding clock. If the time stamp equals the clock value, there has been no write since the last access to the cache line. By DOALL semantics (section 2.1) this also holds for the epoch where the value is written. For an epoch after a write, the cache line will contain its prior time stamp value, but the clock will have been incremented. The cache hardware will find that time stamp < clock, conclude the value is stale, and issue a miss.

Both previous time stamping strategies operate on the whole array level. This is not necessary. It would be possible for time stamping to operate on the section level. However, it would require a separate clock for each section of each array. This would not only require extra clocks but extra bits in the instruction word to specify which clock was relevant.

There is a peculiar limitation to TS. The clocks can overflow. When that happens all cache lines which depend on that clock must be invalidated. This is the same problem extended LSS suffers. Time stamping uses binary counters and the impact is much less. Time stamping ages its cache lines by incrementing clocks on the processor while leaving the cache lines unchanged. Extended LSS ages its cache lines by decrementing counters in the cache line. This distinction will prove useful as explained in section 4.

3.5 A unified view of previous approaches

Despite very different implementations, all of these approaches are variants of the same essential strategy. During epoch e_w location x (some array element) is written on processor p_j; at the end of epoch e_w, processor $p_i, j \neq i$, invalidates location x in its cache. Processor p_i might not know exactly what location x is. It approximates with the smallest set of locations sure to contain x.

FSI and LSS make the pessimistic assumption that x could be anywhere. TS assumes all of the array which x is in could have been written. PEI uses the best available compiler analysis, which is at least as good as the same array analysis of TS. Extended

173

LSS also uses the best available analysis to determine where x could be, but it unions the results over all paths causing it to invalidate more. TS and PEI are concerned only with the run time (inter epoch) path and are in this respect superior to extended LSS.

Dynamic and static strategies both must make the same estimate about how large the set is that encompasses x. Static schemes must also estimate the processor schedule, which means they must assume the worst case. Dynamic schemes, however, know part of the schedule, the part that occurs on the local processor. If x is accessed on p_i in epoch e_w, a dynamic scheme knows that p_j never actually wrote x (section 2.1) regardless of the compile time analysis. It can then avoid the invalidation of x. LSS, TS, and PEI all take advantage of this.

After the end of epoch e_w, if x was not referenced on p_i during e_w, p_i has no run time information about x and it must rely entirely on the compiler's analysis for whether or not p_j might write x in e_w. If the compiler then indicates that p_j appears to write x, a local strategy must invalidate x on p_i before the next read of x on p_i (if the next reference to x on p_i is a write, then it does not matter whether or not x was invalidated). If a strategy invalidates *only* when these two conditions are met (x not referenced on p_i and apparently written on p_j), it is optimal in the sense that no local strategy, with the same granularity of compiler analysis, could have a better hit rate. This is how time-stamping behaves. It is an optimal local strategy. PEI is not optimal because it invalidates before it knows that x is not referenced on p_i. LSS is optimal only in the trivial sense that it uses a know-nothing compiler.

In practice, this utilization of DOALL semantics can make a dramatic difference because it captures reuse when subsequent loops have the same schedule and same reference pattern, for instance a DOALL inside of a serial loop will likely meet this condition. Deliberate attempts to increase loop affinity [13] will further improve the benefit of dynamic strategies.

4 One-Bit Time Stamping

Even though both proposed time-stamping strategies [4, 14] are hit-rate optimal local strategies, they require substantial additional hardware. TS1 achieves the same optimal hit ratio with fewer special bits per cache line and no special bits per instruction word. It also avoids the need for special hardware to load and compare the proper time stamp in a cache line. But, it does require a more sophisticated invalidate.

4.1 Hardware support

TS1 requires a *valid* bit per cache line and an additional bit, the *epoch* bit. In TS1, caches set the *epoch* bit on any reference to that line (read, write, hit, or miss). At the end of a given epoch, e, a special instruction resets the *epoch* bit for every line in the cache. We assume that the cache implementation can do this in

$O(1)$ time by having every cache line respond in parallel. Since all of the *epoch* bits were reset on entry to epoch e from the end of epoch $e-1$, the *epoch* bit reflects which cache lines have been accessed during epoch e.

By the assumed semantics of DOALL loops (section 2.1), any cache line with its *epoch* bit set in epoch e can be left in cache for epoch $e+1$ without causing a stale access. We use this observation in defining a special *invalidate* that operates optimistically. When a particular cache line is the object of an invalidate, it is actually invalidated only if the *epoch* bit is reset, otherwise it remains valid and in cache, i.e. the invalidate copies the *epoch* bit to the *valid* bit.

4.2 Implementation of the invalidate

There are several choices for the actual implementation of the invalidate that trade-off hardware cost for run time efficiency.

A slow but inexpensive implementation would be to have a low level invalidate instruction which could invalidate either a particular line or a particular page. The high level invalidate would then loop over the proper range of pages and lines. Even though this would take $O(|section|)$, acceptable performance could still be achieved. Previously, we examined the efficiency of this kind of invalidate for a static strategy [7].

A faster, but more complex, invalidate could work by using a bit mask to determine which addresses to invalidate. With only '=' comparators and no extra storage, a section could be invalidated in $O(\log(|section|))$ time. Special layouts and strides could reduce this further. This is similar to what PEI does.

Other authors have proposed $O(1)$ time invalidation implementations which work by accessing cache row and column addresses [1].

4.3 Software support

To determine what to invalidate, TS1 uses compile time analysis to determine what is written for each epoch. The compiler makes its best estimate that is sure to include every address actually written. The main task of this analysis is to determine which parts of shared arrays are written. A naive analysis could simply note which arrays appear on the left hand side of an assignment and then conclude that every element of any such array is modified. More sophisticated analysis could try to determine which sections of arrays are actually modified. For every section (or whole array) that is modified, the compiler inserts an invalidate for that range of addresses at the end of the epoch being analyzed. Since schedules are not known, the same set of invalidates is used for every processor.

At run time, for each epoch, some accesses occur, setting the *epoch* bits, then the invalidates are executed as the next to last instruction, removing soon to be stale values, and finally all of the *epoch* bits are reset in preparation for the next epoch.

For a value, x, to be stale for epoch e_r on processor

Operation	Applies to	Bit Assignments	
		Valid Bit	*Epoch* Bit
Read	word	1	1
Write	word	1	1
Invalidate	section	*Epoch* Bit	-
end of epoch	all of cache	-	0

Table 1: Effect of operations on TS1 control bits

State	TS	TS1	
	Time Stamp	Epoch Bit	Valid Bit
just accessed	= clock[+1]	= 1	= 1
not yet stale	= clock	= 0	= 1
stale	< clock	= 0	= 0

Table 2: Possible 'ages' of a cache line

p_i, it must have been written during epoch $e_w, e_w < e_r$ on $p_j, j \neq i$ and have been in p_i's cache on epoch $e_w - 1$. TS1 prevents staleness because x would appear in an invalidate on p_i at the end of epoch e_w. The value in cache in epoch $e_w - 1$ would be removed since p_i did not access x on epoch e_w and left its epoch reset from the end of epoch $e_w - 1$.

If compile time analysis were perfect, TS1 would have the same hit rate as a global scheme. The conservative assumptions that must be made at compile time cause some reuse to be missed. This is the loss that any local scheme must suffer.

4.4 Contrast between TS1 and previous strategies

The best way to understand why TS1 and TS have the same behavior is to return to TS and see it from a different point of view. There are only three states that a cache line can be in with respect to its clock, *just referenced*, *not yet stale*, and *stale* (Table 2). Taking these in reverse order, the *stale* state indicates that for a value x in epoch $e_w + 1$ a new value might have been written in epoch, e_w, after x was loaded in the cache in an earlier epoch, e_a. The *not yet stale* state persists from *after* epoch e_a when x was last accessed *through* epoch e_w which actually makes the line stale (DOALL semantics, section 2.1). The *just accessed* state sets the time stamp so that it will be in the *not yet stale* state in the next epoch. The *just accessed* state persists only for epoch e_a. The time stamp will be either clock+1 or clock depending on whether or not there is a write in epoch e_a.

TS1 implements these same three states by using the *epoch* bit in addition to the *valid* bit. This economy is possible because TS1 invalidates only those locations which could have been written. TS1 ages cache lines explicitly by updating bits in the cache line. TS ages cache lines implicitly by updating a processor clock for later comparison. TS is a lazy strategy.

TS as proposed enforces coherence on the whole array level. TS1 can be used to enforce coherence at the finest available resolution of compiler analysis. This is no worse than the whole array level and often better. TS could in principle do this well too by having a distinct clock for every section of an array which can be recognized at compile time. The cost of that could grow large.

LSS could utilize the same high level of analysis but it makes the pessimistic assumption that all paths are taken. Also, its counters quickly overrun regardless of the path taken. TS1 achieves at least the same hit rate as PEI because both can use the best available compiler analysis.

Another way to view this distinction of different strategies is the manner in which global information is passed. In FSI and LSS, global knowledge is never passed. In TS, global knowledge is passed implicitly by each processor incrementing an array clock for those arrays which might have been modified. In TS1 and PEI, global knowledge is passed implicitly by invalidating a section of memory that could have been written on a different processor. For local strategies, there is no way to avoid the invalidate because it is responsible for conveying the global information. The invalidate can be implicit, explicit, pessimistic, or reasonably precise, but it still has the same function. Table 3 summarizes the costs and capabilities of the different strategies.

4.5 Example

In figure 4, DOALLs are expanded into the worksharing part (PDO) where each processor gets some number of iterations, the common part that all processors execute, and the BARRIER, which is the end of the DOALL. Applying the TS1 compile time phase inserts the *INVALIDATE*'s. For each of the three DOALL epochs, there is an invalidate to cover what was written in that epoch. Table 4 shows the effect on TS1 control bits for the simple schedule, processor 1 gets iteration 1 on each epoch. At line 11, A(1) and B(1,*) have been referenced on p_1 in this epoch. So all cache lines holding these values are valid and have the *epoch* bit set. At line 12, the invalidate removes everything written on p_2 from p_1's cache. If B(2,1) were present on p_1 it would be removed at this point. B(1,1) however has its *epoch* bit set and stays in the cache on p_1. All *epoch* bits are reset at the barrier. At line 21 only B(1,1) has its *epoch* bit set on p_1 since it was the only reference. The invalidate does not reference A or columns of B other than the first. So, all of those stay in cache. The invalidate of B(1,1) finds the *epoch* bit set and leaves it in cache. At line 30, all references are then hits.

Using the same example for TS, the write to B in the second epoch would cause all columns of B to be invalidated. Thus, in the third epoch, all but one element of B would be a miss on p_1.

For LSS, A would suffer the same as the other columns of B and would miss in the third epoch.

For PEI, the second epoch would be handled perfectly by only invalidating the first column of B. How-

	FSI	LSS	PEI	TS	TS1
Inter Epoch Reuse	No	Yes	Yes	Yes	Yes
Granularity of analysis	N/A	whole program	array section	array	array section
bits/cache line	2	3	0	$2 + n_{clock}$	1
bits/instruction	1	2	n	$5 + r_{clock}$ (for reads) $2 + r_{clock}$ (for writes)	0
special bits/processor	0	0	0	$s * n_{clock}$	0
cost of invalidate	O(1)	O(1)	O(1)	O(S)	$O(\sum_{i=1}^{S} \log(s_i))$
handles DOACROSS	No	No	No	Yes	Yes

Notation

n	number of address bits
n_{clock}	number of bits needed to hold clock value
r_{clock}	number of bits to designate a clock
S	number of distinct sections (or arrays) which are written in an epoch
s_i	size of the ith section out of S total sections

Table 3: Comparison of methods

```
      PDO I=1,N
         DO J=1,N
            B(I,J)=A(I)+1
         ENDDO
      ENDDO
11
      CALL INVALIDATE (B(1,1),B(N,N))
      BARRIER
12
      PDO I=1,N
         B(I,1)=0
      ENDDO
21
      CALL INVALIDATE (B(1,1),B(N,1))
      BARRIER
22
      PDO I=1,N
         DO J=1,N
30          C(I,J)=B(I,J)+A(I)
         ENDDO
      ENDDO
      CALL INVALIDATE (C(1,1),C(N,N))
```

Figure 4: Example compiler output for TS1

	Array Element on Processor 1		
Statement	A(1)	B(1,1)	B(1,2)
11	1 , 1	1 , 1	1 , 1
12	1 , 0	1 , 0	1 , 0
21	1 , 0	1 , 1	1 , 0
22	1 , 0	1 , 0	1 , 0
30	hit	hit	hit

Table 4: Example of bit handling in TS1, Entries valid bit, epoch bit

ever, the first epoch would leave only the last column in cache. In the third epoch, the first and last column of B plus all of A would hit. The rest of B would miss.

5 Performance

The execution time of TS versus TS1 depends on two factors, the hit rate and the additional cycles used by a more sophisticated invalidate. We present experimental data on the former. We analyze the latter using reference traces from a real program combined with a hypothetical implementation of an invalidate

We compared TS and TS1 on a small test suite of scientific Fortran programs. These were chosen because they were available, familiar to the authors, and easily convertible to use with simulator. Our methodology was to apply the TS and TS1 algorithms by hand to parallel Fortran programs. For TS1, the same invalidate calls were added at the end of each epoch as the compiler would have produced. We assumed the compiler could recognize only affine subscript expressions. For TS, invalidate calls were applied to whole arrays in an epoch for which the array appeared on the left hand side of an assignment. This has the same effect on hit rate as the suggested TS implementation. These modified programs were then run through the the RPPT [5] simulator. This simulator operates by modifying the assembly code to trap at every global memory reference which is then passed off to a particular architecture simulator.

For identical runs of the test programs, we compared TS, TS1, and hardware coherence. For hardware coherence, we simulated write back caches with an invalidate protocol (WB).

Cyclic work distributions were used. Statistics reflect only shared data and not local data or instruction caching. Caches of sufficient size were simulated

	Procs	Size	TS	TS1	WB
LU	10	100	88.7	89.8	90.8
Heat Flow	20	60	62.6	63.5	63.5
Direct	4	4	97.1	97.1	97.7
Erlebacher	10	20	96.0	97.2	97.6

Table 5: Hit Ratios (%) for different strategies

so that no evictions occurred due to cache size or organization limitations.

Our test programs were:

LU decomposition - a blocked right looking LU decomposition with a blocking factor of 5.

Heat Flow - a simple 2-D heat flow relaxation

Direct - a simplex solver

Erlebacher - a tridiagonal solver for finding derivatives

5.1 Hit rates

Table 5 shows the hit rates for our test suite. Similar relative hit ratios resulted from different combinations of processor and block sizes, except for extreme cases. For larger problem sizes with evictions, the gap narrows.

In both LU and Heat Flow, TS1 managed to find extra hits by not invalidating the whole array in loops that set border elements of the (sub-)arrays. Direct made heavy use of indirection arrays which defeat all attempts at analysis. TS1 could do no better than TS in this case. For Erlebacher, TS1 was able to find substantial benefit because the main computation was distributed through several loops, many of which only modified a small section of a given array.

5.2 Invalidate overhead

Erlebacher is more than a computational kernel (so is Direct, but it showed no improvement). So, we focus on Erlebacher.

To better analyze this case, we looked more carefully at the *miss margin*, the number of extra misses per processor that TS suffers compared to TS1. For a fixed problem size, TS1 does worse as the number of processors increase because the total hit rate is only slightly affected causing the number of misses per processor to drop almost linearly. For a fixed number of processors, TS1 is favored by the same reasoning (for all but the simplest of invalidate implementations). Most importantly, as main memory latency increases TS1 is favored. For an invalidate cost model(section 4.2), we assumed that a contiguous section can be invalidated in $1 + \lfloor \log_2(|section|) \rfloor$ "invalidate cycles" (by "invalidate cycle" we mean the time it takes to invalidate a single, aligned, power-of-2-sized block)

We applied this cost model to a series of Erlebacher runs where the problem size was varied from 2 to 30 as the number of processors varied from 1 to 15. We

Procs	Size	Refs	Miss Margin	Cost	Penalty
		1,000's / processor			
1	2	7.8	0.1	0.8	0.2
2	4	16.2	0.1	1.9	0.3
3	6	31.9	0.3	3.6	0.4
4	8	52.8	0.6	5.6	0.5
5	10	79.2	0.9	8.2	0.5
6	12	110.8	1.3	11.6	0.5
7	14	147.9	1.7	15.0	0.6
8	16	190.3	2.2	19.0	0.7
9	18	238.1	2.8	24.1	0.7
10	20	291.2	3.4	29.1	0.7
11	22	349.7	3.7	34.5	0.8
12	24	413.6	4.8	40.3	0.8
13	26	482.8	5.1	49.0	0.8
14	28	557.45	6.4	56.2	0.9
15	30	637.33	7.4	63.9	0.9

Cost: Invalidate cycles for $\log_2(s_i)$ metric
Penalty: Invalidate cycles for whole array invalidates

Table 6: Erlebacher Profitability

chose this as a natural scalability condition because the hit rate for TS stayed fairly constant with this condition. The raw data is summarized in table 6. For each run, it lists the total shared data references, the miss margin, the invalidate cost (for invalidating precise sections), and worst case TS1 penalty (in invalidate cycles). All of these are normalized to be per processor. Profitability depends on the relative cost of a miss versus the cost of an invalidate cycle. Figure 5 shows the profitability region for some hypothetical miss costs. The profitability is expressed as the percent speed up for a completely memory bound program (compute time is completely overlapped) with the assumption that cache hits take 1 processor cycle and an invalidate cycle takes 2 processor cycles. For different invalidate cycle costs, figure 5 would look essentially the same by scaling the miss cost the same amount. For real machines, we expect the cost of a miss to be 10's of cycles. We expect an implementation of invalidate to be possible where one invalidate cycle takes only 2 processor cycles.

For this test case, if the cost of a miss is almost negligible (1 invalidate cycle) then careful invalidation gains nothing and loses in overhead. If the cost of a miss is 20 cycles, it is a break even proposition. For higher miss costs, TS1 improves performance by paying for the invalidate overhead with time saved from more cache hits.

For miss costs less than 20 cycles, it is possible to switch from a precise invalidate to one which invalidates the whole array. This has the same hit rate as TS, but greatly reduces overhead. For instance, in the 15 processor case the overhead of invalidating whole arrays is about 0.3% (0.9/637*(2 processor cycles/ invalidate cycle)), even if every reference were a hit. The "loss lower bound" line in figure 5 represents this.

TS1 can often perform better than TS. Where it does worse, there is a fall back option, whole array invalidates, to cushion the loss to a tolerable amount.

177

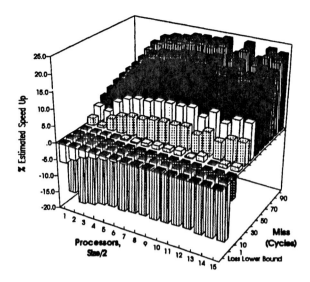

Figure 5: Erlebacher Speed Up

6 Other issues

6.1 DOACROSS

The assumed model for DOACROSS is that later iterations (instances) can wait on earlier iterations. There can be multiple waits on the same previous iterations or several different previous iterations. The compiler cannot necessarily determine anything about the nature of the synchronization. The only guarantee is that no dependences go from later to earlier iterations. A legal schedule for any DOACROSS would be to do the first p iterations with proper posting and waiting, then synchronize all p processors, and do the next p iterations, etc. Unlike DOALL, there can be carried dependence between iterations of a DOACROSS. So, each instance of a DOACROSS epoch must conceptually be treated like a different mini-epoch.

The leverage that local strategies get from the semantics of DOALL (section 2.1) must be abandoned here. For DOACROSS, the *epoch* bit in TS1 indicates that values can be reused on subsequent instances (not epochs). Since two subsequent iterations are almost certain to be scheduled to different processors, the *epoch* bit is useless.

Of the previous strategies surveyed, only Min and Baer's TS [14] handles DOACROSS. It increments the version number for an array at the end of a DOACROSS epoch. To preserve the semantics inside of the DOACROSS, any reference which could be overwritten in a later instance of the same DOACROSS epoch, is marked so that it will be removed at the end of the instance. Conversely, any read which could have been preceded by a write in a previous instance is invalidated on entry to this instance (intra-instance locality is still preserved).

Min and Baer's TS still preserves inter-epoch reuse if it can be proven (via the best available compiler analysis) that a given access will not be over-written on a later instance in the same epoch. Likewise, a read need not be forced to miss if it can be proven that no write on a previous instance of this epoch could reach it. Min and Baer's TS handles this situation with extra bits in the instruction word to specifically mark this condition. This is no longer optimal, even in the restricted sense of local strategies being optimal. Certain kinds of inter-instance intra-epoch reuse could be recognized by a local strategy, but are lost here.

TS1 could work in essentially the same way as TS for DOACROSS by adding the same extra bits. These extra bits could be avoided by changing the invalidation strategy. Instead of invalidating at the end of each epoch, the invalidate could be moved to the start of each instance. The invalidate would then handle those values written since this processor was last scheduled. For instance, if processors are assigned to iterations in strictly cyclic order and there are 5 processors. Then, processor 5, when it gets assigned iteration 11, would invalidate everything written on iterations 7 through 10. Iteration 6 writes were previously performed on processor 5 and do not need to be invalidated. Iterations before 6 were handled when processor 5 was assigned iteration 6. At the end of the DOACROSS, every processor must invalidate writes that occurred since it was last scheduled. This preserves the same inter-epoch reuse as Min and Baer's TS strategy.

In some cases involving DOACROSS, a *live* value is guaranteed to be invalidated before its next reference. In this case, there is no need to allocate a cache line. Read-thru and write-thru could selectively be used to advantage. Min and Baer [14] discuss this at length. This can be done with the bits already present in their strategy. TS1 could accommodate this with extra instruction bits performing the same function as in the Min and Baer strategy.

6.2 Critical sections

For critical section semantics that require inter-instance dependences to be entirely within critical sections, it is a simple matter to maintain coherence. Whatever is written in the critical section must be updated before the end of the section. Whatever is read in the critical section that could be written in another critical section must be invalidated on entry to the critical section.

6.3 Cache line size

Cache lines larger than one word cause aliasing problems. Values are read when they do not appear to be (as seen by the compiler). These values must also be kept coherent. There are several ad hoc methods of dealing with the aliasing problem, e.g. padding of array dimensions, changing layout order, and stripping loops. In truly desperate cases, it may be necessary to always use write-thru or not use caching at all. We assume that such objects are allocated on special cache pages in order to indicate different handling.

7 Conclusions

We believe the proper way to consider coherence strategies is in a framework of local knowledge versus global knowledge, and not as software versus hardware. This paper contributes to that framework.

As local strategies continue to improve their hit rates and decrease their implementation costs, it becomes feasible, at least for scientific codes, to build shared memory multiprocessors which rely on local strategies instead of global strategies for cache coherence. These machines have fewer obstacles to scalability. They may also be less hardware intensive than the sophisticated global strategies which have been proposed for medium and large scale parallelism.

In this paper, we propose a new local strategy, TS1 that improves on the best previously existing local strategy, time-stamping, by achieving better hit ratios, requiring fewer bits per cache line, and no extra bits per instruction. For a given granularity of compiler analysis, no local scheme could ever achieve a higher hit ratio. TS1 requires an *epoch* bit per cache line, a mechanism to invalidate an address range of cache lines, and a compiler that can recognize which array sections are written in a given epoch. If the compiler can only recognize arrays, and not sections, TS1 will have the same hit rate as time-stamping.

Simulation studies show that TS1 almost always has better hit ratios than TS and never worse. TS1 occasionally has slightly worse performance, but often appreciably better performance. An open question is to determine how efficiently a range based invalidate can be implemented. If only inefficient or hardware intensive implementations can be found, TS1 will not be as effective as our data suggest.

Acknowledgments

We would like to thank U. Rajagopalan and S. Dwarkadas for their assistance in modifying the RPPT simulator to handle the specific needs of a local strategy. We would also like to especially thank John Mellor-Crummey for his many useful suggestions on improving this paper.

References

[1] D. A. Abramson, K. Ramamohanarao, and M. Ross. A scalable cache coherence mechanism using a selectively clearable cache memory. *The Australian Computer Journal*, 21(1), Feb. 1989.

[2] L. M. Censier and P. Feautrier. A new solution to coherence problems in multicache systems. *IEEE Transactions on Computers*, C-27(12):1112–1118, Dec. 1978.

[3] H. Cheong. Life-span strategy - a compiler-based approach to cache coherence. In *Proceedings of 1992 International Conference on Supercomputing*, July 1992.

[4] H. Cheong and A. Veidenbaum. Compiler-directed cache management for multiprocessors. *Computer*, 23(6):39–47, June 1990.

[5] R. Covington, S. Dwarkadas, J. Jump, J. Sinclair, and S. Madala. Efficient simulation of paralle computer systems. *International Journal in Comuter Simulation*, 1:31–58, 1991. overview of RPPT.

[6] R. Cytron, S. Karlovsky, and K. McAuliffe. Automatic management of programmable caches. In *Proc. of the 1988 International Conference on Parallel Processing*, pages 229–238, Aug. 1988.

[7] E. Darnell, J. Mellor-Crummey, and K. Kennedy. Automatic software cache coherence through vectorization. In *Proceedings of 1992 International Conference on Supercomputing*, July 1992. Also available as expanded Technical Report CRPC-TR92197, Center for Research on Parallel Computation, January 1992.

[8] D. James, A. Laundrie, S. Gjessing, and G. Sohi. Scalable coherent interface. *Computer*, 23(6), June 1990.

[9] S. Karlovsky. Automatic management of programmable caches: Algorithms and experience. Technical Report 89-8010, Center for Supercomputing Research and Development, University of Illinois, Urbana, IL, July 1989.

[10] L. Lamport. How to make a multiprocessor that correctly executes multiprocess programs. *IEEE Transactions on Computers*, C-28(9), Sept. 1979.

[11] D. Lenoski, J. Laudon, K. Gharachorloo, W. Weber, A. Gupta, J. Hennessy, M. Horowitz, and M. Lam. The Standford DASH multiprocessor. *Computer*, 25(3):63–79, Mar. 1992.

[12] A. Louri and H. Sung. A compiler directed cache coherence scheme with fast and parallel explicit invalidation. In *Proc. of the 1992 International Conference on Parallel Processing*, pages 2–9, Aug. 1992.

[13] E. P. Markatos and T. J. LeBlanc. Using processor affinity in loop scheduling on shared-memory multiprocessors. in *Proceedings of 1992 International Conference on Supercomputing*, pages 104–113, Nov. 1992.

[14] S. Min and J. Baer. Design and analysis of a scalable cache coherence scheme based on clocks and timestamps. *IEEE Transactions on Parallel and Distributed Systems*, 3(1):25–44, Jan. 1992.

[15] S. Min, J. Baer, and H. Kim. An efficient caching support for critical sections in large-scale shared-memory multiprocessors. In *Proc. of the 1990 International Conference on Supercomputing/Computer Architecture News*, pages 4–47, June 1990. Special issue of Computer Architecture News, 18(3), Sept. 1990.

[16] A. Osterhaug, editor. *Guide to Parallel Programming on Sequent Computer Systems*. Sequent Technical Publications, San Diego, CA, 1989.

[17] K. Peterson and K. Li. Cache coherence for shared memory multiprocessors based on virtual memory support. In *Proceedings of the 7th International Parallel Processing Symposium*, Apr. 1993.

[18] D. Schanin. The design and development of a very high speed system bus - the encore multimax nanobus. In *Proceedings of the Fall Joint Computer Conference*, pages 410–418, Nov. 1986.

[19] J. Willis, A. Sanderson, and C. Hill. Cache coherence in systems with parallel communication channels & many processors. In *Supercomputing '90*, pages 554–563, 1990

Chapter 3
Dynamic Software Cache Coherence Schemes

Dynamic software cache coherence schemes detect incoherence conditions and take the appropriate actions to prevent use of the stale cache contents solely at run time. The software mechanisms are built into the operating system kernels, particularly into the operations for processor synchronization and/or the operations for processor mutual exclusion during the shared data access. A virtual multiprocessor machine at the operating system level could be considered as a cache coherent machine; consequently, compiler writers (as well as the application level programmers) could not take care of the coherence maintenance. Dynamic schemes do not suffer from unnecessary preventive activities, as is the case with static schemes. Dynamic software approaches are unsuitable for applications characterized by a high level of sharing, as is the case with numeric applications based on the execution model of parallel loops. Dynamic solutions are suitable for nonnumeric concurrent applications based on a programming model with an explicit management of sharing, as when critical regions or monitors are used. Also, dynamic software cache coherence maintenance has some similarities to the coherence maintenance in DSM (distributed shared memory) systems, as can be seen from the last paper in the chapter and its companions (also by Bennett, Carter, and Zwaenepoel) from the list of papers suggested for further reading. This chapter contains four papers dealing with dynamic software maintenance of cache coherence.

Cheriton, Slavenburg, and Boyle, in the paper "Software-Controlled Caches in the VMP Multiprocessor," propose a combined hardware–software solution for the maintenance of cache coherence in virtually addressed private cache memories. This research was done at Stanford University and was a part of the VMP multiprocessor project. The essence of the solution is in the hardware-based determination of the incoherence conditions and generation of the interrupt request, followed by software-based activities aimed at coherence enforcement. The precise, hardware-based detection of incoherence conditions results in a high restriction of invalidations. However, the size of the cache page (which must be relatively large, so that the interrupts related to private data misses are relatively rare) makes the invalidation poorly selective for shared data of fine granularity (such as synchronization locks).

Smith, in the paper "CPU Cache Consistency with Software Support and Using One Time Identifiers," proposes a solution for dynamic maintenance of cache coherence that is entirely based on the application of operating system level primitive operations for control of exclusive access to critical regions. This research was done at the University of California at Berkeley. The advantage of the OTI scheme is the complete decentralization of the cache coherence maintenance. Coherence is maintained at each processor autonomously, without any communications with other processors in the system. However, the scheme requires relatively complex hardware support (the OTI extension in the translation lookaside buffer and the cache, comparators for the OTI fields, and the like).

The editors of this book in their earlier paper "An Approach to Dynamic Software Cache Consistency Maintenance Based on Conditional Invalidation," propose a class of dynamic software schemes for maintenance of cache coherence based on testing at the entry into a critical region, with a view to avoiding unnecessary invalidations. The work was performed at the University of Belgrade, in cooperation with the NCR Corporation. A simulation analysis has shown the advantages of the restrictively applied invalidation, even if the number of processors is relatively small (up to 16). This was especially the case if the mostly-read shared segments predominate.

Bennett, Carter, and Zwaenepoel, in the paper "Adaptive Software Cache Management for Distributed Shared Memory Architectures," propose a dynamic adaptive software maintenance of cache coherence for the Munin project at Rice University. Munin supports several coherence maintenance mechanisms. Each particular coherence maintenance mechanism is tailored to the appropriate class of shared data objects (the object access dynamics are relevant when making the decision about what specific mechanism to use). The adaptivity of this coherence scheme (based on the dynamic nature of objects) has a very positive impact on the overall performance of the system and the application. The simulation studies have shown that, for a given application (such as Quicksort), this adaptive software method can decrease the bus traffic for more than 50 percent compared to the conventional hardware write-update, and more than 85 percent compared to the write-invalidate mechanism.

Suggestions for Further Reading

Bennett, J.K., Carter, J.B., and Zwaenepoel, W., "Munin: Distributed Shared Memory Based on Type-Specific Memory Coherence," *Proc. 1990 Conf. Principles and Practice of Parallel Programming,* 1990, pp. 168–176.

Carter, J.B., Bennett, J.K., and Zwaenepoel, W., "Implementation and Performance of Munin," *Proc. 13th ACM Symp. Operating System Principles,* ACM Press, New York, N.Y., 1991, pp. 152–164.

Chaiken, D., and Agarwal, A., "Software-Extended Coherent Shared Memory: Performance and Cost," *Proc. 21st Ann. Int'l Symp. Computer Architecture,* IEEE CS Press, Los Alamitos, Calif., 1994, pp. 314–324.

Cox, A.L., et al., "Software Versus Hardware Shared-Memory Implementation: A Case Study," *Proc. 21st Ann. Int'l Symp. Computer Architecture,* IEEE CS Press, Los Alamitos, Calif., 1994, pp. 106–117.

Li, K., and Hudak, P., "Memory Coherence in Shared Virtual Memory Systems," *ACM Trans. Computer Systems,* Vol. 7, No. 4, Nov. 1989, pp. 321–359.

Lo, V., "Operating Systems Enhancements for Distributed Shared Memory," *Advances in Computers,* Vol. 39, Academic Press, Inc., New York, N.Y., 1994, pp. 191–237.

Protić, J., Tomašević, M., and Milutinović, V., "A Survey of Distributed Shared-Memory Systems," *Proc. Hawaii Int'l Conf. System Sciences*, Vol. 1, IEEE CS Press, Los Alamitos, Calif., 1995, pp. 74–84.

Software-Controlled Caches in the VMP Multiprocessor

David R. Cheriton
Stanford University

Gert A. Slavenburg
Philips Research

Patrick D. Boyle
Stanford University

Abstract

VMP is an experimental multiprocessor that follows the familiar basic design of multiple processors, each with a cache, connected by a shared bus to global memory. Each processor has a synchronous, virtually addressed, single master connection to its cache, providing very high memory bandwidth. An unusually large cache page size and fast sequential memory copy hardware make it feasible for cache misses to be handled in software, analogously to the handling of virtual memory page faults. Hardware support for cache consistency is limited to a simple state machine that monitors the bus and interrupts the processor when a cache consistency action is required.

In this paper, we show how the VMP design provides the high memory bandwidth required by modern high-performance processors with a minimum of hardware complexity and cost. We also describe simple solutions to the consistency problems associated with virtually addressed caches. Simulation results indicate that the design achieves good performance providing data contention is not excessive.

This work was sponsored in part by the National Science Foundation Grant DCR-83-52048 and by Philips Research, Bell-Northern Research, ATT Information Systems and NCR.

1 Introduction

VMP is an experimental shared memory multiprocessor being built at Stanford University. It follows the familiar model[4] of multiple processors connected by a shared bus to global memory with per-processor caches to reduce bus traffic.

Our research focuses on the problem of connecting multiple high-performance processors to a shared memory without significant performance degradation, rather than connecting a large number of processors of more modest capabilities[14] or not providing shared memory[17]. By *high-performance*, we mean the 20-30 MIPS microprocessors of modest cost expected in the near future.

This particular focus is motivated by three observations. First, programming parallel applications for shared memory machines is much easier than for networked processors because management of the shared program state is familiar and direct. Second, initial experimentation[7,13] with parallel applications indicates that few, fast processors are more effective than many slow processors, simply because most applications exhibit a low degree of parallelism. Finally, we are interested in medium to high performance workstations with uniprocessor or multiprocessor configurations. For these machines, the processor of choice is obviously the microprocessor of greatest performance within standard VLSI technology.

The performance of future processors will be limited primarily by the memory bandwidth provided. Current conventional processors, such as the Motorola 68020, run at about 75 to 80 percent memory bandwidth utilization. Some RISC processors achieve much higher utilization. Thus, the primary design problem for multiprocessor machines is providing a sufficient memory bandwidth to a shared memory to accommodate multiple processors. This view argues for per-processor caches with very efficient processor-cache coupling.

In the VMP design, each processor has a synchronous, virtually addressed, single master connection to its cache, providing very high memory bandwidth except upon a cache miss. An unusually large cache page size and fast sequential memory copy hardware make it feasible for cache misses to be handled in software, analogously to the handling of virtual memory page faults. Hardware support for cache consistency is limited to a simple state machine that monitors the bus and interrupts the processor when a cache consistency action is required.

We argue that these simple hardware resources, operated under software control, provide memory bandwidth for a very high-performance processor and bring the power of the processor and the flexibility of software management to bear on the cache management (and virtual memory) problem. Simulation results indicate that the design achieves good performance providing data contention is not excessive. We also describe simple solutions to the consistency problems associated with virtually addressed caches. The paper emphasizes the techniques rather than our specific hardware design.

The next section describes the cache miss handling mechanism. Section 3 describes our approach to cache consistency, including consistency with respect to virtual address translation. Section 4 describes additional details of the VMP design. Section 5 provides some indication of expected performance for VMP and raises some software issues with the design. Section 6 compares this design to some other representative multiprocessor designs. We close with a summary of the key points plus an indication of future directions.

2 Cache Access and Cache Miss Handling

The processor is directly connected to a *virtually addressed cache*, as depicted in Figure 1. That is, the cache contents are addressed by virtual address, rather than by physical addresses.[1]

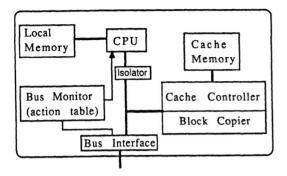

Figure 1: VMP Processor Board Organization

Thus, in the absence of a cache miss, the memory reference is satisfied at maximum speed because the processor is the single master of the cache and it executes synchronously with respect to the cache, i.e. no arbitration is required and there is no virtual-to-physical address translation as part of a cache reference.

The processor is connected to some local memory in the same synchronous, single-master fashion. High-order bits of the address discriminate local memory references from cache references so no significant delay is introduced by having the two memories. Local memory is required for storing the code and data associated with cache miss handling, ensuring there can be no cache miss in the cache miss handling software.

On cache miss, the cache controller signals a processor exception interrupt (bus error) and generates a suggested *cache slot*[2] to use for the missing cache page.

On exception interrupt, the processor saves its state on the supervisor stack in local memory and traps to the cache miss handler routine, also stored in local memory. The processor writes out the cache pag if it has been modifie. It then maps the virtual address that generated the miss to the physical address for the associated cache page. Assuming the virtual memory page is present in the main memory, the processor instructs the block copier to copy the required data from main memory into the cache, specifying the cache flags to be assigned to the cache slot if the copy succeeds. Concurrently with the copy operation the processor updates its data structures describing the current cache contents, returns from the original bus exception and continues execution as soon as the copy operation completes. If the copy operation fails (for instance because it is aborted by one of the bus monitors), the cache flags are left unchanged and the processor traps again in retrying the instruction, causing it to try again. If the required data is not in main memory, the operating system page fault handler is given control.

The virtual-to-physical mapping may be performed in a variety of ways[9]. A two-level page table is the scheme proposed for VMP. With page tables stored in virtual memory, a cache miss may result in additional cache misses as the processor references the page table. Each such miss results in

[1] An address space identifier is included as part of the address presented to the cache so that the cache need not be flushed on context switch.

[2] A *cache slot* is the cache element holding a cache page. The term *cache page* is used the same as *virtual page* is used for conventional virtual memory systems. A *cache page frame* is a portion of main memory corresponding to one cache page.

the processor stacking another level of exception state on the supervisor stack contained in local memory. Some minimum amount of page table information is maintained in local memory (or non-cached global memory) so there is a small bounded depth to page table misses. After handling the cache misses (if any) involved with virtual address translation, the processor returns to handling the original cache miss.

A cache miss can also occur when the processor attempts to write data for which it has not secured write access. In this case, it negotiates write permission using the cache consistency protocol described in Section 3.

Cache miss handling by the processor is facilitated by the hardware providing fast data transfer. This hardware exploits three main techniques for performance:

- **Sequential Memory Access:** Main memory boards are optimized for fast sequential operation by using static column RAM chips (which provide 60 nanosecond access to successive locations). The first access to the memory board takes 300 ns but each subsequent sequential reference takes less than 100 ns.

- **Sequential Bus Protocol:** Bus protocols are optimized for sequential access by issuing a single address for a transfer and then simply strobing the data words across, relying on the source and destination modules to automatically increment the source and destination addresses. This is provided by the VMEbus block transfer mode in our prototype machine.

- **Block Copier:** A specialized block copy mechanism is embedded in the cache controller that allows us to take advantage of the sequential access on the VMEbus and memory board. It also eliminates the instruction fetching overhead which would arise if the processor did the copy.[3] The block copier can operate concurrently with the CPU executing out of local memory.

The block copier significantly reduces the bus occupancy for the transfers as well as the elapsed time. For example, the VMEbus-based VMP block copier should transfer data at 40 megabytes per second, achieving 100 percent VMEbus utilization during the transfer. In contrast, a simple copy loop using the processor can achieve less than 5 megabytes per second at best. The block copier allows some overlap of the copy time with the bookkeeping performed by the processor on cache miss.

Cache miss handling is more complicated with a virtually addressed cache than with a physically addressed cache. A virtually addressed cache requires virtual-to-physical address translation on cache miss and, if page tables are stored in virtual memory, has the possibility of incurring a real page fault as part of cache miss handling.

The software implementation of cache miss handling has the benefit of replacing rather complex cache-control hardware with relatively simple hardware: local memory that holds the cache management software. It also offers the flexibility to experiment with different techniques of virtual-to-physical address translation and cache loading and replacement policies without hardware modification.

[3] The elimination of instruction fetch is secondary in effect compared to the use of sequential access, given that a copy loop fits in the processor's on-chip instruction buffer.

The major concern with software controlled caches is performance. We claim that, by choosing an unconventionally large cache page size (and keeping the number of cache slots and degree of associativity large enough), one reduces the cache miss rate so that the overhead of software cache management is not a problem. The effect of cache page size on cache hit ratio is discussed in Section 5.

It remains to address the problem of maintaining cache consistency. Note that, with a virtually addressed cache, cache consistency is not strictly a multiprocessor issue. A single processor cache can be inconsistent with respect to itself if the same physical memory is mapped to two different virtual addresses and both virtual addresses are represented in the (single) cache.

3 Cache Consistency

There are two cache consistency problems to solve:

- ensuring that all copies of a cache page are consistent across all processors, and

- ensuring that the virtual-to-physical translation implicit in the per-processor caches is consistent with that specified by the system page tables.

We first describe the cache consistency protocol and then how this protocol is implemented with the aid of the bus monitor.

3.1 Cache Consistency Protocol

Cache consistency is maintained by a variant of the distributed ownership protocol described by Frank[11] and Goodman[12]. Main memory is viewed as a sequence of *cache page fames*.[4] For consistency, a cache page must be in one of two states:

- **shared** - Main memory contains the most recently written value of the cache page. Several copies of the block may exist elsewhere, all of them being identical to that in main memory.

- **private** - Some cache i contains the only copy of the page. In this case, cache i is said to *own* this cache page.

The processors use an extended form of read and write bus transactions that specify if ownership is being requested or released. It is up to each processor to observe and respond to bus transactions so as to ensure each page of memory is in one of the two legal states.

There are seven types of bus transactions, one with no associated bus monitor operation (used by DMA devices and CPUs to access device registers), and six with. A processor issues one of these six types of bus transactions, depending on the reason for the bus transaction (the first five are *consistency-related* bus transactions):

- **read-shared** - to acquire a non-exclusive or shared copy of a cache page.

- **read-private** - to acquire an exclusive copy of a cache page. The processor issues this bus transaction when it incurs a cache miss on a write to an address within that cache page but has no copy of that cache page.

- **assert-ownership** - to gain exclusive ownership of a cache page without reading it from main memory. It presumably acquired a shared copy of the cache page earlier using a **read-shared** operation.

- **write-back** - to write the cache page back to main memory, releasing ownership of the page.

- **notify** - to send notification to a processor (described in 5.4)

- **write action table** - to write an entry in the action table (described below).

To allow the processor to execute concurrently with bus transactions, we provide a simple but specialized state machine called a *bus monitor* that monitors the bus and interrupts the processor when either consistency actions are required or notification is signalled.

3.2 Per-Processor Bus Monitor

The bus monitor[5] performs one of four actions on each bus transaction depending on the type of bus transaction, the physical address of the bus transaction and the contents of the bus monitor's action table. The bus monitor's action table contains a two-bit entry per physical cache page frame[6] (of main memory) indicating:

- 00 - do nothing

- 01 - abort bus transaction and interrupt local processor on read-private, assert-ownership (ignore read-shared or notify)

- 10 - abort bus transaction and interrupt local processor on any consistency-related bus transactions (including read-shared)

- 11 - interrupt processor on a notification transaction.

The main function of the bus monitor is to enforce cache consistency, however the action table code 10 can be used to "protect" a page (prevent its modification or a change in its state), and entry 11 can be used for notification (see 5.4).

The action table of the bus monitor associated with a particular CPU is normally updated as a side effect of (and concurrently with) a consistency-related bus transaction issued by that CPU. Thus, in the common cases, checking and updating the action table over the bus does not entail additional bus occupancy. The action table can also be updated by the CPU using the *write action table* bus transaction. Update as part of a consistency-related bus transaction only takes place if the bus transaction is not aborted. The consistency check interval and action table update interval, each of 150 nanoseconds, are overlapped with the block transfer, as shown in Figure 2.

---

[4]Our prototype allows for experimentation with cache page sizes of 128, 256, and 512 bytes.

[5]The main difference between our bus monitor and a "snoop" is that the bus monitor is not connected to the cache (does not share the cache flag matching hardware, the cache tags, or even have a copy of the tags) and thus does not reduce the cpu/cache bandwidth. It can operate at the leisurely pace of our relatively long bus transactions rather than at the memory reference speeds required when using small cache page sizes.

[6]Allowing a maximum of 8 megabytes of physical memory for the prototype with 128 (256, 512) byte pages, each bus monitor has 16 (8, 4) kilobytes of memory for its action table. A larger physical memory would require additional memory for the action table.

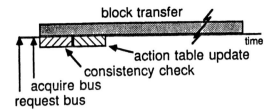

Figure 2: Action Table Update in a Bus Transaction

On abort, the bus transaction is terminated at the end of the current memory reference. The assert-ownership bus transaction is a degenerate form of this behavior since it does not involve block transfer. Updating the action table as part of bus transactions minimizes bus overhead for action table management and avoids the cost of a dual-ported action table, the other solution. Note that completion of a few transfers during the consistency check does not compromise the correctness of main memory because write-back is the only bus transaction that modifies main memory. Write-backs are only issued if a cache is releasing a privately held page and so are never aborted (unless there has been a consistency protocol violation).

The bus monitor is connected to the processor by a non-maskable interrupt and a FIFO queue of interrupt requests. Each time a bus transaction occurs that should interrupt the processor, a word is queued in the FIFO for the processor. The word specifies the type of bus transaction and the physical address associated with the bus transaction. The FIFO provides a maximum of 128 entries, minimizing the likelihood of an interrupt word being lost. However, the FIFO also sets a flag for the processor when an interrupt word is dropped because the FIFO is full.

The bus monitor is a fairly general-purpose hardware resource available to each processor. We plan to explore its use in a variety of settings. However, its primary use is for ensuring cache consistency, as described in the next two subsections.

3.3 Cache Page Consistency

Each processor sets the action table of its bus monitor according to the cache pages its cache holds and acts on bus monitor interrupts so as to enforce this 2-state consistency of cache pages. There are three cases to consider for each cache page frame k in physical memory, corresponding to there being no copy, shared copy or private copy of the page in the processor's cache.

No Copy: The action table entry for cache page k is 00, indicating that the bus monitor can ignore all bus transactions on this cache page.

Shared Copy: The k-th action table entry is set to 01 causing the bus monitor to ignore read-shared transactions, and interrupt on read-private or assert-ownership bus transactions. Write-back operations are protocol violations and result in an abort and interrupt. Note that, due to virtual memory aliasing, the cache may contain multiple copies of this cache page in different cache slots. On interrupt from a read-private or assert-ownership bus transaction, the processor invalidates the cache slots holding this cache page and sets the k-th action table entry to 00. Consequently, when a cache page becomes private, all other cached copies of the page are discarded in parallel.

Private Copy: The k-th action table entry is set to 10 causing the bus monitor to abort the bus transaction and interrupt the processor on all bus transactions on this page (including write-back operations which are protocol violations). On interrupt, the processor writes out the cache page (if dirty). If the bus transaction was read-private (or assert-ownership), it invalidates the cache page and sets the action table entry to 00. If not, it "downgrades" the cache page to read-only and changes the action table entry to that specified for read-shared. The processor issuing the bus transaction detects that the bus transaction was aborted and retries the bus transaction.

This scheme also solves the *alias* consistency problem that arises with a physical cache page mapped to two or more different virtual addresses. Each processor observes the consistency protocol "competing against itself". Thus, for instance, should a processor issue a read-shared for a cache page its cache already owns (referenced by a different virtual address), its own bus monitor will abort the bus transaction and interrupt that CPU. In response to the interrupt, the CPU flushes (or write-back) the owned page. The read-shared bus transaction is then retried.

Using this protocol, a request for a shared copy of a shared cache page is satisfied immediately. A request for a shared copy of a private cache page fails but causes the owner to relinquish ownership, allowing the requestor to succeed on retry. A request for a private copy of a shared cache page succeeds immediately but causes all cache copies of the cache page to be discarded. A request for a private copy of a private cache page fails but causes the owner to relinquish ownership.

Each processor is trusted to set its bus monitor action tables appropriately for the cache pages it holds and to act on interrupts from the bus monitor according to this protocol. Information about the state of each cache page and the mapping from physical address to cache page is maintained by the processor in the local memory.

The consistency scheme is deadlock-free because ownership of cache pages can be preempted (no blocking) and a processor is guaranteed to make at least one successful reference to a newly acquired page before that page is flushed from the cache (non-zero progress). One worst case example is that of two processors simultaneously attempting to acquire a private copy of a cache page. In this case, the first processor to acquire the bus gets the page, then the second issues the read-private resulting in an interrupt to the first processor by its bus monitor leading to subsequent flushing of the page from the first processor's cache, and so on. However, interrupts are only serviced between instructions and the CPU blocks on the cache controller mid-instruction while awaiting the completion of the block transfer. Thus, the first processor makes at least one successful reference so the contention results in performance degradation but not deadlock.

Correctness of consistency maintenance is rendered independent of the processor's ability to keep up with bus monitor interrupts as follows. The interrupt FIFO includes a flag that indicates that an interrupt word was dropped (which only occurs if the processor is unable to keep up with the bus monitor interrupt rate). When this flag is set, the processor recovers by invalidating (or rereading) shared cache entries from main memory and updating its bus monitor action table. Note that loss of the interrupt word for a bus transaction requesting ownership of cache page owned by this processor is not a problem since the bus transaction is aborted by the bus monitor and then retried by the requesting processor until successful.

Dropping an interrupt word in the bus monitor FIFO is extremely unlikely for several reasons. First, the FIFO queue provides considerable buffer space giving the processor time to handle bursts of consistency actions. Second, the only operations that leave the processor unresponsive to these interrupts for a significant time are its block transfers. During the transfer the bus is fully consumed so other bus transactions cannot occur, limiting the rate of accumulation of interrupt words. Finally, the rate of interrupt word generation is no worse than the rate of cache misses, which is assumed to be reasonably low. (Of course, there is no problem with the bus monitor keeping up with the rate of bus transactions.)

The flexibility of the bus monitor allows VME-standard DMA devices to be used i the system. To set up a DMA into a particular area of memory, the operating system code acquires a high-level lock on that area of memory so that it is not accessed by other processors. The cache management software then does an assert-ownership bus transaction on this area of memory, forcing every other processor to discard any cached copies of this memory or write back the private copy, if any. It then sets the bus monitor to abort any consistency-related bus transactions addressing this area (which should not occur in any case). Since DMA operations have no associated consistency operation the DMA completes without abort by a bus monitor. Once the DMA transfer completes, the processor can release its lock on this area of memory at the operating system level and clear the corresponding entries in the bus monitor's action table.

3.4 Virtual Address Translation Consistency

A virtually addressed cache implicitly stores a portion of the virtual-to-physical address mapping specified in the operating system page tables. To ensure consistency, this implicit mapping must be updated when the page tables change. This problem of virtual address translation consistency is handled in a straight-forward fashion in our design, as described below.

The operating system and cache management software ensure that every valid cache slot corresponds to some portion of a virtual memory page currently in main memory. To change the mapping of virtual page vp which currently maps to physical page pp, the processor first issues a read-private for the cache page pt corresponding to the page table entry for vp. If the page table is in virtual memory, obtaining exclusive ownership of pt may entail page faults as well. The processor then issues an assert-ownership on page pp, causing all cached copies to be flushed or written back, depending on whether the copy is shared or private. This flushes the implicit mappings for this virtual page in all other processor caches. The processor then updates the page table entry and relinquishes ownership of the two cache pages. Note that cache page pp need not be read into the cache of the processor performing this mapping operation.

Deletion of an address space can be handled similarly with an assert-ownership on every resident page in the address space.

A similar technique can be used to keep page table reference information consistent with cache page references in the cache. The page-out daemon can periodically use assert-ownership to flush cache pages chosen as candidates for reclamation out of all caches. The processors then update the page table reference

information if they subsequently refer to these cache pages.

The software implementation of address translation in combination with the bus monitor and local memory allows considerable latitude in handling virtual address translation consistency. We have sketched a basic scheme permitting the storage of page tables in either physical memory or virtual memory.

4 Details of VMP

This section provides some details of VMP, the multiprocessor machine we are building to investigate the performance of the cache design described in the previous sections.

The system consists of the following major components:

- A shared central bus (VMEbus) that is used for all communication between processing nodes, memory and I/O devices.

- A central memory connected to the bus. The memory is optimized to do the transfer of cache pages at 40 MBytes/Second.

- I/O units which adhere to the standard VME protocol and can be obtained from external suppliers. Expected I/O units include an Ethernet interface and a framebuffer.

- Several VMP processor boards.

Each VMP processor board consists of a 68020 CPU running at maximum speed (currently 60 nanosecond cycle, 180 nanosecond memory cycle) coupled to a 68881 FPU (Floating Point Coprocessor), local RAM (32 KBytes), a 4-way set associative 256 KByte cache that responds to virtual addresses, a bus monitor (with associated action table), and local devices (UART, timer). The CPU, FPU, local RAM, local devices and bus monitor are connected to a private onboard bus which may be connected to the VME interface through the *bus isolator*. The bus isolator permits concurrent execution of the CPU accessing local memory with transfers between the cache and VME memory. Note the absence of components found in other systems: memory management unit, translation lookaside buffer and reverse translation buffer.

The basic VMP processor board organization is shown in Figure 1. The memory space seen by the CPU is divided into 5 regions. The lowest addressed region (2^{27} bytes or 128 MBytes) maps straight-through to VME address space and is used to access device registers and execute boot ROM code. The next region (128 MB) is set aside for local accesses (local memory, ASID register, bus monitor FIFO, and other local devices). The third region (128 MB) addresses cache control. The fourth region (128 MB) addresses kernel virtual address space. The last region (3.5 Gigabytes) is the user virtual address space, which is extended by an 8 bit Address Space Identifier $ASID$.[7] Accesses to regions other than the user virtual memory require supervisor privilege.[8]

Virtual addresses are mapped into the 4-way set associative cache. The cache page replacement strategy is LRU, with

---

[7]This is similar in function to the context register in the SUN workstation architecture.

[8]This organization allows the kernel space to be part of each user virtual space.

the replacement page "suggested" by the hardware based on references. For each cache page, flags are maintained that indicate: valid, modified, exclusive-ownership, supervisor writable, user readable and user writable. Because the cache matches on <ASID, VirtAddress>, the operating system simply changes the *ASID* to indicate the new address space on each context switch.

The cache in the prototype is configurable for a choice of 128, 256 or 512 byte cache pages to allow us to experiment with a variety of cache page sizes. The number of sets is variable from 1 to 4, and number of pages per set is variable from 16 to 256. In addition to experimenting with different hardware configurations, we are interested in investigating the benefit of software techniques that improve the utilization of large cache blocks.

5 Expected Performance

We are building a prototype of the VMP design that is highly instrumented in order to measure performance and investigate the effects of: different cache page sizes, cache sizes, associativity, modifications to the cache management software, and various software techniques for improving locality and reducing contention. This machine is an initial prototype for the VMP design since the choices of processor (68020 over a RISC-style processor), bus (VMEbus over a much higher-speed bus) and memory boards (commercial sequential-access VME memory over high performance boards) make a significant concession to budget and fast construction over ideal performance. The prototype will allow us to evaluate the expected performance of this design since, as pointed out by Clark[8], trace-driven simulation is frequently a poor indication of real performance. However, since our prototype is not yet operational, we provide some expected performance figures based on: simulation, instruction counts for the key software cache management routines, and timings for hardware components.

In the VMP design, the performance of a processor is degraded by three factors:

- **Cache Misses** - some proportion of the resulting bus transactions are also retried when an ownership conflict arises on the data,

- **Consistency Interrupts** - both for cache data as well as page table updates,

- **Bus Load** - which affects the time for the above two operations.

In this discussion, we first estimate processor performance as a function of the cache miss ratio for different cache page sizes, assuming no consistency interrupts and no bus contention. We then use simulation results (cache miss ratios and bus traffic ratios) to determine the ranges for the cache parameters which will give the desired processor performance. Finally, we calculate bus utilization per processor as a function of the miss ratio to estimate the number of processors that one can feasibly configure without significant bus contention. Consistency interrupts introduce the same overheads as cache misses (and possibly increase the miss ratio by flushing cache entries). Thus, consistency overhead can be incorporated in these performance estimates by hypothesizing a higher miss ratio than that suggested by the simulations.

5.1 Cache Miss Time

The elapsed times for a cache miss (assuming no bus contention and no bus transaction abort) are given in Table 1. These times assume a 16 MHz 68020 running with 0 wait state access to cache memory plus a block copier and memory that perform block transfers in 300 nanoseconds for the first long word (32-bits) and 100 nanoseconds for each subsequent long word. These times were calculated by summing instruction execution times for the cache miss handler and the time to update

Cache Page Size (bytes)	Replaced Page state	Elapsed Time (μsecs)	Bus Time (μsecs)
128	not modified	17	3.5
256	not modified	20	6.6
512	not modified	26	13.0
128	modified	17	7.0
256	modified	23	13.2
512	modified	36	26.0

Table 1: Elapsed Time and Bus Time per Cache Miss

Cache Page Size (bytes)	Elapsed Time (μsecs)	Bus Time (μsecs)
128	17	4.4
256	21	8.3
512	29	16.

Table 2: Average Cache Miss Cost

the cache (one block transfer if the page to be replaced was not modified, two block transfers if it was modified). Block transfer time is overlapped with the CPU processing where possible.

Clearly, the software time associated with miss handling (about 15 μsecs) means that there is limited benefit using in a smaller cache page size. If we assume a mix of different cache miss scenarios with 75 percent of the replaced pages being unmodified then the average cache miss cost is given in Table 2.

Figure 3 plots the processor performance as a function of the miss ratio, assuming the average cache miss cost is incurred on each miss, with data for cache page sizes of 128, 256 and 512 bytes. The processor performance is normalized so that processor performance with no cache misses is 1.[9]

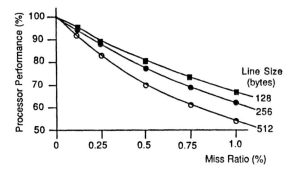

Figure 3: Processor Performance to Cache Miss Ratio

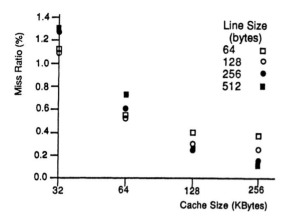

Figure 4: Cache Miss Ratio and Cache Size

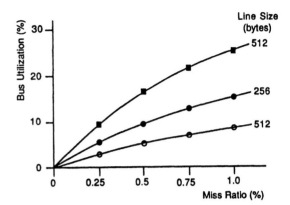

Figure 5: Bus Utilization to Cache Miss Ratio

Note that the miss ratio is a function of the cache page size so it is inappropriate to use this graph to compare the benefits of different cache page sizes.

Next we determine the characteristics of the cache that are required to achieve a sufficiently low miss rate, given the large cache page sizes, to realize reasonable processor performance.

5.2 Cache Miss Ratio and Processor Performance

The ranges of the variable hardware parameters of the VMP prototype (cache size from 64K to 256K bytes, page size of 128, 256 or 512 bytes) were established using four VAX 8200 traces obtained by the ATUM technique[2]. These traces include VMS operating system references and a small degree of multiprogramming. The trace lengths vary from 358,000 to 540,000 four-byte references.

The cold-start simulation results of a 4-way set associative cache for various cache sizes and cache page sizes are summarized in Figure 4. These low miss ratios contrary to most cache measurements published to date. However, with the parameters of our cache, it is better compared to a 4-way associative translation lookaside buffer with 4 kilobyte entries (except that the cache also has the associated data). Smith[19] indicates that .4% miss ratio has been observed with TLB's.

It is interesting to note that the operating system references account for approximately 25% of the references and 50% of the misses, and that the application programs employed no special locality enhancing techniques. So, eventhough traces are always too short and never correspond to the situation at hand, we anticipate that application of appropriate software techniques could lead to even lower miss ratios.

Applying these results, for example, using a 256 byte cache page size and 128 kilobyte total cache size, one would expect a miss ratio of 0.24 giving processor performance of 87% according to Figure 3.

5.3 Bus Utilization and Number of Processors

Each cache miss results in bus traffic. Table 2 provides the bus cost for the "average" cache miss. Figure 5 shows bus utilization as a function of the cache miss ratio for the three cache

page sizes, using this average bus cost per miss.[10] For example, for a 256 byte cache page size, with a miss ratio under 0.6%, the bus utilization by a single processor is under 10%. Using a simple single-server (the bus) multiple-client (several processors, ignoring DMA I/O devices) queuing model, and observing the request service times, we estimate that one can accommodate up to 5 processors on a single bus. Additional processors can be expected to degrade individual processor performance by increasing bus contention as well as possibly increasing the miss ratio because of consistency contention.

5.4 Consistency Overhead and System Software

The effect of consistency interrupts can be incorporated into the above figures by assuming a higher miss ratio. The rate of consistency interrupts and its effect on the cache miss ratio are unknown and highly dependent on the programming of the system and the cache page size. For instance, the straight forward use of test-and-set locks on the same cache pages as the data being modified could result in enormous consistency overhead. Thus, this design requires "good behavior" from the software it is executing to realize its performance, just as the performance of virtual memory systems is highly dependent on program behavior. We are developing software support at the operating system and programming system level that is tuned for the VMP design. In this vein, we are interested in exploring how far the software support can go to ensure good behavior, as opposed to how well the hardware can deal with bad behavior.

For operating system support, we are porting the V kernel[6] to VMP and adding kernel-supported locking and queuing primitives. These primitives can be implemented either using the notification facility offered by the bus monitor, or by using non-cached, globally-addressable physical memory. A process requesting the lock accesses the lock as part of a kernel operation and suspends for a timeout period if the lock is taken. As an additional optimization, the processor can set the action table entry associated with this memory to 11 (notify) so it can wake up the process to retry when the lock is cleared. As another operating system support mechanism, we are planning

---

[9]$performance = (1 + MissRatio * AverageMissCost * RefsPerInstr * InstrExecutionRate)^{-1}$
From MacGregor[16]: RefsPerInstr=1.2 and $InstrExecutionRate = (7clocks/instn * 60nsecs/clock)^{-1} = 2.4$ MIPS

[10]bus utilization is the bus use time during the execution of N instructions divided by the execution time (including miss handling) of N instructions. $Util=(MissRatio * BusTimePerMiss)/((InstrExecutionRate*RefsPerInstr)^{-1} + MissRatio * MissServiceElapsedTime)$

to allow the application to specify whether an area of virtual memory is going to be shared or not. If not, a read cache miss to this area is handled by a read-private bus transaction, eliminating the need to later do an assert-ownership on the first write operation. Since the data is not shared, this should not conflict with other processors and may in fact serve to flush this data from the cache of another processor that was previously running this process. It is interesting to note that the bus monitor can also be used to implement interprocessor messages: the bus monitor would interrupt the processor when a message is written to the cache page corresponding to its mailbox. Other specialized uses are also possible, for example notification locks.

To realize the maximum performance offered by VMP, programming systems need to recognize the importance of clustering related data on cache pages and compiling code and data for high cache page utilization. These demands on software technology are significant but are also a common theme in previous efforts to redefine some of the hardware/software boundaries. We have been exploring a parallel programming paradigm which we call *workform processing*[5] that draws analogy from the processing structure of the (human) office. Determining the quantitative effects of these programming techniques in the VMP prototype is a focus of future research.

6   Related Work

A central focus of our work has been to better understand the proper trade-off between hardware and software. Our design proposes operating system control of the caches with suitable hardware support to make this efficient. An alternative software control scheme proposed for the MIPS-X project[1] is to have the compiler generate cache control instructions to ensure consistency. This relies on using a language that includes explicit constructs for accessing shared data, such as the monitor construct[15], and all data sharing being properly controlled by these constructs. Except for instructions which selectively flush cache entries, this scheme requires no hardware support for consistency. However, the MIPS-X scheme must flush all shared data in anticipation of shared access whereas the VMP scheme only flushes on demand. It remains to be seen which is most expensive and how application-sensitive the behavior is.

The performance of cache memories for single processor machines has been studied extensively[12,19,18]. Much of this work studies much smaller cache page sizes, so the results have limited application. However, as mentioned previously, our expected performance is consistent with that expected and observed with TLB's of comparable size.

There has also been interest in cache consistency protocols for multiprocessor machines[11,12,18,10,3]. The cache consistency algorithm we describe is basically the *ownership* protocol used in the Synapse multiprocessor[11]. The alternative to an ownership protocol is to use a write-broadcast protocol, as used with the snoopy cache schemes.[10] With a write-broadcast protocol, the system bus acts as a sequencer, imposing a total ordering on memory updates consistent with that observed by each processor. However, a write-broadcast scheme requires a data path from the bus to the cache that can update the cache as required at near memory-reference speed. (Replicating cache tags or dual-porting the cache can reduce the contention at some cost in hardware.) It also requires a write-broadcast on every update of (potentially) shared memory at the level of the unit of indivisible memory update, typically a memory word or byte. This precludes the use of the large cache page sizes required for very low cache miss rates. Finally, it requires the cache either be physically addressed with a virtual-to-physical translation between the processor and cache or a physical-to-virtual address translation for use by the bus spy. (Note that the latter translation may be one-to-many unless virtual address aliasing is ruled out.) Thus, a write-broadcast approach requires a multi-master cache together with physical-to-virtual address translation and complex bus spy hardware, all operating at near memory-reference speed.

Most researchers have focused on the performance of different cache consistency protocols, looking only at the bus traffic levels. However, the consistency schemes providing the lowest bus traffic also tend to be the most complex and present a potential bottleneck between processor and cache memory, especially as processor and memory speeds increase. In contrast, we are interested in cache consistency schemes that are simple enough so there is minimal complexity in the processor-to-cache path and so a significant portion of the cache management can be performed in software.

7   Concluding Remarks

We have described the design of VMP, a shared-memory multiprocessor machine that uses software-controlled virtually addressed caches. We have argued that the basic approach of a virtually addressed cache with the processor being its single master provides the high memory bandwidth connection that will be required by processors of the future. Using this high-speed processor in combination with the local memory for cache management software and high-speed block data transfer hardware makes cache miss handling in software efficient. The software implementation provides a high degree of flexibility as well.

There are two major novel aspects of the design. First, an unusually large cache page size is used in combination with a large total cache size and a high-speed block data bus transfer facility, reducing the cache miss ratio so that software control of the caches is feasible. This eliminates the need for a considerable amount of specialized hardware, including memory management unit and cache miss handler. Instead, we simply provide per-processor local memory for the cache management code and data.

Second, the simple *bus monitor* in combination with software control makes it straight forward to solve the consistency problems associated with a virtually addressed cache. In particular, the scheme handles the virtual address aliases or synonyms with no restrictions and virtual address translation consistency. It also allows DMA devices to be accommodated with no special consistency support.

The bus monitor state machine is a hardware resource provided to the processor for cache consistency. However, the generality of the mechanism suggests there may be other uses.

The challenge of the VMP design is in the software. Clearly, the cache management software itself must be highly optimized as well as correct. Moreover, VMP operating system software must provide means of synchronization between processes that does not induce the thrashing that one would expect with conventional test-and-set busy-wait loops on top of the VMP design. Finally, programming systems for the VMP design need to recognize the importance of clustering related data on cache pages and compiling code and data for high cache page utilization. These demands on software technology are significant but also a common theme in previous efforts to redefine some of the hardware/software boundaries.

Finally, there appears to be some issues in designing processors for a VMP-like design. First, the ideal VMP processor is as fast as memory technology allows. Faster processors reduce the speed advantage of implementing complex control logic in hardware. Second, the processor has minimal overhead for taking a bus error (or suitable cache miss signal) trap and returning from the trap, including making some registers available for the trap handler. Fortunately, many of the RISC-style processors appear to being going in these directions.

8 Acknowledgements

The Stanford Center for Integrated Systems and Philips Research made the collaboration among the authors possible. We are grateful to Tim Mann, Michael Stumm, Ross Finlayson and Helen Davis for their critique of the design and early versions of the paper, and Naguine Navab for her work on the consistency software. The comments of the referees were extremely helpful. We thank Anant Agarwal for providing the cache simulation results and to Digital Equipment Corporation for suppplying the instruction traces.

References

[1] A. Agarwal and M. Horowitz.
MIPS-X Internal and External Caches.
Technical Report, Computer Laboratory, Stanford University, 1985.

[2] A. Agarwal, R.L. Sites, and M. Horowitz.
ATUM: A New Technique for Capturing Address Traces Using Microcode.
In Proc. 13th Int. Symp. of Computer Architecture, June 1986.

[3] J. Archibald and J.L. Baer.
An Evaluation of Cache Coherence Solutions in Shared-Bus Multiprocessors.
Technical Report 85-10-05, Computer Science, U. of Washington, October 1985.

[4] C.G. Bell.
Multis: a new class of multiprocessor computers.
Science, 228:462–467, April 1985.

[5] D. Cheriton.
Workform Processing: a model and language for parallel computation.
Stanford University, Computer Science Technical Report, to appear 1985.

[6] D.R. Cheriton.
The V kernel: A Software Base for Distributed Systems.
IEEE Software, 1(2), April 1984.

[7] D.R. Cheriton and M. Stumm.
The Multi-Satellite Star: Structuring Parallel Computations for a Workstation Cluster.
To appear in Distributed Computing.

[8] D. Clark.
Cache Performance in the VAX-11/780.
ACM Trans. on Computer Systems, 1(1), Feb. 1983.

[9] H.M. Deitel.
Introduction to Operating Systems.
Addison-Wesley, 1983.

[10] R. Katz et al.
Implementing a Cache Consistency Protocol.
In Proc. 12th Int. Symp. on Computer Architecture, pages 276–283, ACM SIGARCH, June 1985.
also SIGARCH Newsletter, Volume 13, Issue 3, 1985.

[11] S. Frank.
Tightly-coupled Multiprocessor System Speeds Memory Access Times.
Electronics, 57(1), January 1984.

[12] J.R. Goodman.
Using Cache Memory to Reduce Processor-Memory Traffic.
In Proc. Tenth International Symposium on Computer Architecture, pages 124–131, June 1983.

[13] A. Gupta, C. Forgy, and R. Wedig.
Parallel Algorithms and Architectures for Rule-Based Sytems.
In Proc. 13th Int. Symp. of Computer Architecture, June 1986.

[14] W.D. Hillis.
The Connection Machine.
MIT Press, 1985.

[15] C.A.R. Hoare.
Monitors: An Operating System Structuring Concept.
CACM, 17(10):549–557, October 1974.

[16] D. MacGregor and J. Robinstein.
A Performance Analysis of MC68020-based Systems.
IEEE Micro, 5(6):50–70, December 1985.

[17] C.L. Seitz.
The Cosmic Cube.
CACM, 28(1):22–33, January 1985.

[18] A.J. Smith.
Cache Evaluation and the Impact of Workload Choice.
In Proc. 12th Int. Symp. on Computer Architecture, pages 64–73, ACM SIGARCH, June 1985.
also SIGARCH Newsletter, Volume 13, Issue 3, 1985.

[19] A.J. Smith.
Cache Memories.
Computing Surveys, 14(3), September 1982.

CPU Cache Consistency with Software Support and Using "One Time Identifiers"*

Alan Jay Smith

Computer Science Division
EECS Department
University of California
Berkeley, California 94720
USA

Abstract

Multiprocessors with shared memory are currently viewed as the best way to obtain high (aggregate) performance at moderate or low cost. Shared memory is needed for the efficient and effective cooperation of processes and high performance requires the use of cache memory for each processor. A major problem is to ensure that all processors see exactly the same (consistent) view of those regions of memory that they are referencing; this is the cache consistency problem.

Almost all published and/or implemented solutions to the cache consistency problem have relied solely on hardware, and suffer from cost and performance disadvantages, especially for large numbers of processors. Some of the hardware solutions cannot be made to work at all for large numbers of processors. The generally known software solution for cache consistency requires write-through on all references and cache purging when a shared data area is released; this solution has a performance problem due to the memory bandwidth requirement of write-through.

In this paper, we propose a new software controlled cache consistency mechanism which doesn't require a shared bus and needs only limited hardware support. Shared writeable data is treated as write through in the cache; otherwise the cache is (optionally) copy-back, to minimize memory traffic. Write through ensures that the main memory copy of write-shared regions is always up to date, so that when a processor reads a line from main memory, it always gets the current value. A "one-time identifier" is associated with the TLB entry for each (shared) page and with the address tag for each line of that page that is cache resident; one time identifiers function as unique capabilities. Stale shared cache contents are made inaccessible by changing the one time identifier in the TLB entry for a page, so that the address tag on the cache line no longer matches; this avoids the need to purge the cache whenever write shared regions of memory are passed between processors. Limiting write through to data items to be read by other processors minimizes memory traffic and cache purges are required only when the supply of unique identifiers is exhausted. Our discussion in this paper also includes possible optimizations for this basic idea.

The advantages to the cache consistency mechanism proposed here include the fact that no shared bus is

needed, so that memory interconnection schemes permitting much higher bandwidth are possible. This, then, permits high performance multiprocessors with shared memory to be built with many more processors than shared bus schemes allow.

1. Introduction

The development over the last few years of high performance microprocessors and high performance 'super-minicomputers' has made it very cost effective to obtain high aggregate performance by building multiprocessors [Smit84b]. The performance of the processors in this class is very sensitive to the memory access time, and can also be limited by memory bandwidth; thus cache memories [Smit82,84a] are necessary. The problem is that potentially the contents of the same word of memory can appear in several cache memories at the same time, and unless care is taken, the values for that word held in the caches can differ with each other and with main memory. This is known as the *cache consistency problem*, the problem of ensuring that any and all (legitimate) references to a word of memory at a given time obtain the same value. (We use the word "legitimate" to mean that the computation is deterministic, in the sense of the use of correct synchronization operations.)

Almost all published and/or implemented solutions to the cache consistency problem rely entirely on hardware; we survey those solutions in section 2, below. Those mechanisms have the advantage that consistency is maintained transparently and no software changes are required, but none of those mechanisms are plausible for large numbers of high performance processors: directory methods are expensive and slow, and bus and broadcast methods suffer severe performance bottlenecks for more than a small number of processors.

For large numbers of processors sharing memory, software intervention seems to be necessary to maintain cache consistency, but the standard software solution of write through caches and frequent cache purges also limits performance. The standard software solution to cache consistency functions as follows: by using write through, main memory can be guaranteed to be up to date. Between the time a write shared region is released and the time it is rereferenced by a processor, the cache must be purged, to ensure that no "stale" copies of write-shared data remain; fresh copies are then obtained from the up to date main memory. The use of write through stresses memory bandwidth, which is frequently a system bottleneck, and the purging of cache not only significantly increases the cache miss ratio, but it is difficult to implement efficiently and can be slow. The software solution to cache consistency is discussed further in section

---

*The material presented here is based on research supported in part by the National Science Foundation under grant DCR-8202591, and by the Defense Advance Research Projects Agency (DoD), under Arpa Order No. 4871, Monitored by Naval Electronic Systems Command under Contract No. N00039-84-C-0089.

2.6.

In this paper, we propose a new means of assuring cache consistency through the use of software control and with appropriate hardware support. *Our new mechanism works as follows: We use write through only for shared writeable data, since for read shared data, main memory is always up to date, and for nonshared data, it doesn't matter whether main memory is current. Rather than purge the entire cache in order to avoid using stale data values, we make those values inaccessible: A* **one time identifier (OTI)** *is appended to the TLB entry for a page and to every line within that page which is cache resident; that identifier can be considered to be a* **capability.** *When a line is loaded into the cache, the current one time identifier for that page is placed in its real address tag, and subsequent references require that the one time identifier on the line match that in the TLB entry. Those lines can be made inaccessible by changing the OTI in the TLB entry.* Generating the OTIs is discussed in section 3.4.

The two new features of our design are: *(a) Use write through only for shared writeable data, and use copy back otherwise, thus minimizing memory traffic. (b) Associate with each entry in the TLB and also with each address tag for each cache line a 'one time' identifier; the identifier in the TLB and the one in the line address tag must match in order to reference the cache. When a write-shared memory region is passed from one processor to another, the passing processor makes the shared stale data inaccessible in his own cache by destroying the existing one time identifier.*

There are several advantages to our new mechanism. Primarily, it permits shared memory designs with very large numbers of processors, since no shared bus is needed, and thus memory bandwidth limitations are much less stringent. Avoiding cache purges significantly improves performance, both by improving the cache hit ratio, and by avoiding the real time delays for that purge to occur. The selective write through keeps the memory bandwidth well below what would be needed for write through on all writes, and thus either permits larger numbers of processors to be used or permits an implementation with a lower performance and cheaper memory interconnect.

In the next section of this paper, we survey the existing mechanisms for cache consistency. (For other surveys, see [Smit82, 84a, 85a], [Yen85].) Our new design is presented in section 3, with all relevant details, and with an extensive discussion of the various optimizations possible. The last section provides a brief overview.

2. Survey of Existing Cache Consistency Mechanisms

2.1. Shared Cache

The simplest possible solution to the cache consistency problem is to have only one cache and make all the processors share it; this is illustrated in Figure 1. Just this solution was used in the Amdahl 470, in which I/O was routed through the cache; the original design for the 470 also permitted a second CPU to use the same cache, but that machine version was never built. Another type of shared cache is shown in Figure 2, where the caches are associated with the memories, and are thus shared by all processors. Analyses of aspects of a shared cache appear in [Yeh81], [Yeh83].

There are two factors which make a shared cache design poor. First, the access time to the cache is the

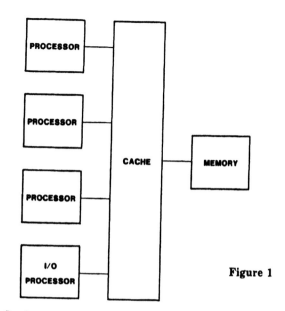

Figure 1

limiting factor in the machine performance for many or most high performance machines, and the access time to a shared cache would have to be greater than for a dedicated cache due to longer (physical) access paths, arbitration delays and access conflicts. Second, it is difficult to make the bandwidth of a shared cache sufficient to support even two high performance processors; this is the reason that the multiprocessor version of the Amdahl 470 was never built.

We do note here that our comments about how many processors a cache or bus can support implicitly assumes that those are high performance processors. If a cache or bus is made fast enough, at considerable expense, and slow (cheap) processors are used, then large numbers of processors can be accommodated. Since our interest is maximum performance at minimum cost, the latter solution is of little interest and we do not consider it further.

2.2. Shared and Private Cache

In this architecture, every processor has its own cache for data local to that processor, and then there is another cache which is shared among all processors. Data tagged as shared would be allocated to the shared cache. Such as scheme is discussed in [Flet83a,b], [IBM85], [Puza83]. Figure 3 illustrates that architecture.

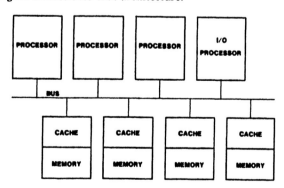

Figure 2

194

This design is feasible although rather inelegant due to the lack of symmetry of reference, but does have some problems. First, it must be possible to identify what data is shared; this is possible and our solution assumes this as well. There are a number of cases, however, (see section 3.3 below) and it is easy to designate far too much as shared. Second, the bandwidth of the shared cache still limits the number of processors. Finally, the slower access time to the shared cache may still affect system performance.

2.3. Broadcast Stores

A solution used in some machines (e.g. the IBM 370/168, 3033) is to broadcast all stores to all machines. The receiving machine then checks its own cache and if the target of the store is found there, then either the target is updated or (as with the 370/168 and 3033) is invalidated. This mechanism is discussed in [Jone76,77].

The problem with this design is that the fraction of the cache bandwidth required to service external updates/invalidates grows (almost) linearly with the number of processors and the resulting memory interference makes this solution implausible for more than 2 to 4 high performance processors, or a dozen or so medium performance processors such as the M68010. (The bandwidth required will grow somewhat less than linearly as cache access contention causes each processor to compute less rapidly and issue fewer writes.)

The use of the broadcast consistency mechanism can be extended to a considerably larger number of processors with the use of a BIAS Filter Memory (BFM) [Bean79]. The BFM remembers the k most recently invalidated lines and filters out repeated requests to invalidate the same cache line. The performance limit is now determined by both the bandwidth of the BFM, which has to handle all stores by all processors, and the interference with the cache by initial invalidates. If the hit ratio in the BFM were 75%, then at most four times as many processors could be used before the cache bandwidth was seriously stressed; this is still a small number of processors. (The BFM bandwidth itself might not be a problem, since it could be interleaved; the cache is generally too expensive to interleave.)

2.4. Directory Methods

The first hardware based consistency mechanism to be described in the literature was that of a centralized directory [Tang76]. In this architecture, main memory maintains a directory which keeps track of which lines are in which caches, and in what status (shared / exclusive). When a processor requests a line for shared access, the main memory controller ensures that no other processor has that line for exclusive access by searching its directory and requiring that any processor holding the line for exclusive access relinquish it. When a processor requests a line for exclusive access (or converts a line from shared to exclusive) the controller invalidates the line in the caches of any processor holding it. Figure 4 shows an architecture of this type, where the "memory controller" holds the directory. Analysis of and improvements to this basic scheme appear in [Arch84], [Cens78], and [Dubo82]. The IBM 3081 uses a version of this algorithm in which the System Controller (SC) maintains a copy of the directory for the cache for each CPU [Gust82]; when the SC is queried, it is called a "cross interrogate." Various

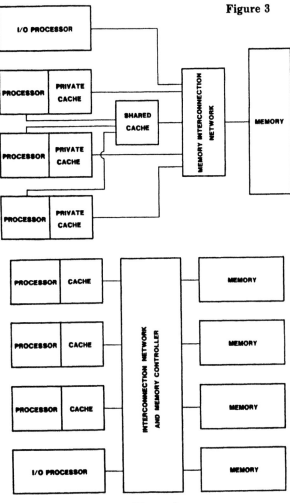

Figure 3

Figure 4

optimizations to the IBM design are discussed in [Bren84], [Flus83], [Hrus82], [Kryg84], and [Knig84].

There are some limitations to the centralized directory method. First, the central controller is expensive and complicated. Second, processing of misses can be slow due to the need to reference the directory and perhaps recall lines from other caches; queueing delays will slow up memory access even further. Finally, the bandwidth of the controller must be sufficient to accommodate all processors at all plausible miss rates.

2.5. Bus Methods

With the availability of high performance, large address space microprocessors, multiprocessor designs in which several microprocessors all share the same main memory bus have become popular; this architecture is illustrated in Figure 5. Because all processors share the same path to main memory, each can monitor misses from all other caches, and the directory method can be implemented straightforwardly in a distributed manner. In one design, a fetch (shared access) from memory will cause any cache holding a dirty copy of the line to provide it to the requesting processor before main memory can respond. A write (exclusive access) miss, or an attempt to write to a line held as shared, will cause all other caches

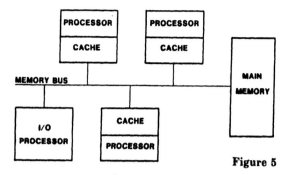

Figure 5

to invalidate their copy of the line.

The first bus consistency method was proposed in [Good83]. Improvements and extensions have appeared in [Fran84], [Papa84], [Rudo84], and [Katz85].

There are several problems with the bus methods, which limit their applicability. First, all processors must share a common bus, which may be difficult due to aggregate memory traffic and other reasons such as bus length, bus loading, physical configuration, etc. Second, the bus traffic limitation sets an upper limit on the number of processors that can be accommodated. Finally, the interface between the cache and the bus must be fairly sophisticated.

2.6. Software Enforced Consistency

In order for a computation to be deterministic, synchronized access to shared resources, such as memory, must be enforced. This implies (although not trivially) that the operating system software knows which areas of memory will be shared and when, and it can issue commands to the various processor caches so that references to that shared memory will be correct.

There are two issues in enforcing consistency:

(1) When a processor requests a line for a read, it must get the latest value; this can be arranged if all misses are serviced from main memory and if main memory is itself guaranteed to be up to date. The use of write through ensures that main memory is current.

(2) When an area of memory is referenced sequentially by processors A, then B, and then A again, we must be sure that the values that A sees are not "stale", through having remaining in A's cache while B modified them. The traditional solution to this problem is to have A purge its own cache when it releases the shared area of memory. This implementation is used by the RP3 [Bran85], and NYU Ultracomputer [Edle85] (both of which also make some shared information uncacheable) and is also discussed in [Maza77].

This traditional way of implementing software consistency causes two performance problems. First, all caches are write through, which burdens main memory with write traffic and may cause processors to block while waiting for writes to complete [Smit79]. Second, the frequent purging of caches when shared areas of memory

are released can significantly increase the overall cache miss ratio. It is also worth noting that purging a cache which is implemented using standard RAM chips is slow; each entry has to be invalidated in turn.

3. New and Efficient Software Solution

3.1. Assumptions and Hardware Support

In order for a software consistency mechanism to work, we have to make some assumptions and have to require certain hardware support. We list those items here:

(1) We assume that memory is paged, that the processors generate virtual addresses and that the caches use real addresses. A TLB (translation lookaside buffer) [Smit82,84a] is used to translate virtual to real addresses. TLBs are one per processor, and are not shared between processors. (The real address cache is needed so that the OTI in the TLB entry can be compared with the OTI part of the line address tag. It is possible to create a design in which operation with a virtual address cache is possible; this is discussed below in section 3.5.) A TLB entry is shown in Figure 6.

(2) We assume that the relevant software (operating system or user) knows which areas of memory are write shared and when control is passed. For simplicity, we assume that access to a write shared region begins with a P(S) (semaphore request) action or its equivalent (e.g. test and set); the access terminates with a V(S) (semaphore release) action. (We assume that there is some indivisible synchronization operation such as P(S) and V(S) or test and set, or compare and swap.) We further assume that the operating system can determine which pages compose the shared region and that each shared region uses an integral number of pages. (I.e. unneeded regions of the last shared page are not allocated to something else. Our mechanism does not support a finer level of granularity of sharing than the page.)

(3) The caching is controlled on a page basis by a two bit field. The first bit (*cacheable bit*) specifies whether a line is cacheable at all, or whether it must be referenced only from main memory. (Uncacheable items would typically include semaphores (synchronization variables) and data that is write-shared with few references by each processor before access is passed. The RP3 and NYU Ultracomputer make some items uncacheable.) The second bit (*write-through bit*) specifies whether the line is to be managed copy-back or write-through. In general, as explained below, shared areas will be managed write-through. When an entry is made in the TLB, the two bit field is copied into the TLB in order to specify the appropriate type of operation on each reference (see Figure 6). We note that the settings of the write through and cacheable bits can be different for different processes, since they reside in the page table for each process. (The availability of copy back is for performance reasons only; write through is sufficient for the correctness of our mechanism.)

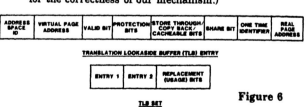

ADDRESS SPACE ID	VIRTUAL PAGE ADDRESS	VALID BIT	PROTECTION BITS	STORE THROUGH/ COPY BACK/ CACHEABLE BITS	SHARE BIT	ONE TIME IDENTIFIER	REAL PAGE ADDRESS

TRANSLATION LOOKASIDE BUFFER (TLB) ENTRY

ENTRY 1	ENTRY 2	REPLACEMENT (USAGE) BITS

TLB SET

Figure 6

(4) A third bit, called the *shared bit*, specifies whether the page is shared between processors. This bit is set by the operating system, either from its own knowledge or by an explicit request from the user. For the optimized versions of the implementation of our consistency mechanism, the shared bit is not always the same as the write through bit; in the simplest implementation, it is always the same.

(5) The TLB real address field and the real address tag for each line each have room for an additional field which we call the *one time identifier* (OTI) field. When the shared bit is on, the OTI fields from the TLB and the line address tag are compared, and if they don't match, the overall match circuitry reports "no match." (If the shared bit is off, the compare does not include the OTI fields.) The function of the OTI is very similar to that of a *capability*, in that it authorizes (permits) reference. See Figures 6 and 7 for an illustration.

(6) There is an *OTI register*, the contents of which are loaded into any new TLB entry for which the shared bit is on. The OTI register is incremented every time it supplies a value. When the OTI register overflows, the entire cache is purged. There must be some mechanism to purge the cache; since it happens seldom, it need not be especially efficient. Generation of OTIs is discussed in more detail in section 3.4, where we also consider the frequency of overflow of the OTI register.

(7) There must be an *Invalidate TLB Entry (ITLBE)* command which will remove an entry from the TLB based on its virtual address. (This can also be accomplished by purging the TLB, but with significant additional performance loss. Also, as discussed below, purging all TLB entries which have the shared bit set is sufficient.)

Although the list above of assumptions and hardware requirements appears to be long, that is the result of an attempt to very clear and explicit about what is needed. In fact, the amount of hardware needed is no more than is required for any of the hardware consistency schemes, and is considerably less than for some.

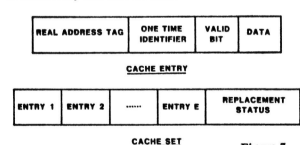

CACHE ENTRY

CACHE SET Figure 7

3.2. The (Basic) Consistency Algorithm

For the basic version of the consistency algorithm given here, we assume that *the shared bit is on for all pages which are write shared between two or more processors* and *any shared page is designated write through.*

Initial Use of Shared Area: The first reference to a write shared region (i.e. one with the shared bit on) or a (re)reference subsequent to the use of the region by another processor, will cause the TLB to be reloaded, automatically, via the hardware, with a new translation entry for any page referenced in that region. This is arranged (see below) by ensuring that there is no current valid TLB entry. Associated with the new TLB entry will be a new one time identifier (OTI) obtained from the OTI register.

Whenever a line is fetched which is within a page marked as shared, the OTI field from the corresponding TLB entry is loaded into the line address tag. The OTI in the TLB entry is compared on all references with that in the cache line. This will prevent access to any line which remains in the cache from previous use, i.e. stale data, since those stale entries will have a different OTI value in their tags. Any lines loaded by virtue of this new TLB entry will have the same new OTI and will be accessible via that new TLB entry.

End of Use of Shared Area: When access to a write shared region is about to be given up (equivalent to V(S)), the TLB entry for every page in that region is invalidated by issuing ITLBE (invalidate TLB entry) commands for each page. This ensures that all data in this region in the cache is now inaccessible and that subsequent references will require new fetches from main memory.

As should be clear, this algorithm avoids the stale data problem without purging the entire cache; only individual TLB entries need to be purged. Memory traffic is minimized by limiting write through to write shared regions.

In Figures 8 and 9, we illustrate the design and operation of the cache, with the special modifications we have proposed.

3.3. What is Shared, and Special Case Optimization

The issue of what is shared is not quite as trivial as it might seem on first inspection. In this section, we list all of the circumstances that lead to the same region of memory being write shared between processors. Some of those cases benefit from special optimizations. We note in particular the distinction between the use of the shared bit and the write through bit. The shared bit is to ensure that when a processor reads a region for which this bit is set, it gets fresh (up to date) data from main memory. The function of the write through bit is to ensure that when a processor with that bit set writes a region, main memory is forced to be current, and thus another processor, when reading the region currently being written to, gets the up to date values. If the use of the shared region is not symmetric, optimizations are possible, as we describe below.

3.3.1. Supervisor Data Structures

The typical shared region of memory would be one containing supervisor data structures such as the job queue. This is handled quite well using the basic algorithm.

3.3.2. Input/Output

Input/output processors (or channels) write directly to main memory, so memory is guaranteed to be current on a read. A processor reading from an input buffer must have the shared bit set for that region to be sure of getting the fresh data from memory. It need not have the write through bit set, since this is an input buffer and no other processor will subsequently read from the area.

197

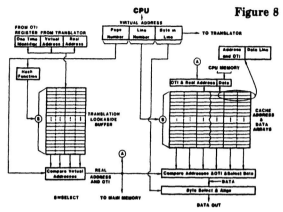

Figure 8

A processor writing to an output buffer must have the write though bit set, so that memory is made up to date. It need not have the shared bit set, since it is not reading from the region.

3.3.3. Message Buffers and Regions

In some systems, processes communicate by passing message buffers, or using mail boxes or pipes. This is one way communication, which means that the sender must use write through and the receiver must use the OTI mechanism, i.e. have the shared bit set.

3.3.4. Forking a Process

If a process is forked off, and the child processes run on the same processor, no special steps need be taken; i.e. neither the write through nor shared bits need to be set in either address space.

If a child process is to run on a different processor, then precautions must be taken. We consider two cases: when the new child has a new copy of the address space, and when the children share the existing address space and physical memory.

If a new address space copy is created, then the program (OS function) making the copy must have the write through bit set in the target pages. The child, which gets a new address space and page table, referencing the physical memory which was the target of the copy, should not have the write through bit set. It does need to have the shared bit set, since although the address space is new, the local cache may contain stale values for that region of main memory.

CACHE OPERATION FLOW CHART

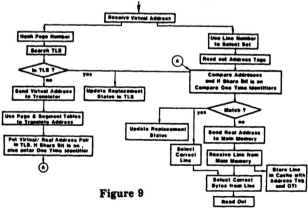

Figure 9

If the child operates in the same address space on the same (shared) physical memory, then access to data must be controlled in the same was as access to shared supervisor data structures.

3.3.5. Semaphores

Semaphores are by definition shared. (By "semaphore", we refer to those variables used for synchronization, including the targets of P(S) and V(S), and test and set instructions.) Since semaphores are only referenced on entry and exit from critical sections, they are likely to be referenced infrequently, and may be made uncacheable; if they are cacheable, they must be placed in a region which is referenced both with the write through bit and shared bit on. Further, it must be possible to operate on semaphores in an indivisible manner so as to accomplish synchronization (i.e. both the cache and main memory are locked and held until the operation is complete); this is a general requirement and is not specific to our consistency mechanism.

3.3.6. Process Migration

Ideally, in a shared memory (tightly coupled) multiprocessor system, we would like to be able to move processes from one processor to another. When memory and all I/O devices are shared between processors, this can be very easy to do, since the process is not bound to any aspect of a specific processor. (Migrating processes in a distributed system in which neither memory or I/O devices are shared is, conversely, very hard, since a process in that case is generally bound to the processor and its I/O devices.) In order for a process to be migratable, it must be treated as if it were a shared data structure: all accesses must be write through, and the processor giving up the process must purge (ITLBE) all relevant TLB entries. This solution, while correct and feasible, because of write through results in a high level of memory traffic and a consequent performance penalty or limitation.

There are two possible ways to minimize the performance penalty here of using write through. One possibility is to create a hardware cache flush mechanism, so that when the process is relinquished, the dirty lines in the cache are immediately expelled and main memory updated. This is straightforward but additional logic is required, and a considerable real time delay can elapse while the cache is flushed.

The second possibility is to create *an architecture with two levels of consistency*, such as that illustrated in Figure 10. There we see a number of busses, with several

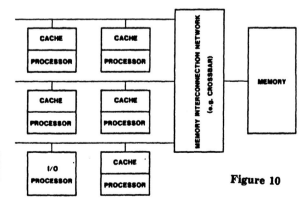

Figure 10

198

processors on each bus. The busses are connected via a crossbar to the main memory. In that architecture, bus-type consistency protocols can be used to ensure that all processors on the same bus have consistent caches; in that case, processes can be moved (only) among the processors on the same bus without using write through. A more extreme version of this approach is to simply forbid process migration; the dispatch queue would be particular to each processor. We believe that the advantages of a bus watch consistency mechanism are substantial, when performance considerations (i.e. bus bandwidth) permit such an architecture. Our proposed design permits the use of a shared bus for small numbers of processors, with our consistency mechanism used only for sharing between processors on different busses.

3.4. One Time Identifiers

Thus far we've given only a very cursory description of the creation and use of the one time identifiers (OTIs); we expand on that here.

The OTI consists of a k-bit field supplied by the OTI register (OTIR). The OTIR is simply a counter, which is incremented every time a value is read from it. The k-bit OTI is kept in every TLB entry and in the address tag field of every cache line. In both cases, the extra storage can be significant in relative terms, although likely not in absolute terms. Assume a machine with 16Mbytes of real storage, 32 bits of virtual address, a 4K page size and a 12 bit OTI (i.e. 4096 different OTIs available). Then a TLB entry consists of 20 bits of virtual address tag, 12 bits of real address field, and 12 bits of OTI. The real address tag on a cache line has expanded from 12 to 24 bits, including the new OTI. (With a reasonable line size [Smit85c], such as 16-bytes (128 bits), the extra 12 bits per line are less than 10% of the total storage to implement the cache.) The comparators that check the real address tags for a match have increased from 12 to 24, plus a new signal line to disable the OTI compare if the share bit is off.

The name "one time identifier" implies that every OTI value is unique and never reused, much like a capability. If it were possible to make the OTI field large enough, e.g. 48 bits, then OTIs could indeed be unique. Because of the need to conserve storage and minimize comparators, however, the size of the OTI needs to be much smaller, which means that eventually the OTIR will overflow or wraparound. If wraparound were to occur, there would be a (very small) chance that a preexisting real address/OTI pair in the TLB could be recreated, leading to a match with stale data still in the cache. The implication is that *when the OTIR overflows, the cache must be purged.*

The cache can be purged in either the foreground or background. A foreground purge means that the machine stops while a small engine (microengine or finite state machine) invalidates each address tag for each line in the cache; because the tags are typically implemented out of standard RAM chips, they can't be invalidated the way a set of flip-flops could be reset. A foreground purge thus requires a real-time halt in processing. We note that only entries with the shared bit on need to be invalidated, but every entry needs to be examined. It might also be possible to purge a cache in software, by writing a code loop guaranteed to cause every current entry in the cache to be pushed. Such a use of software simplifies the hardware, but is likely to be slower. Another difficulty with a software purge is that it must be completely clear

that all existing entries are actually purged, even when traps and interrupts occur during the purge loop.

A cache purge in the background is also possible; i.e. the processor continues processing while spare cache cycles are used to perform the necessary invalidates. We add one more bit to each address tag, which we call the *bank bit* (as in "memory bank"). The bank bit is compared to the *bank flag* on each access, and the real addresses match only if the bank bit matches the bank flag. When an entry is loaded into the cache, the bank bit is always set to the current value of the bank flag. A cache purge can be temporarily accomplished by flipping the bank flag, thus causing every entry in the cache to become invalid. We say "temporarily" because every entry in the cache with the old value of the bank bit must be genuinely invalidated before the bank flag is again flipped; this can be done by an engine using spare cache cycles to invalidate entries.. If the time until the OTIR overflow is reasonably large, as would be the case for a 12 bit OTI, then all invalidations could be easily accomplished in the background. This same mechanism was used in the Amdahl 470 to purge the TLB [Smit82,84a].

It is also possible to implement the valid bits for each cache line as a set of flip flops, rather than as one bit fields within the line address tags. In that case, all of the flip-flops can be reset in one cycle with one signal.

An important issue is the size (number of bits) of the OTI. Because the OTI takes space, we would like to minimize its size. On the other hand, we would like to minimize the frequency of OTIR overflows, since they are costly both in terms of delay to purge the cache and in extra cache misses to reload the cache. As a first approximation, an OTI that is slightly larger than the $\log2$ of the size of the TLB seems to be appropriate. For example, a 512 entry TLB with a 12 bit OTI would at most cause the cache to be purged after 2048 TLB misses, or 4 "TLB-loads". If OTIs are issued only for shared pages, then only a fraction of the TLB misses would use an OTI and overflow would be even less frequent. Since the time to overflow increases exponentially with the size of the OTI, decreasing the size of the OTI by 1 or 2 bits seems to have little payoff due to the increased frequency of overflow (and 1 or 2 bits doesn't save much storage); ·conversely, with an OTI of the indicated size, the frequency of overflow should be low enough that further decreases would have little merit.

3.5. Some Alternatives

For some aspects of our design, there are alternatives. In this section, we list some such which don't naturally fit elsewhere in this paper.

Instead of having the V(S) (release of shared area) function purge one's own TLB entry, it could instead broadcast a TLB entry purge (based on real rather than virtual address) and require that all other caches do a purge. This seems to be less efficient and more difficult to implement.

The ITLBE (invalidate TLB entry) command could instead be given by the P(S) function, when the shared region is acquired, rather than by V(S) when the shared area is released.

Our scheme is compatible with a *virtual address cache design* in one of two possible ways. The first way is to create a TLB that provides only the OTI as an output, instead of both the real address and OTI; the match is then made with the OTI only. This forfeits the access time advantages of a virtual address cache [Smit82,84a]. For the second method, we have to consider how a real address cache works; see Figures 8 and 9 for an illustration. In brief, the high order bits of the virtual address are fed to the TLB which yields the corresponding bits of the real address. The middle bits of the virtual address (which are not translated, and so are the same as the corresponding real bits) are used to select the set in the set-associative cache. The real address tags from that set are then read out and compared with the now available real address. If a match is found, the appropriate portion of the line is selected and read out.

What we can do instead is as follows: we read out the tags from the chosen set and do the select based on a comparison of virtual address tags, and gate out the result if successful. Somewhat (slightly) later, the real address and OTI comparison is performed. If it is successful (i.e. yields the same result as the virtual address comparison), then no action is taken; if it is not successful, then a trap signal is sent and the instruction is restarted after the cache miss is serviced. The important point is that to do this we have to be able to halt the current instruction before it updates registers or memory.

Instead of using write through, it is also possible to have the V(S) action result in a push of all modified lines. This decreases main memory traffic at the cost, as explained above, of examining every cache entry and pushing the dirty ones. Extra hardware is needed, and every such global push causes a significant real time delay. In addition, the burst of writes over the bus or interconnection net to memory can block the other processors.

We noted above that our algorithm uses store through only for shared writeable data. It is possible to use store through for all data, at the cost of increased memory traffic, and thereby avoid the need to implement copy back as well as store through. This doesn't affect the use of the shared bit nor the OTI.

It is worth observing that the OTI mechanism provides an easy way to purge the entire cache. If all TLB entries are invalidated, then all current cache entries become inaccessible, and the cache must be reloaded. Since the TLB is substantially smaller and has fewer entries than the cache, it can be easier to invalidate than the cache itself.

3.6. The Optimized Algorithm

The optimized algorithm is exactly the same as the basic algorithm, but *the shared and write through bits are set differently. The shared bit is set only if the shared region was (or may have been) written by a different processor. The write through bit is set only if the shared region will (may) be read by another processor.* The cases for which this applies are discussed in detail in section 3.3.

These changes substantially reduce the frequency of write through and also the frequency with which OTIs are issued, and therefore the frequency of OTIR overflow and cache purge.

3.7. Costs and Performance

As noted throughout this paper, there are costs associated with our software consistency mechanism. In this section we review those costs.

Extra storage is required in the TLB and in the cache address tags for the OTIs; we estimated less than a 10% increase in cache storage and perhaps 30% increase in TLB storage, using the field sizes from section 3.4. There is also an approximate doubling of signal lines out of the TLB and address tag storage and an approximate doubling of the number of comparators required.

The engine to do a cache purge when the OTIR overflows is needed, unless the valid bits are kept in flip-flops. The additional misses caused by such a cache purge must be accommodated. The number of additional misses, with a reasonable size OTI, overall should be negligible.

The ITLBE (invalidate TLB entry) function must be provided and must be issued by the V(S) operation.

The cache should be able to support both write through and copy back (for best performance), specified on a page by page basis. The memory system must be able to support the extra traffic due to writes to the shared storage. (The amount of such traffic is very sensitive to the software and the algorithms used in the operating system. In some cases, the write through traffic would be negligible; in others, almost all stores would be write through, amounting to 10-20% of all memory references [Smit79,85b]. *This uncertainly in the frequency with which store through would have to be used prevents any detailed and exact performance analysis of the mechanism proposed in this paper.*)

The hardware required to support ITLBE, cache purge, and selectable write through/ copy back seems to be no worse than that required to implement the hardware based consistency protocols. Some extra hardware is needed, however, so a sharp reduction in hardware cost is not the primary advantage of the OTI scheme.

It is important to note that *the efficiency of our algorithm does not decrease significantly with increasing numbers of processors,* provided that the memory bandwidth is otherwise sufficient to support write through. All actions, except the store throughs to main memory, are insensitive to the number of processors. It should be possible to minimize the impact of the store throughs by very selective use of the store through feature. Because unlike the bus consistency algorithms, we can tolerate multiple data paths to memory, as with a banyan or omega network, or crossbar, additional memory traffic can be easily accommodated. (The RP3 system [Bran85] uses an omega network, and can tolerate store through on all writes, with 512 processors.)

4. Conclusions

We have described a new software controlled and hardware supported mechanism to maintain cache consistency in a shared memory (tightly coupled) multiprocessor system. It can be implemented with modest extensions to most machine architectures and with modest additional amounts of hardware to support the consistency mechanism.

The use of OTIs to maintain cache consistency provides a new and significantly improved means to high performance multiprocessing. Because our mechanism does not require a shared bus, nor a complicated central directory, very large numbers of processors can be accommodated. Since we don't require cache purges (except very infrequently) nor do we require write through

200

on all writes, performance should be significantly better than for other software controlled designs (e.g. [Bran85], [Edle85]). We believe that our design should have important applications for tightly coupled multiprocessor systems with large numbers of processors.

Acknowledgements

My thanks to Susan Eggers, Mark Hill, Randy Katz and Howard Sachs for their comments on a draft of this paper. Of course, any remaining errors or omissions are the responsibility of the author.

Bibliography

[Arch84] James Archibald and Jean-Loup Baer, "An Economical Solution to the Cache Coherency Problem", Proc. 11'th Ann. Symp. on Comp. Arch., June, 1984, Ann Arbor, Michigan, pp. 355-362.

[Bean79] Bradford Bean, Keith Langston, Richard Partridge, Kian-Bon Sy, Cache Directories in a Multiprocessor System", United States Patent 4,142,234, February 27, 1979.

[Bran85] W. C. Brantley, K. P. McAuliffe and J. Weiss, "RP3 Processor-Memory Element", Proc. of the 1985 Int. Conf. on Parallel Processing, to appear.

[Bren84] J. G. Brenza, "Cross-Interrogate Directory for a Real, Virtual or Combined Real/Virtual Cache", IBM Tech. Disc. Bull., 26, 11, April, 1984, pp. 6069-6070.

[Cens78] Lucien Censier and Paul Feautrier, "A New Solution to Coherence Problems in Multicache Systems", IEEETC, C-27, 12, December, 1978, pp. 1112-1118.

[Drim81] E.G. Drimak, P. F. Dutton, and W. R. Sitler, "Attached Processor Simultaneous Data Searching and Transfer Via Main Storage Controls and Intercache Transfer Controls", 24, 1A, June, 1981, pp. 26-27.

[Dubo82] Michel Dubois and Faye Briggs, "Effects of Cache Coherency in Multiprocessors", IEEETC, C-31, 11, November, 1982, pp. 1083-1099.

[Edle85] Jan Edler, Allan Gottlieb, Clyde P. Kruskal, Kevin McAuliffe, Larry Rudolph, Marc Snir, Patricia Teller and James Wilson, "Issues Related to MIMD Shared-Memory Computers: the NYU Ultracomputer Approach", Proc. 12'th Int. Symp. on Comp. Arch., Boston, June, 1985, pp. 126-135.

[Flet83a] R. P. Fletcher, R. A. Heller, and D. M. Stein, "MP-Shared Cache with Store-Through Local Caches", IBM Tech. Disc. Bull., 25, 10, March, 1983, pp. 5133-5135.

[Flet83b] R. P. Fletcher, D. M. Stein and I. Wladawsky-Berger, "MP-Shared Processor Memory", IBM Tech. Disc. Bull., 25, 10, March, 1983, pp. 5128- 5132.

[Flus83] Federick O. Flusche, Richard Gustafson, Bruce McGilvray, "Cache Storage Line Sharability Control for a Multiprocessor System", United States Patent 4,394,731, July 19, 1983.

[Fran84] Steven J. Frank, "Tightly Coupled Multiprocessor System Speeds Memory Access Times", Electronics, January 12, 1984, pp. 164-169.

[Good83] James R. Goodman, "Using Cache Memory to Reduce Processor-Memory Traffic", Proc. 10'th Ann. Int. Symp. on Comp. Arch., June, 1983, Stockholm, Sweden, pp. 124-131.

[Gust82] R. N. Gustafson and F. J. Sparacio, "IBM 3081 Processor Unit: Design Considerations and Design Process", IBM J. Res. and Devel., 26, 1, January, 1982, pp. 12-21.

[Hrus82] J. Hrustich and W. R. Sitler, "Dual-Stream Processor Cache Search Synchronization", IBM Tech. Disc. Bull., 25, 7A, December, 1982, pp. 3559-3561.

[IBM85] IBM Corp., "Shared Instruction and/or Data Caches in a Multiprocessing System", IBM Tech. Disc. Bull., 27, 12, May, 1985, pp. 6845-6846.

[Jone76] J. D. Jones, D. M. Junod, R. L. Partridge and B. L. Shawley, "Updating Cache Data Array's with Data Stored by Other CPU's", IBM Tech. Disc. Bull., 19, 2, July, 1976, pp. 594-596.

[Jone77] J. D. Jones and D. M. Junod, "Cache Address Directory Invalidation Scheme for Multiprocessing System", IBM Tech. Disc. Bull., 20, 1, June, 1977, pp. 295-296.

[Katz85] R. H. Katz, S. J. Eggers, D. A. Wood, C. L. Perkins, and R. G. Sheldon, "Implementing a Cache Consistency Protocol", Proc. 12'th Ann. Int. Symp. on Comp. Arch., June, 1985, Boston, Mass, pp. 276-283.

[Knig84] J. W. Knight and L. Liu, "Early Store-Through of XI-Sensitive Data", IBM Tech. Disc. Bull., 27, 2, July, 1984, pp. 1073-1074.

[Kryg84] M. A. Krygowski, "Probabilistic Updating for Store-In Cache Cross Interrogation", IBM Tech. Disc. Bull., 26, 10B, March, 1984, pp. 5504-5505.

[Maza77] Guy Mazare, "A Few Examples of How to Use a Symmetrical Multi-Micro-Processor", Proc. 4'th Ann. Symp. on Computer Architecture, March, 1977, pp. 57-62.

[Nest85] Elliot Nestle and Armond Inselberg, "The Synapse N+1 System: Architectural Characteristics and Performance Data of a Tightly Coupled Multiprocessor System", Proc. 12'th Ann. Int. Symp. on Computer Architecture, June 17-19, 1985, Boston, Mass., pp. 233-239.

[Papa84] Mark Papamarcos and Janak Patel, "A Low-Overhead Coherence Solution for Multiprocessors with Private Cache Memories", Proc. 11'th Ann. Int. Symp. on Comp. Arch., June, 1984, Ann Arbor, Michigan, pp. 348-354.

[Puza83] T. R. Puzak, R. N. Rechtschaffen and K. So, "Managing Targets of Multiprocessor Cross Interrogates", IBM Tech. Disc. Bull., 25, 12, May, 1983, p. 6462.

[Rudo84] Larry Rudolph and Zary Segall, "Dynamic Decentralized Cache Schemes for MIMD Parallel Architectures", Proc. 11'th Ann. Int. Symp. on Comp. Arch., June, 1984, Ann Arbor, Michigan, pp. 340-347.

[Smit79] Alan Jay Smith, "Characterizing the Storage Process and its Effect on the Update of Main Memory by Write-Through", JACM, 26, 1, January, 1979, pp. 6-27.

[Smit82] Alan Jay Smith, "Cache Memories", Computing Surveys, 14, 3, September, 1982, pp. 473-530.

[Smit84a] Alan Jay Smith, "CPU Cache Memories", to appear in Handbook for Computer Designers, ed. Flynn and Rossman.

[Smit84b] Alan Jay Smith, "Trends and Prospects in Computer System Design", part of proceedings of a Seminar on High Technology, at the Korea Institute for Industrial Economics and Technology, Seoul, Korea. June 21-22, 1984. Available as UC Berkeley CS Report UCB/CSD84/219. Verbatim transcript of speech published in "Challenges to High Technology Industries", Korea Institute for Economics and Technology, pp. 79-152.

[Smit85a] Alan Jay Smith, "Problems, Directions and Issues in Memory Hierarchies", Proc. 18'th Annual Hawaii International Conference on System Sciences, January 2-4, 1985, Honolulu, Hawaii, pp. 468-476. Also available as UC Berkeley CS Report UCB/CSD84/220.

[Smit85b] Alan Jay Smith, "Cache Evaluation and the Impact of Workload Choice", Report UCB/CSD85/229, March, 1985, Proc. 12'th International Symposium on Computer Architecture, June 17-19, 1985, Boston, Mass, pp. 64-75.

[Smit85c] Alan Jay Smith, "Line (Block) Size Selection in CPU Cache Memories", June, 1985. Available as UC Berkeley CS Report UCB/CSD85/239.

[Tang76] C. K. Tang, "Cache System Design in the Tightly Coupled Multiprocessor System", Proc. NCC, 1976, pp. 749-753.

[Yeh81] Chi-Chung Yeh, "Shared Cache Organization for Multiple-Stream Computer Systems", Report R-904, January, 1981, University of Illinois Coordinated Science Laboratory.

[Yeh83] Phil Yeh, Janak Patel and Edward Davidson, "Performance of Shared Cache for Parallel-Pipelined Computer Systems", Proc. 10'th Ann. Int. Symp. on Comp. Arch., Stockholm, Sweden, June, 1983, pp. 117-123.

[Yen85] Wei Yen, David Yen, and King-Sun Fu, "Data Coherence Problem in Multicache System", IEEETC, C-34, 1, January, 1985, pp. 56-65.

An Approach to Dynamic Software Cache Consistency Maintenance Based on Conditional Invalidation

Igor Tartalja and Veljko Milutinović

Department of Computer Engineering
School of Electrical Engineering
University of Belgrade

Abstract

This paper introduces a class of software protocols for the maintenance of cache consistency in multiprocessors with shared main memory and private caches. These protocols are designed to be built into the operating system primitives for mutual exclusion. The approach is based on a dynamic decision about invalidation of the shared segment copy residing in the private cache, at the moment of entering into the appropriate critical region.

We gradually introduce here three consistency schemes. They slightly differ in their complexity, and consequently in their rigidity of the invalidation conditions. The most complex and the most rigorous scheme founds on the verification of the shared data segment version ("Version Verification").

In relation to the "Version Control" scheme introduced by Cheong and Veidenbaum, our scheme requires neither a compile-time analysis, nor the comparison of the shared data version for every access to the cache memory. In relation to the "One Time Identifier" scheme introduced by Smith, our scheme is tuned to finer granularity of the shared data, invalidations are conditional, and no complex hardware support is required.

The first simulation results indicate that conditional invalidation increases the hit ratio, and consequently the processing power. Particularly, applied to a workload characterized by the read-mostly access pattern for shared segments, the Version Verification scheme takes an advantage.

1 Introduction

The cache consistency problem is inherent in multiprocessor systems with a shared main memory and private cache memories. The problem appears when two or more processors share changeable data. After one changes the value of a variable in its private cache memory, the values of the same variable in other caches become stale, and reading of these values causes a program malfunction.

This problem is being studied for over a decade now, and most of the solutions introduced so far were on the hardware level. One natural and well accepted classification of hardware schemes divides them in two basic groups: (a) snoopy schemes (see [Archi86] for a survey), and (b) directory schemes, using a centralized or a distributed directory (see [Agarw88] for a survey).

Mailing address: Igor Tartalja, School of Electrical Engineering, University of Belgrade, P.O.B. 816, 11000 Belgrade, Yugoslavia; e-mail: igor@yubgef51.bitnet

Proceedings of the 25-th Hawaii International Conference on System Sciences, HICSS-25, Kauai, Hawaii, U.S.A., January 1992

The major drawback of snoopy schemes is the increased bus traffic, caused by the activities for the consistency maintenance. Consequently, the scalability of these schemes is low, and they can be utilized efficiently only in systems with a relatively small number of processors. On the other hand, the directory schemes have a good scalability, but are complex and expensive to implement.

The major goal of hardware implementations is to make the cache consistency maintenance transparent to the programmer and the system software. Consequently, the cache consistency should be maintained on the individual reference level, i.e. the consistency mechanism have the reference level granularity.

Fortunately, it is not necessary to maintain the consistency on the individual reference level. In realistic parallel programs, the shared data are used in an order which guaranties correct program behavior ("weak ordering" [Duboi86, Adve90]). Therefore, a temporary inconsistency of the cache memory can be tolerated, until the moments when the relevant data are to be used. Consequently, the consistency maintenance can be concentrated in the moments when the processors are to be synchronized for access to shared data. In that way, granularity of the periods between two consecutive consistency maintenance activities becomes coarser. This results in a better efficiency of the system, because the number of consistency activities per time unit decreases. Furthermore, this fact enables that the consistency problem is partially migrated into the system software, which decreases the complexity and the cost of hardware.

The second part of 80s is characterized with a number of research efforts towards the software solutions to the problem [Brant85, Smith85, Veide86, Cheon88, Cytro88, Cheon89, and Benne90]. There is a number of reasons for this trend. First, as already indicated, software methods are less expensive to implement. Second, as we have also seen, software schemes are potentially more efficient than hardware schemes. Third, software schemes are scalable. In most of the software schemes, decisions are partially made statically (during the program translation), and partially dynamically (during the program execution). Therefore, we will use the classification into static schemes (if the decisions are predominantly done at compile time), and dynamic (if the decisions are predominantly done at run time). Static schemes are implemented as a part of the compiler, while the dynamic schemes are implemented in operating system kernels, through the primitive operations of mutual exclusion. In our opinion, two representative solutions are [Cheon89] for static schemes, and [Smith85] for dynamic schemes.

In this work we are especially interested in a class of non-numeric applications characterized by sequences of alternate access of a certain number of processors to a shared data segment, primarily for reading, and rarely for writing. A simple illustration of this class is as follows. A shared segment contains data about the status of a complex process; each processor in the system controls a certain number of subprocesses, frequently using global information about the status of the entire process, which is obtained through the shared segment.

Assuming that subprocesses slowly change the parameters, information about the changes of the relevant parameter is infrequently stored into the shared segment. Consequently, access dynamics to the shared segment are such that processors access it predominantly for reading purposes, and only occasionally for writing purposes. Execution progress of subprocesses controlled by different processors is approximately the same. Consequently, the alternate access (of different processors to the same shared segment) has a relatively high probability.

Accesses to the shared segment (regardless of the fact if the multiprocessor contains private caches or not) is done inside the critical code regions. Logically, if the multiprocessor includes private cache memories, a natural solution is to do a dynamic software consistency maintenance on the entry/exit points of critical regions.

In this paper we (gradually) introduce three schemes for dynamic software maintenance of the consistency. All schemes are based on decisions about invalidation of the shared segment copy residing in the private cache, at the moment of entering into the critical region. The decision is made using information stored in the shared segment table, i.e. using dynamic segment attributes. We refer to the class of schemes as "Selective and Conditional Self-Invalidation Class" (SCSIC) of schemes.

The first scheme is based on an Access Identification (AI) of a processor to a shared segment, while the second one is based on an Authorized Write (AW) to a shared segment. The third one is based on an Verification of the shared segment Version (VV). The third scheme is hardly more complex to implement then the previous two; however, it is provided by the most rigorous condition for invalidation, and is the best suited to the class of applications under consideration. In general, these schemes are relatively independent of the hardware, which implies that they can be implemented with a simple and a limited hardware support, as well as with the more complex hardware for efficient selective cache invalidation.

The structure of the remaining of the paper is as follows. In the next section (2), two existing state-of-the-art approaches for software maintenance of cache consistency are presented. The third section contains the description of the SCSIC of schemes, as well as a short comparison of the SCSIC of schemes with the Smith scheme "One Time Identifier" (OTI) and Cheong-Veidenbaum scheme "Version Control" (VC). Simulation analysis is in progress, but first results related to small scale, bus oriented multiprocessors, under an synthetic workload, are available and described in the fourth section. These results indicate that it is worth using the SCSIC of schemes, specially the VV scheme, in the environments with read-mostly shared data segments.

2 Two Representative State-of-the-Art Software Solutions

As already mentioned, the two representative software solutions to be discussed here are the "One Time Identifier" scheme (OTI) [Smith85], and the "Version Control" scheme (VC) [Cheon89, Cheon90]. The first scheme is representative of the fully dynamic approach, while the second one is representative of the predominantly static approach. Although these two solutions does not cover the entire related space, we have selected them because of the following reasons. Smith s approach is closely related to the operating system level, and it appears as the "starting point" for our research. Static approaches (like those reported in [Veide86, Cheon88, Cytro88, Cheon89]) are not of special interest for the operating system oriented solutions of cache coherence problem, but we find that an idea of shared data version, presented in [Cheon89], can be very useful regardless of the implementation layer, compiler or operating system.

2.1 The One Time Identifier Scheme

The essence of this method is as follows. Each TLB entry and each cache line get extended by the OTI field which contains the temporary unique identifier for the shared data page. Each TLB update is accompanied with a new OTI value written into the OTI field. The new OTI value is obtained from the special incrementer. In the case of the first access to a line in a page, the line is loaded from the main memory, and the value from the TLB entry OTI field is copied into the cache line OTI field. All subsequent references to that line compare the contents of the cache line OTI field and the TLB entry OTI field. If equal, that is a hit; otherwise, that is a miss. After the exit from the critical region, processor invalidates all TLB entries for pages that belong to shared data protected by the critical region being exited. On the first next processor reference to shared data, the corresponding TLB entry is loaded again, using a new value from the OTI register. This approach ensures that each subsequent reference to stale cache lines is treated as a miss, because the contents of the cache line OTI field differs from the corresponding value in the TLB entry.

Furthermore, Smith suggests a selective write-through, where the write of shared data is done as write-through, while the write of private data can be done using the copy-back technique. Write-through ensures that the shared data in main memory are actual. In this way, using invalidation (which causes the next access to be a miss), one forces the access to the actual data.

2.2 The Version Control Scheme

Papers [Veide86], [Cheon88], and [Cheon89] introduce three schemes for the software maintenance of consistency of private cache memories. The three schemes were compared in [Cheon90]. We will describe here only the third scheme, known as the VC scheme, which was shown to be superior to the other two. This scheme introduces the concept of monitoring the version of the shared data item. A similar but different mechanism is employed in the third (VV) of our SCSIC of schemes to be introduced later.

Cheong and Veidenbaum assume an environment typical of parallel numeric applications for which the code was generated either manually, or by a parallelizing compiler. Parallel *DoAll* loop is the basic program structure that expresses parallelism. The program execution model is based on the parallelism in the execution of tasks. Dependency between different tasks can be represented using directed graphs. Two tasks on the same graph level are independent, and they can be executed in parallel on two different processors. On each move from one graph level to another, a synchronization action is needed. One or more iterations of *DoAll* can form a task. No synchronization is needed between these tasks, because they belong to the same graph level.

The essence of the VC scheme is as follows. Each task that writes into a shared variable defines a new "version" of its contents. In case of tasks on the same graph level, as long as this level of task is executed, there is no possibility that the "new version" of a shared variable is needed by another processor. Therefore, between successive synchronization, a temporary inconsistency of the memory system is allowed. However, before the processor progresses through the task-level boundary, one must ensure that the last version of cache data is forwarded to main memory.

Each processor takes a local care about the version of each shared variable in its local memory (CVN - Current Version Number). When moving to the next task level, processors execute instructions to increment the current version number (CVN) for all variables being written during the execution of the previous level tasks. These instructions are generated by the compiler based on the static program analysis. Also, each cache line contains a field called BVN (Birth Version Number). The version number is written into the BVN field at each cache line allocation. After a read miss, and appropriate cache line allocation, BVN is equal to CVN. For every cache line update, the value of CVN + 1 is written into the BVN field. The values of CVN and BVN are compared for every access to shared data in the cache. If BVN is smaller than CVN, the data is stale, and the access is treated as a miss. If BVN is equal to or larger than CVN the access is treated as a hit.

2.3 Discussion of the Presented State-of-the-Art Solutions

Both approaches (OTI and VC) represent an important advance in the state-of-the-art of the field, and in certain conditions represent practically the best solutions. However, both schemes suffer certain disadvantages in some conditions, important from the point of the view of our assumed application.

Basic disadvantages of the OTI scheme are the relatively complex hardware support (the OTI register and the OTI field comparators) and the relatively low selectivity of the invalidation condition. After the exit from the critical region, processor invalidates all cache lines that contain shared data used in the exited region, in spite of the fact that the same processor may be the next user of the same data. In conditions typical of applications under consideration (read-mostly accesses), one disadvantage of the OTI scheme is in its unnecessary preventive invalidation, after every exit from the critical region in which (maybe) a shared data item was read-only.

Basic disadvantages of the VC scheme, in conditions typical of our application, are as follows. The program model oriented to parallel loops is not appropriate for our concurrent application - it is oriented to numeric applications, and the entire method is based in the compiler, while we want to have a consistency mechanism built into the operating system. On the other hand, the VC scheme is characterized with a high level of invalidation selectivity and is provided by a rigorous condition of invalidation. The condition preserves unnecessary invalidations, which is considerable for the read-mostly access pattern characterizing our application workload.

3 The Selective and Conditional Self-Invalidation Class (SCSIC) of Schemes

3.1 The Assumptions

The basic conditions of the analysis to follow are listed here:

(a) A shared memory multiprocessor with private caches is considered, using multitasking on each node. Effects of the migration of tasks are not considered.

(b) The following programming model is considered:

(1) Shared data are accessed exclusively from the critical regions. Critical regions guarantee the mutual exclusion of processes, and consequently of processors, during the access to shared data.

(2) Shared data are stored in segments, i.e. segment is the unit of data sharing, and access to segment has to be protected by the critical region.

(3) Critical regions have their identification. Consequently, different code parts (that access the same shared segment) have the same critical region identification. This enables a mutual exclusion of processes that access a shared segment asymmetrically.

(c) The following applications are considered:

Concurrent software systems with coarser-grained process scheduling. Their processes normally see different address spaces and communicate via messages; however, processes can also use a shared address space when a more efficient communication and a tighter logic interaction is needed. This is typical of some kinds of simulations in real time, process control, and similar. Numerical parallel applications based on the programming model of parallel loops are not considered here. We believe that consistency maintenance methods based on the utilization of compilers (like [Veide86, Cheon88, and Cytro88]) are better suited to that type of applications.

(d) Typical access pattern to shared data is characterized by a sequence of alternate accesses for reading (as indicated in the introductory part of this paper).

(e) Synchronization variables are in the shared memory; they do not get cached in private cache memories.

(f) Primitive operations of the operating system to enter and exit a critical region assume waiting queues. When a process is to enter a critical region, if the region is not free, the process will get suspended, and will be placed into the waiting queue for that region. Upon the exit from the critical region, operating system moves the process from the waiting queue for the critical region, into the queue of ready processes. Primitive operations for synchronization on the lower level (that assume a busy wait, like $P(S)$ and $V(S)$, Test&set and Reset, or similar [Duboi88]) are used only for the mutual exclusion of processes, to access system data used for implementation of upper-level operations like Enter/Exit_region.

3.2 Basic Idea: The Access Identification Scheme

Our approach is based on the fact that the shared segment within a critical region is private to a process, and consequently to the processor running the process. Therefore, it is enough to do the consistency maintenance activities only at the entry and/or exit to/from the critical region.

The other relevant fact is that if the processor which enters the critical region is the processor which was the last one to exit the same critical region, the private cache contents of that processor is actual, and no invalidation of lines that belong to the shared segment is needed. This invalidation condition is sufficient but not necessary. We refer to it as a Selective and Weakly Conditional Self-Invalidation condition (SWCSI). A more rigorous condition, that enables a better selectivity of invalidation, will be introduced later.

Invalidation of potentially stale lines is traditionally done at the exit from the critical region (e.g., in the RP3 [Brant85] and in the NYU Ultracomputer [Edler85]), or in the OTI scheme [Smith85]). Traditional approach is characterized by purging of private cache on exit from a critical region. This prevents stale data in the private cache, when the processor enters into the same critical region next time. Also, traditional approach assumes the write-through policy. It ensures that the contents of shared memory is actual. In the OTI scheme, at the exit from the critical region, the value of the OTI in the corresponding TLB entry is invalidated (although it was mentioned that the invalidation at the entry is also possible).

The schemes which preventively invalidate shared data in a private cache at the exit or the entry point of a critical region will be called the "UnConditional Self-Invalidation" Schemes (UCSI). For example, in the simulation analysis to follows, we will use an UnSelective and UnConditional (USUCSI) scheme, called "Base" scheme, to estimate the lower level of performance. This scheme purges entire data cache at the critical region entry. Also, we will use (for comparison purposes) a Selective and UnConditional Self-Invalidation scheme, called "OTI-like" scheme (in spite of the obvious differences compared to the original OTI scheme). This scheme selectively invalidates the shared data segment to be used at the critical region entry.

Our AI (SWCSI) scheme requires that the invalidation is done at the entry into the critical region, because it is the only moment when one can know if the processor which just exited the critical region is the one to enter it again.

This type of consistency maintenance mechanism can be especially useful in cases when one process (on one processor) that accesses a shared segment in a loop, enters and exits a critical region, without another process (on another processor) accessing the same segment in the meantime. In some considering applications, it is very important that the cache consistency maintenance is done efficiently, when this scenario happens. The basic idea is defined by the pseudo-code that follows:

```
procedure Enter_region(processor);
begin
    Entering activities (e.g., synchronization);
    if (the shared segment has not been accessed last time
        by the processor currently accessing the segment)
    then
        Invalidate cache lines belonging to the shared segment;
        Update the segment access identification;
    end if;
end Enter_region;

procedure Exit_region;
begin
    —— optional, in case of a not-write-through cache ——
    Copy cache lines belonging to
        the shared segment into the main memory
    ────────────────────────────────────
    Releasing activities;
end Exit_region;
```

For every access to a critical region, it is necessary to know which processor was the last one to access that segment. In order to achieve this, it is necessary that each shared segment has an "access id" attribute. Each processor, when entering a region after another processor, is expected to update the "access id" of that segment, by writing into its own (processor s) identification.

Suspending and reactivating of processes is frequent at entry and exit from a region. These operations are relatively time-consuming. Consequently, the time needed for selective invalidation, because it is added to a longer time for the process scheduling, represents a smaller contribution to the overall delay, due to the activity of entering and exiting a critical region.

Entry into a critical region only for reading has no impact on the consistency of other caches in the system. However, this invalidation scheme does not take that fact into account, and it does the invalidation if, between two accesses of a given processor to a shared segment, another processor had accessed the same segment for reading only.

3.3 An Improved Idea: The Authorized Write Scheme

If, at the entry to a critical region, one knows about the intended usage of the segment (read-only, or read-write), a more selective invalidation condition can be constructed. Precisely, the former condition:

(the shared segment has not been *accessed* last time by the processor currently accessing the segment)

can be substituted by another condition:

(the shared segment has not been *modified* last time by the processor currently accessing the segment)

Passing this type of information to the operating system may look like an unnecessary load for the programmer. However, this obligation actually introduces more discipline into the concurrent programming, and probably has similar effects like the introduction of control or data abstraction mechanisms into the sequential programming. Also, the same information can be used at the exit from a region. For example, if a copy-back approach is used, the unnecessary copying can be avoided if it is known that the segment was accessed for reading only.

Implementation of this scheme requires that each shared segment has an attribute that specifies the author of the last modification in the segment. Once a processor enters a critical region to write to a shared segment, it has to update the "author" field, if it was not the author of the last update of the segment.

In comparison to the previous scheme, this one is better suited to the applications where the "authorship" in a segment rarely changes. However, in this scheme we also have unnecessary invalidations, if processors read the shared segment alternatively. Except for the author, all other processors do invalidation on every pass through the critical region. Unfortunately, the application under consideration is characterized exactly with this type of access pattern. Therefore, in our case, a better scheme is needed. It comes next.

3.4 The Full-Blown Concept: The Version Verification Scheme

In essence, a shared segment lines are to be invalidated only if another processor was writing after the last access of the processor which is just about to enter the critical region. With this improvement in invalidation condition we arrive to the "Version Verification" scheme. It has some similarities with the scheme in [Cheon89]. However, as we have mentioned, it has one important difference in relation to [Cheon89]. Our scheme is completely embedded into the operating system and works at run-time. The [Cheon89] scheme is predominantly implemented at compile-time. The following pseudo-code represents the idea of the VV scheme:

```
procedure Enter_region(processor, access_mode);
begin
    Entering activities (e.g., synchronization);
    if (current version of the shared segment is different of the
        last version of the same segment used by the processor)
    then
        Invalidate cache lines belonging to the shared segment;
        if (access_mode = Read_Only) then
            Update private evidence of the shared segment version;
        end if;
    end if;
    if (access_mode = Read_Write) then
        Increment segment version;
        Update private evidence of the shared segment version;
    end if;
end Enter_region;
```

Note that the VV scheme is a Selective and Strongly Conditional Self-Invalidation (SSCSI) scheme.

One of the important implementation details to pay attention to is the fact that only the synchronization data (region semaphores) should not to be cached. All other shared data, including the other elements of the system tables, are being cached. This implies that in all three above protocols an unconditional invalidation of the appropriate segment (or region) table entry is needed, before reading any other segment attributes, including those for consistency maintenance.

3.5 Comparison with State-of-the-Art Solutions

In a former section (2) we gave a list of reasons why the existing software solutions, in spite of their many good features, are not well suited to the application class under consideration here. Now we give a formal list of differences between the approach proposed here, and the existing two approaches.

Differences related to the OTI scheme:

(a) OTI takes into consideration neither the id of the processor that was the last one to use the data, nor the version of the data. Here we take into consideration the processor id, and also the version of the data (in the third scheme).

(b) OTI does invalidation at the exit from the critical region (although [Smith85] mentions the possibility to do the invalidation at the entry of the critical region, too). Here we do it at the entry into the critical region.

(c) OTI assumes selective write-through for the shared data. Here we use copy-back for all data (although we do not exclude the possibility to apply write-through policy, and actually we use the write-through policy in our simulations).

(d) OTI assumes page granularity of the shared data. Here we assume segment granularity.

(e) OTI does not consider critical regions with waiting queues. Here we do consider such regions instead of the primitive synchronization operations exploiting the busy-waiting.

(f) OTI implies more hardware support compared to the scheme proposed here.

(g) OTI requires field comparison for each cache line access. Here we do the consistency related activities only at the entry/exit to/from the critical region.

Differences related to the VC scheme:

(a) VC assumes sequential numerical applications where the parallelization is done primarily for the speed-up reasons. We assume non-numeric inherently concurrent applications.

(b) VC assumes a programming model in which the parallelism is expressed by parallel loops. We assume a model with concurrent processes synchronized using primitive operations of a multiprocessing operating system kernel.

(c) VC assumes a program execution model in which the tasks correspond to one (or several) iteration(s) of a parallel loop. We assume a program execution model in which the tasks (processes) are larger program units (sometimes the *DoForever* loops).

(d) VC algorithm is predominantly static. Our algorithm is fully dynamic.

(e) VC is based on the one cache line granularity of shared data. Our algorithm is based on the shared segment.

(f) VC does the consistency maintenance related activities at the loop exit. We do it at the critical region entry.

(g) VC does the necessary comparisons on every cache access (comparison of CVN and BVN). We have no comparisons at the level

of individual references inside the critical regions.

4 Simulation Analysis

4.1 Assumptions and Conditions

A simulator of a multiprocessor system with shared main memory and private caches was implemented, and results should be treated in regard to the following assumptions and conditions:

1. Details of the processor instruction set are not simulated. The only thing which is important is to distinguish the following instruction types:

   A. Ordinary instructions. According to the memory access method, these instructions are divided into: *No-access*, *Read*, and *Write* instructions.

   B. Cache controller instructions. These are issued to the cache controller, and are divided into: *Invalidate* (selective invalidation) and *Erase* (unselective data cache purge) instructions.

2. The RISC type of processor with one cycle per instruction is assumed.

3. Pipelining is not simulated, but it is assumed that the instruction execution is done in parallel with the fetching of the next instruction. Also, it is assumed that private instruction and data caches are split. Consequently, the instruction fetching and instruction execution do not competing for the private cache.

4. It is assumed that the private instruction cache is large enough to store the entire benchmark program, i.e. the processor does not access the main memory to fetch instructions. With this and previous assumption, the instruction fetch simulation can be avoided. Instead, one can assume that the next instruction is ready in the instruction register, and only its execution has to be simulated.

5. In this stage of the our research, the interconnection network is bus. Details of the bus transfer are not simulated. The bus access is modeled by a FIFO waiting queue (buffered requests). Bus width is 32 bits.

6. The internal organization of the main memory is not considered. It is simulated as a single memory module. In presented simulations we assumed that the entire shared data space is 2 KBytes, and private space is 512 KByte per processor.

7. The private cache memory works similarly as the internal i486 cache. The characteristics are: (1) Write-through, (2) Write-miss-no-allocate, (3) Pseudo-LRU replacement, (4) 4-way set associativity, with 128 lines per set, and four 32-bit words per line.

8. The software workload is simulated with a synthetic benchmark program, which is generated from the given parameter set.

9. The OS is modeled only through the primitive operations for mutual exclusion, which are relevant for the cache consistency maintenance (*Enter/Exit_Region*).

10. There is no process migration, and no preemption of processes in the running state.

4.2 Synthetic Workload

In the previous work, we have used a synthetic workload. Although we are aware of comparative advantages of real trace-driven simulations versus synthetic benchmarks, we believe that synthetic workload based on the parameter values given from the real traces, can produce realistic results. On the other hand, synthetic benchmarks enable more flexible environment for experiments. We think that it is very important in the early stages of research, when understanding of many phenomena is not complete, to be able to observe changes in performance as a result of changing only one parameter in a well defined manner.

Instruction synthesis: It is assumed that an instruction accesses the memory with probability *Paccess*. Initially, if the instruction accesses the memory, it is reading with probability Pread, and writing with probability (1-*Pread*). If the process is in a critical region, and access to the protected segment is characterized as read-only (during this pass through the critical region), the process reads regardless of the value of *Pread*. Also, if the instruction accesses the memory, it accesses the shared data with probability *Pshared*, and the private data with probability (1-*Pshared*).

As typical values for above parameters, we used the following values: (*Paccess* = 30; *Pread* = 75; *Pshared* = 25). Our assumptions are based on the characteristics of samples of real traces, reported in open literature ([Egger88], [Owick89], [Weber89]).

A special attention is payed to the following aspects of the used synthetic benchmark: memory reference address synthesis, critical region handling, and usage of simplified operating system model.

Address synthesis: During the address synthesis we take care about two criterion: (1) temporal locality of references, and (2) spatial locality of references. Also, we indirectly take care about the processor locality. Processor locality will be discussed in the section to follows. As a measure of the temporal locality, we take the probability that a processor accesses at the moment t the same address that was accessed by him at the moment (t-k), where k presents a discrete random variable with a given probability distribution. To simulate temporal locality, we used a mechanism of LRU pseudo-stack, similar to the one described in [Archi86]. As a density function of variable k, we used the function proposed in the [Archi86]. This function favourizes the appearance of small values of k. The main difference in relation to mechanism described in [Archi86] is in the fact that we assumed that the sum of probabilities of k (in the entire range of available values of k) is PTL, where PTL is less then 1.

As a measure of spatial locality, we take the probability that the processor accessing the address A at the moment t, will access the address (A +/- d) at the moment (t+1). The d is a random variable with a given probability distribution, which, also favourizes small values of d. To model the density function of the variable d, we used the same above mentioned function of the variable k. Also, we assumed that the sum of probabilities of different values of d (in the entire range of available values of d) is equal to PSL, where PSL is less then 1.

Initially, an address is generated as an uniformly distributed random address in the appropriate (shared or private) address range. Later, addresses are generated using the criterion of spatial locality, until an enough long-length history to apply the criterion of temporal locality is generated. History of references for shared and private data are separately memorized. After the initialization is completed, the advantage was given to the criterion of temporal locality. The criterion of spatial locality will be applied with probability (1-PTL). However, if the criterion of spatial locality is also omitted (probability of such event is 1-PSL), the address will be generated as an uniformly distributed random address in the appropriate range.

Initialization of the history of private addresses is done only once. However, the history of shared data references will be reset on each entry to the critical region (because it is assumed that the processor will not access the same shared data segment). Such a model has, as a consequence, the fact that references to the private data are mostly affected by the criterion of temporal locality, while the references to the shared data are mostly affected by the criterion of spatial locality.

If a data item is shared, and the processor is in a critical region, the range of addresses corresponds to the segment which is protected by the current region; if the processor is not in a critical region, the range of shared addresses corresponds to the entire shared data space. If the data item is private, the range of addresses corresponds to the private address space of the given processor.

Critical region handling: If the generated address is in the range of shared addresses, and the processor is not already in one of the critical regions, a primitive OS operation is called to implement the entry into the critical region (*Enter_region*). If the entry into the region was successful, the allowed processor run length (APRL) is computed, and the current processor run length (CPRL) is set to zero. The processor run length (PRL) is defined as the number of accesses of the given processor to the shared segment, during an interval when other processors do not access the same segment, i.e. during the critical region pass. The APRL is computed as a uniformly distributed random number in the range [1,MaxRunLength]. If the processor is in the critical region, on each access to the segment, the CPRL is incremented, and compared with the APRL. If CPRL is greater the APRL, an OS primitive for exit from the critical region (*Exit_region*) is invoked.

Parameter MaxRunLength provides a powerful tool for tuning processor locality. We refer to this kind of processor locality as the processor intra-region locality. As a typical value of MaxRunLength we accept 40, relaying on some data published in [Egger88]. Currently, we have no tool for tuning the processor inter-region locality, in spite of the fact that SCSIC of schemes are well suited to workloads with a high level of processor inter-segment locality.

Simplified operating system model: The OS of the system under consideration is simplified, and only the issues relevant for the analysis of cache consistency are supported. The OS kernel is reduced to encompass only the primitive operations for work with critical regions. These operations implement the process scheduling, as well.

It is assumed that each processor executes Ntasks processes. Each process can be in one of the following four states:

LowReady (L): Ready for execution, low priority
HighReady (H): Ready for execution, high priority
Running (R): Currently executed
Waiting (W): Waiting for a critical region

The state transitions are shown by the graph depicted in the Figure 1.

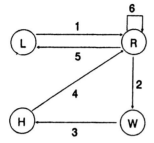

1. when *HighReady* queue is empty &
   a. previously *Running* process Enters the occupied region (2)
   b. previously *Running* process Exits the region (5)
2. currently *Running* process Enters the occupied region
3. previously *Running* process Exits the region (5)
4. <u>when</u> *HighReady* queue is not empty &
   a. previously *Running* process Enters the occupied region (2)
   b. previously *Running* process Exits the region (5)
5. currently *Running* process Exits the region
6. currently *Running* process Enters a free region

Figure 1. Process state transitions graph

After initialization, all processes are in the state L, except the first one, which is in the state R. When the process in the state R requests to enter into the region, if the region is free, the request will be granted, and the process will remain to be in the state R (6). If the region is not free, the process moves into the state W (2), and the next process is activated. The next process is taken from the waiting queue of ready processes of high priority (4), unless this queue is empty. In that case, the next process is taken from the queue of ready processes of the low priority (1), unless this queue is also empty. If both queues are empty, the processor stays in the idle state.

When the processor is in the idle state (which means that all its processes wait to enter the region), it can continue only after the process which is currently in the critical region exits that region. At that time, the first process in the waiting queue will be moved from the W state into the H state (3). The processor in the idle state tries in each cycle to get reactivated by checking if the queue H contains a process ready for execution. If such a process does exist, it will get activated (4).

The access to the critical region is protected by a semaphore. Consequently, if another process requests the entry into the critical region while the process on the processor under consideration was in the H state (because that process already was the first one in the queue for the critical region), the current process of the other processor goes to the W state (2), i.e. into the waiting queue of the processes waiting for that region.

The H state is introduced in order to avoid the preemption of the processes. In other words, at the exit of process A from the region, the process B to be the next one for entry into the region, will not preempt the execution of the process C currently being executed on the home processor of the process B. Process B will wait in the H queue until the C finishes its running state.

At the exit from the critical region, the process goes into the L state (5), and the next process waiting on the region (in the state W), will move into the H state on its home processor. After that, the system checks if the processor which exited the critical region contains the H-state processes. If yes, the first process in the H queue is activated (4), and it automatically gets the control over the critical region. If no, the system checks if the processor which exited the critical region contains the L-state processes; if yes, the first one will

be activated (1). The processor is always active after the exit from the critical region.

4.3 Performance Measures

Conditional invalidation immediately decreases the number of invalidations of the shared data segment per critical region passing. Consequently, it is expected that the overall hit ratio will be increased, and processing power, too. These system performance measures are formally introduced below.

The Processing Power (PP): If the queue of ready processes is empty, the simulated processor is in the idle state and executes the NOP instructions. Note that this would frequently not be the case in realistic systems - the processor would stay in the halted state, waiting for the interrupt that initially activated it. This difference simplifies the analysis, without any impact on the final results. Consequently, the processing power will be defined as:

$$PP = \frac{1}{\text{CPU cycles}} \sum_{i=1}^{N proc} (\text{Ordinary instr.} - \text{Idle NOPs})_i$$

The Hit Ratio (HR) is computed using the following definition:

$$HR = \frac{1}{N proc} \sum_{i=1}^{N proc} \frac{(\text{Read hits} + \text{Write hits})_i}{(\text{Reads} + \text{Writes})_i}$$

where Nproc indicates the number of processors.

The Number of Invalidations per Region Pass (I/R) is defined as a number of executed cache control *Invalidate* (or *Erase*) instructions per satisfied enter region request. Note, it is assumed that in case of selective self-invalidation (SSI) schemes a particular *Invalidate* instruction should be issued preventively and unconditionally to invalidate the copy of the appropriate region/segment table entry. Because of that, the I/R for the SSI schemes is always in the range [1, 2]. The unselective and unconditional self-invalidation (USUCSI) scheme uses an *Erase* - unselective data cache purging instruction, but we will count this instruction as an *Invalidate* instruction. Because of that, the I/R for the USUCSI scheme is always equal to one. A formal definition of I/R is given as follows:

$$I/R = \left(\sum_{i=1}^{N proc} \text{Invalidations}_i \right) / \left(\sum_{i=1}^{N proc} \text{Region passes}_i \right)$$

4.4 Simulation Parameters

The developed simulation tools enable a flexible selection of simulation parameters. Table 1 summarizes the set of parameter values used in simulations for which the results are reported in this paper. Mnemonic "var" denotes that the parameter was changed in simulation.

Nproc:	var	Number of processors
Csize:	8K	Cache size
Nlines:	128	Number of cache lines
Nwords:	4	Number of 32-bit words per cache line
Bwidth:	32	Bus width (in bits)
Paccess:	0.30	Probability that an instruction accesses memory
Pread:	0.75	Probability that an access is a read
Pshared:	0.25	Probability that an access refers to shared data
Pr-o:	var	Probability that a segment is read-only in the region
PTL:	0.95	Probability that the temporal locality criterion is used
PSL:	0.70	Probability that the spatial locality criterion is used
RunLnt:	20	Maximal processor run length
Ntasks:	20	Number of processes (tasks) per processor
Shared:	2K	Overall shared data space
Private:	512K	Private data space per processor
Nshared:	64	Number of shared data segments (of equal lengths)
Cold:	1000	Number of cycles during the "cold start"
Cycles:	11000	Number of cycles during the simulation

Table 1. Description of simulation parameters and values used in our simulation

4.5 Results

In the first stage of our simulation analysis, we wanted to compare the defined performance measures for the following set of consistency schemes: Base (USUCSI), OTI-like (SUCSI), AI (SWCSI), and VV (SSCSI). In all experiments we changed the Nproc parameter in a small-scale range [1, 16]. As a parameter which is expected predominantly to impact the relative performance relation ("key parameter"), we choose the probability that a segment will be treated as read-only in the current region (Pr-o). Figure 2 comparatively presents the performance measures for two extreme values of the Pr-o parameter: 0.05 and 0.95.

4.6 Discussion

As could be expected, small values of the Pr-o parameter almost do not yield improvement to the processing power for the VV (SSCSI) scheme, because the version of shared data segments frequently changes.

On the other hand, the high values of the Pr-o parameter strongly decrease the number of invalidations per critical region pass, in case of the VV (SSCSI) scheme in relation to the AI (SWCSI) scheme, or the OTI-like (SUCSI) scheme. This effect is a result of infrequent changes of the shared segment version, observed only by the VV scheme. Implication is that the hit ratio increases, and consequently the processing power increases. For multiprocessors with 16 processors, the relative processing power improvement for the SSCSI scheme is approximately 5% over the SUCSI scheme.

A very interesting phenomenon should be notified: relative im-

provement of the VV (SSCSI) scheme is increasing with the increased number of processors. This fact is promising, and encourages us for new efforts towards a large-scale multiprocessor simulation analysis.

5 Conclusion

The paper presents a concept of private cache consistency maintenance built into the operating system software. We gradually introduced three selective and conditional self-invalidation schemes of different complexity and different rigidity of the invalidation condition. Common characteristic of all three schemes is that the invalidation condition is placed at the entry of the critical region, immediately before accessing shared data. It enables decreasing of invalidations, in comparison with schemes that propose invalidation at the exit point of the critical region.

Advantages of the proposed approach can be summarized as follows:

(a) No complex hardware support is needed, although further improvements and optimizations are possible, if some specialized hardware is used. These improvements and optimizations are related to effectiveness of the segment invalidation and the segment copying.

(b) An unexpressive reconfigurability is possible. The consistency maintenance schemes can be changed statically, or even dynamically.

(c) The approach is compiler independent. In the case of static software approaches (implemented in compilers, not operating systems), a given consistency maintenance scheme must be developed (from scratch) for each new compiler. This is not convenient for two reasons. First, this implies more work for compiler writers. Second, this type of code is extremely sophisticated to test, which implies even more work. In the case of the schemes embedded into the operating system, the scheme is to be implemented and tested only once, and used for all software layers, including compilers.

First simulation results justified reasons for applying selective and conditional schemes, even in a workload environment without processor inter-region locality, which would be favorable to the schemes. As we expected, the workload with higher probability of read-only shared segment access in a critical region, forces the advantages of the Version Verification (SSCSI) scheme.

Our immediate plans for the future research involves simulation analysis in a general interconnection network environment. We want to consider scalability of the SCSIC of schemes.

6 Acknowledgements

This research was sponsored by the University of Belgrade and the National Science Foundation of Serbia, Belgrade, Yugoslavia. A friendly encouragement was provided by the NCR World Headquarters, Dayton, Ohio, U.S.A., as well as the NCR E+M, Augsburg, Germany.

We would like to thank Professor A. J. Smith of the UC Berkeley, who updated us on the results of his research presented in [Smith85].

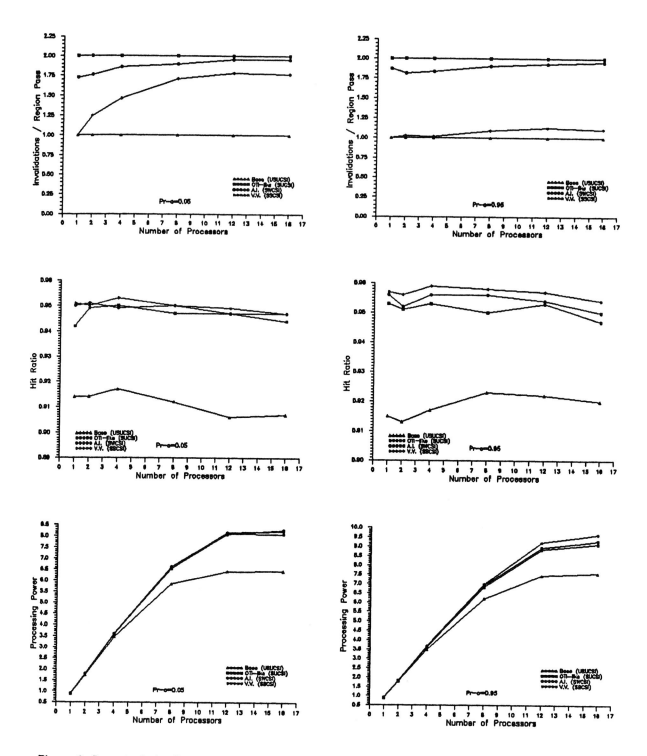

Figure 2. Impact of the Pr-o parameter on performance of the considered cache consistency schemes

7 References

[Agarw88] Agarwal, A., Simoni, R., Hennessy, J., Horowitz, M., "An evaluation of directory schemes for cache coherence," Proceedings of the 15th Annual International Symposium on Computer Architecture, May 1988, pp. 280-289.

[Archi86] Archibald, J., Baer, J.-L., "Cache coherence protocols: evaluation using a multiprocessor simulation model," ACM Transactions on Computer Systems, Vol. 4., No. 4., November 1986, pp. 273-298.

[Adve90] Adve, S. V., Hill, M. D., "Weak ordering - a new definition," Proceedings of the 17th Annual International Symposium on Computer Architecture, June 1990, pp. 2-14.

[Benne90] Bennett, J. K., Carter, J. B., Zwaenepoel, W., "Adaptive software cache management for distributed shared memory architectures," Proceedings of the 17th Annual International Symposium on Computer Architecture, June 1990, pp. 125-134.

[Brant85] Brantley, W. C., McAuliffe, K. P., Weiss, J., "RP3 processor-memory element," Proceedings of the 1985 International Conference on Parallel Processing, August 1985, pp. 782-789.

[Cheon88] Cheong, H., Veidenbaum, A. V., "A cache coherence scheme with fast selective invalidation," Proceedings of the 15th Annual International Symposium on Computer Architecture, May 1988, pp. 299-307.

[Cheon90] Cheong, H., Veidenbaum, A. V., "Compiler-directed cache management in multiprocessors," IEEE Computer, Vol. 23., No. 6., June 1990, pp. 39-47.

[Cytro88] Cytron, R., Karlovsky, S., McAuliffe, K. P., "Automatic management of programmable caches," Proceedings of the 1988 International Conference on Parallel Processing, 1988, pp. 229-238.

[Duboi86] Dubois, M., Sceurich, C., Briggs, F., "Memory access buffering in multiprocessors," Proceedings of the 13th Annual International Symposium on Computer Architecture, June 1986, pp. 434-442.

[Duboi88] Dubois, M., Sceurich, C., Briggs, F., "Synchronization, coherence, and event ordering in multiprocessors," IEEE Computer, Vol. 21., No. 2., February 1988, pp. 9-21.

[Edler85] Edler, J., Gottlieb, A., Kruskal, C. P., McAuliffe, K. P., Rudolph, L., Snir, M., Teller, P., Wilson, J., "Issues related to MIMD shared-memory computers: the NYU Ultracomputer approach," Proceedings of the 12th Annual International Symposium on Computer Architecture, June 1985, pp. 126-135.

[Egger88] Eggers, S. J., Katz, R. H., "A characterization of sharing in parallel programs and its application to coherency protocol evaluation," Proceedings of the 15th Annual International Symposium on Computer Architecture, May 1988, pp. 373-382.

[Owick89] Owicki, S., Agarwal, A., "Evaluating the performance of software cache coherence," Proceedings of the 3rd International Conference on Architectural Support for Programming Languages and Operating Systems, April 1989, pp. 230-242.

[Smith85] Smith, A. J., "CPU cache consistency with software support and using one time identifiers," Proceedings of the Pacific Computer Communication Symposium, Seoul, Korea, October 1985, pp. 142-150.

[Veide86] Veidenbaum, A. V., "A compiler-assisted cache coherence solution for multiprocessors," Proceedings of the 1986 International Conference on Parallel Processing, 1986, pp. 1029-1036.

[Weber89] Weber, W.-D., Gupta, A., "Analysis of cache invalidation patterns in multiprocessors," Proceedings of the 3rd International Conference on Architectural Support for Programming Languages and Operating Systems, April 1989, pp. 243-256.

Adaptive Software Cache Management for Distributed Shared Memory Architectures

*John K. Bennett**

*John B. Carter***

*Willy Zwaenepoel***

*Department of Electrical and Computer Engineering
**Department of Computer Science
Rice University
Houston, TX 77251-1892

Abstract

An *adaptive* cache coherence mechanism exploits semantic information about the expected or observed access behavior of particular data objects. We contend that, in distributed shared memory systems, adaptive cache coherence mechanisms will outperform static cache coherence mechanisms. We have examined the sharing and synchronization behavior of a variety of shared memory parallel programs. We have found that the access patterns of a large percentage of shared data objects fall in a small number of categories for which efficient software coherence mechanisms exist. In addition, we have performed a simulation study that provides two examples of how an adaptive caching mechanism can take advantage of semantic information.

1 Introduction

We are developing Munin [4], a system that will allow programs written for shared memory multiprocessors to be executed efficiently on distributed memory machines. What distinguishes Munin from previous distributed shared memory systems [6, 12, 14] is the means by which memory coherence is achieved. Instead of a single memory coherence mechanism for all shared data objects, Munin will employ several different mechanisms, each appropriate for a different category of shared data object. We refer to this technique of providing multiple coherence mechanisms as *adaptive caching*. Adaptive caching maintains coherence

based on the expected or observed access behavior of each shared object and on the size of cached items. We contend that adaptive caching provides an efficient abstraction of shared memory on distributed memory hardware. Since coherence in distributed shared memory systems is provided in software, we expect the overhead of providing multiple coherence mechanisms to be offset by the increase in performance that such mechanisms will provide.

For adaptive caching to perform well, it must be possible to characterize a large percentage of all accesses to shared data objects by a small number of categories of access patterns for which efficient coherence mechanisms can be developed. In a previous paper [4], we have identified a number of categories, and described the design of efficient coherence mechanism for each. In this paper, we show that these categories capture the vast majority of the accesses to shared data objects in a number of shared memory parallel programs. We also show, through simulation, the potential for performance improvement of adaptive caching compared to static coherence mechanisms.

In Section 2 of this paper, we briefly reiterate the main results of our previous paper [4]. We describe the categories of access patterns, provide examples, and give a brief description of how each category can be handled efficiently. Section 3 describes the programs that we study in this paper, our technique for logging the accesses to shared memory by these programs, the method by which we analyze these logs to discover common access patterns, and the results of our logging study. Section 4 describes a simulation study that provides two examples of how an adaptive caching mechanism can take advantage of semantic information. We discuss previous work in this area in Section 5. Finally, we draw conclusions in Section 6.

This work was supported in part by the National Science Foundation under Grants CDA-8619893 and CCR-8716914.

2 Categories of Sharing

2.1 Intuitive Definitions

We have identified the following categories of shared
data objects: *Write-once, Write-many, Producer-
Consumer, Private, Migratory, Result, Read-mostly,*
and *Synchronization.* We classify all shared data objects that do not fall into one of these categories as
General Read-Write.

Write-once objects are read-only after initialization. *Write-many* objects frequently are modified
by several threads between synchronization points.
For example, in Quicksort, multiple threads concurrently modify independent portions of the array being sorted. *Producer-Consumer* objects are written
(produced) by one thread and read (consumed) by a
fixed set of other threads. *Private* objects, though
declared to be shared data objects, are only accessed
by a single thread. Many parallel scientific programs
exhibit "nearest neighbors" or "wavefront" communication whereby the only communication is the exchange of boundary elements between threads working on adjacent sub-arrays. The boundary elements
are *Producer-Consumer* and the interior elements are
Private. Migratory objects are accessed in phases,
where each phase corresponds to a series of accesses
by a single thread. Shared objects protected by locks
often exhibit this property. *Result* objects collect results. Once written, they are only read by a single thread that uses the results. *Read-mostly* objects are read significantly more often than they are
written. *Synchronization* objects, such as locks and
monitors, are used by programmers to force explicit
inter-thread synchronization points. Synchronization
events include attempting to acquire a lock, acquiring a lock, and releasing a lock. The remaining objects, which we cannot characterize by any of the preceding classes, are called *General Read-Write.* The
categories define a hierarchy of types of shared data
objects. When we identify an object's sharing category, we use the most specific category possible under
the following order (from most specific to least specific): *Synchronization, Private, Write-once, Result,
Producer-Consumer, Migratory, Write-many, Read-
mostly,* and *General Read-Write.*

2.2 Coherence Mechanisms

We have developed memory coherence techniques
that can efficiently support these categories of shared
data objects. A brief description of these mechanisms
may provide insight into why these particular categories are chosen. A separate paper describes our
complete set of coherence mechanisms in more detail [4].

Write-Many objects appear in many parallel programs wherein several threads simultaneously access
and modify a single shared data object between explicit synchronization points in the program. If the
programmer knows that individual threads access independent portions of the data, and the order in
which individual threads are scheduled is unimportant, the program can tolerate a controlled amount
of inconsistency between cached portions of the data.
The programmer uses explicit synchronization (such
as a lock or monitor) to denote the points in the program execution at which such inconsistencies are not
tolerable. We refer to this controlled inconsistency as
loose coherence [4], as contrasted with *strict coherence,* in which no inconsistency is allowed. Strict and
loose coherence are closely related to the concepts of
strong and *weak ordering* of events as described by
Dubois, et al [7]. Strong and weak ordering define
a relation on the ordering of events (such as accesses
to shared memory) in a system, while strict and loose
coherence are operational definitions of the coherence
guarantees that a system provides. Maintaining strict
coherence unnecessarily is inefficient and introduces
false sharing. The effects of false sharing can often
be reduced by algorithm restructuring or careful memory allocation, but these efforts impose significant
additional work on the programmer or compiler, are
not possible for all algorithms, and are architecture
dependent.

Delayed updates, based on loose coherence, allow
Write-many objects to be handled efficiently. When a
thread modifies a *Write-many* object, we delay sending the update to remote copies of the object until
remote threads could otherwise indirectly detect that
the object has been modified. In this manner, by
enforcing only loose coherence, we avoid unnecessary
synchronization that is not required by the program's
semantics, and reduce the number of network packets
needed for data motion and synchronization.

If the system knows that an object is shared in
Producer-Consumer fashion, it can perform *eager object movement.* Eager object movement moves objects to the node at which they are going to be used
in advance of when they are required. In the nearest neighbors example, this involves propagating the
boundary element updates to where they will be required. In the best case, the new values are always
available before they are needed, and threads never
wait to receive the current values.

We propose to handle *Synchronization* objects
with distributed locks. More elaborate synchronization objects, such as monitors and atomic integers,

can be built on top of this. When a thread wants to acquire or test a global lock, it performs the lock operation on a local proxy for the distributed lock, and the local lock server arbitrates with the remote lock servers to perform the lock operation. Each lock has a queue associated with it that contains a list of the servers that need the lock. This queue facilitates efficient exchange of lock ownership. This mechanism is similar to that proposed by Goodman, et al [9].

Several categories of shared data objects can be handled in a straightforward fashion. *Private* objects are only accessed by one thread, so keeping them coherent is trivial. Replication is used for *Write-once* objects. *Read-mostly* objects are also candidates for replication since reads predominate writes. A *Migratory* object can be handled efficiently by migrating a single copy of the object among the processors that access it. *Result* objects are handled by maintaining a single copy and propagating updates to this copy. Finally, *General Read-Write* objects are handled by a standard coherence mechanism.

3 Logging Study

3.1 Programs

We have studied six shared memory parallel programs written in C++ [17] using the Presto programming system [5] on the Sequent Symmetry shared memory multiprocessor [13]. The selected programs are written specifically for a shared memory multiprocessor so that our results are not influenced by the program being written with distribution in mind and accurately reflect the memory access behavior that occurs when programmers do not expend special effort towards distributing the data across processors. Presto programs are divided into an initialization phase, during which the program is single-threaded, and a computation phase.

The six programs are: Matrix multiply, Gaussian elimination, Fast Fourier Transform (FFT), Quicksort, Traveling salesman problem (TSP), and Life. Matrix multiply, Gaussian elimination, and Fast Fourier Transform are numeric problems that distribute the data to separate threads and access shared memory in predictable patterns. Quicksort uses divide-and-conquer to dynamically subdivide the problem. Traveling salesman uses central work queues protected by locks to control access to problem data. Life is a "nearest-neighbors" problem in which data is shared only by neighboring processes.

As a measure of the "quality" of these parallel programs, Figure 3.1 shows a speedup plot for each of the six programs. The programs exhibit nearly linear speedup for small numbers of processors. The decrease in speedup seen for larger numbers of processors is due primarily to the unavailability of processors and the effects of bus contention.

3.2 Logging Technique

We collect logging information for a program by modifying the source and the run-time system to record all accesses to shared memory (13 microseconds to record each access). The program modifications are currently done by hand. A call to a logging object is added to the program source after every statement that accesses shared memory. The Presto run-time system is modified so that thread creations and destructions are recorded, as are all synchronization events. The end of each program's initialization phase is logged as a special event so that our analysis tool can differentiate between the initialization and the computation phase.

A program executed with logging enabled generates a series of log files, one per processor. Each log entry contains an *Object ID*, a *Thread ID*, the *Type of Access*, and the *Time of Access*. Examples of *Type of Access* include creation, read, write, and lock and monitor accesses of various types. *Time of Access* is the absolute time of the access, read from a hardware microsecond clock, so the per-processor logs can be merged to form a single global log.

We can specify the granularity with which to log accesses to objects. The two supported granularities

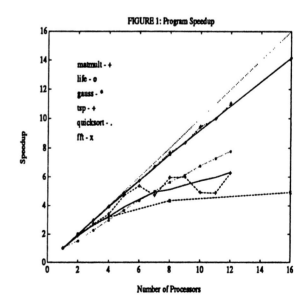

FIGURE 1: Program Speedup

matmult - +
life - o
gauss - *
tsp - +
quicksort - .
fft - x

Speedup

Number of Processors

are *object* and *element*. At object granularity, an access to any part of an object is logged as an access to the entire object. At element granularity, an access to a part of an object is logged as an access to that specific part of the object. For example, the log entry for a read of an element of a matrix object indicates only that the matrix was read at object granularity, but indicates the specific element that was read at element granularity.

Our study of sharing in parallel programs distinguishes itself from similar work [8, 15, 18] in that it studies sharing at the programming language level, and hence is relatively architecture-independent, and in that our selection of parallel programs embodies a wider variation in programming and synchronization styles.

An important difference between our approach and previous methods [1, 16] is that we only log accesses to shared memory, not all accesses to memory. Non-shared memory, such as program code and local variables, generally does not require special handling in a distributed shared memory system. A useful side effect of logging only accesses to shared memory is that the log files are much more compact. This allows us to log the shared memory accesses of relatively long-running programs in their entirety, which is important because the access patterns during initialization are significantly different from those during computation.

Logging in software during program execution combines many of the benefits of software simulation [16] and built-in tracing mechanisms [1], without some of the problems associated with these techniques. As with software simulation, with software logging it is easy to change the information that is collected during a particular run of the program. For example, if only the accesses to a particular object are of interest, such as the accesses to the lock protecting a central queue, only the logging associated with that object need be enabled. On the other hand, software-based logging does not slow down program execution to the extent that software simulation of the program and architecture does. Unlike with address tracing techniques, it is possible to collect higher-order information about particular accesses. For example, we can log an attempt to acquire a monitor, successful acquisition of the monitor, or sleeping on a monitor condition variable. This information is not easily recreated from a standard address trace.

The flexibility, power and low overhead of our system does not come without cost. Only accesses to shared memory performed by the applications program and run-time system are collected, so our system suffers from what Agarwal refers to as *omission*

distortion [1], the inability of a system to record the complete address stream of a running program. The omission distortion is not significant in this study because we are not trying to determine how any particular cache coherence mechanism will perform, but rather are attempting to characterize patterns of sharing that are common in parallel applications programs. Also, because only accesses to shared memory are collected, our logs may experience *temporal distortion* in the sense that periods with frequent accesses to shared memory will be slowed down to a greater extent than periods when accesses to shared memory are infrequent. The temporal distortion is limited by synchronization events, which constrain the relative ordering of events.

3.3 Analysis

We now formalize the intuitive definitions of the different categories of shared data objects given in Section 2 for the purpose of the log analysis.

Objects that are accessed by multiple threads between consecutive synchronization events sufficiently often (default: during 50% of the inter-synchronization periods) are categorized as *Write-Many*. Whenever a thread synchronizes, the analysis program examines each object that the thread has modified since it last synchronized to determine if another thread has accessed the same object during that period.

A producer-consumer phase for a particular object *Obj* is characterized by the following sequence of events. Thread *A* writes *Obj* and synchronizes (thread *A* may access *Obj* additional times). Then some other threads read *Obj* before *A* writes it again. The analysis program counts the number of accesses to an object that occur in producer-consumer phases, and if this number exceeds a specified percentage of all accesses to the object (default: 75%), then the object is declared to be *Producer-Consumer*.

Migratory objects are accessed in long runs. A *run* or *write-run* [8] is a sequence of accesses to a single object by a single thread. For the purposes of our analysis, the minimum length of a long run is variable (default: 8). An object is declared to be migratory if the percentage of all accesses to it that are contained in long runs exceeds a threshold (default: 85%).

Read-Mostly objects are primarily read (default: 75%). *Write-once*, *Result*, *Private*, and *Synchronization* objects can be easily identified using their intuitive definitions (see Section 2.1).

We have developed a tool to analyze the shared memory access logs in the manner just described. The tool detects common access patterns and identifies objects according to the characteristic kind of sharing that they exhibit. It also collects statistics specific to each category of shared data object, such as the average number of consumers for a *Producer-Consumer* object, the average run length of a *Migratory* object, and the average number of accesses to a *Write-Many* object between consecutive synchronization events. We have experimented with different values for the various thresholds, and the results do not appear to be very sensitive to variations in these thresholds.

3.4 Results

The results of our analysis are summarized in Tables 1 through 7. Odd-numbered tables present results from analysis runs where data was logged "by object." Even-numbered runs present results where data was logged "by element."

Tables 1 and 2 give the relative frequency of each type of shared access for each of the programs studied. These tables indicate the potential advantages of a memory coherence mechanism that is able to support both object and element granularity over a mechanism that supports only one level of granularity. With object-level logging, *Write-Many* accesses dominate other forms of shared data access (81.4, 100, 99.1, 99.2, and 47.3 percent), except for Matrix Multiply (only 2.8 percent). The other sharing category into which a large portion of the accesses fall at object-level granularity is *Write-Once* (18.6 percent in FFT, 97.2 percent in Matrix Multiply, and 23.9 percent in TSP). Parallel programs in which the granularity of sharing is fine tend to have their underlying fine grained behavior masked when the logging is performed on a per-object basis. With per-element logging, Matrix Multiply retains its *Write-Once* behavior, indicating that these are the inherent results. However, the access behavior of other programs are considerably different when examined per element. The best example of this unmasking is the Life program, where 82.4 percent of the shared data is in fact *Private* (the interior elements of the board) and 16.8 percent is *Producer-Consumer* (the edge elements).

The results in Tables 1 and 2 can be related to user-level objects in the programs as follows:

- The input arrays in Matrix Multiply exhibit *Write-Once* behavior, and references to these arrays dominate all other forms of access regardless of the granularity of logging. Accesses to the output matrix show up as *Result* when logged by element.

- Edge elements in the Life program exhibit *Producer-Consumer* behavior when shared ac-

Type	FFT	Qsort	Gauss	Life	Mult	TSP
Private						
RdMostly						
WriteOnce	18.6				97.2	23.9
Result						
Prod/Cons						
Migratory						15.0
WriteMany	81.4	100	99.1	99.2	2.8	47.3
Synch			.9	.8		12.4
GeneralRW						1.4

Table 1 Percent of Shared Access (By Object)

Type	FFT	Qsort	Gauss	Life	Mult	TSP
Private	.7	2.8	29.5	82.4	1.6	
RdMostly			30.0			13.2
WriteOnce	17.9		1.7		95.8	25.5
Result			3.7		2.6	
Prod/Cons			10.0	16.8		
Migratory	73.4	.8	2.6			40.8
WriteMany	8.0	96.4	21.6			4.4
Synch			.9	.8		12.0
GeneralRW						4.1

Table 2 Percent of Shared Access (By Element)

cesses are logged by element. Internal elements are *Private*.

- In TSP, the input array containing the path weights is *Write-Once*. At object granularity, the work queue is accessed in a migratory fashion, since it is a single object protected by a lock. The different partially computed tours are treated as one single object, and thus accesses to them are categorized as *Write-Many*. At element granularity, the partially computed tours are treated as independent objects and also exhibit *Migratory* behavior.

- At object granularity, the input coefficient array in Gaussian Elimination exhibits *Write-Many* behavior. At element granularity, access behavior to this array is less well-defined, indicating the different manner in which row, column, and pivot elements are accessed.

- The array being sorted in Quicksort exhibits *Write-Many* sharing at both object and element granularity. This is because of how Quicksort is implemented. The programmer knows that different threads access independent parts of the array, so accesses to the array are not synchronized.

- The input sample array in FFT exhibits *Write-Many* sharing behavior at object granularity. At element granularity, this array exhibits *Migratory* behavior because elements are passed between workers in phases. The ω array, an array of numeric coefficients that is initialized at the start of the algorithm and used extensively thereafter, is *Write-Once*. A temporary array, which is used to re-order the input array (in parallel) so that the elements required by each worker thread are contiguous, is *Write-Many*.

These observations correspond closely to our expectations, based on an informal understanding of how the programs access shared memory.

Tables 3 and 4 illustrate the dramatic differences between element and object granularity. These tables record the average size of the data element being accessed for each type of access for each of the programs. The objects at object granularity are generally arrays or matrices, and are thus relatively large. The 4-byte elements in Quicksort, Gaussian Elimination, Life, and Matrix Multiply are long integers. The 16-byte elements in FFT are complex numbers, represented by a pair of 8-byte double precision floating point numbers. Except for the TSP program, which uses fairly large arrays to store partial solutions, the elements being accessed are quite small. Thus, if coherence is maintained strictly on a per-object basis, the coherence protocol moves much larger units of

memory than the program requires. However, several large objects can be handled easily on a per-object basis. For example, the *Write-Once* (e.g., the input arrays in Matrix Multiply) objects can be replicated. It is therefore advantageous that the coherence protocol knows the size of the shared data objects, and their internal elements, in addition to their sharing behavior.

Tables 5 and 6 present data specific to *Write-Many* objects. The average number of different objects accessed between synchronization points indicates the average number of delayed updates that will be queued up at a time. If this number is small, as the data indicate, managing the queue of delayed updates may not require significant overhead. The remaining *Write-Many* data are also encouraging. *Write-Many* objects are written about one-half as many times as they are read. Large numbers of accesses occur between synchronization points. We call a series of accesses to a single object *by any thread* between two synchronization points in a particular thread a "no-synch run." The large size of the no-synch runs indicate that delayed updates offers substantial performance improvement. No-synch runs differ from Eggers's "write-runs" in that they do not end when a remote thread accesses the object, but rather whenever a thread synchronizes. Intuitively, write-runs end when a standard coherence mechanism, such as write-invalidate and write-update, would ensure consistency. No-synch runs end when the programmer *requires* consistency.

Table 7 presents the data recorded for locks, and contains both good and bad news. The good news is that the same thread frequently reacquires the same lock, which can be handled locally. Another piece of good news is that usually the number of threads

Type	FFT	Qsort	Gauss	Life	Mult	TSP
Private						
RdMostly						
WriteOnce	16K				4.9K	324
Result						
Prod/Cons						
Migratory						12K
WriteMany	32K	4K	2.5K	5K	2.5K	24K
GeneralRW						40

Table 3 Avg Access Size (bytes) (By Object)

Type	FFT	Qsort	Gauss	Life	Mult	TSP
Private	16	4	4	4	4	
RdMostly			4			12
WriteOnce	16		4		4	168
Result			4		4	
Prod/Cons				4	4	
Migratory	16	4	4			114
WriteMany	16	4	4			1.5K
GeneralRW						29

Table 4 Avg Access Size (bytes) (By Element)

	FFT	Qsort	Gauss	Life	Mult	TSP
Avg No Diff Objs Accsd Btwn Synchs	1	2	1.7	1	2	1.5
Avg No of Local Accs Btwn Synchs	8.3K	160	510	3.1K	38	20
Avg No of Loc Writes Btwn Synchs	3.5K	36	110	320	37	12
Avg No of Rmt Accs Btwn Synchs	48K	52K	17K	9.4K	2.4K	47
Avg No of Rmt Writes Btwn Synchs	21K	10K	3.6K	970	12K	28

Table 5 Write-Many Data (By Object)

	FFT	Qsort	Gauss	Life	Mult	TSP
Avg No Diff Objs Accsd Btwn Synchs	96	20	5.5			1.0
Avg No of Local Accs Btwn Synchs	817	127	36			1.3
Avg No of Loc Writes Btwn Synchs	375	35	74			1.1
Avg No of Rmt Accs Btwn Synchs	1.5K	1.5K	1.9K			2.6
Avg No of Rmt Writes Btwn Synchs	750	720	610			2.4

Table 6   Write-Many Data (By Element)

waiting on the same lock is quite small, indicating that lock arbitration will not require excessive network traffic. The bad news, in terms of being able to achieve the same performance on distributed memory multiprocessors as on shared memory multiprocessors, is that we observe small delays between attempts to acquire a lock and lock acquisition. Even an optimized distributed lock scheme requiring only a single message to release and reacquire the lock will be hard pressed to exhibit this small delay for feasible network latencies in a distributed system.

The general results of our analysis can be summarized as follows:

1. There are very few *General Read-Write* objects. Coherence mechanisms exist that can support the other categories of shared data objects efficiently, so a cache coherence protocol that adapts to the expected or observed behavior of each shared object will outperform one that does not.

2. The conventional notion of an object often does not correspond to the appropriate granularity of data decomposition for parallelism. Often it is

	FFT	Qsort	Gauss	Life	Mult	TSP
Avg dt Btwn Lock and Acquire (μsec)			83	1900		350
Pct This Acquire Same Thrd as Last			41	47		25
Avg No of Thrds Waiting on Same Lock			0	.6		.4

Table 7   Lock Data

appropriate to maintain coherence at the object level, but sometimes it is more appropriate to maintain coherence at a level smaller or larger than an object. Thus, a cache coherence protocol that adapts to the appropriate granularity of data decomposition will outperform one that does not.

4   Simulation Study

To test our hypothesis that adaptive caching mechanisms can outperform standard static caching mechanisms, we simulate two memory coherence mechanisms (write-invalidate and write-update) and two coherence mechanisms that are well-suited for particular types of sharing. All simulation runs are fed identical input streams from the logs generated from actual running programs. The simulation model allows us to select the cache coherence mechanism and set the cache line size for each run. It assumes an infinite cache so no replacement is performed except as required for coherence. The simulation collects information such as: the total number of shared memory accesses, the number of transactions, the total amount of data transmitted (bandwidth consumed), and the number of cache misses. For the discussion below, when the term *line size* is used in the context of a distributed shared memory system, it refers to the minimum granularity of memory that the system handles.

In the first simulation, we compare write-invalidate and write-update with our delayed update mechanism. With delayed updates, whenever the updates are propagated, the remote caches are updated rather than invalidated, so the worst case performance of this mechanism should be equivalent to that of a standard write-update cache. However, if multiple accesses to a single shared variable occur between user-specified synchronization points, delayed updates can significantly improve on a standard write-update mechanism.

The delayed update mechanism is particularly useful when the size of the elementary shared data items is smaller than the cache line size, and there can be a significant amount of false sharing. On the other hand, it must be recognized that false sharing can be minimized by prudent memory allocation by the compiler and/or the programmer. Since the programs used in these simulations are not optimized to avoid false sharing, the following results for write-invalidate and write-update must be interpreted as an upper bound on the negative effects of false sharing.

218

Table 8 presents the results of simulating the performance of the parallel Quicksort algorithm. The adaptive caching mechanism significantly reduces the amount of bus traffic required to maintain coherence. Compared to write-invalidate, the delayed update mechanism reduces the amount of bus traffic by 31%, 38%, and 52% for 4, 16, and 64 byte cache lines, respectively. Compared to write-update, the delayed update mechanism reduces the amount of bus traffic by 35%, 73%, and 86% for 4, 16, and 64 byte cache lines, respectively. The improvement is caused by the fact that Quicksort performs many writes to shared data objects between synchronization points, so many updates to the same data object are combined before they are eventually propagated. These results are a conservative estimate of the benefits of a delayed update mechanism, because updates to different data objects being sent to the same remote cache were counted as separate transfers. An efficient delayed update mechanism would coalesce updates to the same cache.

In the second simulation, we compare the standard coherence mechanisms with a write-invalidate mechanism that brings an entire object into the cache whenever any portion of it is accessed. This mechanism helps to alleviate object fragmentation caused by a cache line that is too small to hold an entire object. Both the cache line size and the basic object size that we examine are fairly small, but the results are valid whenever the objects used in a computation are larger than a single cache line. Larger cache line sizes are being proposed, but there will always be problems with very large objects that cannot fit into a single line, such as programs that manipulate rows or columns of a matrix.

Table 9 presents the results of this simulation for the parallel FFT. Since the majority of the data objects accessed by the FFT algorithm are complex variables (consisting of a pair of eight-byte double precision floating point variables), a cache line size of less than 16 bytes is inefficient, but the adaptive mech-

Coherence Mechanism	Linesize	Transfers (1000's)	Data Copied (kilobytes)
Adapts to Object Size	4	11.5	188
	16	11.5	188
	64	3.36	218
Write-Invalidate	4	46.9	188
	16	11.7	188
	64	3.41	218
Write-Update	4	45.2	181
	16	11.3	181
	64	6.00	384

Table 9   Simulation of FFT

anism overcomes this by automatically loading the entire complex data object when any part of it is accessed. The adaptive coherence mechanism requires the same amount of bandwidth as the write-invalidate mechanism, but when the cache line size is 4 bytes, it does so with 25% as many messages (thus, the average message is 4 times as large). The slight differences between write-invalidate and the adaptive scheme for cache line sizes larger than 4 bytes are caused by the relatively few accesses to objects that are even larger than complex variables, such as threads and monitors.

These two examples provide evidence that adaptive cache coherence mechanisms can significantly improve upon the performance of standard cache coherence mechanisms in a distributed shared memory system where all coherence is performed in software and network latencies are relatively high.

5   Related Work

Archibald and Baer discuss a variety of cache coherence protocols [3], most of which are variations of *write-invalidate* and *write-update*. Each works well in some instances and poorly in others. For example, when a single data item is frequently read and written by multiple processors (*fine-grained sharing*), a write-update cache tends to outperform a write-invalidate cache because the data item always resides in the local caches, and the needless cache misses and reloads after each invalidation are avoided. On the other hand, write-invalidate caches outperform write-update caches when one processor is performing most of the reads and writes of a particular data item or when a data item migrates between processors (*sequential sharing*). This is because after the invalidation associated with the first write to a data item, a write-invalidate cache does not needlessly broadcast the new value during subsequent writes.

Coherence Mechanism	Line size	Transfers (1000's)	Data Copied (kilobytes)
Delayed Update	4	19.6	87.7
	16	5.48	78.5
	64	1.65	106
Write-Invalidate	4	28.5	114
	16	8.81	141
	64	3.39	217
Write-Update	4	30.2	121
	16	14.9	239
	64	11.5	734

Table 8   Simulation of Quicksort

Archibald described a cache coherence protocol that attempts to adapt to the current reference pattern and dynamically choose to update or invalidate the other copies of a shared data object depending on how they are being used [2]. His protocol is designed for hardware implementation, and therefore is fairly simple and not as aggressive in its attempts to adapt to the expected access behavior as what we propose. Nevertheless, his simulation study indicates that even a simple adaptive protocol can enhance performance.

Other adaptive caching schemes have been proposed, including competitive snoopy caching [10] and read-broadcast [11]. Each appears to be appropriate for particular types of sharing behavior, and we plan to examine them in more detail as our work continues.

Weber and Gupta attempt to link the observed invalidation patterns back to high-level applications program objects [18]. They distinguished several distinct types of shared data objects: *Code and read-only*, *Mostly-read*, *Migratory*, *Synchronization*, and *Frequently read/written*. The first four of their categories have corresponding categories in our classification and are handled similarly. *Frequently read/written* data had the worst invalidation behavior and their coherence protocols could not handle them efficiently. They advised that this type of data object be avoided if at all possible. Our approach is more aggressive. We have identified two types of shared data objects (*Write-Many* and *Producer-Consumer*) that would fall into Weber-Gupta's *Frequently read/written* category, yet can be handled efficiently by an appropriate protocol.

Eggers and Katz analyze the sharing characteristics of four parallel programs [8]. Two of the applications exhibited a high percentage of *sequential sharing* while the other two exhibited a high degree of *fine-grained sharing*. This indicates that neither write-broadcast nor write-invalidate is clearly better for all applications. The observed low contention for shared data objects led them to conclude that write-invalidate outperforms write-broadcast on the average, but one major cause of their low contention is their programming methodology (SPMD). Each process executes on an independent piece of data, and the only contention occurs at the central task queue. Thus, most computation occurs without contention, which favors write-invalidate.

6 Conclusions

We have characterized several distinct categories of shared data access: *Write-once*, *Write-many*, *Producer-Consumer*, *Private*, *Migratory*, *Result*, *Read-mostly*, *Synchronization*, and *General Read-Write*. We have briefly described efficient memory coherence mechanisms for each of these categories. By studying logs of shared memory accesses of a variety of parallel programs, we have shown that a large percentage of shared memory accesses fall in these categories. These results support our contention that adaptive cache coherence techniques that are designed to exploit the anticipated or observed access behavior of a particular data object can significantly outperform standard cache coherence mechanisms, at least in the context of a distributed shared memory system. We have also described two simulations studies to further support this hypothesis.

Acknowledgements

The authors would like to thank the referees and the members of the Rice computer systems group (Elmootazbellah Elnozahy, Jerry Fowler, David Johnson, Pete Keleher, and Mark Mazina) for their helpful suggestions. Trung Diep assisted with the acquisition and plotting of program speedup data.

References

[1] Anant Agarwal, Richard L. Sites, and Mark Horowitz. ATUM: A new technique for capturing address traces using microcode. In *Proceedings of the 13th Annual International Symposium on Computer Architecture*, pages 119–127, June 1986.

[2] James Archibald. A cache coherence approach for large multiprocessor systems. In *International Conference on Supercomputing*, pages 337–345, November 1988.

[3] James Archibald and Jean-Loup Baer. Cache coherence protocols: Evaluation using a multiprocessor simulation model. *ACM Transactions on Computer Systems*, 4(4):273–298, November 1986.

[4] John K. Bennett, John B. Carter, and Willy Zwaenepoel. Munin: Distributed shared memory based on type-specific memory coherence. In *Proceedings of the 1990 Conference on Principles and Practice of Parallel Programming*, March 1990.

[5] Brian N. Bershad, Edward D. Lazowska, and Henry M. Levy. PRESTO: A system for object-oriented parallel programming. *Software—*

Practice and Experience, 18(8):713-732, August 1988.

[6] Jeffrey S. Chase, Franz G. Amador, Edward D. Lazowska, Henry M. Levy, and Richard J. Littlefield. The Amber system: Parallel programming on a network of multiprocessors. In *Proceedings of the Twelfth ACM Symposium on Operating Systems Principles*, pages 147-158, December 1989.

[7] Michel Dubois, Christoph Scheurich, and Fayé A. Briggs. Synchronization, coherence, and event ordering in multiprocessors. *IEEE Computer*, 21(2):9-21, February 1988.

[8] Susan J. Eggers and Randy H. Katz. A characterization of sharing in parallel programs and its application to coherency protocol evaluation. In *Proceedings of the 15th Annual International Symposium on Computer Architecture*, pages 373-383, May 1988.

[9] James R. Goodman, Mary K. Vernon, and Philip J. Woest. Efficient synchronization primitives for large-scale cache-coherent multiprocessor. In *Proceedings of the 3rd International Conference on Architectural Support for Programming Languages and Systems*, April 1989.

[10] A. R. Karlin, M. S. Manasse, L. Rudolph, and D.D. Sleator. Competitive snoopy caching. In *Proceedings of the 16th Annual IEEE Symposium on the Foundations of Computer Science*, pages 244-254, 1986.

[11] Kai Li. Private communication. March 1990.

[12] Kai Li and Paul Hudak. Memory coherence in shared virtual memory systems. *ACM Transactions on Computer Systems*, 7(4):321-359, November 1989.

[13] Tom Lovett and Shreekant Thakkar. The Symmetry multiprocessor system. In *Proceedings of the 1988 International Conference on Parallel Processing*, pages 303-310, August 1988.

[14] Umakishore Ramachandran and M. Yousef A. Khalidi. An implementation of distributed shared memory. *Distributed and Multiprocessor Systems Workshop*, pages 21-38, 1989.

[15] Richard L. Sites and Anant Agarwal. Multiprocessor cache analysis using ATUM. In *Proceedings of the 15th Annual International Symposium on Computer Architecture*, pages 186-195, June 1988.

[16] K. So, F. Darema-Rogers, D. George, V.A. Norton, and G.F. Pfister. PSIMUL: A system for parallel simulation of the execution of parallel programs. Technical Report RC11674, IBM Research, 1986.

[17] Bjarne Stroustrup. *The C++ Programming Language*. Addison-Wesley, 1987.

[18] Wolf-Dietrich Weber and Anoop Gupta. Analysis of cache invalidation patterns in multiprocessors. In *Proceedings of the 3rd International Conference on Architectural Support for Programming Languages and Systems*, pages 243-256, April 1989.

Chapter 4
Techniques for Modeling and Performance Evaluation of Cache Memories and Cache Coherence Maintenance Mechanisms

This chapter includes some readings that yield a better understanding of methods used in the multiprocessor performance evaluation process. Analytic modeling is a widely used methodology for rough estimation of performance metrics. Petri nets and Marcov chain models give accurate estimations, but are limited to small system evaluation. The MVA (mean value analysis) gives results with satisfactory precision and could be used for large systems as well. Consequently, the Petri nets and the Marcov chains are rarely used, and the MVA is frequently used, in cache coherence performance estimation. Simulation of a multiprocessor system under analysis usually provides a highly precise prediction of the real system performance. If the simulation model of the system is very detailed and a realistic workload behavior is simulated, highly accurate results of simulation can be expected. The most precise performance indexes are obtained when the simulator designer is aware of all structural (architectural and organizational) details and an adequate executable benchmark, written for the multiprocessor under consideration, exists.

Several problems may also be encountered with this approach: first, designing and implementing such a low-level detailed simulator can be a formidable task; second, the representativeness of the benchmark(s) for the general multiprocessor workload behavior is always under question; third, except in the last phases of the multiprocessor development, organizational details may be unknown, and the lack of benchmarks for the multiprocessor under analysis could become a problem. Consequently, the practical simulation model is approximate, and real benchmarks are frequently substituted with adequate address traces (obtained from an existing, but similar, multiprocessor system, driven by a program considered representative for the typical workload of the target multiprocessor). Usually one more problem arises: the real address trace may be extremely long. Various techniques for extracting representative segments with the characteristic workload parameters from a long address trace have to be used. Lately, many research efforts have been invested in multiprocessor workload characterization and modeling. A properly characterized workload behavior would facilitate design of a workload model that is representative and realistic enough to substitute the long address traces, but relatively simple and inexpensive to implement.

This chapter includes seven papers that elucidate the methodologies used in analytic modeling and simulation analysis of caches and cache coherence maintenance schemes. The first two papers introduce the reader to the analytic modeling of private caches in a multiprocessor system (the first paper does not address the coherence maintenance problem). The following two papers discuss the simulation analysis issues (such as the sensitivity of simulation results and acquiring a multiprocessor real address traces). The last three papers deal with the multiprocessor workload characterization and modeling.

In the paper "Analysis of Multiprocessors with Private Cache Memories," Patel assumes a multiprocessor workload in which the incoherence problem does not arise. Nevertheless, this frequently cited paper could be of interest for researchers in the stage of preparing themselves for cache coherence analysis. Patel develops an approximate model for private caches connected to main memory via a crossbar (as well as delta) network, giving an iterative solution for the processor utilization as a performance measure. Analyzing the simulation results, Patel concludes that accuracy of the model is quite satisfactory, particularly in the domain of parameter values and regions of practical interest.

Briggs and Dubois, in the paper "Effectiveness of Private Caches in Multiprocessor Systems with Parallel-Pipelined Memories," published in 1983, analyze the impact of introducing private cache memories on the speed-up of a multiprocessor. They were among the first to take into account the cache coherence problem and proposed an early software solution. In their work, the main memory modules containing noncachable data are separated from the modules containing cachable data. The analyzed multiprocessor is equipped with a crossbar interconnection network and a shared main memory, organized as a two-dimensional LM (L—lines, M—modules) memory structure. The approximate analytical model is developed for the case of a fully-associative cache as well as for the case of a set-associative cache. For each cache organization, the model gives the multiprocessor utilization. Speed-up is computed by comparing the cache-based multiprocessor with a multiprocessor system without caches. Inclusion of cache memories results in a significant speed-up in most cases.

The influence of multiple program runs and program execution dilation (caused by the address trace capturing process) on the simulation results is analyzed in the paper "On the Validity of Trace-Driven Simulation for Multiprocessors," written by Koldinger, Eggers, and Levy. Address traces are collected from the real multiprocessor system (Sequent Symmetry), and experiments are performed using a cache-coherent multiprocessor simulation platform (Charlie). Experiments with several coarse-grained and medium-grained parallel applications show that simulation results of trace-driven simulations are highly stable. Multiple program traces are necessary only if very precise simulation results are needed. To obtain a trend for some performance metric, one program run could be sufficient. The influence of the tracing dilation on the simulation results can be neglected, and the use of software techniques for trace capturing should be encouraged.

In the paper "Multiprocessor Cache Simulation Using Hardware Collected Address Traces," Wilson reported a hardware system for recording the addresses generated during execution. The system was developed at Encore, using one Multimax multiprocessor as a tool to get the address trace from another Multimax executing the program. The main advantage of the proposed method, compared to the software- and microcode-related techniques for trace collection, is realism because the traces are collected exclusively in real time, without any distortion. Although the traces are collected from a multiprocessor with a hardware cache coherence mechanism, this paper is very useful for research and practice in the field of software cache coherence maintenance because the reported methodology for trace collecting is general.

An interesting contribution to understanding the influence of program behavior on system performance is made by Gupta and Weber in the paper "Cache Invalidation Patterns in Shared-Memory Multiprocessors." They recorded the invalidation distribution in multiprocessors with 8, 16, and 32 processors, running real address traces of five applications. Gupta and Weber tried to link the behavior of the invalidation patterns to the high-level data objects causing them. They conclude that, for the considered machines with hundreds or thousands of processors, the extrapolation of high-level data-class behavior gives more accurate results than the extrapolation of the composite behavior of the overall application. Although their research was performed on a hardware directory-based cache coherence maintenance platform, we believe that the results of Gupta/Weber's work will be useful in a significantly wider circle of interest, including different software-based coherence maintenance approaches.

Conte and Hwu propose, in the paper "Benchmark Characterization for Experimental System Evaluation," the methodology for describing program behavior independently of system parameters. Consequently, given program characteristics allow comparisons of different systems to be fair. These authors primarily base benchmark characterization on spatial and temporal locality measures. Instruction and data references are considered separately, and appropriate characteristics of the instruction and data address streams differ. The locality-metrics is formally defined and the mechanism for program characteristics extraction from a real address trace is proposed. Some benchmarks are used to illustrate the proposed methodology, and the derived locality measures are included.

Singh, Stone, and Thiebaut, in the paper "A Model of Workloads and Its Use in Miss-Rate Prediction for Fully Associative Caches," propose an empirically derived analytic model for uniprocessor workload behavior. However, we recommend this paper because it could serve as a very useful foundation for multiprocessor workload modeling. The proposed model for the *footprint function* $u(t,L)$ describing the number of unique lines of size L referenced before time t, includes the parameters that model spatial and temporal locality of the workload reference stream. The cache-miss ratio is evaluated as the time derivative of the footprint function at the point where the function is equal to cache size. This model is highly accurate for large, fully-associative caches.

Suggestions for Further Reading

Agarwal, A., Sites, R.L., and Horowitz, M., "ATUM: A New Technique for Capturing Address Traces Using Microcode," *Proc. 13th Ann. Int'l Symp. Computer Architecture,* IEEE CS Press, Los Alamitos, Calif., 1986, pp. 119-127.

Agarwal, A., and Gupta, A., "Memory-Reference Characteristics of Multiprocessor Applications Under MACH," *Proc. ACM SIGMETRICS Conf.,* ACM Press, New York, N.Y., 1988, pp. 215–225.

Agarwal, A., Horowitz, M., and Hennessy, J., "An Analytical Cache Model," *ACM Trans. Computer Systems*, Vol. 7, May 1989, pp. 184–215.

Agarwal, A., "Performance Tradeoffs in Multithreaded Processors," *IEEE Trans. Parallel and Distributed Systems*, Vol. 3, No. 5, Sept. 1992, pp. 525–539.

Borg, A., Kessler, R.E., and Wall, D.W., "Generation and Analysis of Very Long Address Traces," *Proc. 17th Ann. Int'l Symp. Computer Architecture*, IEEE CS Press, Los Alamitos, Calif., 1990, pp. 270–279.

Eggers, S.J., "Simulation Analysis of Data Sharing in Shared Memory Multiprocessors," PhD dissertation, University of California, Berkeley, April 1989.

Eggers, S.J., and Katz, R.H., "A Characterization of Sharing in Parallel Programs and its Application to Coherence Protocol Evaluation," *Proc. 15th Ann. Int'l Symp. Computer Architecture*, IEEE CS Press, Los Alamitos, Calif., 1988, pp. 373–382.

Eggers, S.J., and Katz, R.H., "The Effect of Sharing on the Cache and Bus Performance of Parallel Programs," *Proc. 3rd Int'l Conf. Architectural Support for Programming Languages and Operating Systems*, ACM Press, New York, N.Y., 1989, pp. 257–270.

Eggers, S.J., et al., "Techniques for Efficient Inline Tracing on a Shared-Memory Multiprocessor," *Proc. Int'l Conf. Measurement and Modeling of Computer Systems*, 1990, pp. 37–46.

Eggers, S.J., "Simplicity Versus Accuracy in a Model of Cache Coherence Overhead," *IEEE Trans. Computers*, Vol. 40, No. 8, Aug. 1991, pp. 893–906.

Grimsrud, K., et al., "BACH: A Hardware Monitor for Tracing Microprocessor Based Systems," *Microprocessor and Microsystems*, Vol. 17, No. 8, Oct. 1993, pp. 443–459.

Heidelberger, P., and Trivedi, K., "Analytic Queuing Models for Programs with Internal Concurrency," *IEEE Trans. Computers*, Vol. C-32, No. 1, Jan. 1983, pp. 73–82.

Marsan, M.A., et al., "Modeling Bus Contention and Memory Interference in a Multiprocessor System," *IEEE Trans. Computers*, Vol. C-32, No. 1, Jan. 1983, pp. 60–72.

Natarajan, C., Sharma, S., and Iyer, R.K., "Measurement-Based Characterization of Global Memory and Network Contention, Operating System and Parallelization Overheads: Case Study on a Shared-Memory Multiprocessor," *Proc. 21st Ann. Int'l Symp. Computer Architecture*, IEEE CS Press, Los Alamitos, Calif., 1994, pp. 71–80.

Patt, Y., "Methodologies for Experimental Research in Computer Architecture and Performance Measurements," *Proc. 23rd Ann. Hawaii Int'l Conf. System Sciences*, Vol. 1, IEEE CS Press, Los Alamitos, Calif., 1990., pp. 2–5.

Singh, J.P., Weber, W.-D., and Gupta, A., "SPLASH: Stanford Parallel Applications for Shared-Memory," *Computer Architecture News*, Vol. 20, No. 1, Mar. 1992, pp. 5–44.

Torrellas, J., Gupta, A., and Hennessy, J., "Characterizing the Caching and Synchronization Performance of a Multiprocessor Operating System," *Proc. 5th Int'l Conf. Architectural Support for Programming Languages and Operating Systems*, ACM Press, New York, N.Y., 1992, pp. 162–174.

Tsuei, T.-F., and Vernon, M.K., "A Multiprocessor Bus Design Model Validated by System Measurement," *IEEE Trans. Parallel and Distributed Systems*, Vol. 3, No. 6, Nov. 1992, pp. 712–727.

Simoni, R., and Horowitz, M., "Modeling the Performance of Limited Pointers Directories for Cache Coherence," *Proc. 18th Ann. Int'l Symp. Computer Architecture*, ACM Press, New York, N.Y., 1991, pp. 309–318.

Vernon M.K., Lazowska, E.D., and Zahorjan, J., "An Accurate and Efficient Performance Analysis Technique for Multiprocessor Snooping Cache-Consistency Protocols," *Proc. 15th Ann. Int'l Symp. Computer Architecture*, IEEE CS Press, Los Alamitos, Calif., 1988, pp. 308–315.

Analysis of Multiprocessors with Private Cache Memories

JANAK H. PATEL, MEMBER, IEEE

Abstract—This paper presents an approximate analytical model for the performance of multiprocessors with private cache memories and a single shared main memory. The accuracy of the model is compared with simulation results and is found to be very good over a broad range of parameters. The parameters of the model are the size of the multiprocessor, the size and type of the interconnection network, the cache miss-ratio, and the cache block transfer time. The analysis is extended to include several different read/write policies such as write-through, load-through, and buffered write-back. The analytical technique presented is also applicable to the performance of interconnection networks under block transfer mode.

Index Terms—Cache memories, crossbar, delta networks, interconnection networks, multiprocessors, parallel memories, performance analysis.

I. INTRODUCTION

WITH the emergence of VLSI technology and low cost processors, multiprocessors are becoming increasingly attractive. Current VLSI designs suffer from a mismatch between internal and external data transfer rates. The data transfer rates on the chip can be made much higher than the transfer rates across chip boundaries, that is, on the pins. This mismatch can be alleviated by placing a private cache on the chip with the processor, and then implementing a multiprocessor organization like that of Fig. 1. In such a design, the traffic across the cache-main memory interface is lower than the traffic across the processor-cache interface. This paper presents analytic and simulation results for the performance of multiprocessors with a two-level memory hierarchy of the type shown in Fig. 1. The first level of memory is a private cache and the second level of the memory is the main memory shared by all processors. The two levels are connected through a switch. In this paper we shall restrict ourselves to switches which are full crossbars or delta networks.

The multiprocessor organization with private cache memories is somewhat restrictive compared to an organization in which all memories are fully shared by each processor. The principal drawback of private cache is that of data consistency, that is, the possibility of creation of several copies of a single variable, where a copy is manipulated in private memory independent of other copies, thus producing inconsistent values among the copies of the same variable. Such problems can be

Manuscript received January 1, 1981; revised May 1, 1981 and December 1, 1981. This work was supported in part by the Joint Services Electronics Program under Contract N00016-79-C-0424.

The author is with the Department of Electrical Engineering and the Coordinated Science Laboratory, University of Illinois, Urbana, IL 61801.

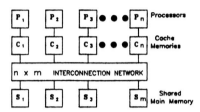

Fig. 1. Multiprocessor organization with private cache memories.

solved through hardware or software interlocks, but only with a substantial penalty in performance [3], [15]. However, there are many applications where the problem of data inconsistency does not arise, for example, in the sharing of reentrant procedures or in the use of read only data. For this paper we shall assume an environment in which data consistency is not a problem.

Design of a cache-based multiprocessor system involves many parameters. These include the cache capacity, the block size and the set size, read and write policies (e.g., write-through and load-through), the size and the type of interconnection network, and the transfer rate between the cache and the main memory. In the absence of an analytical method of performance evaluation, simulation is the only alternative. However, simulation involving so many parameters is truly a formidable task. To reduce the range of parameter values, over which to simulate, even the most rudimentary analysis is of some value. Therefore, an approximate but fairly accurate analysis is of definite help to a designer. The analysis presented in this paper serves such a purpose. In addition, the technique presented is potentially useful for obtaining approximate solutions to many similar problems.

In the next section we present the physical description of the system under study. Following this we develop the analysis of a particularly simple cache organization. This simple cache organization is especially helpful in explaining the development of the approximate analysis. This analysis is evaluated by comparing the results with simulation results. The agreement between the two is within 2 percent in the region of interest. Finally, the analytical method developed for the simple cache organization is applied to more complex cache organizations of practical interest. In particular three organizations, namely, write-through, load-through, and buffered write-back are discussed. As an example, the write-through is evaluated for several different values of the parameters and compared with the simulation results, showing the applicability of the analytical technique to very complex problems.

II. THE PHYSICAL MODEL

A. The Cache

The memory organization assumed here is a two-level memory hierarchy. As the memory speeds and costs continue to change, two-level memory hierarchies may be designed which cannot be classified as a cache/main memory or as a main/secondary memory with their traditional meaning. We shall distinguish these two by several attributes. This is not an attempt to define the two memory systems. However, the distinction is necessary for our analytical model. The model is only discussed in relation to a cache-main memory hierarchy, where a cache-main is assumed to have the following description.

For the purposes of this paper, a cache-main memory hierarchy will be assumed to have a miss ratio less than 0.1 and a block size small enough and/or memories fast enough so that a block transfer time is no greater than about 64 cache cycles. In contrast, a main-secondary memory hierarchy may have fault rates much less than 0.005 and page transfer times far greater than cache block transfer times. In addition, a cache memory is much smaller than the primary memory of a paging hierarchy.

An implication of the above attributes is that in a cache-main memory system it is not profitable to switch processes on a cache miss. This is because a process switching time is comparable to a block transfer time and also because cache is not large enough to hold more than one working set for an acceptable miss ratio. Therefore, we can assume that on a cache miss, the processor is idle while the desired block is being transferred. Thus, the system throughput of a multiprocessor with cache-main memory can be computed directly from the total time spent in doing block transfers, if the processor execution is not overlapped with a block transfer. Note that such an assumption cannot be justified in a main-secondary paging system because the processor execution and the page transfers are almost always overlapped.

B. Cache-Main Interconnection

Two interconnection networks that will be studied here are full crossbars and delta networks [7]. Both networks will be used here in the circuit switching mode. Once a fault occurs in a cache, the fault handling hardware requests a block transfer from a particular main memory module and the network establishes a path between the cache and the main memory module. This path is held until the memory transaction is complete. The path cannot be preempted by any other requests coming from other cache modules. In this description it is assumed that a block resides in a single memory module. However, a memory module itself may be interleaved to increase its bandwidth. The advantage of using circuit switching and storing the block in one memory module is the reduction in block transfer time. Both in the crossbar and delta network there is an initial delay in establishing a path due to arbitration, decoding, and setting of appropriate switches. Once the path is established the data can be transferred at a high rate.

Another advantage of circuit switching is the ease of performing one or more indivisible read/write operations in the main memory. This in turn simplifies the implementation of synchronization and mutual exclusion primitives which are required in most multiprocessing environments.

III. ANALYSIS

A. Simple Cache Model

In this section we develop an analytical model for a very simple cache organization. This will be extended later to include more complex cache organizations. The following assumptions define the simple cache model.

1) Each cache fault involves one block-write to a main memory module followed by one block-read from the same memory module. As a consequence of this, we further assume that once a path is established between the faulting cache and the requested memory module, the transaction (read and write of a block) takes a constant time.

2) Cache requests to main memory are random and uniformly distributed over all main memory modules.

The first assumption is satisfied in a set-associative cache with no write-through or load-through capability by requiring that all blocks that map to a single set be stored in the same memory module. This assumption will be modified later in our treatment of more complex cache organizations.

Thus, in the simple cache model a cache fault generates a request to a main memory module, which is accepted after some wait due to network conflicts. After the request is granted the cache-main memory transaction takes a constant time. Let this time be t time units, where the time unit can be thought of as the processor minor cycle or the unit of the smallest activity in the processor. Thus, all cache and memory cycles are some integral multiples of the CPU minor cycle. Furthermore, we assume that requests from the CPU to the cache are generated at the integral boundaries of the time unit.

The second assumption about the cache-fault behavior is justified for our multiprocessor system. If the processors are not interacting heavily with each other, then very little correlation exists between the address streams of different processors. The uniform distribution assumption is further aided by interleaving the blocks in the main memory, that is, assigning block i to memory module $i \bmod M$, where M is the number of main memory modules. (Note that this does not contradict the earlier assumption of blocks of the same set in a single memory module.) Two successive cache faults of a single processor may be less independent. However, in the time interval between these two faults other cache modules are also faulting. Thus, the requests that a main memory module sees are fairly independent and random.

The miss ratio of a program as a function of cache size, block size, and set size have been measured by several researchers [4], [6], [8], [14], [16]. Also, some analytical models for estimating cache miss ratios exist [5], [9]. From such data it is possible to determine the request rate from a cache to the main memory. Let m be the probability that a cache makes a request to main memory in a given time unit, that is, m is the probability that the processor makes a request to the cache and that it is a fault. m typically would be less than the miss ratio because not every CPU cycle is a memory reference.

To summarize the simple cache model, at each time unit a cache makes a request to the main memory with probability m, after some wait time a transaction between a main memory module and the faulting cache takes place, which lasts for t time units. Throughout this period the processor remains idle.

B. Approximate Analysis of Simple Cache Model

A processor in our multiprocessor is in one of two states. It is either busy doing useful work or it is idle waiting for a cache-fault service to be completed. The throughput of the system is directly proportional to the processor utilization. Therefore, we shall use the processor utilization as a measure of the system performance. This can be computed as follows.

Consider Fig. 2, which shows the effect of cache faults and wait times on the processor activity. Since each processor cycle generates a cache fault with probability m, there are on the average mk faults for k units of useful computation. Let w be the average wait encountered at each request. Since a block transfer takes t time units, the k units of useful processor activity take $k + mk(w + t)$ time units. Assuming N processors and M main memory modules, the following can be computed directly from Fig. 2(c). The processor utilization

$$U = k/[k + mk(w + t)] = 1/[1 + m(w + t)]. \quad (1)$$

The average number of busy main memory modules

$$B = Nmkt/[k + mk(w + t)]$$
$$= Nmt/[1 + m(w + t)]. \quad (2)$$

In terms of utilization U

$$B = NmtU. \quad (3)$$

In the above expressions the only unknown is the average wait time w. It is clear that the wait time depends on several factors, such as request rate m, number of processors N, number of memory modules M, block transfer time t, and the type of the interconnection network. Let us see what are the difficulties involved in computing the average wait time w.

Consider a specific case with $m = 1$ and $t = 1$ and the crossbar as the memory switch. In other words, a request is generated at each time unit. Furthermore, assume that the memory transfer is overlapped with the CPU execution. While this is not a realistic case for our system, it illustrates a point here about the analysis of such problems. This case is identical to the parallel memory model studied by several researchers for the evaluation of memory bandwidth. No exact closed form solution exists to this date for this problem. Given specific numeric values for N and M, exact Markov analysis is possible but involves a large amount of computation. Bhandarkar [2] gave a procedure to carry out such a computation. Others have given approximate analyses for closed form solutions [1], [11]–[13], of which Rau's result [10] comes closest to the exact value.

Now consider our more general case where m and t are not necessarily 1 and the memory transfers are not overlapped with the CPU execution. Exact Markov analysis is always possible for specific numeric values of m, t, N, and M because of the

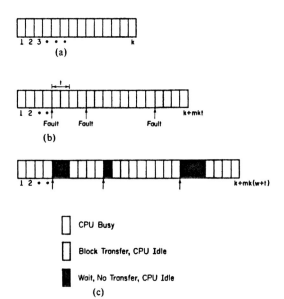

Fig. 2. Effect of cache faults and wait time on CPU utilization. (a) CPU activity with no faults. (b) mk faults with no wait for block transfer. (c) mk faults with average w wait per fault.

finite number of states. However, the state space is much larger than for the often studied case of $m = 1$ and $t = 1$, and therefore computationally far more complex. In the absence of a reasonable analysis, simulation is the only other viable alternative. We have done extensive simulation of the simple cache model. One important outcome of the simulation was an observation that the processor utilization of a given sized multiprocessor system with a specific network (crossbar or delta) can be approximated as a function of the product mt, where m is the probability of a cache to main request and t is the block transfer time. In the terminology of the queueing theory, mt may be described as the offered traffic intensity. Mathematically, the processor utilization most surely will not be a function of the product mt. As a matter of fact, the Markov analysis of a very simple case $N = M = 2$ showed that it is not purely a function of mt. However, the simulation showed that the individual influences of m or t are small compared to the effect of product mt. In other words, the processor utilization depends primarily on the traffic intensity and to a lesser extent on the nature of the traffic. This is the clue we use in obtaining an approximate analysis of the simple cache model. The principle idea behind the analysis is to transform the given simple cache model into an "equivalent" model in which the offered traffic intensity is maintained and for which we also have an approximate solution.

Consider Fig. 2(c) once again which shows the activity of a single processor. While the processor is waiting, the cache is resubmitting the block transfer request again and again until it is accepted by the network; on the average this happens for w time units. After the request is granted, the network holds a path to a memory module for t time units. One can view this as t consecutive requests to the same module, each request requiring one time unit of service. Thus, on each cache fault the network sees an average of $w + t$ consecutive requests for unit service time. Referring to Fig. 2(c), in $k + mk(w + t)$ time units a total of $mk(w + t)$ requests for unit service are made to the network. Therefore, the request rate (for unit service) from a cache module as seen by the network is

$$m' = m(w + t)/[1 + m(w + t)]. \qquad (4)$$

In terms of processor utilization U of (1) we have

$$m' = 1 - U. \qquad (5)$$

The approximation that we introduce here is that $w + t$ consecutive requests to a single memory module can be decomposed into $w + t$ separate requests which are random, independent, and uniformly distributed over all memory modules, without essentially changing the system behavior. Clearly, the transformation is not equivalent to the original system. However, the offered traffic between the cache and the main is maintained as before. Moreover, we do have an approximate analytical solution to the transformed model.

The model that we will analyze is a system of N sources and M destinations; each source generates a request with probability m' in each time unit. The request is independent, random, and uniformly distributed over all destinations. Each request is for one unit service time. Rejected requests are resubmitted as new independent requests and are made part of the new request m'. First, we analyze the system with a crossbar and then with a delta network.

The Crossbar: We already know the average number of busy main memory modules. This from (3) is

$$B = NmtU. \qquad (3)$$

Another way to compute the same quantity assuming the crossbar is as follows. A similar derivation for parallel memory bandwidth was used by Strecker [13].

Each main memory module is addressed with probability m'/M from a cache. The probability that none of the N cache modules make a request to a particular main memory module is $(1 - m'/M)^N$. Therefore, on the average $M[(1 - m'/M)^N]$ modules are not doing any memory transfers, or to put it another way, $M[1 - (1 - m'/M)^N]$ main memory modules are making a memory transfer. Therefore, the average number of busy memory modules is

$$B = M[1 - (1 - m'/M)^N] \qquad (6)$$

substituting for $B = NmtU$ from (3) and $m' = 1 - U$ from (5) we have

$$NmtU - M[1 - (1 - (1 - U)/M)^N] = 0. \qquad (7)$$

The above equation in U can be solved by standard numerical algorithms using iterative techniques. Most of these algorithms require a good initial value for the unknown U. A good initial value for U is obtained by setting wait time $w = 0$ in (1), that is, setting $U = 1/(1 + mt)$, which incidently corresponds to the maximum possible processor utilization.

Note that U in (7) is a function of N, M, and mt. This should be no surprise since our approximation is based on the assumption that the utilization is a function of mt, and not m or t independently.

The Delta Network: A delta network is an n stage network constructed from $a \times b$ crossbar switches with a resulting size

of $a^n \times b^n$. Thus, in our model it is required that $N = a^n$ and $M = b^n$. For a more complete description, see [7]. Functionally, a delta network is an interconnection network which allows any of the N cache modules to communicate with any one of the M main memory modules. However, unlike in a crossbar two requests may collide in the delta network even if the requests were to two different memory modules. Following the analysis in [7], we apply the result of the $a \times b$ crossbar recursively, to each stage of delta network to obtain the average number of busy main memory modules B. It is computed using the following system of equations.

$$B = Mm_n \qquad (8)$$

where

$$m_{i+1} = 1 - (1 - m_i/b)^a \qquad 0 \le i < n$$

and

$$m_0 = m'.$$

Equating this with B of (3) we have

$$NmtU = Mm_n$$

substituting for $m' = 1 - U$ from (5) we have a system of equations for evaluating the utilization U.

$$NmtU - Mm_n = 0 \qquad (9)$$

where

$$m_{i+1} = 1 - (1 - m_i/b)^a \qquad 0 \le i < n$$

and

$$m_0 = 1 - U.$$

Note that in these equations, as in the crossbar, the utilization is a function of the network size $N \times M$ and the product mt. These equations can also be solved numerically. Here too a starting value for $U = 1/(1 + mt)$ is appropriate for iterative solutions.

IV. COMPARISON OF ANALYTICAL AND SIMULATION RESULTS

In this section we present several results obtained using the above approximate analysis and compare these with the simulation results. The results were compared over a wide range of parameters. The parameter ranges were: request rate m from $1/128$ to 1, block transfer time t from 1 to 64 units, and the number of processors and memories from 1 to 128. As an example, Table I shows the CPU utilization obtained through simulation of a 32×32 multiprocessor with a crossbar. The simulation was run for 40 000 time units for each different value of m and t. Table I also lists the confidence intervals for 99 percent confidence level. Each interval was computed using Student's t-distribution, with sample points taken every 1000 time units for a total of 40 points over the simulation run.

The first noticeable thing in the table is the nearly identical values of CPU utilization for a constant mt. The values corresponding to a constant mt can be seen in any forward diagonal of the table. For example, the main diagonal corresponds to the product $mt = 1$. Notice also the small values of the

TABLE I
MEAN CPU UTILIZATION FOR A 32 × 32 MULTIPROCESSOR ± (99 PERCENT CONFIDENCE INTERVAL)

Block Transfer Time t

Request rate m	1	2	4	8	16	32	64
2^0	42.65±.05	25.24±.06	13.69±.05	7.14±.04	3.65±.03	1.82±.03	.91±.02
2^{-1}	62.21±.09	42.57±.09	25.27±.10	13.71±.11	7.17±.09	3.64±.05	1.85±.04
2^{-2}	78.23±.09	62.23±.17	42.58±.23	25.15±.19	13.78±.20	7.07±.16	3.61±.08
2^{-3}	88.28±.08	78.18±.16	62.13±.26	42.43±.32	25.01±.27	13.62±.25	7.22±.18
2^{-4}	93.97±.06	88.27±.12	78.21±.26	62.28±.37	42.55±.44	25.39±.41	13.85±.36
2^{-5}	96.90±.04	93.91±.09	88.34±.14	78.33±.32	62.16±.51	42.48±.61	25.24±.63
2^{-6}	98.45±.03	96.91±.05	93.91±.10	88.21±.24	78.59±.41	62.19±.66	41.82±.85
2^{-7}	99.20±.02	98.45±.04	96.97±.08	93.99±.15	88.36±.36	78.01±.57	62.60±1.09

confidence intervals, indicating that the simulation values are very close to the steady-state values of the system under consideration.

Now let us see the difference between the analytical and simulation results. Table II shows the difference (analytical–simulation) in CPU utilization for the above example of 32 × 32 multiprocessor. The table shows that the analysis overestimates the CPU utilization in most cases, although by a very small amount, an amount comparable to 99 percent confidence interval. If we compute the percentage difference relative to the simulation result, then it is evident that the highest relative differences are 8 to 10 percent, which occur at values of mt near 64. The relative differences are about 2 percent for $mt = 1$. For $mt < 1$ the differences are less than 1 percent and all differences for $mt < 1/2$ are well within the confidence intervals of Table I. In other words, the approximate analysis of the multiprocessor cache organization is quite accurate in the region where $mt < 1$. As we shall see in the following discussion, it is this region which is of practical interest.

Consider Fig. 3, which is a graph of processor utilization over a broad range of parameters. The utilization plotted may be interpreted as simulation results or analytical results, since the differences are so small that they are not visible on the graph with the scale used. Since in the analysis the processor utilization is a function of mt, the parameters m and t are not separated in this and other graphs. The graph shows three different systems: the first is $N = 64$, and $M = 64$ using 64 × 64 crossbar, the second is $N = 64$, $M = 64$ using $2^6 × 2^6$ delta network, and the third is the single processor system $N = M = 1$. Since the wait time is zero in the case of $N = M = 1$ system, the processor utilization from (1) is $1/(1 + mt)$, which serves as the upper bound on the processor utilization. It is clear from the graph that for $mt > 1$ the processor utilization is less than 50 percent. Therefore, in a practical system one must have the product mt much smaller than 1 for an acceptable level of performance. Therefore, the region of interest is $mt < 1$. As pointed out earlier, it is in this region of interest that our approximate analysis is most accurate. Comparing the analytical results with a large number of simulation results, we observed that the differences between analytical and simulation results

TABLE II
THE DIFFERENCE IN CPU UTILIZATION (ANALYTICAL-SIMULATION) FOR A 32 × 32 MULTIPROCESSOR

Block Transfer Time t

Request rate m	1	2	4	8	16	32	64
2^0	.82	1.04	.75	.47	.24	.15	.08
2^{-1}	.43	.90	1.01	.73	.44	.25	.12
2^{-2}	.06	.41	.89	1.13	.66	.54	.28
2^{-3}	.04	.11	.51	1.04	1.27	.82	.39
2^{-4}	-.02	.05	.08	.36	.92	.89	.59
2^{-5}	.03	.04	-.02	-.04	.48	.99	1.04
2^{-6}	.00	.02	.04	.11	-.30	.45	1.65
2^{-7}	.02	.00	-.04	-.04	-.04	.28	.04

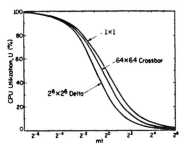

Fig. 3. CPU utilization as a function of mt.

are far less sensitive to the network type (crossbar or delta) and its size, compared to the product mt. This probably is due to the sensitivity of the processor utilization itself, which is much more sensitive to the product mt than the network type or size. Figs. 4 and 5 show the processor utilization in the region of interest. Fig. 4 shows a graph for a 32 × 32 crossbar network and a graph for $2^5 × 2^5$ delta network. Fig. 5 shows the processor utilization as a function of the network size $N × N$ using a crossbar. Both figures are obtained from the analytical model of the previous section.

Other measures of performance may also be evaluated from

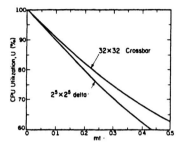

Fig. 4. CPU utilization as a function of mt.

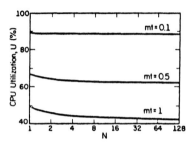

Fig. 5. CPU utilization as a function of the crossbar size $N \times N$.

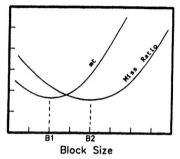

Fig. 6. A typical curve of miss ratio and a hypothetical curve of mt as a function of block size.

the analysis. For example, the average number of busy main memory modules is $NUmt$ from (3). The average wait time w of a request can also be computed in terms of U, mt, and m from (1).

From a designer's perspective the above analysis shows that for optimum performance one must choose mt as small as possible. Recall that m is not the miss-ratio itself but it is directly proportional to the miss ratio, and t is some function of the block size. For example, in an interleaved main memory with access time a and transfer rate c words/time unit, one can express the block transfer time as $t = a + bc$, where b is the block size in words. A typical curve of miss ratio versus block size for a fixed cache size is shown in Fig. 6. The miss-ratio drops when the block size is increased from 1 due to locality in the address stream. However, beyond a certain block size the miss ratio worsens because the additional words fetched in the block are no longer a part of the working set, and furthermore these words occupy valuable cache space by displacing words which are part of the working set. From the graph of miss ratio, one can compute the graph of mt as a function of block size, where m is the probability that the CPU cycle is a memory reference and that it is a miss, and t is the block transfer time. A hypothetical graph of mt versus block size is superimposed on the graph of miss ratio in Fig. 6. From the graph one can choose the optimum block size corresponding to the minimum mt. For a given cache size, the optimum block size for the maximum throughput may or may not correspond to the minimum miss ratio. For the hypothetical example of Fig. 6, block size $B1$ yields the maximum throughput, not the block size $B2$. A similar argument to use mt as a measure of performance rather than m in a uniprocessor system was put forward by Meade [6]. To reduce mt below this value, one can either decrease the miss ratio by choosing a larger cache or reduce the block transfer time by using a faster main memory. Another alternative is to change

the simple cache organization so that some of the block transfer time can be overlapped with the processor execution. This alternative is discussed in the next section.

V. EXTENSIONS OF THE SIMPLE CACHE MODEL

The three most common extensions of a simple cache organization are: 1) write-through, 2) buffered write-back, and 3) load-through. All of these achieve the same objective, namely, overlap of the CPU execution with the data transfers between the cache and the main memory. In this section we apply the analytical technique that we used for the simple cache model in the evaluation of processor utilization. The approximation in each case is to treat the memory traffic as consisting of single cycle requests rather than block requests. Thus, the analysis treats the request rate as unit service requests distributed uniformly over all memory modules. Once the unit request rate is computed, it can be substituted in (6) or (8) to evaluate the cache-main memory traffic, which is also evaluated in another way similar to (2) or (3).

In the following, the write-through cache is discussed in detail with some numeric examples and compared with simulation results. The other two organizations are presented with only the method of analysis. These two organizations are similar in complexity as write-through, and therefore no further numerical evaluation is presented. The following discussion does not concern itself with the evaluation of relative merits of different cache organizations, since our major objective here is to present the technique of analysis, and not an optimum cache design.

Let us describe some notations to be used in the following analyses. Subscript r is used to indicate a read request from cache to main memory for a block transfer, subscript s is used for store (write) of a block into the main memory, subscripts $r1$ and $s1$ represent single word requests for read and store, respectively. The parameters m, t, and w are, as before, the request rate, transfer time, and the wait time, respectively. Thus, some of the variables used have the following meaning; other variables will be defined in the course of the discussion as they are needed.

m_r = probability that there is a read request from the cache to the main memory for a block transfer.

m_{s1} = probability that there is a store request from the cache to the main memory for a single word transfer.

t_r = time to read a block from the main memory into the cache.

232

t_{s1} = time to store a single word into the main memory from the cache.

w_r = average wait time at the network for a block read request.

w_{s1} = average wait time at the network for a one word store request.

For the following analysis, let us assume that the interconnection network gives equal priority to all requests. Thus, the network is unbiased towards the read or write requests and towards the block or single word requests. This is reasonable since to a network a request is for establishing a path between a cache and a main memory module. Once the path is established it can be used for any type of transfers. This implies that average wait time at the network is the same for any request. Let this wait time be w. That is

$$w = w_r = w_{r1} = w_s = w_{s1}. \qquad (10)$$

Write-Through (Store-Through): In this cache organization whenever the processor attempts to write a word in the cache, the word is stored in the main memory, regardless of whether the corresponding block is present in the cache or not. If the block is present in the cache then the word will also be written in the cache. As a consequence, on a read miss the desired block is loaded in the cache and the block being replaced is not required to be written back. If write-through operations are sufficiently buffered, then essentially no penalty exists for successive write-through operations. In practice, this can be satisfied with a small size buffer since the write operations are far less frequent than read operations. For this analysis we shall assume that the write operations are buffered in a buffer of unlimited size.

Since each processor is assumed to have only one communication port to the interconnection network, a read and a write request from the same cache cannot be serviced simultaneously. We shall assume that a read miss from a processor has a higher priority over its own pending write requests. However, once a write request has successfully established a path through the network, it cannot be preempted. Thus, during a write operation to the main memory if a cache miss occurs then the read must wait until the write operation is finished. Let the wait time a read request incurs on a write operation from its own cache be w_r'. After w_r', the read request can be issued to the network. Due to the network conflicts resulting from requests of other processors, the read request will wait on average w_r more time units. Thus, a read miss waits on average $w_r' + w_r$ time units, of which w_r' can be determined as follows.

Recall the definitions of m_r and m_{s1} given earlier in this section. Rephrasing these definitions in the current context of write-through cache, we have m_r as the probability that a processor cycle is a read cycle and that it is a miss; and m_{s1} is the probability that a processor cycle is a write cycle. Thus, in k cycles of processor activity, there are $m_r k$ read requests and $m_{s1} k$ write requests from the cache to the main memory. Given that a write request is in progress between a cache and a main memory, if a read miss occurs in the same cache immediately after the first unit of service of the write request, then the read waits for $(t_{s1} - 1)$ time units before it can be issued to the network, where t_{s1} is the write service time. This event occurs

with a probability m_r. If the read occurred not after the first but after the second time unit, then it waits for $(t_{s1} - 2)$ time units. This happens with a probability $(1 - m_r)m_r$. On the average, each write request will contribute to the wait time of read requests given by the following expression:

$$m_r(t_{s1} - 1) + m_r(1 - m_r)(t_{s1} - 2) + \cdots$$
$$+ m_r(1 - m_r)^{i-1}(t_{s1} - i) + \cdots.$$

Thus, over a run of k useful CPU cycles, $m_{s1} k$ write requests contribute

$$m_{s1} k \sum_{1 \leq i \leq t_{s1}} m_r(1 - m_r)^{i-1}(t_{s1} - i)$$

time units of wait to $m_r k$ read requests. Thus, the average wait suffered by a read request over a write from the same cache is

$$w_r' = m_{s1} \sum_{1 \leq i \leq t_{s1}} (1 - m_r)^{i-1}(t_{s1} - i). \qquad (11)$$

Now we derive the equations involving the other unknowns. Following the method of Fig. 2, we can express the processor utilization U, the average memory bandwidth B, and the unit request rate m' as seen by the network as follows.

$$U = \frac{1}{1 + m_r(w_r' + w_r + t_r)} \qquad (12)$$

$$B = \frac{m_r t_r + m_{s1} t_{s1}}{1 + m_r(w_r' + w_r + t_r)} \qquad (13)$$

$$m' = \frac{m_r(w_r + t_r) + m_{s1}(w_{s1} + t_{s1})}{1 + m_r(w_r' + w_r + t_r)}. \qquad (14)$$

By (10) we have $w_r = w_{s1} = w$, therefore the expression for m' in (14) involves only one unknown w. Substituting this expression for m' in the bandwidth of (6) for crossbar (or (8) for delta network) and then equating it with the bandwidth of (13) above, we have an equation in one unknown, w. The equation in w can be solved iteratively and then used in (12) to obtain the CPU utilization. A suitable starting value for iterative method of solutions is $w = 0$.

The above method of analysis was used in computing the processor utilization for a 4×4 and a 32×32 multiprocessor system with crossbar. Several different values of the parameters m_r, m_{s1}, t_r, and t_{s1} were used for the above analysis and also for the simulation of the write-through cache model. To get a reasonable range of values of these parameters for a typical system, the following reasoning can be used.

Let us say that in a typical processor about 80 percent of all memory references are read operations and 20 percent are write operations. Let us further assume that of the processor cycles available about 75 percent generate memory references. Therefore, the probability that a processor cycle generates a read reference is 0.6. Assuming a cache miss ratio of 10 percent, the probability that a processor cycle results in a read request from the cache to the main memory is $m_r = 0.06$. In the write-through organization every write request generated by the processor also results in a write request from the cache to the main memory. Thus, $m_{s1} = 0.15$. This argument simply establishes what m_r and m_{s1} might look like in a typical system. The range of values we chose for computation is wide enough to cover large variations in the parameter values of the above "typical" system. The analysis and simulation were carried out for all combinations of the following parameters:

$m_r = 0.01, 0.05$ and 0.1 $m_{s1} = 0.1$ and 0.2,

the read block transfer time $t_r = 2, 4, 8$, and 16,

the write word time $t_{s1} = 1, 2$, and 4 with the restriction that t_{s1} is less than t_r.

Table III compares the analytical and simulation results. To keep the table size small not all combinations of the parameters are shown. Each simulation was run for 40 000 time units. The confidence intervals for 99 percent certainty were computed for simulations. No interval was greater than 2 percent, while most were less than 1 percent. Table III again points out the close agreement between our approximate analysis and the simulation results. Considering the complexity of the system, the analysis is remarkably accurate and provides a valuable aid in the design phase of a multiprocessor system.

In the above discussion, the analysis and the simulation both assumed an infinite write buffer. To see the effect of a finite buffer, we also ran simulations with a buffer size of 5 words. Whenever the buffer became full, the processor was made idle until the buffer was no longer full. For the entries in the Table III there was no noticeable change in the performance due to a finite buffer. However, for certain combinations of parameter values which imply a high traffic intensity, the performance was much worse than the infinite buffer case. For example, m_{s1} = 0.2 and $t_{s1} = 4$ implies a traffic intensity of 0.8 just for the write requests. In addition, there are read requests and the network interference. For such cases the system sometimes approached an unstable state with monotonically increasing queue size; and limiting the buffer size resulted in the reduced processor utilization. However, if such cases are indeed frequent in a practical system, then it can be surmised that the system is poorly designed.

Buffered Write Back: On a cache miss the block to be replaced, i.e., written back, is first stored in a high speed buffer. The desired block is then read into the cache module. Following this, the buffer is written back to the main memory module. Assume that the buffer is large enough to handle successive cache faults. For the analysis we shall assume a buffer of unlimited size. The activities of the system can be described quantitatively as follows.

On a cache fault the cache transfers the block to be replaced to the buffer in time t_b, after which the cache issues a read request to the network. The read request is granted after an average wait of w_r time units after which the block is read in time t_r. Thus, the processor is idle during $t_b+w_r+t_r$ time units; after this the buffer issues a store request, which after an average wait of w_s time units is granted and completed in t_s units. During the write back operation the processor is busy. Again let us assume as in the write-through case that once the write operation to the main memory begins, it cannot be preempted and if another cache miss occurs during this operation, then the read request from the cache must wait on average w_r' time units before it can be issued to the network. This wait time can

TABLE III
ANALYTICAL AND SIMULATION RESULTS FOR A WRITE-THROUGH CACHE

m_r	t_r	m_{s1}	t_{s1}	CPU Utilization U% 4 x 4		32 x 32	
				analy.	sim.	analy.	sim.
.01	2	.1	1	97.99	97.92	97.97	97.92
.01	4	.1	2	95.86	95.80	95.79	95.57
.01	8	.1	2	92.25	91.95	92.17	92.01
.01	16	.1	1	86.03	85.27	85.98	85.09
.01	16	.1	2	85.78	85.61	85.67	84.68
.01	2	.2	1	97.94	97.88	97.91	97.89
.01	16	.2	2	85.55	85.06	85.38	83.27
.05	2	.1	1	90.49	90.60	90.36	90.17
.05	8	.1	2	69.11	67.81	68.47	66.32
.05	16	.1	1	53.27	51.00	52.56	48.45
.05	16	.1	2	52.54	50.87	51.66	47.87
.05	4	.2	1	82.48	82.07	82.20	81.22
.05	16	.2	1	53.73	50.80	53.13	48.21
.10	2	.1	1	82.21	81.95	81.87	81.45
.10	4	.1	2	67.97	67.39	67.07	65.66
.10	8	.1	4	48.45	46.01	46.99	44.86
.10	16	.1	4	32.50	30.13	31.23	28.83
.10	2	.2	1	81.93	81.79	81.49	80.58
.10	16	.2	1	35.20	32.29	34.25	29.88

be computed as in the case of write-through and like (10) it is

$$w_r' = m_s \sum_{1 \leq i \leq t_s} (1 - m_r)^{i-1}(t_s - i). \qquad (15)$$

In the current context, the definitions of parameters m_r and m_s can be rephrased as follows. Since every cache miss results in a read request to the main memory, m_r is the probability that the processor cycle generates a memory reference (read or write) and that it is a miss. Since for every cache miss a block must be replaced, the probability m_s of making a write request to the main is the same as m_r. Now following the method of Fig. 2, we can express the processor utilization U, memory bandwidth B, and unit service request rate m' as seen by the network as follows.

$$U = \frac{1}{1 + m_r(t_b + w_r' + w_r + t_r)} \qquad (16)$$

$$B = NU(m_r t_r + m_s t_s) \qquad (17)$$

$$m' = U[m_r(w_r + t_r) + m_s(w_s + t_s)]. \qquad (18)$$

Substituting this m' in the appropriate bandwidth equations for crossbar (6) or delta network (8) and then equating it with the bandwidth of (17), we have an equation in U and w, where $w = w_r = w_s$ from (10). This equation along with the (16) of U and w can be solved iteratively. An appropriate starting value for w is 0.

Two improvements are possible in the basic write-back strategy. One is to overlap the time t_b to write the block in the high speed intermediate buffer with the time $w_r + t_r$ of a block read. This can be done by issuing the read request to the network at the same time when the block to be replaced is being written into the buffer. It is safe to assume that the first word from the memory will not arrive before time t_b. This in essence reduces the time t_b to zero in the above set of equations.

Another improvement in the basic write-back organization is to write back only those blocks which are modified. If the probability of a block being modified is known then it can be reflected in the parameter m_s. This reduces the traffic and therefore the wait time of a request, which in turn improves the processor utilization.

Load-Through: On a cache-miss for a read reference, the desired word is directly loaded into a CPU register from the main memory; after which the whole block containing that word is read into the cache module. This strategy tries to overlap the CPU execution with a block read. Load-through can be combined with either of the two previous strategies of write-back and write-through. As an illustration let us take load-through with write-through. In this analysis we assume that the successive reads to the same block which is not yet fully loaded will not be treated as faults. In practice this assumption does not hold. However, the analysis under this assumption gives a tight upper bound on the system throughput.

Let t_{r1} be the time to load-through a single word and let the other variables be same as in the write-through case. Then

$$U = 1/[1 + m_r(w_{r1} + w_r' + t_{r1})] \tag{19}$$

where w_r' is the same as in (10).

$$B = NU[m_r(t_{r1} + t_r) + m_{s1}t_{s1}] \tag{20}$$

$$m' = U[m_r(w_r + t_{r1} + t_r) + m_{s1}(w_{s1} + t_{s1})]. \tag{21}$$

The above equations can be solved in the same manner as for the other cases. In all of the above analyses the crucial simplifying step was the approximation we proposed earlier in the simple-cache model, namely, breaking up any requests to the main memory into unit requests and then treating them as random, independent, and uniformly distributed requests. If a cache organization does not exactly fit one of the above descriptions, then it can still be analyzed by obtaining the appropriate equations for U, B, and m' along the same lines as one of the above organizations. Although we have not given a theoretical argument to show that our approximation will always give fairly accurate results in similar cases, the experimental data do strongly point in that direction.

VI. Concluding Remarks

In this paper we have presented an approximate analytical model for multiprocessors with private cache memories. The accuracy of the model is remarkably good considering the complexity of the problem. In the region of practical interest the error of the analytical model is less than 1 percent. The same model is useful in computing several different measures of performance, such as the processor utilization, the average wait time of request, and the memory traffic.

The central idea introduced in this paper is that of breaking up a request for a block transfer into several unit requests as well as treating waiting requests as several unit requests for the purpose of the analysis. This idea made the analysis of more complex cache organizations like write-back, write-through, and load-through as easy as the simple cache organization. As a side benefit we now also have a way to evaluate the bandwidths of crossbar and delta networks under asynchronous block transfer mode.

References

[1] F. Baskett and A. J. Smith, "Interference in multiprocessor computer systems and interleaved memory," *Commun. Ass. Comput. Mach.*, vol. 19, pp. 327–334, June 1976.

[2] D. P. Bhandarkar, "Analysis of memory interference in multiprocessors," *IEEE Trans. Comput.*, vol. C-24, pp. 897–908, Sept. 1975.

[3] L. M. Censier and P. Feautrier, "A new solution to coherent problems in multicache systems," *IEEE Trans. Comput.*, vol. C-27, pp. 1112–1118, Dec. 1978.

[4] K. R. Kaplan and R. O. Winder, "Cache based computer systems," *Computer*, pp. 30–36, Mar. 1973.

[5] A. Lehmann, "Performance evaluation and prediction of storage hierarchies," *ACM Sigmetrics, Performance '80*, vol. 9, pp. 43–54, May 1980

[6] R. M. Meade, "On memory system design," in *Proc. Fall Joint Comput. Conf.*, 1970, pp. 33–43.

[7] J. H. Patel, "Performance of processor-memory interconnections for multiprocessors," *IEEE Trans. Comput.*, vol. C-30, pp. 771–780, Oct. 1981.

[8] B. L. Peuto and L. J. Shustek, "An instruction timing model of CPU performance," in *Proc. 4th Symp. Comput. Architecture*, 1977, pp. 165–178.

[9] G. S. Rao, "Performance analysis of cache memories," *J. Ass. Comput. Mach.*, vol. 25, pp. 378–395, July 1978.

[10] B. R. Rau, "Interleaved memory bandwidth in a model of a multiprocessor computer system," *IEEE Trans. Comput.*, vol. C-28, pp. 678–681, Sept. 1979.

[11] C. V. Ravi, "On the bandwidth and interference in interleaved memory systems," *IEEE Trans. Comput.*, vol. C-21, pp. 899–901, Aug. 1972.

[12] C. Skinner and J. Asher, "Effect of storage contention on system performance," *IBM Syst. J.*, vol. 8, no. 4, pp. 319–333, 1969.

[13] W. D. Strecker, "Analysis of the instruction execution rate in certain computer structures," Ph.D. dissertation, Carnegie-Mellon Univ., Pittsburgh, PA, 1970.

[14] ———, "Cache memories for PDP-11 family computers," in *Proc. 3rd Symp. Comput. Architecture*, Jan. 1976, pp. 155–158.

[15] C. K. Tang, "Cache system design in the tightly coupled multiprocessor system," in *Proc. Nat. Comput. Conf.*, 1976, pp. 749–753.

[16] C-C. Yeh, "Shared cache organization for multiple-stream computer systems," Coordinated Sci. Lab., Univ. of Illinois, Urbana, Tech. Rep. R-904, Jan. 1981.

Effectiveness of Private Caches in Multiprocessor Systems with Parallel-Pipelined Memories

FAYÉ A. BRIGGS, MEMBER, IEEE, AND MICHEL DUBOIS, MEMBER, IEEE

Abstract—A possible design alternative for improving the performance of a multiprocessor system is to insert a private cache between each processor and the shared memory. The caches act as high-speed buffers by reducing the effective memory access time, and affect the delays caused by memory conflicts. In this paper, we study the effectiveness of caches in a multiprocessor system. The shared memory is pipelined and interleaved to improve the block transfer rate, and it assumes a two-dimensional organization, previously studied under random and word access. An approximate model is developed to estimate the processor utilization and the speed-up improvement provided by the caches.

Index Terms—Cache memories, memory organization, multicache consistency, multiprocessors, performance evaluation.

I. INTRODUCTION

IN this paper, we present simulation results and an approximate analytical model to evaluate the performance of multiprocessor systems with private caches. An example of such a system with P processors is depicted in Fig. 1. At the first level, each processor has a private cache (PC). The second memory level comprises a two-dimensional memory called the L-M memory organization, which consists of l lines or banks and m memory modules per line [1]. A line is used to denote the address bus within the shared memory (SM). Associated with each line is a direct memory access (DMA) controller which receives a cache request for a block of size B and issues B internal requests (IR) to consecutive modules on the line. In the following discussion, it is assumed that the interconnection network between the private caches and shared memory modules is a full crossbar. The crossbar is symmetric: the delays along all paths from any processor to any memory module are identical. It can be built with multiplexor chips, as described in [26]. The overhead incurred in traversing the switch has two components. First, there is the delay through the arbitration logic, which, for each memory module, selects one request among all the processor requests submitted to the module. This delay is called the switch setup time (t_a), and does not include the waiting time due to conflicts. Second, there are delays through the mutliplexor chips, which connect the selected processor to the memory module. Such a delay is

called the switch transversal time (t_d). In general, t_a and t_d are functions of l, P, and the technology used.

In the architecture of Fig. 1, there is a data coherence problem because several copies of the same block may exist in different caches at any given time. The solution to the coherence problem are *dynamic* or *static*. The dynamic solution consists basically in checking, at run-time, for the presence of the block referenced by the processor in other caches. This can be done by maintaining, dynamically, local and global flags [4], [24]. The dynamic solution is costly and requires conflicting accesses to a central directory shared among all processors. The effects of the enforcement of cache consistency using the dynamic solution have been analyzed in [10].

For the C.mmp [26], the static solution was envisioned but never implemented. In the static solution, each page in shared memory is tagged as *cacheable* or *noncacheable* at compile time. Theoretically, only shared writeable data should be tagged as noncacheable. Examples of noncacheable items are semaphores, process queue and operating system tables. References to noncacheable pages are made directly to the shared memory. Only the blocks contained in cacheable pages are buffered in the private caches. Each page table entry contains a cacheable bit. If the bit is set, the address translation hardware directs the request to the cache. A reset cacheable bit indicates that the data items is to be found in the noncacheable physical space of the shared memory. A similar mechanism was used in the Honeywell 66 Series machines. A modified version of this scheme is proposed for the S-1 multiprocessor system being developed at Lawrence Livermore Laboratory [25]. This scheme works only if a process is not allowed to migrate without the invalidation of its blocks. A similar scheme was introduced [9], in which the noncacheable references are made to a shared cache.

Another method of maintaining multicache consistency may be termed *quasi-dynamic*. In this case, all blocks are initially tagged as cacheable and are stored in the cacheable section of memory. A block which is cached by one processor and is referenced by another processor for a write operation becomes tagged as a shared writeable block. Such a block is "uncached" by transferring the updated block to the noncacheable section of memory where it can be accessed directly by the processors that share the block.

Cacheable and noncacheable data items can be in the same shared memory. Accesses to noncacheable data are made on a word-by-word basis. However, in order to speed-up accesses to noncacheable data the shared memory can be partitioned into cacheable and noncacheable data spaces, where the

Manuscript received February 5, 1982; revised July 22, 1982. This work was supported by the National Science Foundation under Grant ECS 80-16580. Revision of this paper was made while F. A. Briggs was at the IBM Thomas J. Watson Research Center, Yorktown Heights, NY 10598.

F. A. Briggs is with the Department of Electrical Engineering, Rice University, Houston, TX 77001.

M. Dubois is with Thomson-CSF/LCR Domaine de Corbeville, B.P. 10, 91401, Orsay, France.

Reprinted from *IEEE Trans. Computers,* Vol. C-32, No. 1, Jan. 1983, pp. 48–59. Copyright © 1983
by The Institute of Electrical and Electronics Engineers, Inc. All rights reserved.

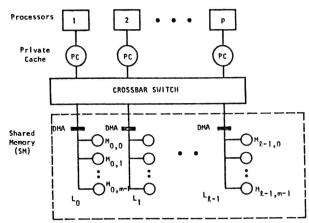

Fig. 1. Cache-based multiprocessor system with L-M shared memory.

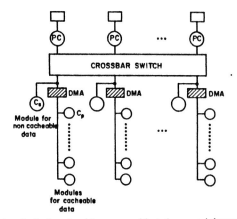

Fig. 2. Cache-based multiprocessor with static or quasi-dynamic coherence check.

noncacheable data are stored in faster memory modules. A typical cache-based multiprocessor system with partitioned shared memory is shown in Fig. 2. The organization of the shared memory will be discussed in Section III.

Most studies to date evaluate the shared memory conflict problem for random-word access [5]. In [2], [3], approximate models were developed to analyze the effect of private caches on the processor utilization. Patel developed a model for a cache-based multiprocessor without pipelined memories [18]. All the above studies ignored the cache coherence problem and thus obtained results that are optimistic. We propose a model which is used to evaluate the degree of memory conflicts in a multiprocessor system with private caches and parallel-pipelined memories. The model developed here incorporates the static and quasi-dynamic coherence checks and hence, is realistic for evaluating the performance of cache-based multiprocessors with software coherence checks. This model permits us to determine the processor utilization and investigate the effects of static and quasi-dynamic cache coherence checks on the performance. Furthermore, we estimate the effect of the caches on the speedup of the multiprocessing system. The performance of the system is a function of the cache hit ratio, h cache organization, processor characteristics and the shared memory characteristics and configuration.

In Section II, we present two cache models, namely, set-associative and fully-associative caches. These models are considered in the analysis to be presented. The organization of the shared memory and its capabilities for handling block transfers are discussed in Section III. Simulation and analytical methodologies are developed in Section IV for the two cache models together with a discussion of the accuracy of the models. Finally, we present an example to illustrate the applicability of the analytical results in the design-decision making phase of the multiprocessor system configuration.

II. The Cache Models

The processor system consists of P identical processors. In each of these processors, we assume that a machine cycle consists of an integer number, d, of cache cycles. An instruction cycle usually consists of an integer number of machine cycles. Typical machine cycles are instruction-fetch, operand-fetch

and execution cycles, which may involve register-register or memory-register references. It is obvious that in some machine cycles of a processor, no cache memory references will occur. Therefore, let θ be the probability that a memory request is issued by a processor to the cache controller in a machine cycle. Thus, the fraction of references made by the processor to the cache controller in each cache cycle is $x = \theta/d$.

When the cacheable data requested by a processor is not in its private cache, a miss occurs that causes the cache controller to issue a shared memory request for a block transfer. The program behavior in a processor will be characterized by its cache hit ratio, h, or its miss ratio, $1 - h$. The hit ratio of a program as a function of cache size, set size, block size and cache replacement policy has been studied by several authors [14], [19], [23]. We assume that no read-through strategy is implemented. However, the model presented here can easily be adapted for read-through strategy. If the cache is full, the cache replacement algorithm is invoked to decide which block-frame to free in order to create space for the new block containing the referenced data.

Cache management algorithms differ basically in the method of resolving write misses [14]. In a *write-through* strategy, a processor always writes directly in the shared memory, and possibly in the cache if the block is present. Consequently, a block is never copied to shared memory when a block-frame is freed. However, such a policy requires buffering of the write requests or results in the blocking of the processor during write operations. The *write-back-write-allocate* strategy is adopted in this paper. In this strategy, if a cache block-frame which has not been modified is to be replaced, it is overwritten with the new block of data. However, a modified block-frame that is to be replaced must be written to the shared memory (SM) before a block-read from the SM is initiated. In this case, two consecutive transfers are made between the cache and SM. We assume that each time a cache miss occurs, a block-write to SM is required, with a probability w_b, followed by a block-read from SM. w_b, which is the probability that the block-frame to be replaced was modified, depends on the program behavior and the cache organization. It is usually larger than w_t, the probability that a reference is a write [22].

Two methods of organizing the cache for block reads and writes are investigated. In one case, it is assumed that the two consecutive block transfers (one block-write followed by one block-read) are made between a processor and the same line. This assumption will be satisfied if a *set-associative* cache is used in which all the blocks that map to the same set are stored on the same line. Hence, in this method a cache miss requires the transfer of a $2B$-word block with a probability w_b and the transfer of a B-word with a probability $1 - w_b$.

A second method of organizing the cache assumes that the two consecutive block-write and block-read requests are considered independent and hence have equal probability of referencing any SM line. This assumption may be valid in a *fully-associative* cache. The effect of making two consecutive and independent block requests from a processor is to increase the effective rate of requests to the SM.

In our models, the hit ratio, h, and the probability w_b that a miss requires a write back are given. Generally the hit ratio depends on the locality property [8] of the program mix, the cache replacement policy, and the block, set and cache sizes. Various studies have addressed this relationship. In [16], a program is characterized by a simplified mathematical model based on its instruction mix and the model is used to estimate the hit ratio. Smith compares different cache replacement policies [21]. Under the assumption of a linear paging model [20], he shows that the ratio of the miss ratios between the set-associative and the fully associative cache is

$$R(i, N) = \frac{i - \frac{1}{N}}{i - 1} \quad \text{for } i \geq 3,$$

where i is the set size (number of blocks in a set) and N is the number of sets. This ratio is always ≥ 1. It tends to 1 when Ni, the cache capacity, increases without limit. This relationship should be considered when comparing the set-associative and fully-associative caches from our models. Strecker presents empirical results for the PDP-11 family computers showing the hit ratio as a function of the cache and block sizes [23]. In [19], an analytical model is proposed. For a *given cache size*, the hit ratio improves as the block size increases from 1, because of the locality of the references to the cache. However, beyond a certain block size, the hit ratio decreases. This is due to the decrease in the usefulness of the extra words in a block as the block size increases. For a given *block size*, the hit ratio increases monotonically with the cache size, for caches with a stack replacement algorithm [6]. If h and w_b can be determined empirically on a uniprocessor machine [23], or theoretically [16], [19], the models given in this paper can then be applied to evaluate the various performance indexes.

For practical purposes, the absolute size of the private cache would be expected to be large enough to accommodate at least the "working set" of the process [8], so that the miss ratio, $1 - h$, is small (in the order of 0.1). Furthermore, we assume that the block transfer time is also small (less than 64 cache cycles). Under these conditions, it is not necessary to perform a task switch on a cache miss to another runnable process. Therefore, in this paper, we shall assume that on a cache miss, the processor enters a *wait state* while waiting for service of the desired block request, and then into a sequence of *transfer states* while the block is being transferred. If a processor is neither in a wait nor a transfer state, it is said to be in an *active state*. Hence, the processor utilization can be computed as the fraction of time the processor is busy processing instructions in an active state. Finally, associated with each DMA controller of a memory line is a buffer which queues the requests for block transfers. The DMA controller schedules these requests to the line, using a first-come-first-served (FCFS) policy.

III. THE SHARED MEMORY ORGANIZATION

The shared memory configuration is derived from the two-dimensional memory organization, which exploits the timing characteristics exhibited by semiconductor memories with address latches [1]. The *address cycle*, or hold time, a_0, which is the minimum duration that the address is maintained on the address bus of the shared memory module for a successful memory operation, is usually less than the shared *memory cycle*, c_0. Throughout this paper, we assume that the basic unit of time is the cache cycle, which is equal to τ s. If the address and shared memory cycles are quantized so that they are expressed as an integer number of cache cycles, then

$$a = \left\lceil \frac{a_0}{\tau} \right\rceil \quad \text{and} \quad c = \left\lceil \frac{c_0}{\tau} \right\rceil$$

so that a set of modules can be multiplexed on a line. In general, $1 \leq a \leq c$. When a memory operation is initiated in a module, it causes the associated line to be active for a units of time, and the module to be active for c units of time.

Recall that the shared memory address space is partitioned into cacheable and noncacheable data spaces. The noncacheable data space (NDS) of shared memory is organized into a set of l interleaved modules, where each module, denoted by ND, is attached to a unique memory line or bank. The memory module characteristic for ND is (a, c_S). The cacheable data space (CDS) of shared memory, which consists of $N = 2^n$ interleaved identical memory modules, is organized in a matrix form in order to exploit the memory module characteristic (a, c_P). Note that each module that stores the cacheable data is denoted by CD and a memory cycle, c_P. As shown in Figs. 1 and 2, a particular memory configuration (l, m) for CDS consists of $l = 2^\beta$ lines and $m = 2^{n-\beta}$ modules of type CD per line, such that $lm = N$, for integer $\beta \geq 0$. The blocks in the memory are interleaved on the lines so that block i is assigned to modules on line $i \bmod l$. It should be noted that this does not contradict the assumption made earlier that blocks of the same set are on the same line for the set-associative cache model. That assumption implies however, that the number of sets is a multiple of the number of lines in SM.

Since the cacheable data space of shared memory is used in the block transfer mode in this paper, we will assume an address cycle of $a = 1$ (i.e., the line holding time is equal to a cache cycle) for the shared memory, in order to obtain a maximum data rate. However, if $a > 1$ for a particular type of memory, the address cycle could be made equal to 1 by incorporating an appropriate address latch in each SM module.

Since $a = 1$, the memory module for cacheable and noncacheable data spaces will be characterized by c_P and c_S respectively. The model developed in [1] is not applicable here, because it was for single-word transfers that are requested by multiple instruction stream pipelined processors.

In order to utilize the SM modules of type CD for the block transfers effectively, the modules on a line are interleaved in a particular fashion, so that the servicing of two SM requests could be overlapped on the same line. The SM modules on a line are interleaved so that a block of data of size $B = 2^b$ is interleaved on consecutive modules on that line. Let line i and module j on that line be referred to as L_i and $M_{i,j}$ respectively for $0 \le i \le l - 1$ and $0 \le j \le m - 1$. Then the kth word of the block of data that exists on line i is in module $k \bmod m$ on that line for $0 \le k \le B - 1$. It is important to note that the first word of a block that exists on line i is in the first module, $M_{i,0}$, on that line. We assume that $B \ge m$. If $B < m$, memory modules $M_{i,B}, M_{i,B+1}, \cdots, M_{i,m-1}$ will not be utilized, because a block starts in module $M_{i,0}$.

When an SM block request is accepted by a line, the DMA controller at the line issues B successive internal requests (IR) to consecutive modules on line i, starting from module $M_{i,0}$. It is assumed that these internal requests are issued at the beginning of every time unit. Therefore, the internal request for the kth word of the block will be issued to module $M_{i,j}$, where $j = k \bmod m$ for $0 \le k \le B - 1$. It is obvious that this set of B internal requests is not preemptible. Note that if $B > m$ or if the cache is set-associative, the $(m + 1)$st internal requests is for module $M_{i,0}$. Consequently, the first IR must be completed by the time the $(m + 1)$st internal request is issued. This constraint is satisifed if $c_P \le m$.

IV. PERFORMANCE ANALYSIS

In this section we present assumptions and develop the models that permit us to evaluate the various performance indicators of the cache-based multiprocessor systems. First, we give a model for the system with static coherence check and from this model obtain results for the degenerate case when no sharing occurs.

A. Simulation Preceded by Analysis

For analytical purposes, it is assumed that cache requests to SM are random and uniformly distributed over all l lines of the SM. Similarly, we assume that memory requests to the non-cacheable segment of memory are random and uniformly distributed over all l lines of the SM. These assumptions are justified by the interleaving of the blocks of CDS and words of NDS across the lines. One inference that can be made directly from the above assumptions is that the probability of a request addressing any line is $1/l$. It is also assumed, for simplicity, that while a noncacheabe data item is being accessed, no other processor can initiate a transfer on the same line. This assumption will result in a pessimistic evaluation. In practice, an address latch could be provided at a module for noncacheable data, allowing a block transfer to take place as soon as the address for the noncacheable data items has been latched.

Recall that there is probability x that each processor submits a request to its cache during a cache cycle. Let us denote by s the probability that such a request is for a noncacheable data item. In this case, the cache controller directs the request to the uncacheable section of shared memory. With probability $1 - s$, the reference is to a cacheable data item, which is first searched for in the cache. It is found in the cache with probability h. Otherwise, a new block is brought into the cache with probability $1 - h$. The handling of this transfer is dependent on the cache organization as described in Section II.

In order to understand the timing characteristics of the servicing of requests for block transfer, we define the time instants t^- and $t+$ as $\lim_{\Delta t \to 0} (t - \Delta t)$ and $\lim_{\Delta t \to 0} (t + \Delta t)$, respectively, for $\Delta t > 0$. A time unit, $\langle t, t + 1 \rangle$, may be thought of as beginning at time t^+ and ending at time $(t + 1)^-$. Hence, as $a = 1$, the successive internal requests which are generated to a line in the servicing of an SM request do not encounter any conflicts.

Recall that when an SM request for a block transfer is accepted, the DMA controller issues B successive IR's. If the request is accepted on line i at time t, then the IR for the kth word of a block of size B is initiated at time $t + k$ to module $M_{i,j}$, for $j = k \bmod m$ and $0 \le k \le B - 1$. As the SM module cycle time is c_P, module $M_{i,j}$ will be busy in the intervals $\langle t + k, t + c_P + k \rangle$ for the values of j.

Since $B = 2^b \ge m = 2^{n-\beta}$, then B/m is an integer ≥ 1. Therefore, each module on a line i which accepts an SM request for block transfer at time t receives B/m internal memory requests. In particular, the last IR to module M_{i0} is made at time $t + (B/m - 1)m = t + B - m$. Thus, the last interval in which module $M_{i,0}$ is busy (during the current block transfer) is $\langle t + B - m, t + B - m + c_P \rangle$. After this period, a new block transfer which addresses line i can be accepted. Because the current block transfer was initiated at time t, all block transfer requests arriving at $t + 1, t + 2, \cdots, t + B - m + c_P - 1$ will find line i busy. Note that to an SM request for block transfer, the line is busy for $B - m + c_P$ time units. We refer to this as the *line service time*. However, the *actual service time* of the SM request is $B + c_P - 1$. This is the time taken to access and transfer a block of size B when the request is accepted. Since we do not implement a read-through policy in the cache model, the processor goes through a sequence of transfer states having total duration $B + c_P - 1$ before returning to the active state. That is, the block transfer must be completed before the processor can become active again. Note that the definition of an active processor includes the interval in which the missed data is requested in the cache after the block transfer has been completed. The pipelining of the successive internal requests increases the block transfer speed at low cost. The alternate solution is to fetch the words in parallel. However, in this case the bus width of each line and of the path through the crossbar must be equal to B words, compared with a data path of one word in our organization.

The cache-based multiprocessor system of Fig. 1 may be modeled by the closed queueing network shown in Fig. 3. This network is not a typical "central server model" because it does not have the basic properties which imply solvability [15]. The servers are the shared memory lines, and the requests are issued by a set of P processing nodes, each of each lumps a processor

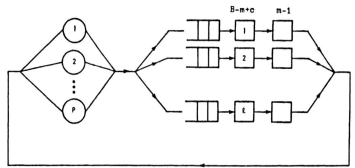

Fig. 3. Central server-like model for the multiprocessor system with private caches.

with its local cache. The two segments of a server model each SM line and reflect the pipeline effect of the L-M memory described above. A similar closed queueing network can be obtained for the system in Fig. 2.

The behavior of each processor in Fig. 2 is illustrated in Figs. 4 and 5 for the set-associative and fully associative cache strategies respectively. Node "A" denotes an active state of the processor and node "W," a waiting state. Node "LT" represents the state for the first part of a transfer during which the line is kept busy (line service time), and "ET," the state in which a transfer is completed without holding a line. These states have to be distinguished because of their different properties. Note that the state graphs, as shown in Figs. 4 and 5, do not constitute Markov graphs, since each state has a different average duration. These average durations are indicated on the graphs. The state of each processor changes asynchronously in an SM request cycle. The SM request cycle C, is the total average time spent in the active state, and the set of transfer states (LT and ET).

When an access to shared memory is made, it can be for one of two reasons: either the reference was for a noncacheable data item (with probability s) or for a cacheable data item absent in the cache [with probability $(1 - s)(1 - h)$]. Hence the fraction of references to SM made to noncacheable data space is $\alpha = s/[s + (1 - h)(1 - s)]$. According to the model assumptions, the visit time (expressed in units of cache cycles) in state A consists of two components. The first component is the processing time during which the processor does not have to reference shared memory. The total probability that a given cache cycle requires an access to the shared memory is $x[s + (1 - h)(1 - s)]$. This can be derived by noting that such an access occurs when a reference is made and the reference is for noncacheable data or is for cacheable data and results in a miss. The mean of the first component of the visit time in state A is thus $1/\{x[s + (1 - h)(1 - s)]\}$, counting the cache cycle in which the access to memory is initiated. The second component of the visit time is the sum of the switch set-up and traversal times in units of cache cycles and is given by ($t_a + t_d$). So, the total duration of a visit to state A in Figs. 4 and 5 is $1/\{x[s + (1 - h)(1 - s)]\} + t_a + t_d$. The visit time in state ET is a constant with value $m - 1$.

For the set-associative cache (Fig. 4), if a block-write is not required (with probability $1 - w_b$) on a cache miss, then the line which accepts the SM block request is busy for $B - m + c_P$ time units. However, if a block-write is required (with

probability w_b) in addition to the block-read, then two consecutive block transfers (each of size B) are made uninterruptedly on the same SM line. In this case, the line that accepts the block request is busy for $2B - m + c_P$ time units.

The case of the fully-associative cache is simpler (Fig. 5): if a cache miss requires a block-write (with a probability w_b) followed by a block-read, the processor submits these requests as two successive and independent requests to transfer a block of size B in each case because these two blocks may not reside on the same line. Each of the two corresponding LT states thus have a constant duration of $B - m + c_P$.

In both cases, each processor goes through "independent" states (states A and ET), followed by "interactive" states (states W and LT). In an independent state, a processor can proceed freely and does not interfere with the progress of other processors. Interactive states are characterized by a potential for conflicts with other processors. The interactive states are framed in Figs. 4 and 5. During any LT state, the SM line is busy and no other processor can access the line. In order to estimate the average visit time in such states, simulations are required. Note that the foregoing analysis that leads to the state graphs of Figs. 4 and 5 simplifies the simulation significantly. Table I is a compilation of some of the simulation results for an example system configuration with fully-associative caches $s = 0$, $w_b = 0.3$, $c_P = 4$, $x = 0.4$, $h = 0.95$, $m = 4$, $P = 16$). The number of lines, l, and the block size, B, are variable. We have assumed that $t_a + t_d = 0$. The performance index is the average processor utilization, U, defined as the average fraction of time spent by each processor processing instructions in an active state. In our study we found that both cache implementations have practically the same performance for the same value of the hit ratio when slow memories ($c_p > 4$) are used. However, the set-associative organization results in a poorer performance for small number of lines ($l \sim 1$) when faster memories are used. Note that a fully-associative cache usually results in a higher hit ratio than set-associative if a given cache size is applied to both cases. The results obtained from such considerations are discussed in Section IV-B(3).

Because these simulations are still expensive, despite the simplification, we have developed an approximate analytical model to estimate the processor utilization.

B. Approximate Analytical Model

The processor's behavior shown in Figs. 4 and 5 is quite complex to model exactly. We propose an approximate ana-

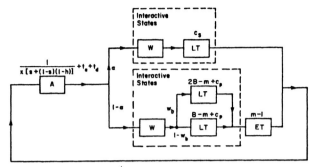

Fig. 4. State graph for set-associative caches system with static or quasi-dynamic coherence check, where $\alpha = s/[s + (1 - s)(1 - h)]$.

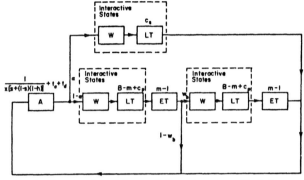

Fig. 5. State graph for fully-associative cache system with static or quasi-dynamic coherence check, where $\alpha = s/[s + (1 - s)(1 - h)]$.

lytical model based on a method applied in [13] for the modeling of random-word accesses in multiprocessor memories. We number the processors from 1 to P and the memory lines from 1 to l. Let

$$I_k(t) = [i_{k,1}(t), i_{k,2}(t), \cdots, i_{k,P}(t)]$$

for $k = 1, \cdots, l$, with $i_{k,j}(t) = 1$ iff processor j is not waiting for or using line k, and $i_{kj}(t) = 0$ iff processor j is waiting for or using line k at time t.

$I_k(t)$ is called the *indicator vector* for line k at time t. Each component, $i_{k,j}(t)$, indicates whether or not processor j is waiting for, or holding line k. Note that a processor waits for or holds a line whenever it is in state W or LT (interactive states), respectively. Let X_s be the probability that a given line is busy and S, the average line service time of a request. Then

X_s = Prob(at least one processor is waiting for, or holding a given line k)

= 1 − Prob[no processor is waiting for, or holding line k]

= 1 − Prob($i_{k,1} \cdot i_{k,2} \cdots i_{k,P} = 1$]

= 1 − $E[i_{k,1} \cdot i_{k,2} \cdots i_{k,P}]$. (1)

This last equality results from the fact that the expectation of a random variable which takes only the values 0 and 1 is equal to the probability of the variable being 1. The rate of *completed* requests by a line is

$$\frac{X_s}{S} \tag{2}$$

TABLE I
PROCESSOR UTILIZATION FOR THE FULLY-ASSOCIATIVE CACHE
($c = 4, w_b = 0.3, m = 4, h = 0.95, P = 16, s = 0$)

l	B	Simulation	Model	Error (%)
1	4	0.596	0.601	+0.8
	8	0.300	0.301	+0.3
	16	0.150	0.150	0.0
	32	0.076	0.075	−1.3
	64	0.038	0.038	0.0
2	4	0.789	0.791	+0.2
	8	0.541	0.579	+7.0
	16	0.286	0.301	+5.2
	32	0.145	0.150	+3.4
	64	0.072	0.075	+4.3
4	4	0.829	0.831	+0.2
	8	0.708	0.721	+1.8
	16	0.475	0.511	+7.6
	32	0.261	0.286	+9.9
	64	0.133	0.145	+10.4
8	4	0.839	0.839	+0.0
	8	0.753	0.754	+0.1
	16	0.598	0.603	+0.8
	32	0.390	0.411	+5.4
	64	0.219	0.238	+8.5
16	4	0.842	0.843	+0.1
	8	0.767	0.768	+0.1
	16	0.640	0.642	+0.3
	32	0.467	0.472	+1.1
	64	0.290	0.300	+3.5

In equilibrium, this rate can be equated to the rate of *submitted* requests to a line. To compute this second member of the equation, we note that a processor submits a request whenever it departs from state A. This occurs, for each processor, whenever a cycle in the networks of Figs. 4 and 5 is completed. Recall that C is the average time taken by such a cycle. The rate of submitted requests to the SM by any one processor is $1/C$. Since there are P requesting processors and each request is submitted randomly to any one of the lines, the average rate of submitted request to a given line k is

$$\frac{1}{C} \cdot \frac{P}{l}$$

Let T be the average time between an exit from an interactive state and a visit to the next interactive state. Let Y be the average fraction of time a given processor is in an independent state. By the ergodic property [15], Y is also the probability of being in such a state. The symmetry of the system implies the same value of Y for all the processors. From the above definitions,

$$Y = \frac{T}{C}.$$

Substituting for $1/C$ in the equation for the average rate of submitted request to a given line, and equating this rate to the rate of completed request in (2), we obtain

$$X_s = Y \cdot \frac{S}{T} \cdot \frac{P}{l}$$

Substituting for X_s in (1), we have

$$E[i_{k,1} \cdot i_{k,2} \cdots i_{k,P}] + \rho Y = 1, \tag{3}$$

where

$$\rho = \frac{S}{T} \cdot \frac{P}{l}.$$

This equation is exact. However, the first term of the left hand side of the equation is very complex to estimate in general. The approximation consists in neglecting the interactions between processors. As a result of the approximation, the components of $I_k(t)$ are not correlated. This approximation performs best for a short and deterministic line service time. Indeed, large instances of the line service time are more likely to result in instantaneous longer queues and more interactions between the processors. Under the noncorrelation conditions,

$$E[i_{k,1} \cdot i_{k,2} \cdots i_{k,P}] = E[i_{k,1}] \cdot E[i_{k,2}] \cdots E[i_{k,P}].$$

If we denote by Z the fraction of time spent by each processor waiting for or holding a given line k, (3) becomes

$$(1 - Z)^P + \rho Y = 1, \qquad (4)$$

because of the symmetry of the system.

On the other hand, since a processor is either in an independent state (A or ET), or in an interactive state (waiting for or holding one of the lines), then by the law of total probability in a system with l lines we have

$$Y + l \cdot Z = 1. \qquad (5)$$

Using (4) with the condition that $1 - \rho Y > 0$,

$$Z = 1 - (1 - \rho Y)^{1/P}.$$

Consequently, by the substitution for Z in (5) and rearranging, we obtain

$$Y = \frac{1}{\rho} \left[1 - \left(\frac{Y + l - 1}{l} \right)^P \right] \qquad (6)$$

with

$$\rho = \frac{P}{l} \cdot \frac{S}{T}.$$

S is the mean line service time and T is the mean time between an exit from an interactive state and a visit to the next interactive state. To compute ρ, we have to distinguish between the two cache implementations. Note that S can be found as the

mean time that a processor spends holding a memory line. Similarly, T is found as the mean time spent *outside* of an interactive state.

Since Y is the average fraction of time spent in state A or ET, the processor utilization, U, which is the fraction of time the processor is busy processing instructions, is given by

$$U = \frac{\dfrac{1}{x[s + (1 - s)(1 - h)]}}{C} = \frac{\dfrac{1}{x[s + (1 - s)(1 - h)]}}{T} Y \qquad (7)$$

Besides being a good approximation for short line service times with low coefficient of variation, the approximation (6) was proven in [11] to have the following desirable properties.

Property 1: when P tends to ∞ (and all other parameters are kept constant), Y tends to $1/\rho$.

Property 2: Equation (6) has a unique real solution between 0 and min $(1, 1/\rho)$.

As a consequence of the first property, the approximation is correct asymptotically, when the traffic at the memory (and thus the interactions between processors) tends to ∞. This can be seen as follows. When the number of processors increases, the system of Fig. 2 tends to saturate [15]. Under saturated conditions, each line is constantly busy, which implies that X_s tends to 1 for all the lines and thus Y tends to $1/\rho$.

1) *Set-Associative Cache (Fig. 4):* From Fig. 4, the mean time spent holding a line is S and can be obtained from the figure as

$$S = c_S \alpha + [B(1 + w_b) - m + c_P](1 - \alpha), \qquad (8)$$

where

$$\alpha = \frac{s}{s + (1 - s)(1 - h)}.$$

The mean time spent in independent states is equal to T and is

$$T = (m - 1)(1 - \alpha) + \frac{1}{x[s + (1 - s)(1 - h)]} + t_a + t_d. \qquad (9)$$

Equation (6) is first solved for Y, with the values of S and T above. This equation can be solved by the Newton's iterative methods [7] with initial value $Y_0 = 0.5$. Alternately, (6) can be solved by finding the zero of the function $f(Y) - Y = 0$ via a zero searching algorithm using Property 2, where $f(Y)$ is given by the right hand side of (6).

The processor utilization is

$$U = \frac{\dfrac{1}{x[s + (1 - s)(1 - h)]}}{T} Y.$$

Or

$$U = \frac{Y}{(m - 1)(1 - h)(1 - s)x + (t_a + t_d)x[s + (1 - s)(1 - h)] + 1}. \qquad (10)$$

2) *Fully-Associative Cache (Fig. 5):* From Fig. 5 the mean time spent holding a memory line is

$$S = \alpha c_S + (1 - \alpha)(1 + w_b)(B - m + c_P), \qquad (11)$$

and

$$T = \frac{1}{x[s + (1 - s)(1 - h)]} + t_a + t_d \\ + (1 - \alpha)(1 + w_b)(m - 1). \qquad (12)$$

Again, (6) is first solved for Y, with these values of S and T. Then, the processor utilization is

$$U = \frac{\dfrac{1}{x[s + (1 - s)(1 - h)]}}{T} Y.$$

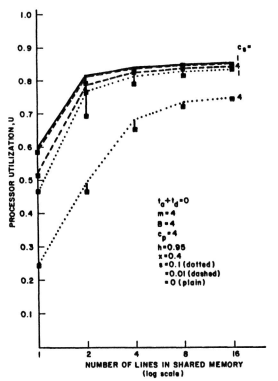

Fig. 6.   Processor utilization for the multiprocessor with set-associative caches and static coherence check.

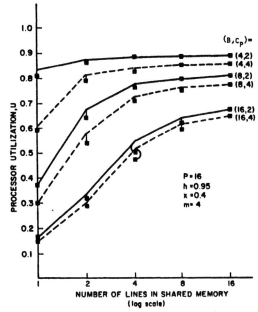

Fig. 7.   Effect of block size and shared memory speed on processor utilization for set-associative caches.

figurations. Assuming that the cache size is adjusted to give the same hit ratio when the block size is increased, an increase in the block size deteriorates the utilization. Again, the simulation points are also linked to their analytical estimates in Fig. 7. In all cases (Figs. 6 and 7), the analytical model tends to overestimate the utilization slightly.

Or

$$U = \frac{Y}{(m - 1)(1 - h)(1 - s)(1 + w_b)x + (t_a + t_d)x[s + (1 - s)(1 - h)] + 1}. \qquad (13)$$

Again, the Newton's iterative or zero searching method can be used to solve for Y.

3) *Accuracy of the Approximate Model:* In order to check the accuracy of approximate model, we have compared it with the simulation. Some typical results that are shown in Table I for the fully-associative case with $s = 0$. The model has been found to be adequate for parameter values corresponding to an effective design, and it is able to detect a poor design.

In order to show the effect of the static coherence check on performance, we display, in Fig. 6, processor utilization curves obtained for the set-associative cache with $B = 4$, $P = 16$, $w_b = 0.3$, and $c_P = 4$, assuming an infinitely fast processor-memory switch. c_S is set to 4 or 1, and s is set to 0.0, 0.01 or 0.1. Note that while $c_S = 1$ and $c_P = 4$ it indicates that noncacheable data space modules are faster than cacheable data space modules. The simulation points (denoted by solid squares) are linked to their analytical estimates. It can be seen that the analytical model approximates the utilization adequately. When the degree of sharing, s, is large ($s = 0.1$), the performance degradations are noticeable. They can be compensated for by using fast modules for the noncacheable data.

The effect of the block size, B, and the shared memory cycle time, c_P, on the processor utilization is illustrated in Fig. 7 for the set-associative cache system with various memory con-

Fig. 8 shows the tradeoffs between the hit ratio, h, and the shared memory cycle time, c_P, for the fully-associative cache system with $s = 0.01$ and $m = B = 8$. Since a change in hit ratio can be due to a change in the cache size, Fig. 8 can be used to study the tradeoffs between cache sizes and memory speeds. In general, as the memory speed decreases, the utilization is reduced. This effect is more pronounced for small l (1 or 2). The diagram shows that a reduction in the memory speed may be compensated for by an appropriate increase in the cache size.

A comparison of set-associative and fully-associative cache systems is shown in Fig. 9. Given the hit ratio, h_{FA}, for a fully-associative cache, we obtained the hit ratio, h_{SA}, for a set associative cache of the same size using the relationship given in Section II for set size $i = 4$ and number of sets, $N = 128$. It can be seen that the hit ratio has a dramatic effect on the processor utilization in both cases.

In order to obtain good estimates with this analytical model, the coefficient of variation of the line service time must be small (say less than 0.5).

For the set-associative cache, the coefficient of variation of the line service time is given by $C_S = \sigma_S/S$, where

$$\sigma_S^2 = \alpha c_S^2 + (1 - \alpha)(2B - m + c_P)^2 w_b$$
$$+ (1 - \alpha)(1 - w_b)(B - m + c_P)^2 - S^2.$$

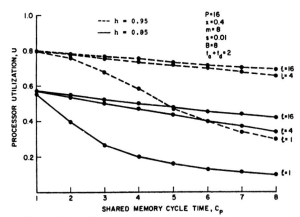

Fig. 8. Effect of block size and shared memory speed on processor utilization for set-associative caches.

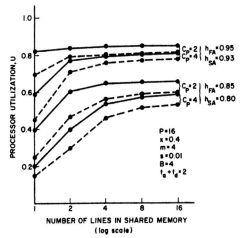

Fig. 9. Comparison of fully-associative and set-associative caches for various memory configurations.

and

$$S = c_S\alpha + [B(1 + w_b) - m + c_P](1 - \alpha),$$

It is interesting to note that the coefficient of variation of the line service time is less than 0.5 in all cases shown except for the case $s = 0.1$ and $c_S = 1$, where it is 0.95.

The coefficient of variation for the worst case of Fig. 7 ($B = 4$, $c_P = 2$) is 0.57. Note that in this case $s = 0$ and hence $\alpha = 0$. The percentage of error is quite small; thus the model is adequate.

For the fully-associative cache model, the coefficient of variation of the line service time is $C_S = \alpha_S/S$, where

$$\sigma_S^2 = \alpha c_S^2 + (1 - \alpha)(1 + w_b)(B - m + c_P)^2 - S^2,$$

and

$$S = \alpha c_S + (1 - \alpha)(1 + w_b)(B - m + c_P).$$

For the fully-associative cache in which $s = 0$, $C_s = 0$ and thus the approximation is very good.

C. Speed-Up of the Cache-Based Multiprocessor

We can derive the speed-up of the cache-based multiprocessor system (called system 1) over another system without caches (called system 2). The system without caches is similar to C.mmp. It consists of a P processor system that has a shared memory with l interleaved modules. The processor and the modules are connected through a crossbar switch. There is no block transfer in system 2, because it is not a cache-based system. The memory modules are interleaved for single-word accesses; i.e., the word with address X is in module $X \mod l$. Each memory reference requires a single-word transfer. Throughout this section, we assume that the degree of sharing is very small and that it can be neglected in order to simplify the computation. Hence $s = 0$ and $\alpha = 0$. Since we assume the same memory parameters, the memory cycle is c_P.

The instruction-mix parameter, θ is the same for both systems. Recall that θ is the probability of a memory request being issued by a processor in a machine cycle. It is important to note that, in system 2, a visit to the SM is part of a useful cycle. The degradation in the processor utilization come uniquely from the waiting time caused by conflicts to the memory.

Because we assume that systems 1 and 2 have identical processors, the absence of the cache in system 2 and the service of each memory reference in the SM elongate the machine cycle time of each processor from T_1 (in system 1) to T_2 (in system 2). It can be easily seen that $T_2 = T_1 - 1 + c_P + t_a + t_d$ time units since every memory reference encounters the delays in the crossbar switch. Note that a cache cycle in system 1 is the time unit. T_1 consists of an integer number, d, of cache cycles. In system 2, a memory reference to SM may encounter a delay in service because of memory conflicts. We denote by A the state in which the processor is active, and by W the state in which the processor is waiting. Furthermore, state M denotes the state of the service of the SM request. From our hypotheses about processor behavior, the number of machine cycles between two successive references to memory are geometrically distributed with parameter θ. The mean number of completed machine cycles between two successive references to memory in system 2 is thus $(1/\theta - 1)$. Fig. 10 depicts the state graph. During a successful memory access, a time c_P is spent in the memory to fetch the requested word. The time spent outside the memory in a successful memory access cycle is thus $T_2 - c_P$. The mean visit time to state A is the mean time spent per cycle through the state graph in the absence of memory conflict, i.e.,

$$\left(\frac{1}{\theta} - 1\right)T_2 + T_2 - c_P = \frac{T_2}{\theta} - c_P.$$

It should be pointed out that the scheduling of requests for single-word transfers in this system is FCFS, as in the system with caches. The model leading to (6) is also applicable to the graph of Fig. 10. Hence

$$Y = \frac{1}{\rho}\left[1 - \left(\frac{Y + l - 1}{l}\right)^P\right],$$

with Y being the fraction of time a given processor is in state A, and

$$\rho = \frac{P}{l} \cdot \frac{S}{T} = \frac{P}{l} \frac{c_P}{\dfrac{T_2}{\theta} - c_P}.$$

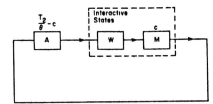

Fig. 10. State graph for the system without caches.

Note that from Fig. 10, $S = c_P$ and T is equal to the mean visit time to state A.

The resulting model is a central server-like model with deterministic servers. In this case, the approximation leading to (6) is accurate, since the coefficient of variation of the memory service time is zero.

The processor utilization, denoted by U_2 is

$$U_2 = \frac{\frac{T_2}{\theta}}{C_2} = \frac{T_2 Y}{T_2 - c_P \theta} ,$$

since $Y = (T_2/\theta - c_P)/C_2$ and C_2 is the request cycle in the system without caches. Fig. 11 shows the processor utilization for different values of c_P, t_a and t_d. The accuracy of the analytical model is guaranteed by the fact that the service time at the memory has a coefficient of variation equal to 0 (this is basically a special case of Hoogendoorn's model [13]). Note that the processor utilization for the system with $t_a + t_d = 0$ is worse than for the system with $t_a + t_d = 2$. Indeed, when the switch is faster, the machine cycle of each processor may be reduced and the traffic to memory is more intense, resulting in increased conflicts and thereby reducing the processor utilization.

Let us represent the utilization of system 1 by U_1. U_1 can be obtained from (10) and (13) for the set-associative and fully-associative cache models respectively. The effective machine cycles for a processor of systems 1 and 2 are T_1/U_1 and T_2/U_2, respectively. Since $T_2 = T_1 + c_P - 1 + t_a + t_d$, and $T_1 = d$, the speed-up for the P processor system is

$$S_P = \frac{T_2/U_2}{T_1/U_1} = \frac{T_2}{T_1} \frac{U_1}{U_2} = \left(1 + \frac{c_P - 1 + t_a + t_d}{d}\right)\frac{U_1}{U_2} .$$

The evaluation of the speed-up permits us to compare the effectiveness of the caches in the multiprocessor system. Certainly, this speed-up is a function of many parameters. The discussion of the results given in the next section exposes the effects of the variability of these parameters on the system performance.

V. DISCUSSION AND CONCLUSION

In the following discussion, we assume that the multiprocessor system consists of $P = 16$ processors with private caches. The machine cycle time of the cache-based system is $d = 2$ (all times are expressed in units of cache cycles), and the instruction-mix parameter, θ is 0.8. For system 1, the shared memory has an L-M configuration with $m = 4$, and l (a power of 2) is between 1 and 16. Thus the total number of modules is variable. Other parameters of the study are B, the block size ($4 \leq B \leq 16$), c_P, the memory cycle time ($2 \leq c_P \leq 4$), h the cache

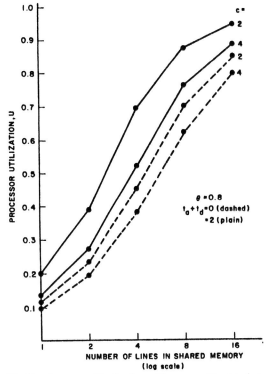

Fig. 11. Processor utilization for multipocessor without caches.

hit ratio ($h = 0.85$ and 0.95), w_b, the probability that a replaced block has been modified ($w_b = 0.3$). Note, however, that for a given cache size, the hit ratio and the block size are not independent, as observed in [23]. In this study, we assume that, for a given block size, a cache with an appropriate size is selected so that the hit ratio is kept constant. We also assume that the degree of sharing is very small ($s \ll 0.01$), so that it can be neglected, as shown in Fig. 6. System 2 does not have any cache, and the shared memory is organized as a set of l interleaved banks.

The processor utilization (U) is a performance index reflecting the degree of matching between the processors and the memory organization. The throughput improvement provided by the introduction of caches is measured by the speed-up (S_p), as defined in Section IV-C. Note that U and S_p are not necessarily related: a system with high speed-up may have an unacceptably low processor utilization. In general, one desires a design with high processor utilization and speed-up to justify the investment in faster processors and expensive cache memories, respectively. For the parameters chosen, there is little difference in the results of the set-associative and fully-associative cache models. Hence, only the results for the set-associative model are given in the figures. To limit the computation cost, the analytical models are used to derive the following curves.

A comparison of Figs. 6 and 11 shows that the caches can have a dramatic effect on processor utilization even when the crossbar delay is neglected ($t_a + t_d = 0$). In general, an increase in the block size or a decrease in the hit ratio causes a significant deterioration of the processor utilization. However, for a reasonable block size (e.g., 4) and high hit ratio (e.g.,

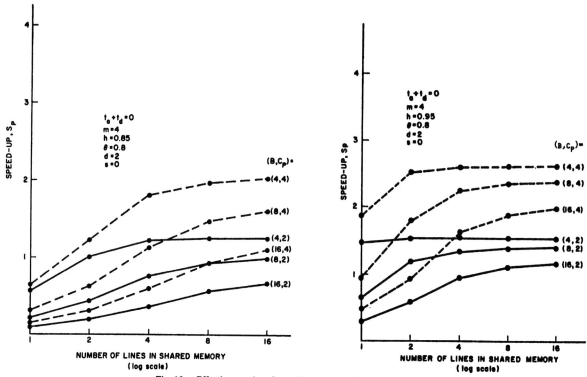

Fig. 12. Effective speed-up for multiprocessor with set-associative caches
assuming infinitely fast crossbar switch. (a) Cache with hit ratio, $h = 0.85$.
(b) Cache with hit ratio, $h = 0.95$.

0.95), the processor utilization for the system with cache is much better than for the system without caches. This observation is particularly true for small values of l, and was shown experimentally by Nesset [17]. The improvement is more dramatic when the memory cycle time, c_P, is large, as shown in Fig. 8.

The following throughput comparisons between two systems emphasize the design alternatives offered by the use of private caches. Both systems consist of 16 processors. In system 1, a private cache is added to each processor and the memory configuration is characterized by $m = 4$ and $1 \leq l \leq 16$. Hence, the cache controllers access the SM via a $16 \times l$ crossbar switch. In system 2, the processors are connected to an interleaved memory with 16 memory banks through a 16×16 crossbar switch. All the other parameters are as described earlier in this section.

The most significant effect of l in a system is the reduction in complexity of the processor-memory interconnection network and hence in the cost. Figs. 12 and 13 show the effective speed-up achieved by the inclusion of cache memories and the simultaneous reduction in the number of lines l. It can be seen that a significant improvement in the system throughput is still achievable by the simultaneous reduction in l and the inclusion of cache memories even for relatively low hit ratios [Figs. 12(a) and 13(a)]. This performance improvement is even more pronounced for large values of c_P and high hit ratios. A possible significant reduction in l gives the designer a choice. If for a small number of lines, $l < 16$, the incorporation of a per-processor cache with small B and high h results in a speed-up, $S_p \geq 1$, the designer can consider trading off low-cost multiport memories for the expensive 16×16 crossbar switch used in

the system without caches. In fact, as is shown in Fig. 12, the incorporation of a per-processor cache results in significant speed-up in most cases, even for small l and when the delay through the crossbar is neglected. This conclusion is much more evident for the case illustrated Fig. 13, in which $t_a + t_d$ has been set to 2.

ACKNOWLEDGMENT

The authors express their gratitude to Dr. O. Ibe of IBM Thomas J. Watson Research Center for his tremendous help in the production of this paper.

REFERENCES

[1] F. A. Briggs and E. S. Davidson, "Organization of semiconductor memories for parallel pipelined processors," *IEEE Trans. Comput.*, vol. C-26, pp. 162–169. Feb. 1977.
[2] F. A. Briggs and M. Dubois, "Performance of cache-based multiprocessors," *Ass. Comput. Mach. Conf. Measurement Modeling Comput. Syst.*, Sept. 1981.
[3] F. A. Briggs and M. Dubois, "Cache effectiveness in multiprocessor systems with pipelined parallel memories," in *Proc. 1981 Int. Conf. Parallel Processing*, Aug. 1981.
[4] L. M. Censier and P. Feautrier, "A new solution to coherence problems in multicache systems," *IEEE Trans. Comput.*, vol. C-27, Dec. 1978.
[5] D. Y. Chang and D. J. Kuck, "On the effective bandwidth of parallel memories," *IEEE Trans. Comput.*, pp. 480–489, May 1977.
[6] E. G. Coffman, Jr. and P. J. Denning, *Operating Systems Theory*. Englewood Cliffs, NJ: Prentice-Hall, 1973.
[7] G. Dahlquist and A. Bjorck, *Numerical Methods*. Englewood Cliffs, NJ: Prentice-Hall, 1974.
[8] P. Denning, "Working sets past and present," *IEEE Trans. Software Eng.*, vol. SE-6, Jan. 1980.
[9] M. Dubois and F. A. Briggs, "Efficient interprocessor communication for MIMD multiprocessor systems," in *Proc. 8th Int. Symp. Comput. Arch.*, May 1981.

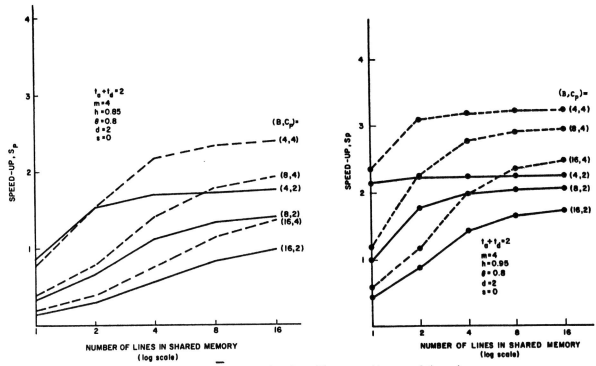

Fig. 13. Effective speed-up for multiprocessor with set-associative caches assuming a finite-speed crossbar switch with $t_a + t_d = 2$. (a) Cache with hit ratio, $h = 0.85$ (b) Cache with hit ratio, $h = 0.95$

[10] M. Dubois and F. A. Briggs, "Effects of cache coherency in multiprocessors," *IEEE Trans. Comput.*, vol. C-31, Nov. 1982.
[11] M. Dubois and F. A. Briggs, "Analytical methodologies for the evaluation of multiprocessing structures," Purdue Univ. Tech. Rep. TR-EE 82-4, Feb. 1982.
[12] M. J. Flynn, "Some computer organizations and their effectiveness," *IEEE Trans. Comput.*, vol. C-21, pp. 998–1005, Sept. 1972.
[13] C. H. Hoogendoorn, "A general model for memory interference in multiprocessors," *IEEE Trans. Comput.*, vol. C-26, pp. 998–1005 Oct. 1977.
[14] K. R. Kaplan and R. O. Winder, "Cache-based computer systems," *Computer*, vol. 6, Mar. 1973.
[15] L. Kleinrock, *Queuing Systems, vols. I and II.* New York: Wiley system.
[16] A. Lehman, "Performance evlauation and prediction of storage hierarchies," *ACM SIGMETRICS Perform. '80*, vol. 9, pp. 43–54, May 1980.
[17] D. M. Nessett, "The effectiveness of cache memories in a multiprocessor environment," *Australian Comput. J.*, vol. 7, Mar. 1975.
[18] J. H. Patel, "Analysis of multiprocessors with private cache memories," *IEEE Trans. Comput.*, vol. C-31, Apr. 1982.

[19] G. S. Rao, "Performance analysis of cache memories," *J. Ass. Comput. Mach.*, vol. 25, pp. 378–395, July 1978.
[20] J. H. Saltzer, "A simple linear model of demand paging performance," *Commun. Ass. Comput. Mach.*, vol. 17, Apr. 1974.
[21] A. J. Smith, "A comparative study of set associative memory mapping algorithms and their use for cache and main memory," *IEEE Trans Software Eng.*, vol. SE-4, pp. 121–130, Mar. 1978.
[22] A. J. Smith, "Characterizing the storage process and its effect on the update of main memory by write through," *J. Ass. Comput. Mach.*, vol. 26, Jan. 1979.
[23] W. D. Streker, "Cache memories for PDP-11 family computers," in *Proc. 3rd Ann. Symp. Comput. Arch.*, Jan. 1976.
[24] C. K. Tang, "Cache system design in the tightly coupled multiprocessor system," *Proc. AFIPS*, 1976.
[25] L. C. Widdoes, "The S-1 project: development of high performance digital computers," *Dig. COMPCON '80*, IEEE Comput. Soc., San Francisco, CA, Feb. 1980.
[26] W. A. Wulf, R. Levin and S. P. Harbison, *Hydra/C.mmp: An Experimental Computer System.* New York: McGraw-Hill, 1981.

On the Validity of Trace-Driven Simulation for Multiprocessors

Eric J. Koldinger, Susan J. Eggers, and Henry M. Levy
Department of Computer Science and Engineering
University of Washington
Seattle, WA 98195

Abstract

Trace-driven simulation is a commonly-used technique for evaluating multiprocessor memory systems. However, several open questions exist concerning the validity of multiprocessor traces. One is the extent to which tracing induced dilation affects the traces and consequently the results of the simulations. A second is whether the traces generated from multiple runs of the same program will yield the same simulation results.

This study examines the variation in simulation results caused by both dilation and multiple runs of the same program on a shared-memory multiprocessor. Overall, our results validate the use of trace-driven simulation for these machines: variability due to dilation and multiple runs appears to be small. However, where small differences in simulated results are crucial to design decisions, multiple traces of parallel applications should be examined.

1 Introduction

Trace-driven simulation is possibly the most common and valuable experimental technique used to explore architectural alternatives. It allows the comparison of many architectural choices quickly and efficiently. It provides more detail than analytical models, and is significantly less expensive and more flexible than building hardware. Among simulation techniques, it produces the most realistic results, since its inputs are derived from actual programs, rather than statistical models.

This work was supported in part by the National Science Foundation under Grants No. CCR-8619663 and PYI Award No. MIP-9058-439, by the Washington Technology Center, and by the Digital Equipment Corporation External Research Program.

In trace-driven simulation, one or more application programs are executed, usually interpretively, and a complete trace is collected from each. The trace typically contains all of the memory addresses referenced, as well as opcodes and possibly timing information. Traces can either be used directly, for example, to evaluate instruction set characteristics [Gross et al. 88, Shustek 78, Wiecek 82], or as input to an architectural simulator to predict the performance of different architectural variants. Such trace-driven simulation is most frequently used to study the behavior of cache memories, for example [Hill 87, Przybylski et al. 88, Smith 82].

The validity of trace-driven simulation relies on a crucial assumption: that perturbations to the trace data caused by the tracing process do not affect the simulation results. Unfortunately, it is nearly impossible to collect traces without perturbing program execution in some way. The most common perturbation is *execution dilation*, i.e., a slowdown in program execution speed. A passive hardware monitor can collect data without dilation, but the limited capacity of hardware monitors typically allows them to collect only relatively short traces. In addition, on-chip caches make it impossible for hardware monitors to capture a complete trace; instead they are only able to gather addresses that leave the chip. For these reasons, software techniques are commonly used. These techniques operate through software traps [Lacy 88, Wiecek 82], microcode modification [Agarwal et al. 86], inline macrocode modification [Eggers et al. 90, Stunkel & Fuchs 89], or compiler-generated tracing code [Borg et al. 90, Larus 90]. All of these techniques cause dilation, from 2 to 3 times for the inline tracing systems to over 1000 times for trap-driven techniques.

Dilation typically affects the behavior of a program by masking the timing differences between instructions. The time spent generating trace data for an instruction can completely overshadow the normal execution time of the instruction, causing all instructions to appear to take the same amount of time. For example, the difference between cache hit and miss times can be camouflaged by dilation.

For the execution of a sequential program in a uniprocessor environment, dilation should cause no problems. In sequential programs, there is only one thread of execution; therefore the slowdown should affect neither which addresses are issued nor the order in which they are issued (except for references caused by real-time events, such as interrupts, which are typically not included in traces).

Unfortunately, the shared-memory multiprocessor environment is much more complex. Parallel programs consist of multiple threads of control that execute concurrently on several processors; the threads communicate with each other and synchronize their execution via shared memory.

In a multiprocessor, dilation can produce a different global execution order.[1] For example, a specific function may be executed by the first processor to reach a particular synchronization point. Dilation can change the relative execution speed of processors with respect to each other, thereby changing the order in which processors reach the synchronization point. This would result in different processors executing code in a different order and, in the most extreme case, executing entirely different sections of code than in an untraced execution.

It is clear that multiprocessor tracing techniques can alter the global execution order of parallel programs; the question then remains whether these disturbances affect the simulation results. Fundamentally, can we trust the validity of simulation results from multiprocessor traces?

Determining the accuracy of multiprocessor traces is further complicated by natural variations that occur between runs of a program. In a uniprocessor, a program will produce identical address sequences each time it is run on the same data (unless it responds to real-time events, or uses randomness in it's algorithms). A multiprocessor program, however, can yield different global execution orders for different runs on the same data. These differences can occur even if identical results are produced each time. Minor variations in the multiprocessor environment, such as when the operating system starts processes relative to each other or how much of the cache needs to be flushed when the program starts, can alter how the processors interact and schedule work between themselves. Medium-grained (multi-threaded) applications can suffer from greater variability, as the schedule of threads onto processors is unlikely to be the same from run to run. Since there are obviously variations between multiple runs of a program, we must ask how these variations affect simulation results. Just how

typical is a "typical run"?

This paper describes a simple study of the variability of trace-driven simulation results for parallel programs executing on shared-memory multiprocessors. The study consists of two parts. The first part examines the variability between multiple runs of parallel programs. The second part examines the impact of tracing-induced dilation. In both cases we produce multiple traces, run the traces through a detailed cache simulator, and then compare the results (e.g., miss ratios and bus utilization) as seen by the simulator.

The paper is structured as follows. The next section describes the environment used for trace generation and simulation, and the benchmark programs that we measured. Sections 3 and 4 present the results of the tracing and simulation experiments. Section 5 summarizes our results.

2 The Measurement Environment

All traces were generated by MPTRACE, a low-dilation, inline tracing system [Eggers et al. 90]. MPTRACE modifies an assembly language program so that the program will save trace data as it executes. It achieves low dilation through two techniques. First, it compiles tracing code directly into the traced program to avoid external interpretation of each instruction. Second, it saves only enough data to reconstruct a complete trace in a postprocessing pass, rather than saving the entire trace at generation time. As a result, MPTRACE-annotated programs see a dilation of only two to three times their normal execution speed. This compares with dilations of about 20 for microcode instrumentation, and 100s to 1000s for trap-driven tracing systems.

To study the effects of dilation, it was necessary to introduce additional dilation into the programs. In MPTRACE, data is collected at *save points*, inserted in each basic block. To introduce additional dilation we added a small loop to these save points. This loop executes a fixed number of times, called the *delay factor*, for each instruction for which the save point records data. Since save points occur every 2–4 instructions, the dilation that we introduce appears evenly distributed throughout the program, much like the dilation that microcode and trap-driven tracing techniques add. By varying the delay factor, we are able to adjust the amount of dilation that the program sees when it runs. In these studies, we used two delay factors, 25 and 250, to model the dilations of microcode modification and a good trap-driven tracer.

All traces were generated on a 20-processor Sequent Symmetry Model B [Lovett & Thakkar 88] running Sequent's Dynix operating system. The traces were then

---

[1] *Global execution order* is the sequence of instructions from all processors, in order of their issue.

simulated with Charlie [Eggers 89], a multiprocessor simulator used for evaluating the SPUR multiprocessor [Hill et al. 86]; Charlie simulates a RISC processor with single-cycle instruction execution. In our experiments, we simulated 128K-byte direct mapped caches with various block sizes, and maintained coherency with the Berkeley Ownership Protocol [Katz et al. 85]. The timing of the bus was similar to the SPURbus [Gibson 88], but accesses to the bus were assigned in round-robin order, rather than in the NuBus order that the SPURbus used. This was done because the NuBus protocol gives priority to certain processors under high bus utilization, resulting in unfair access to the bus [Vernon & Manber 88]. All traces were simulated for several hundred thousand references after a cold start interval (typically 50,000 or 100,000 references).

2.1 The Workload

Table 1 shows the characteristics of the six programs we evaluated, including the percentage of data references and data misses that occurred to shared addresses. These programs fall into two classes of parallel programs: coarse-grained and medium-grained. In coarse-grained programs parallel code is typically scheduled at the Unix process level, one process for each processor. Work (shared data) is divided either statically or dynamically between the assigned processors; in a static division each processor performs only the work originally assigned to it; in a dynamic division work is performed on whatever processor is currently available. Medium-grained programs divide work between multiple dynamically-created threads, where each thread is a "virtual processor"; these threads are then scheduled onto physical processors at runtime. With multi-threaded programs, the order in which threads are scheduled onto processors may differ significantly between runs, and threads can migrate between processors during their lifetime. Fine-grained parallelism, which is often detected by compilers at the loop iteration level rather than explicitly programmed, is not covered in this study.

Three of the programs fall into the coarse-grained category: Pverify, Topopt, and Psim. Pverify [Ma et al. 87] compares boolean circuits to determine if they are functionally identical. The circuits used were combinational benchmarks for evaluating test generation algorithms. Topopt [Devadas & Newton 87] performs topological optimization on VLSI circuits using a parallel simulated-annealing algorithm. The input was a technology independent multi-level logic circuit. Psim simulates switch nodes for a nonshared bus interconnect. Pverify and Psim were run with 12 processors, while Topopt was run with 9. All three programs were compiled by the Sequent C compiler before being modified

by MPTRACE. Psim, which was written in PCP, a variant of C for fork-join programming. Psim was passed through the PCP preprocessor before being compiled.

Two of the medium-grained programs, Grav and Pdsa, were written using the Presto [Bershad et al. 88] parallel programming environment. Presto is a multi-threaded environment for C++ programming, in which the programmer can dynamically create threads for parallelism; the threads are scheduled by a user-level thread scheduler and execute within a single address space that is shared by all processors executing a parallel Presto program. Grav simulates the motion of many bodies interacting through gravity, using the Barnes-Hut $O(n \log n)$ algorithm. The 100 randomly placed bodies were simulated through several iterations of the algorithm. Pdsa [Upton et al. 90] performs topological optimization using a simulated-annealing algorithm. The circuit used was one of the 1990 MCNC benchmarks on placement and routing. The third medium-grained program, FullConn, is a simulation of a fully connected set of processors communicating at random. It uses the SYNAPSE parallel simulation environment [Wagner 89], an environment for conservative parallel simulation that is written on top of the Presto threads package. Two thousand messages in the network were simulated in this trace. All three of these programs were written in C++ and compiled using the C++ 1.2 compiler and the standard Sequent C compiler before being modified by MPTRACE.

To insure that differences in the traces were caused by either scheduling differences or dilation, the runs were kept as identical as possible. For example, all traced runs of a program used the same input. Random number generators (used in the simulated annealing programs Topopt and Pdsa, and in FullConn) were seeded with the same number to provide the same sequence of random numbers in each run. Tracing was turned on at the same point in each run of the programs. This was always after the program had finished it's initialization, and for programs that make several passes over their data (Pdsa, Grav, and Topopt) after the first pass was completed.

3 The Effect of Multiple Runs

Our first experiment investigated the variability among multiple runs of a program, and the significance of these differences. This issue is important to settle prior to running other experiments that require different types of multiple runs, such as the dilation study. In this case we need to know whether variations across dilations are caused by the dilation itself, or are due to variations within the same dilation.

For the multiple run study we traced the same por-

Program Name	Description	Grain	CPUs	Language	Size (Instructions)	References (Per-Processor)	Shared Refs	Shared Misses
Pverify	logic verification	coarse	12	C	7395	300,000	36%	90%
Topopt	topological optimization	coarse	9	C	5916	300,000	42%	99%
Psim	butterfly simulator	coarse	12	PCP	7639	300,000	21%	100%
Grav	physics simulation	medium	10	C++	10501	500,000	95%	99%
Pdsa	simulated annealing	medium	12	C++	10199	500,000	97%	99%
FullConn	network simulator	medium	12	C++	20529	500,000	99%	99%

Table 1: Programs used in dilation studies

tion of each program six times, ran the traces through our cache simulator and compared the results. The graphs that display these results contain miss ratios or bus utilizations over block sizes ranging from 4 to 256 bytes. In each graph the solid line indicates the average values for all six runs of a trace over the block size range. The dotted lines were obtained by computing the 95% confidence interval for the mean of the data (either miss ratio or bus utilization) for each block size, and then connecting the endpoints of those intervals.

Figure 1 shows the miss ratios for the coarse-grained applications, Pverify, Topopt, and Psim; their bus utilizations are shown in Figure 2. The variation among multiple runs for cache miss ratio for these traces is extremely small, as shown by the narrowness of the 95% confidence interval curves. The average deviation from the mean miss ratio for a particular block size is less than 0.01 percentage points, with a maximum of 0.06.

The values for bus utilizations are not as consistent. Pverify and Psim show the same small variation, i.e., an average deviation of 0.55 percentage points; however, Topopt's bus utilization varies over a range of nearly 20 percentage points, with most of the data clustered within 7 percentage points.

Figure 3 shows the miss ratios for the medium-grained applications, FullConn, Grav, and Pdsa. These programs show larger variations in miss ratio than the coarse-grained programs. Individual miss ratios from the six runs differ from their mean by an average of 0.03 percentage points and as much as 0.53 percentage.

Again, bus utilization is not as consistent, especially at smaller block sizes (see Figure 4). The deviation averages 1% of the bus capacity on block sizes less than 64, and in one case (Pdsa with 4 byte blocks) is as high as 8.65% of bus capacity.

Miss ratio and bus utilization curves for the individual runs of a program all follow the same trend; for example all bus utilization values increase with increasing block size, and at approximately the same rate. This demonstrates that the differences in values across block-size cannot be attributed to the variability in the runs, but are due to the change in block size.

From this data it is clear that one trace of an applica-

tion is insufficient to give a completely accurate picture of a program's cache and bus performance. However, whether several runs should be used depends on the precision required by a particular study, and whether one is interested in trends or specific values. For example, if one is interested in charting the *trend* of a metric as a cache parameter varies, and knowing with confidence that changes in the trend are caused by different values of the parameter, then one run is sufficient. In our examples we can definitely say that increases in block size produce the trends observed for both miss ratio and bus utilization. The differences in values across different runs were small compared to the size of the effects we were interested in measuring.

On the other hand, if one is interested in more closely pinpointing the *value* of a metric at a particular parameter value, then more than one run might be necessary, with the mean of the runs used. For example, in designing a small on-chip cache for a 100-MIPS processor, very small changes in miss ratio might have a significant performance impact. In this case, we might need to know as closely as possible the miss ratios of important applications. Therefore, multiple traces would be required. On the other hand, when choosing block-size for a large second-level cache, we may wish to see how blocksize affects miss ratio, but the exact value of the miss ratio is less important. In this case, one trace would be sufficient.

4 Dilation Effects

To determine the effects of dilation, we introduced additional delays into the tracing code and regenerated the traces. Two dilations were used, 25 and 250, as described in Section 2.

Figure 5 depicts the miss ratios for the coarse-grained applications at the three dilation factors, 0 (solid line), 25 (dotted line), and 250 (dashed line). Figure 5 shows the same results for bus utilization. In most cases there is little effect, if any, from dilation.

Results for the medium-grained programs appear in Figures 7 for miss ratios and 8 for bus utilization. For this type of program, increasing dilation appears to increase miss ratio at particular block sizes for all three applications. The effects on bus utilization are varied: the FullConn and Pdsa curves rise with increasing dilation, but those for Grav fall.

A two-sided t-test was used to determine whether the differences exhibited in the simulation results can be attributed to dilation. The two-sided t-test produces a statistic, t, that indicates the difference between the averages in units of the standard error. If the absolute value of t is greater than 2, then, with at least 95% confidence, the differences between the means of the two sets of data are real and caused by dilation. When the absolute value of t is 1, the confidence level decreases to 66%.

Table 2 shows the values of t for miss ratios of all the programs. In all cases but two, the values of t are between -1 and 1. Thus, we cannot say that there is a statistically significant difference between miss ratios from any two dilations, i.e., the differences for individual block sizes across dilations cannot be positively attributed to dilation itself. Table 3 shows the values of t when the test is applied to the bus utilization values. Like miss ratio, there is no statistically significant difference between values from two dilations.

Although the differences are not statistically significant, there is a definite downward trend in the values of em t, particularly for bus utilization. The majority of the t values are negative (74% for the 0–25 dilation comparisons, and 64% for the 0–250 comparisons), indicating that the average bus utilization on traces generated with delay factors of 25 and 250 is greater than that seen with the minimal amount of dilation caused by MPTRACE. The trend is especially pronounced in Topopt and the medium-grained applications. A similar trend is seen in the cache miss statistics, but to a lesser extent.

However, since the t values are small, their downward direction translates into only a slight altering in miss ratio and bus utilization. On average, miss ratios are 0.04 percentage points higher for dilations of both 25 and 250 times. Bus utilization is 1.72 percentage points higher for 25 dilation traces, and 1.26 points higher for the 250 dilation traces; however the actual range of variation is fairly wide (from -1.29 to 10.12 points, and -4.55 to 11.16 points for the two dilations, respectively).

Again, whether or not differences of this magnitude can affect the results of architecture studies depends on the particular study. However, our data indicate that we can make a stronger statement about the effects of dilation than multiple runs. For all programs the dilation effects were extremely slight. Architects can therefore be confident of results produced by most software tracing techniques. In a few cases one might want to be aware of the upward bias caused by dila-

tion. Fortunately the bias is small, and mostly runs in the same direction; from a practical point of view, this bias should not be relevant.

5 Summary

We have examined variability in trace-driven cache simulation results of parallel programs. Our experiments tested variability due to two factors: multiple runs of the same parallel program and tracing-induced dilation. We also evaluated both coarse-grained (process-based) and medium-grained (thread-based) parallel programs. Programs were traced on a Sequent shared-memory multiprocessor and the traces were used to drive a cache simulator.

In general, we found that cache miss ratios varied little between runs of a program. Bus utilizations sometimes differed more, particularly with multi-threaded applications; therefore if exact prediction of bus utilization for parallel applications is critical to a design decision, multiple traces of those applications should probably be examined.

With respect to dilation, our experiments showed little significant difference in the simulation results (miss ratio and bus utilization) between the standard MPTRACE traces and the artifically dilated runs that are 25 and 250 times slower. One plausible explanation hinges on the fact that our metrics measure the aggregate behavior of all processors, rather than any single processor in the machine. For example, which processor accesses the bus is not important for the aggregate metrics as long as some processor accesses it. So, although trace generation-induced dilation affects the global ordering of memory references, it does not affect the aggregate statistics.

From our point of view, these results are positive with respect to the validity of trace-driven simulation of parallel programs. However, we believe that one should still be cautious. In particular, where fine- or medium-grained programs are involved, and where small differences in cache miss ratio or utilization are significant, running multiple traces of some applications should be considered.

The dilation results show that all software trace generation techniques, regardless of the amount of dilation they induce, have comparable accuracy. Unfortunately, they do not indicate how results from these traces compare to the actual performance of the hardware, i.e., we do not know whether any disturbance was caused by the MPTRACE base dilation of 2. Nor do we address the question of whether traces generated on one machine are valid for simulating another machine [Bitar 90]. Both questions require further research.

Program Name	Delay Factors	Blocksize (bytes)						
		4	8	16	32	64	128	256
Pverify	0 & 25	0.19	0.13	0.15	0.08	-0.02	-0.10	-0.39
	0 & 250	0.08	0.06	0.05	0.01	-0.09	-0.41	-0.54
Topopt	0 & 25	0.18	-0.01	-0.17	-0.22	-0.22	-0.34	-0.53
	0 & 250	0.43	0.15	-0.04	-0.16	-0.19	-0.38	-0.64
Psim	0 & 25	0.00	0.00	0.00	-0.10	0.00	0.41	-1.13
	0 & 250	0.00	0.00	-0.17	-0.21	0.16	0.19	0.20
FullConn	0 & 25	-0.50	-0.55	-0.40	-0.43	-0.54	-0.53	-0.15
	0 & 250	-0.50	-0.71	-0.52	-0.46	-0.65	-0.46	-0.38
Grav	0 & 25	-0.54	-0.18	0.16	0.40	0.38	0.25	-0.12
	0 & 250	-0.30	0.27	0.38	0.96	0.89	0.52	-0.05
Pdsa	0 & 25	-0.59	-0.33	-0.31	0.09	-0.23	0.22	0.08
	0 & 250	-0.70	-0.57	-0.45	0.42	0.36	-0.03	-0.04

Table 2: Two valued t-test results for miss ratio

Program Name	Delay Factors	Blocksize (bytes)						
		4	8	16	32	64	128	256
Pverify	0 & 25	0.13	0.03	0.12	0.01	-0.17	-0.07	-0.23
	0 & 250	0.08	0.06	0.07	-0.04	0.03	0.24	-0.32
Topopt	0 & 25	-0.03	-0.14	-0.22	-0.23	-0.29	-0.40	-0.58
	0 & 250	0.04	-0.10	-0.15	-0.23	-0.26	-0.40	-0.70
Psim	0 & 25	0.00	-0.02	0.23	0.02	0.15	-0.05	1.02
	0 & 250	0.00	0.02	-0.01	-0.22	0.22	-0.09	0.28
FullConn	0 & 25	-0.32	-0.39	-0.30	-0.31	-0.33	-0.26	-0.08
	0 & 250	-0.49	-0.75	-0.53	-0.54	-0.58	-0.28	-0.23
Grav	0 & 25	-0.13	0.00	-0.02	0.12	-0.15	-0.50	-0.48
	0 & 250	0.15	0.34	0.19	0.35	0.15	-0.73	-0.75
Pdsa	0 & 25	-0.68	-0.51	-0.65	-0.36	-0.58	-0.40	-0.56
	0 & 250	-0.74	-0.68	-0.98	-0.40	-0.72	-0.51	-0.94

Table 3: Two valued t-test results for bus utilization

6 Acknowledgements

We would like to thank David Keppel for help with Presto and MPTRACE, David Wagner for his assistance with Synapse and FullConn, Werner Stuetzle for statistical consulting and Ed Felten and Michael Upton for allowing us to use Grav and Pdsa, respectively.

References

[Agarwal et al. 86] A. Agarwal, R. L. Sites, and M. Horowitz. ATUM: A new technique for capturing address traces using microcode. In *Proceedings of the 13th International Symposium on Computer Architecture*, pages 119–127, June 1986.

[Bershad et al. 88] B. N. Bershad, E. D. Lazowska, and H. M. Levy. PRESTO: A system for object-oriented parallel programming. *Software – Practice and Experience*, 18(8):713–732, August 1988.

[Bitar 90] P. Bitar. A critique of trace-driven simulation for shared-memory multiprocessors. In *Cache and Interconnect Architectures*, pages 37–52. Kluwer Academic Press, 1990.

[Borg et al. 90] A. Borg, R. Kessler, and D. W. Wall. Generation and analysis of very long address traces. In *Proceedings of the 17th International Symposium on Computer Architecture*, pages 270–279, May 1990.

[Devadas & Newton 87] S. Devadas and A. Newton. Topological optimization of multiple level array logic. *IEEE Transactions on Computer-Aided Design*, November 1987.

[Eggers 89] S. J. Eggers. *Simulation Analysis of Data Sharing in Shared Memory Multiprocessors*. PhD dissertation, University of California, Berkeley, April 1989.

[Eggers et al. 90] S. J. Eggers, D. R. Keppel, E. J. Koldinger, and H. M. Levy. Techniques for efficient inline tracing on a shared-memory multiprocessor. In *Proceedings of the International Conference on Measurement and Modeling of Computer Systems*, pages 37–46, May 1990.

[Gibson 88] G. Gibson. SpurBus specification. Technical report, University of California, Berkeley, December 1988.

[Gross et al. 88] T. R. Gross, J. L. Hennessy, S. A. Przybylski, and C. Rowen. Measurement and evaluation of the MIPS architecture and processor. *Transactions on Computer Systems*, 6(3):229–257, August 1988.

[Hill 87] M. D. Hill. *Aspects of Cache Memory and Instruction Buffer Performance*. PhD dissertation, University of California, Berkeley, November 1987.

[Hill et al. 86] M. Hill, S. Eggers, J. Larus, G. Taylor, G. Adams, B. Bose, G. Gibson, P. Hansen, J.Keller, S. Kong, C. Lee, D. Lee, J. Pendleton, S. Ritchie, D. Wood, B. Zorn, P. Hilfinger, D. Hodges, R. Katz, J. Ousterhout, and D.A.Patterson. SPUR: a VLSI multiprocessor workstation. *IEEE Computer*, 19(11):8–22, November 1986.

[Katz et al. 85] R. Katz, S. Eggers, D. Wood, C. Perkins, and R. Sheldon. Implementing a cache consistency protocol. In *Proceedings of the 12th Annual International Symposium on Computer Architecture*, pages 276–283, June 1985.

[Lacy 88] F. Lacy. An address trace generator for trace-driven simulation of shared memory multiprocessors. Master's thesis, University of California, Berkeley, Computer Science Division, March 1988.

[Larus 90] J. R. Larus. Abstract execution: A technique for efficiently tracing programs. *Software – Practice and Experience*, 1990. To appear.

[Lovett & Thakkar 88] R. Lovett and S. Thakkar. The Symmetry multiprocessoring system. In *Proceedings of the 1988 International Conference on Parallel Processing*, pages 303–310, August 1988.

[Ma et al. 87] H.-K. T. Ma, S. Devadas, R. Wei, and A. Sangiovanni-Vincentelli. Logic verification algorithms and their parallel implementation. In *Proceedings of the 24th Design Automation Conference*, pages 283–290, November 1987.

[Przybylski et al. 88] S. Przybylski, M. Horowitz, and J. Hennessy. Performance tradeoffs in cache design. In *Proceedings of the 15th International Symposium on Computer Architecture*, pages 290–298, May 1988.

[Shustek 78] L. J. Shustek. *Analysis and Performance of Computer Instruction Sets*. PhD dissertation, Stanford University, January 1978.

[Smith 82] A. J. Smith. Cache memories. *ACM Computing Surveys*, 14(3):473–530, September 1982.

[Stunkel & Fuchs 89] C. B. Stunkel and W. K. Fuchs. TRAPEDS: Producing traces for multicomputers via execution driven simulation. In *Proceedings of the International Conference on Measurement and Modeling of Computer Systems*, pages 70–78, May 1989.

[Upton et al. 90] M. Upton, K. Samii, and S. Sugiyama. Integrated placement for mixed standard cell and macro-cell designs. In *Proceedings of the 27th Design Automation Conference*, 1990.

[Vernon & Manber 88] M. K. Vernon and U. Manber. Distributed round-robin and first-come first-serve protocols and their application to multiprocessor bus arbitration. In *Proceedings of the 15th International Symposium on Computer Architecture*, pages 269–279, May 1988.

[Wagner 89] D. B. Wagner. *Conservative Parallel Discrete-Event Simulation: Principles and Practice*. PhD dissertation, University of Washington, September 1989.

[Wiecek 82] C. A. Wiecek. A case study of VAX-11 instruction set usage for compiler execution. In *Proceedings of the Symposium on Architectural Support for Programming Languages and Operating Systems*, pages 177–184, March 1982.

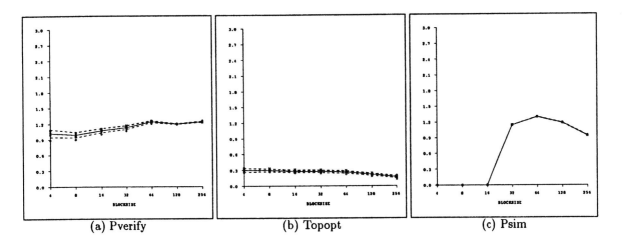

(a) Pverify   (b) Topopt   (c) Psim

Figure 1: Coarse Grained Programs, Miss Ratios

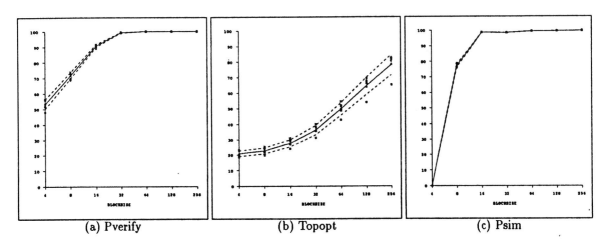

(a) Pverify   (b) Topopt   (c) Psim

Figure 2: Coarse Grained Programs, Bus Utilization

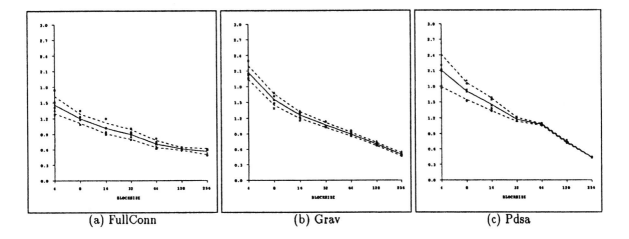

(a) FullConn   (b) Grav   (c) Pdsa

Figure 3: Medium Grained Programs, Miss Ratios

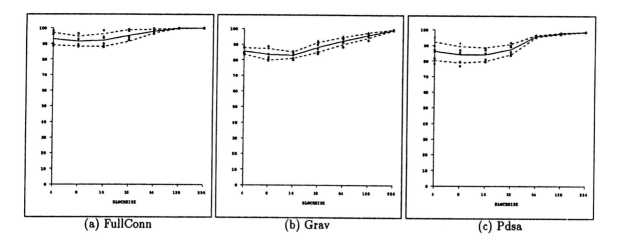

(a) FullConn   (b) Grav   (c) Pdsa

Figure 4: Medium Grained Programs, Bus Utilization

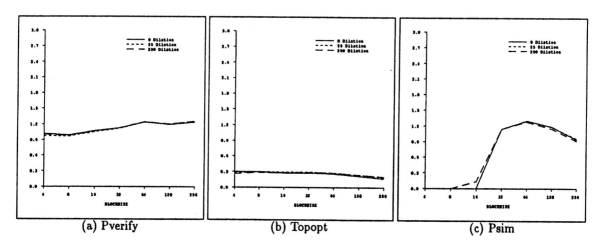

(a) Pverify   (b) Topopt   (c) Psim

Figure 5: Dilation Effects – Coarse Grained Programs, Miss Ratios

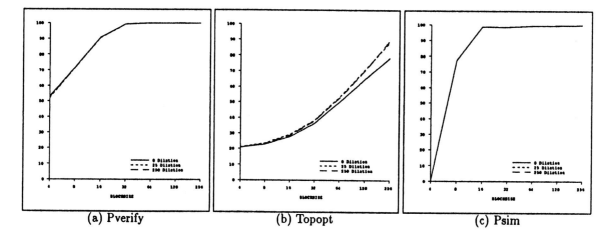

(a) Pverify   (b) Topopt   (c) Psim

Figure 6: Dilation Effects – Coarse Grained Programs, Bus Utilization

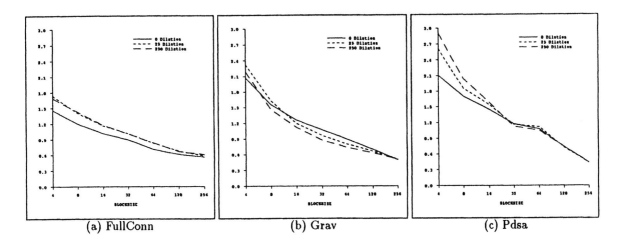

Figure 7: Dilation Effects – Medium Grained Programs, Miss Ratios

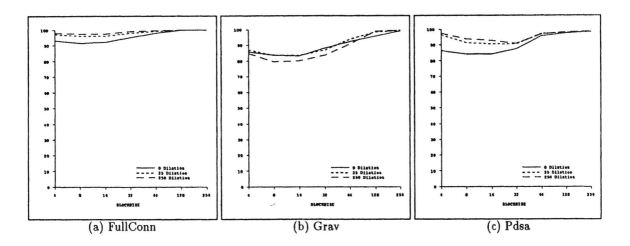

Figure 8: Dilation Effects – Medium Grained Programs, Bus Utilization

Multiprocessor Cache Simulation
Using Hardware Collected Address Traces

Andrew W. Wilson Jr.

Encore Computer Corporation
257 Cedar Hill St.
Marlborough, MA 01752

Abstract

This paper presents an evaluation of the performance of large private caches for multiprocessors using hardware collected address traces. The traces are 14 Million memory references long and were collected from one processor of a multiprocessor in real time using special hardware. Both uniprocessor performance and multiprocessor time sliced performance are simulated. The effects of cache size for large caches, process migration, and cache coherency on hit ratio and bus traffic is measured. A number of conclusions regarding the benefits of large private caches in a timeshared multiprocessor environment are reached.

Introduction

The use of large private caches for Multiprocessors is an idea whose time has come. Much progress has recently been made in the development of efficient algorithms for cache coherency[3] [4] [9], while rapidly increasing memory density makes the implementation of large caches straightforward. A critical issue is just how far caches can go in reducing interconnection utilization for a multiprocessor. Recently researchers have begun to address this question using traces of parallel programs obtained through microcode assisted tracing of a multiprocessor with four processors[1]. The research described in this paper uses large (14 Million reference), address traces which were collected completely unobtrusively through special hardware.

Using these traces, the research attempts to answer the question of how much large caches can help multiprocessor performance. Both miss ratios, which affect effective access time, and transfer ratios, which affect bus utilization are examined. Multiprocessors have an additional source of bus traffic caused by cross invalidations of share data. The effects of one source of this sharing, process migration, are investigated

using a novel technique for simulating process migration in a multiuser multiprocessor.

Hardware Trace Collection Strategy

Many studies of cache performance have been done in the past with traces collected by a variety of software and hardware methodologies[2] [7] [8]. Conventional, software based collection methodologies are highly intrusive and are usually limited to application programs. For uniprocessors the intrusiveness results in a long execution time for the program being traced, typically thousands of times longer than real time, but does not affect the validity of the traces. For programs running on parallel processors, or complete systems on uniprocessors, execution time can critically affect program behavior. For example, I/O operations will appear instantaneous when software tracing is used, thus distorting the behavior of the operating system portion of the trace. Some less intrusive method is required to obtain truly accurate address traces.

A number of attempts have been made to reduce or eliminate the intrusiveness of address tracing. Digital Equipment Corporation has modified the microcode on one of their line of VAX uniprocessors to enable accurate address tracing. With this technique they were able to trace both operating system and user memory accesses for a set of programs running under VAX/VMS and Ultrix. A variety of cache configurations were then traced. A further refinement to the microcoded tracing mechanism was done which allowed a four processor VAX multiprocessor to be traced[1]. While these two trace studies were well done, the size of the traces collected were small (a few million references), only short segments of traces could be taken at a time (400,000 references), and the tracing was still done at slower than real time.

At Encore, acquisition of large address traces collected in real time has recently become possible through modifications to existing equipment. The basic technique is to use one Multimax™ [6] multiprocessor to collect address traces from a second Multimax. A highspeed, mutichannel I/O interface, the Mass Storage Card (MSC), was modified through the addition of some special wiring and a couple of small daughter cards to accept 4 byte addresses sent to it over a parallel cable. This card was plugged into a Multimax 320 ™ system configured with 128 Megabytes of memory. An address capture card was built which connected to the internal bus of the standard Dual Processor Card (DPC) and captured physical addresses generated by the National 32032's MMU chip. The addresses were sent to the modified I/O card in the other Multimax. Figure 1 shows the hardware used, while Figure 2 shows two machines interconnected for tracing.

The research described in this paper is sponsored by the Defense Advanced Research Projects Agency (DOD), DARPA contract DACA76-89-C-0003. The views and conclusions contained in this document are those of the author and should not be interpreted as representing the official policies, either expressed or implied, of the Defense Advanced Research Projects Agency or the US Government.

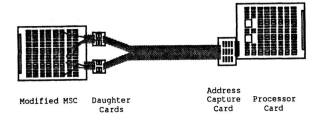

Figure 1: Address Trace Capture Cards

With this arrangement over 100 Megabytes of memory was available to store the collected addresses. Unfortunately, a bug in the operating system limited the size of traces to 56 Megabytes. The bug was not fixed in time to allow full use of the memory for this set of traces. In spite of the reduced size, about 16 seconds of processor execution were captured with each trace.

The procedure used to capture a trace was to start up the workload to be traced, give it a few minutes to get through the initialization phase, then record addresses at full speed until the trace memory is exhausted. At that point the captured addresses were transferred to disk. It took far longer to save the traces to disk (about 1/4 hour) than it did to collect them.

Benchmarks Used

Several different benchmark suits were used to generate traces. For the multiprogramming workload, a set of ten programs typical of those used in other address trace studies[1,3] (and considered to be typical of actual use) were used. Even though the hardware could only trace one processor at a time, it was possible to have more than one processor running and record some aspects of parallel program execution, such as lock contention and context switching, from them. Thus, a couple of traces consisting of one processor of a set of processors running a parallel program were taken. Finally, a script driven simulation of a multiuser timesharing workload was done. The specific programs traced will be discussed next.

The ten programs executed as part of the multiprogramming workload are listed in Table 1. All programs were run as serial programs, even though some have parallel versions. The programs were started in parallel by a shell script, and time multiplexed on the processor(s) by the Unix operating system. Tracing was delayed for about five minutes after initiation of the programs to allow them to reach stable operation.

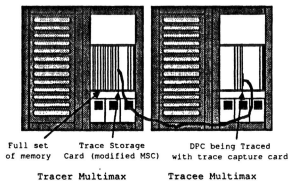

Full set   Trace Storage   DPC being Traced
of memory   Card (modified MSC)   with trace capture card

Tracer Multimax   Tracee Multimax

Figure 2: Tracing Configuration

Quick Sort	Simple quick sort program sorting 32,000 random numbers
NROFF	Execution of the NROFF program formatting a MAN page from the Unix documentation
LISP	A standard LISP benchmark using common lisp
"C" Compile	The Greenhills "C" compiler compiling a short C program
Fortran Compile	The Greenhills Fortran compiler compiling the LINPACK scientific computing benchmark
PCG Pack	Execution of the PCG Pack subroutine library on a sample scientific problem
Spice	Execution of the Spice VLSI circuit simulator on a sample IC circuit description
Molecular Dynamics	Execution of a molecular dynamics package on a sample problem
Ada	Simulation of a battle management scenario written in Ada
ECAS	Simulation of a multiprocessor using the Encore Computer Architecture Simulator

Table 1: List of programs used
for Multiprogramming workload

For parallel program measurements, locally available parallel versions of two of the multiprogramming workload programs were used: ECAS and Ada. Both were run on four processors, though only one processor's execution was actually traced. The Multiuser workload consisted of a set of terminal scripts run on a third Multimax which provided input to a set of jobs on the Multimax being traced. The scripts included delays to simulate user typing speeds and pauses while thinking.

Traces Collected

Eight different traces were collected over a period of three weeks. Even though the actual tracing only took a few minutes, setting up the experiments and saving the results to magnetic tape took quite bit longer (about half a day). The key features of the eight traces are listed in Table 2. The first six traces were done under the Umax 4.2 operating system, a parallel version of Berkeley 4.2 Unix. These consisted of three multiprogramming workload traces, one parallel Ada workload, one parallel ECAS workload, and one multiuser workload. The last two traces were done under Mach, a Unix compatible operating system from Carnegie-Mellon University intended for both distributed and parallel computers, and were both of multiprogramming workloads. Several of the multiprogramming workload programs were omitted from the Mach traces because they hadn't been ported to Mach yet.

Only one processor was traced in each case, even when multiple processors were executing a workload. In the case of the multiprogramming workload, only one set of programs were executed regardless of how many processors were configured. Due to a problem with the operating system on the machine

259

Umax.Mp.1p	Single processor execution of multiprogramming workload under Umax 4.2
Umax.Mp.2p	Dual processor execution of multiprogramming workload under Umax 4.2 (one processor traced)
Umax.Mp.4p	Four processor execution of multiprogramming workload under Umax 4.2 (one processor traced)
Umax.Ada.4p	Four processor execution of parallel Ada workload under Umax 4.2 (one processor traced)
Umax.ECAS.4p	Four processor execution of parallel Computer Architecture Simulator under Umax 4.2 (one processor traced)
Umax.TS.4p	Four processor execution of 30 simulated timesharing sessions under Umax 4.2 (one processor traced)
Mach.Mp.1p	Single processor execution of multiprogramming workload under Mach
Mach.Mp.4p	Four processor execution of multiprogramming workload under Mach (one processor traced)

Table 2: List of Address Traces Recorded

collecting the traces, only 56 Megabytes of traces (14 million references) were collected at a time. This is equivalent to about 16 seconds of a National 32032's execution.

The raw traces were analyzed to obtain some basic statistics about them. Table 3 summarizes these findings. The first three results columns: User Fraction, Write Fraction and Instruction Fraction, are the ratios of memory references in user mode to total references, write references to total references, and instruction references to total references, respectively. Page table walks, which also appear in the address traces, were removed for purposes of these calculations. The data in the Super Calls column is a count of the number of times that the processor switched between supervisor and user mode. Single reference switches, which are due to translations from user virtual to user physical space by the operating system, were not counted. The data in the next two columns were obtained by detecting fetches for the entry points of key operating system subroutines in the address traces. Since the operating system is mapped one-for-one virtual to physical, the occurrence of these addresses indicates that the operating system is performing one of the indicated actions. Finally, Read/Modify/Write Interlocked cycles, which are caused by test and set operations, were counted along with those lock requests which then spun on the lock variable indicating a failed lock attempt. From these numbers the ratio of failed lock attempts was calculated.

Examining some of the data more closely, note that the user fraction generally varied between 85 and 95%, with the exception of one multiprogramming workload trace (Umax.Mp.2p) which was only 55% user. Detailed examination of the Umax.Mp.2p trace indicates that a couple of programs made lengthy system calls, resulting in the low fraction of user mode. This shows how much system and user fractions can vary depending on program

Trace	User Fract.	Write Fract.	Instr. Fract.	Super Calls	Ctx Switches	Page Faults	Fract. Locks Failed
Umax.Mp.1p	.900	.131	.614	4426	286	40	0.000
Umax.Mp.2p	.552	.093	.678	4075	–	–	0.001
Umax.Mp.4p	.885	.130	.602	4290	–	–	0.003
Umax.Ada.4p	.911	.179	.567	888	145	0	0.007
Umax.Ecas.4p	.951	.085	.644	92	97	0	0.071
Umax.TS.4p	.850	.161	.584	4925	228	135	0.007
Mach.Mp.1p	.874	.129	.609	5468	24	40	0.000
Mach.Mp.4p	.867	.123	.614	6903	18	8	0.000

Table 3: Statistics from Address Traces

specifics. However, it is encouraging to see from the Umax.Ada.4p and Umax.Ecas.4p traces that large parallel programs which do not use the operating system will get most of the machine.

Write and instruction fractions can be very useful for estimating system performance. These numbers were quite consistent across all the traces, with an average write fraction of 0.13, and an average instruction fraction of 0.61. These numbers are close to those once obtained directly from a processor card using a logic analyzer by Encore engineering staff (unpublished). The write and instruction fractions are very dependent on processor architecture. It is suspected that a RISC processor, with a larger register set and simpler instructions, would have a lower write fraction and higher instruction fraction. In fact, one RISC manufacturer claims 0.75 instruction fraction.

The number of supervisor calls was determined by counting the switches from user to supervisor mode. User space address translations by the supervisor, which look like switches from super to user and back in one reference, were discarded. interrupt service and page fault handling would also be counted in the supervisor call count, but were not separately counted. Page fault handling and time slice interrupts were counted and have been subtracted out. Other interrupts typically amount to 10 to 30 a second, for at most 450 such interrupts. Supervisor calls were pretty constant for all the multiprogramming traces, and much smaller for the single program traces (as expected). The Mach four processor trace is of the master processor which handles all I/O, and shows a correspondingly higher supervisor call rate (or perhaps interrupt rate).

The occurrence of context switches and page faults was signalled by the detection of specific addresses in the reference stream. Because the two- and four-processor Umax multiprogramming traces were done while running a slightly earlier version of the Umax operating system, and the relevent addresses were not recorded, the correct addresses to monitor were not known. Context switches and page faults in the other traces were reasonably low. Low page faults are especially important, since a fault will cause a section of memory to be written from disk, invalidating the cache entries. While this trace methodology can detect that a page fault happened, it cannot detect which page was replaced, so some locations may still be in the cache and not be purged. The end result would be that the simulated cache hit ratio would be higher than it should. On the other hand, pages which are replaced are those that haven't been used in a long time, so there probably isn't much in the cache anyway.

The final column reports on the percentage of locks which failed. The software normally executes a spin wait when a lock attempt fails, which consists of repeatedly reading and testing the value of the lock. The Address trace will contain a pattern of: test-and-set X, read X, read X, read X, ... , test-and-set X, continue processing. Each time this pattern was observed, it was counted as a failed lock attempt. Locks failed less than one percent of the time for all but the ECAS benchmark. The ECAS benchmark has one key data structure which all the processes frequently access (the event list), which suffers considerable contention. The operating system and the Ada run time have much more finely distributed locks, and suffer almost no contention. Thus lock contention does not appear to be a fundamental problem, but development of better tools to help programmers analyze program behavior and fix heavy contention points would be useful.

To summarize, the statistics gathered from the traces are encouraging. Write and instruction ratios are as expected, the processor is executing in user mode most of the time, and Lock contention is not a major problem. This bodes well for system performance.

Effect of Cache Size on Hit Ratios

One of the key items of interest was the ability of large caches to reduce bus traffic and hide bus latency. Obviously, the more that bus traffic can be reduced, the larger the maximum performance obtainable in a single system becomes. With the fast microprocessors presently available, low average memory latency is critical to achieving reasonable performance. Since memory prices are falling much faster than highspeed backplane prices, a large price advantage can be gained by using large caches instead of fast busses to support high speed multiprocessing.

Early work with traced base cache simulation concluded that there wasn't much benefit to large caches[5], but these studies were limited to short traces of relatively small applications programs. Also, the studies concentrated on hit ratios, which rapidly approach unity as cache size increases and hence do not show much improvement for large caches. When comparing large caches, it is more instructive to compare miss ratios than hit ratios. For example, an increase from 96% hit ratio to 98% does not appear very large, but actually represents a halving of miss ratio. If the miss time is substantially larger than the hit time (as it is with the fast processors currently available), the halving of miss ratio can almost double processor performance.

When longer traces of larger programs, especially multiple time slice programs, are used, the hit ratios for any given size cache are reduced, but there is corespondingly greater room for improvement when large caches are used. Some studies have suggested that the miss ratio continues to improve for caches beyond one megabyte in size[2]. A common rule of thumb is that the miss ratio decreases as one over the square root of the ratio of cache sizes (i.e. a 4 times bigger caches gets 1/2 the miss ratio). One reason for taking these traces was to attempt to verify that figure.

Encore has a computer architecture simulator, ECAS[11], which was used to simulate a simple processor/cache structure for initial analysis of the traces. (ECAS was also used to simulate a small multiprocessor to analyze process migration as discussed in the next section). The cache parameters were picked as: Direct Mapped, eight byte line size, allocate on write miss, and 16K to 1024K cache size. The miss ratios obtained for the eight traces are plotted in Figure 3.

It is very encouraging to note from Figure 3 that the miss ratios for all the traces are trending downward as cache size increases. Also notice how the two large parallel program traces, Ada and ECAS, have a significantly better hit ratio than the other

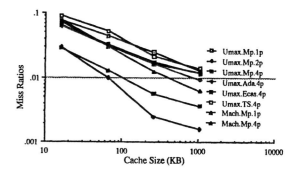

Figure 3: Comparative Miss Ratios for Different Cache Sizes

traces. They also appear to practically fit in the cache at between 64 and 256 kilobytes. These are all effects of having a single parallel program running on the multiprocessor, rather than ten separate serial programs.

Most of the miss ratio curves plotted in the log-log plot of Figure 3 are approximately straight lines. This indicates a power relationship between the variables. It is possible to fit curves of the form $Y = X^n$ to the miss ratio curves, where the exponent n is related to the slope of the log-log plotted curve. The rule of thumb discussed above would yield $n = -1/2$. The multiprogramming traces fall generally a little under that, at about 0.42, but the two single program traces are on or above it. Thus real multiuser and multiprogrammed workloads fall somewhat under the ideal. To get a factor of 8 reduction in miss ratio would require a cache increase factor of 140, rather than 64 as predicted by the square root rule. The rule of thumb is a bit optimistic, but still gets reasonably close even for a large reduction in miss ratio.

There are a couple of other bits of cache folklore that can be explored with these traces: user vs. supervisor miss ratios, instruction vs data miss ratios, and read vs write miss ratios. The cache simulator kept separate track of all these miss ratios. Since the cache size is fairly large, the miss ratios are quite low, typically under 5%. In general, the user miss ratio is lower than the supervisor miss ratio, the instruction miss ratio is lower than the data miss ratio, and the read miss ratio is lower than the write miss ratio. The bar chart in Figure 4 plots miss ratios for 256 Kbyte caches. In general, the plotted data confirm that that user, instruction, and read references cache better than the coresponding supervisor, data and write references.

Figure 4 does show a few exceptions to that rule though. For the two processor Umax multiprogramming trace, the supervisor miss ratio was smaller, while the Ada benchmark showed a much lower write miss ratio than read miss ratio. In fact, the two

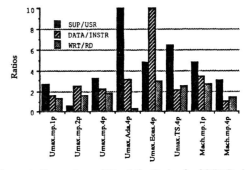

Figure 4: Comparison of Key Miss Ratios for 256K Caches

parallel program traces are markedly different from the other traces. The supervisor miss ratio for Ada was almost 40 times worse than the user miss ratio, while the data miss ratio for ECAS was almost 12 times worse than the instruction miss ratio (i.e. both columns are off the top end of the chart). The average supervisor miss to user miss ratio (ignoring Ada) was 3.7, the average data miss to instruction miss ratio (ignoring ECAS) was 2.3, and the average write miss to read miss ratio was 1.8.

It is often noted in articles on caches[2 8] that miss ratios for supervisor are worse than those for user execution (confirmed by these traces) and that supervisor execution can take up to 50% of the computer's execution time (confirmed by the two processor Umax multiprogramming trace). The conclusion is then reached that traces which only include user execution significantly overstate the hit ratio. But the traces discussed here hint that that conclusion is false, because the one trace which had a high fraction of supervisor references also had a very low supervisor miss ratio. Although a large number of traces would be needed to be sure, it appears that the low hit ratios normally associated with supervisor references are due to their low frequency, not a fundamental difference in cache behavior. As seen from the miss ratio curves of figure 3, all the multiprogramming workloads have similar miss ratios, indicating that differences in supervisor fraction are substantially offset by changes in supervisor hit ratio.

Simulation of Process Migration

In a multiprocessor, additional bus traffic is incurred due to sharing of data between caches. In fact, in the limit as caches reach infinite size, the steady state bus traffic would only be due to sharing effects. These sharing effects come about from two sources: actual sharing between processors executing parallel programs, and effective sharing due to process migration. While most researchers assume a static environment where a single parallel program is running on the multiprocessor, typical commercial multiprocessors see a timesharing workload with a mix of sequential and small parallel programs. In order to keep the workload evenly spread across all processors, migration of processes to under-utilized processors is necessary. The simplest approach is to use a common queue of active processes, with each processor drawing its work from the queue. Other studies have indicated that process migration results in sharing effects that are of the same magnitude as those inherent in the parallel algorithm[4]. This suggests that a multiprocessor designed to operate well when process migration is allowed should have no trouble handling real sharing.

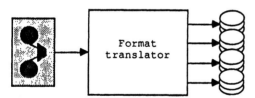

Figure 5: Scheme for Creating Multiple Parallel Traces from a Single Trace to Simulate Process Migration

Since traces were only collected from one processor, process migration had to be simulated. Since process migration occurs at context switch times, and context switching can be detected by observing supervisor mode instruction fetches to particular addresses, simulation of process migration is straightforward. In the Umax 4.2 operating system, processors share a common run queue, picking up a new process whenever the old process is stopped for I/O or its time slice has run out. This behavior was simulated by switching to a different output address trace file

every time a context switch was detected in the reference stream. The new output file that was picked was the one with the least number of references on it in order to keep the amount of simulated work roughly equal between all processors. The end result was that the original trace was split into two or four traces, as indicated in Figure 5.

By splitting the address trace in sections along context switch boundaries, individual processes out of the multiprocessing workload would migrate back and forth between the simulated processors. The effect is similar to that which would occur if a set of processors had been traced in parallel. The multiprogramming workloads had 10 separate programs, while the timesharing workload had 30, giving a high probability that different processes will be running on different simulated processors using the splitting methodology. With the two single parallel program workloads, the simulated process migration is more artificial. Therefore, only the multiprogramming and time shared workloads were split into parallel traces.

The one and two processor Umax multiprogramming workloads, the one processor Mach multiprogramming workload and the timesharing workload were all converted to multiple processor traces as described above. They were then fed into models of Encore's newest dual processor card, which utilizes National 32532 processors. As shown in Figure 6, the caching structure is a two level hierarchy, with small (1.5 Kbyte total) on chip caches and a large 256K byte private cache for each processor.

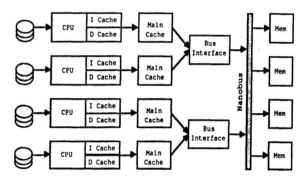

Figure 6: Simulation Models Used to Determine Effect of Process Migration on Cache Behavior

The 256Kbyte caches utilize an explicit ownership write-deferred caching protocol based on one used in the Synapse multiprocessor[3]. In such a protocol, caches use a special read request (called a read-private on Encore's Nanobus) to obtain exclusive ownership of the most recent copy of a location whenever modification of the location is desired. The location can then be modified repeatedly by the processor associated with the cache without any bus traffic. If the location is replaced or another cache requests a copy, the cached contents of the location are written back to main memory or sent to the requesting cache as appropriate.

Encore has extended this protocol with the addition of a "Shared" line on the bus, which indicates on each bus transaction whether other caches already have copies of the line. If no other copies exist, then the requesting cache will take ownership of the location, even if its processor has no intention of modifying the data. This avoids future read-privates for locations that are really not shared (such as stack locations). Of course, process migration will cause non-shared locations to appear shared, defeating this feature of the protocol. Simulations done by the

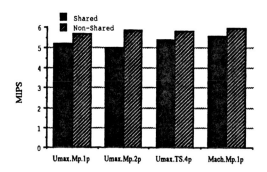

Figure 7: Performance of National 532 Based Processsors
With and Without Sharing Effects

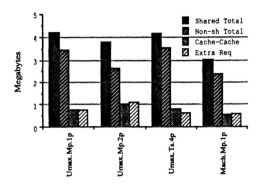

Figure 8: Bus Traffic as a Fraction of Processor Requests

author have shown that the share line can decrease bus traffic as much as 30% in the absence of process migration.

Both processors on a board share a single interface to communicate with the backplane bus. The caches operate independently, with all information transfers utilizing the backplane bus, even if the transfer is actually between caches on the same board. The simulation model records the bus traffic generated, which accurately reflects the traffic which would be generated in the actual multiprocessor system.

To see how much extra traffic is caused by the process migration induced sharing, simulations were done both with and without memory sharing. To disable memory sharing, each processor had its physical addresses mapped to a different area of main memory to preclude any overlap of addresses. The effect is equivelent to disabling snooping, giving "best case" values for traffic and hit ratios. When the non-shared values are subtracted from the shared values, the overhead caused by migration and cross invalidation is revealed.

Simulations of Commercial Processor Cards

Figure 7 shows the simulated processor performance in Vax MIPS achieved for each of the benchmarks. Two National 32532 based processor cards were simulated, for a total of four processors. While the single stream performance reaches 6 MIPS in some cases, there is a small drop in performance when the effects of sharing are included in the simulations. This drop is caused by increased effective memory latency due to increased cache misses and higher cache and bus interface utilization. Of course, the cache has a higher miss rate due to cross invalidations, but in addition there will be cases of writes to shared locations requiring the generation of a bus transaction to invalidate the other copies. Without the modeled sharing, these locations would become privately owned and not require further bus traffic. The higher cache and bus interface utilization comes about because of the extra bus requests just discussed, plus additional traffic necessary to pass data from one cache to another when one of the caches has the only valid copy.

Figure 8 shows the amount of bus traffic generated by a processor card as a function of the memory requests generated by the processor, in other words, the transfer ratio. The first bar in each graph is the transfer ratio for the shared memory case, while the second is the transfer ratio for the non-shared case. The difference in traffic is made up of transmissions of owned data to a another cache (the third bar), and extra requests caused by cache misses (the fourth bar). This graph plots megabytes of data transmitted over the duration of a simulation run. The actual bus

bandwidth utilization would depend on the speed of the bus and other implementation details.

The graph in Figure 8 shows that the amount of cache-to-cache transfers is about the same as the amount of extra traffic produced by cross invalidate caused misses. This approximate equivalence of cache-to-cache transfers and sharing caused traffic can be explained by the sequential nature of the process migration caused sharing being modeled here. When a process moves from one processor to another, many of the locations it owned for writing on the old processor will now be written to from the new processor. This will cause misses in the new cache and cache-to-cache transfers from the old. As the process migrates around the pool of processors, the sequence of misses satisfied by cache-to-cache transfers will repeat, resulting in roughly equal amounts of each.

In these simulations, the extra traffic due to sharing constituted about 1% of the original processor generated traffic. This sets a floor on the transfer rate of at least 1%, no matter how large the cache is made, which limits the maximum performance of a given shared bus multiprocessor. The amount of sharing traffic will not decrease with larger caches, and may even increase. This issue is explored in the next section.

Sensitivity of Sharing Traffic

The preceding section dealt with a fixed cache size (256K bytes) and a fixed number of processors (4). To see how sharing is affected by cache size and number of processors, the simulations were repeated for several values of each. First, the cache size was varied from 128K bytes to 1024K byte with the number of processors fixed at four. Next the number of processors was varied between one and four, with the cache size fixed at 1024K bytes. The larger number of processors and larger cache sizes were picked because they tend to expose the sharing effects more.

Figure 9 plots the amount of sharing caused traffic as a function of cache size for four of the address traces. In general, the sharing effects increase with increasing cache size. Since the replacement rate drops as the cache size is increased, there is a higher probability that a line will still be in the cache at the time a process returns to the cache's processor after migrating to other processors. However, locations in the process's address space which are written to while the process is on a different processor will be invalidated in the old caches. When the process returns to the original processor, these locations will have to be re-fetched, causing an increase in bus traffic over that which would exist in the absence of coherency.

263

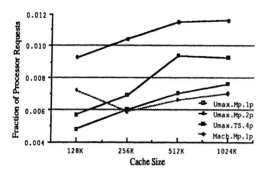

Figure 9: Invalidate Caused Traffic vs. Cache Size

The results shown in Figure 9 indicate that process migration caused sharing is approaching a limiting value as cache sizes increase. In fact, the simulated sharing behavior is the same for all cache sizes so the observed increase is really caused by the dropping intrinsic miss ratio. Figure 10 illustrates this more clearly for a particular address trace, the single processor, multiprogrammed trace under Umax. As the cache size increases, overall traffic drops appreciably, both with and without sharing effects. With the Encore protocol, cache-to-cache traffic does not require additional data bus bandwidth, so it is not included in the shared traffic reported in the top curve. With larger cache sizes, dirty lines are less likely to be written back to main memory before process migration causes their contents to be requested by another cache, so cache-to-cache transfers increase. The additional bus requests caused by the coherency protocol are broken into two component parts. Reads for locations caused by misses which would not have occurred in the absence of sharing (re-reads) and read-privates caused by writes to shared locations which would have been private without sharing (write-signals). The "shared" line included in the cache protocol causes all non-shared locations to be taken private, avoiding the need for a subsequent read-private. The number of re-reads increases with increasing cache size, as expected from the discussion above, while the number of write-signals is relatively constant (though it actually does increase slowly). Since a large fraction of writes are to the stack, and stacks have good locality, the behavior of writes is probably relatively insensitive to cache size.

Figures 9 and 10 indicate a process migration caused sharing of about 1% for the four processor simulations. But much larger numbers of processors are common with many multiprocessors. Splitting the present traces amongst more simulated processors probably would not work, because the length of each trace seen by each cache would be too short to exceed cold start, and because the number of independent processes in each trace was

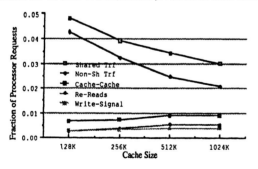

Figure 10: Bus Traffic Sources vs Cache Size for Umax.Mp.1p Trace

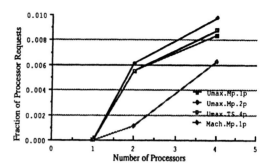

Figure 11: Cache to Cache Transfers vs. Number of Processors

only ten (or less with Mach). Splitting the traces into more than four pieces would result in an increasing potential of having two successive time slices of a process running simultaneously on different simulated cpus, causing a large amount of erroneous sharing as frequently written locations (such as those on the stack) are passed back and forth. In order to get some idea of the trends with increasing numbers of processors, however, one, two and four processor simulations were done.

Figure 11 plots the cache-to-cache transfers caused by process migration. The anomalous behavior of the Mach trace is evident with the extremely small amount of sharing reported for two processors. The Mach trace has fewer independent processes than the other multiprogramming traces, and may have resonated with the alternating placement of processes on the two simulated processors such that little actual process migration occurred. The three Umax traces of Figure 11 all show very similar trends, with an initial increment of cache-to-cache traffic of about 0.6% with two processors, rising to about 0.9% with four. The increase of 50% in cache-to-cache traffic between two and four processors corresponds to the increased probabilities or process migration. The model that fits the data is a burst of cache-to-cache transfers caused by process migration. With two processors, the probability of a process migration between time slices is 50%, it is 75% with four processes. Hence the amount of cache-to-cache traffic increases by 50% going from two to four processes, and should approach twice the value for two processors (1.2%) for large numbers of processors. Since a relatively fixed amount of cache-to-cache traffic seems to be produced by a process migration, increasing the time between process migrations (such as by increasing the time slice interval) will reduce the relative amount of cache-to-cache traffic.

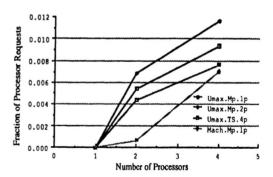

Figure 12: Invalidate Caused Traffic vs. Number of Processors

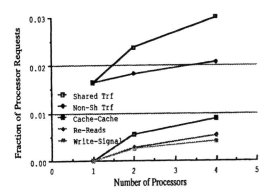

Figure 13: Bus Traffic Sources vs Number of Processors for
Umax.Mp.1p Trace

The extra traffic caused by sharing effects (re-reads due to invalidates and write-signals due to transfer of ownership) is plotted in Figure 12. Note a similar anomalous behavior for the two processor Mach simulation that was evident in Figure 11. The four processor simulations of all four traces are consistent, however. The extra traffic due to sharing effects increases more from two to four processors than with cache-to-cache transfers. The increase is about 70% for all three Umax traces.

A detailed break down of the sources of increased traffic for larger numbers of processors is shown in Figure 13 for the single processor, multiprogrammed Umax trace. Note that there is an increase in intrinsic miss caused traffic as the number of processors increases. There are two likely sources for this increase, process migration causing poorer locality and the shorter length of per processor address trace with the larger numbers of processors causing a larger cold start miss effect. The true, sharing caused increase in traffic is the difference between the shared and non-shared curves. As with Figure 10, the components of shared traffic are broken into cache-to-cache, re-read and write-signal portions. The behavior of cache-to-cache sharing has already been discused with figure 11. The reason that sharing caused excess traffic increases faster than cache-to-cache sharing is indicated in Figure 13, where the re-read component is seen to increase by 90%, while the write-signals only increase by 50%. While write-signals fit the burst of traffic at process migration time model, invalidates of data, which cause re-reads are more pervasive. This component of traffic may become a significant factor with large numbers of processors.

The above analysis indicates that larger caches than one megabye can still reduce bus traffic, but sharing caused traffic is beginning to become a significant fraction of the total bus traffic. Most of the components of this process migration caused traffic are proportional to the frequency of process migration, and can be reduced through control of such migration. However, re-reads seem to increase faster with numbers of processors than just the amount of process migration, which may further restrict the perfomance of large systems.

Conclusions

These trace studies have been quite encouraging for the construction of large, shared bus multiprocessors. They show that large caches do provide significant reductions in bus traffic under real system workloads. Further, while traffic due to sharing effects puts upper limits on the performance achievable with share memory multiprocessors, at least one component (the process migration component) is low enough to allow substantial performance. While process migration is necessary to balance system workloads, a scheduling policy which reduces such migration through processor-process affinity would substantially reduce the sharing traffic. The upper limit to processor performance on a shared bus multiprocessor (100 MBytes/sec bus bandwidth) due to typical process migration as determined by these experiments would be 800 MIPS, provided I/O is ignored. Since both I/O and extra traffic due to intrinsic sharing are expected, the practical limit will probably be around 300 MIPS. Other techniques, such as those presented in[10], or faster busses will be necessary to break that limit.

The amount of simulated context switching may have been overstated by these experiments. The time slicing portion of context switching in these program traces was done every 100 milliseconds at 32032 speeds, which would be every 14 milliseconds at 32532 speeds. Since actual timeslicing will remain at 100 milliseconds, the actual amount of process migration will be less than that reported here.

The lock behavior results are also encouraging. They show that programs can be written in such a way that frequent lock contention does not occur. Of course, it does require some effort to do this, and programs such as ECAS which have not had the effort spent may experience considerable lock contention. Since high lock contention will produce lots of bus traffic, techniques which can reduce lock contention are highly desired.

Acknowledgments

The author would like to thank the following colleagues for their assistance in obtaining the address traces: Jeff Price for designing the trace collection hardware, Terry Kelleher and Alan Langerman for developing the necessary system software, and Peter Fay for helping to collect and run the workload programs.

References

[1] Agarwal, A., and Sites, R.L., "Multiprocessor Cache Analysis Using ATUM", In *Proceedings of the 15th Annual Symposium on Computer Architecture*, pp 186-195, June 1988.

[2] Agarwal, A., Sites, R.L., and Horowitz, M., "ATUM: A New Technique for Capturing Address Traces Using Microcode", In *Proceedings of the 13th Annual Symposium on Computer Architecture*, June 1986, pp 119-127.

[3] Frank, S.J., "A Tightly Coupled Multiprocessor System Speeds Memory-Access Times," *Electronics* 164-169, January, 1984.

[4] Goodman, J.R., "Using Cache Memory to Reduce Processor-Memory Traffic," in *10th Annual Symposium on Computer Architecture*. 1983.

[5] Siewiorek, D.P., Bell, C.G., and Newell, A., "Computer Structure: Principles and Examples", McGraw-Hill 1982, pp 675-677.

[6] Siewiorek, D.P., Anzelmo, A., and Moore, R., "Multiprocessor Computers Expand User Vistas", *Computer Design*, pp. 70-75, August 15, 1985.

[7] Smith, A.J., "Cache Evaluation and the Impact of Workload Choice", In *Proceedings of the 12th Annual Symposium on Computer Architecture*, June 1985, pp 64-73.

[8] Smith, A.J., "Cache Memories", ACM Computing Surveys, Vol. 14, No. 3, September, 1982, pp. 473-530.

[9] Sweazey, P. and Smith, A.J., "A Class of Compatible Cache Consistency Protocols and Their Support by the IEEE Futurebus", The 13th Annual International Symposium on Computer Architecture, pp. 414-423, June, 1986.

[10] Wilson, A.W., "Hierarchical Cache / Bus Architecture for Shared Memory Multiprocessors", In *Proceedings of the 14th Annual Computer Architecture Conference*, June 1987, pp 244-252.

[11] Wilson, A.W., "Parallelization of an Event Driven Simulator for Computer Systems Simulation", *Simulation*, Volume 49, Number 2, August 1987, pp. 72-78.

Cache Invalidation Patterns in Shared-Memory Multiprocessors

Anoop Gupta and Wolf-Dietrich Weber

Abstract—For constructing large-scale shared-memory multiprocessors, researchers are currently exploring cache coherence protocols that do not rely on broadcast, but instead send invalidation messages to individual caches that contain stale data. The feasibility of such directory-based protocols is highly sensitive to the cache invalidation patterns exhibited by parallel programs. In this paper, we analyze the cache invalidation patterns of several parallel applications. Our results are based on multiprocessor simulations with 8, 16, and 32 processors. To provide deeper insight into the observed invalidation behavior, we link the invalidations seen in the simulations to the high-level objects causing them in the programs. To predict what the invalidation patterns would look like beyond 32 processors, we propose a classification scheme for data objects found in parallel programs. The classification scheme provides a powerful conceptual tool to reason about the invalidation patterns of parallel applications. Our results indicate that it should be possible to scale "well-written" parallel programs to a large number of processors without an explosion in invalidation traffic. At the same time, the invalidation patterns are such that directory-based schemes with just a few pointers per entry can be very effective. The paper also explores the variations in invalidation behavior with different cache line sizes. The results indicate that cache line sizes in the 32-byte range yield the lowest data and invalidation traffic.

Index Terms— Cache coherence, cache invalidation patterns, memory traffic, parallel application behavior, shared-memory multiprocessors.

I. INTRODUCTION

A critical issue in the design of shared-memory multiprocessors is the cache coherence strategy. Most existing multiprocessors [10], [15], [19], [25] rely on a shared bus and use a broadcast-based snoopy protocol to keep the caches coherent [12], [20], [22]. However, such multiprocessors are not scalable, since the shared bus soon becomes a bottleneck. As an alternative, researchers have again started looking at cache coherence protocols that do not rely on broadcast, a common example being directory-based protocols [2], [5], [14]. In directory-based protocols the system maintains state about which caches have a copy of each memory block. On a write, invalidation messages are sent only to those specific caches that contain the memory block. The performance of directory-based protocols depends critically on the distribution

Manuscript received September 15, 1989; revised May 5, 1991. A. Gupta and W.-D. Weber are supported by DARPA Contracts N00014-87-K-0828 and N00039-91-C-0138. In addition, A. Gupta is supported by an NSF Presidential Young Investigator Award, and W.-D. Weber is supported by an IBM graduate fellowship.

A. Gupta and W.-D. Weber are with the Computer Systems Laboratory, Stanford University, CA 94305. The electronic mail addresses are gupta@cs.stanford.edu and lupus@sambal.stanford.edu, respectively.

IEEE Log Number 9200197.

of the number of remote caches that need to be invalidated on shared writes. The invalidation distribution is also vital in determining the viability of directory schemes that provide only a limited set of pointers per directory entry [2]. In this paper we investigate the distribution of invalidations, how it relates to data objects in the application, and how it is affected by changes in the number of processors and the cache line size.

Our study is based on the invalidation traffic produced by a set of five application programs. Four of the five applications selected are "real" parallel programs, in that they solve real-world problems and significant effort has gone into obtaining good processor efficiency with them. (These four are also part of the SPLASH parallel applications suite [23].) The remaining application (Maxflow) is smaller, but it is still interesting in that it could form the kernel of larger applications. Our results are based on memory reference streams obtained from the above applications when running with 8, 16, and 32 simulated processors.

While it is valuable to know the invalidation distributions with the relatively small numbers of processors that we can simulate realistically, our ultimate goal is to build machines with hundreds or even thousands of processors [14]. Toward this goal of predicting the invalidation distributions for a much larger number of processors, we link the observed invalidation patterns to the high-level program data structures (objects) that cause them, and present a classification of such objects on the basis of their expected invalidation behavior. We find that it is far more accurate to extrapolate the behavior of each class of data object than to simply extrapolate the composite behavior of an application. For the application types we have considered, our results indicate that it is quite possible to write parallel programs for which the invalidation traffic does not explode as the number of processors is increased. Our results also indicate that directory-based schemes with just three to four pointers per entry should work quite well for executing well-designed parallel programs.

The paper also explores the variations in invalidation behavior and memory system traffic with different cache line sizes. We explore cache line sizes between 4 and 256 bytes. As cache lines are increased in length, we observe a slight shift of invalidation patterns to larger invalidations. With an increase in line size, we also find that the data traffic generally goes up, the coherence traffic comes down, and that the overall traffic is minimum (or close to minimum) when the line size is 32 bytes.

The remainder of the paper is structured as follows. The next section explains our simulation environment and assumptions.

Section III introduces the five applications used in this study and gives a brief overview of their computational behavior. In Section IV we present the basic memory reference characteristics of the applications. Section V presents the proposed classification of shared data objects in parallel programs. In Section VI we provide a detailed analysis of the invalidation behavior of each application and relate the invalidation patterns to specific data objects in the applications. Section VII presents results obtained from experimenting with different cache line sizes. Finally, Section VIII summarizes the results and presents conclusions.

II. SIMULATION ENVIRONMENT

We use a simulated multiprocessor environment to study the behavior of the applications. The simulation environment consists of two parts: 1) a functional simulator that executes the parallel applications and 2) an architectural simulator that models the memory system of the multiprocessor.

The functional simulator used for this study is the Tango multiprocessor reference generator [7]. The Tango system takes a parallel application program and interleaves the execution of its processes on a uniprocessor to simulate a multiprocessor. This is achieved by associating a virtual timer with each process of the application and by always running the process with the lowest virtual time first.

Our architecture simulator assumes shared memory partitioned among the processing nodes, infinite caches, and a directory-based cache-coherence protocol. We have made no special effort to assign a processor's data to memory that is physically close to that processor. Memory pages are simply assigned to memory modules using the lower bits of the virtual page number. Infinite caches are used in the simulator to enable us to study data-sharing effects without any distortions introduced by finite-sized caches. The cache coherence protocol used is an invalidation-based scheme similar to that used by the Stanford DASH multiprocessor [14]. Except when specifically studying the effects of varying the cache line size, the default line size used is 4 bytes. In order to keep the simulator simple and architecture independent, we further assume that all instructions execute in a single cycle.

The simulator gathers statistics on invalidation behavior and message traffic. It also keeps track of each shared write by source code file and line number. This allows us to link the invalidation behavior observed back to the high-level language objects causing it. To observe the behavior of synchronization objects, statistics on locks are maintained by address. At each unlock operation, the number of processors waiting to obtain the lock is recorded. Because of Tango, our current simulation environment is significantly more efficient than the trace-driven environment used in our previous study [27]. We are thus able to run entire programs and can capture the complete invalidation behavior of the applications.

As Torrellas et al. observed [26], the level of compiler optimization makes a significant difference to the ratio between shared and private memory references in an application. Consequently, for this study, all applications were compiled with optimization level 2 (-O2) using the Mips Computer Systems C compiler (version 1.31).

III. APPLICATION PROGRAMS

In this section we describe the data structures and computational behavior of the applications. This is important background for Section VI, where we relate invalidation traffic to high-level objects. The applications were selected to represent a variety of algorithms used in an engineering computing environment. All of the applications are written in C and use the Argonne National Laboratory macro package [16], [17] for synchronization and sharing primitives. The synchronization primitives used include locks and barriers. Further details about four of five the applications can be found in the SPLASH report [23].

A. Maxflow

Maxflow finds the maximum flow in a directed graph. This is a common problem in operations research and many other fields. The program is a parallel implementation of an algorithm proposed by Goldberg and Tarjan [11]. The bulk of execution time in Maxflow is spent in picking activated nodes from the graph, adjusting the flow along these nodes' incoming and outgoing edges, and then activating their successor nodes. Maxflow exploits parallelism at a fine grain.

Maxflow does not assign the nodes of the graph to processors statically. Instead, task queues are used to distribute the load. Each processor has its own local task queue and needs to go to the single global task queue only when its local queue is empty. Tasks are put on to the global queue only when processors are waiting there, and on to the local queue otherwise. Note that the task queues are made up of the nodes themselves, linked together with appropriate pointers. Locks are used to serialize access to each node element, but contention for these is fairly low as there are many more nodes than processors. In Section VI we will see that most cache invalidations are related to the global task queue and the migration of node and edge data from one processor to another. We used a graph with 400 nodes, arranged as a 20x20 grid, for our studies.

B. MP3D

MP3D [18] simulates a three-dimensional wind tunnel using particle-based techniques. It is used to study the shock waves created as an object flies at high speed through the upper atmosphere. A version of MP3D that runs on the Cray-2 is being used extensively at NASA for research.

The overall computation of MP3D consists of evaluating the positions and velocities of molecules over a sequence of time steps, and gathering relevant statistics. During each time step, molecules are picked up and moved according to their velocity vectors, taking into account collisions with the boundaries and other molecules. The main data structures consist of a particle array and a space array. The *particle array* holds the molecules and records their positions, velocities, and other attributes. The *space array* corresponds to a fine grid imposed on the three-dimensional space being modeled. Attributes of the space-array cells specify the boundaries of the tunnel and the location of the physical object. The space array is also used to determine collision partners for molecules and to keep track of statistics (e.g., density and energy of molecules) about the physical space it models.

The simulator is well suited to parallelization because each molecule can be treated independently at each time step. In our program, the molecules are assigned statically to the processors. No locking is employed while accessing cells in the space array as contention is expected to be rare, and occasional errors can be tolerated due to the statistical nature of the computation. A single lock protects the global number of collisions counter. The only other synchronization used is a barrier, which is invoked between the different phases of the program. There are six barrier invocations per time step. MP3D was run for 5 time steps with 10000 molecules and a 14x24x7 space array containing a flat plate object.

C. Water

Water [4] performs an N-body molecular dynamics simulation of the forces and potentials in a system of water molecules. It is used to predict some of the physical properties of water in the liquid state.

The main data structure in Water is a large array of records that is used to store the state of each molecule. As in MP3D, the molecules are statically split among the processors. During each time step, the processors calculate the interaction of the atoms within each molecule, and of the molecules with each other. For each molecule, the owning processor calculates the interactions with only half of the molecules ahead of it in the array. Since the forces between the molecules are symmetric, each pairwise interaction between molecules is thus considered only once. The state associated with the molecules is then updated. We note that while some portions of the molecule state are modified at each interaction, others are changed only between time steps. There are also several variables holding global properties that are updated continuously. Water was run for 2 time steps with 288 molecules.

D. PTHOR

PTHOR [24] is a parallel logic simulator developed at Stanford University. It uses a conservative distributed-time simulation algorithm which is a modified version of the Chandy–Misra algorithm [6].

The primary data structures associated with the simulator are the logic elements (e.g., AND-gates, flip-flops), the nets (the wires linking the elements), and the task queues which contain activated elements. Each element has a preferred task queue to increase data locality. PTHOR alternates between two distinct phases: element evaluation and deadlock resolution. During element evaluation, each processor executes the following loop. It removes an activated element from its task queue (activation list) and determines the changes on the element's outputs. It then looks up the net data structure to determine elements that are affected by the output change and potentially schedules those elements on to other processors' task queues. When a processor's task queue is empty, it steals elements

from other processors' task queues. When all activation lists are empty, a simulation deadlock has been reached and is resolved in a separate phase. During this deadlock resolution phase, more elements are activated. PTHOR was run for a simple RISC processor circuit with 5060 logic elements for 10 clock cycles.

E. LocusRoute

LocusRoute [21] is a global router for VLSI standard cells. It has been used to design real integrated circuits, and offers a high-quality routing.

The LocusRoute program exploits parallelism by routing multiple wires in a circuit concurrently. Each processor executes the following loop: it picks a wire to route from the task queue; it then explores alternative routes; and finally it chooses the best route and places the wire there. The central data structure used in LocusRoute is a grid of cells called the *cost array*. Each row of the cost array corresponds to a routing channel for standard cells. LocusRoute uses the cost array to record the presence of wires at each point, and the congestion of a route is used as a cost function for guiding the placement of new wires. No locking is needed in the cost array, which is accessed and updated simultaneously by several processors, because the effect of occasional contention is tolerable. Each routing task is of a fairly large grain size, which prevents the task queue from becoming a bottleneck. For this study we used the Primary1 circuit consisting of 1266 wires and a 481x18 cell cost array.

IV. PROGRAM CHARACTERISTICS

Table I gives an overview of the characteristics of the five applications when run with 32 processors. For each application, we give the number of data references and the breakdown in terms of reads and writes. We also show the number of shared reads and shared writes. In addition to absolute numbers, the columns also list the number of references in each category as a fraction of all data references. The last two columns give the average number of invalidations caused by each invalidating write, and the number of invalidating writes per 1000 data references. Invalidating writes correspond to write hits to clean data and write misses.

In our study, private and shared references are distinguished as follows. Each application shares data between processes by placing it in a special shared data space. We define *shared blocks* to be those that are in the shared data space. We define *shared references* to be reads and writes to shared blocks. We note that depending on the task distribution strategy used and the dynamics of a particular run, it is possible that some shared blocks are referenced by only one process during the entire run.

From Table I, we see that the proportion of reads and writes is similar to what one might expect in uniprocessor programs—the fraction of reads varies from 62% in MP3D to 83% in LocusRoute. The statistics for shared references, however, vary considerably from application to application. For example, the ratio between shared reads and writes varies from about 1.5:1 for MP3D to about 9:1 for LocusRoute. Overall, considering all applications, shared reads are greatly favored

TABLE I
GENERAL APPLICATION CHARACTERISTICS

Application	num of CPUs	data refs mill	reads mill	reads %	writes mill	writes %	shared reads mill	shared reads %	shared writes mill	shared writes %	avg. invals per inv-write	inv-writes per 1000 refs
Maxflow	32	25.5	18.5	72	7.0	28	12.5	49	2.2	8	1.4	58
MP3D	32	2.3	1.4	62	0.9	38	1.0	46	0.7	30	1.0	221
Water	32	48.0	34.1	71	13.9	29	7.1	15	1.0	2	1.2	11
PTHOR	32	16.6	13.5	81	3.1	19	7.2	43	0.9	5	1.5	32
LocusRoute	32	18.5	15.3	83	3.2	17	8.7	47	1.0	5	1.6	27

over shared writes as compared to uniprocessor programs. As another example, the fraction of shared references varies from about 17% for Water to about 76% for MP3D.[1] In Water, each interaction between molecules requires a fair amount of local calculation. Thus updates to the states of the molecules are relatively infrequent, and the fraction of shared references is very low. In MP3D, on the other hand, most of the data manipulation occurs directly on the shared data, and hence the proportion of shared references is large. While these variations are not unexpected, since they depend closely on the nature of the application and the way in which it is parallelized, they are indicative of the variety in the applications being evaluated.

The second to last column in Table I gives the average number of invalidations per invalidating write. This number is an important metric for directory-based cache coherence schemes because a large value indicates the need for many pointers per directory entry. As we can see, this number is less than two for all applications, even though all runs are with 32 processors. The last column of Table I gives the average number of invalidating writes per 1000 data references. The product of the entries in the last two columns is a good indicator of the amount of invalidation traffic that an application is expected to generate per unit time. We only give average numbers here, and these look quite favorable. However, averages are limited in the information they provide. Consequently, we provide detailed invalidation distributions and their analysis in Section VI.

V. CLASSIFICATION OF DATA OBJECTS

In this section we present our classification of data objects based on invalidation behavior. The classification allows us to explain a given application's invalidation distribution in terms of the underlying high-level data structures of that application. More importantly, it represents a model that enables us to predict the application's invalidation behavior for much larger number of processes than is feasible for us to simulate. We propose to distinguish the following classes of objects:

1) Code and read-only data objects.
2) Migratory objects.
3) Mostly-read objects.
4) Frequently read/written objects.

[1] The fraction of references that are to shared data is somewhat larger than that reported by Eggers [8]. This is most likely due to the fact that we are compiling with the −O2 flag, which tends to reduce local references through register allocation.

5) Synchronization objects.

 • low-contention synchronization objects
 • high-contention synchronization objects

Code and read-only data objects: These objects do not generally pose a problem to directory schemes because they are written only once at the time when the relevant page is first brought into memory, or when the data are initialized. Invalidations are hence *very* infrequent. A fixed database is a good example of read-only data.

Migratory data objects: These objects are manipulated by only one processor at any given time. Shared objects protected by locks often exhibit this property. While such an object is being manipulated by a processor, the object's data resides in the associated cache. When the object is later manipulated by some other processor, the corresponding cache entries in the previous processor are invalidated. Migratory objects occur frequently in parallel programs. The nodes in Maxflow are a good example of migratory data. Each node is looked at by several processors over the complete run, but there is only one processor manipulating each node at any one time. Migratory data usually cause a high proportion of *single* invalidations, irrespective of the number of processors working on the problem.

Mostly-read data objects: These objects are read most of the time, and written only every now and then. An example is the cost array of LocusRoute. It is read frequently, but written only when the best route for a wire is decided. It is a candidate for many invalidations per write, because many reads by different processors occur before each write. However, since only the writes cause invalidations and writes are infrequent, the overall number of invalidations is expected to be quite small.

Frequently read/written objects: These objects are *both* read and written frequently. Although each write causes only a small number of invalidations, writes occur frequently, and so the total number of invalidations can be quite large. An example of a frequently read/written object is the variable that holds the number of processors waiting on the global task queue in Maxflow. It is continually checked by all processes, and is updated whenever a process starts or stops waiting on the global task queue.

Synchronization objects: These objects correspond to the synchronization primitives used in parallel programs, the most frequent examples being locks and barriers. We further divide synchronization objects into two categories, low-contention and high-contention objects, since these two exhibit different invalidation behavior. Low-contention synchronization objects, such as distributed locks that protect access to a collection of shared data objects, usually have very few or no processes waiting on them. As a result, most often they cause zero or a very small number of invalidations. Low-contention locks are thus easy to implement and optimize for in directory-based multiprocessors. High-contention synchronization objects, on the other hand, usually cause frequent invalidations, and the invalidations may be large if there are many contending processes. A lock protecting a highly contended task queue would be an example of such an object. If high-contention locks are treated like regular data objects in limited-pointer directories, their invalidation behavior can have a severe impact on machine performance. Some combination of software techniques (e.g., synchronization trees [28]) and hardware techniques (e.g., queueing lock primitives [13]) are probably required to efficiently support high-contention synchronization objects.

Bennett et al. [3] expand the classification of data objects proposed in our earlier paper [27]. They use their classification to perform adaptive software cache management on distributed shared memory machines. The reason for a finer division of objects is that some differences in object behavior are important to a software cache coherence protocol, while they make no difference in invalidation behavior. For example, the invalidation behavior of Bennett's *producer/consumer* and *read-mostly* types will be indistinguishable for the case of multiple consumers.

VI. APPLICATION CASE STUDIES

In this section we present the results of the detailed analysis of the invalidation traces produced by the applications. For each application, we discuss the overall invalidation patterns, the high-level objects causing the invalidations, the synchronization behavior, and the predicted invalidation behavior beyond 32 processors.

The overall invalidation behavior is presented in terms of a series of graphs as shown in Fig. 1. Parts (a), (c) and (d) are the invalidation distribution graphs for 8, 16, and 32 processors, respectively. These graphs show what proportion of invalidating writes cause 0, 1, 2, or more invalidations.

We distinguish between *large* invalidations and *frequent* invalidations. A large invalidation is caused by a write to a line that is cached by many processors. Frequent invalidations are caused by frequent writes and need not necessarily be large invalidations. Ideally, the invalidation distribution graphs should contain a large proportion of small invalidations, as these can be handled efficiently by directory-based cache schemes. By comparing the invalidation distributions for 8, 16, and 32 processor runs, we can begin to get a feeling for how the invalidations scale with a larger number of processors.

For the 32-processor run we give additional information. Part (e) gives the proportion of reads, writes, shared reads, and shared writes. Part (f) breaks invalidating writes and invalidations down by important data objects found in the application. Part (g) shows the composition of the invalidation distribution of part (d). Each bar of (d) is normalized to 100

and broken down into its data object components. We are thus able to tell, for example, that invalidating writes causing 31 invalidations in Maxflow (0.1% of all invalidating writes) are made up of 80% writes to global values and 20% writes to edge elements of the graph being manipulated [Fig. 1 (g)].

Finally, part (b) presents the synchronization behavior for the 32-processor run. The graph shows the distribution of waiters at all *unlock* operations. For example, low-contention locks should show a very small number of waiters at each unlock operation. Note that the distribution of waiters in these graphs is shown only for locks, since the behavior of waiting processes at barriers depends strongly on the particular barrier implementation chosen (for example, tree-structured versus flat releases). We indicate the number of unlock operations and the number of barriers encountered in text on the graphs.

A. Maxflow

From Figs. 1(a), (c), and (d) we see that a large fraction of the invalidations in Maxflow are single invalidations. These are mostly caused by the manipulation of node and edge data structures, portions of which are good examples of migratory data. What happens is as follows. One processor picks up an active node and pushes flow through it. Later, when the node is reactivated, some other processor picks it up and starts processing it, thus causing a single invalidation. Sometimes, however, the node gets picked up by the same processor as before, in which case we do not see any invalidating writes, because the node data is most likely still in the processor's cache. The likelihood of the same processor picking up a node, however, decreases as more processors are added, and this results in more invalidating writes. The trend is quite clear as one moves from part (a) to (c) to (d) of Fig. 1. The invalidating writes go from 0.93 M to 1.17 M to 1.48 M.

As the number of processors is increased, we also observe that the invalidation distribution slowly shifts to larger invalidations. While with 8 processors only about 9% of shared writes cause more than one invalidation, this figure moves up to 15% with 32 processors. There are three types of data objects causing this shift: 1) data associated with the global task queue, 2) node labels, and 3) edge link pointers. All of these fall into the frequently read/written category. We now consider each of these in turn.

The count of the number of processors waiting for the global task queue to become nonempty is checked frequently by all processors. It is also written frequently, namely whenever a process starts waiting on the global task queue. For the 32-processor run, it has an average of 6 invalidations per invalidating write and the highest number of shared writes to any single data object. The global task queue pointer is a close second. The above two categories are combined in Figs. 1(f) and (g) under *global values*. Here we see, for example, that close to 80% of the writes causing invalidations in all 31 other processors can be attributed to these two data objects.

Node labels are constantly read as processors push flow through nodes, and are also frequently modified. Edge link pointers are traversed whenever flow across an edge is examined, and they are modified whenever an edge becomes

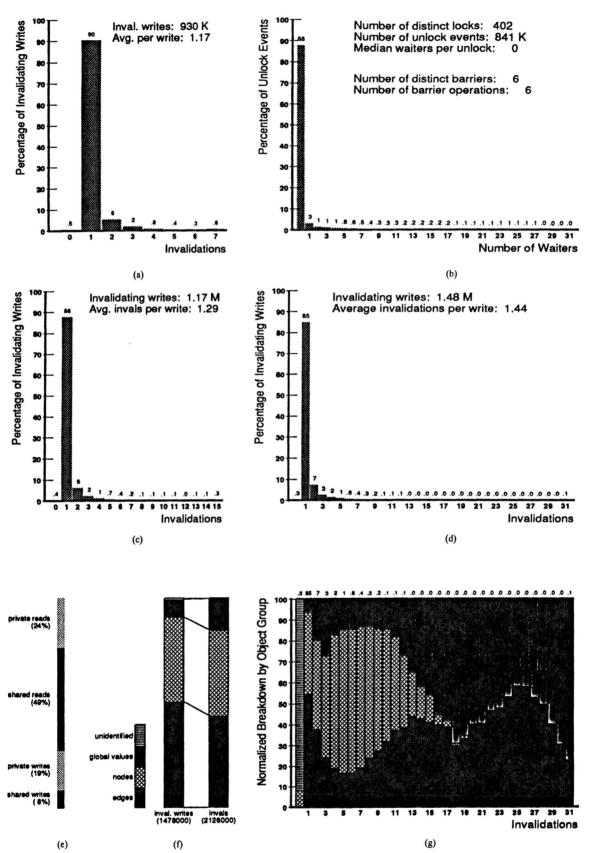

Fig. 1. Behavior of Maxflow.

active or inactive. Since edges connect different nodes, and different nodes are examined by different processors, there are always many different processors traversing the edge lists and modifying the pointers. The node labels and edge link pointers account for most of the increase in small invalidations as we increase the number of processors.

Fig. 1(b) shows the synchronization behavior of Maxflow. There are 402 locks total. Of these, 400 are *distributed* locks, one for each of the 400 graph nodes. These are accessed frequently, but there is very little contention for them. These distributed locks are an excellent example of low-contention locks. The remaining two locks are used to protect access to the global task queue and the variable that counts the number of processors blocked on the global task queue. These two locks incur significant contention and are responsible for the "tail" of large number of waiters in Fig. 1(b). The average number of waiters for these two locks is about 5. We note that there are also six barriers that are exercised once each during the run of the program.

We now use the object classification to see how the invalidation distributions are expected to change as the number of processors is scaled. We expect little change in the invalidations produced by the migratory portions of the graph node and edge structures. They should continue to produce the single invalidations typical of migratory data. The global task queue pointer and block count, on the other hand, are frequently read/written data and are expected to have an increasing average number of invalidations per write. This is also true for the node labels and edge pointers. In addition, we expect to see more waiters at the global queue locks as contention for them increases. If the program is to scale well as number of processors is increased, we must reduce contention for the global task queue and we must partition the graph so that the number of processors sharing the frequently read/written node label and edge pointer objects is small.

B. MP3D

Figs. 2(a), (c), and (d) show the invalidation distributions for the MP3D program, the 3-D particle-based simulator. Here again the distributions are dominated by single invalidations. However, as we increase the number of processors, the invalidation distributions remain essentially the same.

Most accesses to shared data by MP3D consist of updating the properties of a given particle or space array entry. This results in a sequence of reads closely followed by writes to the same locations. Depending on whether the data object was previously accessed by the same processor or not, either a single invalidation or no invalidations result. These data behave in a migratory fashion, with each interval of active use being very short.

From part (g) of Fig. 2 we see that most of the larger invalidations are due to a variable that keeps track of the average probability of collision for each cell in the three-dimensional space array. This variable is read by different processors during a time step as they decide whether or not a collision occurred. It is updated only between time steps. There are also a few global properties that are read by every

processor but again are updated only between time steps. Both of these object groups fall into the mostly-read category.

Part (b) of Fig. 2 shows the synchronization behavior of MP3D. Work is distributed statically in MP3D, and there is very little synchronization overhead. The distribution of waiting processes in Fig. 2(b) is entirely due to one lock that protects the access to a set of global counters. After every time-step each processor updates the global count with its own local count.

The effect of the mostly-read data found in MP3D is minor because of the low frequency of writes to this data. The remaining data behave strictly migratory and we thus expect little change in the invalidation distribution of MP3D as it is scaled to a larger number of processors.

C. Water

Figs. 3(a), (c), and (d) show the invalidation distributions for the Water code. The distributions are made up almost entirely of single invalidations. There is only a slight increase in the number of invalidating writes and in the average invalidations per write as the number of processors is increased.

The main data structure in the Water code is a large array of records, one for each water molecule. Most of the time is spent calculating the pairwise interaction of molecules. At the end of each interaction, a portion of the state of the two molecules is updated. This portion of the molecule data is migratory, and causes only single invalidations. There is another portion of the molecule record that is also read while computing the pairwise interactions, but it is updated only between time steps. Since the molecules allocated to a processor interact with only half of all the other molecules (see Section III-C), at the end of each time step half of the processors have cached this mostly-read data. Consequently the update causes invalidations to half the total number of processors. Part (g) of Fig. 3 illustrates this clearly.

There are also a small number of variables that hold global properties of the water molecule system. These again fall into the mostly-read category. They are read by all processors throughout, and updated between time steps. At each update, invalidations are sent to all processors.

There is very little synchronization in Water, since the work is partitioned statically. There is a set of distributed locks, one for each molecule, and a small number of individual locks to protect the updates of global values. There is very little contention for the distributed locks. While there is some contention for the update of the global values, contention is low enough that it is not a factor in the overall lock waiter distribution [see Fig. 3(b)].

We do not expect the invalidation distribution of the Water code to change significantly as the number of processors is increased, because most of the data is migratory. The mostly-read structures are written very infrequently and thus cause only minor increases in the average number of invalidations per invalidating write.

D. PTHOR

Figs. 4(a), (c), and (d) show the invalidation distributions

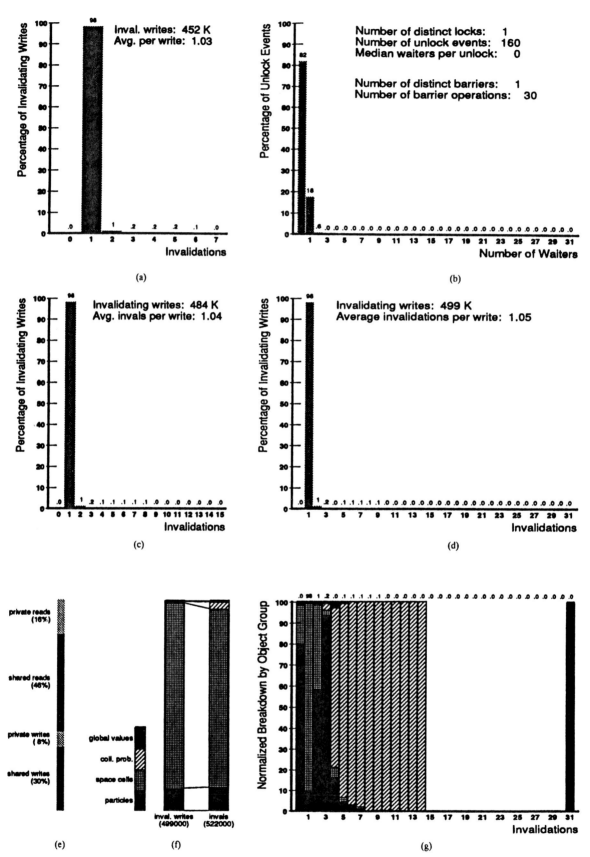

Fig. 2. Behavior of MP3D.

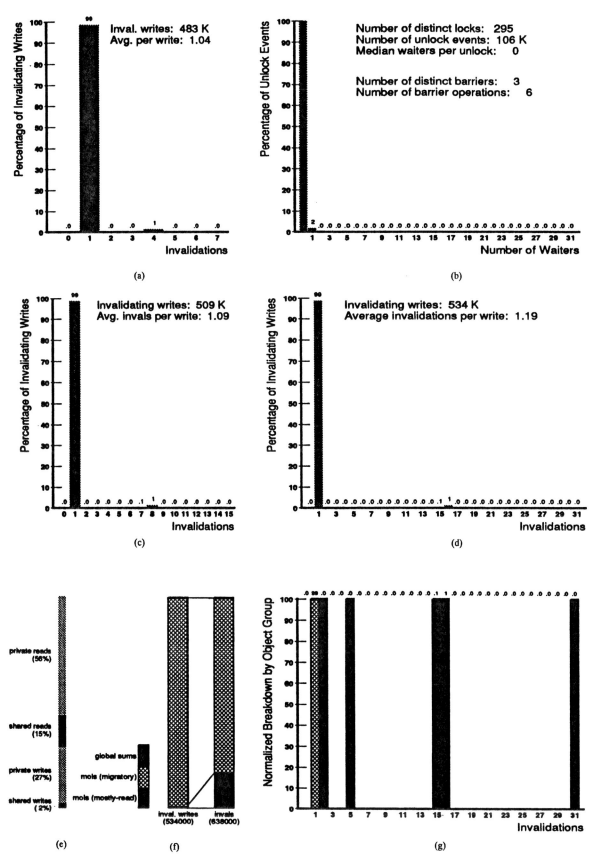

Fig. 3.   Behavior of Water.

275

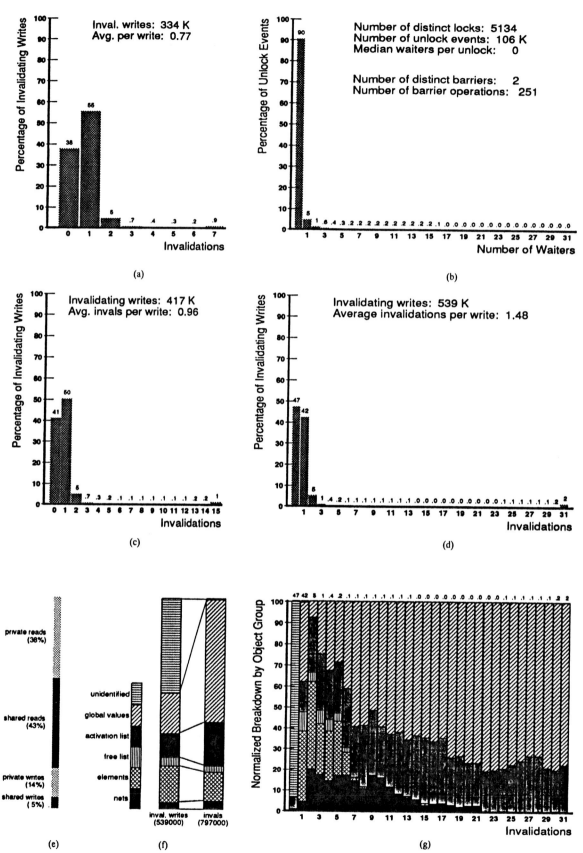

Fig. 4. Behavior of PTHOR.

for PTHOR. We again find that very few of the shared writes cause large invalidations. The basic data objects of PTHOR are the logic elements and net data structures.

In PTHOR, sharing of net data is determined by the connectivity of the circuit. Some nets, such as the clock net, are attached to many elements. They are thus cached by many processors and cause large invalidations when written. Typically though, most nets connect only a few elements and writes to them cause a small number of invalidations.

During the program run, the logic elements behave like migratory objects and we mostly see single invalidations. Some portions of the element data structure, however, are not modified by every processor that references them. These "longer-lived" values, such as the minimum valid time of an element, fit into the mostly-read category and result in larger invalidations when they are updated.

The head pointers of the free lists for data structures are usually migratory. However, the head pointer is checked before taking an item off a given free list. If the list is empty, many processors could cache the head pointer and it becomes mostly-read for a short phase.

The large invalidations in PTHOR are due to mostly-read global data objects. Common examples are the heads of the activation lists (task queues), and the count of number of processors waiting for the deadlock phase. These are checked frequently by most processors, but are changed relatively infrequently. Link pointers in the activation list also fall into the mostly-read category.

Most of the zero invalidations are caused when the element and net data structures are initialized, in parallel, at the beginning of the run.

The synchronization behavior shown in Fig. 4(b) is dominated by element locks. These distributed locks show very little contention. Most of the time there are no waiters when an unlock occurs. The larger number of waiters at unlock operations are almost all due to a single lock that is used to protect the count of processors that have reached the deadlock phase of the Chandy–Misra simulation algorithm.

As the number of processors is scaled, we expect that the invalidations produced by the element data structures would not increase, since they act as migratory objects. The invalidation patterns due to the net data structures should also not change (beyond a point) as the connectivity of the circuit remains the same. We expect larger average invalidations per invalidating write for the mostly-read global objects and the activation list link pointers. Overall, we expect a steady shift of the invalidation distribution toward larger invalidations, unless new locality-enhancing heuristics are added.

E. LocusRoute

Parts (a), (c), and (d) of Fig. 5 show the invalidation distributions for LocusRoute. The largest source of invalidations in LocusRoute is the global cost array. The cost array is a good example of mostly-read data. It is frequently read while testing different routes for a wire, but is written only when the wire route is decided. The average number of invalidations per shared write of the cost array is about 2 with 32 processors,

but some writes can cause up to 17 invalidations. Small invalidations are much more common, because in LocusRoute there is enough locality to keep the number of processors actively sharing a region of the cost array small.

Another large source of invalidating writes is a collection of variables, labeled *misc data* in Figs. 5(f) and (g), that are migratory. The most frequently used ones of this set are the RouteRecords, which are used by the processors as they route a wire. They are reused by other processors for routing other wires, and cause only zero and single invalidations. The data structures related to the wire tasks (labeled *tasks*) are also migratory, while the flag that signals whether the task queue is empty or not (labeled *empty flag*) is mostly-read. Neither one of these last two data structures, however, accounts for a very large fraction of the total invalidations. The group labeled *global values* represents a small number of global variables. These fall into one of two categories: 1) global counts that are updated using read-modify-write operations and act as migratory objects, and 2) global flags that are read by many processors, but modified infrequently and act as mostly-read objects.

Part (b) of Fig. 5 shows the synchronization behavior of LocusRoute. There are a total of 51 locks; 46 of these are distributed locks with very little contention. Of the remaining five, only a mutual exclusion lock used for printing and the lock that controls the task queue from which processors obtain their wire tasks have any noticeable contention. However, they are used infrequently, and thus do not cause problems. The single barrier is used only once to synchronize the start of the slave processes.

As more processors are added, the average number of invalidations per shared write is expected to increase slightly, because more processors are likely to have cached a given portion of the cost array. However, since the cost array is a mostly-read object with infrequent writes, the absolute number of invalidations per data reference is expected to remain small. By exploiting geographic locality, that is by partitioning the cost array into regions and assigning wires in a region to the corresponding processor, it might be possible to further limit the growth in the number of invalidations per shared write.

VII. EFFECT OF CACHE LINE SIZE

We now investigate the effect of different cache line sizes on invalidation patterns and traffic. While larger cache lines are desirable from the point of hardware efficiency and the prefetching they provide in multiprocessors, they can also cause significant increases in message traffic. There are several reasons for this. First, a larger cache line size increases the minimum communication granularity between processes. For example, even if a process wants to communicate a single word of information to another process, the minimum data that is sent across the network is still the whole cache line, thus increasing traffic volume. (This assumes an invalidation-based cache coherence protocol.) Second, parallel programs usually exhibit less spatial locality than sequential programs. For example, if a cache line is large and contains multiple data items (with each data item corresponding to a different

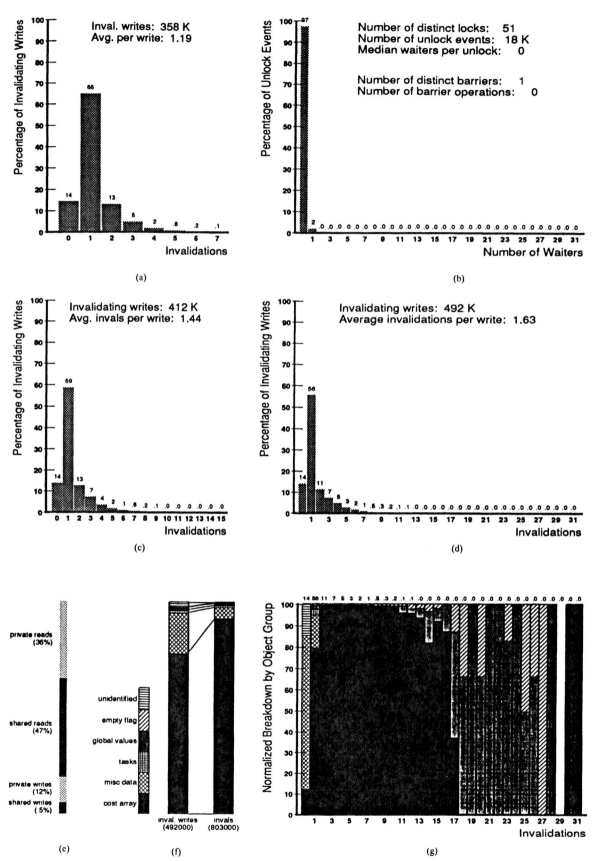

Fig. 5.   Behavior of LocusRoute.

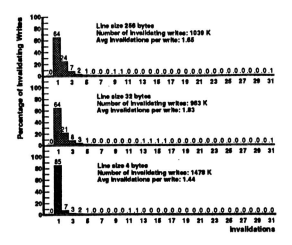
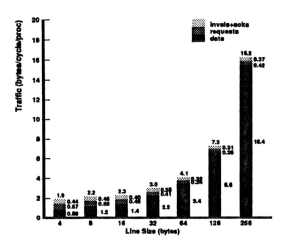

Fig. 6. Maxflow behavior with increasing line size.

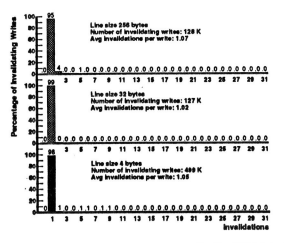
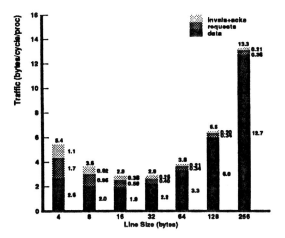

Fig. 7. MP3D behavior with increasing line size.

subtask), in a parallel program those subtasks may be evaluated on different processors. The spatial locality in this case is less than in a sequential version of the program, where all subtasks are processed one after the other by the same processor. Third, the number of invalidating writes and the message traffic may also increase due to *false sharing* [26]. Using the previous example again, if each subtask performs multiple modifications to the corresponding data item, then the cache line will bounce back and forth between the multiple processors, although no real communication is involved.

In the data presented so far we have used a cache line size of 4 bytes. This line size eliminates all false sharing. We now present results for cache line sizes between 4 and 256 bytes. In Figs. 6–10, we show two graphs for each application. The left graph shows the changes in the invalidation distribution as the line size is increased. The right graph shows the amount of message traffic generated and its breakdown into components for different line sizes. The messages correspond to those

that are required by the DASH cache-coherence protocol [14]. To compute traffic, we count three types of messages: invalidations and acknowledgments (7 bytes each), requests (7 bytes), and data messages ($7 + linesize$ bytes). The size of the messages was obtained by assuming 2 bytes for routing, 1 byte for control, and 4 bytes for address. We take the total traffic in bytes and divide it by the product of the total cycles for the run and the number of processors to arrive at the traffic rate in bytes per cycle per processor. Since our simulation runs were done assuming an ideal memory system, where each instruction execution and memory access takes a single cycle, the traffic rate in fact indicates bytes per instruction executed (rather than bytes per clock cycle).

A. Invalidation Patterns

We first examine the left graphs in Figs. 6–10. For line sizes of 4, 32, and 256 bytes the graphs show the invalidation

279

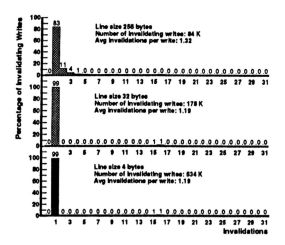

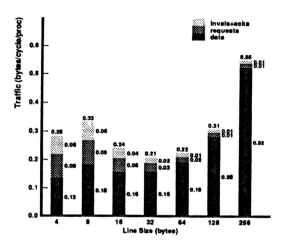

Fig. 8. Water behavior with increasing line size.

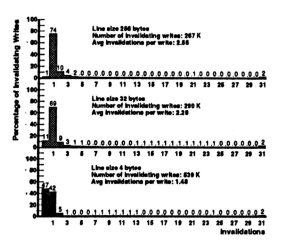

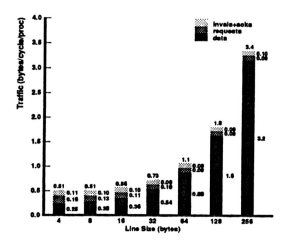

Fig. 9. PTHOR behavior with increasing line size.

distributions, and they list the total number of invalidating writes and the average size of invalidations.

Focusing on the effect of line size on the number of invalidating writes, we observe that the outcome depends on the relative sizes of the data objects in the program and the cache lines. If the typical data objects are larger than the line size, we will need to update several cache lines every time a complete object is written. Consequently, as the line size is increased, fewer lines will be modified, and we should see a decrease in the number of invalidating writes. This effect can be seen in all five applications when the line size is increased from 4 bytes to 32 bytes. For example, for the Water code (Fig. 8), the number of invalidating writes decreases from 534 K with 4-byte lines to 178 K with 32-byte lines. On the other hand, when the line size gets larger than the typical objects, several objects will fit into each cache line, and additional invalidating writes will be generated due to false sharing. Maxflow (Fig. 6) exhibits this trend when going from 32 to

256 byte lines, with the invalidating writes increasing from 963 K to 1039 K. The other applications do not exhibit this trend. For some of these other applications the typical data objects are larger than 256 bytes. For others the apparent object size is increased by reference patterns in which a given processor accesses neighboring objects consecutively.

Considering the effect of line size on the average size of invalidations, there are again several distinct effects that come into play. First, a larger line size is expected to increase the number of processors sharing a cache line (due to false sharing), thus increasing the size of invalidations. Second, depending on the spatial locality exhibited by different classes of objects (e.g., migratory versus mostly-read objects) in the program, an increased line size may reduce the number of invalidating writes causing a single invalidation more than those causing several invalidations, or vice versa. In programs where writes that cause smaller invalidations are reduced by a greater amount, the average size of invalidations will

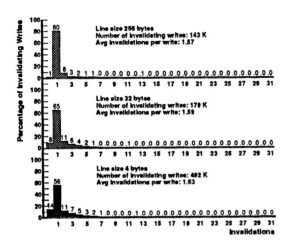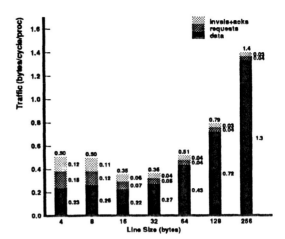

Fig. 10. LocusRoute behavior with increasing line size.

go up. For example, in PTHOR, a large fraction of zero invalidations (with 4-byte lines) are caused during the parallel initialization phase. These initialization accesses show very good locality, and as the line size is increased the number of writes causing zero invalidations diminishes dramatically. The writes causing larger invalidations do not decrease in the same proportion, thus increasing the average number of invalidations per invalidating write. In LocusRoute, on the other hand, the cost array references show good locality. These data are mostly-read and cause many medium-sized invalidations. When the line size is increased the number of invalidating writes due to the cost array decreases, bringing down the average number of invalidations per invalidating write. We see that the effect of line size on invalidation distribution is complex and not easily predicted. In general, though, there is a slight trend toward larger invalidations as the cache line size is increased.

B. Message Traffic

Let us now look at the right graphs in Figs. 6–10. We show the message traffic in bytes per cycle per processor for different line sizes. As the cache line is increased, there are typically fewer messages of each type. As a result, the traffic due to request and invalidation messages decreases, since the message size remains constant regardless of the line size. For data messages, however, the message size increases with line size. This effect tends to offset the reduced number of data messages. Depending on the program, one or the other effect may dominate for a given line size. However, for very large line sizes, the data message size always dominates, and data traffic is largest for all applications. The minimum data traffic is achieved with line sizes as small as 4 bytes for applications with little data locality (such as Maxflow), or as large as 16 bytes for applications with good data locality (such as LocusRoute). When we look at *total* traffic, the minimum is shifted further toward larger cache line sizes, because of the continually decreasing trend of the request and

invalidation message traffic. Overall, traffic is minimum, or close to minimum, for line sizes around 32 bytes.

Several researchers have studied the effect of cache line size on message traffic. In general their data favors cache line sizes smaller than the ones we find best in our study. We now briefly discuss reasons for this apparent discrepancy. Agarwal and Gupta [1] present results for several snoopy coherence schemes using traces obtained from a four processor system. Their traffic data favor smaller block sizes primarily because they simulate bus-based snoopy protocols in contrast to the directory-based protocols studied in this paper. In a bus-based snoopy protocol, the amount of invalidation traffic is quite small, since each invalidating write causes only a single bus transaction. In contrast, in a directory-based protocol the invalidation traffic can be quite large, since separate invalidations must be sent to each processor caching the data and acknowledgments must be received back. Since the benefits of the reduced invalidation traffic (with larger line size) are not so significant for snoopy protocols (as a fraction of total traffic), they favor smaller line sizes. The Agarwal and Gupta study also does not model request traffic (messages to request memory lines from remote processing nodes), and this again favors smaller line sizes. Similar comments apply to the work of Eggers *et al.* [9], who also simulate a bus-based system. Their results are, however, closer to ours. Torrellas *et al.* [26] compute traffic by simply multiplying the number of shared misses by the cache line size, where shared misses include read and write misses as well as write hits to clean data. While this method may provide an accurate traffic estimate for bus-based systems, our model with different message sizes and a fixed message size overhead is more accurate for general interconnects.

VIII. GENERALIZATIONS AND CONCLUSIONS

We have proposed several classes of data objects that can be distinguished by their use in parallel programs and by their invalidation traffic patterns. By merging the invalidation behavior of the individual data objects used in an application, we can gain insight into the overall invalidation behavior of the application. We can also predict the invalidation behavior beyond the 32 processor limit of our current simulation studies.

The code and read-only data objects are, in general, easy to handle. Since they are written very infrequently, they cause very few invalidations. Some directory schemes, however, do not allow a memory location to be present in more caches than there are pointers in the directory entry (for example $Dir_i NB$ schemes in [2]). We would normally expect such schemes to recognize code and handle it differently, thus alleviating part of the problem. However, read-only data is much harder to detect, especially since it is written at least once at initialization time, and it may cause problems for such schemes.

Migratory data objects move from one processor to another as execution progresses, but they are never manipulated by more than one processor at any one time. Migration of the data object causes at most single invalidations, because each processor writes the object before relinquishing control of it. Single invalidations are expected, even as the number of processors is increased. We note that a large number of these invalidations could be avoided if the processors (or the software) were to flush the data items out of their cache when the data were no longer needed.

Mostly-read data have potential for causing a large number of invalidations, since each write is preceded by several reads from multiple processors. The average number of invalidations caused by each write is thus high. Fortunately, writes to this kind of data are infrequent and hence the total invalidation traffic is not very large. With more processors, we expect an increase in the average number of invalidations per shared write, because it is likely that more processors will have touched the data object before a write to it takes place. This effect may be partially mitigated by taking advantage of locality, that is, by partitioning the data set and tasks such that each data portion is referenced by only a small subset of the processors.

Frequently read and written data present a big problem in terms of invalidations. Not only does each write cause several invalidations, but writes are also frequent. Frequently read/written data are expected to show increased invalidations as more processors are used, because more reads and more writes to the data items will take place. If possible, this type of data object should be avoided for parallel applications with a large number of processes. However, as in the case of high-contention synchronization objects, some hardware support such as fetch&op primitives [14], can reduce invalidation traffic.

Synchronization objects are found in all parallel applications. In well-designed applications contention for the critical sections protected by the locks is minimal and thus the invalidation traffic caused by the locks is small. As multiprocessors are scaled, it may not always be possible to avoid high-contention synchronization objects. Invalidation traffic can then be reduced by means of various hardware/software support features. For example, high-contention locks with many processes waiting can be implemented using queueing locks [13]. These locks release waiting processes one by

one without causing large invalidations. Similarly, if the directory has only a few pointers per entry, the compiler may construct fan-in and fan-out trees for implementing barriers, thus reducing both the latency and the frequency with which the pointer overflow mechanism is triggered [28].

Experiments with various cache line sizes indicate that best invalidation behavior is achieved when the cache line matches the size of the data objects being shared. Both line sizes that are too small and line sizes that are too large can drive up the number of invalidations. When the line sizes are too small, each migration of an object causes several invalidations. When they are too large, false sharing may lead to additional invalidations. In terms of overall traffic, we find that the number of messages typically decreases as the line size is increased. However, since data message get larger, there is an intermediate line size that yields minimum overall traffic. Our data show that a line size of 32 bytes is quite reasonable for large-scale multiprocessors. This line size allows efficient transfer of data across a relatively high-latency network, and it is also likely to increase performance due to prefetch. The negative effects of a large line size, namely slightly larger invalidations as well as increased traffic, are still tolerable at this cache line size.

In summary, in this paper we have presented data about the invalidation patterns of five applications using 8, 16, and 32 processor runs. We have introduced a classification of data objects by invalidation behavior. This serves as a conceptual aid for reasoning about and predicting the invalidation behavior of an application. The classification is also useful for predicting the invalidation behavior beyond the number of processors currently simulated. Such extrapolations suggest that the average number of invalidations per invalidating write will remain small for well-designed applications, thus supporting the use of directory-based cache-coherence for large-scale multiprocessors. Effort has to be put into limiting contention over synchronization objects, exploiting locality, and reducing frequently read/written data objects. Finally, line size studies have shown that the overall message traffic is minimum (or close to minimum) when a cache line size of 32 bytes is used.

ACKNOWLEDGMENT

We wish to thank F. Carrasco, J. McDonald, J. P. Singh, L. Soule, and J. Rose for use of their applications, and for explaining the details of the data structures used by them. We are grateful for the feedback given by members of the DASH multiprocessor project at Stanford.

REFERENCES

[1] A. Agarwal and A. Gupta, "Memory reference characteristics of multiprocessor applications under MACH," in *Proc. SIGMETRICS*, May 1988, pp. 215–225.
[2] A. Agarwal, R. Simoni, J. Hennessy, and M. Horowitz, "An evaluation of directory schemes for cache coherence," in *Proc. 15th Int. Symp. Comput. Architecture*, June 1988, pp. 280–289.
[3] J. Bennett, J. Carter, and W. Zwaenepoel, "Adaptive software cache management for distributed shared memory architectures," in *Proc. 17th Int. Symp. Comput. Architecture*, May 1990, pp. 125–134.

[4] M. Berry *et al.*, "The Perfect Club benchmarks: Effective performance evaluation of supercomputers," Tech. Rep. 827, Center for Supercomput. Res. Develop., May 1989.

[5] M. Censier and P. Feautier, "A new solution to coherence problems in multicache systems," *IEEE Trans. Comput.*, vol. C-27, no. 12, pp. 1112–1118, Dec. 1978.

[6] K.M. Chandy and J. Misra, "Asynchronous distributed simulation via a sequence of parallel computations," *Commun. ACM*, pp. 198–206, Apr. 1981.

[7] H. Davis and S. Goldschmidt, "Tango: A multiprocessor simulation and tracing system," Tech. Rep. CSL-TR-90-439, Stanford Univ., July 1990.

[8] S. Eggers and R. Katz, "A characterization of sharing in parallel programs and its application to coherency protocol evaluation," in *Proc. 15th Int. Symp. Comput. Architecture*, June 1988, pp. 373–382.

[9] ——, "The effect of sharing on the cache and bus performance of parallel programs," in *Proc. 3rd Int. Conf. Architectural Support for Programming Languages Oper. Syst.*, Apr. 1989, pp. 257–270.

[10] Encore Computer Corp., *Multimax Technical Summary*, 1986.

[11] A. Goldberg and R. Tarjan, "A new approach to the maximum flow problem," in *Proc. 18th ACM Symp. Theory Comput.*, 1986, pp. 136–146.

[12] J.R. Goodman, "Using cache memory to reduce processor-memory traffic," in *Proc. 10th Int. Symp. Comput. Architecture*, June 1983, pp. 124–131.

[13] J.R. Goodman, M.K. Vernon, and P.J. Woest, "Efficient synchronization primitives for large-scale cache-coherent multiprocessors," in *Proc. 3rd Int. Conf. Architectural Support for Programming Languages Oper. Syst.*, Apr. 1989, pp. 64–75.

[14] D. Lenoski, J. Laudon, K. Gharachorloo, A. Gupta, and J. Hennessy, "The directory-based cache coherence protocol for the DASH multiprocessor," in *Proc. 17th Int. Symp. Comput. Architecture*, May 1990, pp. 148–159.

[15] T. Lovett and S. Thakkar, "The Symmetry multiprocessor system," in *Proc. Int. Conf. Parallel Processing*, vol. I, Aug. 1988, pp. 303–310.

[16] E. Lusk, R. Overbeek, *et al.*, *Portable Programs for Parallel Processors*. New York: Holt, Rinehart, and Winston, 1987.

[17] E. Lusk, R. Stevens, and R. Overbeek. *A Tutorial on the Use of Monitors in C: Writing Portable Code for Multiprocessors*, Argonne National Laboratory, Argonne, IL 60439, 1986.

[18] J. McDonald and D. Baganoff, "Vectorization of a particle simulation method for hypersonic rarified flow," in *Proc. AIAA Thermodynamics, Plasmadynamics and Lasers Conf.*, June 1988.

[19] L. Monier and P. Sindhu, "The architecture of the Dragon," in *Proc. 30th IEEE Int. Conf.*, IEEE, Feb. 1985, pp. 118–121.

[20] R. Katz, S. Eggers, D. Wood, C. Perkins, and R. Sheldon, "Implementing a cache consistency protocol," in *Proc. 12th Int. Symp. Comput. Architecture*, June 1985, pp. 276–283.

[21] J. Rose. "LocusRoute: A parallel global router for standard cells," in *Proc. Design Automat. Conf.*, June 1988, pp. 189–195.

[22] L. Rudolph and Z. Segall, "Dynamic decentralized cache consistency schemes for MIMD parallel processors," in *Proc. 12th Int. Symp. Comput. Architecture*, pp. 355–362, June 1985. Also SIGARCH Newsletter, vol. 13, issue 3, 1985.

[23] J.P. Singh, W.-D. Weber, and A. Gupta, "SPLASH: Stanford parallel applications for shared-memory," Tech. Rep. CSL-TR-91-469, Stanford Univ., Apr. 1991.

[24] L. Soule and A. Gupta, "Characterization of parallelism and deadlocks in distributed logic simulation," in *Proc. 26th Design Automat. Conf.*, June 1989, pp. 81–86.

[25] C. Thacker and L. Stewart. "Firefly: A multiprocessor workstation," in *Proc. 2nd Int. Conf. Architectural Support for Programming Languages Oper. Syst.*, Oct. 1987, pp. 164–172.

[26] J. Torrellas, M. Lam, and J. Hennessy, "Measurement, analysis, and improvement of the cache behavior of shared data in cache-coherent multiprocessors," Tech. Rep. CSL-TR-90-412, Stanford Univ., Feb. 1990.

[27] W.-D. Weber and A. Gupta, "Analysis of cache invalidation patterns in multiprocessors," in *Proc. 3rd Int. Conf. Architectural Support for Programming Languages Oper. Syst.*, Apr. 1989, pp. 243–256.

[28] P.C. Yew, N.F. Tzeng, and D.H. Lawrie, "Distributing hot-spot addressing in large scale multiprocessors," *IEEE Trans. Comput.*, vol. C-36, no. 4, pp. 388–395, Apr. 1987.

Correction to "Cache Invalidation Patterns in Shared-Memory Multiprocessors"[1]

Anoop Gupta and Wolf-Dietrich Weber

Due to difficulties reproducing the figures of the original manuscript, some grey scales were not distinguishable in the graphs as printed in the July 1992 issue. The graphs affected were parts (f) and (g) of Figs. 1–5. They are reprinted here for clarity.

Manuscript received September 4, 1992.

The authors are with the Computer Systems Laboratory, Stanford University, Stanford, CA 94305.

IEEE Log Number 9205228.

[1]A. Gupta and W.-D. Weber, *IEEE Trans. Comput.*, vol. 41, pp. 794–810, July 1992.

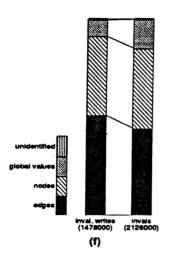

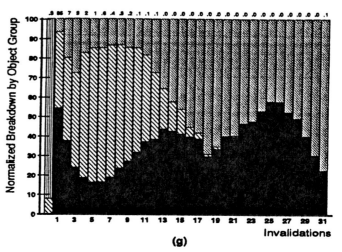

(f)

(g)

Fig. 1. Behavior of Maxflow.

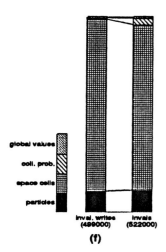

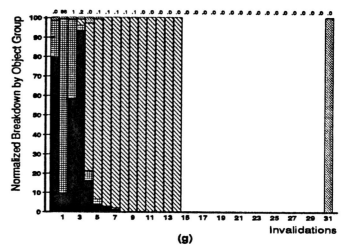

(f)

(g)

Fig. 2. Behavior of MP3D

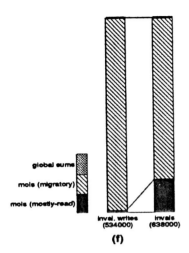
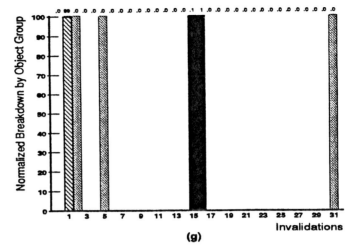

Fig. 3. Behavior of Water

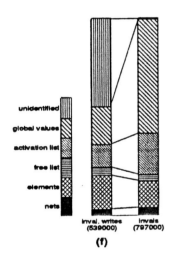
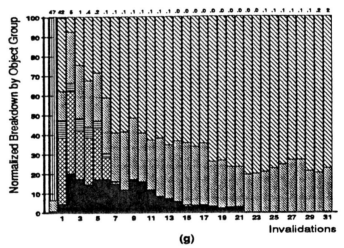

Fig. 4. Behavior of PTHOR.

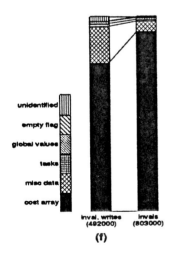
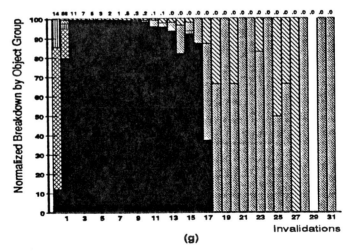

Fig. 5. Behavior of LocusRoute.

285

Benchmark Characterization for Experimental System Evaluation

Thomas M. Conte   Wen-mei W. Hwu

Center for Reliable and High-Performance Computing
University of Illinois
conte@csg.uiuc.edu

Abstract

Benchmarking in its various forms has become a popular approach to evaluating system performance and design decisions. There are at least three levels of behavior of a computer system measured by the benchmarking technique: the level of benchmark program and input set selection, the level of benchmark characteristics, and the level of system behavior in response to the benchmarks. Traditionally, only the system behavior has been measured. In order to make strong conclusion about benchmarking results, however, the nature of the benchmark programs must be characterized. This paper addresses this issue by presenting ways of measuring benchmark characteristics independent of system design. These benchmark characteristics include memory access behavior, control transfer behavior, and data dependencies. Measuring benchmark characteristics independent of the design parameters provides for cross-design and cross-architecture comparisons using the same benchmark set. They also serve as the basis for interpreting benchmarking results. Instruction memory access behavior and control transfer behavior are extracted from real programs and presented in this paper to illustrate the usefulness of benchmark characterization.

1 Introduction

The evaluation of the performance of a computer system typically uses the technique of *benchmarking*. In this technique, the performance of the system is measured for a set of programs, or *benchmarks*, that are executed on the actual system or a simulation of the system. Various forms of benchmarking, such as trace driven simulation, detailed simulation based on executable files, microcode-assisted measurement, hardware monitoring, and software probing, have been used extensively in the evalua-

tion of experimental computer architectures, such as in [1, 2, 3, 4, 5, 6, 7, 8, 9, 10, 11, 12, 13, 14]

Traces are records of the dynamic system behavior in response to benchmarks. These traces are used as the input to simulators that generate system-level performance metrics [2, 3]. The amount of the collected information in these traces often makes measurement of long-term or global system behavior intractable. For example, on a contemporary 5 MIPS machine that accesses memory approximately twice per instruction, a second of real time results in a reference string of length 2 references/inst. × 5 MIPS × 4 bytes/reference $=\sim$ 40Mbytes long. This paper presents behavior measurement techniques based on information that is proportional to the static rather than dynamic program size. Instead of collecting traces, graph and density-function representations of the program are annotated with information from execution. This reduces substantially the amount of storage needed and increases the space of tractable system behavior measurement.

Benchmarking usually involves collecting a set of programs that are believed to be representative of the workload the system will encounter. Since some of these programs might process data, a set of representative inputs for each program is also collected. As each benchmark program is executed, it makes requests of the system that exercise various system features. These requests in turn force the system into certain behavioral patterns. This behavior of the system is then measured and interpreted as its performance. Hence, there are at least three levels of performance of a computer system measured by the benchmarking technique: the level of benchmark input set selection, the level of benchmark characteristics and compiler decisions, and the level of system behavior in response to the benchmarks. Traditionally, only the end-product performance of the system has been measured and this performance has been taken as the performance of the system in general.

This paper addresses this issue by presenting ways of measuring benchmark characteristics separate from system performance.

The performance of the system under benchmarks is often measured in terms of system-level, observable performance metrics, such as throughput and turnaround time [15, 16]. These metrics are functions of the characteristics of the benchmarks used for the performance study. Since they measure the system's performance, the metrics are also a function of the system design parameters. Measuring the characteristics of the benchmarks independent of the design parameters provides for cross-architecture comparisons using the same benchmark set. Additionally, the system-level performance metrics can potentially be approximated using analytical formulas involving the benchmark characteristics and the design parameters. These analytical formulas can provide insight into how benchmark performance and system design parameters impact the system's performance.

The remainder of this paper is divided into three parts. The following section discusses the methodology selected to measure benchmark characteristics. The third section presents implementation issues. An example of the approach is presented in section four. Finally, conclusions and future directions are presented.

2 A Methodology for Benchmark Characterization

This section presents the methodology of benchmark characterization. The benchmark characteristics proposed in this paper are selected to be general, highly architecture-parameter independent rulers by which the system's performance can be estimated. These characteristics, or *General Ruler Independent of Parameters*, (*GRIPs*), are defined below.

2.1 Locality measures

An abstract reference stream of items is a time sequence, $w(t) = r_i$, over a set of possible item values, $r_i \in R$. The items (r_i's) may be the addresses of instructions or data items generated during the execution of a benchmark program, for example. Modern computers exploit the temporal and spatial locality behavior of reference streams by using special fast buffers to achieve high performance (e.g., cache memories) [1]. For this reason, many of the GRIPs presented below are based on locality measures.

Some definitions concerning reference streams will be required below:

DEFINITION 2.1: Define $\text{next}(w(t)) = k$, if k is the smallest integer such that $w(t) = w(t + k)$.
∎

DEFINITION 2.2: The number of unique references between $w(t)$ and $\text{next}(w(t))$, is defined as, $u(w(t)) = \|\{ w(t + k) \mid i \leq k < \text{next}(w(t)) \}\|$.
∎

DEFINITION 2.3: Define $f^T(x)$, the *interreference temporal density function*, $f^T(x)$,, to be the probability of there being x unique references between successive references to the same item,

$$f^T(x) = \sum_t P\left[u(w(t)) = x \right].$$

∎

The interreference temporal density function is a measure of temporal locality of a reference stream. The performance of buffers managed under stacking replacement policies (e.g., LRU) depends directly on this measure of temporal locality. The hit ratio for a fully associative buffer of size N is $h(N) = \sum_{y \leq N} f^T(y)$ (see [17]).

DEFINITION 2.4: The *interreference spatial density function*, $f^S(x)$, is defined as,

$$f^S(x) = \sum_t \sum_{k=1}^{\text{next}(w(t))} P\left[\left|w(t) - w(t + k)\right| = x \right].$$

∎

The interreference spatial density function is a measure of the probability that between references to the same item, a reference to an item x units away occurs. Hence, the function captures the intrinsic interference between items in direct-mapped caches.

Another useful representation of a reference stream of items is as a. How to construct such a graph is illustrated in the following two definitions.

DEFINITION 2.5: The (directed) reference graph, $G = (V, E)$, of a reference stream is defined as $V = R$ and,

$$E = \{ (r_i, r_j) \mid w(t) = r_i \text{ and } w(t+1) = r_j \}.$$

∎

DEFINITION 2.6: Let $n_i(r_i)$ be the number of occurrences $w(t) = r_i$, for $0 \leq t \leq T$. Furthermore, let $n_{ij}(r_i, r_j)$ be the number of occurrences of $w(t + 1) = r_j$, if $w(t) = r_i$. Then, the weighted reference graph, $G' = (V, E)$, is defined such that each node, $r_i \in V$, is weighted with $P[r_i] = n_i/T$, and each edge, $(r_i, r_j) \in E$ is weighted with $P[r_j|r_i] = n_{ij}/n_i$.
∎

Based on these graph definitions, groups of items that are referenced together can be defined. The strongly-connected components of the reference graph, called the *phases*, are such partitions of the reference stream, outlined in the following definition.

DEFINITION 2.7: The set of phases for a reference stream is defined as $\Phi = \{\phi_1, \phi_2, \ldots \phi_i \ldots \phi_p\}$, where

$$\phi_i = \{ r_i \mid \{(r_i, r_{i+1}), (r_{i+1}, r_{i+2}), \\ \ldots, (r_{k-1}, r_k), (r_k, r_i)\} \subseteq E \},$$

and, $\phi_1 \cap \phi_2 \cap \cdots \cap \phi_p = \emptyset$.

∎

In a phase, any node can be reached from any other node through a sequence of edge traversals. During program execution, the items in a newly-encountered phase are guaranteed to not have been referenced before. Intrinsic cold-start buffer behavior can therefore be predicted using phase transitions, since the previous contents of a buffer are useless when a new phase is encountered. The *interphase density function* defined below is intended to capture this phase behavior of benchmarks.

DEFINITION 2.8: The interphase density function, $f^\phi(x)$, is the probability that a phase of size x is encountered in the reference stream,

$$f^\phi(x) = \sum_{\|\phi\| = x} \sum_{r_i \in \phi} P[r_i], \quad \text{for all } \phi \in \Phi.$$

∎

2.2 Control flow GRIPs

The control flow behavior of a benchmark program can be characterized in terms of a reference stream of instructions, $w(t) = i_j, i_j \in I$, and its corresponding weighted reference graph, $G_I = (V_I, E_I)$. The instruction reference stream can be grouped into sets of instructions that must execute sequentially. These sets are called *basic blocks*, and the instruction reference stream can be redefined in terms of them, $w'(i) = B_i, B_i \in \mathcal{B}$. [18]. Some of the GRIPs for control flow are defined below in terms of the benchmark program's basic block weighted reference graph, $G_{BB} = (V_{BB}, E_{BB})$, also called the *weighted control graph* [19].

When the program is mapped into the linear memory space of a computer, the graph nature of the program is preserved using branch instructions. The graph nature still affects the performance of the system, especially for pipelined processors. Methods to reduce the penalty of this mapping have used both hardware and software approaches [10, 11, 12, 6, 13,

14, 8]. Software branch prediction schemes use the weights of the control flow graph to predict a branch's behavior to be either taken or not-taken for the duration of the program's execution [6, 8, 20]. It has been shown that these schemes perform as well as hardware schemes [8], yet the calculation of their performance is architecture-independent. The control flow GRIP *branch prediction accuracy*, A, is a variant of the accuracy of these software schemes.

DEFINITION 2.9: The prediction probability of B_i, $P_p(B_i)$ is defined as,

$$P_p(B_i) = \max\{ P[B_j | B_i] \mid (B_i, B_j) \in E_{BB} \}.$$

∎

DEFINITION 2.10: The branch prediction accuracy, A, is defined as,

$$A = \sum_{i=1}^{N} P(B_i) P_p(B_i).$$

∎

Hence, the branch prediction accuracy is the probability that a prediction based on the most likely behavior of a branch instruction is correct. Since some architectures have separate penalties for incorrectly predicting conditional- and unconditional branches, another GRIP, F_{CB}, is defined as the fraction of dynamic branches that are conditional branches.

The fetching of instructions in modern computers and the hardware-based prediction of branches often involve buffering [11, 6, 8]. The performance of instruction buffering techniques, such as instruction caches and branch target buffers, can estimated using the above locality measures for the instruction reference stream. Hence, $f_I^T(x)$ is defined to be the temporal locality GRIP and $f_I^S(x)$, the spatial locality GRIP for the instruction stream. Also, $f_I^\phi(x)$, the interphase density function, is included as a GRIP. It is important to mention an architecture-specific parameter that maps basic blocks into actual machine instructions. This parameter is the average length of basic blocks, $\overline{L}_{BB}$, and it is measured in terms of machine instructions instructions.

The GRIPs for control flow are summarized in Table 1. These GRIPs will be measured for benchmarks in an example characterization presented in Section 4.

2.3 Data flow GRIPs

The characterization of the data flow behavior of a benchmark program involves the concept of *variables*. A variable is a dynamic instance of a data item. The

Table 1: Control flow GRIPs

GRIP	Benchmark characteristic measured
A	Predictability of branches
F_{CB}	Fraction of conditional branches
$f_I^T(x)$	Instruction stream temporal locality
$f_I^S(x)$	Instruction stream spatial locality
$f_I^\phi(x)$	Instruction stream phase behavior

lifetime of variables, their locality, and the data dependencies that exist between them are the subject of this section.

Variables go through a life cycle in which they are created, used, and then discarded or written out. Register allocation is often performed using the technique of *graph coloring* [21, 22]. In this technique, a register is assigned to two different variables if the two variables are not live (i.e., active) at the same time. In essence, the number of registers required can be estimated by the *variable life density function*.

DEFINITION 2.11: Define the variable life density function, $f^{VL}(n_V)$, as the probability that n_V variables are live at any time during execution of the benchmark program. ∎

Hence, if there are m registers available for allocation by the compiler, then the register utilization will be $\sum_{i \leq m} f^{VL}(i)$, and the amount of spill code required will be $\sum_{i > m} f^{VL}(i)$. (This is similar to an approach described in [23].) The number of live variables can be measured using techniques described in Section 3.

Since buffering is used for data accesses, a set of GRIPs is defined for the locality of data references. Define $f_D^T(x)$ to be the interreference temporal density function, and $f_D^S(x)$ as the interreference spatial density function for the data reference stream. Note that unlike the instruction stream, the variable life density function must be used in conjunction with the locality density functions to predict the performance of buffers after register allocation. Also, phase behavior will be measured with, $f_D^\phi(x)$, the interphase density function for the data reference stream.

The data dependence behavior of a benchmark program can be captured using a *instruction dependence graph*. In this graph, the nodes are the (compiler-intermediate) instructions, $i_j \in I$, and the edges are due to flow dependencies. The following definition states this more formally.

DEFINITION 2.12: If $\mathcal{R}(i_j)$ is the set of variables read by instruction $w(t_1) = i_j$, and $\mathcal{W}(i_k)$ is the set of variables written by instruction $w(t_2) = i_k$, for $i_j, i_k \in I$, and $t_1 < t_2$, then, the instruction dependence graph is a graph, $G_{ID} = (V_I, E_{ID})$, such that $V_I = I$ and

$$E_{ID} = \{ (i_k, i_j) \mid \mathcal{W}(i_j) \cap \mathcal{R}(i_k) \neq \emptyset \}$$

(see [18]). ∎

The dynamic scheduling of instructions using an algorithm such as Scoreboarding or the Tomasulo algorithm is dictated by the structure of the dynamic data dependencies [24, 25, 4, 5]. A possible GRIP to capture the schedulability of a benchmark would be the probability of there being dependencies of distance i intermediate instructions. However, the overlap of dependencies and the branch behavior of the instruction stream is not captured by this GRIP. Emma and Davidson present a set of reductions that can be performed on the instruction dependence graph to eliminate overlap. After these reductions, the probability of a dependence spanning j taken branches while having a distance of i intermediate instructions is sufficient to characterize the performance of out-of-order execution schemes [26, 27]. This statistic is the probability of such a dependence occurring, $p_{i,j}^{DD}$, and can be calculated from the instruction dependence graph after a set of graph reductions are performed [27]. This then will serve as the scheduling GRIP for data flow.

The GRIPs for data flow are summarized in Table 2.

2.4 Other GRIPs

Three areas of benchmark characterization that are not covered in detail in this paper deserve some discussion. These three areas are operating system performance, I/O system performance, and large-grain parallelism.

The performance of a benchmark program under the interruptions and scheduling policies of an operating system is different from that of the program running alone. There are two ways of viewing this

289

Table 2: Data flow GRIPs

GRIP	Benchmark characteristic measured
$f^{VL}(n_v)$	Live variables/register use
$f_D^T(x)$	Data stream temporal locality
$f_D^S(x)$	Data stream spatial locality
$f_D^\phi(x)$	Data stream phase behavior
$p_{i,j}^{DD}$	Data dependence schedulability

interaction. From the operating system viewpoint, the benchmark program is actually an input. Hence, the operating system may be thought of as a meta benchmark program with the characteristics of the benchmarks running under it as its input set. From the benchmark program's viewpoint, the operating system satisfies requests and disturbs buffer usage. These two effects can be characterized using selective flushing of buffers via simulated multitasking, as in [1, 28]. Therefore, an operating system can be viewed as a benchmark and characterized using the same GRIPs. Additionally, the multitasking quantum can be used as a system parameter to modify the role the locality measures play in the approximations of system-level performance parameters.

The I/O system's performance is similar to the operating system in the sense that it views the entire set of benchmark programs as its input set. Since the sequence of references to a peripheral determines its performance, the performance of peripherals has to be modeled for each peripheral architecture. This is analogous to the modeling of cache behavior by locality measures, since cache behavior also depends on reference stream sequencing. Hence, the characterizations are tractable but beyond the scope of this paper.

Large-grain parallelism is usually expressed explicitly by the programmer as a conscious decision. Measuring this parallelism can be done by intercepting the synchronization primitives and then constructing the expressed dynamic parallelism. Again, these characterizations are tractable but beyond the scope of this paper.

3 Implementation issues

Several ways of measuring GRIPs are available. For example, microcode-based measurement techniques exist that modify the microcode of a machine to monitor the instruction stream [2, 3]. In essence, the traces generated by these techniques are reference streams of items. These streams can be analyzed to produce reference graphs and identify phases. However, the length of the traces are excessive.

This paper uses techniques where the reference graph is constructed on-the-fly without the intermediate step of recording the reference string. Previous work has implemented the construction of the control flow graph on-the-fly using the compiler to insert probe instructions at the entrance of each of the program's basic block. As the program executes, the weighted control graph is constructed and stored for later analysis [19, 8, 29].

This paper proposes an extension to the compiler-based profiling technique to measure the instruction dependence graph and the locality measures. Static analysis of dependence information can be done at compile time to produce a list of variables that are born and killed for each basic block [18]. However, static dependence analysis cannot deal efficiently with variables that span function call invocations and aliased pointer references [30]. These instances cause unknowns to appear in the static dependence information. The compiler-based dependence profiler inserts probe instructions at the site of these unknowns to measure their variables. As each basic block is executed, a script describing the birth and death of variables is executed by the profile analyzer. The unknowns are represented as 'wait for variable identity' commands in this script that instruct the analyzer to insert the identity of the variable in its dynamic copy of the script. As each basic block completes execution, the analyzer uses the dynamic copy of the script to update the instruction dependence graph that it builds. Also measured using this technique is the variable life density function, f^{VL}.

After the weighted control graph has been constructed, branch behavior can easily be measured. The branch prediction accuracy, A, can be calculated directly from the weighted control graph using the equation from Section 2.2. The dynamic fraction of conditional branches, F_{CB}, can be calculated by summing the weights of the basic blocks in the weighed control graph that end with conditional branches.

Phases and cycles in the control flow and dependence graphs can be detected during the execution of the program using a stack of recently-seen items. A separate stack maintained using the least-recently-used replacement policy (see [17]) can be employed to find the interreference temporal and spatial density functions. The algorithm for locality measurement

```
Calc_loc_measures(r_i):
 begin
     if  not first time r_i encountered then
     begin
         d ← depth(r_i)
         remove r_i from the stack
         for  all r_j with depth(r_j) < d
         begin
             dist ← |α(r_j) − α(r_i)|
             f̂^S(dist) ← f̂^S(dist) + 1
         end
         f̂^T(d) ← f̂^T(d) + 1
     end
     push(r_i)
 end
```

Figure 1: The algorithm for calculating the locality distributions.

is outlined in Figure 1, where $\alpha(\cdot)$ is the address of a node, and $\mathbf{depth}(\cdot)$ is the stack depth of a node. The approximate distributions, $\hat{f}^S(x)$ and $\hat{f}^T(x)$ are normalized after execution terminates.

4   Example benchmark characterization

As an illustration of the benchmark characterization idea, this section presents the control flow GRIPs for several benchmarks. The benchmark programs were selected to be highly data-driven so as to make their control flow behavior very diverse. The benchmarks are presented in Table 3. A description of the inputs that were used for the programs is also presented.

The GRIPs presented in Table 1 were measured using the techniques outlined in Section 3. The scalar GRIPs, A and F_{CB}, are presented in Table 4. The locality measures, $f_I^T(x)$, $f_I^S(x)$ and $f_I^\phi(x)$ are presented in graph form in Figures 2, 3, 4, and 5.

Table 4: Scalar control flow GRIPs

Benchmark	A	F_{CB}
grep-c	99.0%	30.5%
grep-words	94%	37%
yacc-awk	95%	47%
yacc-make	98%	37%

The value of A shows that all these benchmarks have highly predictable branches. For example, a typical static branch in yacc-awk can be correctly predicted 95% of the time by always choosing the most preferred direction. Hardware or software branch prediction mechanisms should be able to achieve this prediction accuracy. Any result significantly less than this value indicates the existence of system performance problems. In the case of hardware prediction schemes, the problem may be due to either insufficient branch target buffer entries or frequent context switches. The measured instruction-stream locality can then be used to estimate by how much the branch target buffer size should be increased. As for software prediction schemes, the problem may be due to the use of inaccurate profile information. With the A values, one knows what to expect from the measured branch prediction performance. Also, with such a high predictability, software and hardware prediction schemes can be expected to exhibit the same behavior. This is confirmed by the measurements presented in [8].

The spatial locality measure of yacc-awk (Figure 4) indicates that it is highly sequential. The likelihood of a basic block reference being within 30 basic blocks of any other reference is very high. This is of course dependent on the code layout decision made by the compiler. The code layout used in this measurement is intelligently done based on profile information. Therefore, one can expect the spatial locality to be lower for the same benchmark when compiled by a less intelligent compiler. With such a high spatial locality, one can expect the instruction buffers and caches with large blocks to perform well.

The temporal locality of yacc-make indicates that a cache which accommodates approximately 15 basic blocks will accommodate its working set. The entire program consists of almost 1300 basic blocks. With only 1% of the program active at a time, yacc-make has very high locality. With five instructions per basic block and four bytes per instruction, a 0.5KB cache will be adequate for accommodating the working set. Therefore, one expects to find the performance of instruction cache to saturate when the cache size increases beyond 0.5K bytes. Again, one knows what to expect before performing any architecture-parameter-specific measurement.

It is interesting to correlate the spatial and temporal localities. Although the results for grep are not strongly correlated, there is a strong correlation between the spatial and temporal locality measures for yacc-awk and yacc-make. This phenomenon is due in part to the intelligent compiler code layout scheme, trace layout. This scheme emits instructions in the

Table 3: The programs studied

Benchmark	Description	Input description	# Basic blocks
grep-c	*grep*: A general regular-	`grep -c '++' grep.c`	116
grep-words	expression parser	`grep -i '[aeiou]{2,4}' /usr/dict/words`	125
yacc-awk	*yacc*: a LALR(1)	The grammar for *awk*	1307
yacc-make	parser generator	The grammar for *make*	1293

order of their execution based on the program's performance for a large input set [31, 19, 7]. Hence, references a certain distance apart in time tend to be the same distance apart in space.

The comparison of the temporal locality for the same benchmark program using different inputs is also interesting. For example, *grep-c* (Figure 2) has 33% of its references separated by five unique references, whereas *grep-words* has only 11%. On the other hand, *grep-c* has $f_I^T(22) \approx 0$, whereas *grep-words* has $f_I^T(22) \approx 18\%$. Though the temporal localities are input dependent at these two points, buffers of size greater than 50 basic block lengths will perform equally well for both benchmarks. Hence, if a design decision is made to be robust, it will be insensitive to the benchmark program input selection.

Finally, the interphase density functions show a preference for large phases. For example, $f_I^\phi(79) = 99\%$ for *grep-c*. A similar execution probability occurs for a phase of size 513 for *yacc-awk*, and at a size of 74 for *grep-words*. This indicates that the penalty of intrinsic cold-start misses would be very high, but infrequent. However, this also suggests that context switching would have a large impact on buffer performance. Perhaps further subdividing phases by using the weights of the weighted control graph might provide more insight the effect of context switching.

5 Conclusions

This paper presents a method for characterizing benchmark programs. Two key features distinguish the ideas presented in this paper from those presented in the past. One is that all the characteristics are stored as data structures whose sizes are proportional to that of the static size of the benchmark program. In contrast, trace driven simulation is based on the analysis of dynamic execution traces whose size is proportional to the dynamic instruction count of the benchmark program. This makes it possible to characterize each benchmark with many realistic inputs. The other key feature is the separation of benchmark characteristics from architecture-specific parameters. Benchmark characterization is presented as a tech-

nique that can provide some insight into the performance of a system without actually having to simulate the system. This provides a uniform ground for comparing different architectures. It is also a tool to help interpret the results of simulation and measurements.

Several areas of benchmark characterization were presented. Control flow and data flow characterizations were explained in detail. To illustrate the ideas, the results of control flow characterization were presented and discussed. The control flow characteristics presented include branch predictability, instruction stream spatial-, and temporal locality locality. The implication of these characterization results on the evaluation of architecture design decisions were also presented.

A profiler and its supporting software tools are being constructed to implement the ideas presented in this paper. The extraction of control flow GRIPs has been completed and was used to derive the results presented in Section 4. The extraction of data flow GRIPs is under development. Once completed, this profiler will be distributed to the architecture research community.

The authors would like to thank Sadun Anik, David Griffith and all members of the IMPACT research group for their support, comments and suggestions. This research has been supported by the National Science Foundation (NSF) under Grant MIP-8809478, a donation from NCR, the National Aeronautics and Space Administration (NASA) under Contract NASA NAG 1-613 in cooperation with the Illinois Computer laboratory for Aerospace Systems and Software (ICLASS), and the Office of Naval Research under Contract N00014-88-K-0656.

References

[1] A. J. Smith, "Cache memories," *ACM Computing Surveys*, vol. 14, no. 3, pp. 473–530, 1982.

[2] S. W. Melvin and Y. N. Patt, "The use of microcode instrumentation for development, debugging and tuning of operating system kernels,"

in *Proc. ACM SIGMETRICᶜ '88 Conf. on Measurement and Modeling of (›mput. Sys.*, (Santa Fe, NM), pp. 207–214, May 988.

[3] A. Agarwal, R. L. Sites, and M. Horowitz, "ATUM: a new technique for capturing address traces using microcode," in *Proc. 13th Annu. Symp. on Comput. Arch.*, pp. 119–127, June 1986.

[4] N. P. Jouppi and D. W. Wall, "Available instruction-level parallelism for superscalar and superpipelined machines," in *Proc. Third Int'l Conf. on Architectural Support for Prog. Lang. and Operating Systems.*, pp. 272–282, Apr. 1989.

[5] M. D. Smith, M. Johnson, and M. A. Horowitz, "Limits on multiple instruction issue," in *Proc. Third Int'l Conf. on Architectural Support for Prog. Lang. and Operating Systems.*, pp. 290–302, Apr. 1989.

[6] S. McFarling and J. L. Hennessy, "Reducing the cost of branches," in *Proc. 13th Annu. Symp. on Comput. Arch.*, (Tokyo, Japan), pp. 396–403, June 1986.

[7] W. W. Hwu and P. P. Chang, "Achieving high instruction cache performance with an optimizing compiler," in *Proc. 16th Annu. Symp. on Comput. Arch.*, (Jerusalem, Israel), pp. 242–251, June 1989.

[8] W. W. Hwu, T. M. Conte, and P. P. Chang, "Comparing software and hardware schemes for reducing the cost of branches," in *Proc. 16th Annu. Symp. on Comput. Arch.*, (Jerusalem, Israel), pp. 1–1, June 1989.

[9] D. Ferrari, G. Serazzi, and A. Zeigner, *Measurement and tuning of computer systems*. Prentice hall, 1989.

[10] J. E. Smith, "A study of branch predition strategies," in *Proc. 8th Annu. Symp. on Comput. Arch.*, pp. 135–148, June 1981.

[11] J. K. F. Lee and A. J. Smith, "Branch prediction strategies and branch target buffer design," *IEEE Computer*, Jan. 1984.

[12] D. R. Ditzel and H. R. McLellan, "Branch folding in the CRISP microprocessor: reducing branch delay to zero," in *Proc. 14th Annu. Symp. on Comput. Arch.*, pp. 2–9, June 1987.

[13] J. A. DeRosa and H. M. Levy, "An evaluation of branch architectures," in *Proc. 14th. Annu. Symp. on Comput. Arch.*, pp. 10–16, June 1987.

[14] D. J. Lilja, "Reducing the branch penalty in pipelined processors," *IEEE Computer*, July 1988.

[15] J. P. Buzen, "Fundimental operational laws of computer system performance," *Acta Informatica*, vol. 7, pp. 167–182, 1977.

[16] H. M. Levy and D. W. Clark, "On the use of benchmarks for measuring system performance," *Computer architecture news*, Dec. 1982.

[17] R. L. Mattson, J. Gercsei, D. R. Slutz, and I. L. Traiger, "Evaluation techniques for storage hierarchies," *IBM Systems J.*, vol. 9, no. 2, pp. 78–117, 1970.

[18] A. V. Aho, R. Sethi, and J. D. Ullman, *Compilers, principles, techniques, and tools*. Reading, MA: Addison-Wesley, 1986.

[19] W. W. Hwu and P. P. Chang, "Trace selection for compiling large C application programs to microcode," in *Proc. 21st Annu. Workshop on Microprogramming and Microarchitectures*, (San Diego, CA.), Nov. 1988.

[20] W. W. Hwu and P. P. Chang, "Forward Semantic: a compiler-assisted instruction fetch method for heavily pipelined processors," in *Proc. 22st Annu. Workshop on Microprogramming and Microarchitectures*, (Ireland), Nov. 1989.

[21] G. J. Chaitin, M. A. Auslander, A. K. Chandra, and J. Cocke, "Register allocation via coloring," *Computer languages*, vol. 6, pp. 47–57, 1981.

[22] G. J. Chaitin, "Register allocation & spilling via graph coloring," in *Proc. ACM SIGPLAN '82 Symp. on Compiler Construction*, pp. 98–105, 1982.

[23] G. D. McNiven and E. S. Davidson, "Analysis of memory reference behavior for design of local memories," in *Proc. 15th. Annu. Symp. on Comput. Arch.*, pp. 56–63, June 1988.

[24] J. E. Thornton, "Parallel operation in the Control Data 6600," in *Proc. AFIPS FJCC*, pp. 33–40, 1964.

[25] R. M. Tomasulo, "An efficient algorithm for exploiting multiple arithmetic units," *IBM Journal of Research and Development*, vol. 11, pp. 25–33, Jan. 1967.

[26] P. G. Emma, *Discrete-time modeling of pipeline computers under flow perturbations*. PhD thesis,

Department of Electrical and Computer Engineering, University of Illinois, Urbana, Illinois, 1984. Coordinated Science Laboratory Computer Systems Group Report No. CSG-27.

[27] P. G. Emma and E. S. Davidson, "Characterization of branch and data dependencies in programs for evaluating pipeline performance," RC 11733 52535, Computer Science Dept., IBM T. J. Watson Research Center, Yorktown Heights, NY, 1986.

[28] A. Agarwal, M. Horowitz, and J. Hennessy, "An analytical cache model," *ACM Trans. Computer Systems*, vol. 7, pp. 184–215, May 1989.

[29] C. B. Stunkel and W. K. Fuchs, "TRAPEDS: producing traces for multicomputers via execution driven simulation," in *Proc. ACM SIGMETRICS '89 and PERFORMANCE '89 Int'l Conf. on Measurement and Modeling of Comput. Sys.*, (Berkeley, CA), pp. 70–78, May 1989.

[30] J. M. Barth, "A practical interprocedural data flow analysis algorithm," *J. ACM*, vol. 21, pp. 724–736, Sept. 1978.

[31] J. R. Ellis, *Bulldog: a compiler for VLIW architectures.* Combridge, MA: The MIT Press, 1986.

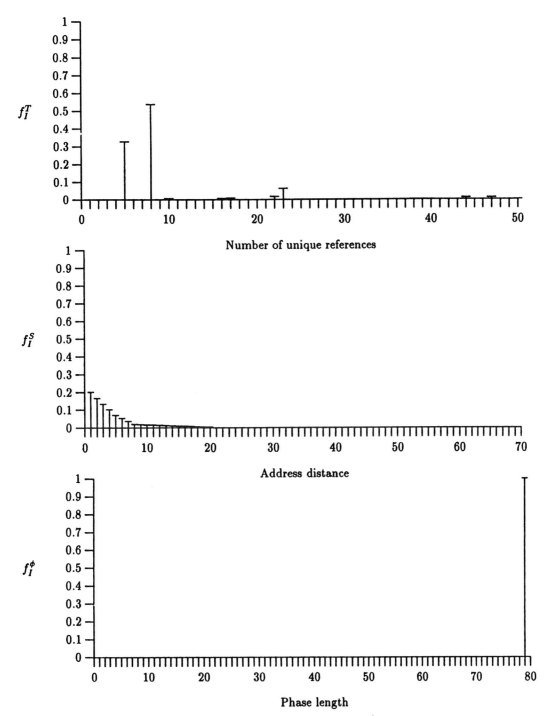

Figure 2: The locality measures, $f_I^T(x)$, $f_I^S(x)$, and $f_I^\phi(x)$, for *grep-c*

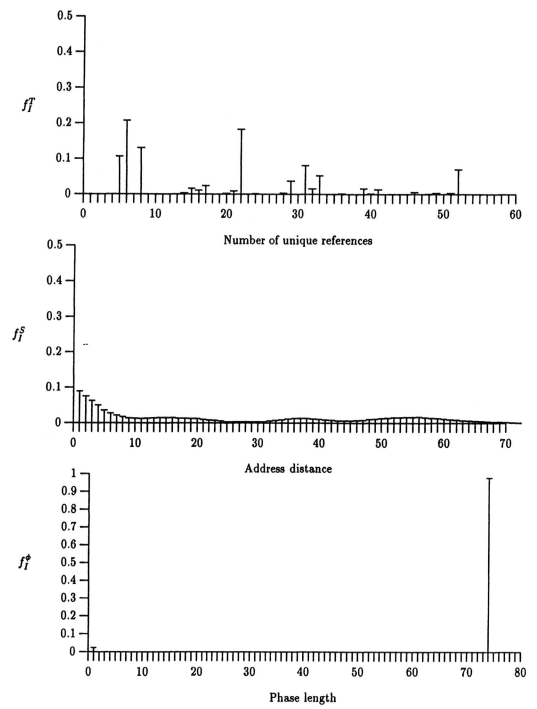

Figure 3: The locality measures, $f_I^T(x)$, $f_I^S(x)$, and $f_I^\phi(x)$, for *grep-words*

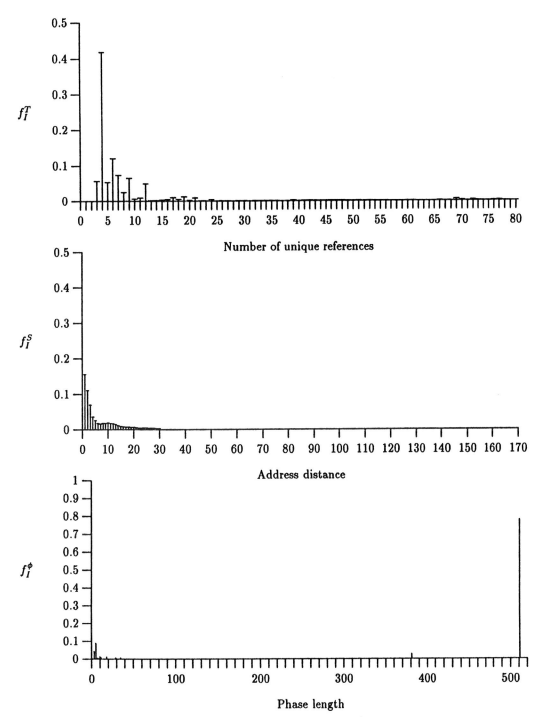

Figure 4: The locality measures, $f_I^T(x)$, $f_I^S(x)$, and $f_I^\phi(x)$, for *yacc-awk*

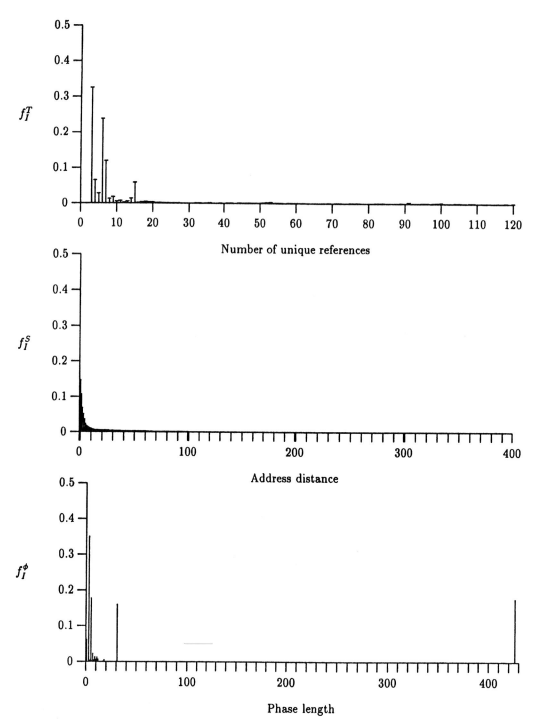

Figure 5: The locality measures, $f_I^T(x)$, $f_I^S(x)$, and $f_I^\phi(x)$, for *yack-make*

A Model of Workloads and Its Use in Miss-Rate Prediction for Fully Associative Caches

Jaswinder Pal Singh, Harold S. Stone, *Fellow, IEEE*, and Dominique F. Thiebaut, *Member, IEEE*

Abstract—We present a mathematical model for the behavior of programs or workloads and extract from it the miss ratio of a finite, fully associative cache (or other first-level memory) using Least-Recently-Used replacement under those workloads. To obtain miss ratios, we first model the function $u(t, L)$ defined to be the number of unique lines of size L referenced before time t. Empirical observations show that this function appears to have the form

$$u(t, L) = W L^a t^b d^{\log L \log t}$$

where W, a, b, d are constants that are related, respectively, to the working set size, locality of references to nearby addresses (spatial locality), temporal locality (locality in time not attributable to spatial locality), and interactions between spatial locality and temporal locality. The miss ratio of a finite fully associative cache can be approximated as the time derivative of $u(t, L)$ evaluated where the function has a value equal to the size of the cache. When the miss ratios from this model are compared to measured miss ratios for a representative trace, the accuracy is high for large caches. For smaller caches, the model is close but not highly precise, although the general shapes of the predicted curves agree with those of the measured curves.

Index Terms—Cache memory, locality, power-law model, miss ratio, miss rate, set associative, spatial locality, temporal locality.

I. INTRODUCTION

AS cache memories evolve in both size and structure, and as the underlying instruction set also evolves with time, the design of cache memories for new machines becomes an interesting challenge. Traditional methods for cache design use trace-driven simulation of systems with caches of various sizes and structures. This method is extremely useful when traces of existing representative workloads are available. When new architectures are in the design stages, no such traces exist. How can a designer estimate the performance of proposed caches in such instances?

In the absence of any other information, the designer can use the extensive curves of Smith [18] collected for a variety of workloads and a variety of machines. However, the cache plays such a critical role in performance that a designer needs to have architecture-specific and workload-specific data available when possible. This paper explores how to model

Manuscript received February 7, 1989; revised March 16, 1990 and October 5, 1991. This work was supported by the IBM Corporation.

J. P. Singh is with the Center for Integrated Systems, Department of Electrical Engineering, Stanford University, Stanford, CA 94305.

H. S. Stone is with the IBM Corporation, Research Division, Yorktown Heights, NY 10598.

D. F. Thiebaut is with the Department of Computer Science, Smith College, Northampton, MA, 01059.

IEEE Log Number 9200186.

workload behavior. The model proposed here appears to yield good enough results to be useful as a design aid when detailed traces are unavailable. However, detailed traces are strongly preferable when the precision of the miss-ratio analysis is of great importance. The parameters of the model reflect characteristics of different applications, and can be obtained by measuring a few different applications executing on similar machines, and by estimating how the parameters change when the applications move to the machine being designed.

For the purposes of this paper, a cache is a buffer memory between a processor and main memory. A cache is accessed associatively to determine if a reference to an item is in the cache or not. If the item is present, the cache honors the memory request. If not, the memory request is honored by main memory, presumably with a greater expenditure of machine cycles. Each replaceable item in the cache is called a *line* (often called *block* in the literature), and the number of bytes in one line is called the *line size*. In physical implementations of caches, associative access is usually approximated by *set-associative* access in which the address space of cache references is logically partitioned into N disjoint spaces, and K cache lines are allocated to each of these spaces. This permits cache accesses to be made by accessing only K of the NK lines of a cache, which is both faster and less costly than accessing all of the lines. A cache with N sets, K-way set associativity, and L bytes per line has a total size of NKL bytes. The cache design problem, in part, is to select the total size of cache and the values of the parameters N, K, and L.

Prior work in modeling cache behavior has been a mixture of analytic and empirical models. The advantage of analytic models is that they are tractable, and yield interesting results quite easily, although the precision of the models may be in question. A model suggested by Rao, for example, uses the analytically tractable "independent reference" model to compute miss ratios for various cache organizations from arithmetic and geometric page reference probabilities [15]. Smith [17] derives miss-ratio curves for set-associative caches using two models—a mixed geometric characterization and the inverse of Saltzer's linear paging model [16]. Both these analyses, however, are only for a fixed line size and do not include the means to parameterize particular workloads.

Other cache models have focused on the transient performance of caches when processes are swapped in and out in a multiprogramming environment [7], [8], [19], [22]. Strecker's model measures the program miss ratios for two different cache sizes and uses parameters derived from these two ratios as the input to a linear paging model in order to obtain miss

Reprinted from *IEEE Trans. Computers*, Vol. 41, No. 7, July 1992, pp. 811–825. Copyright © 1992

ratios for other cache sizes, extending the model to predict the performance with two programs in interleaved execution. While the derived parameters in this model do indirectly characterize the workload, the analysis is again only for a fixed line size. Similar work for a single line size was done by Thiebaut, Stone, and Wolf [23].

A comprehensive and detailed cache model that includes multiprogramming behavior was offered by Agarwal, Horowitz, and Hennessy [2]. This model examines the effects of various cache organizations and characterizes the workload in several ways. One aspect of the model is that it obtains the value of a parameter called the *collision rate* by simulating a small 1-way set-associative cache. The model extends to larger caches by assuming that the collision rate is constant for all other realistic organizations. The advantage of this model is that it is detailed, accurate, and models realistic cache structures. The complementary disadvantage is that it is complex and requires many input parameters that have to be measured from the workload. The many parameters that characterize a workload become a disadvantage when workload information for a new machine has to be extrapolated from a pool of existing information for related but different machines. To design caches under these conditions, it is necessary that a model characterize a workload by as few parameters as possible, and that these parameters bear some natural relationship to workload characteristics.

Two parameters of great importance are

1) (*spatial locality*) the tendency of the workload to cluster references to nearby addresses, and

2) (*temporal locality*) the tendency of the workload to revisit addresses visited recently in time.

The first parameter is useful because it measures the gain in cache hits as line size increases. The second parameter is a useful measure of gain in cache hits as a function of the total size of the cache. The two parameters together help the designer to determine the effects of increasing cache size, and to decide how cache size should be increased as a combination of increases in line size, number of lines, and degree of set associativity.

An empirical model of program-reference behavior that helps characterize temporal locality is the power law observed by Chow [4], [5]. Chow found that the miss ratio of a finite cache almost universally obeys the function $M = AC^B$ where M is the miss ratio, C is the cache size, and A and B are constants. Thiebaut [20], [21] found that a similar function holds for the number of unique references made by a program, at least after its initial working locality is referenced. This result was tested both for a single-user workload and for a multiprogramming workload, and was found to be valid for both. Thiebaut showed that the time derivative of this function provides a good approximation to the miss ratio of a fully associative cache. Thiebaut's model, however, does not include the effects of line size.

The literature contains relatively little on models of line-size effects. Goodman [10] has two curves of line size effects that show nearly straight lines on log / log plots. Such plots imply a power-law relation of the form proposed in this paper.

The present research extends Thiebaut's results [20], [21] to include line-size effects in combination with the temporal effects of his model. The new model was derived from empirical observations on one long representative instruction trace. The model uses the *footprint* function $u(t, L)$, which is defined to be the number of unique memory lines of size L referenced between time 0 and time t. The model shows that $u(t, L)$ is a power-law function of t for fixed L, and a power-law function of L for fixed t. However, the footprint function is not simply the product of the two power-law functions. It also has a term that expresses the interaction of the two parameters. The miss ratio for a particular cache size is obtained by evaluating the time derivative of the footprint function at a point where the value of $u(t, L)$ is equal to the number of lines in the cache. This produces a power-law curve for the miss ratio as a function of cache size, in agreement with Chow's [4] observations. A more complex form is predicted for the miss ratio as a function of line size. The general shapes of the curves obtained for this function agree with the shapes of the curves in the extensive data reported by Smith [18]. Agarwal *et al.* [2] model spatial locality through a function they name $u(B)$, which is defined to be the number of unique cache lines of size B referenced in a time granule of length t. Although their specific mathematical model of this function is different from our mathematical model of the corresponding function, when observed parameters are substituted into both models, the resulting functions are very close to each other for various sizes of caches.

The model developed here has been tested in detail only on the trace cited in the paper. However, we show data from Smith [18] and Agarwal *et al.* [2] that are consistent with the model and explained by it. The model predicts the behavior of programs in large caches, but is not useful for caches too small to hold the initial working set of a program.

The model presented here has several limitations. Cache behavior impacts performance in several ways other than hit ratio. The model in this paper fails to capture the bus traffic generated by writes to cache, and thus fails to distinguish between caches that use a write-through policy as compared to those that use a write-back cache policy. Also, there is no attempt to model traffic generated for cache coherence which is observable in systems in which two or more processors or direct memory-access controllers can write concurrently to a global, shared address space. Finally, the work models fully associative caches, rather than set-associative caches. Set-associative design is used almost universally for processor caches, with fully associative designs relegated to disk caches. Additional research is required in order to overcome these limitations of the model.

Section II of this paper describes the three major trends that were observed in examining the behavior of the footprint function as a function of time and line size. Section III develops the model for the footprint function from these trends, and Section IV derives from this model an expression for the miss ratio of a finite fully associative cache of a given size. Section V discusses the method used to estimate parameters for a workload, and Section VI compares the model's predictions of miss ratios for that workload to observed miss ratios. In

300

Section VII, we show that the new model more accurately characterizes the behavior of programs in large caches than does the model of Agarwal *et al.* [2]. Section VIII reports initial results in an unsuccessful attempt to extend the model to set-associative caches. Finally, Section IX contains a summary and a discussion of open problems.

II. EMPIRICAL OBSERVATIONS

This section describes the three crucial empirical observations from which we build a model for $u(t, L)$, the number of unique lines of length L in a trace of length t. The observations are:

1) The function $u(t, L)$ is a power function of t for fixed L. That is, $\log u(t, L)$ is a linear function of $\log t$.
2) The slope of $\log u(t, L)$ as a function of $\log t$ is a linear function of $\log L$.
3) The function $u(t, L)$ is a power function of L for fixed t.

From these three results we are able to produce in the next section the most general form of $u(t, L)$ that obeys all of these observations. The first of the three observations has been confirmed by independent observations in the literature, but the second and third observations are believed to be new.

A. Unique References as a Function of Total References

The fact that $u(t, L)$ is a power function of t for fixed L was observed by Thiebaut [20], [21], and confirmed by independent observations by Kobayashi and MacDougall [13]. Specifically, let $u(t)$ be the number of unique lines in a trace of length of t for some fixed line size. Then empirical data suggest that $u(t)$ over large regions of time is accurately described by the equation

$$u(t) = Wt^a \qquad (1)$$

where W is a constant related to the initial working-set size and line size of a trace and a is a constant related to the locality of references on the trace. An equivalent way of expressing (1) is

$$\log u(t) = \log W + a \log t. \qquad (2)$$

Our observations of $u(t, L)$ are shown in Fig. 1. This figure plots $u(t, L)$ against t for line sizes varying from 8 to 256 bytes by powers of 2. The trace is of a typical IBM 370 MVS multiprogramming workload and its length is 6 million references. The full trace from which this segment was taken is 200 million references long, and comprises a representative composite sample that includes operating-system activity, compilations, sorts, and various user applications. The trace-generation process was designed to capture a representative sample of IBM 370 workloads, and the full trace been used extensively by IBM for internal studies of processor performance. We do not know which specific activities are present on the 6-million reference sample. Note in Fig. 1 that $u(t, L)$ decreases with increasing line size and that the qualitative behavior as a function of t at different line sizes is similar.

The confirmation of (1) is shown in Fig. 2, which shows the data of Fig. 1 replotted on log / log axes. These curves

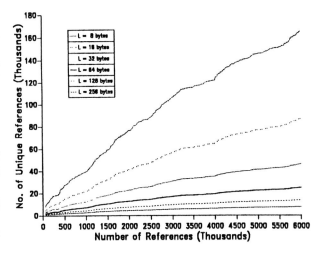

Fig. 1. The function $u(t, L)$ plotted as a function of t, the number of references. L is the line size of the references. The data are plotted from a System/370 trace.

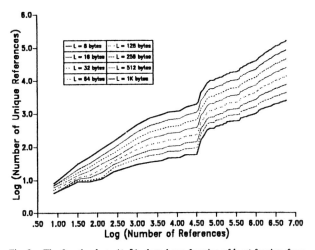

Fig. 2. The function $\log u(t, L)$ plotted as a function of $\log t$ for data from the System/370 trace.

display a strong linear trend for each line size, although their specific details show statistical variations and short-term transient effects. Fig. 3 expands the x-axis of Fig. 2 in the region of the trace between $t = 50\,000$ and $t = 6\,000\,000$. Note how linear the curves are in this region. Thus, for this trace, after a startup transient $u(t, L)$ obeys a power law in t for each line size.

The empirical studies of Thiebaut and of Kobayashi and MacDougall indicate that (1) accurately describes observed data except possibly for an initial transient for small t and a flattening of the trend line for very large t. The initial transient where the formula does not hold may be due to a working-set phenomenon [6]. The working set of a workload at a particular time is the set of lines that receive the bulk of the references, and if cache memory is too small to hold that working set, the rate of cache misses is relatively high. If cache is large enough to hold the working set, the cache miss ratio is relatively low. There is a sharp change in miss ratio as a function of cache

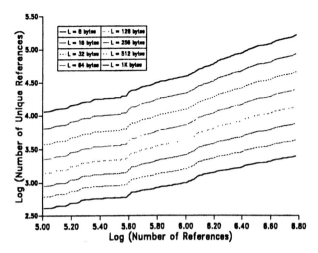

Fig. 3. The function $\log u(t, L)$ plotted as a function of $\log t$ in a stable region of behavior.

size in the region where the cache becomes large enough to hold the working set.

The working set is reflected in empirical data by a fast growth of $u(t)$ for t so small that a trace does not have time to touch the full initial working set. Thiebaut's data [20] shows that $u(t)$ grows at a rate faster than given by (1) until it reaches the curve described by (1), from which point onward it follows (1). The point in time at which $u(t)$ changes its behavior is essentially the point in time at which $u(t)$ has touched the entire initial working set. The transition between the initial behavior of $u(t)$ and its steady-state behavior is typically a smooth transition rather than a sharp change of slope.

Thiebaut [20], [21] argues that the miss rate of a workload in a cache of size C is the time derivative of (1) evaluated at the point where $u(t) = C$. That is,

$$\text{Miss rate}(C) = \frac{du(t)}{dt}\Big|_{u(t)=C} \qquad (3)$$

$$= aW^{1/a}C^{1-1/a}. \qquad (4)$$

This follows because the derivative in (3) is the instantaneous rate at which unique references occur in a trace at the point where the unique references observed so far have just filled a cache of size C. If the miss rate of a finite cache depends only on the size of the cache, then this is the miss rate of a cache with a size of C. Since C is measured in bytes and $u(t)$ is in units of cache lines, (4) gives the basic behavior for a line size of 1 byte. The relation of miss rate to $u(t, L)$ was influenced by mathematical models due to Gillis and Weiss [9] and Mandelbrot [14].

Note that we use the term *miss rate* to express a time derivative whereas the term *miss ratio* expresses the quotient of misses divided by time. Thiebaut's model equates the instantaneous miss rate of a cache to its steady-state miss rate measured over a period of time, which is valid if the miss rate is stable over that period of time. The form of (4) for miss rate agrees with Chow's observations [3]–[5] that the miss ratio M in a cache of size C is given by $M = AC^B$, where A and B are constants.

In (1), the exponent a of t is a measure of locality of reference. If a is small, the rate of observing new references is low, and the reference stream tends to be local in nature. The largest possible value of a is unity. If a were greater, then $u(t)$ would grow faster than linearly in t, which is impossible. As a increases, the corresponding reference stream has a high tendency to access new addresses and the reference stream becomes nonlocal.

Equation (3) expresses the miss rate for caches with a line size of 1 byte. The empirical observations from the literature [4], [17], [10], [21] show that the power law holds at different line sizes, although the exponent may change with line size. Both Smith [17] and Goodman [10] plot some curves on log / log scales, and these curves are straight lines that capture the form of (3).

B. Slope of log u Versus log t as a Function of Line Size

Spatial locality is related to the way the slopes in Fig. 3 change as a function of line size L. Although the slopes of the curves in Fig. 3 appear to be nearly equal, in fact, the slopes decrease with increasing line size. Empirical measurements described in this section show that the power of t in $u(t, L)$ is a linear function of $\log L$, and that the model is accurate for our data over a large range of t and L.

One way of arriving at the spatial locality effect is to obtain a good estimate of the slopes in Fig. 3 and to plot these slopes as a function of line size. We obtained estimates by fitting straight lines to the curves in Fig. 3 using a least-squares fit on the log / log data. Two sets of slopes were computed this way, one for straight lines fitted to the trace region between $t = 2\,000\,000$ and $t = 6\,000\,000$ references and one for the trace region between $t = 300,000$ and $t = 6\,000\,000$ where the curves are not quite as straight as in the first region. The graphs of the slopes plotted against the base 2 logarithm of line size are shown in Fig. 4. Note that both plots are remarkably straight. Also shown in Fig. 4 for comparison purposes are straight lines fitted to the same data. Because the two empirical curves in Fig. 4 are not identical, we conclude that the slope of the curves in Fig. 3 is not constant, but shows a slight decreasing trend as time increases. This effect is small and is not modeled in this paper. How to quantify and use this effect is an open research question.

The observations of Fig. 4 suggest that the appropriate way to modify (1) to show line-size effects is to alter it to the form:

$$u(t, L) = W_L t^{a_L} \qquad (5)$$

where

$$a_L = k_1 + k_2 \log_2 L, \qquad (6)$$

k_1 and k_2 are constants, and W_L is a function of line size. Since, a_L is the slope of a curve in Fig. 3, (6) expresses the fact revealed by Fig. 4 that the slope of $\log u$ versus $\log t$ is a linear function of $\log L$.

The fact that the slopes in Fig. 3 decrease as line size increases indicates that spatial locality behaves in a statistically predictable fashion. When spatial locality is very strong, a doubling of line size produces nearly a factor of 2 reduction

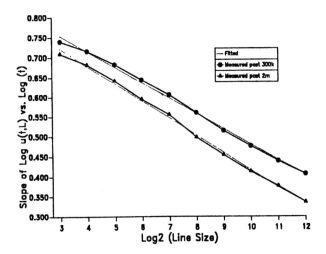

Fig. 4. The slope of curves in Fig. 3 plotted against $\log L$. The slopes are taken in the regions $t \geq 300\,000$ and $t \geq 2\,000\,000$

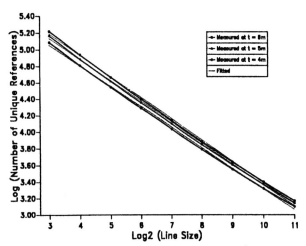

Fig. 5. The function $\log u(t, L)$ plotted against $\log L$.

in the number of unique lines referenced with a corresponding decrease in the slope of $u(t, L)$ when plotted as shown in Fig. 3. Weaker spatial locality produces a smaller change of slope, but the slopes still diminish as line size increases. If spatial locality were negligible, we would see essentially no change of slope in Fig. 3 as line size increases.

C. Unique References as a Function of Line Size

The last observation is that $u(t, L)$ varies as a power of L when t is held fixed, or equivalently, that $\log u$ is a linear function of $\log L$.

Fig. 5 is a $\log / \log$ plot of $u(t, L)$ as a function of L for fixed values of t. Each curve in Fig. 5 plots the points on a vertical slice of Fig. 3. Because the curves in Fig. 5 are very close to linear, the data for $u(t, L)$ for fixed t satisfy

$$\log u(t, L) = k_3 + k_4 \log L \qquad (7)$$

for some constants k_3 and k_4. As a measure of the goodness of fit, Fig. 5 shows plots of fitted straight lines together with the plotted lines. This reveals a very slight curvature in the measured data that is not modeled in this paper.

III. A MODEL FOR THE NUMBER OF UNIQUE REFERENCES

In this section, we develop the most general model for the number of unique references as a function of both the line size and the total number of references that satisfies the three observations of the previous section.

There are three linear relations involving logarithms that must be satisfied. They are

$$\log u(t, L) = \log W_L + a_L \log t \quad \text{for fixed } L, \qquad (8)$$

$$a_L = k_1 + k_2 \log L, \qquad (9)$$

and

$$\log u(t, L) = k_3 + k_4 \log L \quad \text{for fixed } t. \qquad (10)$$

Equations (8) and (10) can be satisfied simultaneously most generally if $\log W_L$ in (8) is itself a linear function of $\log L$.

That is,

$$\log W_L = k_5 + k_6 \log L. \qquad (11)$$

In (9), (10), and (11), the coefficients k_i are constants that are derived empirically and are related to observed spatial and temporal locality.

Substituting (9) and (11) into (8) and grouping coefficients produces

$$\log u(t, L) = k_5 + k_6 \log L + k_1 \log t + k_2 \log L \log t \qquad (12)$$

for some set of coefficients $k_1, k_2, k_5,$ and k_6. Equation (12) shows that $\log u(t, L)$ has a quadratic term involving $\log L$ and $\log t$. The straight lines in Figs. 4 and 5 indicate that the quadratic terms in (12) gives an excellent fit. Higher order terms added to (12) will improve the model to the extent that the model will be better able to capture the curvature in Figs. 4 and 5. However, the curvature is small enough to ignore for our purposes.

To obtain the model in power-law form, we exponentiate (12) to obtain

$$u(t, L) = W L^a t^b d^{\log L \log t} \qquad (13)$$

where the coefficients W, a, b, and d are, respectively, $\log W = k_5$, $a = k_6$, $b = k_1$, and $\log d = k_2$.

Using the relation

$$x^{\log y} = y^{\log x} \qquad (14)$$

we can write (13) as

$$\begin{aligned}
u(t, L) &= W L^a t^b d^{\log L \log t} \\
&= W L^a t^b L^{\log d \log t} = W t^b L^{a + \log d \log t} \qquad (15) \\
&= W L^a t^b t^{\log d \log L} = W L^a t^{b + \log d \log L}. \qquad (16)
\end{aligned}$$

Equations (15) and (16) show that if we hold t fixed while varying L, or hold L fixed while varying t, then $u(t, L)$ varies as a power of the free variable in both cases. Yet the model described by (13) is not simply a multiplicative combination of the two power laws because of the interaction term. If there were no interaction term, then the curves in Fig. 4 would be horizontal.

The model of (13) explains the behavior of the curves in Fig. 1 in the region after the initial working set of the trace has been read. The size of the initial working set is the height of $u(t, L)$ at the knee of the curve where the slope changes from a steep transient to a more shallow steady-state slope. Therefore the segment of the curve to the right of the knee corresponds to the portion of the trace that appears after each line in the initial working set of the trace has been touched at least once. The knees of the curves in Fig. 2 are present, but are not sharply delineated. Hence, the sizes of the respective initial working sets are not well-defined constants. Nevertheless, the figure suggests that if we plotted the curves for a workload with a much larger working set, then the initial transient would last longer, and the steady-state portions of all lines would be displaced upwards. Thus, as the initial working-set size increases so does the y-intercept of Fig. 2. Since the y-intercept is $\log W + a \log L$, the parameter W is related to the working set size.

The spatial locality parameter is the power of L and is equal to $a + \log d \log t$. When L doubles, $u(t, L)$ reduces by as much as a factor of 2. Hence, the power $a + \log d \log t$ in (15) is negative and has a magnitude that does not exceed unity. The closer that this power is to -1, the more local are the address references. Thus, the spatial-locality coefficient a is a measure of locality due to references made to nearby addresses. As its value decreases toward -1, references tend to cluster to nearby addresses.

A similar argument indicates that the power $b + \log d \log L$ in (16) cannot exceed 1, at which point $u(t, L)$ is a linear function of time. If the exponent exceeds 1, then $u(t, L)$ grows faster than linearly in t, and the rate of observing new references will eventually exceed the rate of making references, which is impossible. Locality is lowest for high values of this power and becomes greater as b goes toward 0.

The coefficient d in (13) expresses a second-order interaction. When $d = 1$, $\log d = 0$, and (13) is a purely multiplicative model in which the temporal locality t^b is multiplied by the spatial locality L^a. Note that in this case, $k_2 = 0$ in (12), and (12) becomes a linear function of the logarithms. A nonlinear term in (12) is reflected in (13) as a value of d different from unity, and an interaction between t and L occurs in the exponent of d.

To summarize the model derivation, the proof that we have captured the characteristics of the curves in Figs. 3 through 5 is that we have found ways to plot the data that yield reasonably straight lines. Although Fig. 3 is fairly noisy and subject to error when being modeled by a straight-line fit, the fits in Figs. 4 and 5 are excellent. The key notion that brought out the straight lines is the idea that the model should deal with the function $u(t, L)$ rather than with the less well-behaved miss-ratio function. The straight lines in these curves provide accurate data for finding the coefficients of the model for $u(t, L)$, which we can then use to predict the miss ratios as indicated in the next section.

IV. THE MISS RATIO OF A FINITE FULLY ASSOCIATIVE CACHE

In this section, we use the model for the number of unique line references as a basis for obtaining the miss ratio of a finite fully associative cache.

Thiebaut [20], [21] presents evidence that the miss rate of a cache with C bytes is the time derivative of the $u(t)$ function evaluated where $u(t) = C$. His reasoning is summarized in Section II in the discussion of (3). His argument relies on the assumption that the miss rate of a fully associative cache for a stable trace depends only on the size of the cache. Consequently, the time derivative of $u(t)$ evaluated at $u(t) = C$ is an estimate of the miss ratio of a cache of size C when the input sequence is a trace with a statistically stable reference pattern. The instantaneous miss rate of real workloads varies in time, although it is stationary over long periods of time [24]. The assumption of statistical stability states that miss rates are measured at points in time where the miss process is locally stationary.

In the terminology of this paper, a cache with C bytes composed of C/L L-byte lines fills at the time when $u(t, L)$ reaches the value C/L. The time derivative at this point is therefore an estimate for the miss rate of a fully associative cache of size C bytes with a line size L. Because $u(t, L)$ behaves differently during the transient when the initial working set is loaded as compared to its steady-state behavior, we attempt to model $u(t, L)$ only in the steady-state region, which is equivalent to modeling miss ratios only for caches large enough to hold the initial working set of the workload on the trace.

From the discussion above, we wish to calculate

$$\text{Miss rate}(C, L) = \frac{du(t, L)}{dt} \Big|_{u(t,L)=C/L}. \quad (17)$$

Using (16) we find

$$\text{Miss rate}(C, L) = \frac{1}{\theta_L} (WL^a)^{\theta_L} \left(\frac{C}{L} \right)^{1-\theta_L} \quad (18)$$

where θ_L is the inverse of the exponent of t in (16) and is given by

$$\theta_L = \frac{1}{b + \log d \log L}. \quad (19)$$

We now have an expression for the miss rate in terms of the cache size, the line size, and the four workload parameters W, a, b, and d. We can estimate these parameters from the curves shown in Figs. 3 through 5.

V. ESTIMATION OF WORKLOAD PARAMETERS AND MISS RATIOS

The preceding development of the model tells us what the different parameters represent. We can derive the parameters from the y-intercepts and slopes of the curves in Figs. 3 through 5. In this section we show how to extract those parameters and use them to predict the miss ratio of various fully associative caches.

To aid the visual interpretation of the data, the logarithms of t and u are base 10 logarithms, whereas base 2 is used for logarithms of the line size and cache size. When we measure the slopes and y-intercepts of the graphs, we have to take the base of the logarithm into account, and apply a conversion factor in some cases in order to produce consistent results. In

304

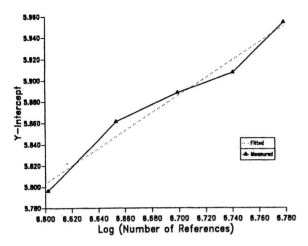

(a)

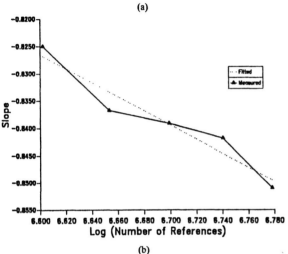

(b)

Fig. 6. Slopes and y-intercepts of Fig. 5 plotted against $\log t$. (a) Plot of y-intercepts versus $\log t$. (b) Plot of slopes versus $\log t$.

the discussion below, the use of the conversion factor between logarithmic bases is made explicit.

The four parameters W, a, b, and d in (15) can all be obtained from Fig. 5. We estimate the parameters by the following procedure:

1) Obtain the y-intercepts and slopes of $\log u(t, L)$ as a function of $\log L$ for fixed t.
2) Obtain the y-intercepts and slopes of $\log u(t, L)$ as a function of $\log t$ for fixed L.
3) Use the four values from Steps 1 and 2 to solve for the four parameters of (15).

Assume that the curves of Fig. 5 are modeled by (15). Then $\log u(t, L)$ as a function of $\log L$ for fixed t has a y-intercept of $\log W + b \log t$ and a slope of $a + \log d \log t$. Fig. 6(a) plots the y-intercepts of the curves in Fig. 5 as a function of $\log t$. In Fig. 6(a), in addition to the points related to the three curves of Fig. 5, points for two other curves have been included in the plot. The two additional curves fall between the ones given in Fig. 5 and have been omitted in that figure for sake of clarity.

The slope of the curve in Fig. 6(a) as a function of $\log t$ is equal to b, and its y-intercept is $\log W$. Although the graph

in Fig. 6(a) ideally should be a straight line, there is some measurement noise evident in that graph as plotted, so that the coefficients derived from it will have some error associated with them. For the curve shown, the fitted straight line has a y-intercept of 0.34208 and a slope of 0.827457, so that $b = 0.827457$, and $W = 10^{0.34208} = 2.19827$.

To find parameters a and d, in Fig. 6(b) we plot the slopes of the graphs in Fig. 5 as a function of $\log t$. Note that the model of (15) indicates that the parameter a is the y-intercept of Fig. 6(b) and the parameter $\log d$ is its slope. As in Fig. 6(a), five points are plotted. The fitted straight line has a y-intercept of 0.033233 and a slope of -0.13025. The y-intercept is the estimated value of a and the slope yields the estimate of the base 10 log of d. Hence, we find $d = 10^{-0.13025} = 0.74088$.

As an independent check of these estimates, we can use the curves in Fig. 4 to estimate b and d Specifically, the y-intercepts of the curves in Fig. 4 approximate b and the slopes approximate $\log d$. (The two curves in Fig. 4 would fall on top of each other if the model were exact, but the curves are slightly separated, indicating a variation of a with time that is not accounted by the model.) The estimates of b are 0.84972 and 0.86916, respectively, for the curves taken past 2 million and 300K, as compared to the estimate of 0.827457 from Fig. 6. The estimates of $\log_{10} d$ (noting that a conversion from a base 2 logarithm is required in Fig. 4) produce respective estimates of -0.14336 and -0.12868 as compared to -0.13025 for $\log d$ produced from Fig. 6. The several estimates are consistent and very close to each other.

This completes the discussion of the extraction of the model's parameters from the trace data. The next section compares the miss ratios predicted by the model to the miss ratios actually observed.

VI. PREDICTED VERSUS ACTUAL MISS RATIOS

In this section, we use the parameters extracted by the method outlined above to predict the miss ratios of caches ranging in size from 8 kilobytes to 1 megabyte with line sizes varying between 8 bytes and 2 kilobytes. The workload is the 370 MVS multiprogramming mix described in Section II-A (6 million references of system activity, compilations, sorts, and other user applications). The results show excellent agreement for large caches, and poor agreement for small caches in regions where we did not attempt to model program behavior.

The model used for $u(t, L)$ for the predictions described below is

$$u(t, L) = W L^a t^b 10^{\log d \log L \log t}$$
$$= 2.19827 L^{0.033233} t^{0.827457} 10^{-0.13025 \log L \log t}.$$

(20)

Fig. 7 compares (20) to the actual data from Fig. 1 at $t = 6\,000\,000$ for varying L. The predictions fit the measurements very well except for the line size of 8 bytes where the predicted point is about 8% smaller than the actual point. The variation is partly due to irregularity in the actual curve for $u(t, L)$ as shown in Fig. 1. The curves in that figure tend to be smoother as the line size increases, but because they are rather noisy we cannot expect a perfect fit at specific points on a curve.

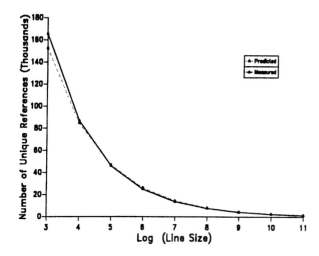

Fig. 7. Comparison of measured and predicted curves for $u(t, L)$ plotted against $\log L$ at $t = 6\,000\,000$.

The quality of the model as a predictor of miss rates is exhibited in Figs. 8 and 9. What we see in general is that the model tends to produce good fits for large caches but poorer fits for small caches. The reason for this is clear from Figs. 2 and 3. The model parameters have been extracted from the slopes of the curves in Fig. 3, but Fig. 2 shows that these slopes tend to characterize the data only for large values of t, but not for small values of t. The miss rate predictions are based on the size of cache that fills at each particular value of time. The parameters derived from the data produce an excellent characterization of the curves at times at which large caches fill, and these caches have roughly 64K to 128K bytes. The parameters, however, produce poor characterizations of the data for small values of time, at which point small caches fill.

The quality of the predictions also depends somewhat on line size. One possible explanation is that the cache-simulation data have a bias due to the shortness of the trace, and the predictions do not have that bias. The bias is due to the initialization misses of a simulated cache becoming a substantial fraction of the total misses recorded during a simulation. This effect appears to be greater for caches with smaller line sizes. This can be explained by the fact that each doubling of line size reduces the number of initialization misses by 2, but does not reduce the remaining number of misses by 2. Hence, the proportion of misses due to initialization is greatest for small line sizes. Therefore, we expect to see distortions due to initialization misses more strongly in caches with small line sizes. Since the initialization miss rate is higher than the steady-state miss rate, for small line sizes the distortion should cause the measured miss rates to be higher than the predicted miss rates.

The miss rates experienced by various caches are shown in Figs. 8(a) and (b). Each figure shows two curves for each cache structure. The dashed curve is the miss rate predicted by (18) and the corresponding solid curve is the miss ratio as measured from the trace. The 16K cache in Fig. 8(a) is too small to be modeled accurately. The model succeeds only in giving the

correct general shape of the miss-ratio curve, and otherwise is not close enough to the true miss ratio to be useful. The 64K cache, however, is just large enough to be in the region where predictions are useful. The prediction fits the measured miss ratio reasonably closely for larger line sizes, but is not useful for smaller line sizes. Note that the general shape of the predicted curve is similar to the shape of the measured curve. Four more caches are plotted in Fig. 8(b), and the fit is excellent for large cache sizes. The smaller caches tend to produce poorer fits, especially at small line sizes.

To give an accurate representation of the relative error in the predicted miss rates, Fig. 8(c) shows the data for four cache sizes with the logarithm of the miss rate plotted against the logarithm of line size. Note that the model is actually quite good for the two large caches, although the relative error tends to increase as line size becomes very long. The model yields a reasonably good approximation to the behavior of the 128K cache at large line sizes, but produces too low an estimate for the miss ratio at small line sizes. The 16K cache is not modeled accurately.

Figs. 9(a) and (b) replot the data in Figs. 8(a) and (b) as a function of cache size rather than of line size. Note that the model tends to be accurate for large cache sizes and moderate line sizes. The least accurate predictions are for the 16-byte line size and the 2K-byte line size. The model tends to produce too small a miss ratio for small line sizes and too large a miss ratio for large line sizes. Fig. 9(c) replots data for three line sizes to show the variation of the logarithm of the miss ratio with respect to changes in cache size. The model predicts that these curves should be straight lines on a log / log plot. The measured curves are not quite straight, so the model is not entirely accurate. However, the measured curves have a strong linear tendency which is captured correctly by the model. For the curves shown, the relative error in the miss ratio is reasonably small throughout the ranges plotted. It is greatest for the 16-byte line size for most caches, and for the 2K-byte line size for small cache sizes.

Note that all data presented here come from a single trace. For the model to be credible, it must hold for all or many traces. Resource limitations prevented us from carrying out the study on other traces to obtain additional confirmation. The work of Kobayashi and MacDougall gives a strong indication that the model holds for fixed line size, but as yet there is no independent confirmation that it captures the effects of line-size variations on other traces. This is an interesting question left open for other researchers.

VII. COMPARISON WITH OTHER RESEARCH

This section compares the new model to data published by Smith [18] and to a model of cache behavior suggested by Agarwal et al. [2], that we call the *AHH model*. Our model is consistent, in general, with prior research, except that it produces a different behavior for large caches from that predicted by the AHH model.

Fig. 10 presents data that demonstrate the validity of the new model for data other than the immediate trace on which it was calibrated. Fig. 10(a) shows Smith's design-target miss-

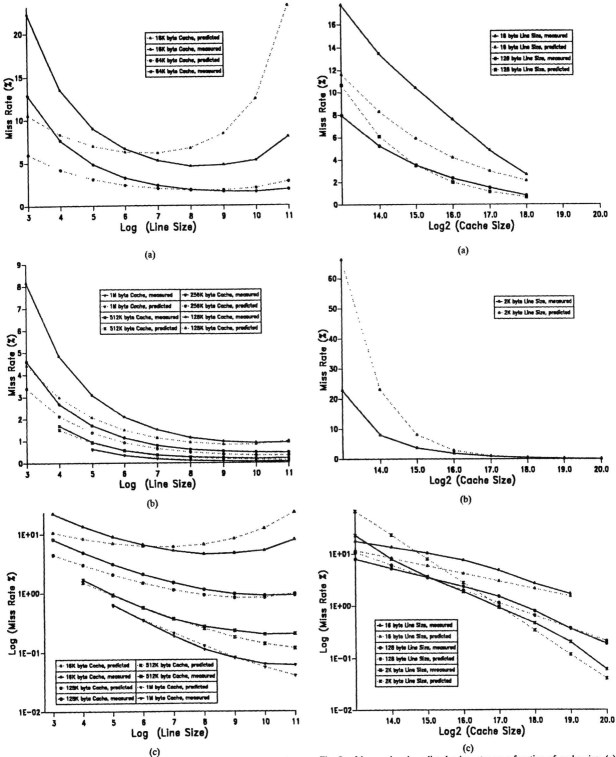

Fig. 8. Comparisons of predicted and measured miss rates. (a) Comparisons of miss rates for small caches as a function of cache size. (b) Comparisons of miss rates for large caches as a function of cache size. (c) Comparisons of miss rates as a function of line size.

Fig. 9. Measured and predicted miss rates as a function of cache size. (a) Miss rates for 16-byte and 128-byte lines sizes. (b) Miss rates for a 2K-byte line size. (c) Plots of log (miss rate) against log (cache size) for several line sizes.

ratios for set-associative caches replotted with respect to cache size instead of line size as it appeared in the original article. What is remarkable about Fig. 10(a) is that the curves are

straight lines on log / log plots, which is precisely the behavior predicted by the model for fully associative caches. In Smith [18] where the data appear, there is no indication that the plots

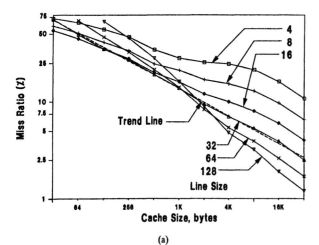

(a)

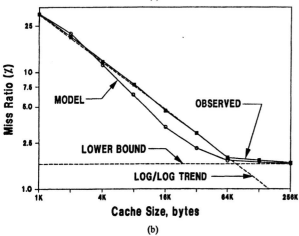

(b)

Fig. 10. Plots of miss rates versus cache size. (a) A log / log plot of design target miss ratios for data references from Smith's data [18]. (b) Trend lines and data from the model of Agarwal, Horowitz, and Hennessy [2].

of the data might produce straight lines when replotted to show miss rate versus cache size. To reveal the straightness of these curves, Fig. 10(a) plots a straight trend line for the curve that corresponds to a 32-byte line size. When straight lines are fitted to the curves in Fig. 10(a), the correlation coefficient for a 4-byte line size exceeds 0.98, and all others exceed 0.99. The curves are average miss ratios taken over a large number of traces for a large number of machines. Smith [18] states that he performed some smoothing of the data from which he produced his design target miss ratios. This may inadvertently have improved the straightness in Fig. 10(a).

Our model also predicts the variation of miss ratio with respect to line size, and the predicted variation is consistent with Smith's data. For example, the curve that describes the 16K cache in Fig. 8(c) follows very closely the curve in Fig. 5 of Smith [18] which shows the variation of design-target miss-ratios with respect to line size. Because Smith's data are intended to be representative of a large class of workloads, the predictions obtained from our model are likely to be consistent with workloads, in general, as characterized by Smith's data.

Fig. 10(b) shows measured and predicted miss ratios for a variety of cache sizes as reported by Agarwal et al. [2]. The

measured data follow a straight line on the log / log graph down to a lower bound, and thereafter become asymptotic to the lower bound as cache size increases. In the range where the data lie on the log / log trend line, they are consistent with our model. In the discussion below, we show that the data that lie on the lower bound asymptote in this case are artifacts of the short trace length and do not give a correct characterization of miss-ratio behavior for large caches. Thus, our model correctly predicts the straightness of the log / log trend of observed data where they are correct, and reveals distortions due to the measurement process where the observations differ from our predictions.

Fig. 10(b) also shows the predicted miss ratios from the model proposed by Agarwal et al. [2]. Since both the AHH model and the new model proposed in this paper predict miss ratios for caches, and both models show line size and cache size effects, it is worthwhile to compare the two to identify how they differ and to indicate their relative advantages and disadvantages. The comparison below treats the following aspects of the models:

1) Scope of application
2) Model components
3) Predictive power
4) Complexity of calibration
5) Method of use.

Scope of application: The AHH model has a broader scope of application because it covers set-associative caches and small caches, neither of which are treated by the new model. When precise analyses of small caches, particularly set-associative caches, are required, we recommend the use of the AHH model.

Model Components: Hill and Smith [12] classify misses into three types—*compulsory, capacity,* and *conflict.* The first reference to each distinct line on a trace produces a compulsory miss. Capacity misses are misses that are experienced by a fully associative cache because the cache is too small to hold all references. *Conflict* misses are misses produced by set-associative caches in excess of those produced by fully associative caches of equal size. Our model estimates the capacity misses because the derivative of $u(t, L)$ is the miss-rate of a fully associative cache at the point it fills. A miss that occurs at this point is due to a limit on cache capacity. Note that the model estimates the capacity misses from the compulsory miss rate. The model does not produce estimates of the conflict misses.

The AHH model includes all three types of misses, but accounts for them in a different way. The AHH model has a term for *startup effects,* which are misses that initially fill a working set, a term for *nonstationary effects,* which accounts for the difference between compulsory misses and startup effects, and a term for *intrinsic interference,* which corresponds to conflict misses. The misses predicted by our model correspond to the sum of the startup and nonstationary misses predicted by AHH, with the compulsory misses subtracted out. The AHH model does not incorporate a relationship equivalent to the relationship of compulsory misses to capacity misses that exists in the our model.

308

Predictive Power: The AHH model is calibrated by measuring the collision-related parameters as a function of cache structure and the other workload parameters individually, and then the model is used to predict the behavior of various cache structures when driven by the given workloads. Its predictive powers are very good, and are illustrated by the closeness of the predicted curve to the measured curve in Fig. 10(b). The maximum error reported in their paper is an estimate about 30% less than the observed miss ratio. However, the predictions are in the form of individual data points, and the AHH model does not show a general behavior by means of a simple formula such as (13).

Consider, for example, the observed data in Fig. 10(b). The AHH model neither predicts nor yields a straight line on the log / log plot, yet the observed data clearly show this behavior. The straight line plot of the observations is predicted by our model, and the AHH observed data generally fall remarkably close to the straight line on all of their plots. Their model is generally a curved line that falls below the straight line, but is close to it. Because the gross characteristics of the prediction curve in Fig. 10(b) are not easily discovered by examining the AHH model, it is difficult to discover the near straight-line behavior of the predicted curve and of the measured data in Fig. 10(b) until the predicted and measured data are plotted. In fact, Agarwal *et al.* make no mention of the straightness of the curves for the observed data in their paper.

Another remarkable aspect of the observed data and the model predictions is the horizontal lower bound on the miss ratio. The lower bound computed by the AHH model is the quotient of the number of unique lines contained in the trace divided by the trace length. This is the miss rate produced by the compulsory misses. If each first reference is treated as a miss, then the miss-ratio observed by a trace-driven simulation cannot fall below the lower bound, regardless of the size and structure of the cache. In the environment in which traces are made, a first reference may be a hit rather than a miss, depending on the contents of the cache when the reference occurs. Trace-driven simulations that treat a first reference as a compulsory miss do so because the cache is uninitialized for the simulation, and the reference does not match the present cache contents.

The observed data for the large caches in Fig. 10(a) may have true miss ratios much less than the observations indicate. To observe the true miss ratios, one must remove the effect of the compulsory misses. One approach to do so is to use a very long trace and exploit the fact that the rate of compulsory misses tends to diminish with increasing trace length. In fact, the rate of such compulsory misses as predicted by our model is $u(t, L)/t$.

What is interesting about the AHH model is that it shows that the compulsory-miss rate accurately models the lower bound of the trace-driven observations, provided that the trace-driven simulation treats each first reference as a miss. The AHH model does not model the true cache behavior when the miss ratio of a cache falls below this lower bound. In Fig. 10(b), for example, a 64K cache has a measured miss ratio very close to the lower bound. Because its miss ratio falls on the log / log trend line, both the measured data and model predictions are accurate for this cache. The 128K and 256K caches are shown to have measured and modeled miss ratios approximately equal to the lower bound. Both of these data points capture only the artifact of the measurement process, namely that the first reference to an cache line uninitialized by the simulator is counted as a miss by the simulation, whereas it could be a hit in a physical environment. The true behavior can lie anywhere below the AHH lower bound, and can, for example, fall on the log / log trend line.

Agarwal [2] replotted the data in Fig. 10(b) with the compulsory misses removed and found that the residual miss rates fall on the straight line trend. Because Agarwal's data are independent of the data used for developing the present model, his results independently show the validity of the straight-line trend predicted by the model.

Because a lower bound on miss rates as exhibited in Fig. 10 has appeared in other published data, there is a question of whether there is a mechanism that produces a lower bound on miss rate in real systems, or whether the published data show a lower bound because of compulsory misses. For example, Hill and Smith [12] published data that show a flattening tendency for large cache sizes. The flattening of miss rate curves that appear in Hill and Smith [12] was later attributed by Hill [11] to compulsory misses.

Given that some data have been published showing a lower bound on miss rate, even though compulsory misses can explain the bound in some cases, a legitimate question is what is the actual miss rate for large caches? Does the miss rate follow the straight-line log/log trend of our model, or does the miss rate reach a lower bound due to some other phenomenon?

In fact, a lower bound can exist for some cache designs. For example, context swaps in multiprogrammed systems provide a mechanism that can flush a cache at regular intervals. These can produce a lower bound on miss rate for large caches if different contexts share the same cache space, regardless of cache size.

An example of a cache design that produces this phenomenon is one that maps virtual addresses to cache sets without including the user ID in the mapping function. Two programs, each beginning at virtual address 0, will map to the same region of the cache, but will be treated as disjoint regions of memory because the address-tag comparisons use both the virtual address and user ID to distinguish their addresses. Periodic context swaps between these programs will produce a miss-rate floor because no matter how large the cache is, the the programs will map onto each other in cache. Thrashing of this form can be avoided by using both user ID and virtual address in the function that maps addresses to cache sets. This permits the programs to map to different regions of the cache and reside there concurrently if a cache is large enough to hold more than one program context.

It is clear that when a cache is sufficiently large to hold all of addressable memory, the miss rate must go to zero in a uniprocessor system, provided that the mapping mechanism maps each distinct line of addressable memory to a distinct cache line. Given a zero miss rate as an asymptotic limit for such a system, a model that produces a nonzero lower bound fails to capture the behavior of caches too large to be initialized by a short trace.

Our trace is an order of magnitude longer than the traces used by Agarwal *et al.* and thus the lower bound produced by compulsory misses for our trace is much smaller than for theirs. This allows us to observe the miss ratios of larger caches with greater accuracy. Our data show that the miss ratios of the large caches that we studied tend to follow the log / log trend line. Our model excludes the effects of compulsory misses, and therefore does not produce the lower bound observed in Fig. 10(b). Hence, our model is not subject to this source of bias, and it produces a a straight line that can be extrapolated to predict large-cache behavior.

We do not know how far the extrapolations can be carried before the model becomes inaccurate. For the trace used in our experiment, the extrapolations are valid for caches up to 1 megabyte, the largest that we simulated. Where the predictions differed from simulations, the differences could well be due to compulsory misses in the cache simulations rather than errors in the model because the traces were too short to obtain accurate measures of miss rates for the largest caches.

Using the AHH model requires traces whose compulsory miss-rates are small compared to the true miss ratios of the caches to be modeled. If we assume that we need at least 10 misses per set of a set-associative cache in order to obtain accurate estimates of miss ratios, and we make reasonable assumptions on the likely miss ratios of large caches, then trace lengths have to be approximately 100 M to 200 M references to evaluate 1-megabyte caches. To evaluate a 4-megabyte cache may require far longer traces, possibly as long as 1 G references. The AHH model yields the observed miss rate of a trace of a given length rather than true cache behavior. This is acceptable for small caches, but fails to produce meaningful information for large caches unless the traces are extremely long. Rather than seek ever larger traces to drive the AHH model, an attractive alternative approach is to alter the AHH model by removing the compulsory misses, for example, or by some similar modification in order to produce a model that accurately predicts miss ratios of large caches.

Complexity of Calibration: The complexity of calibration of the AHH model is greater than that of the new model because the AHH model has more parameters as well as more calculations. The main effort required for our model is the tabulation of the function $u(t, L)$ for various values of L over the length of a given trace. In fact, the work involved for this tabulation is not much more than the tabulation of $u(t, L)$ for the least value of L over the length of the trace. This follows because if a reference is not unique at time t for some line size L, then it is not unique at that time for any larger line size. Hence, $u(t, L)$ should be tabulated at each time t for line sizes in increasing order by size. The computation can be terminated at the first L that produces a nonunique line. After the initialization transient almost all references at the minimum line size are nonunique. The work that remains after the tabulation of $u(t, L)$ is simple curve fitting through a few selected points on the function.

Because the AHH model requires very long traces to eval-

uate large caches, the calibration of the model's parameters is potentially time consuming when used to predict the behavior of such caches. If cache analysis has to be performed from short traces, then the extrapolations produced by our model appear to reflect cache behavior more faithfully than the trends produced by the AHH model. The precision of the characterization grows with the length of the trace data used, but there is no abrupt fall off in precision in our model as there is in the AHH model.

Method of Use: The last characteristic of comparison is the method of use of the two models. The new model is really a model of program behavior rather than a model of cache misses. Because its parameters are directly related to observable program characteristics, it gives a general idea of how program behavior changes as the parameters change, and how the changes in program behavior in turn affect cache behavior. The model can be used to produce cache-behavior estimates when traces are not available, and thus can be used when neither trace-driven simulation nor the AHH model can be exploited.

The locality characteristics of certain classes of workloads have been established in part by studies such as those conducted by Kobayashi and MacDougall [13]. Additional studies of this type can show where different kinds of programs lie in parameter space. We can explore cache behavior for interesting regions of parameter space where traces do not already exist.

For example, we can postulate that the working set size of typical workloads will grow as memory costs diminish. With this assumption, we can use the model to estimate what happens if working set size increases by some factor, while holding other model parameters fixed. Similarly, if trends show that workloads will have less locality, we can model the effects of lower temporal and spatial localities on cache behavior. The AHH model, on the other hand, is most useful for the analysis of the behavior of specific traced workloads on specific caches. It yields more precise results than our model yields. The authors of the AHH model do not provide insight in the use of the model to estimate miss rates for programs whose traces are unavailable, and we believe that this problem still needs to be addressed.

To summarize the comparison, the two models seem to be complementary in that they fulfill different needs and are likely to be used differently. When detailed traces are available, we strongly recommend using the information from the traces, and this approach favors the use of the AHH model. In the absence of detailed traces, when trends and general behavior have to be discovered, but high precision is not important, the new model may prove to be more useful.

As cache designs approach 1 megabyte and 4 megabyte sizes, we believe that trace-driven cache evaluations and models based on trace-driven simulations of caches will be extremely costly to use because of the enormous lengths of the traces required to drive those evaluations. An analytical model that produces reasonably good behavior estimates may be the preferred cache-evaluation technique for practical applications. Experience gained from using both the AHH and the proposed new models may be useful in producing the models that eventually are used in practice.

VIII. The Effect of Set Partitioning

The model proposed is able to predict the miss ratio of fully associative caches, provided that the cache is large enough to hold the initial working set of the trace. Caches are generally not built to be fully associative, but rather are set associative with 1, 2, or 4-way set associativity in typical designs. A set-associative cache with N sets partitions addresses into N disjoint address spaces. If the cache has C bytes with lines of length L bytes, then the cache has C/L lines. These lines are distributed equally among the N disjoint address spaces, thereby producing $K = C/NL$ cache lines per address space. The N sets of lines, each with K lines, form a cache structure said to be a K-way set-associative cache with N sets. A K-way set-associative cache compares a reference address only to the K addresses that lie in one set. The set selected for a reference address is the unique set assigned to the address space that contains the reference address. If the line is in the cache, it must be in that set. If the line is not in the cache, the fact that it is not present can be discovered by searching only the K lines in one set, rather than by searching the full cache of NK lines. This reduces the cost of comparison and increases its speed. As the set associativity increases, the cache miss ratio approaches that of a fully associative cache. An 8-way or 16-way set associative cache has a performance almost indistinguishable from that of a fully associative cache. But 1-way and 2-way caches have miss ratios that fall above those of fully associative caches of comparable size. It would be very useful to predict those miss ratios by using a model of comparable complexity to the model presented in this paper.

Figs. 11(a) through (c) demonstrate that references to individual sets behave more or less similarly to references to a full address space. Fig. 11(a) is a log / log plot of the function $u(t, L)$ for the references to a particular set among 32 sets in a trace that has a line size of 128 bytes. Plots appear for seven different sets among the 32. Time in this figure is virtual time, not real time. The number of references plotted on the x-axis is the number of references made to a particular set. So for a cache with $N = 32$ sets as in Fig. 11(a), the 100th reference to a set is likely to occur roughly 3200 references into the trace. It is recorded as the number 100 (the virtual reference number for the set) rather than the number 3200 when preparing these graphs in Fig. 11(a).

Note that all of the curves in Fig. 11(a) seem to approach the same asymptote after an initial transient phase. Since the slope of this curve is a measure of temporal locality in a trace, we find that each set seems to have the same temporal locality. Figs. 11(b) and (c) are similar plots for different line sizes and different numbers of sets. The data in Figs. 11(a) through (c) are derived by using the first 36 million references of the same trace whose first 6 million references were used to derive the behavior of $u(t, L)$ for the entire address trace.

Table I compares the slopes of the curves in Figs. 11(a) through (c) for set activity in virtual time with set activity of the full trace in real time as plotted in Fig. 4. We show both the mean and median slopes for the set data in the second and third columns, respectively. The two numbers for the slopes given in the column labeled "Full trace" refer to the two slopes

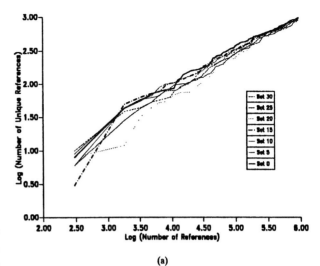

(a)

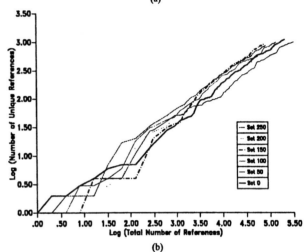

(b)

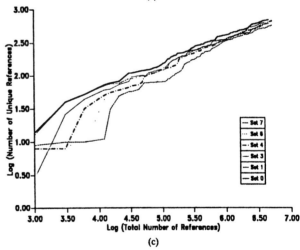

(c)

Fig. 11. Plots of $\log u(t, L)$ against $\log t$ for references to individual sets. (a) Data for a line size of 128 bytes and 32 sets. (b) Data for a line size of 16 bytes and 256 sets. (c) Data for a line size of 1K bytes and 8 sets.

measured from the curves in Fig. 4. The slopes for the full trace are consistently higher than those measured in virtual time for the individual sets. We are not sure at this writing

311

TABLE I
SLOPES OF $u(t, L)$ VERSUS $\log t$ FOR SETS AND FULL CACHES

Cache Structure	Set Mean	Set Median	Full Trace
$L = 128$ 32 Sets	0.47835	0.48948	0.5554 0.6058
$L = 16$ 256 Sets	0.57147	0.56930	0.6818 0.7158
$L = 1K$ 8 Sets	0.37812	0.37355	0.4131 0.4765

how to explain the discrepancy in the measured slopes. One possible explanation is that the slope actually falls off on the full trace as the number of references increases to 36 million. We have not been able to confirm that this is the case, nor have we been able to identify other possible explanations.

Hill and Smith [12] propose a model for comparing the miss ratios of fully associative and set associative caches. The parameters of their model are probability functions that can be computed from the parameters of the model developed in this paper. The combination of our model with the Hill/Smith model remains to be tested and validated, but it appears to be an attractive approach for developing a model of set-associative caches. The data described in this section suggest that the statistics across sets are well behaved, which is a necessary condition for the combination of the Hill/Smith model with the present model to give meaningful results.

IX. SUMMARY AND CONCLUSIONS

Our model of program behavior has only four parameters, one of which is related to the working set of a program, and the other three are measures of locality. The model shows that some locality is due to references that cluster in address space. This is spatial locality. There is a residual locality of reference which is due to revisiting clusters that were visited recently. This is temporal locality. Spatial locality can be exploited by using large line sizes, or equivalently, by prefetching from regions that are close to active regions. Temporal locality is a measure of additional locality within a program that expresses the manner in which a program tends to touch different regions of memory over a period of time. Increases of line size and other prefetching strategies based on address proximity tend to be ineffective for the component of locality due to temporal locality. The interaction coefficient expresses how to combine the two different types of locality.

The novel aspect of the model is that it produces miss ratios by modeling $u(t, L)$, the number of unique lines accessed up to time t for line size L. The advantage of this approach is that $u(t, L)$ is very well behaved, and its parameters can be obtained by fitting straight lines to nearly straight curves.

Our comparison of the model with Smith's data and with the model proposed by Agarwal *et al.* indicates that the straight lines that appear on $\log / \log$ plots have been widely published but not addressed by a specific model. Thiebaut's model [21] produces the straight line and gives a plausible explanation on its origin. The model in this paper shows how line size effects can be incorporated and still produce the straight lines that appear in the literature.

We have demonstrated that the new model is a very good predictor of miss ratios of large fully associative caches. It shows the qualitative behavior of small fully associative caches, but is subject to much higher error for such caches. This is because the model parameters are fitted to regions of curves that specifically relate to large caches and not to small caches. Since there is a relatively strong distinction between the behavior of a program in a cache that holds the initial working set and the program behavior in a cache too small to hold the initial working set, to predict the miss ratio for small caches requires a model that accurately reflects what happens when an initial working set does not fit into cache.

We commented earlier that the model was confirmed by data from a single trace, and that independent confirmation is required if the model is to be used in practice. Specifically, the model of line-size effects has yet to be tested, whereas the literature contains adequate data on the effects of cache size for a fixed line size to create trust in the model.

The value of the model for cache designers is that it enables them to estimate cache miss ratios as a function of parameters that can be varied over ranges of realistic values. Hence, performance estimates can be obtained when traces are not available or are not long enough to produce reliable data. The parameters of the model need to be calibrated for different workloads, but once these are compiled for a sufficient number and variety of workloads, the cache designer will know what regions of parameter space are likely to represent typical workloads. Nevertheless, the model cannot and should not replace the use of trace-driven simulations of representative traces when these are available.

Many problems related to the model are still open. Among them are the following:

1) What is the behavior of programs in small caches?
2) Can the model of program behavior developed here be extended or combined with the Hill/Smith model to predict the behavior of set-associative caches?
3) Is there a range of spatial locality or temporal locality parameters that characterize types of workloads? In other words, can we find ranges for the model parameters for typical scientific programs, for database programs, for Artificial Intelligence programs, and for other types of programs?
4) Does the model characterize accesses to shared data in a multiprocessor? If not, then what model holds for such accesses?
5) The model depends on the slope of $u(t, L)$ with respect to L and with respect to t. The model assumes that the slope is constant when plotted on $\log / \log$ axes. In fact, there is a small curvature, and the slope of $\log u$ versus $\log t$ tends to diminish as t increases. Can we model this curvature? Is it due to the fact that eventually we run out of distinct addresses?

In the current and coming generations of cache designs, the sizes of caches are likely to increase to large fractions of a megabyte and possibly to multiple megabytes. Trace-driven evaluations of such caches may eventually be so costly that the evaluation method of choice is based on workload characterizations and analytic models such as that proposed in this paper.

ACKNOWLEDGMENT

The authors are greatly indebted to Dr. T. R. Puzak of the IBM Research Division for supplying the traces used in this study and for his assistance in the preparation of the programs for analyzing the traces. His efforts contributed substantially to the completion of the research project. The authors also thank the anonymous referees for their perceptive comments and suggestions.

REFERENCES

[1] A. Agarwal, private communication, Jan. 1989.
[2] A. Agarwal, M. Horowitz, and J. Hennessy, "An analytical cache model," *ACM Trans. Comput. Syst.*, vol. 7, no. 2, pp. 184–215, May 1989.
[3] C. K. Chow, "On optimization of storage hierarchy," *IBM J. Res. Develop.*, vol. 18, pp. 194–203, May 1974.
[4] _____, "Determining the optimum capacity of a cache memory," *IBM Tech. Discl. Bull.*, vol. 17, no. 10, pp. 3163–3166, Mar. 1975.
[5] _____, "Determination of a cache's capacity and its matching storage hierarchy," *IEEE Trans. Comput.*, vol. C-25, no. 2, pp. 157–164, Feb. 1976.
[6] P. J. Denning and S. C. Schwartz, "Properties of the working set model," *Commun. ACM*, vol. 15, no. 3, pp. 191–198, Mar. 1972.
[7] M. C. Easton, "Computations of cold-start miss ratios," *IEEE Trans. Comput.*, vol. C-27, no. 5, pp. 404–408, May 1978.
[8] M. C. Easton and R. Fagin, "Cold-start versus warm-start miss ratios," *Commun. ACM*, vol. 21, no. 10, pp. 866–872, Oct. 1978.
[9] J. E. Gillis and G. H. Weiss, "Expected number of distinct sites visited by a random walk with an infinite variance," *J. Math. Phys.*, vol. 11, no. 4, pp. 1307–1312, Apr. 1970.
[10] J. R. Goodman, "Using cache memory to reduce processor-memory traffic," in *Proc. 10th Annu. Symp. Comput. Architecture*, 1983, pp. 124–131.
[11] M. D. Hill, "Correction to 'Evaluating associativity in caches'," *IEEE Trans. Comput.*, vol. 40, no. 3, p. 371, Mar. 1991.
[12] M. D. Hill and A. J. Smith, "Evaluating associativity in caches," *IEEE Trans. Comput.*, vol. 38, no. 12, pp. 1612–1630, Dec. 1989.
[13] M. Kobayashi and M. H. MacDougall, "The stack growth function: Cache line reference models," *IEEE Trans. Comput.*, vol. 38, no. 6, pp. 798–805, June 1989.
[14] B. Mandelbrot, *The Fractal Geometry of Nature.* San Francisco, CA: Freeman, 1983.
[15] G. S. Rao, "Performance analysis of cache memories," *J. ACM*, vol. 25, no. 3, pp. 378–385, July 1978.
[16] J. H. Saltzer, "A simple linear model of demand paging performance," *Commun. ACM*, vol. 17, no. 4, pp. 181–186, Apr. 1974.
[17] A. J. Smith, "A comparative study of set-associative memory mapping algorithms and their use for cache and main memory," *IEEE Trans. Software Eng.*, vol. SE-4, no. 2, pp. 121–130, Mar. 1978.
[18] _____, "Line (block) size choice for CPU cache memories," *IEEE Trans. Comput.*, vol. C-36, no. 9, pp. 1063–1075, Sept. 1987.
[19] W. D. Strecker, "Transient behavior of cache memories," *ACM Trans. Comput. Syst.*, vol. 1, no. 4, pp. 281–293, Nov. 1983.
[20] D. F. Thiebaut, "Influence of program transients in computer cache-memories," Ph.D. dissertation, Univ. Massachusetts, 1989.
[21] _____, "On the fractal dimension of computer programs and its application to the prediction of the cache miss ratio," *IEEE Trans. Comput.* vol. 38, no. 7, pp. 1012–1026, July 1989.
[22] D. F. Thiebaut and H. S. Stone, "Footprints in the cache," *ACM Trans. Comput. Syst.*, vol. 5, no. 4, pp. 305–329, Nov. 1987.
[23] D. F. Thiebaut, H. S. Stone, and J. L. Wolf, "A theory of cache behavior," IBM Res. Rep. RC 13309, Nov. 1987.
[24] J. Voldman et al., "Fractal nature of software-cache interaction," *IBM J. Res. Develop.*, vol. 27, pp. 164–170, Mar. 1983.

Chapter 5
Performance Evaluation Studies
of Software Coherence Schemes

Research efforts dedicated to the evaluation of coherence maintenance overhead merit special attention. Most of these efforts are strictly related to hardware mechanisms, and these papers are excluded from this book. Our selection concentrates primarily on the evaluation of the software coherence mechanisms.

The chapter includes one paper dealing with simulation analysis and two papers based on analytic modeling of software cache coherence maintenance. The small number of papers in this chapter is a consequence of the fact that the number of deep and broad analytic and simulation studies is currently limited in the open literature. On the other hand, the open literature contains a large number of papers dealing with performance evaluation of hardware-based coherence schemes. Representative papers on the evaluation of snoopy and directory schemes, as well as the evaluation of different memory consistency models, are given in the list of Suggestions for Further Reading.

In the paper "A Performance Comparison of Directory-Based and Timestamp-Based Cache Coherence Schemes," Min and Baer compare a hardware scheme based on a centralized full-map directory, developed by Censier and Feautrier, with a static software scheme based on timestamps, developed by Min and Baer. The comparison is based on simulation with three address traces of three different applications in which the model of parallelism is expressed through parallel DoAll loops. The simulation was done both for prescheduled processes and for randomly scheduled processes. As the appropriate performance measures, the following three are obtained through the simulation: miss ratio, write traffic, and network traffic. For the analyzed applications, the miss ratio did not differ significantly between the two schemes, independently of the number of processors. In general, the miss ratio is an increasing function of the number of processors. The write traffic is considerably higher with the software scheme (compared with the hardware scheme) and is fairly independent of the number of processors and the process scheduling policy. The network traffic is larger with the hardware scheme because it is directory-based.

In the paper "Evaluating the Performance of Software Cache Coherence," Owicki and Agarwal use the analytical MVA (mean value analysis) model to compare the performance of multiprocessors supported with four different cache coherence schemes: one without coherence maintenance, two with software coherence maintenance, and one with the hardware coherence maintenance of the snoopy type (Dragon from Xerox, which supports snooping with write broadcast). The developed analytical model includes the system model (described with the number of cycles required for each given operation in hardware), the workload model (described with the frequencies of specific operations), and the contention model (which determines the additional time spent due to contention on the interconnection network). For the common bus case, the analysis has shown that the software schemes are globally characterized with a worse performance compared to the hardware scheme analyzed in the paper. Also, the software schemes are relatively sensitive to changes in the values of some parameters of interest. Only for a relatively low degree of sharing is one of the two software schemes better than the hardware scheme. For the multistage interconnection network case, the analysis has shown that the processing power of the software schemes increases linearly with the number of processors, which is an indication of the high level of scalability of these schemes; this is not the case with the snoopy hardware schemes.

In the paper by S. Adve, V. Adve, Hill, and Vernon, "Comparison of Hardware and Software Cache Coherence Schemes," a performance relation between directory-based hardware schemes and static software schemes is studied. These authors start from a general program behavior model, described by some high-level parameters that specify the access dynamics for various classes of shared data. Some low-level parameters used for comparing the schemes are derived from the same high-level model, enabling the comparison to be fair. Using these low-level parameters as input data, the authors develop the approximate MVA model for the appropriate scheme and compute processor efficiency. For various classes of data objects, the contours of a constant ratio of software to hardware efficiency method are presented. These contours could serve to establish parameter ranges of the performance advantage for the software over the hardware scheme, and vice versa. An interesting conclusion of the evaluation is that, for the workloads characterized by migratory data, the software scheme is always more efficient than the hardware scheme. Workloads primarily characterized by other classes of data objects give the advantage to a software/hardware mechanism, depending on parameter ranges.

Suggestions for Further Reading

Agarwal, A., et al., "An Evaluation of Directory Schemes for Cache Coherence," *Proc. 15th Ann. Int'l Symp. Computer Architecture,* IEEE CS Press, Los Alamitos, Calif., 1988, pp. 280–289.

Archibald, J., and Baer, J.-L., "Cache Coherence Protocols: Evaluation Using a Multiprocessor Simulation Model," *ACM Trans. Computer Systems,* Vol. 4, No. 4, Nov. 1986, pp. 273–298.

Eggers, S.J., and Katz, R.H., "Evaluating the Performance of Four Snooping Cache Coherence Protocols," *Proc. 16th Ann. Int'l Symp. Computer Architecture,* ACM Press, New York, N.Y., 1989, pp. 2–15.

Gharachorloo, K., Gupta, A., and Hennessy, J., "Performance Evaluation of Memory Consistency Models for Shared-Memory Multiprocessors," *Proc. 4th Int'l Conf. Architectural Support for Programming Languages and Operating Systems,* ACM Press, New York, N.Y., 1991, pp. 245–257.

Stenström, P., Joe, T., and Gupta, A., "Comparative Performance Evaluation of Cache-Coherent NUMA and COMA Architectures," *Proc. 19th Ann. Int'l Symp. Computer Architecture,* ACM Press, New York, N.Y., 1992, pp. 80–91.

Tomašević, M., and Milutinović, V., "A Simulation Study of Snoopy Cache Coherence Protocols," *Proc. 25th Ann. Hawaii Int'l Conf. System Sciences,* Vol. 1, IEEE CS Press, Los Alamitos, Calif., 1992, pp. 427–436.

Zucker, R.N., and Baer, J.-L., "A Performance Study of Memory Consistency Models," *Proc. 19th Ann. Int'l Symp. Computer Architecture,* ACM Press, New York, N.Y., 1992, pp. 2–12.

A Performance Comparison of Directory-based and Timestamp-based Cache Coherence Schemes *

Sang Lyul Min[†]
IBM Research Division
Thomas J. Watson Research Center
Yorktown Heights, NY 10598

Jean-Loup Baer
Dept. of Computer Science and Engineering
University of Washington
Seattle, WA 98195

Abstract

This paper reports on preliminary results of a performance comparison between software-assisted and directory-based approaches to enforcing the coherence of multiple private caches in a large-scale shared-memory multiprocessor. The comparison is based on a trace-driven simulation of a timestamp-based scheme [19], whose performance is known to be best among the published software-assisted schemes, and a complete directory-based scheme [6] using actual traces. Statistics are shown for miss ratios, the write traffic, and the network traffic for varying number of processors. The results show that the timestamp-based scheme generally yields miss ratios comparable to those of the directory-based scheme with less network traffic. It is also shown that there is an intrinsic relationship between the way processors are scheduled and the resultant cache performance.

1 Introduction

This paper deals with the evaluation of caching strategies in shared-memory multiprocessors. Attention is focused on large-scale shared-memory multiprocessors where hundreds or thousands of processors and memory modules are interconnected through a multistage interconnection network (MIN). Examples of the above type of architecture include the University of Illinois Cedar machine [11], the BBN Butterfly multiprocessor [4], the NYU Ultracomputer [13], and the IBM RP3 machine [21]. The use of private caches are generally advocated in this type of architecture in order to palliate the slow global memory access. However, the presence of multiple cached copies of the same data introduces the additional burden of maintaining the consistency of the contents of these caches, i.e., the well known cache coherence problem. Solutions to the above problem that have been implemented on bus-based multiprocessors cannot be extended to the MIN-based multiprocessors since these solutions depend on the availability of the *snoopy* mechanism provided by the shared-bus. Software-assisted [8, 16, 17, 19, 22, 25, 26] and directory-based [1, 2, 6, 24, 27] schemes are usually advocated in MIN-based shared-memory multiprocessors.

In this paper, we use a trace-driven simulation as a vehicle to evaluate the relative effectiveness of the last two approaches to enforcing cache coherence in MIN-based shared-memory multiprocessors. In particular, a timestamp-based software-assisted cache coherence scheme, which was previously proposed by the authors in [19] and is known to yield the best performance among the published software-assisted schemes, is used as the representative of the software-assisted schemes. A performance comparison among the software-assisted schemes was made in [20] and is not repeated here.

In this paper, we assume that a parallel program is composed of a set of *epochs* [16] which are either parallel loops (DoAll or DoAcross loops) or serial regions between them. Each epoch consists of a set of instances. Execution of an iteration of a parallel loop constitutes an instance of the epoch of type parallel loop. A serial region is a special type of epoch which has only one instance.

This paper is organized as follows. Section 2 gives a brief survey of cache coherence schemes and provides a description of the two cache coherence schemes that are compared in this paper. In Section 3, the experimental settings are explained. The simulation results are presented and discussed in Section 4. Conclusions are given in Section 5.

2 Cache coherence schemes

Many shared-memory multiprocessors advocate the use of private caches to reduce both the average memory access time and the network traffic. If multiple copies of the same data are allowed to co-exist in the memory hierarchy of a shared-memory multiprocessor, the accesses to these copies should be carefully manipulated and/or coordinated to prevent the possibility of accessing a stale copy. In [6], Censier and Feautrier defined *a memory scheme to be coherent if the value returned on a read is the value given by the most recent store to that address*.

A number of schemes have been proposed and/or implemented to enforce the coherence of multiple private caches. Figure 1 is a taxonomy of the various cache coherence schemes. It is based on whether invalidations are required to enforce the coherence or not and if so, whether the invalidations are done by local processors (i.e., self-invalidation) or by other processors (i.e., induced-invalidation). The schemes are further classified according to whether they require shared resources or not, and if so, what kinds of shared resource are required to enforce the coherence.

The approach taken in the no-invalidation cache coherence scheme used in the C.mmp multiprocessor is to disallow caching of shared read/write data for the entire program [26].

*This work was supported in part by the National Science Foundation (Grants CCR-8619663, CCR-8702915, CCR-8904190), Boeing Computer Services, Digital Equipment Corporation (the Systems Research Center and the External Research Program), and a Fulbright scholarship for Mr. Min.

[†]Research partially performed at the University of Washington.

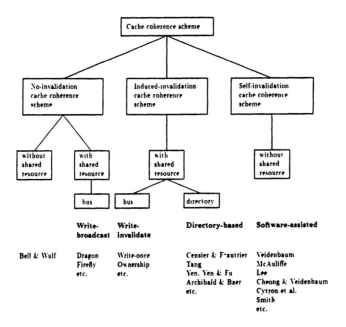

Figure 1: Taxonomy of cache coherence schemes

This is accomplished by a compile-time marking of variables as cacheable or non-cacheable (every shared variable that is writable). The mechanism is simple but inefficient. Every reference to non-cacheable data is forwarded to global memory even though the addressed data could be cacheable during parts of the program where it is either read-only or accessed exclusively by a single processor.

There have been two main approaches to maintaining the cache coherence when the interconnection between processors and memory modules is a shared-bus: write-broadcast and write-invalidate approaches. In write-broadcast cache coherence schemes, private caches are kept coherent by forcing cache controllers to inform other caches in the system on writes so that every cache can update its own copy if such a copy exists. In the write-invalidate counterpart, the cache coherence is maintained by requiring every cache controller to snoop on the bus and, on a write transaction, to invalidate a matching cache entry, if such an entry exists. In [23], Sweazy and Smith proposed a classification scheme for bus-based cache coherence schemes. Their classification scheme encompasses the union of the states used in all existing distributed snoopy protocols. They also proposed a universal scheme that allows the coexistence of different protocols.

The above bus-based cache coherence schemes, however, cannot be extended to the MIN-based shared-memory multiprocessors since they make use of the instantaneous broadcast and "snoopy" mechanisms provided by the shared-bus, features that are not available in a MIN-based multiprocessor.

There are two basic approaches to maintaining cache coherence in MIN-based shared-memory multiprocessors: directory-based and self-invalidation. In a directory-based induced-invalidation cache coherence scheme, a directory entry, which is kept in the memory controller, is associated with each memory block. This entry encodes the state of the block. The state is used to decide whether there is a need for invalidations on a given write transaction to the block and if so, to locate the private caches which have a copy of the block to be invalidated. It is also used to tell whether the corresponding memory block is stale or not and if so, to locate the private cache which is guaranteed to have the most current copy of the block. In addition to the state in the global directory, a local state is usually associated with each cache block in private caches. This local state is used to allow a private cache to service most requests from its associated processor without incurring any global actions.

Even though cache coherence schemes based on central directories can be quite efficient in yielding a high hit ratio because of their ability to dynamically keep track of the status of each block, the network traffic generated for invalidation requests and for the manipulation of local and/or global state information can be substantial. In a self-invalidation cache coherence scheme, cache entries can be invalidated only by local processors and no globally-manipulated information is associated either with cache blocks or with memory blocks. This eliminates the extra network traffic at the expense of less efficient caching. To decide what and when to invalidate in order to correctly maintain cache coherence, self-invalidation cache coherence schemes generally use some knowledge of the referencing structure of the parallel program gathered at compile time. Self-invalidation cache coherence schemes are sometimes referred to as software-assisted cache coherence schemes due

318

to their dependency on the compiler.

In the following, we give a brief description of Censier and Feautrier's scheme (an instance of directory-based schemes) and of the timestamp-based scheme (an instance of software-assisted schemes) that are compared in this paper. These two schemes were chosen since they represent the most efficient protocols in their respective classes of cache coherence schemes in MIN-based architectures. A survey of other directory-based and software-assisted schemes can be found elsewhere and interested readers are referred to [3, 18]. A performance comparison between the timestamp-based scheme and other software-assisted schemes is given by the authors in [20] and is not repeated here.

In Censier and Feautrier's directory-based scheme, each directory entry consists of a dirty bit and an n-bit presence tag, where n is the number of private caches in the system. The ith bit of the presence tag of a memory block is set if the corresponding private cache has a valid copy of the block. The dirty bit tells whether the memory block is up-to-date or not. The local state can be one of the following three states: (1)*invalid*, (2)*clean-shared*, and (3)*dirty-exclusive*.

On a read hit, the requested datum is immediately supplied to the requesting processor and no additional action is required. If there is a write hit and the cache has a *dirty-exclusive* copy of the block, the write can proceed locally without involving any global action. But if there is a write hit and the cache has a *clean-shared* copy of the block, first the cache has to send a request to the memory controller to invalidate copies of the block that might be present in other private caches and then the block can be written and its state is changed to *dirty-exclusive*. On a read miss, the dirty bit and the presence tag associated with the requested memory block are examined to see which private caches, if any, have valid copies of the block. If some private cache has a *dirty-exclusive* copy of the requested block, the block is written back to the global memory and used to supply the data to the requesting cache. The dirty bits of the block are cleared in the global directory and in the local state of the cache that had the dirty copy. The local states in that cache and the requesting one become *clean-shared*. In other cases (i.e., it is not cached or some private caches have *clean-shared* copies of the block), the requested block is supplied by the global memory and is loaded into the cache as *clean-shared*. On a write miss, again the global dirty bit and the presence tag are checked to see if any of the private caches has a valid copy of the requested block. There are three cases to consider. If none of them has a valid copy, the requested block is supplied by the global memory. If at least one private cache has a *clean-shared* copy of the block, all the copies of the block are invalidated and the requested block is supplied by the global memory. If some private cache has a *dirty-exclusive* copy of the block, the dirty copy of the block is written back to the global memory before it is invalidated. The newly updated memory block is used to supply the data to the requesting cache. In all the above three cases, the global dirty bit of the requested memory block is set and the requested block is loaded into the requesting cache as *dirty-exclusive*.

In contrast with Censier and Feautrier's scheme where the cache coherence is maintained solely by the hardware, the timestamp-based scheme prevents stale accesses by the combination of a compile-time analysis and hardware support in the form of counters and tag bits in the cache. Figure 2 shows the approach taken by the timestamp-based scheme to capture localities across different epochs. For a cache entry loaded in an epoch to be used in a different epoch, it must be guaranteed that there is no intervening write reference to the same memory location. This analysis is divided into two parts: intra-epoch analysis and inter-epoch analysis. For a cache entry to be reused in future epochs it should be guaranteed that there is no succeeding write reference to the same memory location in the same epoch. Similarly for a read reference to use a cache entry loaded in past epochs it should be guaranteed that it does not have any preceding write to the same memory location in the same epoch. These intra-epoch analyses are done at compile time in the timestamp-based approach and their results are expressed in terms of various markings of references.

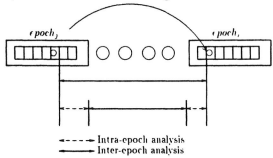

Figure 2: Overall approach to capture inter-epoch localities

To prove that there is no intervening write reference to the same memory location between the epoch in which the cache entry is loaded and the epoch in which the cache entry is accessed, locally maintained clocks (i.e., counters associated with shared variables) and timestamps (i.e., tag bits in the cache) are used. When a cache entry is modified, its timestamp field is set with the current clock value of the associated variable plus one. The clock of a variable is incremented at the end of each epoch in which the variable is modified. The decision as to whether the cache entry is up-to-date or not is made by comparing the clock and the timestamp. If the timestamp is greater than or equal to the current clock value, the cache entry is guaranteed to be up-to-date. Otherwise it may be stale and the request is directed to the global memory. A more detailed description of the timestamp-based scheme and a correctness proof can be found in [18, 19]. A similar scheme has been proposed independently by Cheong and Veidenbaum [7].

3 Multiprocessor cache simulation

The traces used to drive the multiprocessor cache simulator were obtained by executing parallel programs on a single processor. Various kinds of markers were inserted into the parallel programs to facilitate the reconstruction of parallel traces for a given number of processors. The actual gathering of traces was done by using a trace generating program called *tracer* [11]. For each memory reference the corresponding trace record contains fields for the type of reference (e.g., read instruction, read data, write data, etc.), storage segment involved (i.e., data segment, stack segment or instruction segment), the size of the item being referenced, and the memory address.

Three parallel application programs were used to generate the traces. All of them were written based on the same parallel programming paradigm: SPMD (single program multiple data) model of execution expressed in DoAll loops. The first program, *sim* [15], simulates a multistage interconnection network which serves vector load/store requests from processors to memory modules. The second program, *gauss* [9], uses the Gauss elimination technique to solve the following linear system of equations.

$$Ax = b$$

The last application, *mhd*, is a program for the numerical solution of two-dimensional magnetohydrodynamic (MHD) differential equations [12]. Table 1 shows a summary of the characteristics of the three traces used in the experiment.

	sim	*gauss*	*mhd*
number of total references	12829244	8969779	7159598
% instruction references	57.66	49.84	78.58
% data references	42.34	50.16	21.42
% data reads	33.91	42.28	15.19
% data writes	8.43	7.88	6.23
number of epochs	641	201	73
% serial epochs	25.12	50.75	17.81
% parallel epochs	74.88	49.25	82.19
number of epoch instances	26241	5151	2161
% serial epoch instances	0.61	1.98	0.60
% parallel epoch instances	99.39	98.02	99.40
number of shared writes	624387	686435	203701
number of shared reads	1653623	2374210	680349

Table 1: Characteristics of the traces used in the experiment

The actual scheduling of epoch instances on the processors is performed during the simulation and is based on the number of processors provided as a simulation input. Two simple scheduling policies are used: pre-scheduling and random scheduling. In the pre-scheduling policy, the ith iteration of a parallel loop is executed on $processor_{(i \bmod P)+1}$ where P is the number of allocated processors. In this policy, it is also assumed that one designated processor called MASTER always executes all the serial regions in the program. In the random scheduling counterpart, whenever there is an instance of an epoch for execution (including a serial region), a processor is randomly selected to execute it.

In order to make the simulation more manageable and less CPU time-consuming, we will simplify some of its aspects. We assume infinite caches with one-word cache block to eliminate secondary effects due to finite cache storage and *false sharing* [10]. Only shared data references are simulated since requests for instructions and private data can be handled similarly in the two schemes being evaluated. All the performance figures

reported in this paper are averaged over all processors. The above averaging is necessary to accurately capture the impact of inter-cache invalidations on the cache performance in Censier and Feautrier's scheme.

4 Results and Discussions

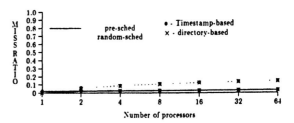

Figure 3.a: Miss ratios vs. Number of processors - Application *sim*

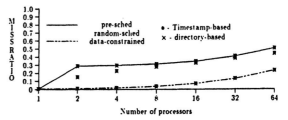

Figure 3.b: Miss ratios vs. Number of processors - Application *gauss*

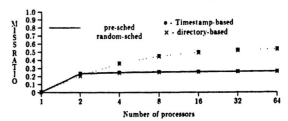

Figure 3.c: Miss ratios vs. Number of processors - Application *mhd*

Figure 3 presents the miss ratios for the shared references of the two schemes as a function of the number of allocated processors for both pre- and random scheduling policies. As can be seen, there is virtually no difference between the miss ratios of the timestamp-based scheme and those of Censier and Feautrier's scheme. This is a consequence of the three applications being simulated and of the particular parallel programming paradigm (i.e., SPMD parallel programming). Since there are no dependencies among instances in the same epoch (i.e., all parallelism is through DoAll loops), the miss ratio of the timestamp-based scheme is identical to that of Censier and Feautrier's scheme. We can also notice that the miss ratios of the two schemes increase with the number of allocated processors. This increase stems from two main reasons. First, the greater the number of allocated processors, the higher the probability that there is at least one intervening write reference by other processors between the time a variable is cached by a processor and the time the variable is subsequently accessed by the same processor. Such an intervening write reference makes the cached variable stale, thus, forcing the subsequent access

320

to be directed to the global memory. As could be expected, the adverse impact of the above intervening write reference on the miss ratio is more apparent in the random scheduling case. Second, as the number of allocated processors is increased, the amount of inter-instance localities due to read-only sharing of variables is reduced, thus yielding higher miss ratios. This effect is most evident in the *gauss* application in which there is a large amount of inter-instance localities due to the read-only sharing of pivot rows. On the other hand, the number of misses due to replacements of useful cache blocks does not decrease as more processors are allocated since we assume infinite caches.

It can also be noticed that the miss ratios of the pre-scheduling case are significantly better than those of the random scheduling counterpart for the *sim* and *mhd* applications. This is a property of the pre-scheduling policy that favors the reuse of cache contents over different epochs. In the *sim* program, each row of the multistage interconnection network is simulated in parallel for each network cycle and the same row is always simulated by the same processor in the pre-scheduling case. This increases the chance of the reuse of the cache contents before they become stale. In the *mhd* application, several huge matrices are used during execution to denote the velocities, the pressure, and the magnetic field at regularly-spaced points within a given rectangular area. If processors are pre-scheduled, each element of the above matrices is always written by the same processor and will be referenced mostly by that processor during the whole execution. Further, the miss ratio gap between the pre-scheduling and random scheduling is increased as more processors are allocated. This results from the proportionally reduced chances of the reuse of cache contents when more processors are random-scheduled.

In the *gauss* application, however, the miss ratios of the pre-scheduling case are worse than those of the random scheduling case. This seemingly anomalous behavior can be best explained by looking carefully inside the reduction step of the Gauss Elimination algorithm. Accesses to each row of the matrix A by processors during the reduction step are shown in Figure 4 assuming three processors are allocated and that they are pre-scheduled naively. In the figure, we can notice that each processor reads the row of the matrix A which was last written by some other processor during the previous step. This drastically reduces the reuse of cache contents since most of the cache contents associated with the matrix A become stale whenever a new step of the reduction is started. In fact, no cache coherence scheme works well in this situation. On the other hand, if we use random scheduling, there is some chance, although small, that elements of the matrix A written by a processor are read by the same processor during the next reduction step. This explains why random scheduling yields slightly better hit ratios than pre-scheduling in the *gauss* application. To see the effects of the scheduling policy on the performance of private caches, the simulation was repeated with the processors scheduled so as to access the matrix A in the way specified in Figure 5. The results are shown in Figure 3.b under *data-constrained*. As might be expected, the new schedule yields better hit ratios than in the pre-scheduling and random scheduling cases since now most of the cache entries associated with the matrix A are re-used over different reduction steps in the new schedule. The above example shows that the performance of private caches in shared-memory multiprocessors is very dependent on how

Matrix A	1st step	2nd step	3rd step
A_1	p_1^r, p_2^r, p_3^r		
A_2	p_1^r, p_1^w	p_1^r, p_2^r	
A_3	p_2^r, p_2^w	p_1^r, p_1^w	p_1^r
A_4	p_3^r, p_3^w	p_2^r, p_2^w	p_1^r, p_1^w

p_i^r: read by p_i
p_i^w: write by p_i

Figure 4: Accesses to matrix A by processors when $p = 3$

Matrix A	1st step	2nd step	3rd step
A_1	p_1^r, p_2^r, p_3^r		
A_2	p_1^r, p_1^w	p_2^r, p_3^r	
A_3	p_2^r, p_2^w	p_2^r, p_2^w	p_3^r
A_4	p_3^r, p_3^w	p_3^r, p_3^w	p_3^r, p_3^w

Figure 5: Accesses to matrix A by processors in the data-constrained schedule

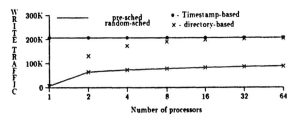

Figure 6.a: Write traffic vs. Number of processors - Application *sim*

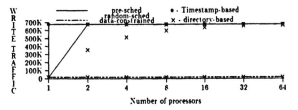

Figure 6.b: Write traffic vs. Number of processors - Application *gauss*

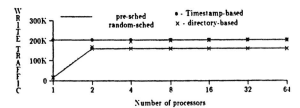

Figure 6.c: Write traffic vs. Number of processors - Application *mhd*

parallel instances are assigned to processors. A study on the generalization of the above scheduling policy, which improves upon a previous study by Callahan [5], is reported in [18].

Figure 6 displays the write traffic of the two schemes with a varying number of processors. The write traffic of the timestamp-based scheme is insensitive both to the scheduling policy and to the number of allocated processors because the scheme uses a limited *write-back* policy where dirty cache entries are written back to the global memory at the end of each epoch instance. The write traffic of Censier and Feautrier's scheme is never larger than that of the timestamp-based scheme, but increases and approaches the traffic of the timestamp-based scheme as more processors are random scheduled. Savings of Censier and Feautrier's scheme over the timestamp-based scheme occur when the same shared variable is written twice by the same processor inside two different epochs without an intervening reference from other processors. The frequency of this situation is reduced as more processors are random scheduled as we can see in Figure 6.

However, there is a substantial number of such savings when the processors are *data-constrained* scheduled. (In the *sim* and *mhd* applications, the pre-scheduling corresponds to the *data-constrained* scheduling.) This is most noticeable in the *gauss* application. In this application, whenever a row of the matrix A is written, the writing processor under the *data-constrained* scheduling policy has a *dirty-exclusive* copy of the row (See Figure 5 for the access pattern to rows of the matrix A by processors when they are *data-constrained* scheduled). Therefore, there is no write traffic generated by write accesses to the matrix A in Censier and Feautrier's scheme. In the *sim* and *mhd* applications, some of these savings occur but to a far limited degree as can be seen in Figure 6.

There are two components in the network traffic of the timestamp-based scheme: one due to misses and the other due to writes. In addition, Censier and Feautrier's scheme has one more component: network traffic due to invalidations. Figure 7 shows the network traffic of the two schemes. The most noticeable point in the figure is that the network traffic of Censier and Feautrier's scheme is significantly higher. This is somewhat surprising since their scheme yields lower miss ratios and less write traffic than the timestamp-based scheme as we noted in Figures 3 and 6. However, an increase in the number of allocated processors usually increases the number of cache entries to be invalidated per write to shared variables in Censier and Feautrier's scheme. Since an invalidation requires a round-trip through the interconnection network, the penalty becomes very severe as soon as more than one invalidation is to be performed. On the other hand, the slight increase in the network traffic for the timestamp-based scheme is solely due to the slightly increased number of misses (see Figure 3 and recall that the write traffic of the timestamp-based scheme remains the same independently of the number of processors).

5 Conclusion

In this paper, we have compared the relative effectiveness of the timestamp-based and directory-based schemes based on hit ratios and network traffic. The results show that the timestamp-

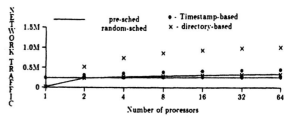

Figure 7.a: Network traffic vs. Number of processors - Application *sim*

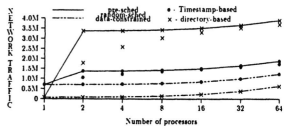

Figure 7.b: Network traffic vs. Number of processors - Application *gauss*

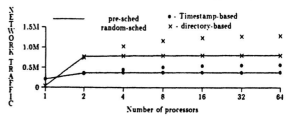

Figure 7.c: Network traffic vs. Number of processors - Application *mhd*

based scheme yields miss ratios comparable to those of the directory-based scheme with less network traffic except in some extreme cases. This result should not be over-generalized since the programming paradigm that we evaluated might favor one scheme over the other. In addition, there are other factors to consider before deciding which scheme is more advantageous in large-scale shared-memory multiprocessors. A distinct advantage of the directory-based scheme over the timestamp-based scheme is that its use is transparent to the programs. In other words, we can improve the performance of a given shared-memory multiprocessor by introducing private caches with a directory-based cache coherence scheme without modifying any existing software. On the other hand, there are some situations which favor the use of the timestamp-based cache coherence scheme. For example, the presence of a *dirty-exclusive* copy of a memory block in the directory-based scheme may increase the service time of read misses by a factor of two when compared to the timestamp-based scheme. It is also possible that the synchronization delay in the directory-based scheme is longer than that in the timestamp-based scheme due to the required invalidations when a write operation is followed by a *signal* operation.

The results also show that there is an intrinsic relationship between the way processors are scheduled and the resultant performance of private caches. This result is general enough to be applied to any cache coherence scheme that can exploit localities over different computational units separated by syn-

322

chronization points. The investigation of more sophisticated scheduling policies that increase the effectiveness of private caches is an interesting topic for further research.

References

[1] A. Agarwal, R. Simoni, J. Hennessy, and M. Horowitz. An evaluation of directory schemes for cache coherence. In *Proceedings of the 15th Annual International Symposium on Computer Architecture*, pages 280–289, June 1988.

[2] J. Archibald and J.-L. Baer. An economical solution to the cache coherence problem. In *Proceedings of the 12th Annual International Symposium on Computer Architecture*, pages 355–362, June 1985.

[3] J. K. Archibald. *The Cache Coherence Problem in Shared-Memory Multiprocessors*. PhD thesis, University of Washington, November 1986.

[4] BBN. *Butterfly Parallel Processor Overview*, version 1 edition.

[5] D. Callahan. *A Global Approach to Detection of Parallelism*. PhD thesis, Rice University, April 1987.

[6] L. M. Censier and P. Feautrier. A new solution to coherence problems in multicache systems. *IEEE Transactions on Computers*, C-27(12):1112–1118, December 1978.

[7] H. Cheong and A. Veidenbaum. A version control approach to cache coherence. In *Proceedings of the 1989 International Conference on Supercomputing*, pages 322–330, June 1989.

[8] H. Cheong and A. V. Veidenbaum. A cache coherence scheme with fast selective invalidation. In *Proceedings of the 15th Annual International Symposium on Computer Architecture*, pages 299–307, June 1988.

[9] G. A. Darmohray and E. D. Brooks III. Gaussian techniques on shared memory multiprocessor computers. Unpublished Technical Report.

[10] S. J. Eggers. *Simulation Analysis of Data Sharing in Shared Memory Multiprocessors*. PhD thesis, University of California, Berkeley, February 1989.

[11] D. Gajski, D. Kuck, D. Lawrie, and A. Sameh. Cedar - a large scale multiprocessor. *Computer Architecture News*, 11(1):7–11, March 1983.

[12] W. Gentzsch. *Vectorization of computer programs with applications to Computational Fluid Dynamics*, volume 8 of *Notes on Numerical Fluid Mechanics*. Friedr. Vieweg & Sohn Verlagsgesellschaft mbH, Braunschweig, 1984.

[13] A. Gottlieb, R. Grishman, C. P. Kruskal, K. P. McAuliffe, L. Rudolph, and M. Snir. The NYU Ultracomputer - Designing a MIMD, Shared-Memory Parallel Machine. In *Proceedings of the 9th Annual International Symposium on Computer Architecture*, pages 27–42, April 1982.

[14] R. R. Henry. Address and instruction tracing for the VAX architecture. Unpublished Technical Report, August 1983.

[15] E. D. Brooks III. Performance of the butterfly processor-memory interconnection in a vector environment. In *Proceedings of the 1985 International Conference on Parallel Processing*, pages 21–24. IEEE, August 1985.

[16] R. L. Lee. The effectiveness of caches and data prefetch buffers in large-scale shared memory multiprocessors. Technical Report CSRD Report. No. 670. Center for Supercomputing Research and Development. University of Illinois, May 1987.

[17] K. P. McAuliffe. *Analysis of Cache Memories in Highly Parallel Systems*. PhD thesis, New York University, May 1986.

[18] S. L. Min. *Memory Hierarchy Management Schemes in Large Scale Shared-Memory Multiprocessors*. PhD thesis, University of Washington, 1989.

[19] S. L. Min and J.-L. Baer. A timestamp-based cache coherence scheme. In *Proceedings of the 1989 International Conference on Parallel Processing. Vol. 1 Architecture*, pages 23–32, August 1989.

[20] S. L. Min and J.-L. Baer. Design and analysis of a scalable cache coherence scheme. Technical Report TR 89-07-08, Department of Computer Science, University of Washington, July 1989. Submitted to the IEEE Transactions on Parallel and Distributed Systems.

[21] G. F. Pfister, W. C. Brantley, D. A. George, S. L. Harvey, W. J. Kleinfelder, K. P. McAuliffe, E. A. Melton, V. A. Norton, and J. Weiss. The IBM Research Parallel Processor Prototype (RP3): Introduction and Architecture. In *Proceedings of the 1985 International Conference on Parallel Processing*, pages 764–771. IEEE, August 1985.

[22] A. J. Smith. CPU cache consistency with software support and using "one time identifiers". In *Proceedings of the Pacific Computer Communications Symposium*, pages 22–24, October 1985.

[23] P. Sweazey and A. J. Smith. A class of compatible cache consistency protocols and their support by the IEEE futurebus. In *Proceedings of the 13th Annual International Symposium on Computer Architecture*, pages 414–423, June 1986.

[24] C. K. Tang. Cache design in the tightly coupled multiprocessor system. In *AFIPS Conference Proceedings National Computer Conference*, pages 749–753, 1976.

[25] A. V. Veidenbaum. A compiler-assisted cache coherence solution for multiprocessors. In *Proceedings of the 1986 International Conference on Parallel Processing*, pages 1029–1036, August 1986.

[26] W. A. Wulf and C. G. Bell. C.mmp - A multi-mini processor. In *Proc. Fall Joint Computer Conference*, pages 765–777, Montvale, New Jersey, December 1972.

[27] W. C. Yen, D. W. L. Yen, and K.-S. Fu. Data coherence problem in a multicache system. *IEEE Transactions on Computers*, C-34(1):56–65, January 1985.

Evaluating the Performance of Software Cache Coherence

Susan Owicki

Systems Research Center

Digital Equipment Corporation

Palo Alto, CA

Anant Agarwal

Laboratory for Computer Science

Massachusetts Institute of Technology

Cambridge, MA

Abstract

In a shared-memory multiprocessor with private caches, cached copies of a data item must be kept consistent. This is called cache coherence. Both hardware and software coherence schemes have been proposed. Software techniques are attractive because they avoid hardware complexity and can be used with any processor-memory interconnection. This paper presents an analytical model of the performance of two software coherence schemes and, for comparison, snoopy-cache hardware. The model is validated against address traces from a bus-based multiprocessor. The behavior of the coherence schemes under various workloads is compared, and their sensitivity to variations in workload parameters is assessed. The analysis shows that the performance of software schemes is critically determined by certain parameters of the workload: the proportion of data accesses, the fraction of shared references, and the number of times a shared block is accessed before it is purged from the cache. Snoopy caches are more resilient to variations in these parameters. Thus when evaluating a software scheme as a design alternative, it is essential to consider the characteristics of the expected workload. The performance of the two software schemes with a multistage interconnection network is also evaluated, and it is determined that both scale well.

1 Introduction

Shared-memory multiprocessors often use per-processor caches to reduce memory latency and to avoid contention on the network between the processors and main memory. In such a system there must be some mechanism to ensure that two processors reading the same address from their caches will see the same value. Most schemes for maintaining this *cache coherence* use one of three approaches: snoopy caches, directories, or software techniques.

Snoopy cache methods [12, 15, 18, 22, 31] are the most commonly used. A snoopy cache-controller listens to transactions between main memory and the other caches and updates its state based on what it hears. The nature of the update varies from one snoopy-cache scheme to another. For example, on hearing that some cache has modified the value of a block, the other caches could either invalidate or update their own copy. Because all caches in the system must observe memory transactions, a shared bus is the typical medium of communication.

Another class of techniques associates a directory entry with each block of main memory; the entry records the current location(s) of each memory block [30, 5, 2]. Memory operations query the directory to determine whether cache-coherence actions are necessary. Directory schemes can be used with an arbitrary interconnection network.

Both snoopy cache and directory schemes involve increased hardware complexity. However, the caches are invisible at the software level, which greatly simplifies programming these machines. As an alternative, cache coherence can be enforced in software, trading software complexity for hardware complexity. Software schemes have been proposed by Smith [29] and Cytron [8] and are part of the design or implementation of the Elxsi System 6400 [24, 23], NYU Ultracomputer [9], IBM RP3 [4, 11], Cedar [6], and VMP [7].

Software schemes are attractive not only because they require minimal hardware support, but also because they can scale beyond the limits imposed by a bus. We will examine two sorts of software schemes in this paper. The simplest approach is to prohibit caching of shared blocks. Shared variables are identified by the programmer or the compiler. They are stored in regions that are marked as non-cachable, typically by a tag or a bit in the page table. Loads and stores to those regions bypass the cache and go directly to main memory, while references to non-shared variables are satisfied in the cache. Such a scheme was used in C.mmp [13] and the Elxsi System 6400 [24, 23]. We refer to this approach as the *No-Cache* scheme.

In another software approach, which we will call *Software-Flush*, shared variables can be removed from the cache by explicit flush instructions. These instructions may be placed in the program by the compiler or the programmer. A typical pattern is to operate on a set of shared variables within a

"Evaluating the Performance of Software Cache Coherence" by S. Owicki and A. Agarwal from *Proc. 3rd Ann. Int'l Conf. Architectural Support for Programming Languages and Operating Systems*, ACM Press, New York, N.Y., 1989, pp. 230–242. Copyright © ACM, Inc. 1989. Reprinted by permission.

critical section and to flush them before leaving the critical section. This will force any modified variables to be written back to memory. Then the next reference to a shared variable in any processor will cause a miss that fetches the variable from memory. A more sophisticated scheme might allow multiple read copies of blocks, and have processes explicitly synchronize and flush cache blocks when performing a write.[1] If the flush instructions are to be inserted by the compiler, it must be possible to detect shared variables and the boundaries of execution within which a shared variable can remain in the local cache. Such regions can be made explicit in the language or detected by compile-time analysis of programs [8]. Except when there is very little shared data, good performance from the Software-Flush scheme places considerable demands on the compiler.

This paper analyses the performance of the No-Cache and Software-Flush schemes. For comparison, we also examine a snoopy-cache scheme, which we call *Dragon*, and the *Base* scheme, which does not take any action to preserve coherence. The questions we address include: What sort of performance can we expect from such schemes? How is their performance effected by scaling? Are there differences in performance between systems based on a bus and a multistage interconnection network? How do variations in the workload affect performance?

We define an analytical multiprocessor cache model, and use it to predict the overhead of the four cache-coherence schemes over a wide range of workload parameters. We chose this approach, rather than simulation, for several reasons. Trace-based simulation was impossible due to the lack of suitable traces. Simulation with a synthetic workload was possible, and would have allowed us to model more detailed features of the coherence schemes. However, there seems to be little benefit in doing this; we can see significant variation among the schemes even without this detail. Evaluating the analytic model is much faster than performing either type of simulation, which allows us to study the schemes over a wide range of workload parameters. This is especially useful for software schemes, where there is as yet little workload data. However, because the results of analytical models are always subject to doubt, we have validated our model against simulation with real address traces from a small multiprocessor system.

We observed that the performance of the software schemes was most affected by the frequency of data references, degree of sharing, and number of references to a shared datum between fetching and flushing. These parameters impact the performance of software schemes much more dramatically than the Dragon scheme. Software caching works well in favorable regions of the above parameters, but does badly in other regions. Therefore, it is critical to estimate the expected range of these parameters when evaluating a software scheme.

Both the Software-Flush scheme and the No-Cache scheme scale to systems with general memory interconnection networks. In such a system, the efficiency of the Software-Flush scheme drops heavily when the workload is

heavy, while the efficiency of the No-Cache scheme becomes abysmal even with moderate workload.

Previous cache-coherence studies have focused on the performance of hardware-based schemes. Archibald and Baer [3] evaluate a number of snoopy-cache schemes using simulation from a synthetic workload. A similar analysis using timed Petri nets was performed by Vernon et al. [32]. A mean value analysis of snoopy cache coherence protocols was presented by Vernon, Lazowska and Zahorjan [33]. They were able to achieve very good agreement between the earlier Petri net simulation and an analytic model that was much less computationally demanding. The approach taken in this last paper is the closest to ours. Greenberg and Mitrani [16] use a slightly different probabilistic model to analyze several snoopy cache protocols. Models characterizing multiprocessor references and their impact on snoopy schemes are presented by Eggers and Katz [10] and Agarwal and Gupta [1]. Directory schemes are evaluated by Agarwal et al. [2] using simulation with multiprocessor address traces.

The rest of the paper is organized as follows: Section 2 presents the cache model for bus-based multiprocessors, and the following section describes its validation. Section 4 performs a sensitivity analysis to determine the critical parameters in the various schemes. The results of the analyses for buses are presented in Section 5. Section 6 gives the model and analysis of a multiprocessor with a multistage interconnection network.

2 The Model

We wish to compare the cost of cache activity in the No-Cache, Software-Flush, Dragon, and Base schemes. Cache overhead consists of the time spent in handling cache misses and implementing cache coherence. Processor utilization U is the fraction of time spent in "productive" (non-overhead) computation. An n-processor machine has *processing power* $n \times U$, and we use processing power as the basis for our comparisons.

An analytic model is used to estimate processing power. It has three components. The *system model* defines the cost of the operations provided by the hardware. The *workload model* gives the frequency with which these operations are invoked, expressed in terms of various workload parameters. From these two models it is possible to determine the average processor and bus time required by an instruction. Additional time is lost to contention for the shared bus or the interconnection network, and this is estimated by the *contention model*. Only the bus model is defined in this section; the network model is defined in Section 6.2.

2.1 System Model

Table 1 lists the operations in the model. In addition to instruction execution, clean miss, and dirty miss, they include specific operations for each coherence scheme. For No-Cache, there are read-through and write-through operations to access a word in main memory rather than a word in the cache. For Software-Flush, a flush instruction in-

---

[1]Some schemes even allow temporary inconsistency to reduce serialization penalties [8].

325

validates a block in the cache and writes the block back to main memory if it is dirty. Finally, the Dragon scheme has write-broadcast, a miss (clean or dirty) satisfied from another cache, and cycle-stealing by the cache controller. Note that executing an instruction corresponds to one or more operations: one for the instruction itself, and possibly others for cache or memory activity.

Table 1 also gives the CPU and bus time, in cycles, for each operation. Here CPU time is the total time required for the operation in the absence of contention, and bus time is the part of that time during which the bus is held. (Bus and CPU cycle time are assumed to be the same.)

Operation	CPU Time	Bus Time
Instruction execution		
(except flush)	1	0
Clean miss (mem)	10	7
Dirty miss (mem)	14	11
Read through	5	4
Write through	2	1
Clean flush	1	0
Dirty flush	6	4
Write broadcast	2	1
Clean miss (cache)	9	6
Dirty miss (cache)	13	10
Cycle stealing	1	0

Table 1: System model: CPU and bus time for hardware operations

The operation costs are based on a hypothetical RISC machine with a combined instruction and data cache. Each instruction takes one cycle, plus the time for any cache operations it triggers. The cost of cache operations is based on a block size of four words. Thus, for example, a load which causes a clean miss from memory needs 7 cycles of bus time, 1 to send the address, 2 for memory access, and 4 to get the 4 words of data. Processor time to detect and process the miss adds 3 CPU cycles for a total of 10. Finally the load itself is performed, adding one more CPU cycle for instruction execution. A read-through takes only 4 cycles of bus time, because only 1 data word is transmitted. It requires 5 cpu cycles: 4 for bus activity, plus 1 for setting up the memory request. The times for other operations are derived in a similar way.

2.2 Workload Model

The workload model determines the frequency of the operations defined in the system model. The operation frequencies are expressed in terms of the parameters listed in Table 2. The "shared data" in this table means slightly different things in the software and Dragon schemes. For No-Cache and Software-Flush, an item is *shared* if it is treated as shared by the cache coherence algorithm; this is determined by the compiler or programmer. For the Dragon scheme, an item is *shared* if it is actually referenced by more

than one processor. These interpretations should not lead to widely differing values.

For all schemes	
ls	probability an instruction is a load or store
msdat	miss rate for data
msins	miss rate for instructions
md	probability a miss replaces a dirty block
shd	probability a load or store refers to shared data
wr	probability a shared load or store is a store
For Software-Flush only	
apl	number of references to a shared block before it is flushed
mdshd	probability a shared block is modified before it is flushed
For Dragon only	
oclean	on miss of a shared block in one cache, probability it is not dirty in another
opres	on reference to a shared block in one cache, probability it is present in another
nshd	on write-broadcast, number of caches containing a shared block

Table 2: Parameters for the Workload Model

Some of these parameters are functions of the underlying system as well as of the program workload. For example, miss rates depend on block size, cache size, and so on. We don't try to model those effects, since they are not relevant to cache coherence. It is enough to consider a range of values for those parameters.

The remainder of this section describes the workloads of the four cache-coherence schemes. The information here, combined with the system model, makes it possible to compute the average rate and service time of bus transactions. Let o denote a hardware operation, $freq_{o,scheme}$ the frequency of that operation in the workload model for $scheme$, cpu_o the CPU time for o, and bus_o the bus time for o in the system model. Then an instruction takes an average of

$$c = \sum_o freq_{o,scheme} \times cpu_o \qquad (1)$$

CPU cycles and

$$b = \sum_o freq_{o,scheme} \times bus_o \qquad (2)$$

bus cycles. Thus bus transactions are generated at an average rate of one every $c - b$ CPU cycles, and each transaction requires an average of b bus cycles. In the contention models, b is the transaction service time, and $1/(c - b)$ is the transaction rate.

2.2.1 Base

The Base scheme, which does not implement coherence, is included to give an upper bound on performance. Its workload is characterized in Table 3.

The formulae give the frequency of clean and dirty misses per instruction. A data miss occurs when a load or store

clean miss	$(ls \times msdat + msins) \times (1 - md)$
dirty miss	$(ls \times msdat + msins) \times md$

Table 3: Workload model: Base scheme

instruction (probability ls) refers to an address that is not present in the cache (probability $msdat$). An instruction miss occurs with probability $msins$. In either case, if the block to be replaced is dirty (probability md) the miss is dirty, if not (probability $1 - md$) it is clean.

2.2.2 No-Cache

In this scheme, shared variables are identified by the programmer or the compiler. They are stored in memory regions that are marked as non-cachable, typically by a tag or a bit in the page table. Loads and stores to those regions bypass the cache and go directly to main memory.

Table 4 gives the frequencies of cache operations for the No-Cache scheme. The probability of a data miss is reduced from the Base scheme by a factor of $1 - shd$, because only unshared data is kept in the cache. In addition, all loads (stores) to shared variables require a read-through (write-through) operation.

clean miss	$(ls \times msdat \times (1 - shd) + msins) \times (1 - md)$
dirty miss	$(ls \times msdat \times (1 - shd) + msins) \times md$
read-thru	$ls \times shd \times (1 - wr)$
write-thru	$ls \times shd \times wr$

Table 4: Workload model: No-Cache

2.2.3 Software-Flush

In this approach, shared variables can be removed from the cache by explicit flush instructions. These instructions may be placed in the program by the compiler or the programmer. A typical pattern is to operate on a set of shared variables within a critical section, and to flush them before leaving the critical section. This will force any variables modified in the critical section to be written back to memory. Then the first reference to a shared variable within the next critical section will cause a miss that fetches the variable from memory. If the flush instructions are to be inserted by the compiler, it must be possible to detect shared variables and the boundaries of execution within which a shared variable can remain locally cached. Such regions can be made explicit in the language or detected by compile-time analysis of programs [8, 6]. A mechanism must also exist to flush all the blocks of a process from a cache if the process migrates to another processor (e.g., purge the entire cache). Our analysis does not consider the effects of process migration, but in general, process migration has a harmful impact on any cache coherence scheme. (See [27] for results on the effect of process migration on snoopy caches).

Table 5 gives the frequency of operations for Software-Flush. Non-shared variables generate the same number of

clean and dirty misses as in the No-Cache scheme. Shared variables are handled by inserting flush instructions at an average rate of one per apl references to shared variables, i.e. with frequency $shd \times ls/apl$. The extra flushes increase operation frequencies in three ways. First, a flush instruction causes a dirty flush with probability $mdshd$ and a clean flush with probability $1 - mdshd$. Second, there is approximately one clean miss for each flush instruction, namely, the miss which brought the flushed block into the cache. This approximation assumes that the probability of the block's being replaced in the cache before it is flushed is low enough to be ignored. Finally, the added flush instructions increase the number of instruction misses: the probability that a flush causes a miss is $msins$. Note that Table 5 reports operation frequencies per non-flush instruction. This is because flush instructions are part of the cache-coherence overhead, and their cost is amortized over the other instructions.

clean miss	$(ls \times msdat \times (1 - shd) + msins)$ $\times (1 - md) + (ls \times shd/apl)$ $+ (ls \times shd/apl) \times msins \times (1 - md)$
dirty miss	$(ls \times msdat \times (1 - shd) + msins) \times md$ $+ (ls \times shd/apl) \times msins \times md$
clean flush	$ls \times shd \times (1 - mdshd)/apl$
dirty flush	$ls \times shd \times mdshd/apl$

Table 5: Workload model: Software-Flush

Both No-Cache and Software-Flush may be available on the same machine. On the Elxsi 6400 [24, 23], the programmer determines whether a particular shared variable is kept coherent by the No-Cache or Software-Flush scheme. In the MultiTitan [17], locks are not cached, and other shared variables are kept coherent by Software-Flush. In the scheme proposed by Cytron [8], the compiler determines which variables are cached.

Although the details of Software-Flush schemes vary, many can be handled by slight modifications of our model. For example, in the scheme proposed by Cytron [8], the compiler uses data-dependence information to determine when to insert instructions for cache management. The instructions are *post*, which writes a block to memory, *invalidate*, which removes a block from the cache, and *flush*, which does both. Let the workload parameter apl be the average number of references to a shared block before it is flushed or invalidated. Let p be the frequency of *post* instructions. Then the workload model for Cytron's scheme is the same as Table 5, with the addition of p full-block write-through operations and $p \times msins$ misses.

Cheong and Veidenbaum [6] propose a somewhat different mechanism for taking advantage of data-dependence information. They use write-through to keep main memory current and an invalidation mechanism that avoids flushing individual lines. Let apl be the average number of references to a shared block each time it is read to the cache from memory. Let inv be the frequency of invalidate and clear instructions. Then for the workload model in Cheong's scheme, *clean miss* $= ls \times msdat \times (1 - shd) + msins + (ls \times shd/apl) + inv \times msins$, and *write-thru* $= ls \times wr$. There are inv invalidate/clear instructions, each costing one cpu cycle; no bus activity is involved. Note that there are no dirty flushes, because of the write-through policy.

2.2.4 Dragon

We have modeled one snoopy bus protocol to provide a comparison point for the software mechanisms. A Dragon-like scheme [22] was selected because Archibald and Baer [3] found its performance to be among the best.

The following is a slightly simplified description of the relevant aspects of the Dragon protocol. From listening to bus traffic, a cache knows if an address is valid in another cache. When a store refers to an address that is in another cache, the address and new value are broadcast on the bus, and any cache that has the address updates its value accordingly. All stores to non-shared addresses are performed in the local cache. On a cache miss, main memory supplies the block unless it is dirty in another cache; in the latter case, that cache supplies the block.

Table 6 gives the frequency of operations for the Dragon model. There are three effects to consider. First, the write-broadcast occurs once per $shd \times opres$ writes. Second, some misses will be satisfied from a cache instead of from main memory; this happens on a miss with probability $shd \times (1 - oclean)$. Finally, a write-broadcast may cause other caches to steal cycles from their processors as they update their own copy of the variable. This occurs with frequency $nshd$ on each write-broadcast. As it happens, the last two effects are small and could have been omitted from the model without significantly affecting our results.

clean miss from mem	$ls \times msdat \times (1 - shd \times (1 - oclean)$ $+ msins) \times (1 - md)$
dirty miss from mem	$ls \times msdat \times (1 - shd \times (1 - oclean)$ $+ msins) \times md$
write broadcast	$ls \times shd \times wr \times opres$
clean miss from cache	$ls \times msdat \times shd \times (1 - oclean)$ $\times (1 - md)$
dirty miss from cache	$ls \times msdat \times shd \times (1 - oclean)$ $\times md$
steal cycle	$ls \times shd \times wr \times opres \times nshd$

Table 6: Workload model: Dragon

2.3 Contention Model

An n-processor system can be modeled as a closed queueing network with a single server (the bus) and n customers (the processors). Such a network is characterized by two parameters: the average service time and average rate of bus transactions.[2] In our system, the average service time is b cycles and the average rate is $1/(c - b)$ transactions per cycle, where c and b are defined in equations 1 and 2 respectively. Solution of the queueing model [21] yields w, the contention cycles per instruction. Thus the total time per instruction is $c + w$. In the absence of cache activity, an

---

[2]If a multistage interconnection network is used, the multistage network is represented as a load-dependent service center characterized by its service rate at various loads.

instruction would take 1 cycle, so the CPU utilization is

$$U = 1/(c + w) \qquad (3)$$

This contention model is very similar to the one used by Vernon et al. [33] in analyzing snoopy-cache protocols.

3 Validation

This section compares model predictions against simulation results for the Base scheme and Dragon schemes. We developed a trace-driven multiprocessor cache and bus simulator, which can compute statistics like cache miss rates, cycles lost to bus contention, and processor utilization, for a variety of coherence schemes, cache sizes and processor numbers.

The address traces used in the validation were obtained using ATUM-2, a multiprocessor tracing technique described in [27]. The traces contain interleaved memory references from the processors. Three of the traces (POPS, THOR, and PERO) were taken on a four-processor VAX 8350 running the MACH operating system. We also used an 8-processor trace of PERO, which was obtained from a parallel tracer that used the VAX T-bit. The four-processor traces include operating system references, and none of the traces include process migration. Sites and Agarwal [27] describe the applications and details of the traces.

We simulated 16K, 64K, and 256K-byte caches with a fixed blocksize of 16 bytes and the same transfer block size. The hardware model used is summarized in Table 1. The model was validated only for the Base and the Dragon schemes. Meaningfully validating the software schemes was not possible because the traces are from a multiprocessor that used hardware for cache coherence. Because the multiprocessor model used in the simulations is different from the traced machine model, the order of references from different processors may be slightly distorted in the simulation. However, we expect that this effect is not large, because the timing differences between the two multiprocessor models affect the address streams from all the processors uniformly. Also, the cache statistics we obtained matched those from simulating a multiprocessor model that retained the exact order of the references in the trace.

For a multiprocessor cache model to be useful, it is important that the parameter values input to the model are valid over the range in which the model is exercised. Variations in input parameters may be modeled, or a parameter value must be input for each point under consideration. In general, we choose parameters that are expected to be nearly constant as the number of processors increases, and verify that they are nearly constant in the trace-driven simulations. The parameters of concern in our model are $oclean$ and $opres$, which can vary with the number of processors in a way that depends on program structure. In our traces, we did observe some random variations in these parameters, but they were small enough that the model was still accurate. A comparative evaluation of snoopy caches should somehow account for the variations in $oclean$ and $opres$.[3]

---

[3]For invalidation-based snoopy caches, the miss rate also falls in this category.

But our focus is on software cache coherence, and we can safely ignore this issue.

The model results closely match simulations in most cases. Figures 1 and 2 present a sampling of our experiments comparing the model predictions to simulations. Figure 1 depicts averages over the four-processor traces, and those in Figure 2 represent the eight-processor trace. We will address potential sources of inaccuracies in the ensuing discussion.

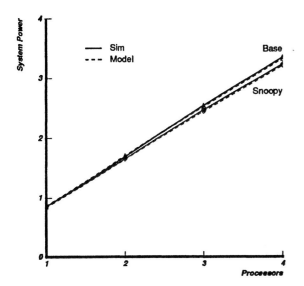

Figure 1: A performance comparison of the Base and the Dragon schemes using simulation and the analytical model for 64K-byte caches.

Figure 1 plots the system power using 64K-byte caches for the Base and Dragon schemes. While the model exactly captures the relative difference between the performance of Base and Dragon schemes, it consistently overestimates bus contention. This is because the bus model is based on exponential service times, while the simulations use fixed bus service times for the different bus operations.

Figure 2 shows the model and simulation results for three cache sizes for the Dragon scheme. Minor inconsistencies between the model and simulation results for single processors can be attributed to the difference in the values of *oclean* and *opres* for one and four processors.

We were unable to validate the Software-Flush schemes because we did not have access to suitable traces. The workload model is straightforward, and seems to adequately capture the costs of the sort of software coherence scheme we assume. The contention model is the same as for Base and Dragon, so their validations can give us some confidence about its use in the Software-Flush scheme. The principle question about its application is that, in Software-Flush, a processor's bus activity is likely to be clustered about the end of critical sections.

To assess the possible impact of this pattern, we simulated a simplified processor-bus system. In this simulation,

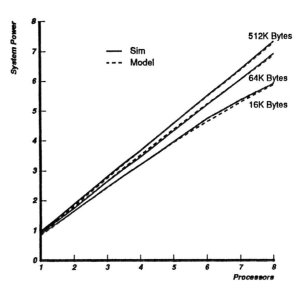

Figure 2: Impact of the cache size on the performance of the Dragon scheme for eight or fewer processors.

processors had bursts of bus activity with exponential interarrival times. Each burst consisted of k bus requests, where k was geometrically distributed. Service times were exponentially distributed. We compared the results to a simulation in which the same number of bus-requests were generated by a simple Poisson process at each processor. Over a variety of parameter values, we found at most a few per-cent difference between response times. Thus we have some reason for confidence that the contention model is valid for Software-Flush.

4 Sensitivity Analysis

The workload model uses a number of parameters to characterize the program's workload. One would expect some of them to be quite important, and others to have little impact on cache performance. This section describes the sensitivity analysis that we used to estimate the importance of each parameter.

The significance of a parameter was assessed from the change in execution time when that parameter was varied and all others were held constant. We chose low, middle, and high values for each parameter, representing the range of values likely to be seen in programs. The ranges are given in Table 7. They were derived from the minimum, average, and maximum values observed in the large-cache traces, except as follows.

There was not enough data in the traces to determine *apl*, so it was estimated by counting the number of references of a cache-line by one processor (at least one of which was a write) between references by another processor. This is an optimistic estimate, so the upper bound of $1/apl$ was taken to be 1, the maximum possible. The values of *md* from the trace were artificially low, because the traces were not long enough to fill up the large caches. The measured high value was 0.25, but 0.5 was used as the high value in the sensitivity analysis; values of this magnitude have been measured by Smith [28]. Finally, the range for *ls* is typical for RISC architectures rather than the CISC machine on which the traces were taken.

Parameter	Low	Middle	High
ls	0.2	0.3	0.4
msdat	0.004	0.014	0.024
msins	0.0014	0.0022	0.0034
md	0.14	0.20	0.50
shd	0.08	0.25	0.42
wr	0.10	0.25	0.40
mdshd	0.0	0.25	0.5
1/apl	0.04	0.13	1.0
oclean	0.60	0.84	0.976
opres	0.63	0.79	0.94
nshd	1.0	1.0	7.0

Table 7: Parameter ranges

Table 8 shows the results of the sensitivity analysis. For each parameter, we computed the per cent change in execution time when the parameter changes from low to high, with all other parameters held constant. (Note that in all cases execution time is greater for the low value of the parameter.) This computation was performed for three settings of the other parameters: low, middle, and high. The maximum per cent change is reported in the table.

Base		No-Cache		Soft-Flush		Dragon	
msdat	17	shd	65	1/apl	88	ls	19
ls	11	ls	48	shd	74	msdat	17
msins	4	msdat	10	ls	49	shd	11
md	4	msins	4	msdat	10	opr	4
		md	1	mdshd	4	msins	4
		wr	<1	msins	4	md	4
				md	1	nshd	4
						wr	3
						oclean	<1

Table 8: Sensitivity to parameter variation, depicted by the per cent change in execution time when the parameter changes from low to high, with all other parameters held constant.

The numbers from the sensitivity analysis must be interpreted with care. The choice of range affects how important a parameter appears. For example, our traces show a small variation in miss rates, and miss rate shows only a modest effect in the sensitivity analysis. Had our traces exhibited greater variation in miss rate, it would have appeared to be much more significant. In addition, changing the miss rate range can change the apparent significance of other parameters, because their effect is estimated at high, low and middle values of miss rate. A wide range may represent a parameter that is observed to vary widely in practice (e.g. *shd*) or a parameter about which we have little information (e.g. *apl*).

In spite of these caveats, certain parameters are clearly more important than others. For the Software-Flush

scheme, *apl* has a huge effect; this is due to both its central importance in the scheme and its wide range. The impact of *shd* is almost as great, and *ls* is significant as well. Miss rate has a noticeably smaller effect, and the other parameters are relatively unimportant. The No-Cache scheme is essentially the same, except that *apl* is not relevant. In the Dragon scheme, the overall hit rate is more important than the level of sharing, even though its range is quite small, because the cost of shared references is relatively low.

In the next section we will analyze the effect of *apl*, *ls* and *shd* in more detail. The effect of *ls* is primarily as a multiplier of *shd* and *msdat*; so the analyses of *ls* and *shd* will be combined by varying them jointly. Parameters *mdshd* and *wr*, which are specific to the Software-Flush and No-Cache schemes, were examined further in spite of their low showing in the sensitivity analysis. When allowed to vary over a wider range, *mdshd* had a small but noticeable effect on the Software-Flush scheme; but *wr* was unimportant even with a wide range.

5 Bus Performance

5.1 Variations among Coherence Schemes

Figures 3 through 5 show the relative performance of the four cache coherence schemes for three settings of *ls* and *shd*. The dotted line is the theoretical upper bound on processing power. It represents the case in which each processor is fully utilized, and there is no delay due to memory activity. All schemes fall below this line, because a processor is delayed when it uses the bus in handling cache misses and references to shared data. With multiple processors the cost of bus operations increases because contention can add a significant delay. For this reason, the incremental benefit of adding a processor is smaller for large systems than small ones.

Comparing the schemes, we find that Base performs best as long as *ls* > 0; this is to be expected, since the others incur overhead in processing shared data. (If *ls* = 0 the schemes are identical.) In most cases Dragon's performance is close to Base. It incurs sharing overhead only when data are simultaneously in the caches of two or more processors, and then only on write operations, i.e. once every *shd* × *opr* × *wr* references. Moreover, the overhead is relatively small, since only one word needs to be transmitted on the bus. No-Cache is much more costly than Dragon, because the processor must go to main memory on every reference to a potentially-shared variable, i. e. once very *shd* references. Software-Flush's performance is drastically affected by the value of *apl*, because there is a main memory operation on every 1/*apl* references to shared data. As will be illustrated in Section 5.3, Software-Flush's performance is usually between Dragon and No-Cache, but it can be better than Dragon or worse than No-Cache.

5.2 Effect of *ls* and *shd*

Parameter *ls* has a significant impact on all schemes, and *shd* is important for all but Base. Both affect the frequency of memory activity. *ls* determines the frequency of data

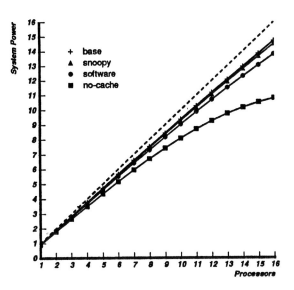

Figure 3: Performance of cache-coherence schemes with low *shd* and *ls*; all other parameters at medium values

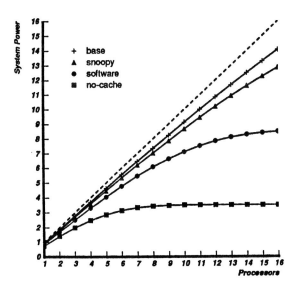

Figure 4: Performance of cache-coherence schemes with medium *shd* and *ls*; all other parameters at medium values

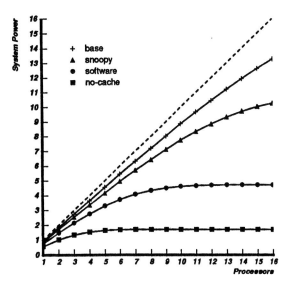

Figure 5: Performance of cache-coherence schemes with high *shd* and *ls*; all other parameters at medium values

references in the instruction stream, while *shd* determines the proportion that go to shared data items. Thus increasing *ls* has a double effect on overhead: it increases both the frequency of misses and the frequency of shared data references.

At low values of *ls* and *shd* (Figure 3), Base, Dragon, and Software-Flush perform well, and there is not much difference between them. (Recall that the Software-Flush scheme is evaluated with a medium *apl* value.) Even No-Cache performs well for a moderate number of processors. Low levels of sharing can be expected in some situations: for example, if a multiprocessor is used as a time sharing system, so that separate processors run unrelated jobs, or if communication is done through messages rather than shared memory [24]. In such environments No-Cache is a viable alternative.

Even with middle values of *ls* and *shd* (Figure 4), No-Cache performs acceptably with a small number of processors. Dragon performs very well even with 16 processors. With medium *apl*, Software-Flush does well with up to 8-10 processors; from then on, adding processors only slightly increases processing power.

With high *ls* and *shd* (Figure 5), Dragon still gives good performance. No-Cache does badly; it saturates the bus with a processing power less than 2. Software-Flush performs acceptably for a small number of processors; it saturates the bus with processing power less than 5. Even in this high sharing region, however, Software-Flush can perform well if *apl* is high.

5.3 Effect of *apl*

The performance of Software-Flush is drastically affected by the value of *apl*. Figure 6 illustrates the variation that can occur. When $apl = 1$, every reference to a shared variable requires a flush (possibly dirty) and a miss. This means that

331

both CPU and bus demands are heavier than for No-Cache, and, indeed, Software-Flush's performance is the worse. On the other hand, very high values of apl make sharing overhead very small, especially if *mdshd* is not high. In this case Software-Flush can perform as well as Dragon, or even better.

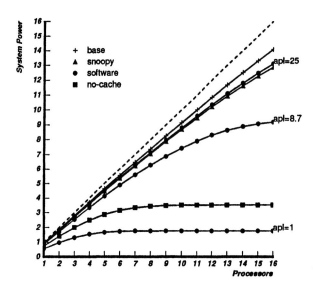

Figure 6: Effect of varying *apl*; other parameters at medium values

Figures 7 and 8 show the variation of processing power with *apl* for two levels of sharing. With low sharing, performance is very sensitive to *apl* at low values, but quickly reaches its maximum as apl is increased. With medium sharing levels, performance is sensitive to variations in *apl* even at relatively high values.

The range for *apl* reported from our traces is optimistic: it assumes that data is flushed only when absolutely necessary. As our measurements show, the number of uninterrupted references to a shared-written object by a processor can be quite large in practice. It remains to be seen whether a compiler can generate code that takes advantage of these long runs. Doing so is crucial if software schemes are to be used in the presence of even moderate amounts of shared data.

6   Interconnection Network Performance

Unlike the snoopy schemes, the software schemes can be used in a network environment where there is no mechanism for a cache to observe all the processor-memory traffic. In this section we explore the scalability of software schemes in such an environment. Some of the questions we address are: Is caching shared data in a network environment worthwhile? Can software schemes scale to a large number of processors?

The analysis uses a multistage interconnection network model to evaluate the system performance of a cache-based

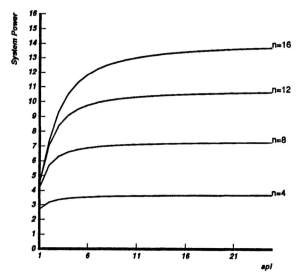

Figure 7: Effect of *apl* with low sharing; other parameters at medium values

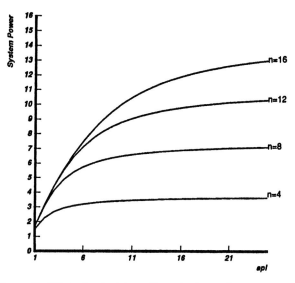

Figure 8: Effect of *apl* with medium sharing; other parameters at medium values

multiprocessor. The workload model is the same as before, and new models for hardware timing and network contention are discussed in the next sections. As in our bus analysis, we first compute the average transaction rate and transaction time for the network, then use the contention model to compute the network delay. From these, system processing power can be computed as before.

6.1 The Network

Our analysis applies to the general class of multistage interconnection networks called Banyan [14], Omega [20], or Delta [26]. For our analysis in this paper we consider an unbuffered, circuit-switched network composed of 2x2 crossbars, with unit dilation factor. (We will also summarize our analytical results for a packet-switched network, with infinite buffering at the switches.) The analysis can be extended easily to dilated networks or crossbar switches with a larger dimension. A request accepted by the network travels through n switch stages (corresponding to a system with 2^n processors) to the memory; the response from the memory returns on the path established by the request. If multiple messages are simultaneously routed to the same output port, a randomly-chosen one is forwarded and the other is dropped. The source is responsible for retransmitting dropped messages. A switch cycle is assumed to be the same as a processor cycle. The network paths are assumed to be one word (4 bytes) wide,[4] and a cache block is 4 words long, as before.

We have tried to keep the network timing model consistent with the bus where possible. Table 9 gives the network timing model. The network delay (without contention) for a cache miss is $6 + 2n$ cycles: n to set up the path, 1 to send the address to memory, 2 for memory access, n for the return of the first data word, and 3 for the remaining 3 words. (We will sometimes refer to the network service time minus $2n$ as the message size.) Similarly, a dirty miss costs $9 + 2n$ cycles: n to set up the path, 1 to send the address to memory, 2 for memory access (overlapped with getting the address of the dirty block and one data word), 3 cycles for the remaining dirty words, n for the return of the first word, and 3 for the remaining 3 words.

Operation	CPU Time	Network Time
Instruction execution		
(Except flush)	1	0
Clean fetch	$9 + 2n$	$6 + 2n$
Dirty fetch	$12 + 2n$	$9 + 2n$
Clean flush	1	0
Dirty flush	$7 + 2n$	$5 + 2n$
Write through	$3 + 2n$	$2 + 2n$
Read through	$4 + 2n$	$3 + 2n$

Table 9: System model for a network with n stages

---

[4]The wide path is one of the reasons we use 2x2 switches, because larger dimension switches will not fit easily into a single chip with current technology.

6.2 The Network Contention Model

Our network analysis uses the model due to Patel [25]. Patel's model has been used extensively in the literature. We are not aware of any validation of this model against multiprocessor traces, although is has been tested using simulations based on synthetic reference patterns.[5]

Our analysis requires certain assumptions for tractability; they are similar to the ones typically made in the literature [25, 19]. We assume that the requests are independent and uniformly distributed over all the memory modules. An average transaction rate m and an average transaction size t is computed for each of the cache coherence schemes; these correspond to $1/(c - b)$ and b from equations 1 and 2 in the bus analysis. The network delay can be estimated using the *unit-request approximation*, in which the transaction rate is taken to be $m \times t$ and the transaction size to be 1. It is as if the processor splits up a t-unit memory request into t independent and uniformly distributed unit-time sub-requests. Patel validates the accuracy of this approximation through simulation.

Let m_i be the probability of a request at a particular input at the nth stage of the network in any given cycle. Then, the effective processor utilization U, and hence system processing power, can be computed using the following system of equations.

$$U = \frac{m_n}{mt}$$
$$m_{i+1} = 1 - (1 - \frac{m_i}{2})^2 \quad 0 \leq i < n$$
$$m_0 = 1 - U$$

In this model, a processor is involved in a network access whenever it is not executing instructions. Using the unit-request approximation, each such cycle corresponds to a request, yielding $m_0 = 1 - U$. The rate m_{i+1} at an output of a level i switch is the probability that at least one of the level i input requests is routed to this port. In the steady state, the request rate at the output of the network (m_n) must equal the rate at which requests are injected into the network by the processor ($U \times m \times t$). The value of m_n in the equations is obtained recursively for successive stages starting with the input request rate of m_0. The equations can be solved using standard iterative numerical techniques.

6.3 Network Performance Results

Before we analyze the network for various ranges of parameter values, it is instructive to compare bus and network performance in small-scale systems (see Figure 9). As reported in the previous section, the Dragon scheme attains near perfect bus performance relative to the Base scheme for fewer than 16 processors and middle parameter ranges, while the Software-Flush and No-Cache schemes saturate

---

[5]We also estimated multiprocessor performance in a manner analogous to our bus analysis by representing the network as a load-dependent service center. The contention delay is computed using the queuing models described in [21]. This model gave virtually the same results as Patel's model.

the bus at 8 and 4 processors respectively. Because the network bandwidth increases with the number of processors, network performance becomes superior to buses when the bus begins to saturate. Both the Software-Flush scheme and the No-Cache scheme scale with the number of processors, though the Software-Flush scheme is clearly more efficient. The No-Cache scheme is poorer despite its smaller message size due to its higher request rate. Still, it scales with the number of processors and is a feasible choice if a designer wants to minimize hardware cost and software complexity. In a circuit-switched network, the request rate plays a more important role than the message size because of the high fixed cost of setting up the path to memory.

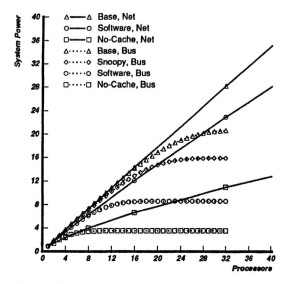

Figure 9: Buses versus networks in the small scale.

Because the network bandwidth scales with the number of processors (to first order), plotting processor utilization for a network of a given size is more interesting than in a bus-based system. Let us consider a network with 256 processors. Figure 10 shows processor utilization with various request rates for several choices of average message sizes. (Note that $2n$ must be added to the message size to get the network time per message.) Nine points are marked on the figure; they correspond to the performance of Base, Software-Flush, and No-Cache schemes with low, middle, and high parameter settings. The first letter in the label (B, S, or N) refers to the scheme, and the second letter (l, m, or h) refers to the range.

The first striking observation is the importance of keeping the network reference rate low. Even for a cache-miss rate as low as 3% in the 256-processor system and a message size of 4 words (corresponding to a unit-time service request rate of $3\% \times (16 + 4) = 60\%$), the processor utilization is halved. In a circuit-switched network, a change in the reference rate impacts system performance more than a proportional change in the blocksize. Of course, using a faster network, or using larger switches, will increase the reference rate at which the network latency begins to increase

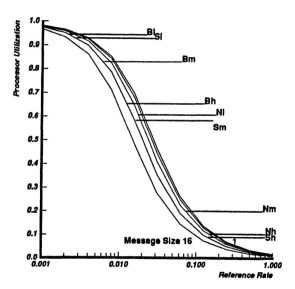

Figure 10: Bus performance for various request rates and with message sizes of 1, 2, 4, 8 and 16 words. The performance of the Base, Software-Flush, and No-Cache schemes is marked with two letter codes, the first letter (B, S, or N) corresponds to the scheme, and the second letter corresponds to a low, middle, or high (l, m, or h) range.

sharply.

The nine points fall into two performance classes. The Base scheme in all ranges, the Software-Flush scheme in its low and middle range, and the No-Cache scheme in its low range, fall into a reasonable performance category, and the other combinations are much poorer. While the Software-Flush scheme is usable even with medium sharing, the No-Cache scheme is efficient only if sharing is very low. Put another way, a system that does not cache shared data (and more so a system that does not cache *any* data) will need to use a much faster network relative to the processor to sustain reasonable performance. The performance of the Software-Flush scheme for the low range approximates the performance of hardware-based directory schemes. If Software-Flush schemes can attain a high value for *apl*, they have the potential to compete with hardware schemes in large-scale networks.

We also modeled buffered packet switched networks for the above three ranges of parameters. We used the model described in [19] to compute the network latency of a memory request for a given processor request rate, and iteratively computed the processor utilization in a manner similar to our circuit-switched network analysis. The relative performance for the nine ranges turns out to be similar to circuit switching, with the difference that the processor utilizations for the No-Cache low range is slightly better than for Base high. In addition, because packet switching favors small packet sizes, the performance of No-cache is generally better than its performance with circuit switching in the three ranges.

In the future we hope to examine reference patterns in large-scale parallel applications, both to get a better understanding of different workloads, and to validate our methodology against simulation. Traditionally, simulations have used synthetically generated traces, but a synthetic trace cannot capture workload-dependent effects such as hot-spot activity (or lack thereof) or locality of references. We are currently working on the generation of large multiprocessor traces and evaluation techniques for these studies. While we focused on a simple network architecture in this paper, we are interested in extending our results to other network architectures as well.

7 Conclusion

Software cache-coherence schemes have been proposed and implemented because they have two advantages over typical hardware schemes: they do not require complex hardware, and they do not have the obvious scalability problem of a shared bus. However, to our knowledge, the performance of software-caching has not been analyzed before. In this paper we used an analytic model to predict caching overhead for several coherence schemes. The model was validated against multiprocessor trace data, and its sensitivity to variations in parameter values was studied.

First let us consider performance on bus-based systems. For almost all workloads, the snoopy cache scheme had the lowest overhead. Its performance was good for all workloads, while the software schemes showed great variation as the workload parameters changed. With a light workload (low memory reference rate and little sharing), the Software-Flush scheme was almost as good as snoopy cache, and even the No-Cache approach was feasible. Performance of the No-Cache method fell off dramatically as the workload increased. The performance of the Software-Flush method also deteriorated, though not as drastically.

We also evaluated the software schemes on a circuit-switched multistage interconnection network. Both software schemes scale well, as expected. Software-Flush does considerably better than No-Cache because it causes fewer memory requests, although the requests are longer. Use of packet-switching would be more favorable to No-Cache.

In both network and bus environments, the performance of Software-Flush is largely determined by the number of references to a block before it is flushed from a cache. This is a affected by program structure and by compiler technology. For example, the compiler can optimize performance by allocating related variables to the same block, and by flushing data as infrequently as possible. But if a shared variable is frequently updated by different processors, it is likely to have about two references per flush, no matter how sophisticated the compiler. At present we lack the workload data and compiler experience that would allow us to predict what is achievable here.

8 Acknowledgements

Dick Sites, Digital Equipment Corporation, lent the ATUM microcode to us, and Roberto Bisiani and the Speech Group at CMU allowed us the use of their VAX 8350 to obtain traces. Forest Baskett of Silicon Graphics suggested analytical modeling of software cache coherence, and Jeremy Dion, Digital Equipment Corporation, gave valuable advice on the software workload model. The T-bit tracer for parallel applications was implemented by Steve Goldschmidt at Stanford. Partial support for the research reported in this paper was provided by DARPA under contract # N00014-87-K-0825.

References

[1] Anant Agarwal and Anoop Gupta. Memory-Reference Characteristics of Multiprocessor Applications under MACH. In *Proceedings of SIGMETRICS 1988*, May 1988.

[2] Anant Agarwal, Richard Simoni, John Hennessy, and Mark Horowitz. An Evaluation of Directory Schemes for Cache Coherence. In *Proceedings of the 15th International Symposium on Computer Architecture*, June 1988.

[3] James Archibald and Jean-Loup Baer. Cache Coherence Protocols: Evaluation Using a Multiprocessor Simulation Model. *ACM Transactions on Computer Systems*, 4(4):273–298, November 1986.

[4] W. C. Brantley, K. P. McAuliffe, and J. Weiss. RP3 Processor-Memory Element. In *Proceedings 1985 Int'l Conference on Parallel Processing*, pages 782–789, 1985.

[5] Lucien M. Censier and Paul Feautrier. A New Solution to Coherence Problems in Multicache Systems. *IEEE Transactions on Computers*, c-27(12):1112–1118, December 1978.

[6] H. Cheong and A. V. Veidenbaum. A Cache Coherence Scheme with Fast Selective Invalidation. In *Proceedings of the 15th International Symposium on Computer Architecture*, June 1988.

[7] David R. Cheriton, Gert A. Slavenberg, and Patrick D. Boyle. Software-Controlled Caches in the VMP Multiprocessor. In *Proceedings of the 13th Annual Symposium on Computer Architecture*, pages 367–374, June 1986.

[8] Ron Cytron, Steve Karlovsky, and Kevin P. McAuliffe. Automatic Management of Programmable Caches. In *Proceedings ICPP*, August 1988.

[9] Jan Edler et al. Issues related to MIMD shared-memory computers: the NYU Ultracomputer Approach. In *Proceedings 12th Annual Int'l Symp. on Computer Architecture*, pages 126–135, June 1985.

[10] S. J. Eggers and R. H. Katz. A Characterization of Sharing in Parallel Programs and Its Application to Coherency Protocol Evaluation. In *Proceedings of the 15th International Symposium on Computer Architecture*, June 1988.

[11] G. F. Pfister et. al. The IBM Research Parallel Processor Prototype (RP3): Introduction and Architecture. In *Proceedings ICPP*, pages 764–771, August 1985.

[12] S. J. Frank. Tightly Coupled Multiprocessor System Speeds Up Memory Access Times. Electronics, 57, 1, January 1984.

[13] S. H. Fuller and S. P. Harbison. *The C.mmp Multiprocessor*. Technical Report, Carnegie-Mellon University, October 1978.

[14] G. R. Goke and G. J. Lipovski. Banyan Networks for Partitioning Multiprocessor Systems. In *Proceedings of the 1st Annual Symposium on Computer Architecture*, pages 21–28, 1973.

[15] James R. Goodman. Using Cache Memory to Reduce Processor-Memory Traffic. In *Proceedings of the 10th Annual Symposium on Computer Architecture*, pages 124–131, June 1983.

[16] Albert G. Greenberg, Isi Mitrani, and Larry Rudolph. Analysis of snooping caches. In *Proceedings of Performance 87, 12th Int'l Symp. on Computer Performance*, December 1987.

[17] Norman P. Jouppi, Jeremy Dion, and Michael J. K. Nielsen. *MultiTitan: four architecture papers*. Technical Report 86/2, Digital Western Research Laboratory, Palo Alto, California, September 1986.

[18] R. H. Katz, S. J. Eggers, D. A. Wood, C. L. Perkins, and R. G. Sheldon. Implementing a Cache Consistency Protocol. In *Proceedings of the 12th International Symposium on Computer Architecture*, pages 276–283, June 1985.

[19] Clyde P. Kruskal and Marc Snir. The Performance of Multistage Interconnection Networks for Multiprocessors. *IEEE Transactions on Computers*, c-32(12):1091–1098, December 1983.

[20] D. H. Lawrie. Access and Alignment of Data in an Array Processor. *IEEE Transactions on Computers*, c-24:1145–1155, 1975.

[21] Edward D. Lazowska, John Zahorjan, G. Scott Graham, and Kenneth C. Sevcik. *Quantitative System Performance*. Prentice Hall, 1984.

[22] E. McCreight. *The Dragon Computer System: An Early Overview*. Technical Report, Xerox Corp., September 1984.

[23] Steve McGrogan, Robert Olson, and Neil Toda. Parallelizing large existing programs - methodology and experiences. In *Proceedings of Spring COMPCON*, pages 458–466, March 1986.

[24] Robert Olson. Parallel Processing in a Message-Based Operating System. *IEEE Software*, July 1985.

[25] Janak H. Patel. Analysis of Multiprocessors with Private Cache Memories. *IEEE Transactions on Computers*, c-31(4):296–304, April 1982.

[26] Janak H. Patel. Performance of Processor-Memory Interconnections for Multiprocessors. *IEEE Transactions on Computers*, c-30(10):771–780, October 1981.

[27] Richard L. Sites and Anant Agarwal. Multiprocessor Cache Analysis using ATUM. In *Proceedings of the 15th International Symposium on Computer Architecture*, June 1988.

[28] Alan Jay Smith. Cache Memories. *ACM Computing Surveys*, 14(3):473–530, September 1982.

[29] Alan Jay Smith. CPU Cache Consistency with Software Support and Using One Time Identifiers. In *Proceedings of the Pacific Computer Communications Symposium*, October 1985.

[30] C. K. Tang. Cache Design in the Tightly Coupled Multiprocessor System. In *AFIPS Conference Proceedings, National Computer Conference, NY, NY*, pages 749–753, June 1976.

[31] Charles P. Thacker and Lawrence C. Stewart. Firefly: a Multiprocessor Workstation. In *Proceedings of ASPLOS II*, pages 164–172, October 1987.

[32] M. K. Vernon and M. A. Holliday. Performance Analysis of Multiprocessor Cache Consistency Protocols Using Generalized Timed Petri Nets. In *Proceedings of SIGMETRICS 1986*, May 1986.

[33] M. K. Vernon, E. D. Lazowska, and J. Zahorjan. An Accurate and Efficient Performance Analysis Technique for Multiprocessor Snooping Cache-Consistency Protocols. In *Proceedings of the 15th International Symposium on Computer Architecture*, June 1988.

Comparison of Hardware and Software Cache Coherence Schemes[†]

Sarita V. Adve, Vikram S. Adve, Mark D. Hill, Mary K. Vernon

Computer Sciences Department
University of Wisconsin-Madison
Madison, WI 53706

ABSTRACT

We use mean value analysis models to compare representative hardware and software cache coherence schemes for a large-scale shared-memory system. Our goal is to identify the workloads for which either of the schemes is significantly better. Our methodology improves upon previous analytical studies and complements previous simulation studies by developing a common high-level workload model that is used to derive separate sets of low-level workload parameters for the two schemes. This approach allows an equitable comparison of the two schemes for a specific workload.

Our results show that software schemes are comparable (in terms of processor efficiency) to hardware schemes for a wide class of programs. The only cases for which software schemes perform significantly worse than hardware schemes are when there is a greater than 15% reduction in hit rate due to inaccurate prediction of memory access conflicts, or when there are many writes in the program that are not executed at runtime. For relatively well-structured and deterministic programs, on the other hand, software schemes perform significantly better than hardware schemes.

Keywords: hardware cache coherence, software cache coherence, mean value analysis, workload model

1. Introduction

In shared-memory systems that allow shared data to be cached, some mechanism is required to keep the caches coherent. Hardware snooping protocols [ArB86] are impractical for large systems because they rely on a broadcast medium to maintain coherence. Hardware directory protocols [ASH88] can be used with a large number of processors, but they are complex to design and implement. An alternative to hardware cache coherence is the use of software techniques to keep caches coherent, as in Cedar [KDL86] and RP3 [BMW85]. Software cache coherence

is attractive because the overhead of detecting stale data is transferred from runtime to compile time, and the design complexity is transferred from hardware to software. However, software schemes may perform poorly because compile-time analysis may need to be conservative, leading to unnecessary cache misses and main memory updates. In this paper, we use approximate Mean Value Analysis [VLZ88] to compare the performance of a representative software scheme with a directory-based hardware scheme on a large-scale shared-memory system.

In a previous study comparing the performance of hardware and software coherence, Cheong and Veidenbaum used a parallelizing compiler to implement three different software coherence schemes [Che90]. For selected subroutines of seven programs, they show that the hit ratio of their most sophisticated software scheme (version control) is comparable to the best possible hit ratio achievable by any coherence scheme.

Min and Baer [MiB90b] simulated a timestamp-based software scheme and a hardware directory scheme using traces from three programs. They also report comparable hit ratios for the two schemes. However, they assume perfect compile-time analysis of memory dependencies, including correct prediction of all conditional branches, which is optimistic for the software scheme.

Owicki and Agarwal [OwA89] used an analytical model to compare a software scheme [CKM88] against the Dragon hardware snooping protocol [ArB86] for bus-based systems. They conclude that the software scheme generally shows lower processor efficiencies than the hardware scheme and is more sensitive to the amount of sharing in the workload. The main drawback of their method is that the principal parameters that determine the performance of the two schemes are specified independently of each other, and therefore *for a given workload* it is difficult to estimate how the schemes would compare. Furthermore, they assume the same miss ratio (0.4-2.4%) for private and shared data accesses in the hardware scheme, which is an optimistic assumption as shown in studies of sharing behavior of parallel programs [EgK89, WeG89].

Our analysis improves on the work by Owicki and Agarwal and complements the simulation studies by quantifying coherence protocol performance as a function of parameters that characterize parallel program behavior and compile-time analysis. Our model permits an equitable comparison of the software and hardware protocols for a chosen workload because we derive the principal parameters for each scheme from a common high-level workload

[†] This work is supported in part by the National Science Foundation (DCR-8451405, MIPS-8957278 and CCR-8902536), A.T.& T. Bell Laboratories, Cray Research Foundation and Digital Equipment Corporation, and by an IBM Graduate Fellowship.

"Comparison of Hardware and Software Cache Coherence Schemes" by S.V. Adve, V.S. Adve, M.D. Hill, and M.K. Vernon from *Proc. 18th Ann. Int'l Symp. Computer Architecture*, ACM Press, New York, N.Y., 1991, pp. 298–308. Copyright © ACM, Inc. 1991. Reprinted by permission.

model. Our workload model captures two important limitations of compile-time analysis that may reduce the performance of software schemes: 1) imperfect knowledge of runtime behavior, such as whether a write under control of a conditional branch will actually be executed, and 2) imperfect knowledge of whether two data references actually refer to the same memory location. Including compile-time and runtime parallel program characteristics in a unified model appears to be essential for comparing software and hardware cache coherence schemes.

From the high-level workload model, we derive two sets of low-level parameters that are used as inputs to queueing network models of the systems with hardware and software coherence. We compare a software coherence scheme similar to one proposed by Cytron et al. [CKM88] to a hardware directory-based Dir_iB protocol [ASH88] for large-scale systems. Our conclusions also hold for the version control and timestamp schemes, as discussed in Sections 5 and 6. The goals of our study are to characterize the workloads for which either the software or the hardware scheme is superior, and to provide intuition for why this is so.

The rest of the paper is organized as follows. In Section 2, we discuss the important issues that can result in performance differences between hardware and software schemes. In Section 3, we describe our common high-level workload model. In Section 4, we first describe the system architecture and cache coherence schemes studied in this paper, and give a brief overview of the Mean Value Analysis models for the systems. We then describe how the low-level workload parameters are derived from the high-level workload model. Section 5 presents the results of our experiments. In Section 6, we discuss the overall results of our study, and comment on some related issues. Section 7 concludes the paper.

2. Performance Issues for Hardware and Software Coherence

In this section we outline the important issues that affect the performance of software and hardware cache coherence schemes. There are two main performance disadvantages of directory-based hardware schemes. First, substantial invalidation or update traffic may be generated on the interconnection network. Second, memory references to blocks that have been modified by a processor but not updated in main memory have to go through the directory to the cache that contains the block.

The performance of software schemes on the other hand is limited by the need to use compile-time information to predict run-time behavior. The limits of this information may force software schemes to be conservative when (1) predicting whether certain sequences of accesses occur at runtime, (2) using multi-word cache lines, and (3) caching synchronization variables.

To detect stale data accesses, the compiler has to identify sequences where one processor reads or writes a memory location, a different processor writes the location,

and the first processor again reads the location. In this case, the compiler has to insert an invalidate before the last reference. To identify when such a sequence can occur, the compiler may need to predict some or all of the following: (a) whether two memory references are to the same location, (b) whether two memory references are executed on different processors, (c) whether a write under control of a conditional will actually be executed, and (d) when a write will be executed in relation to a sequence of reads. If any of these is not precisely known, the compiler has to conservatively introduce invalidation operations, perhaps causing unnecessary cache misses. Note that future advances in compiler technology could permit (a) and (b) above to be predicted accurately, while (c) and (d) involve runtime behavior that cannot be known at compile-time. In our analysis we explicitly model the problems of predicting whether and when a write is executed, and treat them separately from the first two sources of uncertainty in data dependence analysis listed above. In this context, we call a write that executes an *actual write*, whereas we say there is a *potential write* in the program when the compiler for the software coherence scheme has to insert an invalidate for reasons other than inaccurate prediction of memory access conflicts or processor allocation.

Another factor affecting the performance of hardware and software schemes is cache line size. For hardware schemes, it is an open question whether multiple-word cache lines provide higher performance than single-word lines for shared data. On the other hand, no software scheme proposed so far can use multiple-word lines to exploit spatial-locality for shared read-write data. Our workload model includes parameters to account for this factor.

Finally, all the software coherence schemes proposed so far require synchronization variables be uncacheable, whereas many hardware schemes allows such variables to be cached. In the future, the effects of this difference can be mitigated by software techniques [MeSar] that make locks appear more like ordinary shared data. For this reason, we do not model synchronization directly.

3. The High-Level Workload Model

Our high-level workload model partitions shared data objects into classes very similar to those defined by Weber and Gupta [WeG89]. We use five classes, namely, *passively-shared objects, mostly-read objects, frequently read-written objects, migratory objects,* and *synchronization objects.* Passively-shared objects include read-only data as well as the portions of shared read-write objects that are exclusively accessed by a single processor[1]. The latter type of data occurs, for instance, when different tasks of a Single-Program Multiple Data (SPMD) parallel program work on independent portions of a shared array.

---

1. Note that this is a generalization of the read-only class defined by Weber and Gupta.

338

Table 3.1. Parameters of the high-level workload model.

Parameter	Value	Description
Parameters denoting the fractions of references to the various classes		
f_{data}	0.3	fraction of memory accesses that are data references
f_{pvt}	0.75	fraction of data references that are to private data
$f_{PS}, f_{RW}, f_{MR}, f_{MIG}$	0 - 1.0	fraction of shared references that are to passively shared, frequently read-written, mostly-read, and migratory data, respectively ($f_{PS}+f_{RW}+f_{MR}+f_{MIG} = 1$)
Parameters for mostly read data		
$f_{w\|MR}$	≤ 0.1	fraction of accesses to mostly read data that are writes
l_{MR}	≥ 1	runtime average number of read accesses by a processor to a mostly-read data element between consecutive compiler-inserted invalidations executed on that element by the same processor.
n_{MR}	≥ 4	Mean number of processors that access a data element between consecutive (actual) writes to that element.
Parameters for frequently read-written data		
$f_{w\|RW}$	0.1-0.5	fraction of accesses to frequently read-written data that are writes
l_{RW}	≥ 1	average number of read accesses by a processor to a frequently read-written data element between potential writes by other processors
n_{RW}	1-4	Mean number of processors that access a data element between consecutive (actual) writes to that element.
Parameters for migratory data		
l_{MIG}	≥ 2	average number of accesses to a migratory data element by a single processor before an access by another processor

Passively shared data generate no coherence traffic and hence do not cause performance differences between hardware and software coherence schemes.

We use the term *actively shared* to collectively denote all classes of shared data that are not passively shared. Table 3.1 summarizes the high-level workload parameters. (The column of values gives the ranges used in our experiments.) As discussed earlier, we do not model synchronization objects separately, but expect them to behave like ordinary shared data once contention-reducing techniques have been applied [MeSar]. The parameters for mostly-read, frequently read-written and migratory data are further discussed below. These parameters are designed to capture the sharing behavior of the particular data class, so as to reflect the performance considerations discussed in Section 2.

3.1. Mostly-Read Data

Mostly-read objects are those that are written very infrequently, and may be read more than once by multiple processors before a write by some processor. An example is the cost array in a VLSI routing program which is read often by multiple processors, but written when an optimal route for a wire is decided. Even though actual writes to an object of this class are rare, there could be uncertainty in whether and when writes do occur, possibly causing a large number of unnecessary invalidations. We make the assumption that a processor always reads a mostly-read data element before writing it, so that a write always finds the data in the cache.

The parameters $f_{w\|MR}$, l_{MR}, and n_{MR} describe accesses to mostly-read data, and are defined in Table 3.1.

The feasible values of these three parameters are constrained in the following way. Define $ratio_{MR}$ to be the average number of compiler-inserted invalidates that a processor executes on a mostly-read data element in the interval between any two consecutive actual writes to the data element, averaged over the intervals when the processor does execute such invalidates. From the definition, $ratio_{MR} \geq 1$. Since a processor reads a data element l_{MR} times between compiler-inserted invalidates, $l_{MR} \times ratio_{MR} \times n_{MR}$ is approximately the total number of reads on a data element between two actual writes to the element.[2] But the latter is exactly the overall ratio of reads to writes at runtime, $(1-f_{w\|MR})/f_{w\|MR}$. Therefore,

$$ratio_{MR} = \frac{1-f_{w\|MR}}{f_{w\|MR} \times n_{MR} \times l_{MR}} \geq 1. \qquad (3.1)$$

This relationship is significant for two reasons. First, it relates the compile-time and runtime behavior of the program, and therefore the performance of the software and hardware coherence schemes for the given program. Second, it constrains the feasible parameter space to be explored in comparing the two schemes.

---

2. The expression is approximate because the processors that perform the actual writes must be treated somewhat differently in the exact expression for the number of reads between a pair of actual writes.

Table 4.1. Architectural and System Parameters.

Parameter	Value	Description
Architectural Parameters		
N	256	number of processors in the system
$D_{sw}, D_{cache}, D_{mem}$	1.0,1.0,4.0	no contention delay at switch (per packet), cache and memory respectively
L_i	2,8,10,2	number of packets in a message of type i, $i \in \{addr, data, addr+data, invalidate\}$
System Parameters		
ms_{ins}	0.005	fraction of references to instructions that miss
$ms_{pvt\&ps}$	0.01	fraction of references to private and passively-shared data that miss
loc_{hw}, loc_{sw}	1.0	reduction in miss rates to actively shared data due to spatial locality in the hardware and software scheme respectively
$cons$	0.1-1.0	reduction in hit rates to actively shared data due to conservative prediction of memory access conflicts and processor allocation.

3.2. Frequently Read-Written Data

Frequently read-written objects are typically those that show high contention, such as a counter that keeps track of how many processors are waiting on a global task queue. Such data objects are written frequently, and also read by multiple processors between writes. Weber and Gupta show that this type of data can degrade system performance because they cause multiple invalidates relatively frequently. Writes to this type of data may also be executed conditionally, but a relatively high fraction of these writes would be executed compared to the mostly-read data. As for mostly-read data, we assume that a processor always reads a frequently read-written data element before writing it.

$f_{w|RW}$, l_{RW} and n_{RW} are defined in the same fashion as the corresponding parameters for mostly-read data (Table 3.1). By definition, the fraction of writes to this class, $f_{w|RW}$, is expected to be larger than $f_{w|MR}$. Also, n_{RW} is expected to be small. Similar to $ratio_{MR}$, we can define $ratio_{RW}$ and estimate it as

$$ratio_{RW} = \frac{1 - f_{w|RW}}{f_{w|RW} \times n_{RW} \times l_{RW}} \geq 1. \qquad (3.2)$$

3.3. Migratory Data

Migratory data objects are accessed by only a single processor at any given time. Data protected by locks often exhibit this type of behavior, where the processor that is currently in the critical section associated with the lock may read or write the data multiple times before relinquishing the lock and permitting another processor to access the data. Migratory data resides in at most two caches at any time. Again, we assume that a processor always reads a migratory data element before writing it. For migratory data, l_{MIG} is the average number of accesses to a migratory data element by a single processor before an access by another processor.

4. Analysis of the Coherence Schemes

The high-level workload model described in the previous section is used to derive low-level parameters that are inputs to MVA models of the systems being compared. Before describing how the low-level parameters are derived, we state our assumptions about the coherence protocols and the hardware organization, and give a brief overview of the Mean Value Analysis models.

4.1. System Assumptions and Mean Value Analysis

We assume a system consisting of a collection of processing nodes interconnected by separate request and reply networks, each with the geometry of the omega network, with 2×2 switches. We do not believe that the specific choice of network topology should significantly influence the qualitative conclusions of the study. Each node consists of a processor and associated cache, and a part of global shared memory. Messages are pipelined through the network stages. We assume that buffers are associated with the output links of a switch and have unlimited capacity, and that a buffer can simultaneously accept messages from both incoming links. The parameters describing the architecture are given in Table 4.1.

For hardware coherence, we assume a simple directory-based Dir_iB protocol similar to the ones described by Agarwal et al. [ASH88]. A cache miss for a line in global *shared* state is satisfied by main memory, while a miss to a line in *modified* state is forwarded from main memory to the cache that owns the latest copy of the line, and this copy is returned directly to the requesting processor. On a write request to a line in shared state, invalidates are either sent from main memory to some average number of processors or are broadcast to all nodes in the system, consistent with a Dir_iB scheme. The requesting processor is not required to block for the invalidates to complete.[3]

As we will see, one situation where software coherence does better than Dir_iB is when a location is read and

---

3. This implies that the system is not sequentially consistent.

Table 4.2. Low-level workload parameters.

Parameter	Description
Parameters for software cache coherence	
p_r, p_w	fraction of references that are read or write misses respectively
p_{post}, p_{inv}	fraction of references that are posts or invalidates respectively
Parameters for hardware cache coherence	
$p_{r \mid sh}, p_{r \mid mod}$	fraction of references that are read misses to lines in shared or modified state respectively
$p_{w \mid sh}, p_{w \mid mod}$	fraction of references that are write misses to lines in shared or modified state respectively
$p_{ind.inv.}$	probability that invalidations are sent individually (not broadcast)
n_{inv}	average number of processors to which invalidations are sent, when they are sent individually.

then written by a processor. This is because software can use one invalidate whereas Dir_iB may need to take action on both the read and the write. This performance difference can be reduced if hardware supports a *Read-For-Ownership (RFO)* operation [KEW85]. *RFO* is a read operation that procures the requested line in modified state in the processor cache to avoid a directory access on a subsequent write. Since the use of *RFO* could significantly change the performance of Dir_iB relative to software coherence, we model Dir_iB without and with *RFO*.

For software coherence, we model a scheme similar to the one proposed by Cytron et al. [CKM88]. The compiler inserts an *invalidate* instruction before each potential access to stale data, causing the data to be retrieved from main memory. Also, if a write to a shared location is followed by a read by a different processor, the compiler inserts a *post* operation that explicitly writes the line back to main memory. We assume that the processor is blocked for one cycle for each *invalidate* and *post* instruction, i.e. we assume that the processor does not have to block for the post to complete. This is consistent with not requiring a processor to block for invalidates in the hardware scheme. *Read* and *write* misses are identical in behavior as far as the network and main memory are concerned.

We use similar approximate Mean Value Analysis models of the system for both coherence schemes. The shared hardware resources in the system, i.e., the memories and the interconnection network links, are represented as queueing centers in a closed queueing network. The task executing on each processor (representing a single customer) is assumed to be in "steady state," executing locally for a geometrically distributed number of cycles between operations on the global memory. We assume that a global memory operation is equally likely to be directed to each of the nodes in the system, including the node where the request originates. The probabilities of various global memory operations per cycle comprise the low-level work-

load parameters and are defined in Table 4.2. These parameters are derived from the high-level workload model as explained in Section 4.2.

The MVA models used to calculate system performance are similar to models developed by others for the analysis of different types of processor-memory interconnects [VLZ88, WiE90]. The detailed equations of the model are given in [AAH91]. These models can be solved very quickly and have been shown to have high accuracy for studying similar design issues.

The performance metric we use is *processor efficiency*, defined as the average fraction of time each processor spends executing locally out of its cache. This measure includes the effects of hit rate and network interference in each of the schemes.

4.2. Deriving the Low-Level Workload Parameters

The low-level parameters for each coherence scheme are derived from the high-level workload model by calculating the probability that a reference of each class causes each type of global memory operation. The system parameters listed in Table 4.1 are used in this derivation.

For the shared-data classes, the global memory access probabilities are calculated assuming a one-word cache line size, and assuming accurate analysis of memory access conflicts. Then, to account for the reduction in miss rates due to spatial locality, these global memory operation probabilities are reduced by the factor loc_{hw} or loc_{sw}. Also, for the software scheme, the hit ratio of actively shared data is reduced by the factor *cons* to account for inaccurate prediction of memory access conflicts. The approach used in calculating the contributions of each shared class is described here, and the detailed equations for all the low-level parameters are given in Appendix A.

Mostly-Read Data. This type of data is read multiple times (l_{MR} times on the average) by a processor between compiler-inserted invalidates. The first read in each such sequence will be a miss for the software scheme, since it is preceded by an invalidate. Therefore, one in every l_{MR} reads to mostly-read data causes a miss in the software protocol. In the hardware protocol each write causes one read miss for each of n_{MR} processors, on the average. The probability of a read miss is therefore $n_{MR} \times f_{w \mid MR}$. Of these read misses, $1 / n_{MR}$ see the data in modified state (contributing to $p_{r \mid mod}$), while $(n_{MR}-1) / n_{MR}$ see the data in state shared (contributing to $p_{r \mid sh}$).

Writes to mostly-read data do not cause misses with the software protocol, because we assume that they follow a read access. However, each write causes a post operation. In the hardware protocol, all writes to mostly-read data contribute to $p_{w \mid sh}$. Furthermore, we assume that n_{MR} is large enough that broadcast is required for invalidations. This is consistent with Weber and Gupta's findings, which showed that writes to mostly-read data caused an average of 3 to 4 invalidates even for 16 processor systems [WeG89].

Frequently Read-Written Data. The contribution of this class to the probability of read and write misses is calculated in the same manner as for mostly-read data (when RFO is not included). Since this class has a relatively high fraction of actual writes, the assumption that each write finds the data in shared state will be somewhat pessimistic for the hardware scheme because two consecutive writes could be executed by the same processor, with no intervening reads by other processors. This assumption is also somewhat pessimistic for the software scheme, since not all writes would cause a post operation.

Because fewer processors are expected to read between writes for this class (n_{RW} is low), we assume that all writes to data in shared state cause individual invalidates to be sent from main memory. Therefore, the contribution to $p_{ind.inv.}$ is the same as to $p_{w|sh}$. An average of $n_{RW}-1$ invalidates are required for each such write.

When RFO is included, every read sees the data in modified state, writes do not miss, and no invalidations are required.

Migratory Data. For migratory data, the first access in a sequence of l_{MIG} accesses is always a read by assumption. We assume that this type of data is written at least once for each sequence of accesses by a processor. Hence there is a read miss once per l_{MIG} accesses for both protocols. Therefore, for the hardware protocol, the first read by a processor in a sequence always finds the data in modified state. Writes in the software protocol do not miss since they always follow a read. In the hardware protocol without RFO, the first write of the sequence finds the data in shared state, causing a miss and causing an individual invalidate to be sent to exactly one processor. This miss and the invalidate are avoided, however, when RFO is included.

5. Results

We have used our models to perform experiments comparing the hardware and software coherence schemes. The constraints on the high-level workload model parameters discussed in section 3 (equations 3.1 and 3.2) allow us to explore the feasible workload parameter space completely. The ranges of workload parameter values that we consider reflect the characteristics of the shared data classes, and are given in Table 3.1. The system parameters (except *cons*) are held fixed throughout our experiments, and the values are given in Table 4.1. The values of f_{data} and f_{pvt} were chosen to reflect the findings of previous work characterizing parallel applications. [EgK88, OwA89]. Except for loc_{hw} and loc_{sw}, we believe that varying the other parameters will not affect the conclusions of our study. The value of 1 for loc_{hw} and loc_{sw} could be pessimistic for the respective schemes since they assume that spatial locality is not exploited. We will comment on these assumptions at the end of the section. Unless otherwise indicated, the experiments for hardware do not assume RFO.

In Sections 5.1 through 5.3, we study the effect of each class of actively-shared data in isolation, assuming

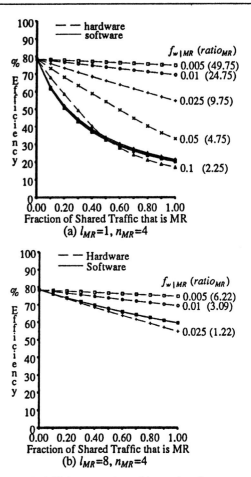

Figure 5.1. Efficiency vs f_{MR} with varying $f_{w|MR}$.

cons = 1. In Section 5.4, we study the effect of smaller values of *cons*. Since the different data classes are independent of each other, their effects in isolation can be combined to draw conclusions about the overall performance of the software and hardware schemes. We discuss the overall performance results in Section 6.

5.1. The Mostly-Read Class

In figures 5.1(a) and (b), we plot the efficiency of the hardware and software coherence schemes as the fraction of shared data references that are to mostly-read data (f_{MR}) is varied from 0 to 1, while all other shared data is passively shared. The hardware scheme is sensitive to $f_{w|MR}$, the fraction of writes to mostly-read data at runtime, and n_{MR}, the mean number of processors that access a mostly-read data element between consecutive writes to the element. n_{MR} is held constant at 4 in both graphs, but the results are similar if $f_{w|MR}$ is held constant and n_{MR} is varied. The software scheme is sensitive to l_{MR}, the mean number of reads by a processor between compiler-inserted invalidates. Figure 5.1(a) shows the results for $l_{MR}=1$, the

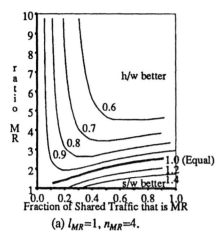

(a) $l_{MR}=1$, $n_{MR}=4$.

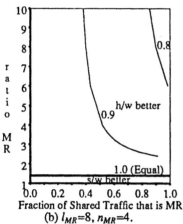

(b) $l_{MR}=8$, $n_{MR}=4$.

Figure 5.2. Contours of constant $\dfrac{\text{Efficiency(software)}}{\text{Efficiency(hardware)}}$.

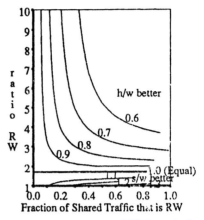

Figure 5.3. Contours of constant $\dfrac{\text{Efficiency(software)}}{\text{Efficiency(hardware)}}$.
$l_{RW} = 1$, $n_{RW} = 2$.

while the hardware scheme is independent of l_{MR}. Note here that the values $f_{w\,|MR} = 0.1$ and $f_{w\,|MR} = 0.05$ are not feasible for Figure 5.1(b) for $n_{MR} = 4$ and $l_{MR} = 8$, since they cause $ratio_{MR}$ to be less than 1. This restricts the region over which software would be superior to hardware.

We next identify the regions in the parameter space over which one of the schemes performs better. For $l_{MR} = 1$ and 8 in figures 5.2(a) and (b) respectively, we plot the contours of constant ratio of software to hardware efficiency over a range of values of $ratio_{MR}$, with the fraction of shared data references that are to mostly-read data varying from 0 to 1. In these experiments, $ratio_{MR}$ is varied by fixing $n_{MR}=4$ and varying $f_{w\,|MR}$. Similar results are obtained when $f_{w\,|MR}$ is fixed and n_{MR} is varied.

For low values of l_{MR}, we observe that the hardware scheme is significantly better (more than 20% better) than the software scheme if more than 20% of the shared data is mostly-read and $ratio_{MR}$ is greater than 3. In this case, the hardware scheme is superior to the software scheme for most of the feasible parameter space. Software coherence is more than 10% better than hardware only for very low $ratio_{MR}$. However, for $l_{MR} \geq 8$, the software scheme becomes competitive with hardware over most of the feasible parameter space.

5.2. The Frequently Read-Written Class

The parameters related to the frequently read-written class of data, l_{RW}, n_{RW} and $f_{w\,|RW}$, are similar to those for mostly-read data, but their values vary over different ranges, thus distinguishing the class.

The contour plots shown in Figure 5.3 give quantitative estimates of the relative performance of software and hardware coherence over the parameter space. As in figure 5.2, we use $ratio_{RW}$ to reflect the relationship between the behavior of the two schemes. Again, we vary $ratio_{RW}$ by holding $n_{RW} = 2$ and $l_{RW} = 1$ constant and varying $f_{w\,|RW}$.

most pessimistic case for the software scheme. 5.1 (b) shows the results for $l_{MR}=8$, where the software scheme has become competitive with the hardware scheme.

In figure 5.1(a) we observe that as $f_{w\,|MR}$ increases, the efficiency of the hardware scheme decreases, while the effect on the software scheme is insignificant. Increasing $f_{w\,|MR}$ while holding n_{MR} and l_{MR} constant decreases $ratio_{MR}$, as shown in the figure. In effect, the number of potential writes in the program (and thus software performance) is held constant, while the fraction of these writes that are executed increases. An increased number of writes that are executed adversely affects the hardware performance in three ways: (1) each write that is executed is an additional miss, (2) the write results in broadcast invalidations causing higher network traffic, and (3) the first read by another processor after the write operation finds the line dirty and has to make an extra hop across the network to fetch the line.

Figure 5.1(b) shows that the software scheme improves significantly for $l_{MR}=8$ as compared with $l_{MR}=1$,

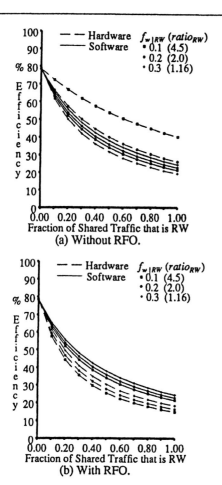

Figure 5.4. The Effect of RFO with Frequently Read-Written Data

parameter range that we explored. The reason for this counterintuitive result is as follows. Without RFO, only the reads that follow an *actual* write incur a miss, requiring a global memory access, and only the first of these requires three traversals of the network. With RFO, every read incurs a miss for $l_{RW} = 1$ (here we assume that a data element is read by some other processor between successive writes by any processor), and requires three traversals of the network since the line is always held in modified state. When even a small fraction of the potential writes are not executed, the loss in efficiency due to the extra misses is not compensated for by the lack of misses when the writes occur, as shown in the plots for $ratio_{RW} = 1.16$ ($f_{w|RW} = 0.3$).

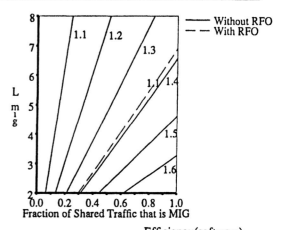

Figure 5.5. Contours of constant $\dfrac{\text{Efficiency(software)}}{\text{Efficiency(hardware)}}$.

As for mostly-read data, the results are similar if n_{RW} is varied instead of $f_{w|RW}$. We observe that the hardware scheme is more than 20% better than the software scheme for $ratio_{RW} \geq 3$ and $f_{RW} > 0.3$. However, we expect that in many programs, less than 20% of shared data references would be to this class ($f_{RW} \leq 0.2$) since it leads to low processor efficiencies for any coherence scheme. Within this range of values, the software scheme is within 20% of hardware coherence in performance. For higher values of l_{RW}, the region for which software is comparable to hardware increases.

Since the RFO optimization may improve the performance of the hardware scheme for frequently read-written data, we examine how the relative performance of the two schemes changes with this optimization. The efficiencies for the cases without and with RFO are shown in Figures 5.4(a) and (b) respectively. Surprisingly, the RFO optimization degrades the performance of the hardware scheme, removing its advantage over the software scheme in regions where it dominates without RFO, for the entire

Another point of interest is that, with RFO, the hardware and software schemes both have the same miss ratios for $l_{RW}=1$, but the software scheme has a lower cost per miss. In general, relative miss ratios do not completely reflect the difference between hardware and software schemes because of differences in network traffic and miss latencies.

5.3. The Migratory Class

The only parameter for migratory data is l_{MIG}, the average length of a sequence of accesses by a single processor. Figure 5.5 shows the contour plots for the relative efficiency of the software and hardware schemes with varying amounts of migratory data and l_{MIG}. The hardware schemes with RFO (solid lines) and without RFO (dashed lines) are shown. All other shared data is assumed to be passively shared. We observe that the hardware scheme consistently performs worse than the software scheme. This is essentially due to the deterministic behavior of this class of data. Without RFO, the difference is more than 20% for a large range of operation. The RFO optimization brings hardware to within 20% of the software scheme over the entire parameter space, but does not make the hardware scheme outperform the software scheme. This is

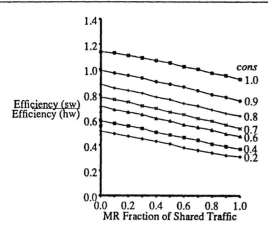

Figure 5.6. The effect of Conservative Analysis of Memory Conflicts, $l_{MIG} = 4$, $l_{MR} = 8$, $ratio_{MR} = 2$, $n_{MR} = 4$.

because, even though the use of RFO avoids the miss on the write for hardware, the read miss requires an extra hop to retrieve the data. Hence, the software scheme is always better than the hardware scheme for migratory data.

5.4. The Effect of Conservative Analysis of Memory Conflicts

The above experiments assume that conflicting memory accesses can be accurately identified at compile time. To analyze the effect of this assumption, we studied the effect of reducing hit rates to actively-shared data in the software scheme due to conservative analysis of conflicting accesses ($cons < 1$). Since the main difference between the hardware and software schemes occurs for mostly-read and migratory data accesses, we assume only these two classes of actively shared data in our experiments. Figure 5.6 plots the ratio of the efficiency of the software scheme to that of the hardware scheme with f_{MR} ranging from 0 to 1, and $f_{MIG} = 1 - f_{MR}$, with separate curves for different values of *cons*. The parameter settings used were those for which software had comparable performance to hardware coherence for *cons* = 1. We find that with up to about 10% reduction in hits due to conservative analysis ($cons \geq 0.9$), the software scheme stays within 10% of hardware. For more than 15% reduction in hit rate, the software scheme becomes more than 20% worse than the hardware scheme.

6. Summary and Discussion of the Results

Our experiments show that if memory access conflicts can be detected accurately at compile time ($cons \geq 0.9$), the software scheme is competitive with the hardware scheme for most cases. The most important case for which hardware coherence significantly outperforms software coherence is for the mostly-read class of data. With a high fraction of this class of data, if less than half of the potential writes detected at compile-time are executed,

the hardware scheme can be more than 30% better than the software scheme. The hardware scheme is also significantly better with high fractions of frequently read-written data, when $ratio_{RW}$ is high. However, we do not expect parallel programs to contain such high proportions of this class of data. Otherwise, the software scheme performs within 10% of the hardware scheme for most cases. For migratory data, the software scheme consistently outperforms the hardware scheme by a significant amount. The RFO optimization for the hardware can substantially reduce this difference, but does not make the hardware scheme perform better than the software scheme.

The chief significance of these results is in showing the effect of various types of sharing behavior on relative hardware and software performance. For data that consists of conditional writes that are performed infrequently at runtime (high values of $ratio_{RW}$ and $ratio_{MR}$), the software scheme performs poorly compared to the hardware scheme. This suggests that if data with many conditional writes occurs frequently in parallel programs, some mechanism to handle these writes is essential for a software scheme to be a viable option. None of the software schemes proposed so far incorporate such a mechanism. Since the result of conditional branches cannot be predicted at compile time, some hardware support appears necessary so that the compiler can optimistically predict branch outcomes, while the hardware takes responsibility for ensuring correctness when a prediction is wrong.

Although we have specifically modeled the scheme described by Cytron et al., we believe our results apply equally to the Fast Selective Invalidation scheme [ChV88] and to the timestamp based [MiB90a] and version control schemes [Che90]. The Fast Selective Invalidation scheme has been shown to be very similar to the Cytron et al. scheme in terms of compile time analysis and exploiting temporal locality. The timestamp-based and version control schemes have been shown to perform better than the scheme by Cytron et al., but our assumption of *cons* = 1 for the Cytron scheme makes it comparable to these more efficient schemes. Furthermore, neither of these schemes can effectively handle potential writes, and hence suffer as much from such conservative compile time predictions as the Cytron scheme.

Finally, all our results have assumed $loc_{hw} = loc_{sw} = 1$, i.e., neither scheme exploits spatial locality for actively-shared data. It is not known if software coherence schemes can effectively use multiple word blocks. It is also not known if multiple word blocks are desirable with hardware coherence schemes in large multiprocessors. If hardware schemes are shown to exploit significantly more spatial locality than the software schemes, our results no longer hold.

7. Conclusions

We have used analytical MVA models to compare the performance of software and hardware coherence schemes for a wide class of programs. Previous studies have yielded seemingly conflicting results about whether software schemes can perform comparably to hardware schemes. The conflict arises because the different studies make varying assumptions about the behavior of parallel programs.

We have characterized the workloads for which each of the two approaches is superior. There are two principal obstacles to such a study: (1) the sharing behavior of parallel programs is not well understood, and (2) for a specific workload, the relative performance of hardware and software schemes depends on the amount of runtime information that can be predicted at compile time. Our approach has been to use a high level workload model in which (1) shared data is classified into independent classes, each of which can be characterized by very few (1-3) parameters and studied in isolation, and (2) the relationship between the compile time and runtime characteristics is captured in a manner that can be related to the high level program, independent of the specific coherence scheme. The high level workload model is used to generate the workload parameters of the MVA model for each of the schemes, thereby allowing an equitable comparison of the schemes.

Quantitative data and intuitive explanations of the results were given in Section 5. The main conclusions of our study (assuming the software and hardware schemes exploit spatial locality equally) are as follows:

- Software schemes perform significantly less well (i.e., have at least 20% lower processor efficiency) than hardware schemes only if: (1) $cons < 0.85$, i.e., the hit ratio to actively-shared data is reduced by more than 15% because of conservative estimates of when two memory accesses conflict, or (2) less than half the potential writes are executed, on the average.

- Software schemes are comparable to hardware schemes (within 10% in terms of processor efficiency) if $cons \geq 0.9$ and if more than half the potential writes in the program are executed.

- Software schemes are more efficient than hardware schemes, up to 20% better in some cases, if $cons \geq 0.95$ and if most of the potential writes are executed.

Several important programs may fall under the category for which software coherence is significantly less efficient than hardware coherence. For example, detecting memory conflicts at compile-time for programs that make heavy use of pointers, such as operating systems and Lisp programs, could be difficult, i.e. $cons$ would be low. On the other hand, for well structured deterministic programs, our results show that software schemes are comparable and in some cases better than hardware schemes. Many scientific programs fall under this class. Our study motivates the need for more work on characterizing parallel program workloads, and the relationship between compile time and runtime parameters of parallel programs. Once such a characterization has been made, our model and its results can be used more effectively.

References

[AAH91]   S. V. ADVE, V. S. ADVE, M. D. HILL and M. K. VERNON, Comparison of Hardware and Software Cache Coherence Schemes, Computer Sciences Technical Report #1012, University of Wisconsin-Madison, March 1991.

[ASH88]   A. AGARWAL, R. SIMONI, M. HOROWITZ and J. HENNESSY, An Evaluation of Directory Schemes for Cache Coherence, *Proc. 15th Annual Intl. Symp. on Computer Architecture*, Honolulu, Hawaii, June 1988, 280-289.

[ArB86]   J. ARCHIBALD and J. BAER, Cache Coherence Protocols: Evaluation Using a Multiprocessor Simulation Model, *ACM Trans. on Computer Systems 4*, 4 (November 1986), 273-298.

[BMW85]   W. C. BRANTLEY, K. P. MCAULIFFE and J. WEISS, RP3 Process-Memory Element, *Intl. Conf. on Parallel Processing*, August 1985, 772-781.

[ChV88]   J. CHEONG and A. V. VEIDENBAUM, A Cache Coherence Scheme With Fast Selective Invalidation, *Proc. of the 15th Annual Intl. Symp. on Computer Architecture 16*, 2 (June 1988), 299-307.

[Che90]   H. CHEONG, Compiler-Directed Cache Coherence Strategies for Large-Scale Shared-Memory Multiprocessor Systems, Ph.D. Thesis, Dept. of Electrical Engineering, University of Illinois, Urbana-Champaign, 1990.

[CKM88]   R. CYTRON, S. KARLOVSKY and K. P. MCAULIFFE, Automatic Management of Programmable Caches, *Proc. 1988 Intl. Conf. on Parallel Processing*, University Park PA, August 1988, II-229-238.

[EgK88]   S. J. EGGERS and R. H. KATZ, A Characterization of Sharing in Parallel Programs and its Application to Coherency Protocol Evaluation, *Proc. 15th Annual Intl. Conf. on Computer Architecture*, Honolulu, HA, May 1988.

[EgK89]   S. J. EGGERS and R. H. KATZ, The Effect of Sharing on the Cache and Bus Performance of Parallel Programs, *Proc. 3rd Intl. Conf. on Architectural Support for Programming Languages and Operating Systems*, Boston, April 1989.

[KEW85]   R. H. KATZ, S. J. EGGERS, D. A. WOOD, C. L. PERKINS and R. G. SHELDON, Implementing a Cache Consistency Protocol, *Proc. 12th Annual Intl. Symp. on Computer Architecture*, Boston, June 1985, 276-283.

[KDL86]   D. J. KUCK, E. S. DAVIDSON, D. H. LAWRIE and A. H. SAMEH, Parallel Supercomputing Today and the Cedar Approach, *Science 231*(28 February 1986), .

[MeSar]   J. M. MELLOR-CRUMMEY and M. L. SCOTT, Algorithms for Scalable Synchronization on Shared-Memory Multiprocessors, *ACM Transactions on Computer Systems*, to appear.

[MiB90a] S. L. MIN and J. BAER, Design and Analysis of a Scalable Cache Coherence Scheme Based on Clocks and Timestamps, *Submitted for Publication*, 1990.

[MiB90b] S. L. MIN and J. BAER, A Performance Comparison of Directory-based and Timestamp-based Cache Coherence Schemes, *Proc. Intl. Conf. on Parallel Processing*, 1990, 1305-1311.

[OwA89] S. Owicki and A. Agarwal, Evaluating the Performance of Software Cache Coherency, *Proc. 3rd Intl. Conf. on Architectural Support for Programming Languages and Operating Systems*, Boston, April 1989.

[VLZ88] M. K. Vernon, E. D. Lazowska and J. Zahorjan, An Accurate and Efficient Performance Analysis Technique for Multiprocessor Snooping Cache-Consistency Protocols, *Proc. 15th Annual Intl. Symp. on Computer Architecture*, June 1988.

[WeG89] W. Weber and A. Gupta, Analysis of Cache Invalidation Patterns in Multiprocessors, *Proc. 3rd Intl. Conf. on Architectural Support for Programming Languages and Operating Systems*, April 1989.

[WiE90] D. L. Willick and D. L. Eager, An Analytic Model of Multistage Interconnection Networks, *Proc. ACM SIGMETRICS Conf. on Measurement and Modeling of Computer Systems 18*, 1 (May 1990), 192-202.

Appendix A

The method used to derive the low-level workload parameters from the high-level workload model is described here. For each low-level workload parameter, we describe the contribution to that parameter by each high-level actively-shared data class in a table. The entries in the table, when weighted by the probabilities of accessing shared data of that particular class, give the total contribution to that parameter by that class.

All private and passively-shared misses are included in p_r for the software scheme and in $p_{r|sh}$ for the hardware scheme. Let $T(param,c)$ denote the table entry in row *param* and column c. Then the equations used to derive the parameters for the software scheme are:

$$p_r = (1-f_{data})\, ms_{ins} + f_{data}\,(f_{pvt}+f_{PS})\, ms_{pvt\&ps}$$

$$+\, 1 - cons \times \left[1 - \frac{f_{data}(1-f_{pvt})}{loc_{sw}} \times \sum_{c \in \{RW,MR,MIG\}} f_c\, T(p_r,c) \right],$$

and for $y \in \{w,inv,post\}$,

$$p_y = 1 - cons \times \left[1 - \frac{f_{data}(1-f_{pvt})}{loc_{sw}} \times \sum_{c \in \{RW,MR,MIG\}} f_c\, T(p_x,c) \right]$$

Similarly, for the hardware scheme:

$$p_{r|sh} = (1-f_{data})\, ms_{ins} + f_{data}\,(f_{pvt}+f_{PS})\, ms_{pvt\&ps}$$

$$+\, \frac{f_{data}(1-f_{pvt})}{loc_{hw}} \times \sum_{c \in \{RW,MR,MIG\}} f_c\, T(p_{r|sh},c),$$

and for $y \in \{w|sh, r|mod, w|mod\}$,

$$p_y = \frac{f_{data}(1-f_{pvt})}{loc_{hw}} \times \sum_{c \in \{RW,MR,MIG\}} f_c\, T(p_x,c).$$

The table entries for the software scheme are given in Table A1, while those for the hardware schemes without and with RFO are given in Tables A2 and A3 respectively.

Table A1. Contribution of actively-shared data classes to software model.

Parameters of Software Model			
Param	Contribution of data class		
	MR	*RW*	*MIG*
p_r	$\dfrac{1-f_{w|MR}}{l_{MR}}$	$\dfrac{1-f_{w|RW}}{l_{RW}}$	$\dfrac{1}{l_{MIG}}$
p_w	0	0	0
p_{inv}	$\dfrac{1-f_{w|MR}}{l_{MR}}$	$\dfrac{1-f_{w|RW}}{l_{RW}}$	$\dfrac{1}{l_{MIG}}$
p_{post}	$f_{w|MR}$	$f_{w|RW}$	$\dfrac{1}{l_{MIG}}$

Table A2. Contribution of actively-shared data classes to hardware model without RFO.

Parameters of Hardware Model (no RFO)			
Param	Contribution of data class		
	MR	*RW*	*MIG*
$p_{r|sh}$	$(n_{MR}-1)f_{w|MR}$	$(n_{RW}-1)f_{w|RW}$	0
$p_{w|sh}$	$f_{w|MR}$	$f_{w|RW}$	$\dfrac{1}{l_{MIG}}$
$p_{r|mod}$	$f_{w|MR}$	$f_{w|RW}$	$\dfrac{1}{l_{MIG}}$
$p_{w|mod}$	0	0	0
$p_{ind.inv.}$	0	$\dfrac{f_{w|RW}}{p_{w|sh}}$	$\dfrac{1}{l_{MIG}p_{w|sh}}$
n_{inv}	0	$\dfrac{f_{w|RW}(n_{RW}-1)}{p_{ind.inv.}}$	$\dfrac{1}{l_{MIG}\,p_{ind.inv.}}$

Table A3. Contribution of actively-shared data classes to hardware model with RFO.

Parameters of Hardware Model (with RFO)			
Param	Contribution of data class		
	MR	*RW*	*MIG*
$p_{r|sh}$	$(n_{MR}-1)f_{w|MR}$	0	0
$p_{w|sh}$	$f_{w|MR}$	0	0
$p_{r|mod}$	$f_{w|MR}$	$1-f_{w|RW}$	$\dfrac{1}{l_{MIG}}$
$p_{w|mod}$	0	0	0
$p_{ind.inv.}$	0	0	0
n_{inv}	0	0	0

About the Authors

Igor Tartalja is currently with the Department of Computer Engineering, School of Electrical Engineering, University of Belgrade. He received the BSEE in 1984 and MSEE in 1989, both from the School of Electrical Engineering, University of Belgrade, Belgrade, Serbia, Yugoslavia. He is in the final phase of finishing his PhD thesis on dynamic software maintenance of cache coherence in shared-memory multiprocessors. From 1984 to 1989 he was with the Laboratory for Computer Engineering, Institute for Nuclear Sciences, Vinča, Serbia, Yugoslavia, working primarily on the development of a real-time computer for applications in biophysics and a distributed operating system for a special-purpose multicomputer. His current research interests include multiprocessor and multicomputer architectures, heterogeneous processing, and system software support for shared-memory multiprocessors and distributed systems.

Veljko Milutinović has been with the Department of Computer Engineering, School of Electrical Engineering, University of Belgrade, Belgrade, Serbia, Yugoslavia since 1990. From 1982 to 1990 he was on the faculty of the School of Electrical and Computer Engineering, Purdue University, West Lafayette, Indiana. He has been active in the RISC field for the last decade and in technology-related research (32-bit GaAs RISC for RCA) and application-related research (multimedia-oriented RISC-based multiprocessors efforts of NCR). He has published 40 papers in IEEE journals and presented over 200 invited talks all over the world. He is a senior member of the IEEE.

IEEE COMPUTER SOCIETY
50 YEARS OF SERVICE •1946-1996

IEEE Computer Society

The IEEE Computer Society advances the theory and practice of computer science and engineering, promotes the exchange of technical information among 100,000 members worldwide, and provides a wide range of services to members and nonmembers.

Membership

All members receive the monthly magazine *Computer*, discounts, and opportunities to serve (all activities are led by volunteer members). Membership is open to all IEEE members, affiliate society members, and others interested in the computer field.

Publications and Activities

Computer Society On-Line: Provides electronic access to abstracts and tables of contents from society periodicals and conference proceedings, plus information on membership and volunteer activities. To access, telnet to the Internet address info.computer.org (user i.d.: guest). The web address is http://www.computer.org.

Computer **magazine:** An authoritative, easy-to-read magazine containing tutorial and in-depth articles on topics across the computer field, plus news, conferences, calendar, interviews, and product reviews.

Periodicals: The society publishes 10 magazines and seven research transactions.

Conference proceedings, tutorial texts, and standards documents: The Computer Society Press publishes more than 100 titles every year.

Standards working groups: Over 200 of these groups produce IEEE standards used throughout the industrial world.

Technical committees: Over 29 TCs publish newsletters, provide interaction with peers in specialty areas, and directly influence standards, conferences, and education.

Conferences/Education: The society holds about 100 conferences each year and sponsors many educational activities, including computing science accreditation.

Chapters: Regular and student chapters worldwide provide the opportunity to interact with colleagues, hear technical experts, and serve the local professional community.

IEEE Computer Society Press Publications

CS Press publishes, promotes, and distributes original and reprint computer science and engineering texts. Original books consist of 100 percent original material; reprint books contain a carefully selected group of previously published papers with accompanying original introductory and explanatory text.

Submission of proposals: For guidelines on preparing CS Press books, write to Manager, Press Product Development, IEEE Computer Society Press, P.O. Box 3014, 10662 Los Vaqueros Circle, Los Alamitos, CA 90720-1264, or telephone (714) 821-8380.

12/13/95

Printed in the United States
1166100001B/127-162